Counseling the Culturally Diverse

SEVENTH EDITION

Counseling the Culturally Diverse

Theory and Practice

Derald Wing Sue | David Sue

WILEY

Library of Congress Cataloging-in-Publication Data:
Sue, Derald Wing.
  Counseling the culturally diverse : theory and practice / Derald Wing Sue, David Sue. – 7th edition.
       pages cm
  Includes bibliographical references and index.
  ISBN 978-1-119-08430-3 (cloth) – ISBN 978-1-119-08437-2 (pdf) – ISBN 978-1-119-08433-4 (epub)
  1. Cross-cultural counseling.   I. Sue, David.   II. Title.
  BF637.C6S85 2016
  158.3–dc23

                                                                                        2015018013

Printed in the United States of America
10 9 8 7 6 5 4 3 2 1

Contents

Preface

Since its publication in 1981, *Counseling the Culturally Diverse: Theory and Practice (CCD)* has become a classic in the field, used in the overwhelming majority of graduate training programs in counseling, counselor education, and clinical psychology, and now forms part of the multicultural knowledge base of licensing and certification exams. It continues to lead the field in the theory, research, and practice of multicultural counseling/therapy and upholds the highest standards of scholarship; it is the most frequently cited text in multicultural psychology and ethnic minority mental health.

Over many decades, feedback from reviewers and readers indicate the success of *CCD* is related to its (a) integrated conceptual framework, (b) up-to-date coverage of research in the field, (c) ability to actively address clinical applications through translating research/concepts to practice, (d) use of numerous examples, vignettes, and case studies that add life and meaning to the material, (e) ability to involve readers in personal self-reflection and exploration, (f) engaging writing style, and (g) passionate style of communication—hard hitting, intense and challenging.

The 13 chapters on specific populations continue to be hailed as among the best thumbnail sketches of how multicultural counseling relates to the various marginalized groups in our society. Adopters have consistently praised the culture-universal and culture-specific balance of the book. The seventh edition of *CCD* does not change the basic formula which has made and continues to make it a success in the academic and clinical markets.

Changes to CCD

In the seventh edition, major changes were made as a result of reviewing three dozen texts on multicultural counseling, general multicultural mental health care, multicultural assessment, multicultural competencies, multicultural supervision, and multicultural consultation. Content coverage, general orientation, philosophical approach, writing style, and pedagogy were analyzed in addition to a 2014 survey conducted by the publisher sent to over 1,300 instructors who each received a copy of the 2013 edition of *CCD*. The survey asked what were the unique challenges to teaching the course, what type of materials would prove helpful to instructors, and what areas needed additional coverage. Based upon a review of competing texts, analysis of the survey, and feedback from past adopters, several findings informed the revision process.

Comprehensiveness

When compared to other texts in the field, *CCD* explores and covers nearly all major multicultural counseling topics in the profession. Indeed, reviewers believed it the most comprehensive of the texts published, and noted that it leads in coverage of microaggressions in counseling, interracial/interethnic counseling, social justice approaches to counseling, the implications of indigenous healing, the sociopolitical nature of counseling, racial identity development, and the cultural use of evidence-based practice. In the reviews, two important observations were made: (a) many competing texts lacked specific coverage of these topics and/or covered these areas superficially, and (b) many competitors relied heavily upon the content of *CCD*, adapting it for their books. This latter observation is certainly flattering, as it indicates that *CCD* continues to be the flagship leader in the field of multicultural counseling by continuing to break new ground in the profession and presenting original cutting-edge research.

Streamlined and Up-to-Date Coverage

In the survey of instructors, there was a notable absence of requests to cover additional topics. We surmise that instructors were satisfied by the comprehensiveness of topical coverage in *CCD*, a conclusion also supported in our review of competing books. Rather than suggesting additional topics, ironically, some adopters noted that *CCD* explores too much material and that it was difficult to cover everything in a single course. Among those who provided this feedback, there were suggestions that *CCD* be shortened. They did not recommend eliminating topics, but rather condensing, summarizing, and streamlining, or eliminating certain subtopics. We have tried our best to do so without violating the integrity of the content. Note that many of the chapters have been retitled because of changes.

Despite our intent to shorten major sections of the text, new advances and important changes in multicultural counseling suggest additional areas that need to be addressed. These include expanded coverage of internalized racism, cultural humility, expansion of microaggression coverage to other marginalized groups, social justice/advocacy skills, recent research and thinking on evidence-based practice, and new approaches to work with specific populations. It goes without saying that the most up-to-date research findings and scholarly works have been integrated into all topics. We have also studied carefully the multicultural guidelines proposed by the American Psychological Association and the 2016 Council for Accreditation of Counseling and Related Educational Programs (CACREP, 2015) to make sure the content conforms to them. Additionally, the American Counseling Association's Multicultural Counseling Competencies Revision Committee has presented a draft proposal of new and integrated *Multicultural and Social Justice Counseling Competencies (MSJCC)* (2015) which is incorporated into the conceptual framework of the text. Thus the text not only represents the most comprehensive coverage of the field, but the most current work of scholars in multicultural counseling and mental health practice.

Emotive Nature of Content

One of the greatest concerns of instructors is the strong emotive reactions of students to the material: grief, anger, depression, and guilt in working through the content. This has been a perennial issue for students and instructors since the first edition was published in 1981. We have been aware from the beginning that *CCD* is very likely to elicit strong emotions among readers because the content of the book challenges racial, gender, and sexual orientation realities, and traditional therapeutic beliefs. On the one hand, *CCD* can be said to accomplish one of its major goals by indicating that cultural competence is more than an intellectual exercise, and that it must include dealing with strong and powerful nested and hidden emotions and biases on the part of the helper. On the other hand, these powerful feelings can become so intense in students (arousing defensiveness, guilt, and anxiety) that they prevent self-exploration (a necessary component of cultural competence in the helping professions).

To aid students in their journey to cultural competence, we have completely rewritten Chapter 1, formerly titled "The Multicultural Journey to Cultural Competence: Personal Narratives." The original intent of this chapter was to present personal narratives of the emotive reactions of a White psychologist in contrast to psychologists of color to the content of *CCD*. It was used to illustrate differences in racial realities of three individuals and to anticipate the emotive reactions of readers and their meanings. Feedback throughout the years indicates that it has been relatively successful in allowing students to link their own emotive reactions with that of the storyteller. But more seemed needed. The one downside to these long narratives was a reliance on students and instructors to distill multicultural lessons from the life stories on their own. Although these lessons seemed obvious to the authors, it was apparently not so obvious for students.

The revision of Chapter 1, now titled "Obstacles to Cultural Competence: Understanding Resistance to Multicultural Training," eliminates the longer narratives in favor of a dozen or more one-paragraph personal statements from a variety of students and people that will illustrate differences in racial realities and emotive reactions that have implications for the students' personal lives, their development as racial/cultural beings, their cultural competence, and their roles as multicultural counselors. Using shorter statements or vignettes will allow us to comment more in depth and help students make sense of their feelings and deconstruct their meanings, and will help them digest the contents of the forthcoming chapters.

Within-Chapter Changes/Additions

We strengthen each chapter by an increased focus on pedagogy, providing instructors with material to facilitate experiential activities and discussion and to help students digest the material. We open every chapter with broad **Chapter Objectives,** followed by more specific and oftentimes controversial **Reflection and Discussion Questions** interspersed throughout. Further, every single chapter opens with a clinical vignette, longer narrative, or situational example that previews the major concepts and issues discussed in the chapter. Many of these are new and serve to anchor the multicultural issues to follow. They add life and meaning to the chapter concepts and research. The Chapter Focus Questions serve as prompts to address the opening "course objectives," and these questions not only preview the content to be covered, but are cast in such a way as to allow instructors and trainers to use them as discussion questions throughout the course or workshop. The specific Reflection and Discussion Questions allow for more concentrated and detailed discussion by students on identifiable topical areas. As in the previous edition, we have retained the **Implications for Clinical Practice** sections and added a new **Summary** after every chapter.

Pedagogical Materials

Plans are under way to strengthen and expand the instructor's handbook so as to provide guidance on teaching the course, anticipating resistances, and overcoming them, and to provide supplementary materials and ideas that the teacher can use, such as case studies, videos/movies, group activities, tours/visits, and other pedagogy that will facilitate learning. In working with the publisher, we are planning an instructor's manual to accompany *CCD* that will actually make suggestions on how to teach the course on a chapter-by-chapter basis. This would be similar to the publication of *Case Studies in Multicultural Counseling and Therapy* edited by Sue, Gallardo, and Neville (2014) intended for use to accompany *CCD*. The instructor's manual would have a similar use, providing advice, suggestions, exercises, and pedagogical tools to use in teaching. Whether this would be a published hard copy or accessible online is currently under consideration.

Book Organization

Much new research and findings in multicultural counseling, cultural competence and the increasing role of using evidence-based interventions have developed over the past few years. In essence, the topical areas covered in each chapter of the book continue to be anchors for multicultural counseling coverage. As a result, while the chapters remain similar to their previous versions, each has undergone major revisions; some are quite extensive in updating of references, introduction of new research and concepts, and discussing future directions in counseling, therapy, and mental health.

We maintain our two-part division of the book with 12 separate chapters in Section One—The Multiple Dimensions of Multicultural Counseling and Therapy, and 13 population-specific chapters in Section Two—Multicultural Counseling and Specific Populations. We spent considerable thought in deciding whether to eliminate certain populations from coverage (to reduce the length of the text) or whether to add others. We felt that adding additional populations was impractical in light of the numerous populations that could be included. We were also conflicted about suggestions that we eliminate some of the population-specific chapters because they were not covered frequently by many instructors. In the end we decided to keep the current ones because they had been developed over time from requests by instructors. Further, most instructors tend to pick and choose the specific populations they desire to cover.

Each population-specific chapter has been thoroughly updated using common topical headings (when possible) that will allow for better cross-comparisons between and among the groups. We attempt to maintain the same length limit for these chapters because further shortening of them would not be educationally sound—they would become checklists rather than integrated chapters.

Appreciation

There is an African American proverb that states, "We stand on the head and shoulders of many who have gone on before us." Certainly, this book would not have been possible without their wisdom, commitment, and sacrifice. We thank them for their inspiration, courage, and dedication and hope that they will look down on us and be pleased with our work. We would like to acknowledge all the dedicated multicultural pioneers in the field who have journeyed with us along the path of multiculturalism before it became fashionable. They are too numerous to name, but their knowledge and wisdom have guided the production of *CCD*. Special thanks go to our editor Rachel Livsey, who supported the revision efforts and constantly encouraged the many new directions exemplified in the seventh edition. We also wish to thank the staff of John Wiley & Sons, especially Patricia Rossi, for the enormous time and effort placed in obtaining, evaluating, and providing us with the necessary data and feedback to produce this edition of *CCD*. Their help was no small undertaking and we feel fortunate in having Wiley as our publisher.

Working on this seventh edition continues to be a labor of love. It would not have been possible, however, without the love and support of our families, who provided the patience and nourishment that sustained us throughout our work on the text. Derald Wing Sue wishes to express his love for his wife, Paulina, his son, Derald Paul, and his daughter, Marissa Catherine. David Sue wishes to express his love and appreciation to his wife, mother, children, and twin grandsons.

We hope that *Counseling the Culturally Diverse: Theory and Practice,* seventh edition, will stand on "the truth" and continue to be the standard bearer of multicultural counseling and therapy texts in the field.

Derald Wing Sue
David Sue

REFERENCES

Counsel for Accreditation of Counseling and Related Educational Programs (2015). *2016 CACREP Standards.* Fairfax, VA: Author

Sue, D. W., Gallardo, M., & Neville, H. (2014). *Case studies in multicultural counseling and therapy.* Hoboken, NJ: Wiley.

About the Authors

Derald Wing Sue is Professor of Psychology and Education in the Department of Counseling and Clinical Psychology at Teachers College, Columbia University. He served as president of the Society for the Psychological Study of Ethnic Minority Issues, the Society of Counseling Psychology, and the Asian American Psychological Association. Dr. Sue continues to be a consulting editor for numerous publications. He is author of over 160 publications, including 19 books, and is well known for his work on racism/antiracism, cultural competence, multicultural counseling and therapy, and social justice advocacy. Three of his books, *Counseling the Culturally Diverse: Theory and Practice, Microaggressions in Everyday Life,* and *Overcoming our Racism: The Journey to Liberation* (John Wiley & Sons) are considered classics in the field. Dr. Sue's most recent research on racial, gender, and sexual orientation microaggressions has provided a major breakthrough in understanding how everyday slights, insults, and invalidations toward marginalized groups create psychological harm to their mental and physical health and create disparities for them in education, employment, and health care. His most recent book, *Race Talk and the Conspiracy of Silence: Understanding and Facilitating Difficult Dialogues on Race,* promises to add to the nationwide debate on racial dialogues. A national survey has identified Derald Wing Sue as "the most influential multicultural scholar in the United States," and his works are among the most frequently cited.

David Sue is Professor Emeritus of Psychology at Western Washington University, where he has served as the director of both the Psychology Counseling Clinic and the Mental Health Counseling Program. He is also an associate of the Center for Cross Cultural Research at Western Washington University. He and his wife, Diane M. Sue, have co-authored the books *Foundations of Counseling and Psychotherapy: Evidence Based Practices for a Diverse Society; Understanding Abnormal Psychology* (11th edition); and *Essentials of Abnormal Psychology.* He is co-author of *Counseling the Culturally Diverse: Theory and Practice.* He received his Ph.D. in Clinical Psychology from Washington State University. His writing and research interests revolve around multicultural issues in individual and group counseling and the integration of multicultural therapy with evidence-based practice. He enjoys hiking, snowshoeing, traveling, and spending time with his family.

Counseling the Culturally Diverse

SECTION ONE

The Multiple Dimensions of Multicultural Counseling and Therapy

Becoming culturally competent in working with diverse populations is a complex interaction of many dimensions that involves broad theoretical, conceptual, research, and practice issues. This section is divided into four parts (each containing a number of chapters) that describe, explain, and analyze the issues that counseling and mental health practitioners must address in the areas of multicultural counseling/therapy, cultural competence, and sociopolitical influences that cut across a spectrum of specific populations.

- Part I: *The Affective and Conceptual Dimensions of Multicultural Counseling and Therapy* makes clear that the journey to cultural competence requires an emotional awakening in the area of one's knowledge, beliefs, attitudes, and behaviors related to race, culture, ethnicity, gender, and other diverse groups. To become culturally competent means developing a broad conceptual framework for viewing diversity and multiculturalism. It also means understanding that multicultural counseling competence applies equally to trainees from dominant and marginalized groups and to helping professionals.

- Part II: *The Impact and Social Justice Implications of Counseling and Psychotherapy* discusses (a) the need to acknowledge the political bases of Western European approaches, (b) the need to recognize that counseling and psychotherapy may represent a microcosm of race relations, gender relations, and other unequal status relations in our larger society, and (c) how modern forms of bias (microaggressions) may affect both the psychological health of socially marginalized groups and our and their standard of living.

- Part III: *The Practice Dimensions of Multicultural Counseling/Therapy* integrates multicultural premises developed from the first two parts into the domain of clinical work. It reviews, analyzes, and points to best practices in working with diverse populations at the individual, familial, group, institutional, and societal levels. The theme of social justice counseling is carried over from Part II and is shown to be balanced with two major new developments in the field: multicultural evidence-based practice and the contributions of non-Western indigenous methods of healing.

- Part IV: *Racial/Cultural Identity Development in Multicultural Counseling and Therapy* has always been a challenging journey for both persons of color and White people. The most recent and up-to-date findings of racial identity development are contained in two chapters. The identities of clinicians and clients as racial/cultural beings and the impact of these identities on the dyadic combinations in therapy can either enhance or negate the therapeutic outcome. Questions such as "Who are you as a racial/cultural being?," "What does it mean to be a person of color?," and "What does it mean to be White?" must be adequately addressed in the journey to cultural competence.

PART I

The Affective and Conceptual Dimensions of Multicultural Counseling and Therapy

Obstacles to Cultural Competence

Understanding Resistance to Multicultural Training

Chapter Objectives

1. Acknowledge and understand personal resistance to multicultural training.

2. Identify how emotional reactions to topics of prejudice, discrimination, and oppression can act as obstacles to *cultural competence*.

3. Understand *worldview* differences between majority and socially devalued group members in this society.

4. Make sense of why majority group members often react differently from marginalized group members when issues of racism, sexism, or heterosexism are discussed.

5. Be cognizant of how *worldviews* may influence the ability to understand, empathize, and work effectively with diverse clients.

6. Realize that becoming an effective multicultural counselor is more than an intellectual exercise and is a lifelong journey.

Reading and digesting the content of this book may prove difficult and filled with powerful feelings for many of you. Students who have taken a course on multicultural counseling/therapy or multicultural mental health issues have almost universally felt both positive and negative feelings that affect their ability to learn about diversity issues. It is important not to allow those emotions to go unacknowledged, or to avoid exploring the psychological meanings they may have for you. As you begin your journey to becoming a culturally competent counselor/mental health professional, the road will be filled with obstacles to self-exploration, to understanding yourself as a racial/cultural being, and to understanding the *worldview* of those who differ from you in race, gender, ethnicity, sexual orientation, and other sociodemographic characteristics.

The subject matter in this book and course requires you to explore your biases and prejudices, a task that often evokes defensiveness and resistance. It is important to recognize personal resistance to the material, to explore its meanings, and to learn about yourself and others. Sometimes what is revealed about you may prove disturbing, but having the courage to continue is necessary to becoming a culturally competent counselor or therapist. This chapter is specifically written to help readers understand and overcome their emotive reactions to the substance of the text, and the course you are about to take. Let us begin by sharing reactions from four past students to reading *Counseling the Culturally Diverse* and discuss their meaning for the students, and the implications for mental health practice.

REACTIONS TO READING *COUNSELING THE CULTURALLY DIVERSE*

Reaction #1

White Female Student: *"How dare you and your fellow caustic co-author express such vitriol against my people? You two are racists, but of a different color. . .I can't believe you two are counselors. Your book does nothing but to weaken our nationalism, our sense of unity and solidarity. If you don't like it here, leave my country. You are both spoiled hate-mongers who take advantage of our educational system by convincing others to use such a propagandistic book! Shame on you. Your book doesn't make me want to be more multicultural, but take ungrateful people like you and export them out of this great land of mine."* (Name withheld)

Analysis: This response reveals immense anger at the content of *CCD*, and especially at the authors, whom she labels "hate mongers" and "racists." It is obvious that she feels the book is biased and propagandistic. The language of her words seems to indicate defensiveness on her part as she easily dismisses the material covered. More important, there is an implicit suggestion in the use of "people like you" and "land of mine" that conveys a perception that only certain groups can be considered "American" and others are "foreigners." This is similar to statements often made to people of color: "If you don't like it here, go back to China, Africa or Latin America." Likewise, the implication is that this land does not belong to persons of color who are U.S. Citizens, but only to White Americans.

Reaction #2
White Male Student: *"I am a student in the field of Professional Counseling and feel compelled to write you because your text is required reading in our program. I am offended that you seem to think that the United States is the only perpetrator of prejudice and horrific acts. Excuse me sir, but racism and oppression are part of every society in the world ad infinitum, not just the United States. I do not appreciate reading biased material that does not take into account all forms of prejudice including those from minorities. You obviously have a bone to grind with White people. Minorities are equally racist. Why do you take such pleasure in attacking whites when we have done so much to help you people?"* (Anonymous)

Analysis: Similar to the first response, the male student is also angry and offended about the content. There is a strong feeling of defensiveness, however, that emanates from his narrative. It appears he feels unjustly accused of being bigoted and that we are implying that only U.S. society and not others are racist. To make himself feel less guilty, he emphasizes that "every society" oppresses "minority" constituents and it is not Whites alone who are prejudiced. These are actually accurate statements, but they mask the defensiveness of the student, and have the goal of exonerating him and other Whites for being prejudiced. If he can get other groups to admit they too are racist, then he feels less guilt and responsibility for his own beliefs and actions.

Reaction #3
Latina Student: *"I am currently embarking on the journey of becoming a Marriage and Family Therapist at a California State University. I just want to thank you for writing* Counseling the Culturally Diverse. *This book has spoken to me and given me so much knowledge that is beyond words to express. Finally, there is someone willing to tell it like it is. You have truly made an impact in*

my life because, being an ethnic minority, I could empathize with many of the concepts that were illustrated. Although some White classmates had difficulty with it, you truly validated much of my experiences. It reaffirmed how I see the world, and it felt good to know that I am not crazy! *Once again thanks for writing the book."* (Name withheld)

Analysis: The reaction from the Latina student is diametrically opposite to that of her White counterparts. She reacts positively to the material, finds the content helpful in explaining her experiential reality, feels validated and reaffirmed, and realizes that she is "not crazy." In other words, she finds the content of the book truthful and empathetic to her situation. The important question to ask is, "Why does she react so differently from the two White students?" After all, the content of the book remains the same, but the perceptions appear worlds apart.

Reaction #4

African American Male Student: *"When I first took this course (multicultural counseling) I did not have much hope that it would be different from all the others in our program, White and Eurocentric. I felt it would be the typical cosmetic and superficial coverage of minority issues. Boy was I wrong. I like that you did not 'tip toe' around the subject. Your book* Counseling the Culturally Diverse *was so forceful and honest that it made me feel liberated . . . I felt like I had a voice, and it allowed me to truly express my anger and frustration. Some of the white students were upset and I could see them squirming in their seats when the professor discussed the book. I felt like saying 'good, it's about time Whites suffer like we have. I have no sympathy for you. It's about time they learned to listen.' Thank you, thank you, and thank you for having the courage to write such an honest book."* (Name withheld)

Analysis: Like the Latina student, the African American male finds the book compelling, honest, and truthful. He describes how it makes him feel liberated, provides him with a voice to describe his experiences, and taps into and allows him to express his anger and frustration, and he thanks the authors for writing *CCD*. He implies that most courses on multicultural psychology are taught from a EuroAmerican perspective, but the book content "tells it like it is." Additionally, the student seems to take pleasure in observing the discomfort of White students, expresses little sympathy for their struggle in the class, and enjoys seeing them being placed on the defensive. (We will return to the meaning of this last point shortly.)

Reading *Counseling the Culturally Diverse: Theory and Practice* (*CCD*) is very likely to elicit strong emotions among readers. These four reactions, two by White students and two by readers of color, reveal the range of emotions and reactions likely to be expressed in classes that use the text. Over the last 35 years we have received literally hundreds of emails, letters, and phone calls from students, trainees, professors, and mental health professionals reacting strongly to the content and substance of *CCD*. Many of the readers praise the book for its honest portrayal of multicultural issues in mental health practice. Indeed, it has become the most widely used and cited text in multicultural psychology, considered a classic in the field (Ponterotto, Fingerhut, & McGuinness, 2013; Ponterotto & Sabnani, 1989), and now forms the knowledge base of licensing and certification exams for counseling and mental health professionals.

Despite the scholarly status that *CCD* has achieved, some readers (generally those from the majority group) find the substance of the book difficult to digest and have reacted very strongly to the content. According to instructors of multicultural counseling/therapy classes, the powerful feelings aroused in some students prevent them from being open to diversity issues, and from making classroom discussions on the topic a learning opportunity. Instead, conversations on diversity become "shouting matches" or become monologues rather than dialogues. These instructors indicate that the content of the book challenges many White students about their racial, gender, and sexual orientation realities, and that the book's writing style (passionate, direct, and hard-hitting) also arouses deep feelings of defensiveness, anger, anxiety, guilt, sadness, hopelessness, and a multitude of other strong emotions in many. Unless properly processed and understood, these emotions act as roadblocks to exploring issues of race, gender, and sexual orientation. Learning about multicultural psychology is much more than an intellectual exercise devoid of emotions.

It would be a mistake, however, to conclude from these examples that White students and students of color respond uniformly in one way. As we will explore in future chapters, many White students react positively to the book and some students of color report negative reactions. But, in general, there are major *worldview* differences and reactions to the material between the two groups. For example, many socially marginalized group members find solace in the book; they describe a deep sense of validation, release, elation, joy, and even feelings of liberation as they read the text. What accounts for these two very different reactions?

For practicing professionals and trainees in the helping professions, understanding the differing *worldviews* of our culturally diverse clients is tantamount to effective multicultural counseling. But understanding our own reactions to issues of diversity, *multiculturalism*, oppression, race, gender, and sexual orientation is equally important to our development as counselors/therapists (Todd & Abrams, 2011). As we will shortly see, that understanding can be quite anxiety provoking, especially when we are asked to confront our own biases, prejudices, and stereotypes. The old adage "counselor or therapist, know thyself" is the basic building block to *cultural competence* in the helping professions. Let us take a few moments here to dissect the reactions of the four readers in our opening narratives and attempt to make meaning of them. This is a task that we encourage you to personally take throughout your educational journey as well. Likewise, as a counselor or therapist working with culturally diverse clients, understanding differences in *worldviews* is an important first step to becoming culturally competent.

EMOTIONAL SELF-REVELATIONS AND FEARS: MAJORITY GROUP MEMBERS

It is clear that the two White students are experiencing strong feelings to the content of *CCD*. As you will shortly see, the book's subject matter (a) deals with prejudice, bias, stereotyping, discrimination, and bigotry; (b) makes a strong case that counseling and psychotherapy may serve as instruments of cultural oppression rather than therapeutic liberation (Sue, 2015; Wendt, Gone, & Nagata, 2015); (c) indicates that well-intentioned mental health professionals are not immune from inheriting the racial and gender biases of the larger society; and (d) suggests therapists and trainees may be unconsciously biased toward clients from marginalized groups (Ratts & Pedersen, 2014).

Although supported by the research literature and by clinical observations and reports, these assertions can be quite disturbing to members of the majority group. If you are a majority group member and beginning the journey to *cultural competence*, it is possible that you may share similar reactions to those of the students. Both White students, for example, are reacting with anger and resentment; they believe that the authors are unjustly accusing U.S. Society and White Americans of racism, and claim the authors are themselves "racist" but of a different color. They have become defensive and are actively resisting and rejecting the content of the book. If these feelings persist throughout the course unabated, they will act as barriers to learning and further self-exploration. But what do these negative reactions mean to the students? Why are they so upset? Dr. Mark Kiselica (Sue & Sue, 2013, pp. 8–9), a White psychologist and now provost of a college in

New York, writes about his own negative emotional reactions to reading the book during his graduate training. His personal and emotional reactions to the book provide us with some clues.

> *I was shaken to my core the first time I read* Counseling the Culturally Different *(now* Counseling the Culturally Diverse*). . . .At the time, I was a doctoral candidate at The Pennsylvania State University's counseling psychology program, and I had been reading Sue's book in preparation for my comprehensive examinations, which I was scheduled to take toward the end of the spring semester. . .*

> *I wish I could tell you that I had acquired Sue's book because I was genuinely interested in learning about multicultural counseling. . .I am embarrassed to say, however, that that was not the case. I had purchased Sue's book purely out of necessity, figuring out that I had better read the book because I was likely to be asked a major question about cross-cultural counseling on the comps. During the early and middle 1980s, taking a course in multicultural counseling was not a requirement in many graduate counseling programs, including mine, and I had decided not to take my department's pertinent course as an elective. I saw myself as a culturally sensitive person, and I concluded that the course wouldn't have much to offer me. Nevertheless, I understood that. . .the professor, who taught the course, would likely submit a question to the pool of materials being used to construct the comps. So, I prudently went to the university bookstore and purchased a copy. . . .because that was the text. . . .used for his course.*

> *I didn't get very far with my highlighting and note-taking before I started to react to Sue's book with great anger and disgust. Early on in the text, Sue blasted the mental health system for its historical mistreatment of people who were considered to be ethnic minorities in the United States. He especially took on White mental health professionals, charging them with a legacy of ethnocentric and racist beliefs and practices that had harmed people of color and made them leery of counselors, psychologists, and psychiatrists. It seemed that Sue didn't have a single good thing to say about White America. I was ticked off at him, and I resented that I had to read his book. However, I knew I had better complete his text and know the subject*

matter covered in it if I wanted to succeed on the examinations. So, out of necessity, I read on and struggled with the feelings that Sue's words stirred in me.

I was very upset as I read and reread Sue's book. I felt that Sue had an axe to grind with White America and that he was using his book to do so. I believed that his accusations were grossly exaggerated and, at least to some extent, unfair. And I felt defensive because I am White and my ancestors had not perpetrated any of the offenses against ethnic minorities that Sue had charged. I looked forward to the day when I would be relieved of him and his writings.

Becoming culturally competent in counseling/mental health practice demands that nested or embedded emotions associated with race, culture, gender, and other sociodemographic differences be openly experienced and discussed. It is these intense feelings that often block our ability to hear the voices of those most oppressed and disempowered (Sue, 2011). How we, as helping professionals, deal with these strong feelings can either enhance or impede a deeper understanding of ourselves as racial/cultural beings and our understanding of the *worldviews* of culturally diverse clients. Because Mark did not allow his defensiveness and anger to get the best of him, he was able to achieve insights into his own biases and false assumptions about people of color. The following passage reveals the internal struggle that he courageously fought and the disturbing realization of his own racism.

I tried to make sense of my emotions—to ascertain why I was drawn back to Sue's book again and again in spite of my initial rejection of it. I know it may sound crazy, but I read certain sections of Sue's book repeatedly and then reflected on what was happening inside of me. . . . .I began to discover important lessons about myself, significant insights prompted by reading Sue's book that would shape the direction of my future. . . . I now realized that Sue was right! The system had been destructive toward people of color, and although my ancestors and I had not directly been a part of that oppressive system, I had unknowingly contributed to it. I began to think about how I had viewed people of color throughout my life, and I had to admit to myself that I had unconsciously bought into the racist stereotypes about African Americans and Latinos. Yes, I had laughed at and told racist jokes. Yes, I had used the "N" word when referring to African Americans. Yes, I had been a racist.

Sue's book forced me to remove my blinders. He helped me to see that I was both a product and an architect of a racist culture. Initially, I didn't want to admit this to myself. That is part of the reason I got so angry at Sue for his book. "His accusations don't apply to me!" was the predominant, initial thought that went through my mind. But Sue's words were too powerful to let me escape my denial of my racism. It was as though I was in a deep sleep and someone had dumped a bucket of ice-cold water onto me, shocking me into a state of sudden wakefulness: The sleep was the denial of my racism; the water was Sue's provocative words; and the wakefulness was the painful recognition that I was a racist. (Sue & Sue, 2013, pp. 9–10)

Years later, Mark Kiselica (1999) talks about his racial awakening and identifies some of the major fears many well-intentioned Whites struggle with as they begin studying racism, sexism, or heterosexism on a personal level. This passage, perhaps, identifies the major psychological obstacle that confronts many Whites as they process the content and meaning of the book.

You see, the subjects I [White psychologist] am about to discuss—ethnocentrism and racism, including my own racism—are topics that most Whites tend to avoid. We shy away from discussing these issues for many reasons: We are racked with guilt over the way people of color have been treated in our nation; we fear that we will be accused of mistreating others; we particularly fear being called the "R" word—racist—so we grow uneasy whenever issues of race emerge; and we tend to back away, change the subject, respond defensively, assert our innocence and our "color blindness," denying that we could possibly be ethnocentric or racist." (p. 14)

It is important to note Kiselica's open admission to racist thoughts, feelings, and behaviors. As a White psychologist, he offers insights into the reasons why many White trainees fear open dialogues on race; they may ultimately reveal unpleasant secrets about themselves. In his own racial/cultural awakening, he realizes that discussing race and racism is so difficult for many Whites because they are racked with guilt about how people of color have been treated in the United States and are fearful that they will be accused of being a racist and be blamed for the oppression of others. Maintaining one's innocence by rejecting and avoiding racial topics are major strategies used to hold on to one's self-image as a good, moral, and decent human being who is innocent of racial bias and discrimination.

Kiselica's reflection is a powerful statement that addresses a major question: Can anyone born and raised in our society not inherit the racial biases of our ancestors and institutions? When we pose this question to our students, surprisingly an overwhelming number say "no." In other words, on an intellectual level they admit that people are products of their social conditioning and that escaping internalizing biases and prejudices is impossible. Yet when racial biases are discussed, these same students have great difficulty entertaining the notion that they have personally inherited racial biases and benefited from the oppression of others, because "racism resides in others, not me!"

Mark's honesty in confronting his own racism is refreshing, and his insights are invaluable to those who wish to become culturally competent counselors and allies in the struggle for equal rights (Chao, Wei, Spanierman, Longo, & Northart, 2015). He is a rarity in academic circles, even rarer because he was willing to put his words on paper for the whole world to read as a means to help others understand the meaning of racism on a human level. Mark's courageous and open exploration of his initial reactions to *CCD* indicates what we have come to learn is a common, intensely emotional experience from many readers. Because *CCD* deals openly, honestly, and passionately with issues of racism, sexism, and homophobia and challenges our belief that we are free of biases, it is likely to evoke defensiveness, resentment, and anger in readers. In Mark's case, he did not allow these reactions to sabotage his own self-exploration and journey to *cultural competence*. And we hope you will not allow your emotional "hot buttons" to deter you from your journey to *cultural competence* as well.

EMOTIONAL INVALIDATION VERSUS AFFIRMATION: FOR MARGINALIZED GROUP MEMBERS

It is clear that the same subject matter in *CCD* often arouses a different emotional response from marginalized group members; for the two students of color, for example, they felt heard, liberated, and validated. They describe the book content as "honest" and "truthful," indicating that their lived experiences were finally validated rather than silenced or ignored. One of the more interesting comments is made by the Latina student that "it felt good to know that I am not crazy." What did she mean by that? Many people of color describe how their thoughts and feelings about race and racism are often ignored, dismissed, negated, or seen as having no basis in fact by majority group members. They are told that they are misreading things, overly sensitive, unduly suspicious or even paranoid when they bring up issues of bias and discrimination; in other words, they are "crazy" to think or feel that way.

As can be seen from the students of color, many marginalized group members react equally strongly as their White counterparts when issues of oppression are raised, especially when their stories of discrimination and pain are minimized or neglected. Their reality of racism, sexism, and homophobia, they contend, is relatively unknown or ignored by those in power because of the discomfort that pervades such topics. Worse yet, many well-intentioned majority persons seem disinclined to hear the personal stories of suffering, humiliation, and pain that accrue to persons of color and other marginalized groups in our society (Sue, 2015). The following quote gives some idea of what it is like for a Black man to live his life day in and day out in a society filled with both covert and overt racist acts that often are invisible to well-intentioned White Americans.

> *I don't think white people, generally, understand the full meaning of racist discriminatory behaviors directed toward Americans of African descent. They seem to see each act of discrimination or any act of violence as an "isolated" event. As a result, most white Americans cannot understand the strong reaction manifested by blacks when such events occur. . . . They forget that in most cases, we live lives of quiet desperation generated by a litany of daily large and small events that, whether or not by design, remind us of our "place" in American society. [Whites] ignore the personal context of the stimulus. That is, they deny the historical impact that a negative act may have on an individual. "Nigger" to a white may simply be an epithet that should be ignored. To most blacks, the term brings into sharp and current focus all kinds of acts of racism—murder, rape, torture, denial of constitutional rights, insults, limited opportunity structure, economic problems, unequal justice under the law and a myriad of. . .other racist and discriminatory acts that occur daily in the lives of most Americans of African descent. (Feagin & Sikes, 2002, pp. 23–24)*

The lived experience of people of color is generally invisible to most White Americans, as this quotation portrays. As we will discuss in Chapter 6, racial, gender, and sexual orientation *microaggressions* are experienced frequently by people of color, women, and LGBTQ persons in their day-to-day interactions with well-intentioned members of the dominant society (Velez, Moradi, & DeBlaere, 2015). _Microaggressions_ are the everyday slights, put-downs, invalidations, and insults directed to socially devalued group members by well-intentioned people who are unaware that they have engaged in such biased and harmful behaviors. A lifetime of _microaggressions_ can have a major harmful impact on the psychological well-being of victims. Note the following narrative provided by an African American man as he describes his day-to-day experiences with _microaggressions_ that label him a dangerous person, a lesser human being, and a potential criminal.

> _It gets so tiring, you know. It sucks you dry. People don't trust you. From the moment I [African American male] wake up, I know stepping out the door, that it will be the same, day after day. The bus can be packed, but no one will sit next to you. . . I guess it may be a good thing because you always get more room, no one crowds you. You get served last . . . when they serve you, they have this phony smile and just want to get rid of you . . . you have to show more ID to cash a check, you turn on the TV and there you always see someone like you, being handcuffed and jailed. They look like you and sometimes you begin to think it is you! You are a plague! You try to hold it in, but sometimes you lose it. Explaining doesn't help. They don't want to hear. Even when they ask, "Why do you have a chip on your shoulder?" Shit . . . I just walk away now. It doesn't do any good explaining. (Sue, 2010, p. 87)_

Here it is important to note the strong and powerful negative emotions and sense of hopelessness that pervades this narrative. The Black man expresses strong anger and resentment toward Whites for how he perceives they are treating him. His daily experiences of racial slights have made him believe that trying to explain to Whites Americans about these indignities would do little good. In fact, he expresses pessimism, rightly or wrongly, that Whites simply do not understand, and worse yet, they do not care to hear his thoughts and feelings about race and racism. He feels hopeless and frustrated about making White Americans understand, and states, "Shit . . . I just walk away now. It doesn't do any good explaining." Although he does not directly mention it, one can surmise that he is also tired and drained at having to constantly deal with the never-ending onslaught of microaggressions. For some people of color, the sense of hopelessness can lead to simply giving up.

Dr. Le Ondra Clark, now an African American psychologist in California, describes her experiences of being one of the few Black students in a graduate program and the feeling of affirmation that flooded her when taking a multicultural counseling course and using *CCD* as the textbook.

I, a native of Southern California, arrived at the University of Wisconsin, Madison, and was eager to learn. I remember the harsh reality I experienced as I confronted the Midwest culture. I felt like I stood out, and I learned quickly that I did. As I walked around the campus and surrounding area, I remember counting on one hand the number of racial and ethnic minorities I saw. I was not completely surprised about this, as I had done some research and was aware that there would be a lack of racial and ethnic diversity on and around campus. However, I was baffled by the paucity of exposure that the 25 members of my master's cohort had to racial and ethnic minority individuals. I assumed that because I was traveling across the country to attend this top-ranked program focused on social justice, everyone else must have been as well. I was wrong.

The majority of my cohort was from the Midwest, and their experiences varied greatly from mine. For example, I remember sitting in my Theories of Counseling course during the first week of the semester. The instructor asked each of us to share about our first exposure to individuals who were racially and ethnically different from ourselves. I thought this was a strange question. . . .I was quite surprised as I listened to what my cohort members shared. I listened to several members share that their first exposure to someone different from them had not occurred until high school and, for some, college. When it came time for me to share, I remember stating that, as a racial and ethnic minority, I had never been in a situation where there was not some type of racial and ethnic diversity. Just sharing this made me feel distant from my cohort, as our different cultural experiences were now plainly highlighted. I remember thinking to myself, "Where am I?" For the first time in my life, I felt as if I was a foreigner, and I badly needed something or someone to relate to.

I did not begin to feel comfortable until I attended the Multicultural Counseling course later that week. Students were assigned a number of textbooks as part of this course, including CCD. . . . *I never imagined a textbook would bring me so much comfort. I vividly remember reading each chapter and vigorously taking notes in the margins. I also remember the energy I felt as I wrote about my reactions to the readings each week. I felt like the book legitimized the experiences of racial and ethnic minorities and helped me understand what I was encountering in my Midwest surroundings. It became a platform from which I could explain my own experience as a racial and ethnic minority from Southern California who was transplanted to the Midwest. The personal stories, concepts, and theories illustrated in* CCD *resonated with me and ultimately helped me overcome my feelings of isolation.* CCD *provided me with the language to engage in intellectual discourse about race, ethnicity, social class, privilege, and disparities. I remember the awareness that swept over the class as we progressed through the textbook. . .I felt that they were beginning to view things through my cultural lens, and I through theirs. We were gaining greater understanding of how our differing cultural realities had shaped us and would impact the work we conducted as therapists. (Sue & Sue, 2013, pp. 17–18)*

Le Ondra's story voices a continuing saga of how persons of color and many marginalized individuals must function in an ethnocentric society that unintentionally invalidates their experiences and enforces silence upon them. She talks about how the text provided a language for her to explain her experiences and how she resonated with its content and meaning. To her, the content of the book tapped into her experiential reality and expressed a *worldview* that is too often ignored or not even discussed in graduate-level programs. Le Ondra found comfort and solace in the book, and she has been fortunate in finding significant others in her life that have validated her thoughts, feelings, and aspirations and allowed her to pursue a social justice direction in counseling. As a person of color, Le Ondra has been able to overcome great odds and to obtain her doctorate in the field without losing her sense of integrity or racial/cultural identity.

A Word of Caution

There is a word of caution that needs to be directed toward students of marginalized groups as they read *CCD* and find it affirming and validating. In teaching the course, for example, we have often encountered students of color who become very contentious and highly outspoken toward White classmates. There are two dangers here that also reveal resistance from students of color to multicultural training. A good example is provided in the reaction of the African American student in the fourth scenario. First, it is clear that the student seems to take delight in seeing his White classmates "squirm" and be uncomfortable. In this respect, he may be taking out his own anger and frustration upon White classmates, and his concern has less to do with helping them understand than hurting them. It is important to express and understand one's anger (it can be healing), but becoming verbally abusive toward another is counterproductive to building rapport and mutual respect. As people of color, for example, we must realize that our enemies are not White Americans, but White supremacy! And, by extension, our enemy is not White Western society, but ethnocentrism.

Second, because the book discusses multicultural issues, some students of color come to believe that multicultural training is only for White students; the implicit assumption is that they know the material already and are the experts on the subject. Although there is some truth to this matter, such a perspective prevents self-exploration and constitutes a form of resistance. As will be seen in Chapter 3, people of color, for example, are not immune from prejudice, bias, and discrimination. Further, such a belief prevents the exploration of interethnic/interracial misunderstandings and biases toward one another. Multicultural training is more than White–African American, White–Latino/a American, White–Asian American, White–Native American, and so on. It is also about African American–Asian American, Asian American–Native American, and Latino/a–Native American relationships; and it includes multiple combinations of other sociodemographic differences like gender, sexual orientation, disability, religious orientation, and so forth. Race, culture, ethnicity, gender, and sexual orientation/identity are about everyone; it is not just a "minority thing."

REFLECTION AND DISCUSSION QUESTIONS

Look at the opening quotes by the four students, then answer these questions.

1. In what ways are the reactions of the White students different from those of students of color? Why do you think this is so?

2. Which of the four reactions can you relate to best? Which reaction can you empathize least with? Why?

3. As you continue reading the material in this text, you are likely to experience strong and powerful reactions and emotions. Being able to understand the meaning of your feelings is the first step to *cultural competence*. Ask yourself, why am I reacting this way? What does it say about my *worldview*, my experiential reality, and my ability to relate to people who differ from me in race, gender, and sexual orientation?

4. As a White counselor working with culturally diverse clients, would you be able to truly relate to the *worldview* being expressed by people of color?

5. As a counselor of color working with White clients, what challenges do you anticipate in the therapeutic relationship with them?

6. What do you think "understanding yourself as a racial/cultural being" means?

RECOGNIZING AND UNDERSTANDING RESISTANCE TO MULTICULTURAL TRAINING

As a counselor or therapist working with clients, you will often encounter psychological resistance or, more accurately, client behaviors that obstruct the therapeutic process or sabotage positive change (Ridley & Thompson, 1999). In therapy sessions, clients may change the topic when recalling unpleasant memories, externalize blame for their own failings, not acknowledge strong feelings of anger toward loved ones, or be chronically late for counseling appointments. All of these client behaviors are examples of resistance or avoidance of acknowledging and confronting unpleasant personal revelations. Oftentimes, these represent unconscious maneuvers to avoid fearful personal insights, to avoid personal responsibility, and to avoid painful feelings. In most cases, resistance masks deeper meanings outside the client's awareness; tardiness for appointments is unacknowledged anger toward therapists, and changing topics in a session is an unconscious deflection of attention away from frightening personal revelations. In many respects, multicultural training can be likened to "therapy" in that trainees are analogous to clients, and trainers are comparable to therapists helping clients with insights about themselves and others.

As we shall see in Chapter 2, the goal of multicultural training is *cultural competence*. It requires trainees to become aware of their own *worldviews*, their assumptions of human behavior, their misinformation and lack of knowledge, and most importantly, their biases and prejudices. Sometimes this journey is a painful one, and trainees will resist moving forward. For trainers or instructors, the job is to help trainees in their self-exploration of themselves as racial/cultural beings, and the meaning it has for their future roles as multicultural counselors. For trainees, being able to recognize, understand, and overcome resistance to multicultural training is important in becoming a culturally competent counselor or therapist.

In the next few sections, we focus upon identifying how resistance manifests itself in training and propose reasons why many well-intentioned trainees find multicultural training disconcerting and difficult to undertake. By so doing, we are hopeful that trainees will attend to their own reactions when reading the text or when participating in classroom dialogues on the subject. Ask yourself the following questions as you continue reading in the next sections and throughout the book.

REFLECTION AND DISCUSSION QUESTIONS

1. What type of reactions or emotions am I feeling as I study the material on multicultural counseling? Am I feeling defensive, angry, anxious, guilty, or helpless? Where are these feelings coming from? Why am I feeling this way, and what does it possibly mean?

2. Does having a different point of view mean I am resisting the multicultural material? List all those reasons that support your stance. List all those reasons that do not support it.

3. How applicable are the resistances outlined in the following sections to me?

4. In what ways may these emotions affect my ability to understand the *worldview* of clients who differ from me, and how might that affect my work?

In work with resistance to diversity training, research reveals how it is likely to be manifested in three forms: *cognitive resistance, emotional resistance,* and *behavioral resistance* (Sue, 2015). Recognizing the manifestation and hidden meanings of resistance is one of the first priorities of multicultural training for both trainees and trainers. For trainees it is finding the courage to confront their own fears and apprehensions, to work through the powerful emotions they are likely to experience, to explore what these feelings mean for them as racial/cultural beings, to achieve new insights about themselves, and to develop multicultural skills and behaviors in their personal lives and as mental health professionals. For trainers it means understanding the nature of trainee resistance, creating a safe but challenging environment for self-exploration, and using intervention strategies that facilitate difficult dialogues on race, gender, sexual orientation, and other topics in the area of diversity.

Cognitive Resistance—Denial

> To date, my biggest discovery is that I didn't really believe that people were being discriminated against because of their race. I could hear them say it, but in my head, I kept running a parallel reason from the White perspective. A Chinese lady says that her party had to wait longer while Whites kept getting seated in front of them. I say, other people had made reservations. A black man says that the receptionist was rude, and made him wait longer because he's Black. I say she had a bad day, and the person he was there to see was busy. A Puerto Rican couple says that the second they drove into Modesto. . .a cop started tailing them, and continued to do so until they reached their hotel, which they opted to drive right on by because they didn't feel safe. I say, there's nothing to be afraid of in Modesto. It's a nice little town. And surely the cop wasn't following you because you're Puerto Rican. I bet your hotel was on his way to the station. I know that for every story in which something bad happens to someone because of their race, I can counter it with a White interpretation. And while I was listening with a sympathetic ear, I silently continued to offer up alternative explanations, benign explanations that kept my world in equilibrium. (Rabow, Venieris & Dhillon, 2014, p. 189)

This student account reveals a pattern of entertaining alternative explanations to the stories told by persons of color about their experiences of prejudice and discrimination. Although the author describes "listening sympathetically," it was clear that he or she silently did not believe that these were instances of racism; other more plausible and "benign" explanations could account for the events. This is not an atypical response for many White trainees when they listen to stories of discrimination from classmates of color (Young, 2003). Because of a strong belief that racism is a thing of the past, that we live in a post-racial society, and that equal access and opportunity are open to everyone, people of color are seen as exaggerating or misperceiving situations. When stories of prejudice and discrimination are told, it directly challenges these cherished beliefs. The student's quote indicates as much when he says that his "benign explanations" preserves his racial reality ("kept my world in equilibrium").

The fact that the student chose not to voice his thoughts is actually an impediment to learning and understanding. In many classrooms, teachers have noted how silence is used by some White students to mask or conceal their true thoughts and feelings about multicultural issues (Sue, 2010; Sue, Torino, Capodilupo, Rivera, & Lin, 2010; van Dijk, 1992). Denial through disbelief, unwillingness to consider alternative scenarios, distortion, fabrication, and rationalizations are all mechanisms frequently used by some trainees during racial conversations to prevent them from thinking about or discussing topics of race and racism in an honest manner (Feagin, 2001; Sue, Rivera, Capodilupo, Lin, & Torino, 2010; van Dijk, 1992). In our teaching in multicultural classes, we have observed many types of denials that work against honest diversity discussions. There are denials that students are prejudiced, that racism still exists, that they are responsible for the oppression of others, that Whites occupy an advantaged and privileged position, that they hold power over people of color, and even denial that they are White (Feagin & Vera, 2002; McIntosh, 2002; Sue, 2010; Tatum, 1992; Todd & Abrams, 2011). This latter point (Whiteness and White privilege) is an especially "hot topic" that will be thoroughly discussed in Chapter 12. As a trainee in this course, you will be presented with opportunities to discuss these topics in greater detail, and explore what these denials may mean about you and your classmates. We hope you will actively participate in such discussions, rather than passively dealing with the material.

Emotional Resistance

Emotional resistance is perhaps the major obstacle to multicultural understanding because it blocks a trainee's ability to acknowledge, understand, and make meaning out of strong and powerful feelings associated with multicultural or diversity topics. The manifestation and dynamics of emotional resistance are aptly described by Sara Winter (1977, p. 24), a White female psychologist. She also provides some insights as to why this occurs; it serves to protect people from having to examine their own prejudices and biases.

> When someone pushes racism into my awareness, I feel **guilty** (that I could be doing so much more); **angry** (I don't like to feel like I'm wrong); **defensive** (I already have two Black friends. . .I worry more

about racism than most whites do—isn't that enough); **turned off** *(I have other priorities in my life with guilt about that thought);* **helpless** *(the problem is so big—what can I do?). I HATE TO FEEL THIS WAY. That is why I minimize race issues and let them fade from my awareness whenever possible.*

The Meaning of Anxiety and Fear

Anxiety is the primary subjective emotion encountered by White trainees exposed to multicultural content and its implications. In one study, it was found that when racial dialogues occurred, nearly all students described fears of verbal participation because they could be misunderstood, or be perceived as racist (Sue et al., 2010). Others went further in describing having to confront the realization that they held stereotypes, biases, and prejudices toward people of color. This insight was very disturbing and anxiety-provoking to them because it directly challenged their self-image of themselves as good, moral, and decent human beings who did not discriminate. Facing this potential awareness creates high levels of anxiety, and often results in maneuvers among students to avoid confronting their meanings.

> *I have a fear of speaking as a member of the dominant group. . . .My feelings of fear stem from not wanting to be labeled as being a racist. I think that fear also stems from the inner fear that I do not want to know what happens to people of color every day. I may not directly be a racist, but not reacting or speaking up to try to change things is a result of my guilt. . . . This is a frightening prospect because I do not want to see the possibility that I have been a racist. Awareness is scary. (Rabow et al., 2014, p. 192)*

In the above quote, the student talks about "fear" being a powerful force in preventing him or her from wanting to learn about the plight of people of color. The strong emotions of guilt and fear, and possibly "being racist" are too frightening to consider. For many students, these feelings block them from exploring and attempting to understand the life experience of people of color. In one major study, for example, silence or not participating in diversity discussions, denials of personal and societal racism, or physically leaving the situation were notable avoidant ploys used by students. The apprehensions they felt affected them physically as well (Sue et al., 2010; Sue, Torino, et al., 2010). Some students described physiological reactions of anxiety like a pounding heart, dry mouth, tense muscles and perspiration. One student stated, *"I tried hard to say something thoughtful and it's hard for me to say, and my heart was pounding when I said it."* Others described feeling intimidated in the discussions, stammering when trying to say something, being overly concerned about offending others, a strong sense of confusion as to what was going on, censoring thoughts or statements that could be misunderstood, reluctance in expressing their thoughts, being overwhelmed by the mix of emotions they felt, and the constriction they heard in their own voices.

These thoughts, feelings, and concerns blocked participants from fully participating in learning and discussing diversity issues because they became so concerned about themselves (turning inward) that they could not freely be open and listen to the messages being communicated by socially devalued group members. Indeed, their whole goal seemed to be to ward off the messages and meanings being communicated to them, which challenged their *worldviews*, and themselves as racial beings, and highlighted their potential roles as oppressors.

The Meaning of Defensiveness and Anger

Although defensiveness and anger are two different emotions, studies seem to indicate a high relationship between the two (Apfelbaum, Sommers, & Norton, 2008; Sue, Torino, et al., 2010; Zou & Dickter, 2013). One represents a protective stance and the other an attempt to strike back at the perpetrator (in many cases statements by people of color). In the opening quotes for this chapter, note that both White students became angry at the authors and accused them of being racist and propagandistic. In absorbing diversity content, many White students described feeling defensive (unfairly accused of being biased or racist, blamed for past racial injustices, and responsible for the current state of race relations). *"I'm tired of hearing 'White people this. . .White people that'. . .why are we always blamed for everything?"*

When the text discusses bias and bigotry, or when classmates of color bring up the issue, for example, some White students seem to interpret these as a personal accusation, and rather than reach out to understand the content, respond in a defensive and protective posture. In many cases, even statements of racial facts and statistics, such as definitions of racism, disparities in income and education, segregation of neighborhoods, hate crime figures, and so forth, arouse defensiveness in many White students. Their defense response to a racial dialogue is seen as protection against (a) criticism ("You just don't get it!"), (b) revealing personal shortcomings ("You are racist!"), or (c) perceived threat to their self-image and egos ("I'm not a racist—I'm a good person."). Because of this stance, we have observed that many White students who feel attacked may engage in behaviors or argumentative ploys that present denials and counterpoints because they view the racial dialogue as a win-lose proposition. Warding off the legitimacy of the points raised by people of color becomes the primary goal rather than listening and attempting to understand the material or point of view.

When White students feel wrongly accused, they may respond with anger and engage in a counterattack when a racial topic arises. It appears that anger stems from two sources: (a) feeling unfairly accused (defensiveness) and/or (b) being told the substance or stance they take is wrong. Many White students may feel offended and perceive the allegations as a provocation or an attack that requires retaliation. Anger may be aroused when students feel offended ("How dare you imply that about me?") or wronged ("I am deeply hurt you see me that way"), or that their good standing is denied ("Don't associate me with racists!"). Unlike defensiveness, which defends one's own stance, anger turns its attention to attacking the threatening behavior of others. Given the choice of the fight-or-flight response, some White students make a choice to take verbal action in stopping the threatening accusations. The strategy used is to discredit the substance of an argument and/or to derogate the communicator, often through a personal attack ("he or she is just an angry Black man or woman"). In many respects, anger and defensiveness may become so aroused that one loses control of one's self-monitoring capacities and the ability to accurately assess the external environment. These latter two abilities are extremely important for effective multicultural counseling.

The Meaning of Guilt, Regret, and Remorse

When discussing diversity issues, many White trainees admit to feeling guilty, although most tend to say that they "are made to feel guilty" by people of color, especially when unjustly accused (Sue, 2003). This statement actually suggests a distancing strategy in localizing guilt as external to oneself rather than one rightfully residing and felt internally. Guilt as an emotion occurs when we believe we have violated an internal moral code, and have compromised our own standards of conduct. The question becomes, why should White trainees feel guilty when topics of race, racism, or Whiteness are discussed? If indeed they are not racist, not responsible for the racial sins of the past, and not responsible for current injustices, then neither would they feel guilt nor could they be made to feel guilty.

Some have coined the term "White guilt" to refer to the individual and collective feelings of culpability experienced by some Whites for the racist treatment of people of color, both historically and currently (Goodman, 2001; Spanierman,

Todd, & Anderson, 2009; Tatum, 1992). In diversity discussions, many White trainees find guilt extremely uncomfortable because it means that they have violated a moral standard and are disinclined to acknowledge their violation. What is that moral standard? Being a good, moral, and decent human being who does not discriminate, being a *nonracist*, living a life that speaks to equality and justice, and being a humane person who treats everyone with respect and dignity are the positive standards that are being breached. Compromising these moral standards and beliefs and acting in ways that violate them bring on bad feelings of guilt and remorse.

Behavioral Resistance

> All the white people I know deplore racism. We feel helpless about racial injustice in society, and we don't know what to do about the racism we sense in our own groups and lives. Persons of other races avoid our groups when they accurately sense the racism we don't see. . . . Few white people socialize or work politically with people of other races, even when our goals are the same. We don't want to be racist—so much of the time we go around trying not to be, by pretending we're not. Yet white supremacy is basic in American social and economic history, and this racist heritage has been internalized by American white people of all classes. We have all absorbed white racism; pretense and mystification only compound the problem. . . . We avoid black people because their presence brings painful questions to mind. Is it OK to talk about watermelon or mention "black coffee?" Should we use black slang and tell racial jokes? How about talking about our experiences in Harlem, or mentioning our black lovers? Should we conceal the fact that our mother still employs a black cleaning lady?. . . We're embarrassedly aware of trying to do our best, but to "act natural" at the same time. No wonder we're more comfortable in all-White situations where these dilemmas don't arise. (Winter, 1977, p. 1)

Although helplessness and hopelessness can rightly be classified as emotions, they also border on providing direct excuses for inaction. Students studying diversity topics often describe two emotions that vary from helplessness (feeling powerless) to hopelessness (despair) when diversity topics are discussed. These feelings are expressed in the quote above by the author when she realizes the vastness and magnitude of individual, institutional and societal racism; how they make themselves felt in all facets of human life; and how deeply racism is ingrained in the individual psyches of people and in the entire nation. Like many students who read *CCD* and take this course, the author's denial of her own biases has begun to crumble, and her self-awareness places her in a very uncomfortable position. Trainees who have come to recognize and own their biased beliefs and prejudices, their roles in perpetuating racism, the pain their obliviousness has inflicted on people of color, and their privileged and advantaged position in society may feel overwhelmed by the magnitude of the problem. This may cause paralysis or inaction. Taking steps to make the "invisible" visible and to eradicate bias and discrimination requires concrete action. As long as the person feels helpless and hopeless, inaction will result.

Although guilt continues over realizing their potential culpability over past deeds, it is compounded by the knowledge that continued inaction on their part allows for the perpetuation of racism in the self and others. Thus taking action is a means to alleviate feelings of guilt. The emotions of helplessness and hopelessness make themselves felt in two different arenas: one is internal (personal change) and the other is external (system change). In becoming aware of one's racial/cultural identity, for example, White students at this juncture of development may begin to ask two primary questions:

First is the question, "How does one change?" What needs to be changed? How does one become a *nonracist* **or an unbiased person**? How do I break the shackles of social conditioning that have taught me that some groups are more worthy than others, and that other groups are less worthy? Many trainees often make these comments: "I don't know where to begin." "If I am not aware of my racism, how do I become aware of it?" "Tell me what I must do to rid myself of these prejudices." "Should I attend more workshops?" "I feel so confused, helpless, impotent, and paralyzed."

The second question is "What must I do to eradicate racism in the broader society?" While self-change requires becoming a *nonracist* person, societal change requires becoming an *antiracist* one. Impacting an ethnocentric mental health delivery system falls into this category. This role means becoming an advocate and actively intervening when injustice makes its presence felt at the individual level (for example, objecting to a racist joke or confronting friends, neighbors, or colleagues about their prejudices) and at the institutional level (for example, opposing biased mental health practices, supporting civil rights issues, making sure a multicultural curriculum is being taught in schools, or openly supporting social justice groups).

Helplessness that is felt by White students in diversity studies, unless adequately deconstructed as to what it means, can easily provide an excuse or rationalization for inaction. What good would it do? I'm only one person, how can I make any difference? The problem is so big, whatever I do will only be a drop in the bucket. Feeling helpless and hopeless are legitimate feelings unless used as an excuse to escape responsibility for taking any form of action. Helplessness is modifiable when these students are provided options and strategies that can be used to increase their awareness and personal growth, and when they are provided with the tools to dismantle racism in our society. Hopefully, this course and the readings will provide you with suggestions of where to begin, especially in mental health practice.

Hopelessness is a feeling of despair and of giving up, a self-belief that no action will matter and no solution will work. Helplessness and hopelessness associated with the need for change and action can be paralytic. The excuse for inaction, and thus the avoidance of racial exploration, does not necessarily reside simply in not knowing what to do, but in very basic fears eloquently expressed by Tatum (2002):

> Fear is a powerful emotion, one that immobilizes, traps words in our throats, and stills our tongues. Like a deer on the highway, frozen in the panic induced by the lights of an oncoming car, when we are afraid it seems that we cannot think, we cannot speak, we cannot move. . . . What do we fear? Isolation from friends and family, ostracism for speaking of things that generate discomfort, rejection by those who may be offended by what we have to say, the loss of privilege or status for speaking in support of those who have been marginalized by society, physical harm caused by the irrational wrath of those who disagree with your stance? (pp. 115–116)

In other words, helplessness and hopelessness are emotions that can provide cover for not taking action. It allows many of us to not change for fear that our actions will result in the negative consequences expressed above. Becoming a multiculturally competent counselor or therapist requires change.

CULTURAL COMPETENCE AND EMOTIONS

There are many other powerful emotions often experienced by students during the journey to *cultural competence*. They include sadness, disappointment, humiliation, blame, invalidation, and so on. These feelings, along with those already discussed, can make their appearance in dialogues on *multiculturalism* or diversity.

The unpleasantness of some emotions and their potentially disturbing meanings makes for avoidance of honest multicultural dialogues and hence a blockage of the learning process. Rather than seeing emotions as a hindrance and barrier to mutual understanding, and rather than shutting them down, allowing them to bubble to the surface actually frees the mind and body to achieve understanding and insight. The cathartic relationship between memories, fears, stereotypic images, and the emotional release of feelings is captured in this passage by Winter (1977, p. 28), who describes her own racial awakening:

> Let me explain this healing process in more detail. We must unearth all the words and memories we generally try not to think about, but which are inside us all the time: "nigger," "Uncle Tom," "jungle bunny," "Oreo"; lynching, cattle prods, castrations, rapists, "black pussy," and black men with their huge penises, and hundreds more. (I shudder as I write.). We need to review three different kinds of material: (1) All our personal memories connected with blackness and black people including everything we can recall hearing or reading; (2) all the racist images and stereotypes we've ever heard, particularly the grossest and most hurtful ones; (3) any race-related things we ourselves said, did or omitted doing which we feel bad about today. . . Most whites begin with a good deal of amnesia. Eventually the memories crowd in, especially when several people pool recollections. Emotional release is a vital part of the process. Experiencing feelings seems to allow further recollections to come. I need persistent encouragement from my companions to continue.

We are aware that the content of this chapter has probably already pushed hot emotional buttons in many of you. For trainees in the dominant group, we ask the following questions: Are you willing to look at yourself, to examine your assumptions, your attitudes, your conscious and unconscious behaviors, the privileges you enjoy as a dominant group member, and how you may have unintentionally treated others in less than a respectful manner? For socially marginalized group members, we ask whether you are willing to confront your own biases and prejudices toward dominant group members, be honest in acknowledging your own biases toward other socially devalued group members, and work to build bridges of mutual understanding and respect for all groups.

Trainees who bravely undertake the journey to *cultural competence* eventually realize that change is a lifelong process, and that it does not simply occur in a workshop, classroom, or singular event. It is a monumental task, but the rewards are many when we are successful. A whole body of literature supports the belief that encountering diverse points of view, being able to engage in honest diversity conversations, and successfully acknowledging and integrating differing perspectives lead to an expansion of critical consciousness (Gurin, Dey, Hurtado, & Gurin, 2002; Jayakumar, 2008). On a cognitive level, many have observed that cross-racial interactions and dialogues, for example, are a necessity to increase racial literacy, expand the ability to critically analyze racial ideologies, and dispel stereotypes and misinformation about other groups (Bolgatz, 2005; Ford, 2012; Pollock, 2004; Stevens, Plaut, & Sanchez-Burks, 2008). On an emotional level, trainees of successful diversity training report less intimidation and fear of differences, an increased compassion for others, a broadening of their horizons, appreciation of people of all colors and cultures, and a greater sense of belonging and connectedness with all groups (APA Presidential Task Force, 2012; Bell, 2002; President's Initiative on Race, 1999; Sue, 2003).

In closing, we implore you not to allow your initial negative feelings to interfere with your ultimate aim of learning from this text as you journey toward *cultural competence*. Sad to say, this empathic ability is blocked when readers react with defensiveness and anger upon hearing the life stories of those most disempowered in our society. We have always believed that our worth as human beings is derived from the collective relationships we hold with all people; that we are people of emotions, intuitions, and spirituality; and that the lifeblood of people can be understood only through lived realities. Although we believe strongly in the value of science and the importance psychology places on empiricism, *Counseling the Culturally Diverse* is based on the premise that a profession that fails to recognize the heart and soul of the human condition is a discipline that is spiritually and emotionally bankrupt. As such, this book not only touches on the theory and practice of multicultural counseling and psychotherapy, but also reveals the hearts and souls of our diverse clienteles.

 IMPLICATIONS FOR CLINICAL PRACTICE

1. Listen and be open to stories of those most disempowered in this society. Counseling has always been about listening to our clients. Don't allow your emotional reactions to negate their voices because you become defensive.

2. Know that although you were not born wanting to be racist, sexist, or hetero-sexist, or to be prejudiced against any other group, your cultural conditioning has imbued certain biases and prejudices in you. No person or group is free from inheriting the biases of this society.

3. Understand and acknowledge your intense emotions and what they mean for you. *CCD* speaks about unfairness, racism, sexism, and prejudice, making some feel accused and blamed. The "isms" of our society are not pleasant topics, and we often feel unfairly accused.

4. It is important that helping professionals understand how they may still benefit from the past actions of their predecessors and continue to reap the benefits of the present social/educational arrangements.

5. Understand that multicultural training requires more than book learning. In your journey to *cultural competence*, it is necessary to supplement your intellectual development with experiential reality.

6. Don't be afraid to explore yourself as a racial/cultural being. An overwhelming number of mental health practitioners believe they are good, decent, and moral people. Because most of us would not intentionally discriminate, we often find great difficulty in realizing that our belief systems and actions may have oppressed others.

7. Open dialogue—to discuss and work through differences in thoughts, beliefs, and values—is crucial to becoming culturally competent. It is healthy when we are allowed to engage in free dialogue with one another. To a large extent, unspoken thoughts and feelings serve as barriers to open and honest dialogue about the pain of discrimination and how each and every one of us perpetuates bias through our silence or obliviousness.

8. Finally, continue to use these suggestions in reading throughout the text. What emotions or feelings are you experiencing? Where are they coming from? Are they blocking your understanding of the material? What do these reactions mean for you personally and as a helping professional?

SUMMARY

Students who take a course on multicultural counseling and mental health issues have almost universally felt both positive and negative feelings that affect their ability to learn about diversity issues. Those from marginalized groups often feel validated by the content while majority group members often feel a range of emotions like defensiveness, anxiety, anger, and guilt. It is important not to allow these nested or embedded emotions to go unacknowledged, or to avoid exploring the psychological meanings they may have for trainees. The journey to becoming culturally competent therapists is filled with obstacles to self-exploration, to understanding oneself as a racial/cultural being, and to understanding the *worldview* of those who differ from others in terms of race, gender, ethnicity, sexual orientation and other sociodemographic dimensions. The subject matter in this book requires students to explore their biases and prejudices, a task that often evokes strong resistance from both majority and oppressed group members.

It is important to recognize personal resistance to the material, to explore its meaning, and to learn about yourself and others. Sometimes what is revealed about you may prove disturbing, but having the courage to continue is necessary to becoming a culturally competent counselor or therapist. Recognizing the manifestation and hidden meanings of resistance is one of the first priorities of multicultural training for both trainees and trainers. For trainees it is finding the courage to confront their own fears and apprehensions, to work through the powerful emotions they are likely to experience, to explore what these feelings mean for them as racial/cultural beings, to achieve new insights about themselves, and to develop multicultural skills and behaviors in their personal lives and as mental health professionals. For trainers it means understanding the nature of trainee resistance, creating a safe but challenging environment for self-exploration, and using intervention strategies that facilitate difficult dialogues on race, gender, sexual orientation, and other sociodemographic dimensions. This chapter is specifically written to help readers understand and overcome their emotive reactions to the substance of the text and the course they are about to take.

GLOSSARY TERMS

Antiracist

Behavioral resistance (to multicultural training)

Cognitive resistance (to multicultural training)

Cultural competence

Emotional affirmation

Emotional invalidation

Emotional resistance (to multicultural training)

Emotional self-revelation

Microaggressions

Multiculturalism

Nested/Embedded emotions

Nonracist

Self-reflection

Worldview

REFERENCES

American Psychological Association (APA) Presidential Task Force on Preventing Discrimination and Promoting Diversity. (2012). *Dual pathways to a better America: Preventing discrimination and promoting diversity.* Washington, DC: American Psychological Association.

Apfelbaum, E. P., Sommers, S. R., & Norton, M. I. (2008). Seeing race and seeming racist: Evaluating strategic colorblindness in social interaction. *Journal of Personality and Social Psychology, 95,* 918–932.

Bell, L. A. (2002). Sincere fictions: The pedagogical challenges of preparing White teachers for multicultural classrooms. *Equity and Excellence in Education, 35,* 236–244.

Bolgatz, J. (2005). *Talking race in the classroom.* New York, NY: Educators College Press.

Chao, R. C., Wei, M., Spanierman, L., Longo, J., & Northart, D. (2015). White racial attitudes and white empathy: The moderation of openness to diversity. *Counseling Psychologist, 43,* 94–120.

Feagin, J. R. (2001). *Racist America: Roots, current realities, and future reparations.* New York, NY: Routledge.

Feagin, J. R., & Sikes, M. P. (1994). *Living with racism.* Boston, MA: Bacon.

Feagin, J. R., & Vera, H. (2002). Confronting one's own racism. In P. S. Rothenberg (Ed.), *White privilege* (pp. 121–125). New York, NY: Worth.

Ford, K. A. (2012). Shifting White ideological scripts: The educational benefits of inter- and intraracial curricular dialogues on the experiences of White college students. *Journal of Diversity in Higher Education, 5,* 138–158.

Goodman, D. J. (2001). *Promoting diversity and social justice: Educating people from privileged groups.* Thousand Oaks, CA: Sage.

Gurin, P., Dey, E. L., Hurtado, S., & Gurin, G. (2002). Diversity and higher education: Theory and impact on educational outcomes. *Harvard Educational Review, 72,* 330–366.

Jayakumar, U. M. (2008). Can higher education meet the needs of an increasingly diverse and global society? Campus diversity and cross-cultural workforce competencies. *Harvard Educational Review, 78,* 615–651.

Kiselica, M. S. (1999). Confronting my own ethnocentrism and racism: A process of pain and growth. *Journal of Counseling and Development, 77,* 14–17.

McIntosh, P. (2002). White privilege: Unpacking the invisible knapsack. In P. S. Rothenberg (Ed.), *White privilege* (pp. 97–101). New York, NY: Worth.

Pollock, M. (2004). *Colormute: Race talk dilemmas in an American high school.* Princeton, NJ: Princeton University Press.

Ponterotto, J. G., Fingerhut, E. S., & McGuinness, R. (2013). Legends of the field: Influential scholars in multicultural counseling. *Psychological Reports, 111*(2), 364–382.

Ponterotto, J. G., & Sabnani, H. B. (1989). "Classics" in multicultural counseling: A systematic five-year content analysis. *Journal of Multicultural Counseling and Development, 17,* 23–37.

President's Initiative on Race. (1999). *Pathways to one America in the 21st century.* Washington, DC: U.S. Government Printing Office.

Rabow, J., Venieris, P. Y., & Dhillon, M. (2014). *Ending racism in America: One microaggression at a time.* Dubuque, IA: Kendall Hunt.

Ratts, M. J., & Pedersen, P. B. (2014). *Counseling for multiculturalism and social justice.* Alexandria, VA: American Counseling Association.

Ridley, R. R., & Thompson, C. E. (1999). Managing resistance to diversity training: A social systems perspective. In M. S. Kiselica (Ed.), *Prejudice and racism* (pp. 3–24). Alexandria, VA: American Counseling Association.

Spanierman, L. B., Todd, N. R., & Anderson, C. J. (2009). Psychosocial costs of racism to Whites: Understanding patterns among university students. *Journal of Counseling Psychology, 56,* 239–252.

Stevens, F. G., Plaut, V. C., & Sanchez-Burks, J. (2008). Unlocking the benefits of diversity. *Journal of Applied Behavioral Science, 44,* 116–133.

Sue, D. W. (2003). *Overcoming our racism: The journey to liberation.* San Francisco, CA: Jossey-Bass.

Sue, D. W. (2010). *Microaggressions in everyday life: Race, gender, and sexual orientation.* Hoboken, NJ: Wiley.

Sue, D. W. (2011). The challenge of White dialectics: Making the "invisible" visible. *Counseling Psychologist, 39,* 414–423.

Sue, D. W. (2015). *Race talk and the conspiracy of silence. Understanding and facilitating difficult dialogues on race.* Hoboken, NJ: Wiley.

Sue, D. W., & Sue, D. (2013). *Counseling the culturally diverse: Theory and practice* (6th ed.). Hoboken, NJ: Wiley.

Sue, D. W., Rivera, D. P., Capodilupo, C. M., Lin, A. I., & Torino, G. C. (2010). Racial dialogues and White trainee fears: Implications for education and training. *Cultural Diversity and Ethnic Minority Psychology, 16,* 206–214.

Sue, D. W., Torino, G. C., Capodilupo, C. M., Rivera, D. P., & Lin, A. I. (2010). How White faculty perceive and react to classroom dialogues on race: Implications for education and training. *Counseling Psychologist, 37,* 1090–1115.

Tatum, B. D. (1992). Talking about race, learning about racism: The application of racial identity development theory in the classroom. *Harvard Educational Review, 62,* 1–24.

Tatum, B. D. (2002). Breaking the silence. In P. S. Rothenberg (Ed.), *White privilege* (pp. 115–120). New York, NY: Worth.

Todd, N. R., & Abrams, E. M. (2011). White dialectics: A new framework for theory, research and practice with White students. *Counseling Psychologist, 39,* 353–395.

van Dijk, T. A. (1992). Discourse and the denial of racism. *Discourse and Society, 3,* 87–118.

Velez, B. L., Moradi, B., & DeBlaere, G. (2015). Multiple oppressions and the mental health of sexual minority Latina/o individuals. *Counseling Psychologist, 43,* 7–38.

Wendt, D. C., Gone, J. P., & Nagata, D. K. (2015). Potentially harmful therapy and multicultural counseling: Bridging two disciplinary discourses. *Counseling Psychologist, 43,* 334–358.

Winter, S. (1977). Rooting out racism. *Issues in Radical Therapy, 17,* 24–30.

Young, G. (2003). Dealing with difficult classroom dialogues. In P. Bronstein & K. Quina (Eds.), *Teaching gender and multicultural awareness* (pp. 360–437). Washington, DC: American Psychological Association.

Zou, L. X., & Dickter, C. L. (2013). Perceptions of racial confrontation: The role of color blindness and comment ambiguity. *Cultural Diversity and Ethnic Minority Psychology, 19,* 92–96.

The Superordinate Nature of Multicultural Counseling and Therapy

Chapter Objectives

1. Compare and contrast similarities and differences between "traditional counseling/clinical practice" and culturally sensitive counseling.

2. Understand the *Etic* and *Emic* orientation to *multicultural counseling*.

3. Become cognizant of differences between counseling/clinical competence and *multicultural counseling* competence.

4. Identify Eurocentric assumptions inherent in our standards of clinical practice.

5. Discuss and understand the characteristics of the three levels of personal identity.

6. Develop awareness of possible differences in counseling culturally diverse clients who differ in race, gender, sexual orientation, and other group identities.

7. Provide examples of ways that other special populations may constitute a distinct cultural group.

8. Define *multicultural counseling and therapy, cultural competence*, and *cultural humility*.

9. Explain how *cultural humility* is different from *cultural competence*.

The following is the third counseling session between Dr. D. (a White counselor) and Gabriella, a 29-year-old single Latina, who was born and raised in Brazil but came to the United States when she was 10 years old.

Dr. D: So how did it go last week with Russell (White boyfriend of 6 months).

Gabriella: Okay, I guess (seems withdrawn and distracted).

Dr. D: You don't sound too sure to me.

Gabriella: What do you mean?

Dr. D: Well, from the last session, I understood that you were going to talk to him [Russell] about your decision to live together, but that you wanted to clarify what moving into his apartment meant for him.

Gabriella: I didn't get a chance to talk about it. I was going to bring it up, but I had another attack, so I didn't get a chance. It was awful (begins to fidget in the chair)! Why does this always happen to me?

Dr. D: Tell me what happened.

Gabriella: I don't know. I had a disagreement with him, a big stupid argument over Jennifer Lopez's song "Booty".

Dr. D: "Booty"?

Gabriella: Yeah, he kept watching the video over and over on the computer. He loves the song, but I find it vulgar.

Dr. D: Lots of songs press the limits of decency nowadays. . . .Tell me about the attack.

Gabriella: I don't know what happened. I lost control and started screaming at him. I threw dishes at him and started to cry. I couldn't breathe. Then it got really bad, and I could feel the heat rise in my chest. I was scared to death. Everything felt unreal and I felt like fainting. My mother used to suffer from similar episodes of *ataques*. Have I become like her?. . . .God I hope not!

Dr. D: Sounds like you had another panic attack. Did you try the relaxation exercises we practiced?

Gabriella: No, how could I? I couldn't control myself. It was frightening. I started to cry and couldn't stop. Russell kept telling me to calm down. We finally made up and got it on.

Dr. D: I'm glad things got smoothed over. But you always say that you have no control over your attacks. We've spent lots of time on learning how to manage your panic attacks by nipping them in the bud. . . before they get out of control. Maybe some medication might help.

Gabriella: Yes, I know, but it doesn't seem to do any good. I just couldn't help it.

Dr. D: Did you try?

Gabriella: Do you think I enjoy the attacks (shouts)? How come I always feel worse when I come here? I feel blamed. . .Russell says I'm a typical emotional Latina. What am I to do? I come here to get help, and I just get no understanding (stated with much anger).

Dr. D: You're angry at me because I don't seem to be supportive of your predicament, and you think I'm blaming you. But I wonder if you have ever asked yourself how you contribute to the situation as well. Do you think that fighting over a song is the real issue here?

Gabriella: Maybe not, but I just don't feel like you understand.

Dr. D: Understand what?

Gabriella: Understand what it is like to be a Latina woman dealing with all those stereotypes. My parents don't want me living with Russell. . .they think he benefits from having sex with no commitment to marriage, and that I'm a fool. They think he is selfish and just wants a Latina. . . .like a fetish. . . .

Dr. D: I think it's more important what **you** think and want for yourself, not what your parents would like you to do. Be your own person. And we've talked about cultural differences before, in the first session, remember? Cultural differences are important, but it's more important to recognize that we are all human beings. Granted, you and I are different from one another, but most people share many more similarities than differences.

Gabriella: Yes, but can you really understand what's it like to be a Latina, the problems I deal with in my life? Aren't they important?

Dr. D: Of course I can. And of course they [differences] are. . .but let me tell you, I've worked with many Latinos in my practice. When it comes right down to it, we are all the same under the skin.

Gabriella: (period of silence)

Dr. D: Now, let's go back and talk about your panic attacks and what you can do to prevent and reduce them.

REFLECTION AND DISCUSSION QUESTIONS

1. What are your thoughts and feelings about the counseling encounter between Dr. D. and Gabriella?

2. Do you think that Dr. D. demonstrated cultural awareness? Is this an example of "good counseling"? If not, why not?

3. When Gabriella described her episodes as *ataques*, do you know what is meant?

4. What are the potential counseling and cultural issues in this case?

5. Is it important for the counselor to know what the song "Booty" is about?

6. When the parents suggest that their daughter might be a "fetish," what could they possibly mean? Is it important?

7. What images of Latinas exist in our society? How might they affect Gabriella's relationship with Russell?

8. If you were the counselor, how would you have handled the situation?

Culturally competent care has become a major force in the helping professions (American Psychological Association, 2003; Arredondo, Toporek, Brown, Jones, Locke, Sanchez, & Stadler, 1996; CACREP, 2015; Cornish, Schreier, Nadkarni, Metzger, & Rodolfa, 2010; D. W. Sue, Arredondo, & McDavis, 1992). The therapy session between Dr. D. and Gabriella illustrates the importance of cultural awareness and sensitivity in mental health practice. There is a marked *worldview* difference between that of the White therapist and the Latina client. In many cases, these differences reflect the therapist's (a) belief in the universality of the human condition, (b) belief that disorders are similar and cut across societies, (c) lack of *knowledge* of Latina/o culture, (d) task orientation, (e) failure to pick up clinical clues provided by the client, (f) not being aware of the influence of sociopolitical forces in the lives of marginalized group members, and (g) lack of openness to professional limitations. Let us briefly explore these factors in analyzing the previous transcript.

CULTURE-UNIVERSAL (ETIC) VERSUS CULTURE-SPECIFIC (EMIC) FORMULATIONS

First and foremost, it is important to note that Dr. D. is not a bad counselor per se, but like many helping professionals is culture-bound and adheres to Euro-American assumptions and values that encapsulate and prevent him from seeing beyond his Western therapeutic training (Comas-Diaz, 2010). One of the primary issues raised in this case relates to the *etic* (culturally universal) versus *emic* (culturally specific) perspectives in psychology and mental health. Dr. D. operates from the former position. His training has taught him that disorders such as panic attacks, depression, schizophrenia, and sociopathic behaviors appear in all cultures and societies; that minimal modification in their diagnosis and treatment is required; and that Western concepts of normality and abnormality can be considered universal and equally applicable across cultures (Arnett, 2009; Howard, 1992; Suzuki, Kugler, & Aguiar, 2005). Many multicultural psychologists, however, operate from an *emic* position and challenge these assumptions. In Gabriella's case, they argue that lifestyles, cultural values, and *worldviews* affect the expression and determination of behavior disorders (Ponterotto, Utsey, & Pedersen, 2006). They stress that all theories of human development arise within a cultural context and that using the EuroAmerican values of normality and abnormality may be culture-bound and biased (Locke & Bailey, 2014). From this case, we offer six tentative cultural/clinical observations that may help Dr. D. in his work with Gabriella.

Cultural Concepts of Distress

It is obvious that Dr. D. has concluded that Gabriella suffers from a panic disorder and that her attacks fulfill criteria set forth in the *Diagnostic and Statistical Manual of Mental Disorders* (*DSM-5*, American Psychiatric Association, 2013). When Gabriella uses the term *ataques* to describe her emotional outbursts, episodes of crying, feeling faint, somatic symptoms ("heat rising in her chest"), feeling of depersonalization (unreal) and loss of control, a Western-trained counseling/mental health professional may very likely diagnose a panic attack. Is a panic attack diagnosis the same as *ataques*? Is it simply a Latin American translation of an anxiety disorder? We now recognize that *ataque de nervios* ("attack of the nerves") is a cultural syndrome, occurs often in Latin American countries (in individuals of Latina/o descent), and is distinguishable from panic attacks (American Psychiatric Association, 2013). Cultural syndromes that do not share a one-to-one correspondence with psychiatric disorders in *DSM-5* have been found in South Asia, Zimbabwe, Haiti, China, Mexico, Japan, and other places. Failure to consider the cultural context and manifestation of disorders often result in inaccurate diagnosis and inappropriate treatment (D. Sue, Sue, Sue, & Sue, 2016). Chapter 10 will discuss these cultural syndromes and treatments in greater detail.

Acknowledging Group Differences

Dr. D. seems to easily dismiss the importance of Gabriella's Latina/o culture as a possible barrier to their therapeutic work together. She wonders aloud, for example, whether he can understand her as a Latina (being a racial/cultural being), and the unique problems she faces as a person of color. Dr. D. attempts to reassure Gabriella that he can in several ways. He stresses (a) that people are more similar than different, (b) that we are all "human beings," (c) that he has much experience in working with Latinos, and (d) that everyone is the "same under the skin." Although there is much truth to these statements, he has unintentionally negated the racialized experiences of Gabriella, and the importance that she places on her racial/ethnic identity. In *multicultural counseling*, this response often creates an impasse to therapeutic relationships (Arredondo, Gallardo-Cooper, Delgado-Romero, & Zapata, 2014). Note the long period of silence by Gabriella, for example, after Dr. D's response. He apparently misinterprets the silence as agreement. We will return to this important point shortly.

Being Aware of Collectivistic Cultures

It is obvious that Dr. D. operates from an individualistic approach and values individualism, autonomy, and independence. He communicates to Gabriella that it is more important for her to decide what she wants for herself than being concerned about her parents' desires. Western European concepts of mental health stress the importance of independence and "being your own person" because it leads to healthy development and maturity, rather than dependency (in Gabriella's case "pathological family enmeshment"). Dr. D. fails to consider that in many collectivistic cultures such as Latino or Asian American, independence may be considered undesirable and interdependence is valued (Ivey, Ivey, & Zalaquett, 2014; Kail & Cavanaugh, 2013). When the norms and values of Western European concepts of mental health are imposed universally upon culturally diverse clients, there is the very real danger of cultural oppression, resulting in "blaming the victim."

Attuning to Cultural and Clinical Clues

There are many cultural clues in this therapeutic encounter that might have provided Dr. D. with additional insights into Latina/o culture and its meaning for culturally competent assessment, diagnosis, and treatment. We have already pointed out his failure to explore more in depth Gabriella's description of her attacks (*ataques de nervios*), and her concern about her parents' approval. But many potential sociocultural and sociopolitical clues were present in their dialogue as well. For example, Dr. D. failed to follow up on why the song "Booty" by Jennifer Lopez precipitated an argument, and what the parents' use of the term "fetish" shows us about how Russell may view their daughter.

The 4-minute music video *Booty* shows Jennifer Lopez and Iggy Azalea with many anonymous beauties grinding their derrieres (booties) in front of the camera while chanting "Big, big booty, big, big booty" continuously. It has been described as provocative, exploitative and "soft porn." Nevertheless, the video has become a major hit. And while Dr. D. might be correct in saying that the argument couldn't possibly be over a song (implying that there is a more meaningful reason), he doesn't explore the possible cultural or political implications for Gabriella. Is there meaning in her finding the song offensive and Russell's enjoyment of it? Is there a relationship between the sexiness of big butts to the terms "fetish" and "emotionality" that upset Gabriella? We know, for example, that Latina and Asian women are victims of widespread societal stereotyping that objectifies them as sex objects. Could this be something that Gabriella is wrestling with? At some level, does she suspect that Russell is only attracted to her because of these stereotypes, as her parents' use of the word "fetish" implies? In not exploring these issues, or worse yet, not being aware of them, Dr. D. may have lost a valuable opportunity to help Gabriella gain insight into her emotional distress.

Seeing the Forest through the Trees

These important questions are left unanswered because the therapist fails to see the forest through the trees. Dr. D. appears to suffer from "tunnel vision" and seems more task oriented than people oriented. His major goal seems to be "identify the problem (panic attacks) and solve it (relaxation exercises, medication, etc.)." Who Gabriella is as a flesh and blood person seems less important than the problem. In its attempt to mimic the physical sciences, the discipline of mental health practice has often stressed the importance of objectivity, rational thinking, and problem solving—identify the problem and solve it. Although valuable in many respects, this approach may clash with the Latina/o concept of *personalismo*, in which people relationships are equally if not more important than tasks. Many Latina/o, for example, have described Western-trained counselors or therapists as "remote," "aloof," or "cold" (Arredondo et al. 2014; Comas-Diaz, 2010). There are some indications that Gabriella may view Dr. D. in this manner. His task orientation regardless of what she does or says makes her concerns remain invisible; he fails to explore the many clues provided to him by Gabriella. For example, he mistakes her silence for agreement, fails to inquire into the video-song, *Booty*, dismisses her cultural concerns in favor of finding solutions, and implies that she is responsible for her plight. An interesting observation of how his rigid goal-directness blinds him to what Gabriella says is seen in the description of the aftermath of her attack: "We finally made up and got it on." The therapist interprets the statement as Gabriella and Russell "smoothing things over," but is there more to this statement? What does she mean by "got it on"?

Balancing the Culture-Specific and Culture-Universal Orientations

Throughout our analysis of Dr. D., we have made the point that culture and life experiences affect the expression of abnormal behavior and that counselors need to attune to these sociodemographic variables. Some have even proposed the use of culture-specific strategies in counseling and therapy (Ivey, Ivey, & Zalaquett, 2014; Parham, Ajamu, & White, 2011). Such professionals point out that current guidelines and standards of clinical practice are culture bound and often inappropriate for racial/ethnic minority groups. Which view is correct? Should treatment approaches be based on cultural universality or *cultural relativism*? Few mental health professionals today embrace the extremes of either position, although most gravitate toward one or the other.

Proponents of cultural universality focus on disorders and their consequent treatments and minimize cultural factors, whereas proponents of *cultural relativism* focus on the culture and on how the disorder is manifested and treated within it. Both views have validity. It would be naive to believe that no disorders cut across different cultures or share universal characteristics. Likewise, it is naive to believe that the relative frequencies and manners of symptom formation for various disorders do not reflect the dominant cultural values and lifestyles of a society. Nor would it be beyond our scope to entertain the notion that various diverse groups may respond better to culture-specific therapeutic strategies. A more fruitful approach to these opposing views might be to address the following two questions: (a) What is universal in human behavior that is also relevant to counseling and therapy? and (b) What is the relationship between cultural norms, values, and attitudes, on the one hand, and the manifestation of behavior disorders and their treatments, on the other?

THE NATURE OF MULTICULTURAL COUNSELING COMPETENCE

Clinicians have oftentimes asserted that "good counseling is good counseling" and that good clinical practice subsumes *cultural competence*, which is simply a subset of good clinical *skills*. In this view, they would make a strong case that if Dr. D. had simply exercised these therapeutic *skills*, he would have worked effectively with Gabriella. Our contention, however, is that *cultural competence* is superordinate to counseling competence. How Dr. D. worked with Gabriella contains the seeds of a therapeutic bias that makes him susceptible to cultural errors in therapy. Traditional definitions of counseling and psychotherapy are culture bound because they are defined from a primarily White Western-European perspective (Gallardo, 2014). Let us briefly explore the rationale for our position.

The Harm of Cultural Incompetence

Although there are disagreements over the definition of *cultural competence*, many of us know *cultural incompetence* when we see it; we recognize it by its horrendous outcomes or by the human toll it takes on our marginalized clients. For some time now, multicultural specialists have described Western-trained counseling/mental health professionals in very unflattering terms: (a) They are insensitive to the needs of their culturally diverse clients; do not accept, respect, and understand cultural differences; are arrogant and contemptuous; and have little understanding of their prejudices (Ridley, 2005; Thomas & Sillen, 1972); (b) clients of color, women, and gays and lesbians frequently complain that they feel abused, intimidated, and harassed by nonminority personnel (Atkinson, Morten, & Sue, 1998; President's Commission on Mental Health, 1978); (c) discriminatory practices in mental health delivery systems are deeply embedded in the ways in which the services are organized and in how they are delivered to minority populations and are reflected in biased diagnoses and treatment, in indicators of dangerousness, and in the type of people occupying decision-making roles (Parham et al., 2011; Cross, Bazron, Dennis, & Isaacs, 1989); and (d) mental health professionals continue to be trained in programs in which the issues of ethnicity, gender, and sexual orientation are ignored, regarded as deficiencies, portrayed in stereotypic ways, or included as an afterthought (Ponterotto et al., 2006; Ratts & Pedersen, 2014).

From our perspective, counseling/mental health professionals have difficulty functioning in a culturally competent manner. Rather, they have functioned in a monoculturally competent manner with only a limited segment of the population (White, male, and straight Euro-Americans), but even that has become a topic of debate (Ridley & Mollen, 2011). We submit that much of the current therapeutic practice taught in graduate programs derives mainly from clinical experience and research with middle- to upper-class Whites (Ridley, 2005). Even though our profession has advocated moving into the realm of evidence-based practice (EBP), little evidence exists that they are applicable to racial/ethnic minorities (Atkinson, Bui, & Mori, 2001; D. W. Sue, 2015). A review of studies on EBP reveals few, if any, on racial minority populations, which renders assumptions of external validity questionable when applied to people of color (Atkinson et al., 1998; Hall, 2001; S. Sue, 1999). If we are honest with ourselves, we can conclude only that many of our standards of professional competence are derived primarily from the values, belief systems, cultural assumptions, and traditions of the larger (Eurocentric) society. We will, however, in Chapter 9 attempt to summarize multicultural evidence-based practices that have recently begun to work their way into the scientific literature.

The Superordinate Nature of Cultural Competence

As we have discussed, values of individualism and psychological mindedness and using rational approaches to solve problems have much to do with how competence is defined. Many of our colleagues continue to hold firmly to the belief that "good counseling is good counseling," dismissing in their definitions the centrality of culture. The problem with traditional definitions of counseling, therapy, and mental health practice is that they arose from monocultural and ethnocentric norms that excluded other cultural groups. Mental health professionals must realize that "good counseling" uses White EuroAmerican norms that exclude most of the world's population. In a hard-hitting article, Arnett (2009) indicates that psychological research, which forms the *knowledge* base of our profession, focuses on Americans who constitute only 5 percent of the world's population. He concludes that the *knowledge* of human behavior neglects 95 percent of the world's population and is an inadequate representation of humanity. Thus it is clear to us that the more superordinate and inclusive concept is that of *multicultural counseling* competence, not merely clinical or counseling competence. Standards of helping derived from such a philosophy and framework are inclusive and offer the broadest and most accurate view of *cultural competence*.

A TRIPARTITE FRAMEWORK FOR UNDERSTANDING THE MULTIPLE DIMENSIONS OF IDENTITY

All too often, counseling and psychotherapy seem to ignore the group dimension of human existence. For example, a White counselor who works with an African American client might intentionally or unintentionally avoid acknowledging the racial or cultural background of the person by stating, "We are all the same under the skin" or "Apart from your racial background, we are all unique." We have already indicated possible reasons why this happens, but such avoidance tends to negate an intimate aspect of the client's group identity (Apfelbaum, Sommers, & Norton, 2008; Neville, Gallardo & Sue, in press). Dr. D.'s responses toward Gabriella seem to have had this effect. These forms of microinvalidations will be discussed more fully in Chapter 6. As a result of these invalidations, a client of color might feel misunderstood and resentful toward the helping professional, hindering the effectiveness of the counseling. Besides unresolved personal issues arising from counselors, the assumptions embedded in Western forms of therapy exaggerate the chasm between therapists and culturally diverse clients.

First, the concepts of counseling and psychotherapy are uniquely EuroAmerican in origin, as they are based on certain philosophical assumptions and values that are strongly endorsed by Western civilizations. On the one side are beliefs that people are unique and that the psychosocial unit of operation is the individual; on the other side are beliefs that clients are the same and that the goals and techniques of counseling and therapy are equally applicable across all groups. Taken to its extreme, this latter approach nearly assumes that persons of color, for example, are White, and that race and culture are insignificant variables in counseling and psychotherapy (D. W. Sue, 2010). Statements such as "There is only one race, the human race" and "Apart from your racial/cultural background, you are no different from me" are indicative of the tendency to avoid acknowledging how race, culture, and other group dimensions may influence identity, values, beliefs, behaviors, and the perception of reality (Lum, 2011; D. W. Sue, 2015). Indeed, in an excellent conceptual/analytical article proposing a new and distinct definition of *counseling competence*, Ridley, Mollen, and Kelly (2011) conclude that "counseling competence is multicultural counseling competence" and that "competent counselors consistently incorporate cultural data into counseling, and they must be careful never to relegate cultural diversity to the status of a sidebar" (p. 841).

Second, related to the negation of race, we have indicated that a most problematic issue deals with the inclusive or exclusive nature of *multiculturalism*. A number of psychologists have indicated that an inclusive definition of *multiculturalism* (one that includes gender, ability/disability, sexual orientation, and so forth) can obscure the understanding and study of race as a powerful dimension of human existence (Carter, 2005; Helms & Richardson, 1997). This stance is not intended to minimize the importance of the many cultural dimensions of human identity but rather emphasizes the greater discomfort that many psychologists experience in dealing with issues of race rather than with other sociodemographic differences (D. W. Sue, Lin, Torino, Capodilupo, & Rivera, 2009). As a result, race becomes less salient and allows us to avoid addressing problems of racial prejudice, racial discrimination, and systemic racial oppression. This concern appears to have great legitimacy. We have noted, for example, that when issues of race are discussed in the classroom, a mental health agency, or some other public forum, it is not uncommon for participants to refocus the dialogue on differences related to gender, socioeconomic status, or religious orientation.

On the other hand, many groups often rightly feel excluded from the multicultural debate and find themselves in opposition to one another. Thus enhancing multicultural understanding and sensitivity means balancing our understanding of the sociopolitical forces that dilute the importance of race, on the one hand, and our need to acknowledge the existence of other group identities related to social class, gender, ability/disability, age, religious affiliation, and sexual orientation, on the other (Anderson & Middleton, 2011; D. W. Sue, 2010).

There is an old Asian saying that goes something like this: "All individuals, in many respects, are (a) like no other individuals, (b) like some individuals, and (c) like all other individuals." Although this statement might sound confusing and contradictory, Asians believe these words to have great wisdom and to be entirely true with respect to human development and identity. We have found the tripartite framework shown in Figure 2.1 (D. W. Sue, 2001) to be useful in exploring and understanding the formation of personal identity. The three concentric circles illustrated in Figure 2.1 denote individual, group, and universal levels of personal identity.

FIGURE 2.1 Tripartite Development of Personal Identity

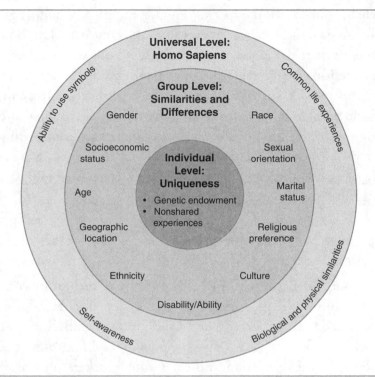

Individual Level: "All Individuals Are, in Some Respects, Like No Other Individuals"

There is much truth in the saying that no two individuals are identical. We are all unique biologically, and recent breakthroughs in mapping the human genome have provided some startling findings. Biologists, anthropologists, and evolutionary psychologists had looked to the Human Genome Project as potentially providing answers to comparative and evolutionary biology that would allow us to find the secrets to life. Although the project has provided valuable answers to many questions, scientists have discovered even more complex questions. For example, they had expected to find 100,000 genes in the human genome, but only about 20,000 were initially found, with the possible existence of another 5,000—only two or three times more than are found in a fruit fly or a nematode worm. Of those 25,000 genes, only 300 unique genes distinguish us from the mouse. In other words, human and mouse genomes are about 85 percent identical! Although it may be a blow to human dignity, the more important question is how so relatively few genes can account for our humanness.

Likewise, if so few genes can determine such great differences between species, what about within the species? Human inheritance almost guarantees differences because no two individuals ever share the same genetic endowment. Further, no two of us share the exact same experiences in our society. Even identical twins, who theoretically share the same gene pool and are raised in the same family, are exposed to both shared and nonshared experiences. Different experiences in school and with peers, as well as qualitative differences in how parents treat them, will contribute to individual uniqueness. Research indicates that psychological characteristics, behavior, and mental disorders are more affected by experiences specific to a child than are shared experiences (Bale et al., 2010; Foster & MacQueen, 2008).

Group Level: "All Individuals Are, in Some Respects, Like Some Other Individuals"

As mentioned earlier, each of us is born into a cultural matrix of beliefs, values, rules, and social practices. By virtue of social, cultural, and political distinctions made in our society, perceived group membership exerts a powerful influence over how society views sociodemographic groups and over how its members view themselves and others. Group markers such as race and gender are relatively stable and less subject to change. Some markers, such as education, socioeconomic status, marital status, and geographic location, are more fluid and changeable. Although ethnicity is fairly stable, some argue that it can also be fluid. Likewise, debate and controversy surround the discussions about whether sexual orientation is determined at birth and whether we should be speaking of sexuality or sexualities (D. Sue et al., 2016). Nevertheless, membership in these groups may result in shared experiences and characteristics. Group identities may serve as powerful reference groups in the formation of *worldviews*. On the *group level of identity*, Figure 2.1 reveals that people may belong to more than one cultural group (e.g., an Asian American female with a disability), that some group identities may be more salient than others (e.g., race over religious orientation), and that the salience of cultural group identity may shift from one to the other depending on the situation. For example, a gay man with a disability may find that his disability identity is more salient among the able-bodied but that his sexual orientation is more salient among those with disabilities.

Universal Level: "All Individuals Are, in Some Respects, Like All Other Individuals"

Because we are members of the human race and belong to the species *Homo sapiens*, we share many similarities. Universal to our commonalities are (a) biological and physical similarities, (b) common life experiences (birth, death, love, sadness, and so forth), (c) self-awareness, and (d) the ability to use symbols, such as language. In Shakespeare's *Merchant of Venice*, Shylock attempts to acknowledge the universal nature of the human condition by asking, "When you prick us, do we not bleed?" Again, although the Human Genome Project indicates that a few genes may cause major differences between and within species, it is startling how similar the genetic material within our chromosomes is and how much we share in common.

REFLECTION AND DISCUSSION QUESTIONS

1. Select three group identities you possess related to race, gender, sexual orientation, disability, religion, socioeconomic status, and so forth. Of the three you have chosen, which one is more salient to you? Why? Does it shift or change? How aware are you of other sociodemographic identities?

2. Using the tripartite framework just discussed, can you outline ways in which you are unique, share characteristics with only certain groups, and share similarities with everyone?

3. Can someone truly be color-blind? What makes seeing and acknowledging differences so difficult? In what ways does a color-blind approach hinder the counseling relationship when working with diverse clients?

INDIVIDUAL AND UNIVERSAL BIASES IN PSYCHOLOGY AND MENTAL HEALTH

Psychology—and mental health professionals in particular—have generally focused on either the individual or the *universal levels of identity*, placing less importance on the group level. There are several reasons for this orientation. First, our society arose from the concept of rugged individualism, and we have traditionally valued autonomy, independence, and uniqueness. Our culture assumes that individuals are the basic building blocks of our society. Sayings such as "Be your own person, (à la Dr. D.)," "Stand on your own two feet," and "Don't depend on anyone but yourself" reflect this value. Psychology and education represent the carriers of this value, and the study of individual differences is most exemplified in the individual intelligence testing movement that pays homage to individual uniqueness (Suzuki et al., 2005).

Second, the universal level is consistent with the tradition and history of psychology, which has historically sought universal facts, principles, and laws in explaining human behavior. Although this is an important quest, the nature of scientific inquiry has often meant studying phenomena independently of the context in which human behavior originates. Thus therapeutic interventions from which research findings are derived may lack external validity (Chang & Sue, 2005).

Third, we have historically neglected the study of identity at the group level for sociopolitical and normative reasons. As we have seen, issues of race, gender, sexual orientation, and disability seem to touch hot buttons in all of us because they bring to light issues of oppression and the unpleasantness of personal biases (Lo, 2010; Zetzer, 2011). In addition, racial/ethnic differences have frequently been interpreted from a deficit perspective and have been equated with being abnormal or pathological (Guthrie, 1997; Parham et al., 2011). We have more to say about this in Chapter 4.

Disciplines that hope to understand the human condition cannot neglect any level of our identity. For example, psychological explanations that acknowledge the importance of group influences such as gender, race, culture, sexual orientation, socioeconomic class, and religious affiliation lead to more accurate understanding of human psychology. Failure to acknowledge these influences may skew research findings and lead to biased conclusions about human behavior that are culture bound, class bound, and gender bound.

Thus it is possible to conclude that all people possess individual, group, and universal levels of identity. A holistic approach to understanding personal identity demands that we recognize all three levels: individual (uniqueness), group (shared cultural values and beliefs), and universal (common features of being human). Because of the historical scientific neglect of the *group level of identity*, this text focuses primarily on this category.

Before closing this portion of our discussion, we would like to add a caution. Although the concentric circles in Figure 2.1 might unintentionally suggest a clear boundary, each level of identity must be viewed as permeable and ever-changing in salience. In counseling and psychotherapy, for example, a client might view his or her uniqueness as important at one point in the session and stress commonalities of the human condition at another. Even within the *group level of identity*, multiple forces may be operative. As mentioned earlier, the *group level of identity* reveals many reference groups, both fixed and nonfixed, that might impact our lives. Being an elderly, gay, Latino male, for example, represents four potential reference groups operating on the person. The culturally competent helping professional must be willing and able to touch all dimensions of human existence without negating any of the others.

THE IMPACT OF GROUP IDENTITIES ON COUNSELING AND PSYCHOTHERAPY

Accepting the premise that race, ethnicity, and culture are powerful variables in influencing how people think, make decisions, behave, and define events, it is not far-fetched to conclude that such forces may also affect how different groups define a helping relationship (Herlihy & Corey, 2015). Multicultural psychologists have long noted, for example, that different theories of counseling and psychotherapy represent different *worldviews*, each with its own values, biases, and assumptions about human behavior (Geva & Wiener, 2015). Given that schools of counseling and psychotherapy arise from Western European contexts, the *worldview* that they espouse as reality may not be shared by racial/ethnic minority groups in the United States, or by those who reside in different countries (Parham et al., 2011). Each cultural/racial group may have its own distinct interpretation of reality and offer a different perspective on the nature of people, the origin of disorders, standards for judging normality and abnormality, and therapeutic approaches.

Among many Asian Americans, for example, a self-orientation is considered undesirable, whereas a group orientation is highly valued (Kim, 2011). The Japanese have a saying that goes like this: "The nail that stands up should be pounded back down." The meaning seems clear: Healthy development is considering the needs of the entire group, whereas unhealthy development is thinking only of oneself. Likewise, relative to their EuroAmerican counterparts, many African Americans value the emotive and affective quality of interpersonal interactions as qualities of sincerity and authenticity (West-Olatunji & Conwill, 2011). Euro-Americans often view the passionate expression of affect as irrational, impulsive, immature, and lacking objectivity on the part of the communicator. Thus the autonomy-oriented goal of counseling and psychotherapy and the objective focus of the therapeutic process might prove antagonistic to the *worldviews* of Asian Americans and African Americans, respectively.

It is therefore highly probable that different racial/ethnic minority groups perceive the competence of the helping professional differently than do mainstream client groups. Further, if race/ethnicity affects perception, what about other group differences, such as gender and sexual orientation? Minority clients may see a clinician who exhibits therapeutic *skills* that are associated primarily with mainstream therapies as having lower credibility. The important question to ask is, "Do such groups as racial/ethnic minorities define *cultural competence* differently than do their Euro-American counterparts?" Anecdotal observations, clinical case studies, conceptual analytical writings, and some empirical studies seem to suggest an affirmative response to the question (Fraga, Atkinson, & Wampold, 2002; Garrett & Portman, 2011; Guzman & Carrasco, 2011; McGoldrick, Giordano, & Garcia-Preto, 2005; Nwachuku & Ivey, 1991).

WHAT IS MULTICULTURAL COUNSELING/THERAPY?

In light of the previous analysis, let us define *multicultural counseling/therapy* (MCT) as it relates to the therapy process and the roles of the mental health practitioner:

> *Multicultural counseling and therapy can be defined as both a helping role and a process that uses modalities and defines goals consistent with the life experiences and cultural values of clients; recognizes client identities to include individual, group, and universal dimensions; advocates the use of universal and culture-specific strategies and roles in the healing process; and balances the importance of individualism and* collectivism *in the assessment, diagnosis, and treatment of client and client systems. (D. W. Sue & Torino, 2005)*

This definition often contrasts markedly with traditional views of counseling and psychotherapy. A more thorough analysis of these characteristics is described in Chapter 7. For now, let us extract the key phrases in our definition and expand their implications for clinical practice.

1. *Helping role and process.* MCT broadens the roles that counselors play and expands the repertoire of therapy *skills* considered helpful and appropriate in counseling. The more passive and objective stance taken by therapists in clinical work is seen as only one method of helping. Likewise, teaching, consulting, and advocacy can supplement the conventional counselor or therapist role.

2. *Consistent with life experiences and cultural values.* Effective MCT means using modalities and defining goals for culturally diverse clients that are consistent with their racial, cultural, ethnic, gender, and sexual orientation backgrounds. Advice and suggestions, for example, may be effectively used for some client populations.

3. *Individual, group, and universal dimensions of existence.* As we have already seen, MCT acknowledges that our existence and identity are composed of individual (uniqueness), group, and universal dimensions. Any form of helping that fails to recognize the totality of these dimensions negates important aspects of a person's identity.

4. *Universal and culture-specific strategies.* MCT believes that different racial/ethnic minority groups might respond best to culture-specific strategies of helping. For example, research seems to support the belief that Asian Americans and Latino/a Americans are more responsive to directive/active approaches (Guzman & Carrasco, 2011; Kim, 2011) and that African Americans appreciate helpers who are authentic in their self-disclosures (Parham et al., 2011). Likewise, it is clear that common features in helping relationships cut across cultures and societies as well.

5. *Individualism and collectivism.* MCT broadens the perspective of the helping relationship by balancing the individualistic approach with a collectivistic reality that acknowledges our embeddedness in families, relationships with significant others, communities, and cultures. A client is perceived not just as an individual, but as an individual who is a product of his or her social and cultural context.

6. *Client and client systems.* MCT assumes a dual role in helping clients. In many cases, for example, it is important to focus on individual clients and to encourage them to achieve insights and learn new behaviors. However, when problems of clients of color reside in prejudice, discrimination, and racism of employers, educators, and neighbors or in organizational policies or practices in schools, mental health agencies, government, business, and society, the traditional therapeutic role appears ineffective and inappropriate. The focus for change must shift to altering client systems rather than individual clients.

WHAT IS CULTURAL COMPETENCE?

Consistent with the definition of MCT, it becomes clear that culturally competent healers are working toward several primary goals (American Psychological Association, 2003; D. W. Sue et al., 1992; D. W. Sue et al., 1998). First, culturally competent helping professionals are ones who are actively in the process of becoming aware of their own values, biases, assumptions about human behavior, preconceived notions, personal limitations, and so forth. Second, culturally competent helping professionals are ones who actively attempt to understand the *worldview* of their culturally diverse clients. In other words, what are the client's values and assumptions about human behavior, biases, and so on? Third, culturally competent helping professionals are ones who are in the process of actively developing and practicing appropriate, relevant, and sensitive intervention strategies and *skills* in working with their culturally diverse clients. These three attributes make it clear that *cultural competence* is an active, developmental, and ongoing process and that it is aspirational rather than achieved. Let us more carefully explore these attributes of *cultural competence*.

Competency 1: Therapist Awareness of One's Own Assumptions, Values, and Biases

In almost all human service programs, counselors, therapists, and social workers are familiar with the phrase "Counselor, know thyself." Programs stress the importance of not allowing our own biases, values, or hang-ups to interfere with our ability to work with clients. In most cases, such a warning stays primarily on an intellectual level, and very little training is directed at having trainees get in touch with their own values and biases about human behavior. In other words, it appears to be easier to deal with trainees' cognitive understanding of their own cultural heritage, the values they hold about human behavior, their standards for judging normality and abnormality, and the culture-bound goals toward which they strive.

As indicated in Chapter 1, what makes examination of the self difficult is the emotional impact of attitudes, beliefs, and feelings associated with cultural differences, such as racism, sexism, heterosexism, able-body-ism, and ageism. For example, as a member of a White EuroAmerican group, what responsibility do you hold for the racist, oppressive, and discriminating manner by which you personally and professionally deal with persons of color? This is a threatening question for many White people. However, to be effective in MCT means that one has adequately dealt with this question and worked through the biases, feelings, fears, and guilt associated with it. A similar question can be asked of men with respect to women and of straights with respect to gays.

Competency 2: Understanding the Worldviews of Culturally Diverse Clients

It is crucial that counselors and therapists understand and can share the *worldviews* of their culturally diverse clients. This statement does not mean that providers must hold these *worldviews* as their own, but rather that they can see and accept other *worldviews* in a nonjudgmental manner. Some have referred to the process as cultural role taking: Therapists acknowledge that they may not have lived a lifetime as a person of color, as a woman, or as a lesbian, gay, bisexual, or trans-gendered person (LGBT). With respect to race, for example, it is almost impossible for a White therapist to think, feel, and react as a racial minority individual. Nonetheless, cognitive empathy, as distinct from affective empathy, may be possible. In cultural role taking, the therapist acquires practical *knowledge* concerning the scope and nature of the client's cultural background, daily living experience, hopes, fears, and aspirations. Inherent in cognitive empathy is the understanding of how therapy relates to the wider sociopolitical system with which minorities contend every day of their lives.

Competency 3: Developing Culturally Appropriate Intervention Strategies and Techniques

Effectiveness is most likely enhanced when the therapist uses therapeutic modalities and defines goals that are consistent with the life experiences and cultural values of the client. This basic premise will be emphasized throughout future chapters. Studies have consistently revealed that (a) economically and educationally marginalized clients may not be oriented toward "talk therapy"; (b) self-disclosure may be incompatible with the cultural values of Asian Americans, Hispanic Americans, and American Indians; (c) the sociopolitical atmosphere may dictate against self-disclosure from racial minorities and gays and lesbians; (d) the ambiguous nature of counseling may be antagonistic to life values of certain diverse groups; and (e) many minority clients prefer an active/directive approach over an inactive/nondirective one in treatment. Therapy has too long assumed that clients share a similar background and cultural heritage and that the same approaches are equally effective with all clients. This erroneous assumption needs to be challenged.

Because groups and individuals differ from one another, the blind application of techniques to all situations and all populations seems ludicrous. The interpersonal transactions between the counselor and the client require different approaches that are consistent with the client's life experiences (Choudhuri, Santiago-Rivera, & Garrett, 2012; Ratts & Pedersen, 2014). It is ironic that equal treatment in therapy may be discriminatory treatment! Therapists need to understand this. As a means to prove discriminatory mental health practices, racial/ethnic minority groups have in the past pointed to studies revealing that minority clients are given less preferential forms of treatment (medication, electroconvulsive therapy, etc.). Somewhere, confusion has occurred, and it was believed that to be treated differently is akin to discrimination. The confusion centered on the distinction between equal access and opportunities versus equal treatment. Racial/ethnic minority groups may not be asking for equal treatment so much as they are asking for equal access and opportunities. This dictates a differential approach that is truly nondiscriminatory. Thus to be an effective multicultural helper requires *cultural competence*. In light of the previous analysis, we define *cultural competence* in the following manner:

> *Cultural competence is the ability to engage in actions or create conditions that maximize the optimal development of client and client systems. Multicultural counseling competence is defined as the counselor's acquisition of awareness, knowledge, and skills needed to function effectively in a pluralistic democratic society (ability to communicate, interact, negotiate, and intervene on behalf of clients from diverse backgrounds), and on an organizational/societal level, advocating effectively to develop new theories, practices, policies, and organizational structures that are more responsive to all groups. (D. W. Sue & Torino, 2005)*

This definition of *cultural competence* in the helping professions makes it clear that the conventional one-to-one, in-the-office, objective form of treatment aimed at remediation of existing problems may be at odds with the sociopolitical and cultural experiences of the clients. Like the complementary definition of MCT, it addresses not only clients (individuals, families, and groups) but also client systems (institutions, policies, and practices that may be unhealthy or problematic for healthy development). Addressing client systems is especially important if problems reside outside rather than inside the client. For example, prejudice and discrimination such as racism, sexism, and homophobia may impede the healthy functioning of individuals and groups in our society.

Second, *cultural competence* can be seen as residing in three major domains: (a) attitudes/beliefs component—an understanding of one's own cultural conditioning and how this conditioning affects the personal beliefs, values, and attitudes of a culturally diverse population; (b) knowledge component—understanding and knowledge of the *worldviews* of culturally diverse individuals and groups; and (c) *skills* component—an ability to determine and use culturally appropriate intervention strategies when working with different groups in our society. Box 2.1 provides an outline of *cultural competencies* related to these three domains.

BOX 2.1 MULTICULTURAL COUNSELING COMPETENCIES

I. Cultural Competence: *Awareness*

   1. Moved from being culturally unaware to being aware and sensitive to own cultural heritage and to valuing and respecting differences.

   2. Aware of own values and biases and of how they may affect diverse clients.

   3. Comfortable with differences that exist between themselves and their clients in terms of race, gender, sexual orientation, and other sociodemographic variables. Differences are not seen as deviant.

   4. Sensitive to circumstances (personal biases; stage of racial, gender, and sexual orientation identity; sociopolitical influences; etc.) that may dictate referral of clients to members of their own sociodemographic group or to different therapists in general.

   5. Aware of their own racist, sexist, heterosexist, or other detrimental attitudes, beliefs, and feelings.

II. Cultural Competence: *Knowledge*

   1. Knowledgeable and informed on a number of culturally diverse groups, especially groups with whom therapists work.

   2. Knowledgeable about the sociopolitical system's operation in the United States with respect to its treatment of marginalized groups in society.

   3. Possess specific *knowledge* and understanding of the generic characteristics of counseling and therapy.

   4. Knowledgeable of institutional barriers that prevent some diverse clients from using mental health services.

III. Cultural Competence: *Skills*

1. Able to generate a wide variety of verbal and nonverbal helping responses.

2. Able to communicate (send and receive both verbal and nonverbal messages) accurately and appropriately.

3. Able to exercise institutional intervention *skills* on behalf of clients when appropriate.

4. Able to anticipate the impact of their helping styles and of their limitations on culturally diverse clients.

5. Able to play helping roles characterized by an active systemic focus, which leads to environmental interventions. Not restricted by the conventional counselor/therapist mode of operation.

Sources: D. W. Sue et al. (1992), and D. W. Sue et al. (1998). Readers are encouraged to review the original 34 multicultural competencies, which are fully elaborated in both publications.

Third, in a broad sense, this definition is directed toward two levels of *cultural competence*: the personal/individual and the organizational/system levels. The work on *cultural competence* has generally focused on the micro level, the individual. In the education and training of psychologists, for example, the goals have been to increase the level of self-awareness of trainees (potential biases, values, and assumptions about human behavior); to acquire knowledge of the history, culture, and life experiences of various minority groups; and to aid in developing culturally appropriate and adaptive interpersonal *skills* (clinical work, management, conflict resolution, etc.). Less emphasis is placed on the macro level: the profession of psychology, organizations, and the society in general (Lum, 2011; D. W. Sue, 2001). We suggest that it does little good to train culturally competent helping professionals when the very organizations that employ them are monocultural and discourage or even punish psychologists for using their culturally competent knowledge and *skills*. If our profession is interested in the development of *cultural competence*, then it must become involved in impacting systemic and societal levels as well.

Fourth, our definition of *cultural competence* speaks strongly to the development of alternative helping roles. Much of this comes from recasting healing as involving more than one-to-one therapy. If part of *cultural competence* involves systemic intervention, then such roles as consultant, change agent, teacher, and advocate supplement the conventional role of therapy. In contrast to this role, alternatives are characterized by the following:

- Having a more active helping style

- Working outside the office (home, institution, or community)

- Being focused on changing environmental conditions, as opposed to changing the client

- Viewing the client as encountering problems rather than having a problem

- Being oriented toward prevention rather than remediation

- Shouldering increased responsibility for determining the course and the outcome of the helping process

It is clear that these alternative roles and their underlying assumptions and practices have not been historically perceived as activities consistent with counseling and psychotherapy.

CULTURAL HUMILITY AND CULTURAL COMPETENCE

Can anyone ever be completely culturally competent in working with diverse clients? Are the *awareness*, knowledge, and skills of *cultural competence* the only areas sufficient to be an effective multicultural helping professional? The answers to these questions are extremely important not only to the practice of counseling/therapy, but to the education and training of counselors and therapists. The answer to the first question is an obvious "no." It is impossible for anyone to possess sufficient knowledge, understanding, and experience of the diversity of populations that inhabit this planet. Indeed, those who have developed and advocated *multicultural counseling* competencies have repeatedly stressed that "*cultural competence*" is an aspirational goal, that no single individual can become completely competent, and that the journey toward *cultural competence* is a lifelong process (D. W. Sue et al., 1992; Cornish et al., 2010).

With respect to the second question, it appears that the dimensions of awareness, knowledge, and *skills* may be necessary, but not sufficient conditions to work effectively with diverse clients. Other attributes, like openness to diversity (Chao, Wei, Spanierman, Longo, & Northart, 2015) and *cultural humility* seem central to effective multicultural counseling (Gallardo, 2014). The concept of *cultural humility* was first coined in medical education, where it was associated with an open attitudinal stance or a multicultural open orientation to diverse patients, and found to be quite different from *cultural competence* (Tervalon & Murray-Garcia, 1998). The term has found its way into the field of *multicultural counseling*, where it also refers to an openness to working with culturally diverse clients (Hook, Davis, Owen, Worthington, & Utsey, 2013; Owen et al., 2014). But exactly how does it differ from *cultural competence* and what evidence do we have that it is an important component?

Cultural humility appears more like a "way of being" rather than a "way of doing," which has characterized *cultural competence* (Owen, Tao, Leach, & Rodolfa, 2011). In the former, we are referring to the virtues and dispositions inherent in the attitudes that counselors hold toward their clients, while the latter refers more to the acquisition of knowledge and skills used in working with clients. The attitudinal components of respect for others, an egalitarian stance, and diminished superiority over clients means an "other-orientation" rather than one that is self-focused (concern with one's expertise, training, credentials, and authority). Recall again the therapeutic encounter between Dr. D. and Gabriella. When asked by Gabriella whether he could understand what it's like to be Latina, and the unique issues she must cope with, his response was "*Of course I can*" and "*I've worked with many Latinos in my practice.*" In many respects, the definition of *cultural humility* is *humbleness*; thus therapists acknowledging that they may be limited in their knowledge and understanding of clients' cultural concerns may actually strengthen the therapeutic relationship. Dr. D.'s response, however, suggests he is self-oriented ("I am the therapist and I know best"), while *cultural humility* would entertain the possibility that the therapist *may not* understand. A therapeutic response that would indicate *cultural humility* would be: "*I hope I can, let's give it a try, okay?*" Hook et al. (2013) make the following observations about cultural humility:

> *Culturally humble therapists rarely assume competence (i.e., letting prior experience and even expertness lead to overconfidence) for working with clients just based on their prior experience working with a particular group. Rather, therapists who are more culturally humble approach clients with respectful openness and work collaboratively with clients to understand the unique intersection of clients' various aspects of identities and how that affects the developing therapy alliance. (p. 354)*

Although *cultural humility* may appear difficult to define and measure, researchers have been able to begin construction of an instrument to quantify it (Hook et al., 2013; Owen et al., 2014). In a therapeutic context, *cultural humility* of therapists was (a) considered very important to many socially marginalized clients, (b) correlated with a higher likelihood of continuing in treatment, (c) strongly related to the strength of the therapeutic alliance, and (d) related to perceived benefit and improvement in therapy. Thus *cultural humility* as a dispositional orientation may be equally important as *cultural competence* (awareness, knowledge, and skills) in *multicultural counseling* and therapy.

SOCIAL JUSTICE AND CULTURAL COMPETENCE

Recently, the Multicultural Counseling Competencies Revision Committee of the American Counseling Association (Ratts, Singh, Nassar-McMillan, Butler, & McCullough, 2015) has presented an important draft document, *Multicultural and Social Justice Counseling Competencies* (MSJCC) that proposes to revise the multicultural counseling competencies devised by D. W. Sue et al. (1992). As indicated in Chapter 4, at the heart of the revision is integration of *social justice* competencies with multicultural competencies. Acknowledging that *multiculturalism* leads to *social justice* initiatives and actions, they propose a conceptual framework that includes *quadrants* (privilege and oppressed statuses), *domains* (counselor self-awareness, client *worldview*, counseling relationships, and counseling and advocacy interventions), and *competencies* (attitudes and beliefs, knowledge, skills, and action).

Perhaps the most important aspect of the proposed MSJCC is seen in the *quadrants* category, where they identify four major counseling relationships between counselor and client that directly address matters of power and privilege: (1) privileged counselor working with an oppressed client, (2) privileged counselor working with a privileged client, (3) oppressed counselor working with a privileged client, and (4) oppressed counselor working with an oppressed client. In other words, when applied to racial/ethnic counseling/therapy, various combinations can occur: (a) White counselors working with clients of color, (b) counselors of color working with White clients, (c) counselors of color working with clients of color, and (d) White counselors working with White clients. Analysis and research regarding these dyadic combinations have seldom been addressed in the multicultural field. Further, little in the way of addressing counseling work with interracial/interethnic combinations is seen in the literature. We address this topic in the next chapter. We will also cover the issues raised in the MSJCC framework more thoroughly in Chapters 3, 4, and 5. In Chapter 3 we focus on enumerating the quadrants of power and privilege relationships between counselor and client, in Chapter 4 we address the importance of *social justice* advocacy and action on behalf of the client, and in Chapter 5 we deal with individual and systems level work.

REFLECTION AND DISCUSSION QUESTIONS

1. If the basic building blocks of *cultural competence* in clinical practice are *awareness, knowledge*, and *skills,* how do you hope to fulfill competency one, two, and three? Can you list the various educational and training activities you would need in order to work effectively with a client who differs from you in terms of race, gender, or sexual orientation?

2. What are your thoughts regarding *cultural humility*? How important is this attitude or stance in your work with culturally diverse clients?

3. Look at the six characteristics that define alternative roles for helping culturally diverse clients. Which of these roles are you most comfortable playing? Why? Which of these activities would make you uncomfortable? Why?

 ## IMPLICATIONS FOR CLINICAL PRACTICE

1. Know that the definition of *multiculturalism* is inclusive and encompasses race, culture, gender, religious affiliation, sexual orientation, age, disability, and so on.

2. When working with diverse populations, attempt to identify culture-specific and culture-universal domains of helping.

3. Be aware that persons of color, gays/lesbians, women, and other groups may perceive mental illness/health and the healing process differently than do Euro-American men.

4. Do not disregard differences and impose the conventional helping role and process on culturally diverse groups, as such actions may constitute cultural oppression.

5. Be aware that EuroAmerican healing standards originate from a cultural context and may be culture-bound. As long as counselors and therapists continue to view EuroAmerican standards as normative, they may judge others as abnormal.

6. Realize that the concept of *cultural competence* is more inclusive and superordinate than is the traditional definition of *clinical competence*. Do not fall into the trap of thinking "good counseling is good counseling."

7. If you are planning to work with the diversity of clients in our world, you must play roles other than that of the conventional counselor.

8. Use modalities that are consistent with the lifestyles and cultural systems of clients.

9. Understand that one's multicultural orientation, *cultural humility*, is very important to successful multicultural counseling.

SUMMARY

Traditional definitions of counseling, therapy, and mental health practice arise from monocultural and ethnocentric norms that may be antagonistic to the life styles and cultural values of diverse groups. These Western worldviews reflect a belief in the universality of the human condition, a belief that disorders are similar and cut across societies, and a conviction that mental health concepts are equally applicable across all populations and disorders. These *worldviews* also often fail to consider the different cultural and sociopolitical experiences of marginalized group members. As a result, counseling and therapy may often be inappropriate to marginalized groups in our society, resulting in cultural oppression. The movement to redefine counseling/therapy, and identify aspects of *cultural competence* in mental health practice has been advocated by nearly all multicultural counseling specialists

Multicultural counseling and therapy is defined as both a helping role and a process that uses modalities and defines goals consistent with the life experiences and cultural values of clients; recognizes client identities to include individual, group, and universal dimensions; advocates the use of universal and culture-specific strategies and roles in the healing process; and balances the importance of individualism and *collectivism* in the assessment, diagnosis, and treatment of client and client systems. Thus *cultural competence* is the ability to engage in actions or create conditions that maximize the optimal development of client and client systems.

On a personal developmental level, *multicultural counseling competence* is defined as the counselor's acquisition of *awareness*, *knowledge*, and *skills* needed to function effectively in a pluralistic democratic society (ability to communicate, interact, negotiate, and intervene on behalf of clients from diverse backgrounds); on an organizational/societal level, it is defined as advocating effectively to develop new theories, practices, policies, and organizational structures that are more responsive to all groups. Another attribute, *cultural humility* seems central to effective *multicultural counseling*. *Cultural humility* appears more like a "way of being" rather than a "way of doing." The attitudinal components of respect for others, an egalitarian stance, and diminished superiority over clients means an "other-orientation" rather than one that is self-focused. Finally, it appears that there is a strong need to integrate social justice competencies with that of *cultural competence*. Becoming culturally competent is a lifelong journey but promises much in providing culturally appropriate services to all groups in our society.

GLOSSARY TERMS

Awareness

Collectivism

Cultural competence

Cultural humility

Cultural incompetence

Cultural relativism

Culture-bound syndromes

Emic (culturally specific)

Etic (culturally universal)

Group level of identity

Individual level of identity

Knowledge

Multicultural counseling/therapy

Multiculturalism

Personalismo

Skills

Social justice

Universal level of identity

Worldview

REFERENCES

American Psychiatric Association. (2013). *Diagnostic and statistical manual of mental disorders* (5th ed.). Arlington, VA: Author.

American Psychological Association. (2003). Guidelines on multicultural education, training, research, practice, and organizational change for psychologists. *American Psychologist, 58,* 377–402.

Anderson, S. H., & Middleton, V. A. (Eds.). (2011). *Explorations in diversity: Examining privilege and oppression in a multicultural society* (2nd ed.). Belmont, CA: Thomson Brooks/Cole.

Apfelbaum, E. P., Sommers, S. R., & Norton, M. I. (2008). Seeing race and seeming racist: Evaluating strategic colorblindness in social interaction. *Journal of Personality and Social Psychology*, 95, 918–932.

Arnett, J. J. (2009). The neglected 95%: Why American psychology needs to become less American. *American Psychologist*, 63, 602–614.

Arredondo, P., Gallardo-Cooper, M., Delgado-Romero, E. A., & Zapata, A. L. (2014). *Culturally responsive counseling with Latinas/os.* Alexandria, VA: American Counseling Association.

Arredondo, P., Toporek, M. S., Brown, S., Jones, J., Locke, D. C., Sanchez, J., & Stadler, H. (1996). *Operationalization of the multicultural counseling competencies.* Alexandria, VA: Association of Multicultural Counseling and Development.

Atkinson, D. R., Bui, U., & Mori, S. (2001). Multiculturally sensitive empirically supported treatments—an oxymoron? In J. G. Ponterotto, J. M. Casas, L. A. Suzuki, & C. M. Alexander (Eds.), *Handbook of multicultural counseling* (pp. 542–574). Thousand Oaks, CA: Sage.

Atkinson, D. R., Morten, G., & Sue, D. W. (1998).*Counseling American minorities: A cross-cultural perspective* (5th ed.). Dubuque, IA: Wm. C. Brown.

Bale, T. L., Baram, T. Z., Brown, A. S., Goldstein, J. M., Insel, T. R., McCarthy, M. M., . . . & Nestler, E. J. (2010). Early life programming and neurodevelopmental disorders. *Biological Psychiatry*, 68, 314–319.

Carter, R. T. (Ed.). (2005). *Handbook of racial-cultural psychology and counseling.* Hoboken, NJ: Wiley.

Chang, J., & Sue, S. (2005). Culturally sensitive research: Where have we gone wrong and what do we need to do now? In M. G. Constantine & D. W. Sue (Eds.), *Strategies for building multicultural competence in mental health and educational settings* (pp. 229–246). Hoboken, NJ: Wiley.

Chao, R. C., Wei, M., Spanierman, L., Longo, J., & Northart, D. (2015). White racial attitudes and White empathy: The moderation of openness to diversity. *Counseling Psychologist*, 43, 94–120.

Choudhuri, D. D., Santiago-Rivera, A. L., & Garrett, M. T. (2012). *Counseling and diversity.* Belmont, CA: Cengage.

Comas-Diaz, L. (2010). On being a Latina healer: Voice, conscience and identity. *Psychotherapy Theory, Research, Practice, Training*, 47, 162–168.

Cornish, J.A.E., Schreier, B. A., Nadkarni, L. I., Metzger, L. H., & Rodolfa, E. R. (2010). *Handbook of multicultural counseling competencies.* Hoboken, NJ: Wiley.

Cross, T. L., Bazron, B. J., Dennis, K. W., & Isaacs, M. R. (1989). *Towards a culturally competent system of care.* Washington, DC: Child and Adolescent Service System Program Technical Assistance Center.

Counsel for Accreditation of Counseling and Related Educational Programs (CACREP). (2015). *2016 CACREP Standards.* Fairfax, VA: Author.

Foster, J. A., & MacQueen, G. (2008). Neurobiological factors linking personality traits and major depression. *La Revue Canadienne de Psychiatrie*, 53, 6–13.

Fraga, E. D., Atkinson, D. R., & Wampold, B. E. (2002). Ethnic group preferences for multicultural counseling competencies. *Cultural Diversity and Ethnic Minority Psychology*, 10, 53–65.

Gallardo, M. E. (2014). *Developing cultural humility.* Thousand Oaks, CA: Sage.

Garrett, M. T., & Portman, T.A.A. (2011). *Counseling Native Americans.* Belmont, CA: Cengage.

Geva, E., & Wiener, J. (2015). *Psychological assessment of culturally and linguistically diverse children and adolescents.* New York, NY: Springer.

Guthrie, R. V. (1997). *Even the rat was White: A historical view of psychology* (2nd ed.). New York, NY: Harper & Row.

Guzman, M. R., & Carrasco, N. (2011). *Counseling Latino/a Americans*. Belmont, CA: Cengage.

Hall, G.C.N. (2001). Psychotherapy research with ethnic minorities: Empirical, ethical, and conceptual issues. *Journal of Counseling and Clinical Psychology, 69*, 502–510.

Helms, J. E., & Richardson, T. Q. (1997). How multiculturalism obscures race and culture as different aspects of counseling competency. In D. B. Pope-Davis & H.L.K. Coleman (Eds.), *Multicultural counseling competencies* (pp. 60–79). Thousand Oaks, CA: Sage.

Herlihy, B., & Corey, G. (2015). *Boundary issues in counseling*. Alexandria, VA: American Counseling Association.

Hook, J. N., Davis, D. E., Owen, J., Worthington, E. L., & Utsey, S. O. (2013). Cultural humility: Measuring openness to culturally diverse clients. *Journal of Counseling Psychology, 60*, 353–366.

Howard, R. (1992). Folie à deux involving a dog. *American Journal of Psychiatry, 149*, 414.

Ivey, A. E., Ivey, M. B., & Zalaquett, C. P. (2014). *Intentional interviewing and counseling* (8th ed.). Belmont, CA: Brooks/Cole.

Kail, R. V., & Cavanaugh, J. C. (2013). *Human development: A life-span view* (6th ed.). Belmont, CA: Brooks/Cole.

Kim, B.S.K. (2011). *Counseling Asian Americans*. Belmont, CA: Cengage.

Lo, H.-W. (2010). My racial identity development and supervision: A self-reflection. *Training and Education in Professional Psychology, 4*, 26–28.

Locke, D. C., & Bailey, D. F. (2014). *Increasing multicultural understanding*. Thousand Oaks, CA: Sage.

Lum, D. (2011). *Culturally competent practice*. Belmont, CA: Cengage.

McGoldrick, M., Giordano, J., & Garcia-Preto, N. (2005). *Ethnicity and family therapy*. New York, NY: Guilford Press.

Neville, H. A., Gallardo, M. E., & Sue, D. W. (in press). *What does it mean to be color-blind? Manifestation, dynamics and impact*. Washington, DC: American Psychological Association.

Nwachuku, U., & Ivey, A. (1991). Culture specific counseling: An alternative approach. *Journal of Counseling and Development, 70*, 106–111.

Owen, J., Jordan, T. A., Turner, D., Davis, D. E., Hook, J. N., & Leach, M. M. (2014). Therapists' multicultural orientation: Client perceptions of cultural humility, spiritual/religious commitment, and therapy outcomes. *Journal of Psychology and Theology, 42*, 91–98.

Owen, J., Tao, K., Leach, M. M., & Rodolfa, E. (2011). Clients' perceptions of their psychotherapists' multicultural orientation. *Psychotherapy, 48*, 274–282.

Parham, T. A., Ajamu, A., & White, J. L. (2011). *The psychology of Blacks. Centering our perspectives in the African consciousness*. Boston, MA: Prentice Hall.

Ponterotto, J. G., Utsey, S. O., & Pedersen, P. B. (2006). *Preventing prejudice: A guide for counselors, educators, and parents*. Thousand Oaks, CA: Sage.

President's Commission on Mental Health. (1978). *Report from the President's Commission on Mental Health*. Washington, DC: U.S. Government Printing Office.

Ratts, M. J., & Pedersen, P. B. (2014). *Counseling for multiculturalism and social justice*. Alexandria, VA: American Counseling Association.

Ratts, M. J., Singh, A. A., Nassar-McMillan, S., Butler, K., & McCullough, R. J. (2015). *Multicultural and social justice counseling competencies*. The Multicultural Counseling Competencies Revision Committee of the American Counseling Association, Draft Report.

Ridley, C. R. (2005). *Overcoming unintentional racism in counseling and therapy* (2nd ed.). Thousand Oaks, CA: Sage.

Ridley, C. R., & Mollen, D. (2011). Training in counseling psychology: An introduction to the major contribution. *Counseling Psychologist, 39,* 793–799.

Ridley, C. R., Mollen, D., & Kelly, S. M. (2011). Beyond microskills: Toward a model of counseling competence. *Counseling Psychologist, 39,* 825–864.

Sue, D. W. (2001). Multidimensional facets of cultural competence. *Counseling Psychologist, 29,* 790–821.

Sue, D. W. (2010). *Microaggressions in everyday life: Race, gender, and sexual orientation.* Hoboken, NJ: Wiley.

Sue, D. W. (2015). *Race talk and the conspiracy of silence: Understanding and facilitating difficult dialogues on race.* Hoboken, NJ: Wiley.

Sue, D. W., Arredondo, P., & McDavis, R. J. (1992). Multicultural competencies/standards: A call to the profession. *Journal of Counseling and Development, 70*(4), 477–486.

Sue, D. W., Carter, R. T., Casas, J. M., Fouad, N. A., Ivey, A. E., Jensen, M., & Vazquez-Nutall, E. (1998). *Multicultural counseling competencies: Individual and organizational development.* Thousand Oaks, CA: Sage.

Sue, D. W., Lin, A. I., Torino, G. C., Capodilupo, C. M., & Rivera, D. P. (2009). Racial microaggressions and difficult dialogues on race in the classroom. *Cultural Diversity and Ethnic Minority Psychology, 15,* 183–190.

Sue, D., Sue, D. W., Sue, D. M., & Sue, S. (2016). *Understanding abnormal behavior.* Stamford, CT: Cengage.

Sue, D. W., & Torino, G. C. (2005). Racial cultural competence: Awareness, knowledge and skills. In R. T. Carter (Ed.), *Handbook of racial-cultural psychology and counseling* (pp. 3–18). Hoboken, NJ: Wiley.

Sue, S. (1999). Science, ethnicity and bias: Where have we gone wrong? *American Psychologist, 54,* 1070–1077.

Suzuki, L. A., Kugler, J. F., & Aguiar, L. J. (2005). Assessment practices in racial-cultural psychology. In R. T. Carter (Ed.), *Handbook of racial-cultural psychology and counseling* (pp. 297–315). Hoboken, NJ: Wiley.

Tervalon, M., & Murray-Garcia, J. (1998). Cultural humility versus cultural competence: A critical distinction in defining physician training outcomes in multicultural education. *Journal of Health Care for the Poor and Underserved, 9,* 117–125.

Thomas, A., & Sillen, S. (1972). *Racism and psychiatry.* New York, NY: Brunner/Mazel.

West-Olatunji, C. A., & Conwill, W. (2011). *Counseling African Americans.* Belmont, CA: Cengage.

Zetzer, H. A. (2011). White out: Privilege and its problems. In S. H. Anderson & V. A. Middleton (Eds.), *Explorations in diversity: Examining privilege and oppression in a multicultural society* (pp. 11–24). Belmont, CA: Cengage.

Multicultural Counseling Competence for Counselors and Therapists of Marginalized Groups

Chapter Objectives

1. Learn the importance of cultural competence and cultural humility for trainees of color, and other marginalized group trainees.

2. Identify the major obstacles that prevent honest dialogue between and among groups of color and other *socially marginalized group* members.

3. Describe the types of stereotype that people of color have toward one another.

4. Learn how the historical relationships between groups of color affect their current attitudes toward one another.

5. Identify group differences that may serve as barriers to *multicultural counseling*.

6. Become aware of how attitudes and beliefs between groups of color can interfere with interracial/interethnic counseling.

7. Identify therapeutic barriers likely to arise between a counselor of color and a White client.

8. Identify therapeutic barriers likely to arise between a counselor of color and a client of color.

As a professor of color who has taught many courses on *multicultural counseling/ therapy* and conducted numerous workshops on race relations, I [Derald Sue] have always been aware that my teaching and training were primarily directed at educating White trainees and counselors to their own biases and assumptions about human behavior. I operated from the assumption that people of color knew much of the material on oppression, discrimination, and stereotyping. After all, I reasoned, we were members of the oppressed group and had experiential knowledge of how racism harmed us.

Yet in the back of my mind, I knew that I was shortchanging my trainees of color by making this supposition. I knew that they also had biases and prejudices toward one another and that oftentimes their strong negative reactions toward White fellow students (albeit often justified) could prevent their development toward cultural competence (Ratts & Pedersen, 2014). I knew that much of my trepidation in addressing interracial and interethnic relations had to do with presenting a united front among people of color, and I erroneously operated from a "common enemy" perspective (Sue, 2015). I knew that by taking this stance, I was perpetuating the belief that only Whites needed to change. I also knew that avoiding broader discussions of interethnic relations blocked the ability of people of color to more deeply explore their own biased beliefs about one another. With this realization, I became more active in addressing these issues in my classes and workshops, often pushing emotional hot buttons in some participants of color. The following journal entry made by a former African American student illustrates this point.

> *I've been angry at Professor Sue for this whole semester. I wish that they would have had a Black professor teach the class. How could he possibly have given me a B– in the midterm [racial counseling lab course]? I'll bet the White students got better grades. As a Black woman I know racism firsthand. They [White students] don't get it and still get better grades. And then we have to keep this stupid journal so he [professor] can have the TA help us process our feelings. I don't care if you read this stupid journal or not. . . . I know what I feel and why. . . . Well, I'm angry and furious that you gave me a low grade. . . . I'm angry at the White students who hide their racism and just say the right things in class. They are phonies. They are scared to death of me. . . . I just won't put up with their lies and I don't care if I make them cry. . . . I'm sure they think I'm just an angry Black woman. . .*

Why am I not getting an A in the course? I know why. It has to do with our role-play last week. The class thought I should have been more empathetic with Sandy [Asian American female who played the role of a client]. They said I couldn't relate to her and didn't explore her feelings of discrimination as an Asian. Well, I did. But you can't tell me that she suffers like Blacks do. I felt like saying. . .good, now you know what it feels like!!!!. . .

Then, Dr. Sue had to stop us from continuing and made process observations. He said I seemed to have difficulty being empathic with the client and believing her. What does he know? How does he know what's going on inside my head? But truth be told, Sandy doesn't have anything to complain or whine about. She doesn't understand what discrimination really is. . .maybe she has been treated poorly. . . but. . .but. . .well, I don't consider Asians people of color anyway. How can they claim to be oppressed when they are so successful? On this campus, they are everywhere, taking slots away from us. Sometimes I think they are whiter than Whites. I'll probably get an even worst grade because of what I'm saying, but who cares.

Interracial/Interethnic Biases

It took much class time and several individual meetings to finally get the student to begin examining her reactions to fellow White students and her images and prejudices toward Asians and Asian Americans. I [Derald Sue] tried to focus the discussion on the meaning of her extreme reactions to other group members and what significance it would have if they were her clients. Although the student did not change significantly because of her classroom experience, the lessons that came out from that role-play provided an opportunity for the entire class to enter a discussion of interracial/interethnic counseling topics. Some important themes are the following.

Impact on Interracial Counseling Relationships

First, we must not blame the victim (African American student) for the strong and emotive feelings of anger, resentment, and bitterness emanating from her. It is important to understand and be empathic to the fact that these reactions are most likely the result of cumulative years of prejudice and discrimination directed toward her as a socially devalued group member (Parham, Ajamu, & White, 2011; Ridley, 2005). Is she justified in her anger? The answer is probably "yes." But is her anger and bitterness misdirected and likely to cause her difficulty in working with Asian American and White clients? Again, the answer is probably "yes."

In working with White clients, members of oppressed groups might (a) be unable to contain their anger and rage toward majority group clients, as they are viewed as the oppressor, (b) have difficulty understanding the worldview of their clients, (c) be hindered in their ability to establish rapport, (d) be pulled between opposing tendencies of helping and harming their clients, and (e) be guilty of imposing their racial realities upon clients. The following quote indicates that this type of dilemma can occur in any marginalized-dominant therapeutic relationship. In this case, the female therapist echoes this challenging dilemma in working with a male client.

> *My challenge has been in my work with men. I have always felt somewhat constrained with my male clients and did not like the impact it had on our therapy. I had talked to other women therapists about my difficulties and found that they had similar experiences. My problems became most evident to me when issues related to privilege, gender, and power needed to be discussed. I found myself caught between being too adversarial and challenging on one hand and the "all-giving" protector trained to soothe pain on the other. (Kort, 1997, p. 97)*

Stereotypes Held by Socially Marginalized Group Members

Second, the African American student possesses many stereotypes and inaccurate beliefs about Asian Americans. She seems to operate from the assumptions that Asian Americans "are not people of color," that they know little about racism and discrimination, and that they are like Whites. These statements and her desire that a Black professor should teach the course rather than an Asian American reflect these beliefs. As you will see shortly in Chapter 16, headlines in the national press such as "Asian Americans: Outwhiting Whites" and "Asian Americans: The Model Minority" have perpetuated the success myth and belief that Asians are a "*model minority*" and somehow immune to prejudice and racism (D. W. Sue, 2010b).

These false stereotypes of Asian Americans have often played into major misunderstandings and conflicts between the African American and Asian American communities (Kim & Park, 2013). The issue here is the stereotypes that various racial/ethnic groups hold toward one another. For example, in one study, it was found that more than 40 percent of African Americans and Hispanics believe that Asian Americans are unscrupulous, crafty, and devious in business (National Conference of Christians and Jews, 1994). How do these beliefs affect interethnic relations, and how do they affect the counseling/therapy process? No racial/ethnic group is immune from inheriting biased beliefs, misinformation, and stereotypes of other groups. This is a reality often not discussed in courses on diversity and multiculturalism.

The Who-Is-More-Oppressed Game

Third, we have some flavor of the "*who's more oppressed*?" trap being played out in the mind of the African American student. She believes that Sandy can in no way equate her experiences of discrimination and prejudice with the Black experience. And perhaps she is right! There is little doubt that a racial hierarchy exists in our society in which various groups can be ordered along a continuum. The fact that African Americans have historically been and continue to be in the national forefront of the civil rights debate must be acknowledged and appreciated by all.

There is also, however, little doubt that each group—whether Native American, African American, Latino/a American, or Asian American—can claim that it has suffered immensely from racism. But what we need to realize is that all oppression is damaging and serves to separate rather than unify. Playing the "who is more oppressed?" game is destructive to group unity and counterproductive to combating racism. If we understand our own group's oppression, shouldn't it be easier to recognize the oppression of another? To use one group's oppression to negate that of another group is to diminish, dismiss, or negate the claims of another. This leads to separation rather than mutual understanding.

COUNSELORS FROM MARGINALIZED GROUPS WORKING WITH MAJORITY AND OTHER MARGINALIZED GROUP CLIENTS

Counseling the Culturally Diverse has never shied away from tackling controversial issues and topics, especially when they are central to the education and training of culturally competent mental health professionals. Persons of color, for example, have major hesitations and concerns about publicly airing *interracial/interethnic conflicts*, differences, and misunderstandings because of the possible political ramifications for group unity. But it appears that cultural competency and cultural humility objectives are equally applicable to therapists of color and to other clinicians from marginalized groups.

There is legitimacy, however, as to why greater emphasis has been placed on the education of White trainees: (a) the majority of counseling and mental health providers are White or members of the majority group; (b) the theories and practices of counseling/therapy arise from a predominantly White, Western perspective and form the educational foundations of our graduate programs; and (c) White, male, and straight EuroAmericans continue to control and hold power in being able to determine the definitions of normality and abnormality and to define mental health reality for marginalized groups. Even if counselors and therapists of color work with other culturally diverse groups, they are generally educated in White, Western ways of describing, explaining, diagnosing, and treating mental disorders. Thus there is great justification for continuing to focus primarily upon the education and training of those who control the gateways to the delivery of mental health services to socially devalued client populations.

On the other hand, it is clear that all groups can benefit from learning to work with one another. Being a helping professional or trainee of color does not automatically denote cultural competence in working with other clients of color or with White clients. Being a member of an oppressed or marginalized group (e.g., a gay and/or a woman therapist) does not mean you are more effective in treating other culturally diverse clients than if you were a straight or male therapist. It is important to recognize that in the area of racial interactions, multicultural counseling and therapy is more than White–Black, White–Asian, or White–Latino/a. To be a truly multicultural discipline, we must also recognize that MCT involves multiple combinations such as Asian–Black, Latino/a–Native American, Black–Latino/a, and so on.

The American Counseling Association has begun to recognize in their proposed Multicultural and Social Justice Counseling Competencies (MSJCC) that the dimensions of privilege and oppressed statuses vary in the therapeutic relationship between counselors and clients (Ratts, Singh, Nassar-McMillan, Butler, & McCullough, 2015). Most discussions of *multicultural counseling* focus upon White therapists (privileged status) and clients of color (oppressed status) and little emphasis is placed on other combinations: counselors of color (oppressed status) working with White clients (privileged status) or counselors of color (oppressed status) working with clients of color (oppressed status).

> ## REFLECTION AND DISCUSSION QUESTIONS
>
> 1. How does a counselor of color work with a White client who expresses racist thoughts and feelings in the therapeutic session? Should he or she confront the client about these biased attitudes? Is this therapeutic?
>
> 2. What biases and prejudices do people of color have toward one another?
>
> 3. What advantages and disadvantages do you foresee in counselors of color working with clients of color?

We address these issues from a number of perspectives: sociopolitical group relationships, cultural differences, *racial identity* development, and practice implications. We start with the assumption that people in the United States, regardless of race and ethnicity, are exposed to the racial, gender, and sexual orientation socialization processes of this society and also inherit racial, gender, and sexual orientation biases about various populations. We focus primarily on racial/ethnic combinations, but similar analysis using gender, sexual orientation, disability, social class, and other combinations are also important to consider. We are hopeful that these other relationships may be explored further in your classes and workshops.

THE POLITICS OF INTERETHNIC AND INTERRACIAL BIAS AND DISCRIMINATION

People of color generally become very wary about discussing interethnic and interracial misunderstandings and conflicts between various groups for fear that such problems may be used by those in power to

- assuage their own guilt feelings and excuse their racism—"People of color are equally racist, so why should I change when they can't even get along with one another?"

- divide and conquer—"As long as people of color fight among themselves, they can't form alliances to confront the establishment," and

- divert attention away from the injustices of society by defining problems as residing between various racial minority groups.

Further, readers must understand that prejudice toward other groups occurs under an umbrella of White racial superiority and supremacy; although members of socially devalued groups may discriminate, they do not have the systemic power to oppress on a large-scale basis (Spradlin & Parsons, 2008; Sue, 2015). In other words, although they may be able to hurt one another on an individual basis and to individually discriminate against White Americans, they possess little power to cause systemic harm, especially to White Americans. Some people of color have even suggested that interethnic prejudice among minorities serves to benefit only those in power.

As a result, people of color are sometimes cautioned not to "air dirty laundry in public." This admonition speaks realistically to the existence of miscommunications, disagreements, misunderstandings, and potential conflicts between and among groups of color. When they constituted a small percentage of the population, it was to their advantage to become allies in a united front against sources of injustice. Avoiding or minimizing interethnic group differences and conflicts served a functional purpose: to allow them to form coalitions of political, economic, and social power to effect changes in society. Although this solidarity may have been historically beneficial on a political and systemic level, the downside has been neglected in dealing with interracial differences that have proven to become problematic. This issue is even more pressing when, for example, one considers that people of color will become a numerical majority in the next several decades.

People of color have always known that they, too, harbor prejudicial and detrimental beliefs about one another and about majority group members. Feminists have acknowledged difficulty in relating to men who hold traditional beliefs about appropriate female gender roles.

> *I know that I'm a good therapist, but it galls me to have to work with men that are so dense about their own sexism. Last week I was doing marital counseling, and the husband kept interrupting his wife and berating her for not having his dinner on time when he returned from work, not having the home tidy, and keeping the kids quiet. He said she did not appreciate how hard he worked to keep food on the table. Well, I thought, what a chauvinistic attitude. What about his poor wife? Doesn't he have any idea of what it's like for her to raise the three kids? Does he think she has been lying on the couch and eating bon bons all day? I nearly blew up at him when he dismissed my observations about his behavior. He was treating me like his wife. I was furious at him. [His wife] would be better off getting a divorce. (female therapist)*

LGBT groups describe negative reactions to straights who voice beliefs that gay sex is immoral, that marriage should be between a man and a woman, or that their religion condemns LGBT lifestyles.

> *My greatest difficulty is working with patients who are strongly homophobic. You see, I am gay, an invisible minority. People assume I'm heterosexual, so in therapy they give voice to many anti-gay beliefs. I'm often conflicted about what to say or do. By ignoring the comments or allowing them to go unchallenged, am I perpetuating such beliefs? Is it my role to challenge them? (gay male therapist)*

If we also look at the relationships between groups of color, misunderstandings and mistrust become very obvious. In the early 1990s, the racial discourse in urban America was dominated by African American boycotts of Korean mom-and-pop grocery stores, which was followed by looting, firebombing, and mayhem that engulfed Los Angeles (Chang, 2001). Many in the Black community felt that Koreans were exploiting their communities as had White businesses. Instances of Hispanic and Black conflicts in the inner cities have also been reported throughout the country. As Latinos have surpassed Blacks in numbers, they have increasingly demanded a greater voice in communities and in the political process. Since Latinos and Blacks tend to gravitate toward the same inner-city areas and compete for the same jobs, great resentment has grown between the groups (Wood, 2006).

On November 20, 2014, President Obama single-handedly issued an executive order protecting some estimated 5 million undocumented immigrants from being deported, an action that created a huge outcry from many White Americans. The immigration issue has also historically sparked fierce debate within the Latino and Black communities, as some Blacks believe jobs are being lost to the huge influx of Latinos (Behnken, 2011). In essence, the discourse of race that once was confined to Black–White relations has become increasingly multiethnic and multiracial. Several national surveys (Jones, 2013a, b; National Conference of Christians and Jews, 1994; Pew Research Center, 2008, 2012) found the following:

- More than 40% of African Americans and Hispanics, and one of every four Whites, believe that Asian Americans are "unscrupulous, crafty, and devious in business."

- Nearly half the Hispanic Americans surveyed and 40% of African Americans and Whites believe Muslims "belong to a religion that condones or supports terrorism."

- Blacks think they are treated far worse than Whites and worse than other minority groups when it comes to getting equal treatment in applying for mortgages, in the media, and in job promotions.

- Although an overwhelming number of people rate racial/ethnic relations between racial group combinations as positive, the most favorable ratings are Whites/Asians (80%) with Blacks/Hispanics in last place.

- Nearly 50% of African Americans believe Latino immigrants reduce job opportunities for them, while fewer than 40% of Latinos agree.

- Approximately 70% of Asian Americans rate their relations with Hispanics as good and 60% say that of Blacks. Interestingly and consistent with our earlier analysis, 50% of Korean Americans have negative views of their relationships with Blacks.

- Most Blacks and Latinos view their relationships positively, but Hispanics are less likely to say that the two groups get along well.

- Only 10% of African Americans—a staggeringly low number—believe the police treat them as fairly as other groups.

- African Americans believe that everyone else is treated with more equality and especially that Asian Americans are doing better.

- There is tremendous resentment of Whites by all minority groups.

- Two-thirds of minorities think Whites "believe they are superior and can boss people around," "are insensitive to other people," "control power and wealth in America," and "do not want to share it with non-Whites."

Three primary conclusions are noteworthy here: First, racial/ethnic groups harbor considerable mistrust, envy, and misunderstandings toward one another. Surprisingly, African Americans and Latinos held stronger negative beliefs about Asian Americans than did White Americans (40% versus 25%). Second, and not surprisingly, people of color continue to hold beliefs and attitudes toward Whites that are very negative and filled with resentments, anger, and strong mistrust. Third, dialogue between people of color must come out of the closet in order to make important and long-lasting progress toward mutual respect and understanding rather than a relationship simply based upon political convenience.

REFLECTION AND DISCUSSION QUESTIONS

1. What effect does interethnic bias on the part of therapists of color have upon their culturally diverse clients?

2. If an African American therapist works with an Asian American client or vice versa, what therapeutic issues are likely to arise?

3. Likewise, in light of the strong negative feelings expressed by all groups of color against Whites, how might a therapist of color react intentionally and unintentionally toward a White client?

Some might argue that a therapist of color working with a White client may be different from a therapist of color working with a client of color because power differentials still exist on a systemic level for White clients. Little in the way of research or conceptual scholarly contributions has addressed these questions. It may not be far-fetched, however, to surmise that these racial combinations may share some similar dynamics and clinical issues to White therapist/client-of-color dyads. Some increased understanding of these issues may come from a brief review of the historical analysis of interracial/interethnic relationships between groups of color in other venues of their lives.

THE HISTORICAL AND POLITICAL RELATIONSHIPS BETWEEN GROUPS OF COLOR

There is a paucity of literature that focuses specifically on interracial interactions between counselors and clients of different racial/ethnic minority groups (e.g., Asian, Black, Latino/a, or Native American). This may falsely convey that there is limited tension between groups of color and that discrimination and stereotyping does not occur between these groups. Given the history of the United States, it is apparent that discrimination and stereotyping does occur between all racial groups.

During the civil rights movement, people of color banded together to combat economic and social injustices that were against them. As a result, people of color have avoided public dialogue (on both individual and group levels) about historical and existing tensions among their groups. Because individuals of color have experienced racism throughout their lives, it may prove difficult for them to understand the biases they hold toward other groups. Some people of color believe that they would not be able to discriminate, stereotype, or pass judgment on others because they themselves have been racially victimized. Other people of color may recognize their biases but may believe that because they do not have any systemic power their biases are excusable or insignificant. Regardless of these perspectives, examining the history of interracial/interethnic relations may prove enlightening.

African American and Asian American Relationships

The conflicting relationships between African Americans and Asian Americans remained relatively unspoken until the Los Angeles Riots in 1992, in which some Black Americans looted Korean American businesses. The riot occurred when African Americans were outraged at the acquittal of four White officers from the Los Angeles Police Department in the beating of Rodney King, a Black motorist. Of the 4,500 stores that were looted and burned, however, 2,300 were Korean-owned (Yoon, 1997). Although hard feelings existed prior to the riots, this experience led to overt tension between the groups throughout the United States (K. Kim, 1999).

In interviews with several Korean American business owners, it was clear that they stereotyped Black American customers as likely to steal or become violent; likewise, some Black Americans who acted out against Korean businesses stereotyped Asian Americans as being racist and hostile toward them and thought that they took economic advantage of their communities. This may have even led to overt racist behaviors toward one another, in which Asian American store owners would blatantly refuse business from Black American patrons or follow them around stores, and Black Americans might blatantly use racial slurs such as "Chinaman" or "chink" when speaking to Korean workers (Myers, 2001).

Asian and Latino/a Americans

The historical relationship between Asian Americans and Latino/a Americans is almost never discussed and is usually invisible in discussions of race (De Genova, 2006). However, there are several ways in which these two groups may share a sense of camaraderie with one another along with divisive tension. Both groups share the experience of immigration; the majority of Asian Americans and Latino/a Americans are first- or second-generation Americans (De Genova, 2006; B.S.K. Kim, 2011). This shared history may lead to similar experiences of biculturalism (maintaining both Asian or Latino/a and American values) and culture conflicts, similar linguistic concerns (bilingualism), and similar experiences of pursuing the American dream. One of the dominant similarities between the two groups is their shared experience of being treated like foreigners in their own country (particularly those who were born and raised in the United States); another is that both groups are often left out of the Black–White racial paradigm debate.

When issues or matters of race are discussed in the news media, for example, the dialogue is usually Black–White and seldom includes Asian Americans or Latino/a Americans. This invisibility as groups of color in the racial debate has often created hard feelings in these two groups toward African Americans. Because these groups may feel invisible, they may compete with each other in order to have their voices heard. Historically there was a moment, during the Chicano-Filipino United Farm Workers Movement in the 1930s, in which Mexican and Filipino Americans worked cohesively for farm workers' rights in California. Yet they disbanded when the groups could not agree upon common interests (Scharlin & Villanueva, 1994). Currently, this may be exemplified with U.S. politics in which Asian and Latino Americans may run against each other in local elections instead of working harmoniously to form a unified alliance.

Latino/a Americans and Black Americans

The history between Latino/a Americans and Black Americans also has both solidarity and discord. Historically, there has been solidarity between the two groups, particularly in their quest for equality during the civil rights era (Behnken, 2011). Traditionally, both groups recognized each other as oppressed minority groups, understanding that the other may experience racism, be subjected to widespread stereotyping, and be denied equal access and opportunities given to White people. However, there are also points of contention between these two groups.

First, similar to the relationships between Asians and Latinos, there may be tension between Latinos and Blacks as a result of each group fighting for the sociopolitical issues and needs for its own group. In recent years, Latino/a Americans have overwhelmingly exceeded Black Americans in regard to population; this has led to Latinos gaining more visibility in politics and education (Wood, 2006). The rise of Latino/a demands has also created tension amongst Latinos and Blacks because they now find themselves competing for jobs, which has forced some Black Americans to oppose many Latino/a Americans in the immigration debate (Behnken, 2011). This competition for jobs has often resulted in problems related to a lack of alliance between the two groups, particularly when it comes to advocacy in government, education, and community organizing (Samad et al., 2006).

Second, it is important to recognize that racism within the Latino/a community has historical roots as a result of Spanish colonialism in Latin America. The term *Latino/a* is an ethnic designator and not a racial one. Hence Latinos may be members of any racial grouping. As a result, they may range from phenotypically appearing Black to White, with many appearing to be somewhere in between (Bautista, 2003). However, because of the colonial mentality, *mestizos,* or light-skinned Latinos, are valued more highly than darker-skinned Latinos, who may be viewed as inferior, unintelligent, or unattractive (*colorism*) (Patrinos, 2000). This may lead to a hierarchy within the Latino/a community, in which light-skinned groups, such as Argentineans, Colombians, or Cubans, may view themselves as superior to darker-skinned groups, such as Dominicans or Mexicans. This colonial mentality may transcend a Latino/a individual's view of a Black American; this observation is supported by studies showing that Latinos hold negative stereotypes of Black Americans as being lazy and untrustworthy, whereas Black Americans do not feel the same way about Latinos (McClain et al., 2006).

Native Americans and Black, Latino/a, and Asian Americans

The relationship between Native Americans and Black, Latino/a, and Asian Americans may not be discussed or known, due to the small numbers of Native Americans in the United States. Black Americans, Latinos, and Asians may have little interaction with Native Americans, which may lead to less obvious tension or dynamics between Native Americans and another racial group. Concurrently, because 40 percent of the Native American population may be of mixed racial background (U.S. Census Bureau, 2005), many Native Americans may physically look like members of other racial groups, causing others to perceive them and treat them in different ways. However, a Native American interacting with members of these racial groups may share similarities or experience tensions with individuals of other races, perhaps empathizing with a Black American's experiences of oppression or bonding with a Latino/a's or an Asian's feelings of being an invisible minority. At the same time, a Black, a Latino/a, or an Asian individual who does not recognize the Native American's *racial identity*, realities, history, or experiences may cause the Native American to feel dismissed, ignored, or invalidated.

DIFFERENCES BETWEEN RACIAL/ETHNIC GROUPS

To further understand interracial/interethnic dynamics, it is important to recognize that groups of color may hold values, beliefs, and behaviors unique to their cultures. Many of these differences in *cultural values* are addressed in Chapter 7. Specifically, previous literature has found that racial/ethnic groups have differences in worldviews and *communication styles*. These groups may have different views of therapy, based on cultural stigma and the group's historical experiences with mental health institutions. Knowledge of these cultural differences may aid mental health practitioners to better understand the types of dynamics that occur in a therapeutic relationship. Let us explore a few of these differences.

Cultural Values

Shared and nonshared values held by groups of color may lead to an experience of camaraderie or to one of tension and antagonism. For example, although many White Americans typically believe that people have mastery and control over the environment, persons of color typically believe that people and nature are harmonious with one another (Chen, 2005; McCormick, 2005). Additionally, whereas Whites adhere to the value of individualism, Asian, Native, Black, and Latino/a Americans may maintain the values of collectivism, in which the needs of the group/family/community are paramount. Within collectivism, emphasis is placed on the family, what Latinos call *familialism* or *familismo*; a high value is placed on family loyalty and unity (Arredondo, Gallardo-Cooper, Delgado-Romero, & Zapata, 2014; Guzman & Carrasco, 2011). If a Latino/a counselor ascribes to familismo and works with a client of color who does not place the same central importance on the family, the counselor may inadvertently interpret this person to be emotionally disconnected and isolated.

Although sharing a cultural value may lead to a therapeutic working relationship between two different individuals of color, its expression may potentially cause a misunderstanding in therapy as well. For example, respect for elders is a value traditionally held by both Asian Americans (Kim & Park, 2013) and African Americans (Evans, 2013). However, expression of this value may differ among members of each racial group. In some Asian American cultures, respect is shown by not talking unless spoken to and by averting one's eyes and thus not making direct eye contact with the elder or respected person (Nadal, 2011). An African American counselor may misinterpret an avoidance of eye contact by an Asian American client to be a sign of disrespect, avoidance, or even deceitfulness. In fact, during the Los Angeles riots, this major cultural difference created much animosity between Black patrons and Korean American shop owners; the former saw Koreans as unable to be truthful about prices in the store because they wouldn't "look you in the eye." Conversely, the Korean shop owner saw the African American customer as rude, demanding, and aggressive.

Communication Styles

The previous examples lead to our discussion of differences in *communication styles* between various racial/ethnic groups. Communication style differences (see Chapter 8) displayed by therapists can impact the expectations or responsiveness of clients from different backgrounds. Native Americans, for example, are more likely to speak softly, use an indirect gaze, and interject less frequently, whereas White Americans are more likely to speak loudly, have direct eye contact, and show a direct approach (Duran, 2006). These same characteristics may be displayed by therapists when they interact with clients. Hence therapists need to be aware of their verbal and nonverbal styles and to determine how they may either facilitate or act as a barrier to the formation of a therapeutic alliance.

Communication styles may include overt verbal communication that may occur between two people (content of what is said) but may also include nonverbal communication (body language, tone of voice, volume of speech, what is not said, and the directness of speech), which is equally as important as the spoken word. African American communication style tends to be direct, passionate, and forthright (an indication of sincerity and truthfulness) (Kochman, 1981; Parham et al., 2011). However, Asian culture highly prizes a person's subtlety and indirectness in communication, as it is considered a sign of respect to the other person (B.S.K. Kim, 2011). Even when disagreements are present, differences are discussed tactfully, avoiding direct confrontation.

Native Americans and Latino/a Americans may be nonconfrontational like Asian Americans, but their communication styles may change depending on the varying levels of authority between two people (Garrett & Portman, 2011). For example, Latino/a children are expected to respect their parents, to speak only when spoken to, to have younger siblings defer to older ones, and to yield to the wishes of someone with higher status and authority. Latino/a students, thus, may feel uncomfortable challenging or speaking directly to their teachers (Santiago-Rivera, Arredondo, & Gallardo-Cooper, 2002). This value may also conflict with the White American value of egalitarianism, where children are encouraged to freely express their thoughts and feelings. Although African American *commu-nication styles* may be egalitarian as well, they are likely to be more animated and interpersonal, generating much emotion, affect, and feeling (Hecht, Jackson, & Ribeau, 2002; Weber, 1985). Given this, if an African American counselor com-municates in a more animated and passionate fashion, it may negatively impact Latino/a or Asian American clients.

Issues Regarding Stage of Ethnic Identity

The processes of assimilation and acculturation for various racial/ethnic minority groups in the United States are powerful forces in the development of identity. Studies continue to indicate that as groups of color are exposed to the values, beliefs, and standards of the larger society, many become increasingly Western-ized. This process is described more fully in Chapter 11, so we will not elaborate here. People of color who are born and raised in the United States may continue to value their traditional racial/ethnic group heritage, actively reject it in favor of an "American identity," or form an integrated new identity. Depending on where they may fall on this continuum, their reactions to other people of color (both within and outside their own group) and to majority individuals may differ con-siderably. The stage of identity of ethnic minority therapists is likely to affect their work with clients.

COUNSELORS OF COLOR AND DYADIC COMBINATIONS

The analysis in this chapter indicates how important sociopolitical factors, historical relationships between racial/ethnic minority groups, differences in *cultural values*, and racial identity of counselors and clients can serve either to enhance or to under-mine the counseling process (Comas-Diaz & Jacobsen, 1995; Ratts & Pedersen, 2014). Little actual research has been conducted on the challenges and difficulties that counselors of color face when working with other culturally diverse groups. Less yet has been done on the subject of cultural competence as it relates to therapists of color. Nevertheless, the foregoing analysis would imply several situational challenges that therapists and trainees of color might expect on their journey to cultural com-petence. Table 3.1 outlines five common challenges therapists of color encounter as they work with White clients and five for working with clients of color.

TABLE 3.1   Ten Common Challenges Counselors of Color Face When Working with White Clients and Clients of Color

Counselor of Color and White Client Dyads

1. Challenging the Competency of Counselors of Color
2. Needing to Prove Competence
3. Transferring Racial Animosity toward White Clients
4. Viewing the Counselor of Color as a Super Minority Therapist
5. Dealing with Client Expressions of Racism

Counselor of Color and Client of Color Dyads

1. Overidentification with the Client
2. Encountering Clashes in Cultural Values
3. Experiencing Clashes in Communication and Counseling Styles
4. Receiving and Expressing Racial Animosity
5. Dealing With the Stage of Racial Identity of the Client or Counselor

Challenges Associated with Counselor of Color and White Client Dyads

When working with White clients, a counselor of color is likely to operate in a situation of power reversal (Comas-Diaz, 2012; Comas-Diaz & Jacobsen, 1995). When the counselor is White and the client is a person of color, the power relationship is congruent with historical and sociopolitical racial roles and structures in our society. The roles of colonizer-colonized, master-slave, and oppressor-oppressed have defined relationships of who are leaders and followers, who is superior and inferior, and who is given higher or lower status (Ratts & Pedersen, 2014). When the counselor is a person of color, however, it fosters a role reversal because the status of therapist denotes a person who possesses a set of expertise that surpasses that of the White client. In this case, the White client is in need of help, and the counselor of color is in a position to provide it (to diagnose, treat, advise, teach, and guide). Many White clients may find this dependent role very disturbing and manifest it in various ways. Some may, however, find the new relationship exotic or even a positive development. Counselors of color may also misuse the power reversal to harm or to deny appropriate help to their White clients.

Situation 1: Challenging the Competency of Counselors of Color

Whether White clients are conscious of it or not, they may directly or indirectly engage in maneuvers that challenge the credibility of the counselor of color, question the counselor's competence, negate the counselor's insights and advice, and undermine the therapeutic process (D. W. Sue, 2010a). Such challenges are not necessarily conscious to the client or expressed overtly. They may be manifested through an excessive interest in seeking greater information about the counselor's training and background, type of degrees received, place of training, and number of years in clinical practice. Or, they may be expressed through a tendency to be hypercritical of even the smallest omissions, oversights, and mistakes of the counselor. Behind these resistant behaviors is a presumption that therapists of color are less qualified than White ones—that therapists of color achieved their positions not through their own internal attributes (intelligence and abilities) or efforts (motivation and actions) but through external circumstance, such as attending lesser qualified schools or being recipients of affirmative action programs. A study exploring both White and African American therapists' experiences in working with White clients supports these observations. Ethnic minority therapists consistently reported being the recipient of greater hostility, resistance, and mistrust in cross-racial practice than their White counterparts (Davis & Gelsomino, 1994).

For counselors of color, there are no easy answers or solutions to dealing with challenges to their credibility. A decision to explore or confront a White client's resistance to the counselor of color depends on many internal and contextual factors: (a) the counselor of color's comfort with his or her racial/cultural identity, (b) clinical significance of the behavior, (c) timeliness of the intervention, (d) strength of the relationship, and (e) the form in which the intervention would take place. Regardless, several overarching guidelines might prove helpful here. First and foremost, a challenge to one's competence is not a pleasant thing, especially if it is tinged with racial overtones. Although the counselor may become upset with the client, become defensive, and allow the defensiveness to dictate actions in the therapeutic session, these reactions are counterproductive to helping the client. Second, before an effective intervention can take place, a counselor must recognize the resistance for what it is. This means an accurate diagnosis separating out behaviors such as questioning one's qualifications from other clinical motivations. Third, a decision to intervene must be dictated by timeliness: it should occur at an opportune time that would maximize the insight of the client. Last, as the therapist of color will need to address racial issues, he or she must feel comfortable with engaging in a difficult dialogue on race.

Situation 2: Needing to Prove Competence

The fact that some Whites may consciously and unconsciously harbor beliefs that persons of color are less capable than Whites may affect people of color in two ways: (a) they may internalize these beliefs and stereotypes about themselves and their own group, or (b) they can become victims of *stereotype threat*, despite not believing in their own inferiority (Steele, 1997). The former may be especially true for therapists who have not resolved issues surrounding their *racial identity* and have accepted and adopted the standards and beliefs of mainstream society (Helms, 1995). In these cases, counselors of color may be trapped in the need to prove their competence and capabilities; unfortunately, this proof must come from White society, other White helping professionals, and even from White clients. In the counseling session, this type of conflict may be played out in seeking affirmation from White clients and abdicating their roles as experts in the relationship. They may also have a disinclination to see clients of color because it may bring to mind their own internalized racism that creates discomfort for them. In such cases, counselors of color may be paralyzed in discussing racial dynamics, experience extreme anxiety when racial issues arise, and allow their clients to take the lead in the sessions.

Even if a counselor of color has a healthy *racial identity* and does not believe the stereotypes of his or her own group's inferiority, that therapist may experience *stereotype threat* (Steele, 2003; Steele, Spencer, & Aronson, 2002). Research on *stereotype threat* suggests that persons of color are oftentimes placed in a position in which they fear confirming a mistaken notion about themselves. For example, Black students taking a math test and being told that it was a measure of intelligence have been found to perform more poorly than their White counterparts, despite possessing equal skills and abilities. Yet when given the identical task but instructed that the test was not a measure of intelligence, the performance of Black students equaled that of Whites. These researchers concluded that the fear of confirming a stereotype (e.g., Blacks are less intelligent than Whites and lack higher-order abstract conceptual ability) created emotional threat and tension, hence Black students worked hard to disconfirm stereotypes, which drained energies away from the task at hand. The result was underperformance in problem solving.

It is not too far-fetched to imagine how *stereotype threat* might also affect a counselor of color's performance in therapy. The counselor may repeatedly feel pressure to disconfirm stereotypes, to enhance credibility, and to prove to White clients and White mental health professionals that he or she is capable and competent. For example, an African American woman found herself placing on her office wall every professional certificate that she had received during her working career. When a colleague commented to her that her office's walls were appearing cluttered, the therapist was able to identify this behavior with the onset of her working with White patients (Comas-Diaz & Jacobsen, 1995, p. 102).

Situation 3: Transferring Racial Animosity toward White Clients

This situation is likely to arise through a process of countertransference where the counselor of color transfers feelings of resentment, anger, and antagonism toward White society to the client. In general, the therapist of color is unable to separate out the experiences of racism, discrimination, and prejudice experienced through years of oppression from those of the client. The White client may become a symbol of the inherent mistrust that exists in majority-minority interpersonal relationships; thus the counselor/therapist may harbor negative feelings that infect and distort the counseling relationship. In most cases these grudges do not operate at a conscious level, but they are likely to present themselves in various forms: (a) dismissing or diluting the pain and suffering of their White clients, (b) being unable to form a working alliance, (c) having difficulty in being empathetic to the client's plight, (d) being ultrasensitive to potential racial slights, (e) distorting or misinterpreting the client's actions to include a racial motivation, and (f) possessing an unconscious desire to harm rather than help White clients. This is potentially a toxic situation and is best resolved within therapists of color prior to clinical practice.

Situation 4: Viewing the Counselor of Color as a Super Minority Counselor

It may appear contradictory, but evidence exists, in the form of counselor preference studies and clinical narratives, that some White clients actually prefer a therapist of color over a White one (Sue & Sue, 2013). It has been found, for example, that some White college students actually indicate a preference for seeing a Black helping professional. The reason behind such a preference flies in the face of traditional race relations and is difficult to explain. In our own work with White clients and in speaking to colleagues of color, however, several possibilities have arisen.

First, many White clients may possess an exaggerated sense of the therapist of color's qualifications, reasoning that to have achieved the status of therapist would require a nearly superhuman effort against the forces of discrimination. His or her accomplishments could come only from high intelligence, outstanding abilities, and high motivation. Thus the therapist of color is seen as immensely superior and likely to better help the client. Second, many clients, regardless of race, often feel rejected, invalidated, misunderstood, and put down, and suffer from pangs of inferiority and feelings of worthlessness. White clients may possess a mistaken notion that a therapist of color (who him- or herself has suffered from racism and stigmatization) may be able to sympathize and empathize better with the client. Third, the therapist of color may be perceived as an expert on race relations, and some Whites may be consciously or unconsciously attempting to deal with their own racial attitudes. At times the White client may be coping either with a conscious interracial relationship (e.g., dating a person of another race) or with more subtle unconscious personal dilemmas (e.g., White guilt and issues of privilege).

There is certainly a seductive quality to being perceived in such a favorable light, being viewed as an expert, and being accorded such high respect. This challenge is particularly difficult for therapists of color who in their daily lives outside of therapy sessions are not easily accorded the respect and dignity given to others. Yet to allow the "super minority counselor" image to persist is to perpetuate the false illusion of White clients and to potentially harm therapeutic progress. In this situation, the White clients may abdicate responsibility for their own improvements and become overly dependent on the counselor for answers to their problems. Counselors of color need to have a good sense of themselves as racial/cultural beings and not fall into the all-omnipotent trap.

Situation 5: Dealing with Client Expressions of Racism

It goes without saying that counselors/therapists of color often encounter racist, sexist, and heterosexist statements and reactions from their clients. Whereas many LGBT people may remain invisible, people of color represent a visible racial/ethnic minority with distinguishable physical features. Counselors of color, through appearance, speech, or other characteristics, generate reactions. These perceived differences may influence the development of a therapeutic relationship. As Asian American therapists, we've had clients make statements such as, "I like Chinese food" or "The Chinese are very smart and family-oriented," or they exhibit some discomfort when meeting us for the first time. In one study (Fuertes & Gelso, 2000), male Hispanic counselors who spoke with a Spanish accent were rated lower in expertise by EuroAmerican students than those counselors without an accent. This phenomenon may also exist for therapists with other accents and may need to be discussed in therapy to allay anxiety in both the therapist and the client. One graduate student from Bosnia would discuss her accent and would let clients know that English was her second language. Although her command of English was good, this explanation helped establish a more collaborative relationship.

Acknowledging differences or investigating the reasons for client reactions is important since they may affect the therapeutic process. In one instance, an African American psychology intern working with a man in his 70s noticed that the client persisted in telling stories about the "Negro fellas" that he served with in the army.

He made positive comments about his Black comrades and talked about their contributions to the unit. The intern responded by saying, "I guess you noticed I'm Black" (Hinrichsen, 2006, p. 31). This response led to a discussion of client concerns that he would say something that might be considered offensive. He also worried about whether the intern could understand the experience of an older White man.

White counselors facing an ethnic minority client often struggle with whether to ask, "How do you feel working with a White helping professional?" This situation is also faced by counselors of color working with White clients. When differences between therapist and client are apparent (e.g., ethnicity, gender, ability, age) or revealed (e.g., religion, sexual orientation), acknowledging them is important. Both African American and White American students revealed a stronger preference for openness and self-disclosure when asked to imagine a counselor of a different ethnicity (Cashwell, Shcherbakova, & Cashwell, 2003). Self-disclosure, or the acknowledgment of differences, may increase feelings of similarity between therapist and client and reduce concerns about differences. In this respect, the same might apply when both the therapist and the client are persons of color but are from different racial/ethnic groups.

Challenges Associated with Counselor of Color and Client of Color Dyads

Many of the challenges facing therapists of color working with White clients can also make their appearance in counseling dyads where both are from marginalized groups. Like their White counterparts, people of color are socialized into the dominant values and beliefs of the larger society. As a result, they may inherit perceptions and beliefs about other racial/ethnic minority groups. In this case, the biases and stereotypes held about other groups of color may not be all that different from those held by White Americans. A Latino/a American client can harbor doubts about the qualifications of a Native American counselor; an Asian American client can act out racist attitudes toward an African American counselor, and an African American counselor may downplay the role that prejudice and discrimination play in the life of Asian Americans. Other interethnic/interracial specific challenges may also make their appearance in the counseling dyad.

Situation 1: Overidentification with the Client

Overidentification with clients of color, whether with in-group or outgroup dyadic counseling racial relationships, is often manifested through countertransference.

Although it is accepted that the transference of symbolic feelings, thoughts, and experiences of the client of color can occur in relation to the counselor, an equally powerful countertransference can occur from therapist to client, especially in interracial and interethnic dyadic combinations.

> Years ago, one of the authors was supervising a young African American male trainee in the college counseling center. He was meeting for the first time with an African American male student-athlete who came to the clinic complaining of "not being played enough" in the football games and spending more time warming the bench than most of his fellow White students. He described experiencing racial taunts from fans on the opposing teams and described how he felt isolated from his own teammates and believed his White coach and his staff was prejudiced. He was fearful of being dropped by the team and losing his scholarship. The experience of discrimination was so disturbing, according to the student, that he was unable to concentrate on his studies and was depressed. By the end of the first session, the African American trainee agreed to contact his professors to obtain an extension in taking further finals, speak to the coach about the many racist incidents he was being subjected to, and contact the ombudsperson about the plight of the student. In fact, the two even discussed possible legal action that could be taken on behalf of the student.

Although it would appear admirable that the African American trainee was willing to engage in all these advocacy actions, there was only one thing wrong: He accepted the story of the client without exploration or corroboration from other sources. As it turned out, the African American football player had equal, if not greater, playing time than his White teammates; his supposed isolation was due to his own disinclination to mix with other students; and his poor school performance was evident even prior to these supposed incidents. In fact, the coach stated that the student was an outstanding tight end and that it would be a serious blow to the prospects of the team should he be unable to play. He emphatically emphasized that the student was in no danger of being dropped from the team, unless his academic performance made such a decision inevitable. In processing the situation with the African American counselor, it became apparent that he overidentified with the Black client. He too had been a football player in high school and experienced hearing racial epithets directed at him during games. When he heard the tale of the Black client, he experienced rage and anger. He was too quick to accept the story of the client and became immersed in the situation. Because emotional hot buttons were pushed in him, his own experiences were transferred to the student, producing tunnel vision that prevented him from entertaining other perspectives.

It is said that people of color share a sense of peoplehood in that, despite cultural differences, they know what it is like to live and deal with a monocultural society. They have firsthand experience with prejudice, discrimination, stereotyping, and oppression. It is a constant reality in their lives. They know what it is like to be "the only one," to have their thoughts and feelings invalidated, to have their sons and daughters teased because of their differences, to be constantly seen as inferior or lesser human beings, and to be denied equal access and opportunity (Sue, 2010a). For these reasons, countertransference among counselors of color working with clients of color is a real possibility. Thus, although therapists of color must work hard not to dismiss the stated experiences of their clients, they must work equally hard to separate out their own experiences from those of their clients.

Situation 2: Encountering Clashes in Cultural Values

As we have mentioned earlier, cultural differences can impact the way we perceive events. This was clearly seen in a study involving Chinese American and White American psychiatrists (Li-Repac, 1980). Both groups of therapists viewed and rated recorded interviews with Chinese and White patients. When rating White patients, White therapists were more likely to use terms such as *affectionate, adventurous,* and *capable,* whereas Chinese therapists used terms such as *active, aggressive,* and *rebellious* to describe the same patients. Similarly, White psychiatrists described Chinese patients as *anxious, awkward, nervous,* and *quiet,* whereas Chinese psychiatrists were more likely to use the terms *adaptable, alert, dependable,* and *friendly.* It is clear that both majority and minority therapists are influenced by their ethnocentric beliefs and values.

Many cultural value differences between groups of color are as great and prone to misinterpretation and conflict as are those among groups of color and White Americans. In the previous study it was clear that the Chinese psychiatrists made such evaluations based upon a number of *cultural values.* They saw the more active and direct expressions of feeling as aggressive, hostile, and rebellious and the more controlled, sedate, and indirect expressions of emotion as indicative of dependable and healthy responding. A prime example of how different cultural dictates affect interpersonal behavior and interpretation is seen in the ways that emotions are expressed among Asian Americans, Latino/a Americans, and African

Americans. Restraint of strong feelings is considered a sign of maturity, wisdom, and control among many Asian cultures. The wise and mature "man" is considered able to control feelings (both positive and negative). Thus Asian Americans may avoid overtly displaying emotions and even discussing them with others (Kim & Park, 2013). This is in marked contrast to many Latinos, who value emotional and physical closeness when communicating with each other (Guzman & Carrasco, 2011). Likewise, African Americans operate from a cultural context in which the expression of affect and passion in interpersonal interactions is a sign of sincerity, authenticity, and humanness (Parham et al., 2011).

Therapists of color who operate from their own worldview without awareness of the different worldviews held by other clients of color may be guilty of cultural oppression, imposing their values and standards upon culturally diverse clients. The outcome can be quite devastating and harmful to clients of color. Let us use the example of a potential misunderstanding likely to occur between an African American counselor and an Asian American client (both holding the values described earlier). As the African American counselor encounters an Asian American client who values restraint of strong feelings, several potential culture-clash scenarios are likely to occur in a situation where the expression of feelings seems called for: First, the Asian American client's reluctance to express feelings in an emotional situation (loss of a job, death of a loved one, etc.) might be perceived as denial, or as emotionally inappropriate or unfeeling. Second, in a situation where the feelings are being discussed and the client does not desire to, or appears unable to, express them, the counselor may potentially interpret the client as resistant, unable to access emotions, repressed, or inhibited. These potentially negative misinterpretations have major consequences for the client, who may be misdiagnosed and treated inappropriately. It is clear that counselors of color, when working with clients of color, must be aware of their own worldviews and those of their diverse clients.

Situation 3: Experiencing Clashes in Communication and Counseling Styles

One area of a possible clash in *communication styles* is that of how groups use personal space when speaking to one another. Africans, Black Americans, and Latinos, as a rule, have a much closer conversing distance with one another than either White Americans or Asian Americans (Jensen, 1985; Nydell, 1996). How culture dictates conversation distances is well defined, and varies according to many sociodemographic differences, including race, ethnicity, and gender. Whereas a

Black therapist may value proximity to an Asian American client in therapy (e.g., sitting closer or learning forward), the latter may feel quite uncomfortable and find such close conversing distances to be an intrusion of personal space. Worse yet, the client may interpret the counselor as aggressive, rude, or disrespectful. The Black therapist, on the other hand, may view the Asian American client as cold, unfeeling, and evasive. Further, major differences may be exaggerated by the manner of communication. Blacks tend to be more direct in their *communication styles* (thoughts and feelings), whereas Asian Americans tend to be more indirect and subtle in communication; an Asian American client may feel uncomfortable with a Black American who expresses him- or herself in such a forthright and open manner.

Therapy is a context in which communication is paramount, and there are many ways that these differences in *communication styles* across races and cultures manifest in the therapeutic relationship. First, because Asian Americans, Latino/a Americans, and Native Americans may be indirect in their *communication styles* and may avoid eye contact when listening and speaking, they are often pathologized as being resistant to therapy (D. W. Sue, 2010a). At the same time, because Black Americans are stereotyped as being quick to anger and prone to violence and crime, they are often viewed as threatening and can trigger fear in people (D. W. Sue, 2010b). The combination of these two contrary types of communication can lead to various tensions in a therapeutic relationship. Again, counselors of color must (a) understand their communication and therapeutic styles and the potential impact they have on other clients of color, (b) be aware of and knowledgeable about the *communication styles* of other groups of color, and (c) be willing to modify their intervention styles to be consistent with the cultural values and life experiences of their culturally diverse clients.

Situation 4: Receiving and Expressing Racial Animosity

A counselor of color may be the object of racial animosity from clients of color simply because he or she is associated with the mental health system. Many people of color have viewed mental health practice and therapy as a White middle-class activity with values that are often antagonistic to the ones held by groups of color. African Americans, for example, may have a negative view of therapy, often holding a "historical hostility" response because of the history of oppression of Blacks in the United States (Ridley, 2005). Therapy is highly stigmatizing among many in the Asian American community, who often view it as a source of shame and disgrace (Kim & Park, 2013). Latino/a Americans may react similarly, believing that therapy is not only stigmatizing but that "talk therapies" are less appropriate and helpful than concrete advice and suggestions (de las Fuentes, 2006). Native Americans may vary in their views of therapy, depending on their level of assimilation; traditional Native Americans may view Westernized institutions and practices as not trustworthy or as ineffective in comparison to spiritual healing or indigenous practices (Duran, 2006).

Given these different views of therapy and mental health practices, there are several dynamics that can occur between racial groups. Black American clients may view therapy as a symbol of political oppression and may perceive a Latino/a American therapist or even a Black counselor as a sellout to the broader society. Or because traditional forms of therapy oftentimes emphasize insight through the medium of verbal self-exploration, many Asian and Latino/a clients may view the process as inappropriate and question the qualifications of the therapist. Native American clients who value nontraditional counseling or spiritual healing may not seek or continue therapy, especially if a counselor of any race does not recognize alternatives to Western practices. All of these factors may influence the dynamics in a counseling relationship in which the therapist of color is responded to as a symbol of oppression and as someone who cannot relate to the client's problems. The therapist's credibility and trustworthiness are suspect, and will be frequently tested in the session. These tests may vary from overt hostility to other forms of resistance.

We have already spent considerable time discussing the racial animosity that has historically existed between racial groups and how it may continue to affect the race relations between groups of color. Like Situations 3 and 5 therapists of color working with White clients, similar dynamics can occur between racial/ethnic minority individuals in the therapy sessions. Therapists of color may be either targets or perpetrators of racial animosity in therapy sessions. This is often exaggerated by differences in *cultural values* and *communication styles* that trigger stereotypes that affect their attitudes toward one another. Thus, if Latino/a clients hold stereotypes (consciously or unconsciously) toward Black counselors (e.g., believing them violent, dangerous, and aggressive), these beliefs may reinforce the hostility they feel toward Black Americans. Clinically, like work with White clients, counselors of color may transfer their animosity toward minority clients; or, similar to hostility from White clients, they may receive racial animosity from clients of color. Our clinical analysis and suggestions in those situations would be similar for counselors of color working with clients of color.

Situation 5: Dealing with the Stage of Racial Identity of Counselors and Clients

We have already stressed the importance of considering the racial/cultural identity stage of both therapists of color and clients of color. We explore this issue in detail in Chapter 11, "Racial/Cultural Identity Development in People of Color: Counseling Implications." How it affects within-group and between-group racial/ethnic minority counseling is extremely important for cultural competence. Thus we will defer our discussion for now, until we reach that point. Suffice it to say that the degree of assimilation/acculturation and *racial identity* of both the counselor and the client of color can result in dyadic combinations that create major conflicts.

REFLECTION AND DISCUSSION QUESTIONS

1. What are some of the therapeutic issues that face counselors of color working with members of their own group or with another minority group member?

2. As a counselor of color, which other minority group member do you anticipate would be most difficult to work with? Why?

3. If you were a client of color and had to choose the race of the counselor, whom would you choose? Why?

4. As a White person, would working with a minority group counselor bother you? What reactions or thoughts do you have about this question?

5. For each of the challenges noted in this chapter, can you provide suggestions of how best to handle these situations? What are the pros and cons of your advice?

It is clear that cultural competence goals do not apply only to White helping professionals. All therapists and counselors, regardless of race, culture, gender, and sexual orientation, need to (a) become aware of their own worldviews and their biases, values, and assumptions about human behavior; (b) understand the worldviews of their culturally diverse clients; and (c) develop culturally appropriate intervention strategies in working with culturally diverse clients.

IMPLICATIONS FOR CLINICAL PRACTICE

1. Working toward cultural competence and cultural humility are functions of everyone, regardless of race, gender, sexual orientation, religious preference, and so on.

2. Marginalized group members are not immune from having biases and prejudices toward majority group members and one another.

3. Because all oppression is damaging and serves to separate rather than unify, playing the "I'm more oppressed" game is destructive to group unity and counterproductive to combating racism.

4. In order to improve interracial/interethnic counseling relationships, we must face the fact that there is also much misunderstanding and bias among and between groups of color.

5. Be aware that not all bad things that happen to people of color are the results of racism. Although we need to trust our intuitive or experiential reality, it is equally important that we do not externalize everything.

6. Despite sharing similar experiences of oppression, cultural differences may infect the therapeutic process and render your attempts to help the client ineffective.

7. Realize how your communication style (direct versus subtle, passionate versus controlled) and nonverbal differences may impact the client.

8. Therapists must evaluate their own and the client's stage of identity and determine how these factors might impact work with clients of the same or different ethnicity.

9. Addressing ethnic or other differences between the therapist and the client can be useful in facilitating a helping relationship.

10. Counselors of color should be aware of and prepared to deal with the many therapeutic challenges they are likely to encounter when working with White clients and clients of color.

SUMMARY

Persons of color have major hesitations and concerns about publicly airing interracial/interethnic conflicts, differences, and misunderstandings because of the possible political ramifications for group unity. But it appears that cultural competency and cultural humility objectives are applicable both to therapists of color and to other clinicians from marginalized groups. In addition to historical relationships and sociopolitical factors that have created possible animosity between groups, differences in *cultural values, communication styles* and racial/cultural identity development also contribute to misunderstanding and conflict. Little actual research has been conducted on the challenges and difficulties that counselors of color face when working with other culturally diverse groups. Less yet has been done on the subject of cultural competence as it relates to therapists of color.

In working with White clients, however, members of oppressed groups might (a) be unable to contain their anger and rage toward majority group clients, as they are viewed as oppressors, (b) have difficulty understanding the worldview of their clients, (c) be hindered in their ability to establish rapport, (d) be pulled between opposing tendencies of desiring to help and to harm their clients, and (e) be guilty of imposing their racial realities upon clients. The five challenges counselors of color are likely to encounter are (1) questioning their competence, (2) a desire to prove competence, (3) controlling racial animosity toward White clients, (4) clients viewing therapists of color as super minorities, and (5) dealing with client expressions of racism.

Many of the challenges facing therapists of color working with White clients can also make their appearance in counseling dyads where both are from marginalized groups. Like their White counterparts, people of color are socialized into the dominant values and beliefs of the larger society. As a result, they may inherit the perceptions and beliefs of other racial/ethnic minority groups as well. In this case, the biases and stereotypes held for other groups of color may not be all that different from that of White Americans. Other interethnic/interracial–specific challenges may also make their appearance in the counseling dyad and include over-identification with the client, encountering clashes in *cultural values*, experiencing clashes in communication and therapeutic styles, receiving and expressing racial animosity, and dealing with the stage of racial identity of counselors and clients.

GLOSSARY TERMS

Communication styles	Interracial/interethnic discrimination
Cultural values	Interracial/interethnic group relations
Historical stereotypes	Model minority
Interracial/interethnic bias	Multicultural counseling
Interracial/interethnic conflict	Racial/Ethnic identity

Socially marginalized groups

Who's more oppressed game

Stereotype threat

REFERENCES

Arredondo, P., Gallardo-Cooper, M., Delgado-Romero, E. A., & Zapata, A. L. (2014). *Culturally responsive counseling with Latinas/os*. Alexandria, VA: American Counseling Association.

Bautista, E. M. (2003). The impact of context, phenotype, and other identifiers on Latina/o adolescent ethnic identity and acculturation. *Dissertation Abstracts International: Section B: The Sciences and Engineering, 63*(7-B), 3464.

Behnken, B. D. (2011). *Fighting their own battles: Mexican Americans, African Americans, and the struggle for civil rights in Texas*. Charlotte, NC: University of North Carolina Press.

Cashwell, C. S., Shcherbakova, J., & Cashwell, T. H. (2003). Effect of client and counselor ethnicity on preference for counselor disclosure. *Journal of Counseling and Development, 81*, 196–201.

Chang, E. T. (2001). Bitter fruit: The politics of Black-Korean conflict in New York City (Review). *Journal of Asian American Studies, 4*(3), 295–298.

Chen, C. P. (2005). Morita therapy: A philosophy of Yin/Yang coexistence. In R. Moodley & W. West (Eds.), *Integrating traditional healing practices into counseling and psychotherapy* (pp. 221–232). Thousand Oaks, CA: Sage.

Comas-Diaz, L. (2012). *Multicultural care: A clinician's guide to cultural competence*. Washington, DC: American Psychological Association.

Comas-Diaz, L., & Jacobsen, F. M. (1995). Ethnocultural transference and countertransference in the therapeutic dyad. *American Journal of Orthopsychiatry, 61*, 392–402.

Davis, L. E., & Gelsomino, J. (1994). An assessment of practitioner cross-racial treatment experiences. *Social Work, 39*, 116–123.

De Genova, N. (2006). *Racial transformations: Latinos and Asians remaking the United States*. Durham, NC: Duke University Press.

de las Fuentes, C. (2006). Latina/o American populations. In M. G. Constantine (Ed.), *Clinical practice with people of color* (pp. 46–60). Hoboken, NJ: Wiley.

Duran, E. (2006). *Healing the soul wound*. New York, NY: Teachers College Press.

Evans, K. M. (2013). Culturally alert counseling with African Americans. In G. McAuliffe & Associates (Eds.), *Culturally alert counseling* (2nd ed., pp. 125–155). Thousand Oaks, CA: Sage.

Fuertes, J. N., & Gelso, C. J. (2000). Hispanic counselors' race and accent and Euro Americans' universal-diverse orientation: A study of initial perceptions. *Cultural Diversity and Ethnic Minority Psychology, 6*, 211–219.

Garrett, M. T., & Portman, T.A.A. (2011). *Counseling Native Americans*. Belmont, CA: Cengage.

Guzman, M. R., & Carrasco, N. (2011). *Counseling Latino/a Americans*. Belmont, CA: Cengage.

Hecht, M. L., Jackson, R. L., & Ribeau, S. A. (2002). *African American communication: Exploring identity and culture* (2nd ed.). Mahwah, NJ: Erlbaum.

Helms, J. E. (1995). An update of Helms's White and people of color racial identity models. In J. G. Ponterotto, J. M. Casas, L. A. Suzuki, & C. M. Alexander (Eds.), *Handbook of multicultural counseling* (pp. 181–191). Thousand Oaks, CA: Sage.

Hinrichsen, G. A. (2006). Why multicultural issues matter for practitioners working with older adults. *Professional Psychology: Research and Practice, 37*, 29–35,

Jensen, J. V. (1985). Perspective on nonverbal intercultural communication. In L. A. Samovar & R. E. Porter (Eds.), *Intercultural communication: A reader* (pp. 256–272). Belmont, CA: Wadsworth.

Jones, J. M. (2013a, July 17). *Americans rate racial and ethnic relations in U.S. positively.* Retrieved from http://www.gallup.com/poll/163535 /americans-rate-racial-ethnic-relations-posi-tively.aspx?

Jones, J. M. (2013b, August 2). Race always matters! *Diversity Us.* Retrieved from http://sites.udel .edu/csd/2013/08/02/race-always-matters-2/

Kim, B.S.K. (2011). *Counseling Asian Americans.* Belmont, CA: Cengage.

Kim, B.S.K., & Park, Y. S. (2013). Culturally alert counseling with East and Southeast Asian Americans. In G. McAuliffe & Associates (Eds.), *Culturally alert counseling* (pp. 157–183). Thousand Oaks, CA: Sage.

Kim, K. (1999). *Koreans in the hood: Conflict with African-Americans.* Baltimore, MD: Johns Hopkins University Press.

Kochman, T. (1981). *Black and White styles in conflict.* Chicago, IL: University of Chicago Press.

Kort, B. (1997). Female therapist, male client: Challenging beliefs—a personal journey. *Women and Therapy, 20,* 97–100.

Li-Repac, D. (1980). Cultural influences on clinical perception: A comparison between Caucasian and Chinese-American therapists. *Journal of Cross-Cultural Psychology, 11, 327–342.*

McClain, P. D., Carter, N., DeFrancesco, V., Lyle, M., Nunnally, S. C., & Cotton, K. D. (2006). Racial distancing in a southern city: Latino immigrants' views of Black Americans. *Journal of Politics, 68,* 3–23.

McCormick, R. (2005). The healing path: What can counselors learn from aboriginal people about how to heal? In R. Moodley & W. West (Eds.), *Integrating traditional healing practices into counseling and psychotherapy* (pp. 293–304). Thousand Oaks, CA: Sage.

Myers, E. R. (2001). African-American perceptions of Asian-American merchants: An exploratory study. In E. R. Myers (Ed.), *Challenges of a changing America: Perspectives on immigration and multiculturalism in the United States* (2nd ed., pp. 171–179). San Francisco, CA: Caddo Gap Press.

Nadal, K. L. (2011). *Filipino American psychology.* Hoboken, NJ: Wiley.

National Conference of Christians and Jews. (1994). *Taking America's pulse: A summary report of the national survey report of intergroup relations.* New York: Author.

Nydell, M. K. (1996). *Understanding Arabs: A guide for Westerners.* Yarmouth, ME: Intercultural Press,

Parham, T. A., Ajamu, A., & White, J. L. (2011). *Psychology of Blacks: Centering our perspectives in the African consciousness.* Boston, MA: Prentice Hall.

Patrinos, H. A. (2000). The cost of discrimination in Latin America. *Studies in Comparative International Development, 35*(2), 3–17.

Pew Research Center. (2008). *Do Blacks and Hispanics get along?* Washington, DC: Author.

Pew Research Center. (2012). *The rise of Asian Americans.* Washington, DC: Author.

Ratts, M. J., & Pedersen, P. B. (2014). *Counseling for multiculturalism and social justice.* Alexandria, VA: American Counseling Association.

Ratts, M. J., Singh, A. A., Nassar-McMillan, S., Butler, K., & McCullough, R. J. (2015). *Multicultural and social justice counseling competencies.* The Multicultural Counseling Competencies Revision Committee of the American Counseling Association, Draft Report.

Ridley, C. R. (2005). *Overcoming unintentional racism in counseling and therapy* (2nd ed.). Thousand Oaks, CA: Sage.

Samad, L., Tate, A. R., Dezateaux, C., Peckham, C., Butler, N., & Bedford, H. (2006). Differences in risk factors for partial and no immunisation in the first year of life: Prospective cohort study. *British Medical Journal, 332,* 1312–1313.

Santiago-Rivera, A., Arredondo, P., & Gallardo-Cooper, M. (2002). *Counseling Latinos and la familia: A guide for practitioners.* Thousand Oaks, CA: Sage.

Scharlin, C., & Villanueva, L. V. (1994). *Philip Vera Cruz: A personal history of Filipino immigrants and the farmworkers movement.* Seattle: University of Washington Press.

Spradlin, I. K., & Parsons, R. D. (2008). *Diversity matters.* Belmont, CA: Thompson Wadsworth.

Steele, C. M. (1997). A threat in the air: How stereotypes shape intellectual identity and performance. *American Psychologist, 52,* 613–629.

Steele, C. M. (2003). Race and the schooling of Black Americans. In S. Plous (Ed.), *Understanding prejudice and discrimination* (pp. 98–107). New York, NY: McGraw-Hill.

Steele, C. M., Spencer, S. J., & Aronson, J. (2002). Contending with group image: The psychology of stereotype and social identity threat. In M. Zanna (Ed.), *Advances in experimental social psychology* (Vol. 23, pp. 379–440). New York, NY: Academic Press.

Sue, D. W. (2010a). *Microaggressions in everyday life: Race, gender, and sexual orientation.* Hoboken, NJ: Wiley.

Sue, D. W. (2010b). *Microaggressions and marginality: Manifestations, dynamics, and impact.* Hoboken, NJ: Wiley.

Sue, D. W. (2015). *Race talk and the conspiracy of silence: Understanding and facilitating difficult dialogues on race.* Hoboken, NJ: Wiley.

Sue, D. W., & Sue, D. (2013). *Counseling the culturally diverse: Theory and practice,* 6th ed. Hoboken, NJ: Wiley.

U.S. Census Bureau. (2005). *Statistical abstract of the United States: 2004–2005. The national data book.* American Indian, Alaska Native tables. Retrieved from http://www.census.gov/statab/www/sa04aian.pdf

Weber, S. N. (1985). The need to be: The sociocultural significance of Black language. In L. A. Samovar & R. E. Porter (Eds.), *Intercultural communication: A reader* (pp. 244–253). Belmont, CA: Wadsworth.

Wood, D. B. (2006, May 25). Rising black-Latino clash on jobs. *Christian Science Monitor.* Retrieved from http://www.csmonitor.com/2006/0525/p01s03-ussc.html

Yoon, I. (1997). *On my own: Korean business and race relations in America.* Chicago, IL: University of Chicago Press.

PART II

The Impact and Social Justice Implications of Counseling and Psychotherapy

The Political and Social Justice Implications of Counseling and Psychotherapy

AN OPEN LETTER TO BROTHERS AND SISTERS OF COLOR

In 1997, I, Derald Wing Sue, was privileged to testify before President Clinton's Race Advisory Board on the President's Initiative on Race (1998) about the impact of racism on people of color. The televised public testimony evoked strong negative reactions from primarily White viewers, who claimed my colleagues and I were simply exaggerating, and that racism was now a thing of the past. In reaction to those criticisms, I published an open letter to brothers and sisters of color in 2003. A brief portion is reproduced here.

Dear Brothers and Sisters of Color:

I write . . . to you and to those White folks who have marched with us against racism and shown that their hearts are in the right place. Throughout our people's histories, we have had to contend with invalidation, oppression, injustice, terrorism, and genocide. Racism is a constant reality in our lives. It is a toxic force that has sought to

- *strip us of our identities,*

- *take away our dignity,*

- *make us second-class citizens,*

- *destroy our peoples, cultures, and communities,*

- *steal our land and property,*

- *torture, rape, and murder us,*

- *imprison us on reservations, concentration camps, inferior schools, segregated neighborhoods, and jails,*

- *use us as guinea pigs in medical experiments, and*

- *blame our victimization upon the faults of our own people.*

Attempts to express these thoughts have generally been met with disbelief and/or incredulity by many of our well-intentioned White brothers and sisters. We have been asked, "Aren't you distorting the truth? Where is your proof? Where is your evidence?"

When we attempt to provide it, we are interrogated about its legitimacy, told that we are biased or paranoid, and accused of being dishonest in how we present the facts. After all, they say, "Our nation is built upon life, liberty, and the pursuit of happiness. It was founded upon the principles of freedom, democracy, and equality." Yet, these guiding principles seem intended for Whites only! In the classic book, Animal Farm *(Orwell, 1945), when the issue of inequality arose, the character in a position of power justified the treatment by stating, "Some are more equal than others." Rather than offer enlightenment and freedom, education and healing, and rather than allowing for equal access and opportunity, historical and current practices in our nation have restricted, stereotyped, damaged, and oppressed persons of color.*

For too long people of color have not had the opportunity or power to express their points of view. For too long our voices have not been heard. For too long our worldviews have been diminished, negated, or considered invalid. For too long we have been told that our perceptions are incorrect, that most things are well with our society, and that our concerns and complaints are not supported. For too long we have had to justify our existence, and to fight for our dignity and humanity. No wonder that we are so tired, impatient, and angry. Yet, as people of color, we cannot let fatigue turn into hopelessness, nor anger into bitterness. Hopelessness is the forerunner to surrender, and bitterness leads to blind hatred. Either could spell our downfall!

(D. W. Sue, 2003, pp. 257–259)

IMPACT OF POLITICAL OPPRESSION

Multicultural counseling/therapy means understanding the worldviews and life experience of diverse groups in our nation. To be culturally competent means to understand the history of oppression experienced by marginalized groups in our society. The stories of discrimination and pain of the oppressed are often minimized and neglected. Many, for example, contend that the reality of racism, sexism, and homophobia is relatively unknown or ignored by those in power because of the discomfort that pervades such topics. Vernon E. Jordan, Jr., an African American attorney and former confidant of President Bill Clinton, made this point about racism in startling terms. In making an analogy between the terrorist attacks of September 11, 2001, and the racism directed at African Americans, Jordan stated:

None of this is new to Black people. War, hunger, disease, unemployment, deprivation, dehumanization, and terrorism define our existence. They are not new to us. Slavery was terrorism, segregation was terrorism, and the bombing of the four little girls in Sunday school in Birmingham was terrorism. The violent deaths of Medgar, Martin, Malcolm, Vernon Dahmer, Chaney, Shwerner, and Goodman were terrorism. And the difference between September 11 and the terror visited upon Black people is that on September 11, the terrorists were foreigners. When we were terrorized, it was by our neighbors. The terrorists were Americans. (Excerpted from a speech by Vernon E. Jordan, June 2002)

Likewise, in speaking about the history of psychological research conducted on ethnic minority communities by White social scientists, the late Charles W. Thomas (1970), a respected African American psychologist, voiced his concerns even more strongly:

White psychologists have raped Black communities all over the country. Yes, raped. They have used Black people as the human equivalent of rats run through Ph.D. experiments and as helpless clients for programs that serve middle-class White administrators better than they do the poor. They have used research on Black people as green stamps to trade for research grants. They have been vultures. (p. 52)

To many people of color, the "Tuskegee experiment" represents a prime example of the allegation by Thomas. The Tuskegee experiment was carried out from 1932 to 1972 by the U.S. Public Health Service; more than 600 Alabama Black men were used as guinea pigs in the study of what damage would occur to the body if syphilis were left untreated. Approximately 399 were allowed to go untreated, even when medication was available. Records indicate that 7 died as a result of syphilis, and an additional 154 died of heart disease that may have been caused by the untreated syphilis! In a moving ceremony in 1997, President Clinton officially expressed regret for the experiment to the few survivors and apologized to Black America.

Likewise, in August 2011, a White House bioethics panel heard about American-run venereal disease experiments conducted on Guatemalan prisoners, soldiers, and mental patients from 1946 to 1948: The United States paid for syphilis-infected Guatemalan prostitutes to have sex with prisoners. Approximately 5,500 Guatemalans were enrolled, 1,300 were deliberately infected, and 83 died (McNeil, 2011). The aim of the study was to see whether penicillin could prevent infection after exposure. When these experiments came to light, President Obama apologized to President Alvaro Colom of Guatemala. Dr. Amy Gutman, the chairwoman of the bioethics panel and president of the University of Pennsylvania, described the incident as a dark chapter in the history of medical research. Experiments of this type are ghastly and give rise to suspicions that people of color arc being used as guinea pigs in other medical and social experiments as well.

REFLECTION AND DISCUSSION QUESTIONS

1. Are these beliefs by people of color accurate?

2. Aren't they simply exaggerations from overly mistrustful individuals?

3. Aren't people of color making a mountain out of a molehill?

4. As indicated in Chapter 1, what might be emotional roadblocks you are now feeling? What meaning do you impute to them?

5. What has all this to do with counseling and psychotherapy?

Because the worldviews of culturally diverse clients are often linked to the historical and current experiences of oppression in the United States (American Psychological Association Presidential Task Force on Preventing Discrimination and Promoting Diversity 2012; Ponterotto, Utsey, & Pedersen, 2006), it is necessary to understand the worldview of culturally diverse clients from both a cultural and a political perspective (Ridley, 2005). Clients of color, for example, are likely to approach counseling and therapy with a great deal of healthy skepticism regarding the institutions from which therapists work and even the conscious and unconscious motives of the helping professional.

The main thesis of this book is that counseling and psychotherapy do not take place in a vacuum, isolated from the larger sociopolitical influences of our societal climate (Constantine, 2006; Katz, 1985; Liu, Hernandez, Mahmood, & Stinson, 2006). Counseling people of color, for example, often mirrors the nature of race relations in the wider society as well as the dominant-subordinate relationships of other marginalized groups (lesbian, gay, bisexual, and transgendered [LGBT] people; women; and the physically challenged). It serves as a microcosm, reflecting

Black–White, Asian–White, Hispanic–White, and American Indian–White relations. But as we saw in Chapter 3, it also mirrors interethnic/interracial relations as well.

We explore the many ways in which counseling and psychotherapy have failed with respect to providing culturally appropriate mental health services to disempowered groups in our society. We do this by using people of color as an example of the damaging oppressor–oppressed relationships that historically characterize many other marginalized groups. Many readers may have a very powerful negative reaction to the following material. However, only by honestly confronting these unpleasant social realities and accepting responsibility for changing them will our profession be able to advance and grow (D. W. Sue, 2010a; D. W. Sue, 2015). Jones (2010) cites an African proverb: "The true tale of the lion hunt will never be told as long as the hunter tells the story." In other words, the story of racial, ethnic, and cultural groups (people of color) is largely a hunter's story (White Americans). To learn about the hunter (White Americans) and the hunt (balanced history), the story of the lion must be told regardless of how unpleasant.

THE EDUCATION AND TRAINING OF COUNSELING/ MENTAL HEALTH PROFESSIONALS

While national interest in the mental health needs of people of color has increased, the human service professions have historically neglected this population. Evidence reveals that these groups, in addition to the common stresses experienced by everyone else, are more likely to encounter problems such as immigrant status, poverty, cultural racism, prejudice, and discrimination (Choudhuri, Santiago-Rivera, & Garrett, 2012; West-Olatunji & Conwill, 2011). Yet studies continue to reveal that American Indians, Asian Americans, African Americans, and Latino/Hispanic Americans tend to underutilize traditional mental health services in a variety of contexts (Kearney, Draper, & Baron, 2005; Owen, Imel, Adelson, & Rodolfa, 2012; Wang & Kim, 2010).

Some researchers have hypothesized that people of color underutilize and prematurely terminate counseling/therapy because of the biased nature of the services themselves (Kearney et al., 2005). The services offered are frequently antagonistic or inappropriate to the life experiences of culturally diverse clients; they lack sensitivity and understanding, and they are oppressive and discriminating toward clients of color (Cokley, 2006). Many believed that the presence of ill-prepared mental health professionals was the direct result of a *culture-bound and biased training system* (Mio, 2005; Utsey, Grange, & Allyne, 2006).

Most graduate programs continue to give inadequate treatment to the mental health issues of persons of color (Ponterotto & Austin, 2005; Utsey et al., 2006). Cultural influences affecting personality formation, career choice, educational development, and the manifestation of behavior disorders are infrequently part of mental health training or are treated in a tangential manner (Parham, Ajamu, & White, 2011; Vazquez & Garcia-Vazquez, 2003). When the experiences of socially devalued groups are discussed, they are generally seen and analyzed from the White, EuroAmerican, middle-class perspective. In programs where these experiences have been discussed, the focus tends to be on pathological lifestyles and/or maintenance of false stereotypes. The result is twofold: (a) professionals who deal with mental health problems of people of color lack understanding and knowledge about ethnic values and their consequent interaction with a racist society, and (b) mental health practitioners are graduated from our programs believing that persons of color are inherently pathological and that therapy involves a simple modification of traditional White models.

This *ethnocentric* bias has been highly destructive to the natural help-giving networks of ethnic/racial communities (Duran, 2006). Oftentimes mental health professionals operate under the assumption that groups of color never had such a thing as "counseling" and "psychotherapy" until it was "invented" and institutionalized in Western cultures. For the benefit of those people, the mental health movement has delegitimized natural help-giving networks that have operated for thousands of years by labeling them as unscientific, supernatural, mystical, and not consistent with "professional standards of practice." Mental health professionals are then surprised to find that there is a high incidence of psychological distress in communities of color, that their treatment techniques do not work, and that some culturally diverse groups do not utilize their services.

Contrary to this *ethnocentric* orientation, we need to expand our perception of what constitutes valid mental health practices. Equally legitimate methods of treatment are nonformal or natural support systems (e.g., family, friends, community self-help programs, and occupational networks), folk-healing methods, and indigenous formal systems of therapy (Gone, 2010; Moodley & West, 2005). Instead of attempting to destroy these practices, we should be actively trying to find out why they may work better than Western forms of counseling and therapy (Trimble, 2010). We cover indigenous healing in Chapter 10.

DEFINITIONS OF MENTAL HEALTH

Counseling and psychotherapy tend to assume universal *(etic)* applications of their concepts and goals to the exclusion of culture-specific *(emic)* views (Choudhuri et al., 2012). Likewise, graduate programs have often been accused of fostering *cultural encapsulation,* a term first coined by Wrenn (1962). The term refers specifically to (a) the substitution of modal stereotypes for the real world, (b) the disregarding of cultural variations in a dogmatic adherence to some universal notion of truth, and (c) the use of a technique-oriented definition of the counseling process. The results are that counselor roles are rigidly defined, implanting an implicit belief in a universal concept of "healthy" and "normal."

If we look at criteria used by the mental health profession to judge normality and *abnormality*, this *ethnocentricity* becomes glaring. Several fundamental approaches that have particular relevance to our discussion have been identified (D. Sue, Sue, Sue, & Sue, 2016): (a) normality as a statistical concept, (b) normality as ideal mental health, and (c) *abnormality* as the presence of certain behaviors (research criteria).

Normality as a Statistical Concept

First, statistical criteria equate normality with those behaviors that occur most frequently in the population. *Abnormality* is defined in terms of those behaviors that occur least frequently. Despite the word *statistical*, however, these criteria need not be quantitative in nature: Individuals who talk to themselves, disrobe in public, or laugh uncontrollably for no apparent reason are considered abnormal according to these criteria simply because most people do not behave in that way. Statistical criteria undergird our notion of a normal probability curve, so often used in IQ tests, achievement tests, and personality inventories. Statistical criteria may seem adequate in specific instances, but they are fraught with hazards and problems. For one thing, they fail to take into account differences in time, community standards, and cultural values. If deviations from the majority are considered abnormal, then many ethnic and racial minorities that exhibit strong cultural differences from the majority have to be so classified. When we resort to a statistical definition, it is generally the group in power that determines what constitutes normality and *abnormality*. For example, if African Americans were to be administered a personality test and it was found that they were more suspicious than their White counterparts, what would this mean?

Some psychologists and educators have used such findings to label African Americans as paranoid. Statements by Blacks that "The Man" is out to get them may be perceived as supporting a paranoid delusion. This interpretation, however, has been challenged by many Black psychologists as being inaccurate (Grier & Cobbs, 1968, 1971; Parham et al., 2011). In response to their heritage of slavery and a history of White discrimination against them, African Americans have adopted various behaviors (in particular, behaviors toward Whites) that have proved important for survival in a racist society. "Playing it cool" has been identified as one means by which Blacks, as well as members of other groups of color, may conceal their true thoughts and feelings. A Black person who is experiencing conflict, anger, or even rage may be skillful at appearing serene and composed. This tactic is a survival mechanism aimed at reducing one's vulnerability to harm and to exploitation in a hostile environment.

Personality tests that reveal Blacks as being suspicious, mistrustful, and paranoid need to be understood from a larger sociopolitical perspective. Marginalized groups who have consistently been victims of discrimination and oppression in a culture that is full of racism have good reason to be suspicious and mistrustful of White society. In their classic book *Black Rage*, Grier and Cobbs (1968) point out how Blacks, in order to survive in a White racist society, have developed a highly functional survival mechanism to protect them against possible physical and psychological harm. The authors perceive this *"cultural paranoia"* as adaptive and healthy rather than dysfunctional and pathological. Indeed, some psychologists of color have indicated that the absence of a *paranorm* (healthy suspiciousness and vigilance of others' motives) among people of color may be more indicative of pathology than its presence. The absence of a *paranorm* may indicate either poor reality testing (denial of oppression/racism in our society) or naiveté in understanding the operation of racism.

Normality as Ideal Mental Health

Second, humanistic psychologists have proposed the concept of ideal mental health as the criteria of normality (Cain, 2010). Such criteria stress the importance of attaining some positive goal like consciousness-insight, self-actualization/creativity, competence, autonomy, resistance to stress, and psychological mindedness. The biased nature of such approaches is grounded in the belief in a universal application (all populations in all situations) and reveals a failure to recognize the value base from which the criteria are derived. The particular goal or ideal used is intimately linked with the theoretical frame of reference and values held by the practitioner (psychodynamic, humanistic/existential, or cognitive/behavioral).

For example, the psychoanalytic emphasis on *insight* as a determinant of mental health is a value in itself (London, 1988).

It is important for the mental health professional to be aware, however, that certain socioeconomic groups and people of color may not particularly value insight. Furthermore, the use of self-disclosure as a measure of mental health tends to neglect the earlier discussion presented on the *paranorm*. One characteristic often linked to the healthy personality is the ability to talk about the deepest and most intimate aspects of one's life: to self-disclose. This orientation is very characteristic of our counseling and therapy process, in which clients are expected to talk about themselves in a very personal manner. The fact that many people of color are initially reluctant to self-disclose can place them in a situation where they are judged to be mentally unhealthy and, in this case, paranoid (Parham, 2002).

Definitions of mental health such as competence, autonomy, and resistance to stress are related to White middle-class notions of individual maturity (Ahuvia, 2001; Triandis, 2000). The mental health professions originated from the ideological milieu of individualism (Ivey, D'Andrea, Ivey, & Simek-Morgan, 2007). Individuals make their lot in life. Those who succeed in society do so because of their *own* efforts and abilities. Successful people are seen as mature, independent, and possessing great ego strength. Apart from the potential bias in defining what constitutes competence, autonomy, and resistance to stress, the use of such a person-focused definition of maturity places the responsibility on the individual. When people fail in life, it is because of their own lack of ability, interest, or maturity, or some inherent weakness of the ego. If, on the other hand, we see minorities as being subjected to higher stress factors in society and placed in a one-down position by virtue of racism, then it becomes quite clear that the definition will tend to portray the lifestyle of minorities as inferior, underdeveloped, and deficient. Ryan (1971) was the first to coin the phrase "blaming the victim" to refer to this process. Hence a broader system analysis would show that the economic, social, and psychological conditions of people of color are related to their oppressed status in America.

Abnormality as the Presence of Certain Behaviors

Third, an alternative to the previous two definitions of *abnormality* is a research one. For example, in determining rates of mental illness in different ethnic groups, "psychiatric diagnosis," "presence in mental hospitals," and scores on "objective psychological inventories" are frequently used (D. Sue et al., 2016). Diagnosis and hospitalization present a circular problem. The definition of normality/*abnormality* depends on what mental health practitioners say it is! In this case, the race or ethnicity of mental health professionals is likely to be different from that of clients of color. Bias on the part of the practitioner with respect to diagnosis and treatment is likely to occur (Constantine, Myers, Kindaichi, & Moore, 2004). The inescapable conclusion is that clients of color tend to be diagnosed differently and to receive less preferred modes of treatment (Paniagua, 2005).

Furthermore, the political and societal implications of psychiatric diagnosis and hospitalization were forcefully pointed out nearly 40 years ago by Laing (1967, 1969) and Szasz (1970, 1971). Although it appears that minorities underutilize outpatient services, they also appear to face greater levels of involuntary hospital commitments (Snowden & Cheung, 1990). Laing believes that individual madness is but a reflection of the madness of society. He describes schizophrenic breakdowns as desperate strategies by people to liberate themselves from a "false self" used to maintain behavioral normality in our society. Attempts to adjust the person back to the original normality (sick society) are unethical. Szasz states this opinion even more strongly:

> In my opinion, mental illness is a myth. People we label "mentally ill" are not sick, and involuntary mental hospitalization is not treatment. It is punishment. . . . The fact that mental illness designates a deviation from an ethical rule of conduct, and that such rules vary widely, explains why upper-middle-class psychiatrists can so easily find evidence of "mental illness" in lower-class individuals and why so many prominent persons in the past fifty years or so have been diagnosed by their enemies as suffering from some type of insanity. Barry Goldwater was called a paranoid schizophrenic. . . . Woodrow Wilson, a neurotic. . . . Jesus Christ, according to two psychiatrists. . .was a born degenerate with a fixed delusion system. (1970, pp. 167–168)

Szasz (1987, 1999) views the mental health professional as an inquisitor, an agent of society exerting social control over those individuals who deviate in thought and behavior from the accepted norms of society. Psychiatric hospitalization is believed to be a form of social control for persons who annoy or disturb us. The label *mental illness* may be seen as a political ploy used to control those who are different, and therapy is used to control, brainwash, or reorient the identified victims to fit into society. It is exactly this concept that many people of color find frightening. For example, many Asian Americans, American Indians, African Americans, and Hispanic/Latino Americans are increasingly challenging the concepts of normality and *abnormality*. They believe that their values and lifestyles are often seen by society as pathological and thus are unfairly discriminated against by the mental health professions (Constantine, 2006).

In addition, the use of "objective" psychological inventories as indicators of maladjustment may also place people of color at a disadvantage. Many are aware that the test instruments used on them have been constructed and standardized according to White middle-class norms. The lack of culturally unbiased instruments makes many feel that the results obtained are invalid. Indeed, in a landmark decision in the State of California (*Larry P. v. California*, 1986), a judge ruled in favor of the Association of Black Psychologists' claim that individual intelligence tests, such as versions of the WISC, WAIS, and Stanford Binet, could not be used in the public schools on Black students. The improper use of such instruments can lead to an exclusion of minorities from jobs and promotion, to discriminatory educational decisions, and to biased determination of what constitutes pathology and cure in counseling/therapy (Samuda, 1998).

Further, when a diagnosis becomes a label, it can have serious consequences. First, a label can cause people to interpret all activities of the affected individual as pathological. No matter what African Americans may do or say that breaks a stereotype, their behaviors will seem to reflect the fact that they are less intelligent than others around them. Second, the label may cause others to treat individuals differently, even when they are perfectly normal. Third, a label may cause those who are labeled to believe that they do indeed possess such characteristics (Rosenthal & Jacobson, 1968) or that the threats of being perceived as less capable can seriously impair their performance (Steele, 2003).

Curriculum and Training Deficiencies

It appears that many of the universal definitions of mental health that have pervaded the profession have primarily been due to severe deficiencies in training programs. Educators (Chen, 2005; Mio & Morris, 1990; D. W. Sue, 2010b) have asserted that the major reason for ineffectiveness in working with culturally diverse populations is the lack of culturally sensitive material taught in the curricula. It has been ethnocentrically assumed that the material taught in traditional mental health programs is equally applicable to all groups. Even now, when there is high recognition of the need for multicultural curricula, it has become a battle to infuse such concepts into course content (Vera, Buhin, & Shin, 2006). As a result, course offerings continue to lack a non-White perspective, to treat cultural issues as an adjunct or add-on, to portray cultural groups in stereotypic ways, and to create an academic environment that does not support their concerns, needs, and issues (Turner, Gonzalez, & Wood, 2008).

Further, a major criticism has been that training programs purposely leave out *antiracism*, antisexism, and antihomophobia curricula for fear of requiring students to explore their own biases and prejudices (Carter, 2005; Vera et al., 2006). Because multicultural competence cannot occur without students or trainees confronting these harmful and detrimental attitudes about race, gender, and sexual orientation, the education and training of psychologists remain at the cognitive and objective domain, preventing self-exploration (D. W. Sue, 2015). This allows students to study the material from their positions of safety. An effective curriculum must enable students to understand feelings of helplessness and powerlessness, low self-esteem, and poor self-concept and how they contribute to low motivation, frustration, hate, ambivalence, and apathy. Each course should contain (a) a *consciousness-raising* component, (b) an *affective/experiential* component, (c) a *knowledge* component, and (d) a *skills* component. Importantly, the American Psychological Association (2006) recommended that psychology training programs at all levels provide information on the political nature of the practice of psychology and that professionals need to "own" their value positions.

COUNSELING AND MENTAL HEALTH LITERATURE

Many psychologists have noted how the social science literature, and specifically research, has failed to create a realistic understanding of various ethnic groups in America (Cokley, 2006; Guthrie, 1997). In fact, certain practices are felt to have done great harm to persons of color by ignoring them, maintaining false stereotypes, and/or presenting a distorted view of their lifestyles. Mental health practice may be viewed as encompassing the use of social power and functioning as a handmaiden of the status quo (Halleck, 1971; Katz, 1985). Social sciences are part of a culture-bound social system, from which researchers are usually drawn; moreover, organized social science is often dependent on the status quo for financial support. People of color frequently see the mental health profession in a similar way—as a discipline concerned with maintaining the status quo

(Ponterotto, Utsey, & Pedersen, 2006). As a result, the person collecting and reporting data is often perceived as possessing the social bias of his or her society (Ridley, 2005).

Social sciences, for example, have historically ignored the study of Asians in America (Hong & Domokos-Cheng Ham, 2001; Nadal, 2011). This deficit has contributed to the perpetuation of false stereotypes, which has angered many younger Asians concerned with raising consciousness and group esteem. When studies have been conducted on people of color, research has been appallingly unbalanced. Many social scientists (Cokley, 2006; Jones, 2010) have pointed out how "White social science" has tended to reinforce a negative view of African Americans among the public by concentrating on unstable Black families instead of on the many stable ones. Such unfair treatment has also been the case in studies on Latinos that have focused on the psychopathological problems encountered by Mexican Americans (Falicov, 2005). Other ethnic groups, such as Native Americans (Sutton & Broken Nose, 2005) and Puerto Ricans (Garcia-Preto, 2005), have fared no better. Even more disturbing is the assumption that the problems encountered by people of color are due to intrinsic factors (racial inferiority, incompatible value systems, etc.) rather than to the failure of society (D. W. Sue, 2003). Although there are many aspects of how persons of color are portrayed in social science literature, two seem crucial for us to explore: (a) people of color and pathology and (b) the role of *scientific racism* in research.

Pathology and Persons of Color

When we seriously study the "scientific" literature of the past relating to people of color, we are immediately impressed with how an implicit equation of them with pathology is a common theme. The historical use of science in the investigation of racial differences seems to be linked with White supremacist notions (Jones, 1997, 2010). The classic work of Thomas and Sillen (1972) refers to this as *scientific racism* and cites several historical examples to support their contention:

- Census figures (fabricated) from 1840 were used to support the notion that Blacks living under unnatural conditions of freedom were prone to anxiety.

- Influential medical journals presented fantasies as facts, supporting the belief that anatomical, neurological, or endocrinological aspects of Blacks were always inferior to those of Whites.

- The following misconceptions were presented as facts:

- ○ Mental health for Blacks was contentment with subservience.

- ○ Psychologically normal Blacks were faithful and happy-go-lucky.

- ○ Black persons' brains were smaller and less developed.

- ○ Blacks were less prone to mental illness because their minds were so simple.

- ○ The dreams of Blacks were juvenile in character and not as complex as those of Whites.

More frightening, perhaps, is a survey that found that many of these stereotypes continue to be accepted by White Americans: 20% publicly expressed a belief that African Americans are innately inferior in thinking ability, 19% believe that Blacks have thicker craniums, 23.5% believe they have longer arms than Whites, 50% believe Blacks have achieved equality, and 30% believe problems of Blacks reside in their own group (Astor, 1997; Babbington; 2008; Pew Research Center, 2007; Plous & Williams, 1995). One wonders how many White Americans hold similar beliefs privately but because of social pressures do not publicly voice them.

Furthermore, the belief that various human groups exist at different stages of biological evolution was accepted by G. Stanley Hall. He stated explicitly in 1904 that Africans, Indians, and Chinese were members of adolescent races and in a stage of incomplete development. In most cases, the evidence used to support these conclusions was fabricated, extremely flimsy, or distorted to fit the belief in non-White inferiority (A. Thomas & Sillen, 1972). For example, Gossett (1963) reports that when one particular study in 1895 revealed that the sensory perception of Native Americans was superior to that of Blacks and that of Blacks was superior to that of Whites, the results were used to support a belief in the mental superiority of Whites: "Their reactions were slower because they belonged to a more deliberate and reflective race than did the members of the other two groups" (p. 364). The belief that Blacks are "born athletes," as opposed to scientists or statesmen, derives from this tradition. The fact that Hall was a well-respected psychologist, often referred to as "the father of child psychology," and first president of the American Psychological Association did not prevent him from inheriting the racial biases of the times.

The Genetically Deficient Model

The portrayal of people of color in literature has generally taken the form of stereotyping them as deficient in certain desirable attributes. For example, de

Gobineau's (1915) *The Inequality of the Human Races* and Darwin's (1859) *On the Origin of Species by Natural Selection* were used to support the belief in the genetic intellectual superiority of Whites and the genetic inferiority of the "lower races." Galton (1869) wrote explicitly that African "Negroes" were "half-witted men" who made "childish, stupid, and simpleton-like mistakes," while Jews were inferior physically and mentally and only designed for a parasitical existence on other nations of people. Terman (1916), using the Binet scales in testing Black, Mexican American, and Spanish Indian families, concluded that they were uneducable.

The *genetically deficient model* is present in the writings of educational psychologists and academicians. In 1989, Professor Rushton of the University of Western Ontario claimed that human intelligence and behavior were largely determined by race, that Whites have bigger brains than Blacks, and that Blacks are more aggressive (Samuda, 1998). Shockley (1972) has expressed fears that the accumulation of weak or low intelligence genes in the Black population will seriously affect overall intelligence. Thus he advocates that people with low IQs should not be allowed to bear children—they should be sterilized. Allegations of *scientific racism* can also be seen in the work of Cyril Burt, eminent British psychologist, who fabricated data to support his contention that intelligence is inherited and that Blacks have inherited inferior brains. Such an accusation is immensely important when one considers that Burt is a major influence in American and British psychology, is considered by many to be the father of educational psychology, was the first psychologist to be knighted, and was awarded the American Psychological Association's Thorndike Prize, and that his research findings form the foundation for the belief that intelligence is inherited.

A belief that race and gender dictate intelligence continues to be expressed in modern times and even by our most educated populace. In 2005, then–Harvard President Larry Summers (former director of President Obama's National Economic Council) suggested that innate differences between the sexes might help explain why relatively few women become professional scientists or engineers. His comments set off a furor, with demands that he be fired. Women academicians were reported to have stormed out of the conference in disgust as Summers used "innate ability" as a possible explanation for sex differences in test scores. Ironically, Summers was lecturing to a room of the most accomplished women scholars in engineering and science in the nation.

The questions about whether there are differences in intelligence between races are both complex and emotional. The difficulty in clarifying these questions is compounded by many factors. Besides the difficulty in defining *race*, questionable assumptions exist regarding whether research on the intelligence of Whites can be generalized to other groups, whether middle-class and lower-class ethnic minorities grow up in environments similar to those of middle- and lower-class Whites, and whether test instruments are valid for both minority and White subjects. More important, we should recognize that the average values of different populations tell us nothing about any one individual. Heritability is a function of the population, *not* a trait. Ethnic groups all have individuals in the full range of intelligence, and to think of any racial group in terms of a single stereotype goes against all we know about the mechanics of heredity. Yet much of social science literature continues to portray people of color as being *genetically deficient* in one sense or another.

The Culturally Deficient Model

Well-meaning social scientists who challenged the genetic deficit model by placing heavy reliance on environmental factors nevertheless tended to perpetuate a view that saw people of color as culturally disadvantaged, deficient, or deprived. Instead of a biological condition that caused differences, the blame now shifted to the lifestyles or values of various ethnic groups. The term *cultural deprivation* was first popularized by Riessman's widely read book, *The Culturally Deprived Child* (1962). It was used to indicate that many groups perform poorly on tests or exhibit deviant characteristics because they lack many of the advantages of middle-class culture (education, books, toys, formal language, etc.). In essence, these groups were culturally impoverished!

While Riessman was well-intentioned in trying to not attribute blame to "genes" and intended to improve the condition of African Americans in America, some educators strenuously objected to the term. First, the term *culturally deprived* means to lack a cultural background (e g , enslaved Blacks arrived in America culturally naked), which is incongruous, because everyone inherits a culture. Second, such terms cause conceptual and theoretical confusions that may adversely affect social planning, educational policy, and research; for example, the oft-quoted Moynihan Report (Moynihan, 1965) asserts that "at the heart of deterioration of the Negro society is the deterioration of the Black family. It is the fundamental source of the weakness in the Negro community" (p. 5). Action was thus directed toward infusing White concepts of the family into those of Blacks. Third, cultural deprivation is used synonymously with deviation from and superiority of White middle-class values. Fourth, these deviations in values become equated with pathology, in which a group's cultural values, families, or lifestyles transmit the pathology. Thus the term "cultural deprivation" provides a convenient rationalization and alibi for the perpetuation of racism and the inequities of the socioeconomic system.

The Culturally Diverse Model

Many now maintain that the *culturally deficient* model serves only to perpetuate the myth of people of color inferiority. The focus tends to be one of blaming the person, with an emphasis on pathology and a use of White middle-class definitions of desirable and undesirable behavior. The social science use of a common, standard assumption implies that to be different is to be deviant, pathological, or sick. Is it possible that intelligence and personality scores for minority children really measure how Anglicized a child has become? To arrive at a more accurate understanding, people of color should no longer be viewed as deficient, but rather as *culturally diverse*. The goal of society should be to recognize the legitimacy of alternative lifestyles, the advantages of being bicultural (capable of functioning in two different cultural environments), and the value of differences.

REFLECTION AND DISCUSSION QUESTIONS

1. What reactions are you experiencing in learning that the history of the mental health movement was filled with racist formulations? As a White trainee, what thoughts and feelings are you experiencing? As a trainee of color (or a member of a marginalized group), what thoughts and feelings do you have?

2. Go back to Chapter 1 and reread the reactions to this book. Do the reactions in that chapter provide insights about your own thoughts and feelings?

3. Given the preceding discussion, in what ways may counseling and psychotherapy represent instruments of cultural oppression? How is this possibly reflected in definitions of normality and *abnormality*, the goals you have for therapy, and the way you conduct your practice with marginalized groups in our society?

THE NEED TO TREAT SOCIAL PROBLEMS— SOCIAL JUSTICE COUNSELING

DARYL

Daryl Cokely (a pseudonym) is a 12-year-old African American student attending a predominantly White grade school in Santa Barbara, California. He was referred for counseling by his homeroom teacher because of "constant fighting" on the school grounds, inability to control his anger, and exhibiting "a potential to seriously injure others." In addition, his teachers reported that Daryl was doing poorly in class and was inattentive, argumentative toward authority figures, and disrespectful. He appeared withdrawn in his classroom and seldom participated, but when Daryl spoke, he was "loud and aggressive." Teachers would often admonish Daryl "to calm down."

The most recent problematic incident, an especially violent one, required the assistant principal to physically pull Daryl away to prevent him from seriously injuring a fellow student. He was suspended from school for 3 days and subsequently referred to the school psychologist, who conducted a psychological evaluation. Daryl was diagnosed with a conduct disorder, and the psychologist recommended immediate counseling to prevent the untreated disorder from leading to more serious antisocial behaviors. He worried that Daryl was on his way to developing an antisocial personality disorder. The recommended course of treatment consisted of medication and therapy aimed at eliminating Daryl's aggressive behaviors and "controlling his underlying hostility and anger."

Daryl's parents, however, objected strenuously to the school psychologist's diagnosis and treatment recommendations. They described their son as a "normal child" when at home and not a behavior problem before moving from Los Angeles to Santa Barbara. They described him as feeling isolated, having few friends, being rejected by classmates, feeling invalidated by teachers, and feeling "removed" from the content of his classes. They also noted that all of the "fights" were generally instigated through "baiting" and "name-calling" by his White classmates, that the school climate was hostile toward their son, that the curriculum was very Eurocentric, and that school personnel and teachers seemed naive about racial or multicultural issues. They hinted strongly that racism was at work in the school district and enlisted the aid of the only Black counselor in the school, Ms. Jones. Although Ms. Jones seemed to be understanding and empathic toward Daryl's plight, she seemed reluctant to intercede on behalf of the parents. Being a recent graduate from the local college, Ms. Jones feared being ostracized by other school personnel.

CASE STUDY

The concerns of Daryl's parents were quickly dismissed by school officials as having little validity. In fact, the principal was quite incensed by these "accusatory statements of possible racism." He indicated to the parents that "your people" do not have a history of academic pursuit and that discipline in the home was usually the culprit. School officials contended that Daryl needed to be more accommodating, to reach out and make friends rather than isolating himself, to take a more active interest in his schoolwork, and to become a good citizen. Further, they asserted that it was not the school climate that was hostile, but that Daryl needed to "learn to fit in." "We treat everyone the same, regardless of race. This school doesn't discriminate," stated the principal. He went on to say, "Perhaps it was a mistake to move to Santa Barbara. For the sake of your son, you should consider returning to L.A. so he can better fit in with his people." These statements greatly angered Daryl's parents.

Adapted from D. W. Sue & Constantine, 2003, pp. 214–215.

If you were a counselor, how would you address this case? Where would you focus your energies? Traditional clinical approaches would direct their attention to what they perceive as the locus of the problem—Daryl and his aggressive behavior with classmates, his inattentiveness in class, and his disrespect of authority figures. This approach, however, makes several assumptions: (a) that the locus of the problem resides in the person, (b) that behaviors that violate socially accepted norms are considered maladaptive or disordered, (c) that remediation or elimination of problem behaviors is the goal, (d) that the social context or status quo guides the determination of normal versus abnormal and healthy versus unhealthy behaviors, and (e) that the appropriate role for the counselor is to help the client "fit in" and become "a good citizen."

But as we have just seen, mental health assumptions and practices are strongly influenced by sociopolitical factors. An enlightened approach that acknowledges potential oppression in the manifestation, diagnosis, etiology, and treatment is best accomplished by taking a social justice approach (Flores et al, 2014; McAuliffe & Associates, 2013). In the new proposed ACA Multicultural and Social Justice Counseling Competencies (Ratts, Singh, Nassar-McMillan, Butler, & McCullough, 2015), a strong case is made that multiculturalism is intimately related to social justice and counselors must engage in actions that require both individual- and systems-level work. Such an approach might mean challenging the traditional assumptions of therapy and even reversing them as follows:

1. The locus of the problem may reside in the social system (other students, hostile campus environment, alienating curriculum, lack of minority teachers/staff/students, etc.) rather than in the individual.

2. Behaviors that violate social norms may not be disordered or unhealthy.

3. The social norms, prevailing beliefs, and institutional policies and practices that maintain the status quo may need to be challenged and changed.

4. Although remediation is important, the more effective long-term solution is prevention.

5. Organizational change requires a macrosystems approach involving other roles and skills beyond the traditional clinical ones.

Along with these five assumptions, implementing *social justice counseling* means recognition that interventions can occur at four different foci, as illustrated in Figure 4.1 on page 129. A basic premise of *social justice counseling* is that culturally competent helping professionals must not confine their perspectives to just individual treatment but must be able to intervene effectively at the professional, organizational, and societal levels as well.

THE FOCI OF COUNSELING INTERVENTIONS: INDIVIDUAL, PROFESSIONAL, ORGANIZATIONAL, AND SOCIETAL

Focus 1: Individual

To provide culturally effective and sensitive counseling/mental health services, helping clients acquire changes in personal beliefs, attitudes, emotions, and behaviors has always been a major goal in counseling and therapy. This is especially true when attempting to help clients achieve new insights and to have them acquire new and adaptive behaviors. Most traditional forms of counseling and psychotherapy fall within this category.

Focus 2: Professional

It is clear that our profession has developed from a Western European perspective. As a result, how we define *psychology* (the study of mind and behavior) may be biased and at odds with different cultural groups. Further, if the professional standards and codes of ethics in mental health practice are culture bound, then they must be changed to reflect a multicultural worldview. As we will see in future chapters, oftentimes it is these professional codes of conduct that require change in order to help a diverse population.

Focus 3: Organizational

Since clients often work for and are influenced by organizations, it is important to realize that institutional practices, policies, programs, and structures may, especially if they are monocultural, be oppressive to certain groups. If organizational policies and practices deny equal access and opportunity for different groups or oppress them (redlining in home mortgages, laws against domestic partners, inequitable mental health care, etc.), then those policies and practices should become the targets for change. In other words, the causes of disorders may not reside in the individual, but in systems of organizational oppression.

Focus 4: Societal

If social policies (racial profiling, misinformation in educational materials, inequities in health care, etc.) are detrimental to the mental and physical health of minority groups, for example, does not the mental health professional have a responsibility to advocate for change? Our answer, of course, is affirmative.

*   *   *

Often, psychologists treat individuals who are the victims of failed systemic processes. Intervention at the individual level is primarily remedial when a strong need exists for preventive measures. Because psychology concentrates primarily on the individual, it has been deficient in developing more systemic and large-scale change strategies. Using the case of Daryl, let us illustrate some social justice principles as they apply to multicultural counseling.

Principle 1: A Failure to Develop a Balanced Perspective between Person and System Focus Can Result in False Attribution of the Problem.

It is apparent that school officials have attributed the locus of the problem—that he is impulsive, angry, inattentive, unmotivated, disrespectful, and a poor student—to reside in Daryl. He is labeled as having a conduct disorder with potential antisocial personality traits. Diagnosis of the problem is internal; that is, it resides in Daryl. When the focus of therapy is primarily on the individual, there is a strong tendency to see the locus of the problem as residing solely in the person (Cosgrove, 2006; Ratts & Pedersen, 2014) rather than in the school system, curriculum, or wider campus community. As a result, well-intentioned counselors may mistakenly blame the victim (e.g., by seeing the problem as a deficiency of the

FIGURE 4.1 Levels of Counseling Interventions

person) when, in actuality, the problem may reside in the environment (prejudice, discrimination, racial/cultural invalidation, etc.) (Metzl & Hansen, 2014).

We would submit that it is highly probable that Daryl is the victim of (a) a monocultural educational environment that alienates and denigrates him (Davidson, Waldo, & Adams, 2006); (b) a curriculum that does not deal with the contributions of African Americans or portrays them in a demeaning fashion; (c) teaching styles that may be culturally biased (Cokley, 2006); (d) a campus climate that is hostile to minority students (perceives them as less qualified) (D. W. Sue et al., 2011); (e) support services (counseling, study skills, etc.) that fail to understand the minority student experience; and (f) the lack of role models (presence of only one Black teacher in the school) (Alexander & Moore, 2008). For example, would it change your analysis and focus of intervention if Daryl gets into fights because he is teased mercilessly by fellow students who use racial slurs (nigger, jungle bunny, burr head, etc.)? In other words, suppose there is good reason that this 12-year-old feels isolated, rejected, devalued, and misunderstood.

Principle 2: A Failure to Develop a Balanced Perspective between Person and System Focus Can Result in an Ineffective and Inaccurate Treatment Plan Potentially Harmful to the Client.

Failure to understand how systemic factors contribute to individual behavior can result in an ineffective and inaccurate treatment plan; the treatment itself may be potentially harmful (Ali & Sichel, 2014). A basic premise of a broad ecological approach is the assumption that person–environment interactions are crucial to diagnosing and treating problems (J. Goodman, 2009; L. A. Goodman et al., 2004). Clients, for example, are not viewed as isolated units but as embedded in their families, social groups, communities, institutions, cultures, and major systems of our society (Vera & Speight, 2003). Behavior is always a function of the interactions or transactions that occur between and among the many systems that comprise the life of the person. For example, a *micro* level of analysis (the individual) may lead to one treatment plan, whereas a *macro* analysis (the social system) would lead to another (Toporek & Worthington, 2014). In other words, how a helping professional defines the problem affects the treatment focus and plan. If Daryl's problems are due to internal and intrapsychic dynamics, then it makes sense that therapy be directed toward changing the individual. The fighting behavior is perceived as dysfunctional and should be eliminated through Daryl's learning to control his anger or through medication that may correct his internal biological dysfunction.

But what if the problem is external? Will having Daryl stop his fighting behavior result in the elimination of teasing from White classmates? Will it make him more connected to the campus? Will it make him feel more valued and accepted? Will he relate more to the content of courses that denigrate the contributions of African Americans? Treating the symptoms or eliminating fighting behavior may actually make Daryl more vulnerable to racism.

Principle 3: When the Client Is an Organization or a Larger System and Not an Individual, a Major Paradigm Shift Is Required to Attain a True Understanding of Problem and Solution Identification.

Let us assume that Daryl is getting into fights because of the hostile school climate and the invalidating nature of his educational experience. Given this assumption, we ask the question "Who is the client?" Is it Daryl or the school? Where should we direct our therapeutic interventions? In his analysis of schizophrenia, R. D. Laing (1969), an existential psychiatrist, once asked the following question: "Is schizophrenia a sick response to a healthy situation, or is it a healthy response to a sick situation?" In other words, if it is the school system that is dysfunctional (sick) and not the individual client, do we or should we adjust that person to a sick situation? In this case, do we focus on stopping the fighting behavior? Or if we view the fighting behavior as a healthy response to a sick situation, then eliminating the unhealthy situation (teasing, insensitive administrators and teachers, monocultural curriculum, etc.) should receive top priority for change (Lee, 2007). In other words, rather than individual therapy, social therapy may be the most appropriate and effective means of intervention. Yet mental health professionals are ill-equipped and untrained as social change agents (Ali & Sichel, 2014; Lopez-Baez & Paylo, 2009).

Principle 4: Organizations Are Microcosms of the Wider Society from Which They Originate. As a Result, They Are Likely to Be Reflections of the Monocultural Values and Practices of the Larger Culture.

As we have repeatedly emphasized, we are all products of our cultural conditioning and inherit the biases of the larger society (D. W. Sue, 2015). Likewise, organizations are microcosms of the wider society from which they originate. As a result, they are likely to be reflections of the monocultural values and practices of the larger culture. In this case, it is not far-fetched to assume that White students, helping professionals, and educators may have inherited the racial biases of their forebears. Further, multicultural education specialists have decried the biased nature of the traditional curriculum. Although education is supposed to liberate and convey truth and knowledge, we have seen how it has oftentimes been the culprit in perpetuating false stereotypes and misinformation about various groups in our society. It has done this, perhaps not intentionally, but through omission, fabrication, distortion, or selective emphasis of information, designed to enhance the contributions of certain groups over others (Cokley, 2006). The result is that institutions of learning become sites that perpetuate myths and inaccuracies about certain groups in society, with devastating consequences to students of color. Further, policies and practices that claim to "treat everyone the same" may themselves be culturally biased. If this is the institutional context from which Daryl is receiving his education, little wonder that he exhibits so-called problem behaviors. Again, the focus of change must be directed at the institutional level.

Principle 5: Organizations Are Powerful Entities That Inevitably Resist Change and Possess Many Ways to Force Compliance among Workers. Going against the Policies, Practices, and Procedures of the Institution, for Example, Can Bring about Major Punitive Actions.

Let us look at the situation of Ms. Jones, the Black teacher. There are indications in this case that she understands that Daryl may be the victim of racism and a mono-cultural education that invalidates him. If she is aware of this factor, why is she so reluctant to act on behalf of Daryl and his parents? First, it is highly probable that, even if she is aware of the true problem, she lacks the knowledge, expertise, and skill to intervene on a systemic level. Second, institutions have many avenues open to them, which can be used to force compliance on the part of employees. Voicing an alternative opinion against prevailing beliefs can result in ostracism by fellow work-ers, a poor job performance rating, denial of a promotion, or even an eventual firing (D. W. Sue et al., 2011). This creates a very strong ethical dilemma for mental health workers or educators when the needs of their clients differ from those of the organi-zation or employer. The fact that counselors' livelihoods depend on the employing agency (school district) creates additional pressures to conform. How do counselors handle such conflicts? Organizational knowledge and skills become a necessity if the therapist is to be truly effective (Toporek, Lewis, & Crethar, 2009). So even the most enlightened educators and counselors may find their good intentions thwarted by their lack of systems intervention skills and their fears of punitive actions.

Principle 6: When Multicultural Organizational Development Is Required, Alternative Helping Roles That Emphasize Systems Intervention and Advocacy Skills Must Be Part of the Repertoire of the Mental Health Professional.

Alternative helping roles that emphasize systems intervention must be part of the repertoire of the mental health professional. Because the traditional counseling/therapy roles focus on one-to-one or small-group relationships, they may not be productive when dealing with larger ecological and systemic issues. Competence in changing organizational policies, practices, procedures, and structures within insti-tutions requires a different set of knowledge and skills that are more action oriented. Among them, consultation and advocacy become crucial in helping institutions move from a monocultural to a multicultural orientation (Davidson et al., 2006). Daryl's school and the school district need a thorough cultural audit, institutional change in the campus climate, sensitivity training for all school personnel, increased racial/ethnic personnel at all levels of the school, revamping of the curriculum to be more multicultural, and so on. This is a major task that requires multicultural awareness, knowledge, and skills on the part of the mental health professional.

Principle 7: Although Remediation Will Always Be Needed, Prevention Is Better.

Conventional practice at the micro level continues to be oriented toward remediation rather than prevention. Although no one would deny the important effects of biological and internal psychological factors on personal problems, more research now acknowledges the importance of sociocultural factors (inadequate or biased education, poor socialization practices, biased values, and discriminatory institutional policies) in creating many of the difficulties encountered by individuals (Flores et al., 2014). As therapists, we are frequently placed in a position of treating clients who represent the aftermath of failed and oppressive policies and practices. We have been trapped in the role of remediation (attempting to help clients once they have been damaged by sociocultural biases). Although treating troubled clients (remediation) is a necessity, our task would be an endless and losing venture unless the true sources of the problem (stereotypes, prejudice, discrimination, and oppression) are changed. Would it not make more sense to take a proactive and preventive approach by attacking the cultural and institutional bases of the problem?

REFLECTION AND DISCUSSION QUESTIONS

1. Exactly how do organizational policies and practices oppress?

2. What do you need to know in order to effectively be a social-change agent?

3. Is organizational change difficult?

4. If individual counseling/therapy is ineffective in systems intervention, what alternative roles would you need to play?

SOCIAL JUSTICE COUNSELING

The case of Daryl demonstrates strongly the need for a social justice orientation to counseling and therapy (Neville, 2015). Indeed, multicultural counseling/therapy competence is intimately linked to the values of social justice (Koch & Juntunen,

2014; Ratts et al., 2015). If mental health practice is concerned with bettering the life circumstances of individuals, families, groups, and communities in our society, then social justice is the overarching umbrella that guides our profession. The welfare of a democratic society very much depends on equal access and opportunity, fair distribution of power and resources, and empowering individuals and groups with a right to determine their own lives (Ratts & Hutchins, 2009). J. M. Smith (2003) defines a socially just world as having access to

> *adequate food, sleep, wages, education, safety, opportunity, institutional support, health care, child care, and loving relationships. "Adequate" means enough to allow [participation] in the world. . .without starving, or feeling economically trapped or uncompensated, continually exploited, terrorized, devalued, battered, chronically exhausted, or virtually enslaved (and for some reason, still, actually enslaved). (p. 167)*

Bell (1997) states that the goal of social justice is

> *full and equal participation of all groups in a society that is mutually shaped to meet their needs. Social justice includes a vision of society in which the distribution of resources is equitable and all members are physically and psychologically safe and secure. (p. 3)*

Given these broad descriptions, we propose a working definition of social justice counseling/therapy:

> Social justice counseling/therapy *is an active philosophy and approach aimed at producing conditions that allow for equal access and opportunity; reducing or eliminating disparities in education, health care, employment, and other areas that lower the quality of life for affected populations; encouraging mental health professionals to consider micro, meso, and macro levels in the assessment, diagnosis, and treatment of client and client systems; and broadening the role of the helping professional to include not only counselor/therapist but advocate, consultant, psychoeducator, change agent, community worker, and so on.*

Thus social justice counseling/therapy has the following goals:

1. Aims to produce conditions that allow for equal access and opportunity;

2. Reduces or eliminates disparities in education, health care, employment, and other areas, that lower the quality of life for affected populations;

3. Encourages mental health professionals to consider micro, meso, and macro levels in the assessment, diagnosis, and treatment of clients and client systems;

4. Broadens the role of the helping professional to include not only counselor/therapist but advocate, consultant, psychoeducator, change agent, community worker, and so on.

Advocacy for Organizational Change

All helping professionals need to understand two things about mental health practice: (a) They often work within organizations that may be monocultural in policies and practices, and (b) the problems encountered by clients are often due to organizational or systemic factors. This is a key component of the ecological or person-in-environment perspective (Fouad, Gerstein, & Toporek, 2006). In the first case, the policies and practices of an institution may thwart the ability of counselors to provide culturally appropriate help for their diverse clientele. In the second case, the structures and operations of an organization may unfairly deny equal access and opportunity (access to health care, employment, and education) for certain groups in our society. It is possible that many problems of mental health are truly systemic problems caused by racism, sexism, and homophobia. Thus understanding organizational dynamics and possessing multicultural institutional intervention skills are part of the social justice framework (Pieterse, Evans, Risner-Butner, Collins, & Mason, 2009). Making organizations responsive to a diverse population ultimately means being able to help them become more multicultural in outlook, philosophy, and practice.

Social justice counseling (a) takes a social change perspective that focuses on ending oppression and discrimination in our society (e.g., within organizations, communities, municipalities, governmental entities); (b) believes that inequities that arise within our society are due not necessarily to misunderstandings, poor communication, lack of knowledge, and so on, but to monopolies of power; and (c) assumes that conflict is inevitable and not necessarily unhealthy. Diversity trainers, consultants, and many industrial-organizational (I/O) psychologists increasingly endorse multicultural change, based on the premise that organizations vary in their awareness of how racial, cultural, ethnic, sexual orientation, and gender issues impact their clients or workers. Increasingly, leaders in the field of counseling psychology have indicated that the profession should promote the general welfare of society; be concerned with the development of people, their communities, and their environment; and promote social, economic, and political equity consistent with the goals of social justice (Toporek, Gerstein, Fouad, Roy-sircar, & Israel, 2006).

Thus *social justice counseling* includes social and political action that seeks to ensure that all people have equal access to the resources, employment, services, and opportunities they require to meet their basic human needs and to develop fully (Goodman et al., 2004). If mental health professionals are concerned with the welfare of society, and if society's purpose is to enhance the quality of life for all persons, then these professionals must ultimately be concerned with the injustices and obstacles that oppress, denigrate, and harm those in our society (Warren & Constantine, 2007). They must be concerned with issues of classism, racism, sexism, homophobia, and all the other "isms" that deny equal rights to everyone. As mentioned previously, counselors/therapists practice at three levels: micro—where the focus is on individuals, families, and small groups; meso—where the focus is on communities and organizations; and macro—where the focus is on the larger society (e.g., statutes and social policies).

Advocacy Counseling Roles

To achieve these conditions is truly an uphill battle. But, just as the history of the United States is the history of racism, it is the history of *antiracism* as well. There have always been people and movements directed toward the eradication of racism, including abolitionists, civil rights workers, private organizations (Southern Poverty Law Center, NAACP, and B'nai Brith), political leaders, and especially people of color. Racism, like sexism, homophobia, and all forms of oppression, must be on the forefront of social justice work. Efforts must be directed at social change in order to eradicate bigotry and prejudice. In this respect, psychologists must use their knowledge and skills to (a) impact the channels of socialization (e.g., education, media, groups, organizations) to spread a curriculum of multiculturalism, and (b) aid in the passage of legislation and social policy (e.g., affirmative action, civil rights voting protections, sexual harassment laws) (Goodman, 2009; Lopez-Baez & Paylo, 2009; Ratts, 2010). To accomplish these goals, we need to openly embrace the systems intervention roles identified by Atkinson, Thompson, and Grant (1993): advocate, change agent, consultant, adviser, facilitator of indigenous support systems, and facilitator of indigenous healing methods. In closing, we include the words of Toporek (2006, p. 496) about the social justice agenda and its implications for psychologists:

> *The vastness of social challenges facing humanity requires large-scale intervention. Although the expertise of counseling psychologists is well*

suited to individual empowerment and local community involvement, likewise, much of this expertise can, and should, be applied on a broad scale. Public policy decisions such as welfare reform, gender equity, same-sex marriage and adoption, and homelessness must be informed by knowledge that comes from the communities most affected. Counseling psychologists, with expertise in consulting, communicating, researching, and direct service, are in a unique position to serve as that bridge.

IMPLICATIONS FOR CLINICAL PRACTICE

1. The mental health profession must take the initiative in confronting the potential political nature of mental health practice. The practice of counseling/therapy and the knowledge base that underlies the profession are not morally, ethically, and politically neutral.

2. We must critically reexamine our concepts of what constitutes normality and *abnormality*, begin mandatory training programs that deal with these issues, critically examine and reinterpret past and continuing literature dealing with socially marginalized groups in society, and use research in such a manner as to improve the life conditions of the researched populations.

3. The study of marginalized group cultures must receive equal treatment and fair portrayal at all levels of education.

4. The education and training of psychologists have, at times, created the impression that its theories and practices are apolitical and value free.

5. Psychological problems of marginalized group members may reside not within but outside of our clients.

6. Too much research has concentrated on the mental health problems and pathologies of groups of color, while little has been done to determine the advantages of being bicultural and the strengths and assets of these groups.

7. Psychological disturbances and problems in living are not necessarily caused by internal attributes (low intelligence, lack of motivation, character flaws, etc.) but may result from external circumstances, such as prejudice, discrimination, and disparities in education, employment, and health care.

8. *Social justice counseling* may dictate social and political actions that seek to ensure that all people have equal access to the resources, employment, services, and opportunities they require to meet their basic human needs.

9. Social justice advocacy dictates playing roles that involve advocating on behalf of clients who are victimized by the social system that creates disparities in health care, education, and employment.

SUMMARY

Mental health practice is strongly influenced by historical and current sociopolitical forces that impinge on issues of race, culture, and ethnicity. The therapeutic session is often a microcosm of race relations in our larger society; therapists often inherit the biases of their forebears; and therapy represents a primarily EuroAmerican activity. These failures can be seen in (a) the education and training of mental health professionals, (b) biased mental health literature, and (c) an equation of pathology with differences. The *genetic* and *culturally deficient* models have perpetuated these failures by graduating mental health practitioners from programs believing that people of color are lacking the right genes or the right White middle class values to succeed in this society. The *culturally diverse model*, however, no longer views people of color as deficient, but recasts differences as alternative lifestyles and addresses the advantages of being bicultural and the inherent value of differences.

Social justice counseling recognizes that problems do not necessarily reside in individuals but may be externally located in organizations and the social system. As a result, mental health professionals must be prepared to direct their foci of interventions to the individual, professional, organizational, and societal levels. Specifically, when organizational interventions are required, seven principles are identified. Students are encouraged to study them thoroughly. All stress the importance of understanding how systemic factors (person–environment interactions) contribute to individual behavior, and are necessary for accurate assessment, diagnosis, and treatment. Clients are not viewed as isolated units but as embedded in their families, social groups, communities, institutions, cultures, and in major systems of our society.

If mental health practice is concerned with bettering the life circumstances of individuals, families, groups, and communities in our society, then social justice is the overarching umbrella that guides our profession. The welfare of a democratic society very much depends on equal access and opportunity, fair distribution of power and resources, and empowering individuals and groups with a right to determine their own lives. To accomplish this goal, therapists must be prepared to treat social and systemic problems and play alternative helping roles that have not traditionally been considered therapy. Advocacy roles in counseling fall into this category.

GLOSSARY TERMS

Abnormality	Etic
Antiracism	Emic
Cultural encapsulation	Ethnocentricity
Culture-bound training	Genetically deficient model
Cultural paranoia	Levels of intervention
Cultural deprivation	Paranorm
Culturally deficient model	Scientific racism
Culturally diverse model	Social justice counseling

REFERENCES

Ahuvia, A. (2001). Well-being in cultures of choice: A cross-cultural perspective. *American Psychologist, 56*(1), 77.

Alexander, R., & Moore, S. E. (2008). The benefits, challenges, and strategies of African American faculty teaching at predominantly White institutions. *Journal of African American Studies, 12,* 4–18.

Ali, A., & Sichel, C. (2014). Structural competency as a framework for training in counseling psychology. *Counseling Psychologist, 42,* 901–918.

American Psychological Association. (2006)

American Psychological Association Presidential Task Force on Preventing Discrimination and Promoting Diversity. (2012). *Dual pathways to a better America: Preventing discrimination and promoting diversity.* Washington, DC: American Psychological Association.

Astor, C. (1997). Gallup poll: Progress in Black/White relations, but race is still an issue. *U.S. Society & Values.* Retrieved from http://usinfo.state.gov/journals/itsv/089//ijse/ gallup.htm

Atkinson, D. R., Thompson, C. E., & Grant, S. K. (1993). A three-dimensional model for counseling racial/ethnic minorities. *Counseling Psychologist, 21,* 257–277.

Babbington, C. (2008). *Poll shows gap between Blacks and Whites over racial discrimination.* Retrieved from https://groups.yahoo.com /neo/groups/VaUMCTalk/conversations /topics/4286

Bell, L. A. (1997). Theoretical foundations for social justice education. In M. Adams, L. A. Bell, & P. Griffin (Eds.), *Teaching for diversity and social justice: A sourcebook* (pp. 3–15). New York, NY: Routledge.

Cain, D. J. (2010). *Person-centered psychotherapies.* Washington, DC: APA Press.

Carter, R. T. (Ed.). (2005). *Handbook of racial-cultural psychology and counseling.* Hoboken, NJ: Wiley.

Chen, C. P. (2005). Morita therapy: A philosophy of Yin/Yang coexistence. In R. Moodley & W. West (Eds.), *Integrating traditional healing practices into counseling and psychotherapy* (pp. 221–232). Thousand Oaks, CA: Sage.

Choudhuri, D. D., Santiago-Rivera, A. L., & Garrett, M. T. (2012). *Counseling and diversity.* Belmont, CA: Cengage.

Cokley, K. (2006). The impact of racialized schools and racist (mis)education on African American students' academic identity. In M. G. Constantine & D. W. Sue (Eds.), *Addressing racism* (pp. 127–144). Hoboken, NJ: Wiley.

Constantine, M. G. (2006). Institutional racism against African Americans. In M. G. Constantine & D. W. Sue (Eds.), *Addressing racism* (pp. 33–41). Hoboken, NJ: Wiley.

Constantine, M. G., Myers, L. J., Kindaichi, M., & Moore, J. L. (2004). Exploring indigenous mental health practices: The roles of healers and helpers in promoting well-being in people of color. *Counseling and Values, 48,* 110–125.

Cosgrove, L. (2006). The unwarranted pathologizing of homeless mothers: Implications for research and social policy. In R. L. Toporek, L. H. Gerstein, N. A. Fouad, G. Roysircar, & T. Israel (Eds.), *Handbook for social justice in counseling psychology* (pp. 200–214). Thousand Oaks, CA: Sage.

Darwin, C. (1859). *On the origin of species by natural selection.* London, UK: Murray.

Davidson, M. M., Waldo, M., & Adams, E. M. (2006). Promoting social justice through preventive interventions in schools. In R. L. Toporek, L. H. Gerstein, N. A. Fouad, G. Roysircar, & T. Israel (Eds.), *Handbook for social justice in counseling psychology* (pp. 117–129). Thousand Oaks, CA: Sage.

de Gobineau, A. (1915). *The inequality of human races.* New York, NY: Putnam.

Duran, E. (2006). *Healing the soul wound.* New York, NY: Teachers College Press.

Falicov, C. J. (2005). Mexican families. In M. McGoldrick, J. Giordano, & N. Garcia-Preto (Eds.), *Ethnicity and family therapy* (2nd ed., pp. 229–241). New York, NY: Guilford Press.

Flores, M. P., De La Rue, L., Neville, H. A., Santiago, S., Rakemayahu, K., Garite, R., . . . Ginsburg, R. (2014), Developing social justice competencies: A consultation training approach. *Counseling Psychologist, 46,* 998–1020.

Fouad, N. A., Gerstein, L. H., & Toporek, R. L. (2006). Social justice and counseling psychology in context. In R. L. Toporek, L. H. Gerstein, N. A. Fouad, G. Roysircar, & T. Israel (Eds.), *Handbook for social justice in counseling psychology* (pp. 1–16). Thousand Oaks, CA: Sage.

Galton, F. (1869). *Hereditary genius: An inquiry into its laws and consequences.* London, UK: Macmillan.

Garcia-Preto, N. (2005). Puerto Rican families. In M. McGoldrick, J. Giordano, & N. Garcia-Preto (Eds.), *Ethnicity and family therapy* (2nd ed., pp. 242–255). New York, NY: Guilford Press.

Gone, J. P. (2010). Psychotherapy and traditional healing for American Indians: Exploring the prospects for therapeutic integration. *Counseling Psychologist, 38,* 166–235.

Goodman, J. (2009). Starfish, salmon, and whales: An introduction to the special section. *Journal of Counseling and Development, 87,* 259.

Goodman, L. A., Liang, B., Helms, J. E., Latta, R. E., Sparks, E., & Weintraub, S. (2004). Training counseling psychologists as social justice agents: Feminist and multicultural perspectives. *Counseling Psychologist, 32,* 793–837.

Gossett, T. F. (1963). *Race: The history of an idea in America.* Dallas, TX: Southern Methodist University Press.

Grier, W., & Cobbs, P. (1968). *Black rage.* New York, NY: Basic Books.

Grier, W., & Cobbs, P. (1971). *The Jesus bag.* San Francisco, CA: McGraw-Hill.

Guthrie, R. V. (1997). *Even the rat was White: A historical view of psychology* (2nd ed.). New York, NY: Harper & Row.

Hall, G. S.(1904). *Adolescence, its psychology, and its relation to physiology, anthropology, sociology, sex, crime, religion and education.* New York, NY: Appleton.

Halleck, S. L. (1971, April). Therapy is the handmaiden of the status quo. *Psychology Today, 4,* 30–34, 98–100.

Hong, G. K., & Domokos-Cheng Ham, M. (2001). *Psychotherapy and counseling with Asian American clients.* Thousand Oaks, CA: Sage.

Ivey, A. E., D'Andrea, M., Ivey, M. B., & Simek-Morgan, L. (2007). *Theories of counseling and psychotherapy: A multicultural perspective* (2nd ed.). Boston, MA: Allyn & Bacon.

Jones, J. M. (1997). *Prejudice and racism* (2nd ed.). Washington, DC: McGraw-Hill.

Jones, J. M. (2010). I'm White and you're not: The value of unraveling ethnocentric science. *Psychological Science, 5,* 700–707.

Jordan, V. L. (2002, June). Speech given at Howard University's Rankin Memorial Chapel, Washington, DC.

Katz, J. (1985). The sociopolitical nature of counseling. *Counseling Psychologist, 13,* 615–624.

Kearney, L. K., Draper, M., & Baron, A. (2005). Counseling utilization of ethnic minority college students. *Cultural Diversity and Ethnic Minority Psychology, 11,* 272–285.

Koch, J. M., & Juntunen, C. L. (2014). Nontraditional teaching methods that promote

social justice: Introduction to the Special Issue. *Counseling Psychologist, 42,* 894–900.

Laing, R. D. (1967). *The divided self.* New York, NY: Pantheon.

Laing, R. D. (1969). *The politics of experience.* New York, NY: Pantheon.

Lee, C. C. (2007). *Counseling for social justice.* Alexandria, VA: American Counseling Association.

Liu, W. M., Hernandez, J., Mahmood, A., & Stinson, R. (2006). Linking poverty, classism, and racism in mental health: Overcoming barriers to multicultural competency. In M. G. Constantine & D. W. Sue (Eds.), *Addressing racism* (pp. 65–86). Hoboken, NJ: Wiley.

London, P. (1988). *Modes and morals of psychotherapy.* New York, NY: Holt, Rinehart & Winston.

Lopez-Baez, S. I., & Paylo, M. J. (2009). Social justice advocacy: Community collaboration and systems advocacy. *Journal of Counseling and Development, 87,* 276–283.

McAuliffe, G., & Associates. (2013). *Culturally alert counseling.* Thousand Oaks, CA: Sage.

McNeil, D. G. (2011, August 30). Panel hears grim details of venereal disease tests. *New York Times.* Retrieved from http://www.nytimes.com/2011/08/31/world/americas/31syphilis.html?scp=1&sq=McNeil%20syphilis&st=cse

Metzl, J., & Hansen, H. (2014). Structural competency: Theorizing a new medical engagement with stigma and inequality. *Social Science and Medicine, 103,* 126–133.

Mio, J. S. (2005). Academic mental health training settings and the multicultural guidelines. In M. G. Constantine & D. W. Sue (Eds.), *Strategies for building multicultural competence in mental health and educational settings* (pp. 129–144). Hoboken, NJ: Wiley.

Mio, J. S., & Morris, D. R. (1990). Cross-cultural issues in psychology training programs: An invitation for discussion. *Professional Psychology: Theory and Practice, 21,* 434–441.

Moodley, R., & West, W. (Eds.). (2005). *Integrating traditional healing practices into counseling and psychotherapy.* Thousand Oaks, CA: Sage.

Moynihan, D. P. (1965). Employment, income and the ordeal of the Negro family. *Daedalus, 140,* 745–770.

Nadal, K. L. (2011). *Filipino American psychology.* Hoboken, NJ: Wiley.

Neville, H. A. (2015). Social justice mentoring: Supporting the development of future leaders for struggles, resistance, and transformation. *Counseling Psychologist, 43,* 157–169.

Orwell, G. (1945). *Animal farm.* London, UK: Secker and Warburg.

Owen, J., Imel, Z., Adelson, J., & Rodolfa, E. (2012). "No-show": Therapist racial/ethnic disparities in client unilateral termination. *Journal of Counseling Psychology, 29,* 314–320.

Paniagua, F. A. (2005). *Assessing and treating culturally diverse clients: A practical guide* (3rd ed.). Thousand Oaks, CA: Sage.

Parham, T. A. (2002). *Counseling persons of African descent.* Thousand Oaks, CA: Sage.

Parham, T. A., Ajamu, A., & White, J. L. (2011). *The psychology of Blacks. Centering our perspectives in the African consciousness.* Boston, MA: Prentice Hall.

Pew Research Center. (2007). *Blacks see growing values gap between poor and middle class.* Washington, DC: Author.

Pieterse, A. I., Evans, S. A., Risner-Butner, A., Collins, N. M., & Mason, L. B. (2009). Multicultural competence and social justice training in counseling psychology and counselor education: A review and analysis of a sample of multicultural course syllabi. *Counseling Psychologist, 37,* 93–115.

Plous, S., & Williams, T. (1995). Racial stereotypes from the days of American slavery: A continuing legacy. *Journal of Applied Social Psychology, 25,* 795–817.

Ponterotto, J. G., & Austin, R. (2005). Emerging approaches to training psychologists to be culturally competent. In R. T. Carter (Ed.), *Handbook of racial-cultural psychology and counseling* (pp. 19–35). Hoboken, NJ: Wiley.

Ponterotto, J. G., Utsey, S. O., & Pedersen, P. B. (2006). *Preventing prejudice: A guide for counselors, educators, and parents.* Thousand Oaks, CA: Sage.

President's Initiative on Race. (1998). *One America in the twenty-first century.* Washington, DC: U.S. Government Printing Office.

Ratts, M. J. (2010). Multiculturalism and social justice: Two sides of the same coin. *Journal of Multicultural Counseling and Development, 39,* 24–37.

Ratts, M. J., & Hutchins, A. M. (2009). ACA advocacy competencies: Social justice advocacy at the client/student level. *Journal of Counseling and Development, 87,* 269–275.

Ratts, M. J., & Pedersen, P. B. (2014). *Counseling for multiculturalism and social justice.* Alexandria, VA: American Counseling Association.

Ratts, M. J., Singh, A. A., Nassar-McMillan, S., Butler, K., & McCullough, R. J. (2015). *Multicultural and social justice counseling competencies.* The Multicultural Counseling Competencies Revision Committee of the American Counseling Association, Draft Report.

Ridley, C. R. (2005). *Overcoming unintentional racism in counseling and therapy* (2nd ed.). Thousand Oaks, CA: Sage.

Riessman, F. (1962). *The culturally deprived child.* New York, NY: Harper & Row.

Rosenthal, R., & Jacobson, L. (1968). *Pygmalion in the classroom.* New York, NY: Holt, Rinehart & Winston.

Rushton, J. P. (1989). The evolution of racial differences: A response to Lynn. *Journal of Research in Personality, 23,* 441–452.

Ryan, W. (1971). *Blaming the victim.* New York, NY: Pantheon.

Samuda, R. J. (1998). *Psychological testing of American minorities.* Thousand Oaks, CA: Sage.

Shockley, W. (1972). Determination of human intelligence. *Journal of Criminal Law and Criminology, 7,* 530–543.

Smith, J. M. (2003). *A potent spell: Mother love and the power of fear.* Boston, MA: Houghton Mifflin.

Snowden, L. R., & Cheung, F. H. (1990). Use of inpatient mental health services by members of ethnic minority groups. *American Psychologist, 45,* 347–355.

Steele, C. M. (2003). Race and the schooling of Black Americans. In S. Plous (Ed.), *Understanding prejudice and discrimination* (pp. 98–107). New York: McGraw-Hill.

Sue, D., Sue, D. W., Sue, D. M., & Sue, S. (2016). *Understanding abnormal behavior.* Stamford, CT: Cengage.

Sue, D. W. (2003). *Overcoming our racism: The journey to liberation.* San Francisco, CA: Jossey-Bass.

Sue, D. W. (2010a). *Microaggressions in everyday life: Race, gender, and sexual orientation.* Hoboken, NJ: Wiley.

Sue, D. W. (2010b). *Microaggressions and marginality: Manifestations, dynamics, and impact.* Hoboken, NJ: Wiley.

Sue, D. W. (2015, March 20). Therapeutic harm and cultural oppression. *Counseling Psychologist.* doi: 0011000014565713

Sue, D. W., & Constantine, M. G. (2003). Optimal human functioning in people of color in the United States. In W. B. Walsh (Ed.), *Counseling psychology and optimal human functioning* (pp. 151–169). Mahwah, NJ: Erlbaum.

Sue, D. W., Rivera, D. P., Watkins, N. L., Kim, R. H., Kim, S., & Williams, C. D. (2011). Racial dialogues: Challenges faculty of color face in the classroom. *Cultural Diversity and Ethnic Minority Psychology, 17*(3), 331–340.

Sutton, C. T., & Broken Nose, M. A. (2005). American Indian families: An overview. In M. McGoldrick, J. Giordano, & N. Garcia-Preto (Eds.), *Ethnicity and family therapy* (2nd ed., pp. 43–54). New York, NY: Guilford Press.

Szasz, T. S. (1970). The crime of commitment. In *Readings in clinical psychology today* (pp. 167–169). Del Mar, CA: CRM Books.

Szasz, T. S. (1971). *The myth of mental illness.* New York, NY: Hoeber.

Szasz, T. S. (1987). The case against suicide prevention. *American Psychologist, 41,* 806–812.

Szasz, T. S. (1999). *Fatal freedom: The ethics and politics of suicide.* Westport, CT: Praeger.

Terman, L. M. (1916). *The measurement of intelligence.* Boston, MA: Houghton Mifflin.

Thomas, A., & Sillen, S. (1972). *Racism and psychiatry.* New York, NY: Brunner/Mazel.

Thomas, C. W. (1970). Different strokes for different folks. *Psychology Today, 4,* 49–53, 80.

Toporek, R. L. (2006). Social action in policy and legislation. In R. L. Toporek, L. H. Gerstein, N. A. Fouad, G. Roysircar, & T. Israel (Eds.), *Handbook for social justice in counseling psychology* (pp. 489–497). Thousand Oaks, CA: Sage.

Toporek, R. L., Lewis, J. A., & Crethar, H. C. (2009). Promoting systemic change through the ACA advocacy competencies. *Journal of Counseling and Development, 87,* 260–268.

Toporek, R. L., & Worthington, R. L. (2014). Integrating service learning and difficult dialogues pedagogy to advance social justice training. *Counseling Psychologist, 46,* 919–945.

Triandis, H. C. (2000). Cultural syndromes and subjective well-being. In E. Diener & E. M. Suh (Eds.), *Culture and subjective well-being* (pp. 13–36). London, UK: MIT Press.

Trimble, J. E. (2010). The virtues of cultural resonance, competence, and relational collaboration with Native American Indian communities: A synthesis of the counseling and psychotherapy literature. *Counseling Psychologist, 38,* 243–256.

Turner, C.S.V., Gonzalez, J. C., & Wood, J. L. (2008). Faculty of color in academe: What 20 years of literature tells us. *Journal of Diversity in Higher Education, 1*, 139–168.

Utsey, S. O., Grange, C., & Allyne, R. (2006). Guidelines for evaluating the racial and cultural environment of graduate training programs in professional psychology. In M. G. Constantine & D. W. Sue (Eds.), *Addressing racism* (pp. 213–232). Hoboken, NJ: Wiley.

Vazquez, L. A., & Garcia-Vazquez, E. (2003). Teaching multicultural competence in the counseling curriculum. In D. B. Pope-Davis, H.L.K. Coleman, W. M. Liu, & R. L. Toporek (Eds.), *Handbook of multicultural competencies in counseling and psychology* (pp. 546–561). Thousand Oaks, CA: Sage.

Vera, E. M., Buhin, L., & Shin, R. Q. (2006). The pursuit of social justice and the elimination of racism. In M. G. Constantine & D. W. Sue (Eds.), *Addressing racism* (pp. 271–287). Hoboken, NJ: Wiley.

Vera, E. M., & Speight, S. L. (2003). Multicultural competence, social justice, and counseling psychology: Expanding our roles. *Counseling Psychologist, 31*, 253–272.

Wang, S., & Kim, B.S.K. (2010). Therapist multicultural competence, Asian American participants' cultural values, and counseling process. *Journal of Counseling Psychology, 57*, 394–401.

Warren, A. K., & Constantine, M. G. (2007). Social justice issues. In M. G. Constantine (Ed.), *Clinical practice with people of color* (pp. 231–242). New York, NY: Teachers College Press.

West-Olatunji, C. A., & Conwill, W. (2011). *Counseling African Americans.* Belmont, CA: Cengage.

Wrenn, C. G. (1962). The culturally encapsulated counselor. *Harvard Educational Review, 32*, 444–449.

The Impact of Systemic Oppression

Counselor Credibility and Client Worldviews

The true tale of the lion hunt will never be told as long as the hunter tells the story.

—African proverb as cited in J. M. Jones (2010)

CASE STUDY

MALACHI

I [White male] have worked with very few African American clients during my internship at the clinic, but one particular incident left me with very negative feelings. A Black client named Malachi was given an appointment with me. Even though I'm White, I tried not to let his being Black get in the way of our sessions. I treated him like everyone else, a human being who needed help.

At the onset, Malachi was obviously guarded, mistrustful, and frustrated when talking about his reasons for coming. While his intake form listed depression as the problem, he seemed more concerned about nonclinical matters. He spoke about his inability to find a job, about the need to obtain help with job-hunting skills, and about advice in how best to write his résumé. He was quite demanding in asking for advice and information. It was almost as if Malachi wanted everything handed to him on a silver platter without putting any work into our sessions. Not only did he appear reluctant to take responsibility to change his own life, but I felt he needed to go elsewhere for help. After all, this was a mental health clinic, not an employment agency.

Confronting him about his avoidance of responsibility would probably prove counterproductive, so I chose to focus on his feelings. Using a humanistic-existential approach, I reflected his feelings, paraphrased his thoughts, and summarized his dilemmas. This did not seem to help immediately, as I sensed an increase in the tension level, and he seemed antagonistic toward me.

After several attempts by Malachi to obtain direct advice from me, I stated, "You're getting frustrated at me because I'm not giving you the answers you want." It was clear that this angered Malachi. Getting up in a very menacing manner, he stood over me and angrily shouted, "Forget it, man! I don't have time to play your silly games." For one brief moment, I felt in danger of being physically assaulted before he stormed out of the office. This incident occurred several years ago, and I must admit that I was left with a very unfavorable impression of Blacks. I see myself as basically a good person who truly wants to help others less fortunate than myself. I know it sounds racist, but Malachi's behavior only reinforces my belief that Blacks have trouble controlling their anger, like to take the easy way out, and find it difficult to be open and trusting of others. If I am wrong in this belief, I hope this workshop [multicultural counseling/therapy] will help me better understand the Black personality.

> ## REFLECTION AND DISCUSSION QUESTIONS
>
> 1. What do you think is the source of Malachi's anger?
>
> 2. How may the therapist and the therapeutic process be contributing to Malachi's frustration and anger?
>
> 3. Was the therapist in physical danger or was his fear based on *stereotypes*?
>
> 4. Might not this potential misinterpretation be due to differences in communication styles?
>
> 5. Is giving advice and suggestions, helping clients prepare a résumé, or helping them find a job part of therapy?

The clinical tale being told here was supplied at an in-service training workshop by a White male therapist, and is used here to illustrate the meaning of the lion hunt proverb. In this case, we question neither the sincerity of the White therapist nor his desire to help the African American client. We do, however, wish to tell "the rest of the story."

THE REST OF THE STORY

It is obvious to us that the therapist is part of the problem and not the solution. The male therapist's preconceived notions and *stereotypes* about African Americans appear to have affected his definition of the problem, assessment of the situation, and therapeutic intervention. Let us analyze this case in greater detail from the perspective of "the lion."

Stereotyping the Client

Statements about Malachi's wanting things handed to him on a "silver platter," his "avoidance of responsibility," and his "wanting to take the easy way out" are characteristic of social *stereotypes* that Blacks are lazy and unmotivated. The therapist's statements that African Americans have difficulty "controlling their anger," that Malachi was "menacing," and that the therapist was in fear of being assaulted seem to paint the picture of the hostile, angry, and violent Black male—again an image of African Americans to which many in this society consciously and unconsciously subscribe. Although it is always possible that the client was unmotivated and prone to violence, studies suggest that White Americans continue to cling to the image of the dangerous, violence-prone, and antisocial Black man (Babbington, 2008; J. M. Jones, 2010).

Blaming the Client

Mental health practice has been characterized as primarily a White middle-class activity that values rugged individualism, individual responsibility, and autonomy (Ivey, Ivey, & Zalaquett, 2014). Because people are seen as being responsible for their own actions and predicaments, clients are expected to make decisions on their own and to be primarily responsible for their fate in life. The traditional therapist's role should be to encourage self-exploration so that the client can act on his or her own behalf (Lum, 2011). The individual-centered approach tends to view the problem as residing within the person. If something goes wrong, it is the client's fault. Many problems encountered by clients of color reside external to them (bias, discrimination, prejudice, etc.) and they should not be faulted for the obstacles they encounter. To do so is to engage in *victim blaming* (Ratts & Pedersen, 2014; Ryan, 1971).

Objectifying the Client

Therapists are expected to avoid giving advice or suggestions and disclosing their thoughts and feelings not only because they may unduly influence their clients and block individual development, but also because they may become emotionally involved, lose their objectivity, and blur the boundaries of the helping relationship (Parham & Caldwell, 2015). Parham (1997) states, however, that a fundamental African principle is that human beings realize themselves only in moral relations to others (collectivity, not individuality): "Consequently, application of an African-centered *worldview* will cause one to question the need for objectivity absent emotions, the need for distance rather than connectedness, and the need for dichotomous relationships rather than multiple roles" (p. 110). In other words, from an African American perspective, the helper and the helpee are not separated from one another but are bound together both emotionally and spiritually. The EuroAmerican style of objectivity encourages distancing and separation that may be interpreted by Malachi as uninvolved, uncaring, insincere, and dishonest—that is, "playing silly games."

Being Nondirective with the Client

The more active and involved role demanded by Malachi goes against what the helping profession considers therapy. Studies indicate that clients of color prefer a therapeutic relationship in which the helper is more active, self-disclosing, and not adverse to giving advice and suggestions when appropriate (Bemak & Chung, 2015; Choudhuri, Santiago-Rivera, & Garrett, 2012). The therapist in this scenario fails to entertain the possibility that requests for advice, information, and suggestions may be legitimate and not indicative of pathological responding. The therapist has been trained to believe that his role as a therapist is to be primarily nondirective; therapists do therapy, not provide job-hunting information. This has always been the conventional counseling and psychotherapy role, one whose emphasis is a one-to-one, in-the-office, remedial relationship aimed at self-exploration and the achievement of insight (Atkinson, Thompson, & Grant, 1993).

Pathologizing the Client

In almost every introductory text on counseling and psychotherapy, lip service is paid to the axiom, "Counselor, know thyself." In other words, therapeutic wisdom endorses the notion that we become better therapists the more we understand our own motives, biases, values, and assumptions about human behavior. We are taught to look at our clients, to analyze them, and to note their weaknesses, limitations, and pathological trends; less often do we either look for positive healthy characteristics in our clients or question our conclusions (Choudhuri et al., 2012). When the therapist ends his story by stating that he hopes the workshop will "help me better understand the Black personality," his *worldview* is clearly evident. The assumption is that multicultural counseling/therapy simply requires the acquisition of knowledge, and good intentions are all that is needed. This statement represents one of the major obstacles to self awareness and dealing with one's own biases and prejudices. Without awareness, differences are equated with deviancy and the client is pathologized.

Seeing Race as the Problem

The therapist states that he tried not to let Malachi's "being Black get in the way" of the session and that he treated him like any other "human being." This is a very typical statement made by Whites who unconsciously subscribe to the belief that people of color are problem people. In reality, color is not the problem, but society's perception of color is! In other words, the locus of the problem (racism, sexism, and homophobia) resides not in marginalized groups but in the society at large. Often this view of race is manifested in the myth of color blindness: If color is the problem, let's pretend not to see it (Neville, Gallardo, & Sue, in press). Our contention, however, is that it is nearly impossible to overlook the fact that a client is Black, Asian American, Hispanic, and so forth. When operating in this manner, *color-blind* therapists may actually be obscuring their understandings of who their clients really are. To overlook one's racial group membership is to deny an intimate and important aspect of one's identity.

Perceiving the Client as "Paranoid"

Central to the thesis of this chapter is the statement made by the counselor that Malachi appears guarded and mistrustful and has difficulty being open (self-disclosing). In essence, he is paranoid. We have mentioned several times that a counselor's inability to establish rapport and a relationship of trust with culturally diverse clients is a major therapeutic barrier. When the emotional climate is negative, and when little trust or understanding exists between the therapist and the client, therapy can be both ineffective and destructive. Yet if the emotional climate is realistically positive and if trust and understanding exist between the parties, the two-way communication of thoughts and feelings can proceed with optimism. This latter condition is often referred to as rapport and sets the stage on which other essential conditions can become effective. One of these, self-disclosure, is particularly crucial to the process and goals of counseling because it is the most direct means by which individuals make themselves known to others. This chapter discusses trust–mistrust and *worldviews* as they relate to marginalized groups.

EFFECTS OF HISTORICAL AND CURRENT OPPRESSION

Persons of color and other marginalized groups (women, gays/lesbians, and those with disabilities) live under a societal umbrella of individual, institutional, and cultural forces that often demean them, disadvantage them, and deny them equal access and opportunity (Toporek & Worthington, 2014). Experiences of prejudice and discrimination are a social reality for many marginalized groups and affect the perception of the helping professional in multicultural counseling (Parham & Caldwell, 2015). Thus mental health practitioners must become aware of the sociopolitical dynamics that form not only their clients' *worldviews*, but their own as well. As in the clinical case presented earlier, racial/cultural dynamics may intrude into the helping process and cause misdiagnosis, confusion, pain, and a reinforcement of the biases and *stereotypes* that both groups have of one another.

It is important for the therapist to realize that the history of race relations in the United States has influenced us to the point where we are extremely cautious about revealing to strangers our feelings and attitudes about race. In an interracial encounter with a stranger (i.e., therapy), each party will attempt to discern gross or subtle racial attitudes of the other while minimizing vulnerability. *Ethnocentric monoculturalism* lies at the heart of oppressor–oppressed relationships that affect trust–mistrust and self-disclosure in the therapeutic encounter.

Ethnocentric Monoculturalism

Most mental health professionals have not been trained to work with anyone other than mainstream individuals or groups. This is understandable in light of the historical origins of education, counseling/guidance, and our mental health systems, which have their roots in EuroAmerican or Western cultures (Arredondo, Gallardo-Cooper, Delgado-Romero, & Zapata, 2014). As a result, American (U.S.) psychology has been severely criticized as being ethnocentric, monocultural, and inherently biased against racial/ethnic minorities, women, gays/lesbians, and other culturally diverse groups (Constantine & Sue, 2006; Ridley, 2005). In light of the increasing diversity of our society, mental health professionals will inevitably encounter client populations that differ from themselves in terms of race, culture, and ethnicity. Such differences, however, are believed to pose no problems as long as psychologists adhere to the notion of an unyielding, universal psychology that is applicable across all populations.

Although few mental health professionals would voice such a belief, in reality the very policies and practices of mental health delivery systems do reflect such an ethnocentric orientation. The theories of counseling and psychotherapy, the standards used to judge normality-abnormality, and the actual process of mental health practice are culture bound and reflect a monocultural perspective of the helping professions (Highlen, 1994; J. M. Jones, 2010). As such, they are often culturally inappropriate and antagonistic to the lifestyles and values of diverse groups in our society. Indeed, some mental health professionals assert that counseling and psychotherapy may be "handmaidens of the status quo," instruments of oppression, and transmitters of society's values (Halleck, 1971; Thomas & Sillen, 1972).

We believe that *ethnocentric monoculturalism* is dysfunctional in a pluralistic society such as the United States. It is a powerful force, however, in forming, influencing, and determining the goals and processes of mental health delivery systems. Hence it is very important for mental health professionals to unmask or deconstruct the values, biases, and assumptions that reside in it. *Ethnocentric monoculturalism* combines what Wrenn (1962) calls *cultural encapsulation* and what J. M. Jones (1997) refers to as *cultural racism*. Five components of *ethnocentric monoculturalism* have been identified (Sue, 2004).

Belief in Superiority of Dominant Group

First, there is a strong belief in the superiority of one group's cultural heritage (history, values, language, traditions, arts/crafts, etc.). The group norms and values are seen positively, and descriptors may include such phrases as "more advanced" and "more civilized." Members of the society may possess conscious and unconscious feelings of superiority and feel that their way of doing things is the best way. In our society, White EuroAmerican cultures are seen as not only desirable but normative as well. Physical characteristics such as light complexion, blond hair, and blue eyes; cultural characteristics such as a belief in Christianity (or monotheism), individualism, Protestant work ethic, and capitalism; and behavioral characteristics such as standard English, control of emotions, and the written tradition are highly valued components of EuroAmerican culture (Anderson & Middleton, 2011; Katz, 1985). People possessing these traits are perceived more favorably and often are allowed easier access to the privileges and rewards of the larger society (Furman, 2011).

Belief in the Inferiority of Others

Second, there is a belief in the inferiority of the cultural heritage of persons of color, which extends to its customs, values, traditions, and language (J. M. Jones, 1997). Other societies or groups may be perceived as less developed, uncivilized, primitive, or even pathological. The groups' lifestyles or ways of doing things are considered inferior. Physical characteristics such as dark complexion, black hair, and brown eyes; cultural characteristics such as belief in non-Christian religions (Islam, Confucianism, polytheism, etc.), collectivism, present-time orientation, and the importance of shared wealth; and linguistic characteristics such as bilingualism, nonstandard English, speaking with an accent, use of nonverbal and contextual communication, and reliance on the oral tradition are usually seen as less desirable by the society (Sue, 2010). Studies consistently reveal that individuals who are physically different, who speak with an accent, and who adhere to different cultural beliefs and practices are more likely to be evaluated more negatively in our schools and workplaces. Culturally diverse groups may be seen as less intelligent, less qualified, and less popular, and as possessing more undesirable traits.

Power to Impose Standards

Third, the dominant group possesses the power to impose their standards and beliefs on the less powerful group (Ratts & Pedersen, 2014; Ridley, 2005). This third component of *ethnocentric monoculturalism* is very important. All groups are to some extent ethnocentric; that is, they feel positive about their cultural heritage and way of life. Persons of color can be biased, can hold stereotypes, and can strongly believe that their way is the best way. Yet if they do not possess the power to impose their values on others, then hypothetically they cannot oppress. It is power or the unequal status relationship between groups that defines *ethnocentric monoculturalism*. *Ethnocentric monoculturalism* is the individual, institutional, and cultural expression of the belief in the superiority of one group's cultural heritage over another, combined with the possession of power to impose those standards broadly on less powerful groups. Since marginalized groups do not possess a share of economic, social, and political power equal to that of Whites in our society, they are generally unable to discriminate on a large-scale basis (Ponterotto, Utsey, & Pedersen, 2006). The damage and harm of oppression is likely to be one-sided, from dominant to marginalized group.

Manifestation in Institutions

Fourth, the ethnocentric values and beliefs are manifested in the programs, policies, priorities, structures, and institutions of the society. For example, chain-of-command systems, training and educational systems, communications systems, management systems, and performance-appraisal systems often dictate and control our lives. Ethnocentric values attain untouchable and godfather-like status in an organization. Because most systems are monocultural in nature and demand compliance, persons of color and women may be oppressed. J. M. Jones (1997) labels *institutional racism* as a set of policies, priorities, and accepted normative patterns designed to subjugate and oppress individuals and groups, and force their dependence on a larger society. It does this by sanctioning unequal goals, unequal status, and unequal access to goods and services. *Institutional racism* has fostered the enactment of discriminatory statutes, the selective enforcement of laws, the blocking of economic opportunities and outcomes, and the imposition of forced assimilation/acculturation on the culturally diverse.

The Invisible Veil

Fifth, since people are all products of cultural conditioning, their values and beliefs (*worldviews*) represent an *invisible veil* that operates outside the level of conscious awareness (Neville, Gallardo, & Sue, in press). As a result, people assume universality: that regardless of race, culture, ethnicity, or gender, everyone shares the nature of reality and truth. This assumption is erroneous but is seldom questioned because it is firmly ingrained in our *worldview*. It is well-intentioned individuals who consider themselves moral, decent, and fair-minded who may have the greatest difficulty in understanding how their belief systems and actions may be biased and prejudiced. It is clear that no one is born wanting to be racist, sexist, or homophobic. Misinformation related to culturally diverse groups is not acquired by our free choice but rather is imposed through a painful process of social conditioning; all of us were taught to hate and fear others who are different in some way (Sue, 2003). Likewise, because all of us live, play, and work within organizations, those policies, practices, and structures that may be less than fair to minority groups are invisible in controlling our lives. Perhaps the greatest obstacle to a meaningful movement toward a multicultural society is our failure to understand our unconscious and unintentional complicity in perpetuating bias and discrimination via our personal values/beliefs and our institutions. The power of racism, sexism, and homophobia is related to the invisibility of the powerful forces that control and dictate our lives.

Historical Manifestations of Ethnocentric Monoculturalism

The European American *worldview* can be described as possessing the following values and beliefs: rugged individualism, competition, mastery and control over nature, a unitary and static conception of time, religion based on Christianity, separation of science and religion, and competition (Katz, 1985; Ratts & Pedersen, 2014). It is important to note that *worldviews* are neither right or wrong, nor good or bad. They become problematic, however, when they are expressed through the process of *ethnocentric monoculturalism*. In the United States, the historical manifestations of this process are quite clear. The European colonization efforts toward the Americas, for example, operated from the assumption that the enculturation of indigenous peoples was justified because European culture was superior. Forcing the colonized to adopt European beliefs and customs was seen as civilizing them. In the United States, this practice was clearly evident in the treatment of Native Americans, whose lifestyles, customs, and practices were seen as backward and uncivilized, and attempts were made to make over the "heathens" (Duran, 2006; Gone, 2010).

Monocultural ethnocentric bias has a long history in the United States and is even reflected as early as the uneven application of the Bill of Rights, which favored White immigrants/descendants over minority populations (Barongan et al., 1997). More than 200 years ago, Britain's King George III accepted a Declaration of Independence from former subjects who moved to this country. This proclamation was destined to shape and reshape the geopolitical and sociocultural landscape of the world many times over. The lofty language penned by its principal architect, Thomas Jefferson, and signed by those present was indeed inspiring: *"We hold these truths to be self evident, that all men are created equal."*

Yet as we now view the historic actions of that time, we cannot help but be struck by the paradox inherent in those events. First, all 56 of the signatories were White males of European descent, hardly a representation of the current racial and gender composition of the population. Second, the language of the declaration suggests that only men were created equal; what about women? Third, many of the founding fathers were slave owners who seemed not to recognize the hypocritical personal standards that they used because they considered Blacks to be subhuman. Fourth, the history of this land did not start with the Declaration of Independence or the formation of the United States of America. Nevertheless, our textbooks continue to teach us an ethnocentric perspective ("Western Civilization") that ignores the natives of this country. Last, it is important to note that those early Europeans who came to this country were immigrants attempting to escape persecution (oppression), who in the process did not recognize their own role in the oppression of indigenous peoples (American Indians) who had already resided in this country for centuries.

While *ethnocentric monoculturalism* is much broader than the concept of racial oppression, it is race and color that have been primarily used to determine the social order. The White race has been seen as superior and White culture as normative. Thus a study of U.S. history must include a study of racism and racist practices directed at people of color. The oppression of the indigenous people of this country (Native Americans), enslavement of African Americans, widespread segregation of Hispanic Americans, passage of exclusionary laws against the Chinese, and the forced internment of Japanese Americans are social realities. Telling "the rest of the story" is important. Thus it should be of no surprise that our racial/ethnic minority citizens may view EuroAmericans and our institutions with considerable mistrust and suspicion. Likewise, in counseling and psychotherapy, which demand a certain degree of trust among therapist and client, an interracial encounter may be fraught with historical and current psychological baggage related to issues of discrimination, prejudice, and oppression.

Surviving Systemic Oppression

Many multicultural specialists (Parham, Ajamu, & White, 2011; Ponterotto et al., 2006) have pointed out how African Americans, in responding to their forced enslavement, our history of discrimination, and America's reaction to their skin color, have adopted toward Whites behavior patterns that are important for survival in a racist society. These behavior patterns may include indirect expressions of hostility, aggression, and fear. During slavery, to rear children who would fit into a segregated system and who could physically survive, African American mothers were forced to teach them (a) to express aggression indirectly, (b) to read the thoughts of others while concealing their own, and (c) to engage in ritualized accommodating/subordinating behaviors designed to create as few waves as possible. This process involves a "mild dissociation" whereby African Americans may separate their true selves from their roles as "Negroes" (Boyd-Franklin, 2010; J. M. Jones, 1997). In this dual identity the true self is revealed to fellow Blacks, while the dissociated self is revealed to meet the expectations of prejudiced Whites. From the analysis of African American history, the dissociative process may be manifested in two major ways.

First, "*playing it cool*" has been identified as one means by which African Americans or other minorities may conceal their true feelings (Boyd-Franklin, 2010; Cross, Smith, & Payne, 2002; Grier & Cobbs, 1971; A. C. Jones, 1985). This behavior is intended to prevent Whites from knowing what the minority person is thinking or feeling and to express feelings and behaviors in such a way as to prevent offending or threatening Whites (C. Jones & Shorter-Gooden, 2003; Ridley, 2005). Thus a person of color who is experiencing conflict, explosive anger, and suppressed feelings may appear serene and composed on the surface. This is a defense mechanism aimed at protecting people of color from harm and exploitation. Second, the *Uncle Tom syndrome* may be used by Blacks to appear docile, nonassertive, and happy-go-lucky. Especially during slavery, Blacks learned that passivity was a necessary survival technique. To retain the most menial jobs, to minimize retaliation, and to maximize survival of the self and loved ones, many minorities have learned to deny their aggressive feelings toward their oppressors. The overall result of the experiences of minorities in the United States has been to increase their vigilance and sensitivity to the thoughts and behaviors of Whites in society.

In summary, it becomes all too clear that past and present discrimination against certain culturally diverse groups is a tangible basis for distrust of the majority society (McAuliffe & Associates, 2013). White people are perceived as potential oppressors unless proved otherwise. Under such a sociopolitical atmosphere, marginalized groups may use several adaptive devices to prevent Whites from knowing their true feelings. Because multicultural counseling may mirror the sentiments of the larger society, these modes of behavior and their detrimental effects may be reenacted in the sessions. The fact that many marginalized clients are suspicious, mistrustful, and guarded in their interactions with White therapists is certainly understandable in light of the foregoing analysis. Despite their conscious desires to help, White therapists are not immune from inheriting racist attitudes, beliefs, myths, and *stereotypes* about Asian American, African American, Latino/Hispanic American, and American Indian clients (Sue, 2004). For example, White counselors often believe that Blacks are nonverbal, paranoid, and angry and that they are most likely to have character disorders (Carter, 1995; A. C. Jones, 1985) or to be schizophrenic (Pavkov, Lewis, & Lyons, 1989). As a result, they view African Americans as unsuitable for counseling and psychotherapy. Mental health practitioners and social scientists who hold to this belief fail to understand the following facts:

1. As a group, African Americans tend to communicate nonverbally more than their White counterparts and to assume that nonverbal communication is a more accurate barometer of one's true thoughts and feelings. E. T. Hall (1976) observed that African Americans are better able to read nonverbal messages (high context) than are their White counterparts and that they rely less on verbalizations than on nonverbal communication to make a point. Whites, on the other hand, tune in more to verbal messages than to nonverbal messages (low context). Because they rely less on nonverbal cues, Whites need greater verbal elaboration to get a point across (Sue, Ivey, & Pedersen, 1996). Being unaware of and insensitive to these differences, White therapists are prone to feel that African Americans are unable to communicate in complex

ways. This judgment is based on the high value that therapy places on intellectual/verbal activity.

2. Rightfully or not, White therapists are often perceived as symbols of the Establishment, who have inherited the racial biases of their forebears. Thus socially marginalized clients are likely to impute all the negative experiences of oppression to them. This may prevent clients from responding to helping professionals as individuals. While therapists may be possessed of the most admirable motives, clients may reject helping professionals simply because they are White. Thus communication may be directly or indirectly shut off.

3. Some culturally diverse clients may lack confidence in the counseling and therapy process because White counselors often propose White solutions to their concerns (Atkinson, Kim, & Caldwell, 1998). Many pressures are placed on clients of color to accept an alien value system and reject their own. We have already indicated how counseling and psychotherapy may be perceived as instruments of oppression whose function is to force assimilation and acculturation. As some racial/ethnic minority clients have asked, "Why do I have to become White in order to be considered healthy?"

4. The "*playing it cool*" and Uncle Tom responses of many people of color are present also in the therapy sessions. As pointed out earlier, these mechanisms are attempts to conceal true feelings, to hinder self-disclosure, and to prevent the therapist from getting to know the client. These adaptive survival mechanisms have been acquired through generations of experience with a hostile and invalidating society. The therapeutic dilemma encountered by the helping professional in working with a client of color is how to gain trust and break through this maze. What therapists ultimately do in sessions will determine their *trustworthiness*.

In closing, culturally diverse clients entering counseling or therapy are likely to experience considerable anxiety about ethnic/racial/cultural differences. Suspicion, apprehension, verbal constriction, unnatural reactions, open resentment and hostility, and passive or cool behavior may all be expressed. Self-disclosure and the possible establishment of a working relationship can be seriously delayed or prevented from occurring. In all cases, the therapist's *trustworthiness* may be put to severe tests. Culturally effective therapists are ones who (a) can view these behaviors in a nonjudgmental manner (i.e., they are not necessarily indicative of pathology but are a manifestation of adaptive survival mechanisms), (b) can avoid personalizing any potential hostility expressed toward them, and (c) can adequately resolve challenges to their *credibility*. Thus it becomes important for us to understand those dimensions that may enhance or diminish the culturally different client's receptivity to self-disclosure.

COUNSELOR CREDIBILITY AND ATTRACTIVENESS

Counselors who are perceived by their clients as credible (expert and trustworthy) and attractive (similar) are better able to establish rapport with them than those therapists lacking such attributes (Heesacker & Carroll, 1997). Regardless of the counseling orientation (psychodynamic, humanistic, behavioral, etc.), therapists' effectiveness depends on client perceptions of their *expertness, trustworthiness,* and *attractiveness.* Most studies on social influence and counseling, however, have dealt exclusively with a White population (Heesacker, Conner, & Pritchard, 1995; Strong, 1969). Thus counselor attributes traditionally associated with *credibility* and *attractiveness* may not be so perceived by culturally diverse clients. It is entirely possible that *credibility*, as defined by professional credentials or advanced degrees, might only indicate to a Latino/a client that the White therapist has no knowledge or expertise in working with Latinos. It seems important, therefore, for helping professionals to understand what factors/conditions may enhance or negate counselor *credibility* and *attractiveness* when working with diverse clients.

Understanding Client Mind-Sets

The therapist's *credibility* and *attractiveness* depend very much on the mind-set or frame of reference of culturally diverse clients. Understanding a client's psychological mind-set may facilitate the therapist's ability to exert social influence in counseling. The conceptual categories that can be used to understand people's perception of communicator (counselor) *credibility* and *attractiveness* are drawn from social psychology (Collins, 1970). We apply those categories with respect to the therapy situation. Note that race, ethnicity, and the experience of discrimination often affect the type of mind-set operative in the clinical encounter.

1. *The problem-solving set.* In the problem-solving set, the client is concerned about obtaining correct information (solutions and skills) that has adaptive value in the real world. The client accepts or rejects information from the therapist on the basis of its perceived truth or falsity: Is it an accurate representation of reality? The processes that are used tend to be rational and logical

in analyzing and attacking the problem. First, the client may apply a consistency test and compare the new facts with earlier information. For example, a White male therapist might try to reassure an Asian American client that he is not against interracial marriage but might hesitate in speech and tense up whenever the topic is broached (Utsey, Gernat, & Hammar, 2005). In this case, the verbal or content message is inconsistent with nonverbal cues, and the *credibility* and social influence of the therapist are likely to decline.

Second, the Asian client may apply a corroboration test by actively seeking information from others for comparison purposes. If he or she hears from a friend that the therapist has racial hang-ups, then the therapist's effectiveness is again likely to be severely diminished. The former test makes use of information that the individual already has (understanding of nonverbal meanings), while the latter requires him or her to seek out new information (asking a trusted Asian American friend). Through their experiences, clients of color may have learned that many Whites have little expertise when it comes to their lifestyles and that the information or suggestions that they give are White solutions.

2. *The consistency set.* People are operating under the *consistency set* whenever they change an opinion, belief, or behavior to make it consistent with other opinions, beliefs, or behaviors. For example, since therapists are supposed to help, we naturally believe that they would do nothing to harm us. A therapist who is not in touch with personal prejudices or biases may send out conflicting messages to a minority client. The counselor may verbally state, "I am here to help you," but at the same time indicate racist attitudes and feelings nonverbally. This can destroy the counselor's *credibility* very quickly, for example, in the case of a Latino client who accurately applies a *consistency set* such as, "White people say one thing, but do another. You can't believe what they tell you." Culturally diverse clients will actively seek out disclosures on the part of the therapist to compare them with the information they have about the world. If the therapist passes the test, new information may be more readily accepted.

3. *The identity set.* An individual who strongly identifies with a particular group is likely to accept the group's beliefs and to conform to behaviors dictated by the group. If race or ethnicity constitute a strong reference group for a client, then a counselor of the same race/ethnicity is likely to be more influential

than one who is not. It is believed that racial/ethnic similarity may actually increase willingness to return for therapy and facilitate effectiveness. The findings on this matter are quite mixed, as there is considerable evidence that membership group similarity may not be as effective as belief or attitude similarity. It has also been found that the stage of cultural or racial identity affects which dimensions of similarities will be preferred by the racial/ethnic minority client (Cross, Smith, & Payne, 2002). We have much more to say about cultural identity development later in Chapter 11. It is obvious, however, that racial differences between counselor and client make bridging this gap a major challenge.

4. *The economic set*. In the *economic set*, the person is influenced because of the perceived rewards and punishments that the source is able to deliver. In this set, a person performs a behavior or states a belief in order to gain rewards and avoid punishments. In the counseling setting, this means that the therapist controls important resources that may affect the client. For example, a therapist may decide to recommend expulsion of a student from school or deny a positive parole recommendation to a client who is in prison. In less subtle ways, the therapist may ridicule or praise a client during a group counseling session. In these cases, the client may decide to alter his or her behavior because the therapist holds greater power. The major problem with the use of rewards and punishments to induce change is that although it may assure *behavioral compliance*, it does not guarantee *private acceptance*. For culturally diverse clients, therapy that operates primarily on the *economic set* is more likely to prevent the development of trust, rapport, and self-disclosure.

5. *The authority set*. Under this set, some individuals are thought to have a particular position that gives them a legitimate right to prescribe attitudes or behaviors. In our society, we have been conditioned to believe that certain authorities (police officers, chairpersons, designated leaders, etc.) have the right to demand compliance. This occurs via training in role behavior and group norms. Mental health professionals, such as counselors, are thought to have a legitimate right to recommend and provide psychological treatment to disturbed or troubled clients. This psychological set legitimizes the counselor's role as a helping professional. Yet for many minorities, these roles in society are exactly the ones that are perceived as instruments of institutional oppression and racism.

* * *

It should be clear at this point that characteristics of the influencing source (therapist) are of the utmost importance in eliciting types of changes. In addition, the type of mental or psychological set placed in operation often dictates the permanency and degree of attitude/belief change. While these sets operate similarly for majority and marginalized clients, their manifestations may be quite different. Obviously, a client may have great difficulty identifying with a counselor from another race or culture (identity set). Also, what constitutes *credibility* to minority clients may be far different from what constitutes *credibility* to a majority client.

Counselor Credibility

Credibility (which elicits the problem-solving, consistency, and *identity sets*) may be defined as the constellation of characteristics that makes certain individuals appear worthy of belief, capable, entitled to confidence, reliable, and trustworthy. *Credibility* has two components—expertness and *trustworthiness*. Expertness is an *ability variable*, whereas *trustworthiness* is a *motivation variable*. Expertness depends on how well informed, capable, or intelligent others perceive the communicator (counselor/therapist) to be. *Trustworthiness* is dependent on the degree to which people perceive the communicator as motivated to make valid or invalid assertions. The weight of evidence supports our commonsense beliefs that the helping professional who is perceived as expert and trustworthy can influence clients more than can one who is perceived to be lower on these traits.

Expertness

Clients often go to a therapist not only because they are in distress and in need of relief but also because they believe the counselor is an expert, and has the necessary knowledge, skills, experience, training, and tools to help (*problem-solving set*). Perceived *expertness* is typically a function of (a) reputation, (b) evidence of specialized training, and (c) behavioral evidence of proficiency/competency. For clients seeing a therapist of a different race/culture, the issue of therapist *expertness* seems to be raised more often than when clients go to a therapist of their own culture and race. The fact that therapists have degrees and certificates from prestigious institutions (*authority set*) may not enhance perceived *expertness*. This is especially true of socially marginalized clients who are aware that institutional bias exists in training programs. Indeed, it may have the opposite effect, by reducing *credibility*! Additionally, reputation-expertness (*authority set*) is unlikely to impress diverse clients unless the favorable testimony comes from someone of their own group.

Thus behavior-expertness, or demonstrating the ability to help a client, becomes the critical form of *expertness* in effective multicultural counseling (*problem-solving set*). It appears that using counseling skills and strategies appropriate to the life values of the culturally diverse client is crucial. We have already mentioned evidence that certain minority groups prefer a much more active approach to counseling. A counselor playing a relatively inactive role may be perceived as being incompetent and unhelpful. The following example shows how the therapist's approach lowers perceived *expertness*.

Asian American Male Client:	It's hard for me to talk about these issues. My parents and friends. . .they wouldn't understand. . .if they ever found out I was coming here for help. . .
White Male Therapist:	I sense it's difficult to talk about personal things. How are you feeling right now?
Asian American Client:	Oh, all right.
White Therapist:	That's not a feeling. Sit back and get in touch with your feelings. [pause] Now tell me, how are you feeling right now?
Asian American Client:	Somewhat nervous.
White therapist:	When you talked about your parents and friends not understanding and the way you said it made me think you felt ashamed and disgraced at having to come. Was that what you felt?

Although this exchange appears to indicate that the therapist could (a) see the client's discomfort and (b) interpret his feelings correctly, it also points out the therapist's lack of understanding and knowledge of Asian cultural values. Although we do not want to be guilty of *stereotyping* Asian Americans, many believe that publicly expressing feelings to a stranger is inappropriate. The therapist's persistent attempts to focus on feelings and his direct and blunt interpretation of them may indicate to the Asian American client that the therapist lacks the more subtle skills of dealing with a sensitive topic or that the therapist is shaming the client.

Furthermore, it is possible that the Asian American client in this case is much more used to discussing feelings in an indirect or subtle manner. A direct response from the therapist addressed to a feeling may not be as effective as one that deals with it indirectly. In many traditional Asian groups, subtlety is a highly prized art, and the traditional Asian client may feel much more comfortable when dealing with feelings in an indirect manner.

Many educators claim that specific therapy skills are not as important as the attitude one brings into the therapeutic situation. Behind this statement is the belief that universal attributes of genuineness, love, unconditional acceptance, and positive regard are the only things needed. Yet the question remains: How does a therapist communicate these things to culturally diverse clients? While a therapist might have the best of intentions, it is possible that his or her intentions might be misunderstood. Let us use another example with the same Asian American client.

Asian American Client:	I'm even nervous about others seeing me come in here. It's so difficult for me to talk about this.
White Therapist:	We all find some things difficult to talk about. It's important that you do.
Asian American Client:	It's easy to say that. But do you really understand how awful I feel, talking about my parents?
White Therapist:	I've worked with many Asian Americans, and many have similar problems.

Here we find a distinction between the therapist's intentions and the effects of his comments. The therapist's intentions were to reassure the client that he understood his feelings, to imply that he had worked with similar cases, and to make the client feel less isolated (i.e., that others have the same problems). The effects, however, were to dilute and dismiss the client's feelings and concerns and to take the uniqueness out of the situation.

Trustworthiness

Perceived trustworthiness encompasses such factors as sincerity, openness, honesty, and perceived lack of motivation for personal gain. A therapist who is perceived as trustworthy is likely to exert more influence over a client than one who is not. In our society, many people assume that certain roles, such as minister, doctor, psychiatrist, and counselor, exist to help people. With respect to minorities, self-disclosure is very much dependent on this attribute of perceived trustworthiness. Because mental health professionals are often perceived by minorities to be agents of the Establishment, trust is something that does not come with the role (*authority set*). Indeed, many minorities may perceive that therapists cannot be trusted unless otherwise demonstrated. Again, the role and reputation that the therapist has as being trustworthy must be evidenced in behavioral terms. More than anything, challenges to the therapist's trustworthiness will be a frequent theme blocking further exploration and movement until it is resolved to the satisfaction of the client. These verbatim transcripts illustrate the trust issue.

White Male Therapist:	I sense some major hesitations. . .It's difficult for you to discuss your concerns with me.
Black Male Client:	You're damn right! If I really told you how I felt about my [White] coach, what's to prevent you from telling him? You Whities are all of the same mind.
White Therapist [angry]:	Look, it would be a lie for me to say I don't know your coach. He's an acquaintance but not a personal friend. Don't put me in the same bag with all Whites! Anyway, even if he were a close friend, I hold our discussion in strictest confidence. Let me ask you this question: What would I need to do that would make it easier for you to trust me?
Black Client:	You're on your way, man!

This verbal exchange illustrates several issues related to trustworthiness. First, the African American client is likely to test the therapist constantly regarding issues of confidentiality. Second, the onus of responsibility for proving trustworthiness falls on the therapist. Third, to prove that one is trustworthy requires, at times, self-disclosure on the part of the mental health professional. That the therapist did not hide the fact that he knew the coach (openness), became angry about being lumped with all Whites (sincerity), assured the client that he would not tell the coach or anyone else about their sessions (confidentiality), and asked the client how he could work to prove he was trustworthy (genuineness) were all elements that enhanced his trustworthiness.

Handling the "prove to me that you can be trusted" ploy is very difficult for many therapists. It is difficult because it demands self-disclosure on the part of the helping professional, something that graduate training programs have taught us to avoid. It places the focus on the therapist rather than on the client and makes many uncomfortable. In addition, it is likely to evoke defensiveness on the part of many mental health practitioners. Here is another verbatim exchange in which defensiveness is evoked, destroying the helping professional's trustworthiness.

Black Female Client:	Students in my drama class expect me to laugh when they do "Stepin Fechit" routines and tell Black jokes. . . . I'm wondering whether you've ever laughed at any of those jokes.
White Male Therapist:	[long pause] Yes, I'm sure I have. Have you ever laughed at any White jokes?
Black Client:	What's a White joke?
White Male Therapist:	I don't know [nervous laughter]; I suppose one making fun of Whites. Look, I'm Irish. Have you ever laughed at Irish jokes?
Black Client:	People tell me many jokes, but I don't laugh at racial jokes. I feel we're all minorities and should respect each other.

Again, the client tested the therapist indirectly by asking him if he ever laughed at racial jokes. Since most of us probably have, to say "no" would be a blatant lie. The client's motivation for asking this question was to find out (a) how sincere and open the therapist was and (b) whether the therapist could recognize his racist attitudes without letting it interfere with therapy. While the therapist admitted to having laughed at such jokes, he proceeded to destroy his trustworthiness by becoming defensive. Rather than simply stopping with his statement of "Yes, I'm sure I have" or making some other similar remark, he defends himself by trying to get the client to admit to similar actions. Thus the therapist's trustworthiness is seriously impaired. He is perceived as motivated to defend himself rather than to help the client.

The therapist's obvious defensiveness in this case has prevented him from understanding the intent and motive of the question. Is the African American female client really asking the therapist whether he has actually laughed at Black jokes before? Or is the client asking the therapist if he is a racist? Both of these speculations have a certain amount of validity, but it is our belief that the Black female client is actually asking the following important question of the therapist: "How open and honest are you about your own racism, and will it interfere with our session here?" Again, the test is one of trustworthiness, a motivational variable that the White male therapist has obviously failed.

REFLECTION AND DISCUSSION QUESTIONS

1. Think about yourself, your characteristics, and your interaction style. Think about your daily interactions with friends, coworkers, colleagues, or fellow students. How influential are you with them? What makes you influential?

2. As a counselor or therapist, what makes you credible with your clients? Using the psychological sets outlined earlier, how do you convey *expertness* and trustworthiness?

3. What do you believe would stand in the way of your trustworthiness with clients of color? How would you overcome it?

FORMATION OF INDIVIDUAL AND SYSTEMIC WORLDVIEWS

The dimensions of trust–mistrust and *credibility* in the helping professions are strongly influenced by *worldviews*. *Worldviews* determine how people perceive their relationship to the world (nature, institutions, other people, etc.), and they are highly correlated with a person's cultural upbringing and life experiences (Koltko-Rivera, 2004). Put in a much more practical way, not only are *worldviews* composed of our attitudes, values, opinions, and concepts, but they also affect how we think, define events, make decisions, and behave. For marginalized groups in America, a strong determinant of *worldviews* is very much related to the subordinate position assigned to them in society. Helping professionals who hold a *worldview* different from that of their clients and who are unaware of the basis for this difference are most likely to impute negative traits to clients and to engage in *cultural oppression*. To understand this assertion, we discuss two different psychological orientations considered important in the formation of *worldviews:* (a) *locus of control* and (b) *locus of responsibility.*

Locus of Control

Locus of control can be conceptualized as having two dimensions (Rotter,1966). *Internal control* (IC) refers to the belief that reinforcements are contingent on our own actions and that we can shape our own fate. *External control* (EC) refers to the belief that reinforcing events occur independently of our actions and that the future is determined more by chance and luck. Research suggests that high internality is associated with multiple positive attributes such as higher achievement motivation, belief in mastery over the environment, superior intellect, superior coping skills, and so on (Lefcourt, 1966; Rotter, 1966, 1975). These attributes are highly valued by U.S. society and seem to constitute the core features of Western mental health.

On the other hand, it has been found that people of color, women, and people from low socioeconomic status score significantly higher on the external end of the locus-of-control continuum (Sue, 1978; Koltko-Rivera, 2004). Using the I-E dimension as a criterion of mental health would mean that people of color and poor or female clients would be viewed as possessing less desirable attributes. Thus a clinician who encounters a minority client with a high external orientation ("It's no use trying," "There's nothing I can do about it," and "You shouldn't rock the boat") may interpret the client as being inherently apathetic, procrastinating, lazy, depressed, or anxious about trying. The problem with an unqualified application of the I-E dimension is that it fails to take into consideration different cultural and social experiences of the individual. This failure may lead to highly inappropriate and destructive applications in therapy. It seems plausible that different cultural groups, women, and people from a lower SES have learned that control in their lives operates differently from how it operates for society at large (American Psychological Association, 2007; Ridley, 2005). For example, externality related to impersonal forces (chance and luck) is different from that ascribed to cultural forces and from that ascribed to powerful others.

Externality and Culture

Chance and luck operate equally across situations for everyone. However, the forces that determine *locus of control* from a cultural perspective may be viewed by the particular ethnic group as acceptable and benevolent. In this case, externality is viewed positively. American culture, for example, values the uniqueness, independence, and self-reliance of each individual. It places a high premium on self-reliance, individualism, and status achieved through one's own efforts. In contrast, the situation-centered Chinese culture places importance on the group, on tradition, social roles expectations, and harmony with the universe (Kim, 2011; Ratts & Pedersen, 2014). Thus the cultural orientation of the more traditional Chinese tends to elevate the external scores. In contrast to U.S. society, Chinese society highly values externality.

Externality and Sociopolitical Factors

Likewise, high externality may constitute a realistic sociopolitical presence. A major force in the literature dealing with *locus of control* is that of powerlessness. *Powerlessness* may be defined as the expectancy that a person's behavior cannot determine the outcomes or reinforcements that he or she seeks. For example, low SES individuals and Blacks are not given an equal opportunity to obtain the material rewards of Western culture. Because of racism, African Americans may perceive, in a realistic fashion, a discrepancy between their ability and attainment. In this case, externality may be seen as a malevolent force to be distinguished from the benevolent cultural ones just discussed. Focusing on external forces may be motivationally healthy if it results from assessing one's chances for success against real systematic and external obstacles rather than unpredictable fate. The I-E continuum is useful for therapists only if they make clear distinctions about the meaning of the external control dimension. High externality may be due to (a) chance/luck, (b) cultural dictates that are viewed as benevolent, and (c) political forces (racism and discrimination) that represent malevolent but realistic obstacles.

Locus of Responsibility

Another important dimension in world outlooks is the concept of *locus of responsibility* (J. M. Jones, 1997). In essence, this dimension measures the degree of responsibility or blame placed on the individual or system. In the case of Latino Americans, their lower standard of living may be attributed to either their personal shortcomings or to racial discrimination and lack of opportunities. The former orientation blames the individual, while the latter explanation blames the system.

The degree of emphasis placed on the individual as opposed to the system in affecting a person's behavior is important in the formation of life orientations. Those who hold a person-centered orientation believe that success or failure is attributable to the individual's skills or personal inadequacies, and that there is a strong relationship between ability, effort, and success in society. In essence, these people adhere strongly to the Protestant ethic that idealizes rugged individualism.

On the other hand, situation-centered or system-blame people view the sociocultural and sociopolitical environment as more potent than the individual. Social, economic, and political forces are powerful; success or failure is generally dependent on the social forces and not necessarily on personal attributes. Defining the problem as residing in the person enables society to ignore the influence of external factors, and to protect and preserve social institutions and belief systems. Thus the individual/system blame continuum may need to be viewed differentially for socially devalued groups. An internal response (acceptance of blame for one's failure) might be considered normal for the White middle class, but for minorities it may be extreme and intropunitive.

FORMATION OF WORLDVIEWS

The two psychological orientations, *locus of control* and *locus of responsibility*, are independent of one another. As shown in Figure 5.1, both may be placed on the continuum in such a manner that they intersect, forming four quadrants: internal locus of control–internal locus of responsibility (IC-IR), external locus of control–internal locus of responsibility (EC-IR), external locus of control–external locus of responsibility (EC-ER), and internal locus of control–external locus of responsibility (IC-ER). Each quadrant represents a different *worldview* or orientation to life.

FIGURE 5.1 Graphic Representation of Worldviews

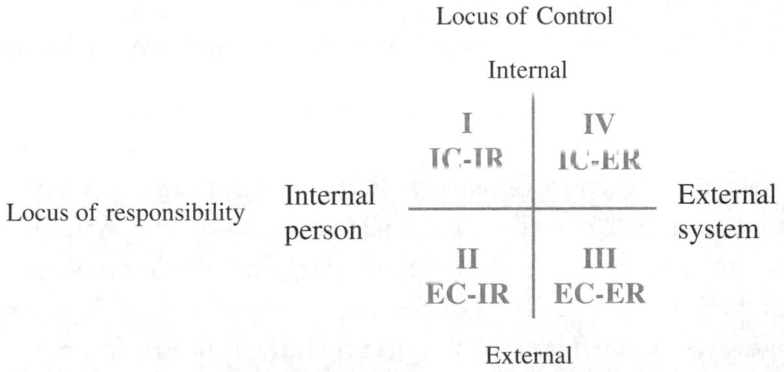

Locus of Control

Internal

	I IC-IR	IV IC-ER	
Locus of responsibility	Internal person		External system
	II EC-IR	III EC-ER	

External

Source: D. W. Sue (1978), "Eliminating Cultural Oppression in Counseling: Toward a General Theory," *Journal of Counseling Psychology, 25,* p. 422. Copyright © 1978 by the *Journal of Counseling Psychology.* Reprinted by permission.

Internal Locus of Control (IC)–Internal Locus of Responsibility (IR)

As mentioned earlier, individuals high in internal personal control (IC) believe that they are masters of their fate and that their actions do affect the outcomes. Likewise, people high in internal *locus of responsibility* (IR) attribute their current status and life conditions to their own unique attributes; success is due to one's own efforts, and lack of success is attributed to one's shortcomings or inadequacies. Perhaps the greatest exemplification of the IC-IR philosophy is U.S. society. American culture can be described as the epitome of the individual-centered approach that emphasizes uniqueness, independence, and self-reliance. A high value is placed on personal resources for solving all problems; self-reliance; pragmatism; individualism; status achievement through one's own effort; and power or control over others, things, animals, and forces of nature. Democratic ideals such as "equal access to opportunity," "liberty and justice for all," "God helps those who help themselves," and "fulfillment of personal destiny" all reflect this *worldview*. The individual is held accountable for all that transpires. Most members of the White upper and middle class would fall within this quadrant.

Counseling Implications

Most Western-trained therapists are of the opinion that people must take major responsibility for their own actions, and that they can improve their lot in life by their own efforts. Clients who occupy this quadrant tend to be White middle-class clients, and for these clients such approaches might be entirely appropriate. In working with clients from different cultures, however, such an approach might be inappropriate. *Cultural oppression* in therapy becomes an ever-present danger.

External Locus of Control (EC)–Internal Locus of Responsibility (IR)

Individuals who fall into this quadrant are most likely to accept the dominant culture's definition for self-responsibility but to have very little real control over how they are defined by others. The term *marginal man* (person) was first coined by Stonequist (1937) to describe a person living on the margins of two cultures and not fully accommodated to either. Marginal individuals deny the existence of racism; believe that the plight of their own people is due to laziness, stupidity, and a clinging to outdated traditions; reject their own cultural heritage and believe that their ethnicity represents a handicap in Western society; evidence racial self-hatred; accept White social, cultural, and institutional standards; perceive physical features of White men and women as an exemplification of beauty; and are powerless to control their sense of self-worth because approval must come from an external source. As a result, they are high in person-focus and external control.

Counseling Implications

The psychological dynamics for the EC-IR minority client are likely to reflect his or her marginal status and self-hate or internalized racism. For example, White therapists might be perceived as more competent and preferred than are therapists of the client's own race. To EC-IR individuals, focusing on feelings may be very threatening because it ultimately may reveal the presence of self-hate. A culturally encapsulated White counselor or therapist who does not understand the sociopolitical dynamics of the client's concerns may unwittingly perpetuate the conflict. For example, the client's preference for a White therapist, coupled with the therapist's implicit belief in the values of U.S. culture, becomes a barrier to effective counseling. Culturally competent therapists need to help clients (a) understand the particular dominant-subordinate political forces that have created this dilemma and (b) distinguish between positive attempts to acculturate and a negative rejection of one's own cultural values.

External Locus of Control (EC)–External Locus of Responsibility (ER)

A person high in system blame and external control feels that there is very little one can do in the face of oppression. In essence, the EC response might be a manifestation of (a) having given up or (b) attempting to placate those in power. In the former, individuals internalize their impotence even though they are aware of the external basis of their plight. In its extreme form, oppression may result in a form of learned helplessness. When marginalized groups learn that their responses have minimal effect on the environment, the resulting phenomenon can best be described as an expectation of helplessness. People's susceptibility to helplessness depends on their experience with controlling the environment. In the face of continued oppression, many may simply give up in their attempts to achieve personal goals.

The dynamics of the placater, however, are not related to the response of giving up. Rather, social forces in the form of prejudice and discrimination are seen as too powerful to combat at that particular time. The best one can hope to do is to suffer the inequities in silence for fear of retaliation. The phrases that most describe this mode of adjustment include "Don't rock the boat," "Keep a low profile," and "Survival at all costs." Life is viewed as relatively fixed, and there is little that the individual can do. Passivity in the face of oppression is the primary reaction of the placater. Slavery was one of the most important factors shaping the sociopsychological functioning of African Americans. Interpersonal relations between Whites and Blacks were highly structured and placed African Americans in a subservient and inferior role. Those Blacks who broke the rules or did not show proper deferential behavior were severely punished. The spirits of most African Americans, however, were not broken. Conformance to White EuroAmerican rules and regulations was dictated by the need to survive in an oppressive environment. Direct expressions of anger and resentment were dangerous, but indirect expressions were frequent.

Counseling Implications

EC-ER African Americans are very likely to see the White therapist as symbolic of any other Black–White relations. They are likely to show "proper" deferential behavior and not to take seriously admonitions by the therapist that they are the masters of their own fate. As a result, an IC-IR therapist may perceive the culturally different client as lacking in courage and ego strength and as being passive. A culturally effective therapist, however, would realize the basis of these adaptations. Unlike EC-IR clients, EC-ER individuals do understand the political forces that have subjugated their existence. The most helpful approach on the part of the therapist would be (a) to teach the clients new coping strategies, (b) to have them experience successes, and (c) to validate who and what they represent.

Internal Locus of Control (IC)–External Locus of Responsibility (ER)

Individuals who score high in internal control and system-focus believe that they are able to shape events in their own life if given a chance. They do not accept the idea that their present state is due to their own inherent weakness. However, they also realistically perceive that external barriers of discrimination, prejudice, and exploitation block their paths to the successful attainment of goals. There is a considerable body of evidence to support this contention. Recall that the IC dimension was correlated with greater feelings of personal efficacy, higher aspirations, and so forth, and that ER was related to collective action in the social arena. Hence we would expect that IC-ER people would be more likely to participate in civil rights activities and to stress racial identity and militancy. Pride in one's racial and cultural identity is most likely to be accepted by an IC-ER person. The low self-esteem engendered by widespread prejudice and racism is actively challenged. There is an attempt to redefine a group's existence by stressing consciousness and pride in their own racial and cultural heritage. Such phrases as "Black is beautiful" represent a symbolic relabeling of identity from "Negro" and "colored" to Black or African American. To many African Americans, *Negro* and *colored* are White labels symbolic of a warped and degrading identity given them by a racist society. As a means of throwing off these burdensome shackles, the Black individual and African Americans as a group are redefined in a positive light.

Counseling Implications

Much evidence indicates that people of color are becoming increasingly conscious of their own racial and cultural identities as they relate to oppression in U.S. society. If the evidence is correct, it is also probable that more and more persons of color are likely to hold an IC-ER *worldview*. Thus therapists who work with the culturally different will increasingly be exposed to clients with an IC-ER *worldview*. In many respects, these clients pose the most difficult problems for the White IC-IR therapist. These clients are likely to raise challenges to the therapist's *credibility* and trustworthiness. The helping professional is likely to be seen as a part of the establishment that has oppressed minorities. Self-disclosure on the part of the client is not likely to come quickly; more than any other *worldview*, an IC-ER orientation means that clients are likely to play a much more active part in the therapy process and to demand action from the therapist.

IMPLICATIONS FOR CLINICAL PRACTICE

1. Understand and apply the concepts of *ethnocentric monoculturalism* to the wider society and to marginalized groups; understand how it may manifest and affect the dynamics in dominant-subordinate counseling relationships.

2. Distinguish between behaviors indicative of a true mental disorder and those that result from oppression and survival tactics.

3. Do not personalize the suspicions a client may have of your motives. If you become defensive, insulted, or angry with the client, your effectiveness will be seriously diminished.

4. Be willing to understand and overcome your *stereotypes*, biases, and assumptions about other cultural groups.

5. Know that expertness and trustworthiness are important components of any therapeutic relationship, but that it may be affected by experiences of oppression.

6. Know that your *credibility* and *trustworthiness* will be tested when working with culturally diverse clients. Tests of *credibility* may occur frequently in the therapy session, and the onus of responsibility for proving expertness and *trustworthiness* lies with the therapist.

7. Understanding the worldviews of culturally diverse clients means understanding how they are formed.

8. Know that traditional counseling and therapy operates from the assumption of high internal *locus of control* and responsibility. Be able to apply and understand how Western therapeutic characteristics may detrimentally interact with other *worldviews*.

SUMMARY

It is important to realize that the history of race relations in the United States has influenced us to the point where we are extremely cautious about revealing to strangers our feelings and attitudes about race. In an interracial encounter with a stranger (i.e., therapy), each party will attempt to discern gross or subtle racial attitudes of the other while minimizing vulnerability. *Ethnocentric monoculturalism* lies at the heart of oppressor–oppressed relationships that affect trust–mistrust and self-disclosure in the therapeutic encounter. The five components of *ethnocentric monoculturalism* are belief in the superiority of one group over another, belief in inferiority of all other groups, the power to impose standards on socially devalued groups, manifestation and support of institutions, and the invisibility of the imposition process.

It is clear that past and present discrimination against certain culturally diverse groups is a tangible basis for minority distrust of the majority society. Majority group members are perceived as potential oppressors unless proved otherwise. Under such a sociopolitical atmosphere, marginalized groups may use several adaptive behaviors to prevent Whites from knowing their true feelings. Because multicultural counseling may mirror the sentiments of the larger society, these modes of behavior and their detrimental effects may be reenacted in the sessions. The fact that many marginalized clients are suspicious, mistrustful, and guarded in their interactions with White therapists is certainly understandable in light of the foregoing analysis.

Counselors who are perceived by their clients as *credible* (expert and trustworthy) and *attractive* (similar) are better able to establish rapport with them than those therapists lacking such attributes. Social psychologists have identified the "psychological mind-sets" of people that work toward establishing communicator and therapist *credibility*. In multicultural counseling, client tests of trustworthiness and expertness are likely to enhance or negate the counselor's *credibility*. Many of these tests are likely to prove challenging to well-intentioned therapists. Cultural competence means understanding the *worldviews* of diverse clients. *Locus of control* (people's beliefs that they can shape their own fate—IC, or that chance or luck determines outcomes—EC) and *locus of responsibility* (causation resides in the person—IR, or system—ER) interact to form four major *worldviews* that explain possible majority and diverse client perceptions and interactions: IC–IR, EC–IR, EC–ER, and IC–ER. We summarize therapeutic implications for each of these dimensions of *worldviews*.

GLOSSARY TERMS

Attractiveness	The authority set
Color blindness	The consistency set
Credibility	The economic set
Cultural oppression	The identity set
Ethnocentric monoculturalism	The problem-solving set
Expertness	Trustworthiness
Institutional racism	Uncle Tom Syndrome
Invisible veil	Unintentional racism
Locus of control	Victim blaming
Locus of responsibility	White privilege
Playing it cool	Worldview
Stereotyping	

REFERENCES

American Psychological Association. (2007). Guidelines for the psychological practice with girls and women. *American Psychologist, 62*, 949–979.

Anderson, S. H., & Middleton, V. A. (2011). *Explorations in diversity.* Belmont, CA: Cengage.

Arredondo, P., Gallardo-Cooper, M., Delgado-Romero, E. A., & Zapata, A. L. (2014). *Culturally responsive counseling with Latinas/os.* Alexandria, VA: American Counseling Association.

Atkinson, D. R., Kim, B.S.K., & Caldwell, R. (1998). Ratings of helper roles by multicultural psychologists and Asian American students: Initial support for the three-dimensional model of multicultural counseling. *Journal of Counseling Psychology, 45*, 414–423.

Atkinson, D. R., Thompson, C. E., & Grant, S. K. (1993). A three-dimensional model for counseling racial/ethnic minorities. *Counseling Psychologist, 21*, 257–277.

Babbington, C. (2008). *Poll shows gap between Blacks and Whites over racial discrimination.* Retrieved from https://groups.yahoo.com/neo /groups/VaUMCTalk/conversations/topics /4286

Barongan, C., Bernal, G., Comas-Diaz, L., Iijima Hall, C. C., Nagayama Hall, G. C., LaDue, R. A., & Root, M.P.P. (1997). Misunderstandings of multiculturalism: Shouting fire in crowded theaters. *American Psychologist, 52*, 654–655.

Bemak, F., & Chung, R. C. (2015). Cultural boundaries, cultural norms: Multicultural and social justice perspectives. In B. Herlihy & G. Corey (Eds.), *Boundary issues in counseling* (pp. 84–92). Alexandria, VA: American Counseling Association.

Boyd-Franklin, N. (2010). Incorporating spirituality and religion into the treatment of African American clients. *Counseling Psychologist, 38*, 976–1000.

Carter, R. T. (1995). *The influence of race and racial identity in psychotherapy.* New York, NY: Wiley.

Choudhuri, D. D., Santiago-Rivera, A. L., & Garrett, M. T. (2012). *Counseling and diversity.* Belmont, CA: Cengage.

Collins, B. E. (1970). *Social psychology.* Reading, MA: Addison-Wesley.

Constantine, M. G., & Sue, D. W. (2006). *Addressing racism.* Hoboken, NJ: Wiley.

Cross, W. E., Smith, L., & Payne, Y. (2002). Black identity. In P. B. Pedersen, J. G. Draguns, W. J. Lonner, & J. E. Trimble (Eds.), *Counseling across cultures* (pp. 93–108). Thousand Oaks, CA: Sage.

Duran, E. (2006). *Healing the soul wound.* New York, NY: Teachers College Press.

Furman, R. (2011). White male privilege in the context of my life. In S. H. Anderson & V. A. Middleton (Eds.), *Explorations in diversity: Examining privilege and oppression in a multicultural society* (pp. 33–37). Belmont, CA: Cengage.

Gone, J. P. (2010). Psychotherapy and traditional healing for American Indians: Exploring the prospects for therapeutic integration. *Counseling Psychologist, 38*, 166–235.

Grier, W., & Cobbs, P. (1971). *The Jesus bag.* San Francisco, CA: McGraw-Hill.

Hall, E. T. (1976). *Beyond culture.* New York, NY: Anchor Press.

Halleck, S. L. (1971, April). Therapy is the handmaiden of the status quo. *Psychology Today, 4*, 30–34, 98–100.

Heesacker, M., & Carroll, T. A. (1997). Identifying and solving impediments to the social and counseling psychology interface. *Counseling Psychologist, 25*, 171–179.

Heesacker, M., Conner, K., & Pritchard, S. (1995). Individual counseling and psychotherapy: Allocations from the social psychology of attitude change. *Counseling Psychologist, 23,* 611–632.

Highlen, P. S. (1994). Racial/ethnic diversity in doctoral programs of psychology: Challenges for the twenty-first century. *Applied and Preventive Psychology, 3,* 91–108.

Ivey, A. E., Ivey, M. B., & Zalaquett, C. P. (2014). *Intentional interviewing and counseling* (8th ed.). Belmont, CA: Brooks/Cole.

Jones, A. C. (1985). Psychological functioning in Black Americans: A conceptual guide for use in psychotherapy. *Psychotherapy, 22,* 363–369.

Jones, C., & Shorter-Gooden, K. (2003). *Shifting: The double lives of Black women in America.* New York, NY: HarperCollins.

Jones, J. M. (1997). *Prejudice and racism* (2nd ed.). Washington, DC: McGraw-Hill.

Jones, J. M. (2010). I'm White and you're not: The value of unraveling ethnocentric science. *Psychological Science, 5,* 700–707.

Katz, J. (1985). The sociopolitical nature of counseling. *Counseling Psychologist, 13,* 615–624.

Kim, B.S.K. (2011). *Counseling Asian Americans.* Belmont, CA: Cengage.

Koltko-Rivera, M. E. (2004). The psychology of worldviews. *Review of General Psychology, 8,* 3–58.

Lefcourt, H. (1966). Internal versus external control of reinforcement: A review. *Psychological Bulletin, 65,* 206–220.

Lum, D. (2011). *Culturally competent practice.* Belmont, CA: Cengage.

McAuliffe, G., & Associates. (2013). *Culturally alert counseling.* Thousand Oaks, CA: Sage.

Neville, H. A., Gallardo, M. E., & Sue, D. W. (in press). *What does it mean to be color-blind? Manifestation, dynamics and impact.* Washington, DC: American Psychological Association.

Parham, T. A. (1997). An African-centered view of dual relationships. In B. Herlihy & G. Corey (Eds.), *Boundary issues in counseling* (pp. 109–112). Alexandria, VA: American Counseling Association.

Parham, T. A., & Caldwell, L. D. (2015). Boundaries in the context of a collective community: An African-centered perspective. In B. Herlihy & G. Corey (Eds.), *Boundary issues in counseling* (2nd ed., pp. 96–100). Alexandria, VA: American Counseling Association.

Parham, T. A., Ajamu, A., & White, J. L. (2011). *The psychology of Blacks. Centering our perspectives in the African consciousness.* Boston, MA: Prentice Hall.

Pavkov, T. W., Lewis, D. A., & Lyons, J. S. (1989). Psychiatric diagnosis and racial bias: An empirical investigation. *Professional Psychology: Research & Practice, 20,* 364–368.

Ponterotto, J. G., Utsey, S. O., & Pedersen, P. B. (2006). *Preventing prejudice: A guide for counselors, educators, and parents.* Thousand Oaks, CA: Sage.

Ratts, M. J., & Pedersen, P. B. (2014). *Counseling for multiculturalism and social justice.* Alexandria, VA: American Counseling Association.

Ridley, C. R. (2005). *Overcoming unintentional racism in counseling and therapy* (2nd ed.). Thousand Oaks, CA: Sage.

Rotter, J. (1966). Generalized expectancies for internal versus external control of reinforcement. *Psychological Monographs, 80,* 1–28.

Rotter, J. (1975). Some problems and misconceptions related to the construct of internal versus external control of reinforcement. *Journal of Consulting and Clinical Psychology, 43,* 56–67.

Ryan, W. (1971). *Blaming the victim.* New York, NY: Pantheon.

Stonequist, E. V. (1937). *The marginal man.* New York, NY: Scribner's.

Strong, S. R. (1969). Counseling: An interpersonal influence process. *Journal of Counseling Psychology, 15,* 215–224.

Sue, D. W. (1978). Eliminating cultural oppression in counseling: Toward a general theory. *Journal of Counseling Psychology, 25,* 419–428.

Sue, D. W. (2003). *Overcoming our racism: The journey to liberation.* San Francisco, CA: Jossey-Bass.

Sue, D. W. (2004). Whiteness and ethnocentric monoculturalism: Making the invisible visible. *American Psychologist, 59,* 761–769.

Sue, D. W. (2010). *Microaggressions and marginality: Manifestations, dynamics, and impact.* Hoboken, NJ: Wiley.

Sue, D. W., Ivey, A. E., & Pedersen, P. B. (1996). *A theory of multicultural counseling and therapy.* Pacific Grove, CA: Brooks/Cole.

Thomas, A., & Sillen, S. (1972). *Racism and psychiatry.* New York, NY: Brunner/Mazel.

Toporek, R. L., & Worthington, R. L. (2014). Integrating service learning and difficult dialogues pedagogy to advance social justice training. *Counseling Psychologist, 46,* 919–945.

Utsey, S. O., Gernat, C. A., & Hammar, L. (2005). Examining White counselor trainees' reactions to racial issues in counseling and supervision dyads. *Counseling Psychologist, 33,* 449–478.

Wrenn, C. G. (1962). The culturally encapsulated counselor. *Harvard Educational Review, 32,* 444–449.

Microaggressions in Counseling and Psychotherapy

Christina M. Capodilupo Ph. D.

Teachers College, Columbia University

Chapter Objectives

1. Define and describe *microaggressions*.

2. Differentiate between the intentions (by the aggressor) and the impact (on the victim) of *microaggressions*.

3. Understand the psychological impact of *microaggressions* on marginalized groups.

4. Describe the various psychological dynamics involved in *microaggressions*.

5. Apply knowledge of *microaggressions* to understanding therapeutic process and client/counselor dynamics.

CAN ANYBODY SEE ME? THE CASE OF KIANA

Kiana is a 34-year old multiracial bisexual woman living in a large metropolitan city. Her father is African American and her mother is biracial: Korean and Italian American. Kiana has medium skin tone and wears her hair very short and natural. She is currently an administrative assistant at a large university where she has worked for three years. Kiana works in this position while pursuing her Master's degree in Fine Arts. She performs and choreographs modern dance. Kiana has felt marginalized in her place of work and also recently ended a long-term romantic relationship. She struggles with managing her work environment and with re-entering the dating scene. She has also had some trouble getting out of bed in the morning and generally feels melancholy. She asked a friend to recommend a therapist, hoping it might help her feel more energetic and motivated to meet a new partner.

Kiana's friend referred her to a psychoanalyst she had been seeing for years: Alan, a White male in his late 50s. Kiana had some reservations about therapy; her mother felt it was disgraceful and inappropriate to tell a stranger about personal problems and her father felt it was for "crazy" people. In the first therapy session, Kiana described the difficulties she was having meeting other single people in the city. Alan asked Kiana if she might be contributing to her inability to meet men by having an "unapproachable air." Kiana was surprised by his question and asked him what he meant by "unapproachable"? He shared his first impression of her, which was that her body language seemed closed and she appeared angry. Kiana paused, as this was not the first time someone had perceived her as an "angry Black woman." She did not have the energy to explore this with him, and so accepted his observation and tried to change the subject by pointing out that she is attracted to both men and women.

Alan was curious about Kiana's bisexuality and how she understands it. He offered an interpretation of bisexuality as being a phase during which a person is trying to find their sexual identity. He asked her if identity issues had been an ongoing theme in her life and wondered aloud about her ethnicity. Once again, the kind of curiosity Alan was expressing was a familiar experience to Kiana, but she did not want to waste her time in therapy educating Alan about her sexuality or her ethnicity. She agreed with him that identity issues were an ongoing theme in her life and moved the discussion to her workplace.

Kiana shared with Alan that in her current role as administrative assistant, she experiences persistent feelings of invisibility. She relayed multiple incidents in which she would be sitting at her desk and people would look right past her, act as if she was not there, and generally treat her as unimportant. Further, though she was in this job to support her Master's degree studies, she felt she was often treated by professors and students as a "second class citizen": there to serve them. She frequently noted looks of surprise and shock when she revealed that she was a Master's candidate. For example,

a professor from a different department had recently come in to inquire about prerequisites for a particular course. Though the professor hadn't directed her question to her, Kiana spoke up, saying that she had taken the course and the student should be fine even with a limited background in the subject matter. The professor looked somewhat stunned and thanked Kiana tentatively before asking, "Why did you take the course? Is it free for staff?"

Kiana shared an office space with another administrative assistant named Michelle, who was a younger White female and newer to the job. When a colleague would come into their office with a policy or inventory question, they always directed it to Michelle. When a delivery person or tech would come in, they would address Michelle, and if Michelle was not at her desk (but Kiana was), they would simply walk out, as if no one were in the office. She shared with Alan that she sometimes wonders: can anybody see me? While exploring this, Alan wondered if Kiana was "making a mountain out of a mole hill." For example, he asked if Michelle's desk was positioned closer to the door in the office, implying that she is the "first line" for inquiries. He also asked how Michelle greets people: was she smiling and cheerful? Pleasant and warm? Alan felt it was important for Kiana to consider where these feelings of invisibility may be coming from, and invited her to consider if she felt that she was not worthy of others' attention and admiration. He then began to ask her how her relationship was with her parents as a child, with particular interest in how she felt about her father.

These questions frustrated Kiana, but she was aware that Alan was already experiencing her as closed and angry. Actually, she *was* feeling angry, and it felt very similar to the anger she experienced in her workplace. She felt caught in that moment between sharing her authentic reaction and being type cast as an angry Black woman and holding in her true feelings to avoid the stereotype. It was a familiar scenario. Alan interpreted Kiana's silence as resistance to the therapeutic process. Kiana responded that she had come to therapy to deepen her self-awareness; however, she could see that there were going to be too many barriers between herself and Alan for her to be able to authentically share herself. Alan expressed regret about this and asked if Kiana would consider coming to another session the next day. He felt that Kiana's desire to terminate their work prematurely was a defense mechanism; a common reaction for those who are new to therapy. Somehow, this did not resonate for Kiana and she did not return for a second session.

REFLECTION AND DISCUSSION QUESTIONS

1. What are some of the assumptions that Alan makes about Kiana? Why might he be making these?

CASE STUDY

2. Can you describe the psychological impact these assumptions may be having on Kiana?

3. How may race, gender, age, and sexuality be affecting the therapeutic relationship between Kiana and Alan?

4. If you were Kiana's therapist, how would you approach your work with her? What sociocultural dynamics would exist between you, and how might they influence the therapeutic process?

5. What could Alan do to repair this therapeutic rupture with Kiana? What role might cultural mistrust play in this process?

There is clearly misunderstanding and miscommunication between Kiana and Alan. Kiana was attending therapy in hopes of deepening her self-understanding; however, her initial session has served as a microcosm for her experiences in society at large where she feels invisible. Alan seems to relate to Kiana as a stereotype ("angry Black woman") and explains her feelings of invisibility as being self-imposed (rather than being caused by the environment and larger climate of *racism* and sexism). Kiana's feelings and experience are unknowingly invalidated, negated, and dismissed by the therapist. This anecdote illustrates how racial, gender, and sexual orientation *microaggressions* can have a detrimental impact upon marginalized groups and also undermine the therapeutic process. Let us briefly review Kiana's interactions with others from her perspective.

In her workplace, Kiana experiences persistent feelings of invisibility. She feels she is often overlooked by others and is generally taken to be less important and qualified than her younger and less experienced White officemate. Yet she is placed in an unenviable position of not being absolutely certain that colleagues are reacting to her race. Further, she is keenly aware of the stereotype of the "angry Black woman" and does not want to be typecast should she express her frustrations. She is aware that if she is experienced as hostile and angry, then people may avoid her in the future, only compounding her feelings of invisibility. Therefore, Kiana feels a persistent need to monitor her authentic reactions and her tone of voice, impeding her ability to be her true self (and using a lot of psychic energy!) while at work.

Although the therapist may be attempting to help Kiana by asking her to look inside herself for the cause of these feelings of invisibility (a common psychodynamic intervention is to explore intrapsychic dynamics) he actually undermines and invalidates Kiana's experiential reality. Instead of exploring the workplace environment and considering that *racism* and sexism cause people to see a Black woman such as Kiana as less capable, intelligent, and important, Alan immediately locates the problem within Kiana ("blaming the victim"). He does the same thing when asking her about dating. He uses his own experience of her in therapy (closed body language, angry expression) and asks her about an "unapproachable air"; again locating the problem within Kiana. Alan also makes a heteronormative assumption about Kiana's sexuality when he asks her why she is having difficulty meeting men. Then, when Kiana responds that she is interested in men *and* women, he has difficulty owning up to his lack of awareness and instead interprets bisexuality as a phase, thereby invalidating Kiana's sexual identity. He goes on to further alienate his client by suggesting that Kiana struggles with identity issues, given her multiple ethnic identities. Being multiethnic, Kiana has faced questions her entire life about "what she is" and even though she has a strong understanding of herself as a racial being, Alan has enacted the idea that she must be confused and unsure of her identity.

The incidents experienced by Kiana are examples of *microaggressions*. The term *racial microaggressions* was originally coined by Chester Pierce to describe the subtle and often automatic put-downs that African Americans face (Pierce, Carew, Pierce-Gonzalez, & Willis, 1978; Pierce, 1995). Since then, the definition has expanded to apply to any marginalized group. *Microaggressions* can be defined as brief, everyday exchanges that send denigrating messages to a target group, such as people of color; religious minorities; women; people with disabilities; and gay, lesbian, bisexual, and transgendered individuals (Sue, 2010; Sue, Capodilupo, et al., 2007). These *microaggressions* are often subtle in nature and can be manifested in the verbal, nonverbal, visual, or behavioral realm. They are often enacted automatically and unconsciously (Pierce et al., 1978; Solórzano, Ceja, & Yosso, 2000), although the person who delivers the *microaggression* can do so intentionally or unintentionally (Sue, Capodilupo, et al., 2007). Investigators have recently introduced the term *hierarchical microaggressions*, defined as "everyday slights found in higher education that communicate systemic valuing (or devaluing) of a person because of the institutional role held by that person" (Young, Anderson & Stewart, 2015, p. 66). Consistent with Kiana's experiences, participants in that study felt that staff were devalued and made to feel unimportant.

When colleagues and service workers seek answers only from Kiana's coworker and ignore Kiana, they are sending a nonverbal message (walking out of the office) that they do not believe Kiana is competent to handle the task at hand. When the professor is surprised to learn that Kiana has taken a graduate course and assumes it is free for staff, she is sending a nonverbal (look of surprise) and verbal message that Kiana does not belong in the advanced academic environment. The underlying thought process seems to be that Black people are less qualified, less competent, and less educated. As we shall see, *microaggressions* may seem innocent and innocuous, but their cumulative nature can be extremely harmful to the victim's physical and mental health. In addition, they create hostile work environments such as Kiana's where she may be denied opportunities and have difficulties advancing because of unconscious biases and beliefs held by the colleagues.

To help in understanding the effects of *microaggressions* on marginalized groups, we will be (a) reviewing related literature on contemporary forms of oppression (e.g., *racism*, sexism, *heterosexism*, *ableism*, and *religious discrimination*); (b) presenting a framework for classifying and understanding the hidden and damaging messages of *microaggressions*; and (c) presenting findings from studies that have explored people's lived experiences of *microaggressions*.

CONTEMPORARY FORMS OF OPPRESSION

Most people associate *racism* with blatant and overt acts of discrimination that are epitomized by White supremacy and hate crimes. Studies suggest, however, that what has been called "old-fashioned" *racism* has seemingly declined (Dovidio & Gaertner, 2000). However, the nature and expression of *racism* (see Chapter 4) has evolved into a more subtle and ambiguous form, perhaps reflecting people's belief that overt and blatant acts of *racism* are unjust and politically incorrect (Dovidio, Gaertner, Kawakami, & Hodson, 2002). In a sense, *racism* has gone underground, has become more disguised, and is more likely to be covert. A similar process seems to have occurred with sexism as well. Three types of sexism have been identified: overt, covert, and subtle (Swim & Cohen, 1997). *Overt sexism* is blatant unequal and unfair treatment of women. *Covert sexism* refers to unequal and harmful treatment of women that is conducted in a hidden manner (Swim & Cohen, 1997); for example, a person may endorse a belief in gender equality but engage in hiring practices that are gender biased. The third type, *subtle sexism*, represents "unequal and unfair treatment of women that is not recognized by many people because it is perceived to be normative, and therefore does not appear unusual" (Swim, Mallett, & Stangor, 2004, p. 117). Whereas *overt* and *covert sexism* are intentional, *subtle sexism* is not deliberate or conscious. An example of *subtle sexism* is sexist language, such as the use of the pronoun *he* to convey universal human experience.

In many ways, *subtle sexism* contains many of the features that define *aversive racism*, a form of subtle and unintentional racism (Dovidio & Gaertner, 2000). *Aversive racism* is manifested in individuals who consciously assert egalitarian values but unconsciously hold anti-minority feelings; therefore, "aversive racists consciously sympathize with victims of past injustice, support the principles of racial equality, and regard themselves as nonprejudiced. At the same time, however, they possess negative feelings and beliefs about historically disadvantaged groups, which may be unconscious" (Gaertner & Dovidio, 2006, p. 618). Inheriting such negative feelings and beliefs about members of marginalized groups (e.g., people of color, women, and lesbian, gay, bisexual, or transgendered person [LGBT] populations) is unavoidable and inevitable due to the socialization process in the United States (Sue, 2004), where biased attitudes and stereotypes reinforce group hierarchy (Gaertner & Dovidio, 2006).

Subtle sexism is very similar to *aversive racism* in that individuals support and actively condone gender equality, yet unknowingly engage in behaviors that contribute to the unequal treatment of women (Cundiff, Zawadzki, Danube, & Shields, 2014). Much like *aversive racism, subtle sexism* devalues women, dismisses their accomplishments, and limits their effectiveness in a variety of social and professional settings (Calogero & Tylka, 2014). Researchers have begun to underscore the importance of these daily experiences of *subtle sexism*, arguing that they are in fact harmful and need to be recognized as such (Becker & Swim, 2012; Cundiff et al., 2014).

Researchers have used the templates of modern forms of *racism* and sexism to better understand the various forms of modern *heterosexism* (Smith & Shin, 2014; Walls, 2008) and modern *homonegativity* (M. A. Morrison & T. G. Morrison, 2002). *Heterosexism* and anti-gay harassment has a long history and is currently prevalent in the United States. Recent studies find the following for LGBT persons in the workplace: (a) 15–43 percent experience discrimination or harassment; (b) 7–41 percent report verbal or physical abuse or had their workplace vandalized; and (c) 10–28 percent were not promoted because they were gay or transgender (Burns & Krehely, 2011). *Anti-gay harassment* can be defined as "verbal or physical behavior that injures, interferes with, or intimidates lesbian women, gay men, and bisexual individuals" (Burn, Kadlec, & Rexler, 2005, p. 24).

Although anti-gay harassment includes comments and jokes that convey that LGB individuals are pathological, abnormal, or unwelcome, authors identify subtle *heterosexism* by the indirect nature of such remarks (Burn et al., 2005). For example, blatant *heterosexism* would be calling a lesbian a dyke, whereas subtle *heterosexism* would be referring to something as gay to convey that it is stupid. For sexual minorities, hearing this remark may result in a vicarious experience of insult and invalidation (Burn et al., 2005; Marzullo & Libman, 2009). It may also encourage individuals to remain closeted, as the environment can be perceived as hostile.

The discriminatory experiences of transgendered people have been very rarely studied in psychology (Nadal, Rivera, & Corpus, 2010), yet there is evidence to suggest that the pervasive daily discrimination faced by this population is associated with an elevated risk for suicide (Marzullo & Libman, 2009). One term used to define prejudice against transgendered individuals is *transphobia*, "an emotional disgust toward individuals who do not conform to society's gender expectations" (Hill & Willoughby, 2005, p. 533). There is recent evidence to suggest that the *microaggressions* experienced by transgender individuals are distinct from those experienced by lesbian, gay, and bisexual people (Nadal, Skolnik, &Wong, 2012).

Although it is increasingly considered politically incorrect to hold racist, sexist, and, to some extent, heterosexist beliefs, gender roles and expectations tend to be rigid in the United States, and people may feel more justified in adhering to their transphobic views (Nadal, Issa, Griffin, Hamit, & Lyons, 2010; Nadal et al., 2012). Another area that has received limited attention in the psychological literature is *religious discrimination*, despite a high prevalence of religious-based hate crimes in the United States (Nadal et al., 2010). The largest percentage of religious harassment and civil rights violations in the United States are committed against Jewish and Muslim individuals (Nadal et al., 2010). Some commonly held anti-Semitic beliefs are that Jews (a) are more loyal to Israel than to the United States, (b) hold too much power in the United States, and (c) are responsible for the death of Jesus Christ (Nadal et al., 2010).

The prejudice experienced by Muslim individuals is often referred to as *Islamaphobia* and has been well documented in Western European countries both before and after the September 11, 2001, terrorist attacks (Nadal et al., 2010). The media tends to depict Muslims as religious fanatics and terrorists (James, 2008), and one study reveals that Americans hold both implicit and explicit negative attitudes toward this group (Rowatt, Franklin, & Cotton, 2005). Finally, though discriminatory practices toward people with disabilities (PWD) is long-standing in the United States and even believed to be increasing in frequency and intensity (Leadership Conference on Civil Rights Education Fund [LCCREF], 2009, as cited in Keller & Galgay, 2010), *ableism* is rarely included in discussions about modern forms of oppression (Keller & Galgay, 2010). The expression of *ableism* "favors people without disabilities and maintains that disability in and of itself is a negative concept, state, and experience" (Keller & Galgay, 2010, p. 242).

What makes this phenomenon of subtle discrimination particularly complex is that ambiguity and alternative explanations obscure the true meaning of the event not only for the person who engages in this behavior, but also for the person on the receiving end of the action. This is the central dilemma created by *microaggressions*, which are manifestations of these subtle forms of oppression.

EVOLUTION OF THE "ISMS": MICROAGGRESSIONS

Microaggressions are "brief and commonplace daily verbal or behavioral indignities, whether intentional or unintentional, that communicate hostile, derogatory, or negative racial slights and insults that potentially have a harmful or unpleasant psychological impact on the target person or group" (Sue, Bucceri, Lin, Nadal, & Torino, 2007). *Microaggressions* can also be delivered environmentally through the physical surroundings of target groups, where they are made to feel unwelcome, isolated, unsafe, and alienated. For example, a prestigious Eastern university conducts new faculty orientations in their main conference room, which displays portraits of all past presidents of the university. One new female faculty of color mentioned that during the orientation she noticed that every single portrait was that of a White male. She described feelings of unease and alienation. To her, the all-White-male portraits sent powerful messages: "Your kind does not belong here," "You will not be comfortable here," and "If you stay, there is only so far you can rise at this university!" Environmental *microaggressions* can occur when there is an absence of students or faculty of color on college campuses, few women in the upper echelons of the workplace, and limited or no access for disabled persons in buildings (e.g., only stairs and no ramp; no Braille in elevators).

Research suggests that the socialization process culturally conditions racist, sexist, and heterosexist attitudes and behaviors in well-intentioned individuals and that these biases are often automatically enacted without conscious awareness, particularly for those who endorse egalitarian values (Dovidio & Gaertner, 2000). Based on the literature on subtle forms of oppression, one might conclude the following about *microaggressions*: They (a) tend to be subtle, unintentional, and indirect; (b) often occur in situations where there are alternative explanations; (c) represent unconscious and ingrained biased beliefs and attitudes; and (d) are more likely to occur when people pretend not to notice differences, thereby denying that race, sex, sexual orientation, religion, or ability had anything to do with their actions (Sue, Capodilupi, et al., 2007). Three types of *microaggressions* have been identified: *microassault*, *microinsult*, and *microinvalidation*.

Microassault

The term *microassault* refers to a blatant verbal, nonverbal, or environmental attack intended to convey discriminatory and biased sentiments. This notion is related to overt *racism*, sexism, *heterosexism*, *ableism*, and *religious discrimination* in which individuals deliberately convey derogatory messages to target groups. Using epithets like *spic, faggot, or kyke;* hiring only men for managerial positions; requesting not to sit next to a Muslim on an airplane; and deliberately serving disabled patrons last are examples. Unless we are talking about White supremacists, most perpetrators with conscious biases will engage in overt discrimination only under three conditions: (a) when some degree of anonymity can be insured, (b) when they are in the presence of others who share or tolerate their biased beliefs and actions, or (c) when they lose control of their feelings and actions.

Two past high-profile examples exemplify the first condition: (a) Paula Deen's use of the N-word and racial harassment to employees of color (caught on tape), and (b) Justin Bieber's use of the N-word and racial jokes (caught on video). There are also high-profile examples of the last condition: (a) actor Mel Gibson made highly inflammatory anti-Semitic public statements to police officers when he was arrested for driving while intoxicated, and (b) comedian Michael Richards, who played Kramer on *Seinfeld*, went on an out-of-control rant at a comedy club and publicly insulted African Americans by hurling racial epithets at them and by demeaning their race. Gibson and Richards denied being anti-Semitic or racist and issued immediate apologies, but it was obvious both had lost control. Because *microassaults* are most similar to old-fashioned *racism*, no guessing game is likely to occur as to their intent: to hurt or injure the recipient. Both the perpetrator and the recipient are clear about what has transpired. We submit that *microassaults* are in many respects easier to deal with than those that are unintentional and outside the perpetrator's level of awareness (*microinsults* and *microinvalidations*).

Microinsult

Microinsults are unintentional behaviors or verbal comments that convey rudeness or insensitivity or demean a person's racial heritage/identity, gender identity, religion, ability, or sexual orientation identity. Despite being outside the level of conscious awareness, these subtle snubs are characterized by an insulting hidden message. For example, when a person frantically rushes to help a person with a disability onto public transportation, the underlying message is that disabled people are in constant need of help and dependent on others. When the coworkers in the case study at the beginning of this chapter look past Kiana to answer workplace-related questions, they were conveying a hidden message: Black females are less competent and capable.

African Americans consistently report that intellectual inferiority is a common communication they receive from Whites in their everyday experiences (Sue, Capodilupo, & Holder, 2008). Latinos also report a variety of incidences in which their academic success is questioned or they are assumed to be less qualified (Ramirez, 2014; Rivera, Forquer, & Rangel, 2010). Native Americans also report constant, continual, and cumulative experiences of *microinsults* (Jones & Galliher, 2015). A recent investigation of *microaggression* experiences on college campuses indicates that Black and Latina/o students experience significantly more *microaggressions* where they are treated as inferiors than their White and Asian counterparts. Further, Black participants reported more experiences of being treated as second-class citizens than all other groups (Nadal, Wong, Griffin, Davidoff, & Sriken, 2014). Similarly, when teachers in a classroom consistently call on male students rather than females to answer questions, the hidden message is that men are brighter and more capable than women.

Microinvalidation

Microinvalidations are verbal comments or behaviors that exclude, negate, or dismiss the psychological thoughts, feelings, or experiential reality of the target group. Like *microinsults*, they are unintentional and usually outside the perpetrator's awareness. When Alan dismissed Kiana's bisexuality as a "phase," he negated the client's sexual identity. The hidden message delivered to Kiana is that she is confused and working through her sexual preference, thereby denying that she can be attracted to both sexes. Because Alan is in a position of power as a White therapist, he is able to not only define Kiana's experiential reality but also direct the course of therapy. While Kiana entered therapy to deepen her self-understanding, the therapy has quickly become about Alan's understanding of Kiana—through his racialized, gendered, and sexual assumptions about her. Thus, the entire experience of therapy is *microinvalidation* for Kiana.

Another common *microinvalidation* is when individuals claim that they do not see religion or color but instead see only the human being. Common statements such as "there is only one race: the human race" negate the lived experiences of religious and ethnic minorities in the United States. Such statements have been coined by researchers as "color-blind" attitudes and new research shows that among White adults in a workplace setting, higher color-blind attitudes are associated with lower likelihoods of perceiving *microaggressions* (Offermann et al., 2014; Sue, 2010). To further illustrate the concepts of *microinsults* and *microinvalidations*, Table 6.1 provides examples of comments, actions, and situations, as well as accompanying hidden messages and assumptions. There are 16 distinct categories represented in this table: alien in one's own land; ascription of intelligence; assumption of abnormality; color blindness; criminality/assumption of criminal status; denial of individual *racism*/sexism/*heterosexism*/religious prejudice; myth of meritocracy; pathologizing cultural values/communication styles; second-class status; sexual objectification; use of sexist/heterosexist language; traditional gender role prejudice and stereotyping; helplessness; denial of personal identity; exoticization; and assumption of one's own religion as normal. Some of these categories are more applicable to certain forms of *microaggressions* (racial, gender, religion, ability, or sexual orientation), but they all seem to share commonalities.

REFLECTION AND DISCUSSION QUESTIONS

1. In looking at Table 6.1, can you identify how you may have committed *microaggressions* related to race, gender, sexual orientation, religion, or ability?

2. Compile a list of possible *microaggressions* you may have committed. Can you explore the potential hidden messages they communicate to the recipients?

3. What do your *microaggressions* tell you about your unconscious perception of marginalized groups?

4. If *microaggressions* are mostly outside the level of conscious awareness, what must you do to make them visible? What steps must you take to personally stop *microaggressions*?

5. What solutions can you offer that would be directed at individual change, institutional change, and societal change?

TABLE 6.1   Examples of Microaggressions

Themes	Microaggression	Message
Alien in Own Land When Asian Americans and Latino Americans are assumed to be foreign-born	"Where are you from?" "Where were you born?" "You speak good English"	You are not American.
A person asking an Asian American to teach them words in their native language	You are a foreigner.	
Ascription of Intelligence Assigning intelligence to a person of color or a woman based on his or her race/gender	"You are a credit to your race."	People of color are generally not as intelligent as Whites.
	"Wow! How did you become so good in math?"	It is unusual for a woman to be smart in math.
	Asking an Asian person to help with a math or science problem	All Asians are intelligent and good in math/sciences.
	"You only got into college because of affirmative action."	You are not smart enough on your own to get into college.
Color Blindness Statements that indicate that a White person does not want to acknowledge race	"When I look at you, I don't see color."	Denying a person of color's racial/ethnic experiences.
	"America is a Melting Pot."	Assimilate/acculturate to dominant culture.
	"There is only one race: the human race."	Denying the individual as a racial/cultural being.
Criminality/Assumption of Criminal Status A person of color is presumed to be dangerous, criminal, or deviant based on their race	A White man or woman clutching their purse or checking their wallet as a Black or Latino approaches or passes.	You are a criminal/You are dangerous.
	A White person waits to ride the next elevator when a person of color is on it.	You are dangerous.
Use of Sexist/Heterosexist Language Terms that exclude or degrade women and LGB persons	Use of the pronoun "he" to refer to all people.	Male experience is universal. Female experience is meaningless.
	Though a male-to-female transgendered employee has consistently referred to herself as "she," coworkers continue to refer to "he."	Our language does not need to change to reflect your identity, your identity is meaningless.
	Two options for Relationship Status: Married or Single.	LGB partnerships do not matter/are meaningless.
	An assertive woman is labeled a "bitch."	Women should be passive.
	A heterosexual man who often hangs out with his female friends more than his male friends is labeled a "faggot."	Men who act like women are inferior (women are inferior)/gay men are inferior.

(Continued)

TABLE 6.1 *(Continued)*

Themes	Microaggression	Message
Denial of Individual Racism/ Sexism/Heterosexism/Religious Discrimination A statement made when bias is denied	"I'm not racist. I have several Black friends."	I am immune to racism because I have friends of color.
	"I am not prejudiced against Muslims. I am just fearful of Muslims who are religious fanatics."	I can separate Islamaphobic social conditioning from my feelings about Muslim people in general.
	"As an employer, I always treat men and women equally."	I am incapable of sexism.
Myth of Meritocracy Statements that assert that race or gender does not play a role in life successes	"I believe the most qualified person should get the job."	People of color are given extra unfair benefits because of their race.
	"Men and women have equal opportunities for achievement."	The playing field is even; so if women cannot make it, the problem is with them.
Pathologizing Cultural Values/ Communication Styles The notion that the values and communication styles of the dominant/White culture are ideal	Asking a Black person: "Why do you have to be so loud/animated? Just calm down."	Assimilate to dominant culture.
	Dismissing an individual who brings up race/culture in work/school setting	Leave your cultural baggage outside.
Second-Class Citizen Occurs when a target group member receives differential treatment from the power group	Person of color mistaken for a service worker	People of color are servants to Whites. They couldn't possibly occupy high-status positions.
	Female doctor mistaken for a nurse	Women occupy nurturing roles.
	Having a taxi cab pass a person of color and pick up a White passenger	You are likely to cause trouble and/or travel to a dangerous neighborhood.
	Being ignored at a store counter as attention is given to the White customer behind you	Whites are more valued customers than people of color.
	A lesbian woman is not invited out with a group of girlfriends because they thought she would be bored if they were talking to men.	You don't belong.
Traditional Gender Role Prejudicing and Stereotyping Occurs when expectations of traditional roles or stereotypes are conveyed	When a female student asked a male professor for extra help on a chemistry assignment, he asks, "What do you need to work on this for anyway?"	Women are less capable in math and science.
	A person asks a woman her age and, upon hearing she is 31, looks quickly at her ring finger.	Women should be married during child-bearing ages because that is their primary purpose.
	A woman is assumed to be a lesbian because she does not put a lot of effort into her appearance.	Lesbians do not care about being attractive to others.

Sexual Objectification Occurs when women are treated like objects at men's disposal	A male stranger puts his hands on a woman's hips or on the swell of her back to pass by her.	Your body is not yours.
	Whistles and catcalls as a woman walks down the street.	Your body/appearance is for men's enjoyment and pleasure.
	Students use the term *gay* to describe a fellow student who is socially ostracized at school.	People who are weird and different are "gay."
Assumption of Abnormality Occurs when it is implied that there is something wrong with being LGBT	Two men holding hands in public receiving stares from strangers.	You should keep your displays of affection private because they are offensive.
	"Did something terrible happen to you in your childhood?" to a transgendered person.	Your choices must be the result of a trauma and not your authentic identity.
Helplessness[1] Occurs when people frantically try to help people with disabilities (PWDs)	Someone helps you onto a bus or train, even when you need no help.	You can't do anything by yourself because you have a disability.
	People feel they need to rescue you from your disability.	Having a disability is a catastrophe.
Denial of Personal Identity[2] Occurs when any aspect of a person's identity other than disability is ignored or denied	"I can't believe you are married!"	Your life is not normal or like mine. The only thing I see when I look at you is your disability.
Exoticization Occurs when an LGBT, women of color, or a religious minority is treated as a foreign object for the pleasure/entertainment of others	"I've always wanted an Asian girlfriend! They wait hand and foot on their men."	Asian American women are submissive and meant to serve the physical needs of men.
	"Tell me some of your wild sex stories!" to an LGBT person.	Your privacy is not valued; you should entertain with stories.
	Asking a Muslim person incessant questions about his/her diet, dress, and relationships.	Your privacy is not valued; you should educate me about your cultural practices, which are strange and different.
Assumption of One's Own Religion as Normal[3]	Saying "Merry Christmas" as a universal greeting	Your religious beliefs are not important; everyone should celebrate Christmas.
	The sole acknowledgment of Christian holidays in work and school.	Your religious holidays need to be celebrated on your time; they are unimportant.

[1] Adapted from Sue et al., 2007.
[2] Themes and examples are taken from Keller & Galgay, 2010.
[3] Themes and examples are taken from Nadal et al., 2010.

THE DYNAMICS AND DILEMMAS OF MICROAGGRESSIONS

Let us use the case of Kiana to illustrate some of the dynamics and dilemmas presented by *microaggressions*. Research on subtle forms of *racism* (Dovidio et al., 2002; Ridley, 2005), sexism (Swim et al., 2004), and *heterosexism* (Morrison & Morrison, 2002) provide evidence that they operate in individuals who endorse egalitarian beliefs, adamantly deny that they are biased, and consider themselves to be moral, just, and fair. What people consciously believe or say (e.g., "I have no gay bias"), however, is oftentimes at odds with what they actually do (e.g., avoiding sitting next to an ostensibly gay man). Further, those who purport to not see race but rather see all people as equal (i.e., color-blind attitude) are significantly less likely to recognize and perceive racial *microaggressions* (Offermann et al., 2014).

Proving that one's actions or comments stem from an unconsciously held set of negative beliefs toward the target group is virtually impossible when alternative explanations exist. Because Whites who engage in *microaggressions* truly believe they acted without racial bias toward persons of color, for example, they will disclaim any racist meaning. Not only is the subtle and insidious nature of racial *microaggressions* outside the level of awareness of perpetrators but also recipients find their ambiguity difficult to handle. Victims are placed in an unenviable position of questioning not only perpetrators, but themselves as well (e.g., "Did I misread what happened?"). Victims often replay the incident over and over again to try to understand its meaning.

A study of Black undergraduates summarizes the energy that can go into the interpretation of *microaggressions*: "Participants also typically reported trying to balance responding to or educating others about *racism*, while not 'overthinking' these incidents or placing too much energy on [these] encounters" (Watkins, Labarrie, & Appio, 2010, p. 35). We see this very dynamic when Kiana chooses not to respond to Alan's questions about her sexual and ethnic identity. Though she feels marginalized by him as she has in her daily experiences in society, she chooses not to educate Alan in that moment, since her experience in therapy is meant to be about and for her. Qualitative narratives speak to the idea that bisexual women have to work to "make their identity understood, seen and accepted, not only by strangers—but by their loved ones" (Bostwick & Hequembourg, 2014, p. 499); consistently having to "prove" one's identity certainly represents an emotional burden.

In the face of *microaggressions*, many members of historically marginalized groups describe feeling a vague unease that something is not right and that they were insulted or disrespected. In this respect, overt acts of *racism*, sexism, or *hetero-sexism* may be easier to handle than *microaggressions* because the intent and meaning of the event are clear and indisputable (Solórzano et al., 2000; Sue, 2004). In support of this, recent studies found that racial *microaggressions* were more impactful, harmful, and distressing to African Americans and Asian Americans than everyday hassles (Utsey, Giesbrecht, Hook, & Stanard, 2008; Wang, Leu, & Shoda, 2011). *Microaggressions* toward marginalized groups, however, pose special problems. Four psychological dilemmas have been identified when *microaggressions* occur (Sue et al., 2007).

Dilemma 1: Clash of Sociodemographic Realities

For Kiana, one major question was, "Were people looking past her and ignoring her because of her race?" Although lived experience tells her that many Whites devalue Black women, chances are that her workplace colleagues would be offended at such a suggestion. They would likely deny they possessed any stereotypes and might point to Kiana's own demeanor (not "friendly enough") as being responsible for her being overlooked (as Alan did). In other words, they would emphasize that they and their organizations do not discriminate on the basis of color, sex, sexual orientation, or creed. The question becomes, "Whose reality is the true reality?"

Oftentimes the perceptions held by the dominant group differ significantly from those of marginalized groups in our society. For example, studies show that many Whites believe that *racism* is no longer prevalent in society and not important in the lives of people of color (Sue, 2010), that heterosexuals believe that homophobia is a "thing of the past" and that anti-gay harassment is on the decline (Nadal, 2013), and that men (and women) assert that women have achieved equal status and are no longer discriminated against (Cundiff et al., 2014; Swim & Cohen, 1997). Most important, individuals in power positions do not consider themselves capable of discrimination based on race, gender, or sexual orientation because, they believe, they are free of bias.

On the other hand, people of color perceive Whites to be racially insensitive, enjoy holding power over others, and think they are superior (Sue et al., 2007). LGB individuals consider *homonegativity* and anti-gay harassment to be a crucial aspect of their everyday existence (Burn et al., 2005; Nadal, 2013), and women contend that sexism is alive and well in social and professional settings. Although research supports the fact that those most disempowered are more likely to have a more accurate perception of reality, it is groups in power that have the ability to define reality. Thus, people of color, women, and LGB individuals are likely to experience their perceptions and interpretations being negated or dismissed. This becomes particularly salient in the therapeutic encounter, which represents an unequal power dynamic.

For Kiana, who has had countless experiences of being taken as an "angry Black woman" when she expresses a strong opinion, she is clear that she needs to monitor and edit her point of view at work. Alan, however, has not experienced this racial reality and tries to "objectively" reason that Kiana may be reading too much into or misinterpreting the situation, or even contributing to others' perceptions of her as angry by not smiling or being "friendly." Further, Alan invalidates Kiana's sexual identity by referring to bisexuality as a "phase" and he eliminates a healthy space for her to explore her feelings about trying to find a partner.

Microaggressions that dismiss a bisexual identity "reinforce the myth of monosexuality, wherein persons can only be understood to occupy one of two mutually exclusive categories (heterosexual versus homosexual)" (Bostwick & Hequembourg, 2014, p. 494). A recent study of lesbian, gay, bisexual, and transgendered clients revealed that "clients were left feeling doubtful about the effectiveness of therapy, the therapists' abilities, and the therapists' investment in the therapeutic process when therapists minimized their sexual reality" (Shelton & Delgado-Romero, 2011, p. 217).

Dilemma 2: The Invisibility of Unintentional Expressions of Bias

Although Kiana did not ask colleagues about their persistent behavior of ignoring her, nor their treating of her as a second-class citizen (as opposed to an equal), one can imagine that they might feel stunned and surprised to learn how Kiana feels. Especially in a place of higher education where many consider themselves to be liberal and egalitarian, they would likely dismiss Kiana's interpretations and deny their behavior. To Kiana, being ignored and undervalued in the academic community reflected a common experience for her of people seeming surprised that she is articulate, well educated, and intellectually competent.

How could Kiana "prove" that colleagues doubted her intelligence or worth? Her only evidence is her felt experience and interpretation, which are easily explained away and disregarded by coworkers, students, and professors with alternative explanations. For example, Alan wonders if colleagues simply approach Kiana's White officemate first because her desk is closer to the door.

Further compounding the situation is the idea that Kiana is experiencing these *microaggressions* in her place of work and school: an environment that should be fostering and supporting her intellectual growth. Kiana's academic achievements may be hampered by the stress she is experiencing on campus or she may perceive further education (i.e., pursuit of a doctorate) to be an impossibility for her. Research on *microaggressions* in higher education showed participants "to take on an identity associated with their status at the university" (Young et al., 2015, p. 69). That the *microaggression* is essentially invisible to the perpetrator creates a psychological dilemma for victims that can leave them frustrated, feeling powerless, and even questioning their own sanity (Bostwick & Hequembourg, 2014; Sue, Capodilupo, et al., 2007; Watkins et al., 2010).

Dilemma 3: Perceived Minimal Harm of Microaggressions

Oftentimes, when perpetrators are confronted about *microaggressions*, they accuse the victim of overreacting or being hypersensitive or touchy. Because the *microaggressions* are often invisible to the perpetrators, they cannot understand how the events could cause any significant harm to the victims. They see the events as innocent and innocuous and often feel that victims are "making a mountain out of a mole hill" (à la Alan). Trivializing the impact of racial *microaggressions* by some White people can be an automatic, defensive reaction to avoid feeling blamed and guilty (Sue, Capodilupo, Nadal, & Torino, 2008). Despite a lack of acknowledgment by majority groups that everyday experiences of discrimination can be harmful to minorities, research is mounting to suggest otherwise: a large-scale meta-analysis reveals that perceived discrimination has cumulative and harmful effects on psychological well-being (Schmitt, Branscombe, Postmes, & Garcia, 2014).

Racism and racial/ethnic discrimination cause significant psychological distress (Fang & Meyers, 2001; Krieger & Sidney, 1996, Sue, Capodilupo, et al. 2008; Sue, Capodilupo, & Holder, 2008; Watkins et al., 2010), depression (Comas-Diaz & Greene, 1994; Kim, 2002), and negative health outcomes (Harrell, Hall, & Taliaferro, 2003). Researchers have even coined the terms *racism-related stress* (Harrell, 2000) and *minority stress framework* (for sexual minorities) (Meyer, 2003). Recent qualitative work with bisexual women revealed that "*microaggressions* that render bisexual women's identity claims faulty or, worse, false and inauthentic, burden bisexual women with additional identity work, which is both cognitively and emotionally taxing" (Bostwick & Hequembourg, 2014, p. 499).

One study that looked at racial *microaggressions* in the lived experience of African Americans found that the cumulative effect of these events was feelings of self-doubt, frustration, and isolation (Solórzano et al., 2000). Another study found that consequences of *microaggressions* for African Americans included feelings of powerlessness, invisibility, and loss of integrity (Sue, Capodilupo, et al., 2008; Sue, Capodilupo, & Holder, 2008).

In a 2-week daily diary study of Asian American college students' experiences of *microaggressions*, it was found that 78 percent experienced at least one micro-aggression, and the reporting of such events predicted higher negative affect and more somatic symptoms (Ong, Burrow, Fuller-Rowell, Ja, & Sue, 2013). This supports earlier qualitative work that reported Asian Americans feel belittled, angry, invalidated, invisible, and trapped by their experiences of racial *microaggressions* (Sue, Capodilupo, Nadal, & Torino, 2007). Multiple studies suggest that Latino/a and Chicano/a students feel marginalized and frustrated by microaggressive experiences in educational settings (Huber & Cueva, 2012; Nadal, Mazzula, Rivera, & Fujii-Doe, 2014; Ramirez, 2014) and investigations link the experience of *microaggressions* on college campuses with serious behavioral and psychological consequences. For example, college students of color who experienced greater numbers of *microaggressions* were at increased risk for higher anxiety and binge drinking (Blume, Lovato, Thyken, & Denny, 2012). In another study, the experience of *microaggressions* was significantly associated with low self-esteem (Nadal, Wong, et al., 2014b). Specifically, *microaggressions* experienced in educational and workplace settings were found to be especially harmful to participants' self-esteem (Nadal, Wong, et al., 2014). Likewise, homonegative *microaggressions* are associated with lower self-esteem, negative feelings about one's sexual orientation identity, and obstacles to developing one's sexual identity (Wright & Wegner, 2012). In fact, anti-gay slurs and related hostilities on campus are significantly related to psychological distress, anxiety, and post-traumatic stress disorder symptoms not only for the target of said incidents but also for those who indirectly experience these incidents (e.g., third-party observation) (Nadal, Issa, et al., 2011; Woodford, Han, Craig, Lim, & Matney, 2013).

Dilemma 4: The Catch-22 of Responding to Microaggressions

When a *microaggression* occurs, the recipient is often placed in an unenviable position of deciding what to do. This is compounded with numerous questions likely to go through the mind of the recipient: Did what I think happened really happen? If it did, how can I possibly prove it? How should I respond? Will it do any good if

I bring it to the attention of the perpetrator? If I do, will it affect my relationship with coworkers, friends, or acquaintances? Many well-intentioned perpetrators are unaware of the exhausting nature of these internal questions as they sap the spiritual and psychic energy of victims. Kiana was obviously caught in a conflict, asking herself: Should I voice my concerns of being unimportant and overlooked, or should I bother to respond at all?

As a multiracial bisexual female, Kiana has probably experienced many *microaggressions* throughout her lifetime, and so microaggressive comments from coworkers do not feel random (Ridley, 2005). On the other hand, White colleagues who have not faced similar experiences are unable to see a pattern running throughout incidents encountered by people of color—hidden bias associated with race. People of color, for example, use context and experiential reality to interpret the meaning of *microaggressions*. The common thread operating in multiple situations is that of "race." Whites, however, see such situations as "isolated incidents," so the pattern of *racism* experienced by persons of color is invisible to them.

The fundamental issue is that responding to a *microaggression* can have detrimental consequences for the victim. In work settings, hiring and firing practices hang in the balance. In school settings, academic performance can be impacted. Sometimes consequences of responding to *microaggressions* are relational. Consider when Alan assumed Kiana was heterosexual and asked why she is having difficulty meeting men. Kiana explained her attraction to both sexes only to then have Alan suggest that her sexual identity is a "phase." In an effort to avoid an uncomfortable exchange with Alan, or to waste her own therapy time explaining her identity, Kiana moves the conversation elsewhere.

If Kiana responds to Alan with frustration or anger over his assumption, she risks being perceived as the "angry Black woman" and potentially jeopardizing their therapeutic relationship. Kiana might feel compelled to avoid this label and to simply forgo the hassles. Unfortunately, it has been found that such a reaction takes a psychological toll on the recipient because it requires her to suppress and obscure her authentic thoughts and feelings in order to avoid further discrimination (Franklin, 2004). Authors have referred to this process as self-silencing and have linked it to "compromising women's success by heightening feelings of alienation and reducing motivation" (London, Downey, Romero-Canyas, Rattan, & Tyson, 2012, p. 219).

Confronting sexual orientation *microaggressions* is further complicated for LGB individuals who may not necessarily be out of the closet. The reality of looming anti-gay harassment and differential (unequal) treatment may prevent LGB persons from coming out in a variety of settings, especially when there is evidence to suggest that the environment is heterosexist. Anti-gay slurs and pervasive use of the word "gay" to communicate that someone or something is inferior, stupid, or abnormal (Nadal, 2013) all contribute to hostile educational and workplace environments. The therapeutic room can be equally unwelcoming and hostile: qualitative work reports that "fear of being seen as different had a suppressive and muting effect on some participants' disclosure of their sexual orientation to their therapists" (Shelton & Delgado-Romero, 2013, p. 66).

By not confronting or processing these experiences, marginalized groups are forced to shoulder the burden themselves with detrimental mental health consequences. In one study, African American participants revealed some strategies for dealing with this catch-22: (a) empowering and validating the self and (b) sanity check. *Empowering and validating the self* refers to a process of interrupting the *racism* by "calling it what it is" and staying true to one's thoughts and feelings that the incident is related to one's race. *Sanity check* refers to a process of checking in with like-minded and same-race people about microaggressive incidents. Talking about the incident with someone who has faced similar discrimination helps participants to feel validated in their experience that the incident is racially motivated (Sue, Capodilupo, et al., 2008; Sue, Capodilupo, & Holder, 2008). In another study, Black undergraduates identified support systems, such as family, friends, religious faith, club involvement, journal writing, and academic leadership positions, as being factors that promote resilience in the face of racial *microaggressions* (Watkins et al., 2010).

COUNSELING IMPLICATIONS

We have repeatedly emphasized that clients of color tend to prematurely terminate counseling and therapy at a 50% rate after only the first initial contact with a mental health provider (à la Kiana). We submit that racial *microaggressions* may lie at the core of the problem. Take, for example, a recent study which found that more than half of racial and ethnic minority clients at a college counseling center reported experiencing a *microaggression* from their therapist (Owen, Tao, Imel, Wampold, & Rodolfa, 2014). There is growing evidence to suggest that racial, gender, and sexual orientation *microaggressions* have a detrimental effect on the therapeutic alliance for clients of color (Owen et al., 2014), women (Owen, Tao, & Rodolfa, 2010) and LGBT individuals (Shelton & Delgado-Romero, 2011,

2013). In counseling and psychotherapy, the credibility of the therapist is paramount in determining whether clients stay or leave sessions (Strong, 1969). As we have seen in Chapter 5, credibility is composed of two dimensions: expertness and trustworthiness. *Expertness* is a function of how much knowledge, training, experience, and skills clinicians possess with respect to the population being treated; it is an *ability component.* *Trustworthiness*, however, is a *motivational component* that encompasses trust, honesty, and genuineness. Although expertness is always important, trustworthiness becomes central in multicultural counseling and therapy.

Effective counseling is likely to occur when both therapist and client are able to form a working relationship, therapeutic alliance, or some form of positive coalition. In mental health practice there is a near universal belief that effective and beneficial counseling requires that clients trust their counselors (Corey, 2012; Day, 2004). Research supports the idea that the therapeutic alliance is a key component in therapy work and is correlated with successful outcomes (Lui & Pope-Davis, 2005). Recent work supports the idea that clients' perceptions of racial *microaggressions* are negatively associated with therapeutic alliance (Owen et al., 2014).

Specifically, "*microaggressions* can be thought of as a special case of ruptures in therapy, wherein experiences of discrimination and oppression from the larger society are recapitulated, which places the therapeutic relationship under duress and strain" (Owen et al., 2014, p. 287). Qualitative work supports a similar finding for work with LGBT clients, where the therapeutic alliance and process has been shown to be diminished and negatively impacted by the presence of sexual orientation *microaggressions*: "affective consequences of sexual orientation *microaggressions* included clients feeling uncomfortable, confused, powerless, invisible, rejected, and forced or manipulated to comply with treatment" (Shelton & Delgado-Romero, 2013, p. 66).

Because all people inherit bias about various identity groups through cultural conditioning in the United States, no one, including helping professionals, is free from these biases (Ridley, 2005). This fact poses a unique dilemma in therapy for several reasons: Helping professionals are supposed to work for the welfare of all groups, be trained to be "objective," and be inclined to see problems as internally situated, and are usually in positions of power over the client. The fact that therapists possess unconscious biases and prejudices is problematic, especially when they sincerely believe they are capable of preventing them from entering sessions. Counselors often find themselves in positions of power in their ability to define their client's experiential reality (i.e., interpretation), which may prove harmful, especially if counselors adamantly deny the presence of *microaggressions* both inside and outside of the therapy situation. Recent research suggests that prejudice and bias continue to be manifested in the therapeutic process, despite the good intentions of mental health professionals (Owen et al., 2010, 2014; Shelton & Delgado-Romero, 2011, 2013; Utsey, Gernat, & Hammar, 2005).

Manifestations of Microaggressions in Counseling/Therapy

The importance of understanding how *microaggressions* manifest in the therapeutic relationship cannot be understated, especially as this phenomenon may underlie the high prevalence of drop-out rates among people of color and other marginalized groups. Let us use the case of Kiana to illustrate how *microaggressions* may operate in the counseling process.

1. Kiana revealed to Alan her experiences of racial, gender, and sexual orientation *microaggressions*, using therapy as a space for deeper exploration of a meaningful issue. Because Kiana and Alan are not the same race, gender, or sexuality, they do not share similar racial realities (Dilemma 1: clash of sociodemographic realities) or worldviews. The therapist has minimal understanding of what constitutes racial or sexual orientation *microaggressions*, how they make their appearance in everyday interactions, how he himself may be guilty of microaggressive behaviors, the psychological toll they take on minorities, and the negative effects they have on the therapeutic relationship. We have emphasized earlier that cultural competence requires helping professionals to understand the worldviews of their culturally diverse clients.

2. The therapist tends to minimize the importance of Kiana's feelings of invisibility and being overlooked, believes these feelings are trivial, and cannot relate to the negative impact these *microaggressions* have on his client. Even though the workplace feels hostile to Kiana, the therapist concludes that Kiana needs to explore intrapsychic dynamics to better understand her feelings of alienation; the emotional and psychological impact of these experiences on Kiana is thereby minimized (Dilemma 3: minimal harm). For Kiana, on the other hand, the experience of being ignored and the subsequent looks of surprise when she does speak up represent one of many cumulative messages of intellectual inferiority about her race. She is placed in an ongoing state of vigilance in maintaining her sense of integrity in the face of constant invalidations and insults. Racial, gender, and sexual *microaggressions* are a constant reality for people of color, assailing

group identities and experiences. White people seldom understand how much time, energy, and effort are expended by people of color to retain some semblance of worth and self-esteem.

3. Another major detrimental event in the first session is that the therapist locates the source of problems within Kiana by insinuating that she is unapproachable. While there may be some legitimacy to this interpretation, Alan is unaware that he has engaged in person-blame and that he has invalidated Kiana's experiential reality by dismissing race and sexuality as important factors. As a mental health professional, Alan probably considers himself unbiased and objective. However, he has cut off meaningful exploration for Kiana by removing the salience of race and sexuality from the conversation (Dilemma 2: invisibility). For example, had he asked Kiana more questions about the dating scene for bisexuals in her city, he might have learned that bisexuals often have to navigate the LGBT community differently from other sexual minorities, frequently experiencing rejection not only from mainstream society but also from those who identify as gay and lesbian (Bostwick & Hequembourg, 2014).

4. As a client, Kiana is caught in a catch-22—a "damned if you do and damned if you don't" conflict (Dilemma 4: catch-22). Both inside and outside of therapy, Kiana is probably internally wrestling with a series of questions: Did what I think happened really happen? Was this a deliberate act or an unintentional slight? How should I respond: Sit and stew on it or confront the person? What are the consequences if I do? If I bring up the topic, how do I prove it? These questions take a tremendous psychological toll on many marginalized groups. If Kiana chooses to do nothing, she may suffer emotionally by having to deny her own experiential reality or allow her sense of integrity to be assailed. Feelings of powerlessness, alienation, and frustration may take not only a psychological toll but also a physical toll on her. If she chooses to raise issues with the coworkers, students, or professors, she risks being isolated by others, seen as oversensitive or angry.

Table 6.2 provides several more therapy-specific examples of *microaggressions*, using the same organizing themes presented in Table 6.1. We ask that you study these themes and ask if you have ever engaged in these or similar actions. If so, how can you prevent your own personal *microaggressions* from impairing the therapy process?

TABLE 6.2   Examples of Microaggressions in Therapeutic Practice

Themes	Microaggression	Message
Alien in Own Land When Asian Americans and Latino Americans are assumed to be foreign-born	A White client does not want to work with an Asian American therapist because she "will not understand my problem."	You are not American.
	A White therapist tells an American-born Latino client that he/she should seek a Spanish-speaking therapist.	
Ascription of Intelligence Assigning a degree of intelligence to a person of color or a woman based on race or gender	A school counselor reacts with surprise when an Asian American student had trouble on the math portion of a standardized test.	All Asians are smart and good at math.
	A career counselor asking a Black or Latino student, "Do you think you're ready for college?"	It is unusual for people of color to succeed.
	A school counselor reacts with surprise that a female student scored high on a math portion of a standardized test.	It is unusual for women to be smart and good in math.
Color Blindness Statements that indicate that a White person does not want to acknowledge race	A therapist says, "I think you are being too paranoid. We should emphasize similarities, not people's differences," when a client of color attempts to discuss her feelings about being the only person of color at her job and feeling alienated and dismissed by her coworkers.	Race and culture are not important variables that affect people's lives.
	A client of color expresses concern in discussing racial issues with her therapist. Her therapist replies, "When I see you, I don't see color."	Your racial experiences are not valid.
Criminality/Assumption of Criminal Status A person of color is presumed to be dangerous, criminal, or deviant based on their race	When a Black client shares that she was accused of stealing from work, the therapist encourages the client to explore how she might have contributed to her employer's mistrust of her.	You are a criminal.
	A therapist takes great care to ask all substance-abuse questions in an intake with a Native American client and is suspicious of the client's nonexistent history with substances.	You are deviant.
Use of Sexist/Heterosexist Language Terms that exclude or degrade women and LGB groups	During the intake session, a female client discloses that she has been in her current relationship for one year. The therapist asks how long the client has known her boyfriend.	Heterosexuality is the norm.
	When an adult female client explains she is feeling isolated at work, her male therapist asks, "Aren't there any girls you can gossip with there?"	Application of language that implies to adolescent females or to adult females "your problems are trivial."

Denial of Individual Racism/Sexism/Heterosexism	A client of color asks his/her therapist about how race affects their working relationship. The therapist replies, "Race does not affect the way I treat you."	Your racial/ethnic experience is not important.
A statement made when a member of the power group renounces their biases	A client of color expresses hesitancy in discussing racial issues with his White female therapist. She replies, "I understand. As a woman, I face discrimination also."	Your racial oppression is no different from my gender oppression.
	A therapist's nonverbal behavior conveys discomfort when a bisexual male client is describing a recent sexual experience with a man. When he asks her about it, she insists she has "no negative feelings toward gay people" and says it is important to keep the conversation on him.	I am incapable of homonegativity, yet I am unwilling to explore this.
Myth of Meritocracy	A school counselor tells a Black student that "if you work hard, you can succeed like everyone else."	People of color/women are lazy and/or incompetent and need to work harder. If you don't succeed, you have only yourself to blame (blaming the victim).
Statements that assert that race or gender does not play a role in succeeding in career advancement or education	A female client visits a career counselor to share her concerns that a male coworker was chosen for a managerial position over her, despite the fact that she was better qualified and in the job longer. The counselor responds that "he must have been better suited for some of the job requirements."	
Pathologizing Cultural Values/Communication Styles	A Black client is loud, emotional, and confrontational in a counseling session. The therapist diagnoses her with borderline personality disorder.	Assimilate to dominant culture.
The notion that the values and communication styles of the dominant/White culture are ideal	A client of Asian or Native American descent has trouble maintaining eye contact with his therapist. The therapist diagnoses him with a social anxiety disorder.	
	Advising a client, "Do you really think your problem stems from racism?"	Leave your cultural baggage outside.
Second-Class Citizen	A male client calls and requests a session time that is currently taken by a female client. The therapist grants the male client the appointment without calling the female client to see if she can change times.	Males are more valued than women.
Occurs when a member of the power group is given preferential treatment over a target group member	Clients of color are not welcomed or acknowledged by receptionists.	White clients are more valued than clients of color.

(Continued)

TABLE 6.2 *(Continued)*

Themes	Microaggression	Message
Traditional Gender Role Prejudicing and Stereotyping Occurs when expectations of traditional roles or stereotypes are conveyed	A therapist continually asks the middle-aged female client about dating and "putting herself out there" despite the fact that the client has not expressed interest in exploring this area.	Women should be married, and dating should be an important topic/part of your life.
	A gay male client has been with his partner for 5 years. His therapist continually probes his desires to meet other men and be unfaithful.	Gay men are promiscuous. Gay men cannot have monogamous relationships.
	A therapist raises her eyebrows when a female client mentions that she has had a one-night stand.	Women should not be sexually adventurous.
Sexual Objectification Occurs when women are treated like objects at men's disposal	A male therapist puts his hands on a female client's back as she walks out of the session.	Your body is not yours.
	A male therapist is looking at his female client's breasts while she is talking.	Your body/appearance is for men's enjoyment and pleasure.
Assumption of Abnormality Occurs when it is implied that there is something wrong with being LGBT	When discussing the client's bisexuality, the therapist continues to imply that there is a "crisis of identity."	Bisexuality represents a confusion about sexual orientation.
	A lesbian comes in for career counseling, but the therapist continually insists that she needs to discuss her sexuality.	Your sexual orientation represents pathology.
	The therapist of a 20-year-old lesbian inadvertently refers to sexuality as a "phase."	Your sexuality is something that is not stable.

Adapted from Sue, Capodilupo, et al., 2007.

 IMPLICATIONS FOR CLINICAL PRACTICE

1. Be aware that racial, gender, and sexual orientation *microaggressions* are a constant reality in the lives of culturally diverse groups. They take a major psychological toll on members of marginalized groups.

2. Be aware that everyone has engaged and continues to engage in unintentional *microaggressions*. For helping professionals, these *microaggressions* may serve as impediments to effective multicultural counseling and therapy.

3. Entertain the notion that culturally diverse groups may have a more accurate perception of reality than you do, especially when it comes to issues of *racism*,

sexism, or *heterosexism*. Try to understand worldviews and sociocultural realities, and don't be quick to dismiss or negate racial, gender, or sexual orientation issues.

4. If your culturally different client implies that you have engaged in a microaggressive remark or behavior, engage in a nondefensive discussion and try to clarify the situation by showing you are open and receptive to conversations on race, gender, or sexual orientation. Remember, it's how the therapist recovers, not how he or she "covers up," that makes for successful multicultural counseling.

SUMMARY

Microaggressions represent daily stressors in the lives of marginalized groups in the United States. The literal explosion of research on *microaggressions* in the last five years has grown to include cultural identities beyond race, gender, and sexual orientation, such as transgender, bisexual, biracial, gender nonconforming, ability, and religion. In addition, researchers have begun to explore the impact of *microaggressions* on mental health outcomes, behaviors, and functioning. These studies lend support to the previous generation of qualitative investigations, which suggested that *microaggressions* are frustrating, psychologically taxing, and emotionally harmful to those who experience them.

Clients trust mental health professionals to take an intimate and deeply personal journey of self-exploration with them through the process of therapy. They grant these professionals the opportunity to look into their inner world and also invite them to walk where they live in their everyday lives. Therapists and counselors have an obligation to their clients, especially when their clients differ from them in terms of race, gender, ability, religion, and/or sexual orientation, to work to understand their experiential reality. There is evidence to suggest that *microaggressions* are everyday experiences too innumerable to count. The therapeutic relationship is not immune from these experiences; however, research suggests that when therapist and client are able to successfully discuss the *microaggression*, the therapeutic alliance can be restored. Therefore therapists must be open to the idea that they can commit *microaggressions* against their clients and be willing to examine their role in this process.

There is much work to be done to better understand the nuances and processes involved in this very complex phenomenon. Therapists and counselors are in a position to learn from their clients about *microaggressions* and their relationship to the clients' presenting concerns and developmental issues. It is imperative to encourage clients to explore their feelings about incidents that involve their race, gender, and sexual orientation so that the status quo of silence and invisibility can be destroyed.

GLOSSARY TERMS

Ableism	Microinsult
Aversive racism	Microinvalidation
Covert sexism	Overt sexism
Heterosexism	Racism
Homonegativity	Religious discrimination
Islamaphobia	Subtle sexism
Microaggression	Transphobia
Microassault	

REFERENCES

Becker, J. C., & Swim, J. K. (2012). Reducing endorsement of benevolent and modern sexist beliefs: Differential effects of addressing harm versus pervasiveness of benevolent sexism. *Social Psychology, 43*, 127–137.

Blume, A. W., Lovato, L. V., Thyken, B. N., & Denny, N. (2012). The relationship of microaggressions with alcohol use and anxiety among ethnic minority college students in a historically White institution. *Cultural Diversity and Ethnic Minority Psychology, 18*(1), 45–54.

Bostwick, W., & Hequembourg, A. (2014). "Just a little hint": Bisexual-specific microaggressions and their connection to epistemic injustices. *Culture, Health and Sexuality, 16*(5), 488–503.

Burn, S. M., Kadlec, K., & Rexer, B. S. (2005). Effects of subtle heterosexism on gays, lesbians, and bisexuals. *Journal of Homosexuality, 49*, 23–38.

Burns, C., & Krehely, J. (2011). *Gay and transgender people face high rates of workplace discrimination and harassment.* Retrieved from https://www.americanprogress.org/issues/lgbt /news/2011/06/02/9872/gay-and-transgender -people-face-high-rates-of-workplace-discrimi nation-and-harassment/

Calogero, R. M., & Tylka, T. L. (2014). Sanctioning resistance to sexual objectification: An integrative system justification perspective. *Journal of Social Issues, 70*, 763–778.

Comas-Diaz, L., & Greene, B. (1994). Women of color with professional status. In L. Comas-Diaz & B. Greene (Eds.), *Women of color: Integrating ethnic and gender identities in psychotherapy* (pp. 347–388). New York, NY: Guilford Press.

Corey, G. (2012). *Theory and practice of counseling and psychotherapy*, 9th ed. Belmont, CA: Brooks/Cole.

Cundiff, J. L., Zawadzki, M. J., Danube, C. L., & Shields, S. A. (2014). Using experiential learning to increase the recognition of everyday sexism as harmful: The WAGES intervention. *Journal of Social Issues, 70*, 703–721.

Day, S. X. (2004). *Theory and design in counseling and psychotherapy.* Boston, MA: Houghton Mifflin.

Dovidio, J. F., & Gaertner, S. L. (2000). Aversive racism and selective decisions: 1989–1999. *Psychological Science, 11*, 315–319.

Dovidio, J. F., Gaertner, S. L., Kawakami, K., & Hodson, G. (2002). Why can't we all just get along? Interpersonal biases and interracial distrust. *Cultural Diversity and Ethnic Minority Psychology, 8*, 88–102.

Fang, C. Y., & Meyers, H. F. (2001). The effects of racial stressors and hostility on cardiovascular reactivity in African American and Caucasian men. *Health Psychology, 20*, 64–70.

Franklin, A. J. (2004). *From brotherhood to manhood: How Black men rescue their relationships and dreams from the invisibility syndrome.* Hoboken, NJ: Wiley.

Gaertner, S. L., & Dovidio, J. F. (2006). Understanding and addressing contemporary racism: From aversive racism to the common ingroup. *Journal of Social Issues, 61*(3), 615–639.

Harrell, J. P. (2000). A multidimensional conceptualization of racism-related stress: Implications for the well-being of people of color. *American Journal of Orthopsychiatry, 70*, 42–57.

Harrell, J. P., Hall, S., & Taliaferro, J. (2003). Physiological responses to racism and discrimination: An assessment of the evidence. *American Journal of Public Health, 93*, 243–248.

Hill, D. B., & Willoughby, B.L.B. (2005). The development and validation of the genderism and transphobia scale. *Sex Roles, 53*(7/8), 531–544.

Huber, L. P., & Cueva, B. M. (2012). Chicana/Latina testimonios on effects and responses to microaggressions. *Equity & Excellence in Education, 45*(3), 392–410.

James, E. (2008). Arab culture and Muslim stereotypes. *World and I, 23*(5), 4.

Jones, M. L., & Galliher, R. V. (2015). Daily racial microaggressions and ethnic identification among Native American young adults. *Cultural Diversity and Ethnic Minority Psychology, 21*, 1–9.

Keller, R. M., & Galgay, C. E. (2010). Microaggressive experience of people with disabilities. In D. W. Sue (Ed.), *Microaggressions and marginality* (pp. 241–267). Hoboken, NJ: Wiley.

Kim, J.G.S. (2002). *Racial perceptions and psychological wellbeing in Asian and Hispanic Americans.* Retrieved from Dissertation Abstracts International, *63*(2-B), 1033B.

Krieger, N., & Sidney, S. (1996). Racial discrimination and blood pressure: The CARDIA study of young Black and White adults. *American Journal of Public Health, 86*, 1370–1378.

London, B., Downey, G., Romero-Canyas, R., Rattan, A., & Tyson, D. (2012). Gender-based rejection sensitivity and academic self-silencing in women. *Journal of Personality and Social Psychology, 102*(5), 961–979.

Lui, W. M., & Pope-Davis, D. B. (2005). The working alliance, therapy ruptures and impasses, and counseling competence: Implications for counselor training and education. In R. T. Carter (Ed.), *Handbook of racial-cultural psychology and counseling* (pp. 148–167). Hoboken, NJ: Wiley.

Marzullo, M. A., & Libman, A. J. (2009). *Research overview: Hate crimes and violence against lesbian, gay, bisexual and transgender people.* Report for the Human Rights Campaign Foundation. Retrieved from http://www.hrc.org/resources/entry/hate-crimes-and-violence-against-lgbt-people

Meyer, I. H. (2003). Prejudice, social stress, and mental health in lesbian, gay, and bisexual populations: Conceptual issues and research evidence. *Psychological Bulletin, 129,* 674–697.

Morrison, M. A., & Morrison, T. G. (2002). Development and validation of a scale measuring prejudice toward gay men and lesbian women. *Journal of Homosexuality, 43,* 15–37.

Nadal, K. L. (2013). *That's so gay! Microaggressions and the lesbian, gay, bisexual, and transgender community.* Washington, DC: American Psychological Association.

Nadal, K. L., Issa, M., Griffin, K. E., Hamit, S., & Lyons, O. B. (2010). Religious microaggressions in the United States. In D. W. Sue (Ed.), *Microaggressions and marginality* (pp. 287–310). Hoboken, NJ: Wiley.

Nadal, K. L., Issa, M., Leon, J., Meterko, V., Wideman, M., & Wong, Y. (2011). Sexual orientation microaggressions: "Death by a thousand cuts" for lesbian, gay, and bisexual youth. *Journal of LGBT Youth, 8,* 234–259.

Nadal, K.L., Mazzula, S.L., Rivera, D.P., & Fujii-Doe, W. (2014). Microaggressions and Latina/o Americans: An analysis of nativity, gender, and ethnicity. *Journal of Latina/o Psychology, 2*(2), 67–78.

Nadal, K. L., Rivera, D. P., & Corpus, J. H. (2010). Sexual orientation and transgender microaggressions. In D. W. Sue (Ed.), *Microaggressions and marginality* (pp. 217–240). Hoboken, NJ: Wiley.

Nadal, K. L., Skolnik, A., & Wong, Y. (2012). Interpersonal and systemic microaggressions toward transgender people: Implications for counseling. *Journal of LGBT Issues in Counseling, 6*(1), 55–82.

Nadal, K. L., Wong, Y., Griffin, K., Davidoff, K., & Sriken, J. (2014). The adverse impact of racial microaggressions on college students' self-esteem. *Journal of College Student Development, 55*(5), 461–474.

Offermann, L. R., Basford, T. E., Graebner, R., Jaffer, S., De Graaf, S. B., & Kaminsky, S. E. (2014). See no evil: Colorblindness and perceptions of subtle racial discrimination in the workplace. *Cultural Diversity and Ethnic Minority Psychology, 20*(4), 499–507.

Ong, A. D., Burrow, A. L., Fuller-Rowell, T. E., Ja, N. M., & Sue, D. W. (2013). Racial microaggressions and daily well-being among Asian Americans. *Journal of Counseling Psychology, 60*(2), 188–199.

Owen, J., Tao, K. W., Imel, Z. E., Wampold, B. E., & Rodolfa, E. (2014). Addressing racial and ethnic microaggressions in therapy. *Professional Psychology: Research and Practice, 45*(4), 283–290.

Owen, J., Tao, K., & Rodolfa, E. (2010). Microaggressions and women in short-term therapy: Initial evidence. *Counseling Psychologist, 38*(7), 923–946.

Pierce, C. (1995). Stress analogs of racism and sexism: Terrorism, torture, and disaster. In C. Willie, P. Rieker, B. Kramer, & B. Brown (Eds.), *Mental health, racism, and sexism* (pp. 277–293). Pittsburgh, PA: University of Pittsburgh Press.

Pierce, C., Carew, J., Pierce-Gonzalez, D., & Willis, D. (1978). An experiment in racism: TV commercials. In C. Pierce (Ed.), *Television and education* (pp. 62–88). Beverly Hills, CA: Sage.

Ramirez, E. (2014). Que estoy haciendo aqui? (What am I doing here?): Chicanos/Latinos(as) navigating challenges and inequalities during their first year of graduate school. *Equity & Excellence in Education, 47*(2), 167–186.

Ridley, C. R. (2005). *Overcoming unintentional racism in counseling and therapy* (2nd ed.). Thousand Oaks, CA: Sage.

Rivera, D. P., Forquer, E. E., & Rangel, R. (2010). Microaggressions and the life experience of Latina/o Americans. In D. W. Sue (Ed.), *Microaggressions and marginality* (pp. 59–83). Hoboken, NJ: Wiley.

Rowatt, W. C., Franklin, L. M., & Cotton, M. (2005). Patterns and personality correlates of implicit and explicit attitudes toward Christians and Muslims. *Journal for the Scientific Study of Religion, 44*(1), 29–43.

Schmitt, M. T., Branscombe, N. R., Postmes, T., & Garcia, A. (2014). The consequences of perceived discrimination for psychological well-being: A meta-analytic review. *Psychological Bulletin, 140*(4), 921–948.

Shelton, K., & Delgado-Romero, E. A. (2011). Sexual orientation microaggressions: The experience of lesbian, gay, bisexual, and queer clients in psychotherapy. *Journal of Counseling Psychology, 58*(2), 210–221.

Shelton, K., & Delgado-Romero, E. A. (2013). Sexual orientation microaggressions: The experience of lesbian, gay, bisexual, and queer clients in psychotherapy. *Psychology of Sexual Orientation and Gender Diversity, 1*(S), 59–70.

Smith, L. C., & Shin, R. Q. (2014). Queer blindfolding: A case study on difference "blindness" toward persons who identify as lesbian, gay, bisexual and transgender. *Journal of Homosexuality, 61*, 940–961.

Solórzano, D., Ceja, M., & Yosso, T. (2000). Critical race theory, racial microaggressions, and campus racial climate: The experiences of African American college students. *Journal of Negro Education, 69*(1/2), 60–73.

Strong, S. R. (1969). Counseling: An interpersonal influence process. *Journal of Counseling Psychology, 15*, 215–224.

Sue, D. W. (2004). Whiteness and ethnocentric monoculturalism: Making the invisible visible. *American Psychologist, 59*, 761–769.

Sue, D. W. (2010). *Microaggressions in everyday life: Race, gender, and sexual orientation.* Hoboken, NJ: Wiley.

Sue, D. W., Bucceri, J., Lin, A. I., Nadal, K. L., & Torino, G. C. (2007). Racial microaggressions and the Asian American experience. *Cultural Diversity and Ethnic Minority Psychology, 13*, 72–81. doi: 10.1037/1099–9809.13.1.72

Sue, D. W., Capodilupo, C. M., & Holder, A.M.B. (2008). Racial microaggressions in the life experience of Black Americans. *Professional Psychology: Research and Practice, 39*, 329–336. doi: 10.1037/0735–7028.39.3.329

Sue, D. W., Capodilupo, C. M., Nadal, K. L., & Torino, G. C. (2008). Racial microaggressions and the power to define reality. *American Psychologist, 63*, 277–279.

Sue, D. W., Capodilupo, C. M., Torino, G. C., Bucceri, J. M., Holder, A.M.B., Nadal, K. L., & Esquilin, M. (2007). Racial microaggressions in everyday life: Implications for clinical practice. *American Psychologist, 62*, 271–286. doi: 10.1037/0003–066X.62.4.271

Swim, J. K., & Cohen, L. L. (1997). Overt, covert, and subtle sexism. *Psychology of Women Quarterly, 21*, 103–118.

Swim, J. K., Mallett, R., & Stangor, C. (2004). Understanding subtle sexism: Detection and use of sexist language. *Sex Roles, 51*, 117–128.

Utsey, S. O., Gernat, C. A., & Hammar, L. (2005). Examining white counselor trainees' reactions to racial issues in counseling and supervision dyads. *Counseling Psychologist, 33*, 449–478.

Utsey, S. O., Giesbrecht, N., Hook, J., & Stanard, P. M. (2008). Cultural, sociofamilial, and psychological resources that inhibit psychological distress in African Americans exposed to stressful life events and race related stress. *Journal of Counseling Psychology, 55*, 49–62.

Walls, N. E. (2008). Toward a multidimensional understanding of heterosexism: The changing nature of prejudice. *Journal of Homosexuality, 55*(1), 1–51.

Wang, J., Leu, J., & Shoda, Y. (2011). When the seemingly innocuous "stings": Racial microaggressions and their emotional consequences. *Personality and Social Psychology Bulletin, 37*(12), 1666–1678.

Watkins, N. L., Labarrie, T. L., & Appio, L. M. (2010). Black undergraduates' experiences with perceived racial microaggressions in predominately White colleges and universities. In D. W. Sue (Ed.), *Microaggressions and marginality* (pp. 25–51). Hoboken, NJ: Wiley.

Woodford, M. R., Han, Y., Craig, S., Lim, C., & Matney, M. M. (2013). Discrimination and mental health among sexual minority college students: The type and form of discrimination does matter. *Journal of Gay & Lesbian Mental Health, 18*, 142–163.

Wright, A. J., & Wegner, R. T. (2012). Homonegative microaggressions and their impact on LGB individuals: A measure validity study. *Journal of LGBT Issues in Counseling, 6*, 34–54.

Young, K., Anderson, M., & Stewart, S. (2015). Hierarchical microaggressions in higher education. *Journal of Diversity in Higher Education, 8*(1), 61–71.

PART III

The Practice Dimensions of Multicultural Counseling/Therapy

Barriers to Multicultural Counseling and Therapy

Individual and Family Perspectives

Chapter Objectives

1. Identify the basic values, beliefs, and assumptions that characterize U.S. society, and how these are manifested in counseling practice.

2. Determine how the generic characteristics of counseling and psychotherapy may be barriers to culturally diverse clients.

3. Describe how cultural values of diverse populations may affect the counseling process.

4. Describe how socioeconomic class issues may impact mental health services.

5. Understand *linguistic barriers* likely to arise in working with clients whose first language is not English.

6. Learn how Western definitions of the family may detrimentally impact counseling and therapy with diverse families.

Whereas the previous three chapters dealt with the sociopolitical dynamics affecting multicultural counseling/therapy, this chapter discusses the cultural barriers that may render the helping professional ineffective, thereby denying help to culturally diverse clients. The following case study illustrates important multicultural issues that are related to both individual and family counseling approaches.

THE MARTINEZ FAMILY

Elena Martinez is the second oldest of four siblings, ages 15, 12, 10, and 7. The father is an undocumented immigrant from Mexico, and the mother a naturalized citizen. The family resides in a blue-collar Mexican American neighborhood in San Jose, California. Elena, the identified client, has been reported as having minor problems in school even prior to the "drug-selling incident" that resulted in her referral to the counselor's office. For example, she has "talked back to teachers," refused to do homework assignments, and had "fought" with other students. Because of the seriousness of the drug allegations, the school contacted the parents immediately.

Mrs. B., the counselor, called the parents to set up a day and time to meet at the school. In her conversation with Mrs. Martinez, the mother, Mrs. B. indicated that Elena had been caught by a police officer selling drugs on the school premises, and taken to the vice-principal's office rather than into police custody. After the explanation, Mrs. B. indicated that they should make immediate arrangements for a meeting to have a parent-teacher conference, and determine an appropriate course of action.

According to the counselor, however, Elena's mother seemed hesitant about choosing a time to come and, when pressed by Mrs. B., excused herself from the phone. The counselor reported hearing some whispering on the other end, and then the voice of Mr. Martinez came on the line. She found it difficult to understand Mr. Martinez because he spoke with such a heavy accent and had poor command of English. He immediately asked how his daughter was, and expressed his consternation over the entire incident. The counselor stated she understood his feelings, but it would be best to set up an appointment for tomorrow to discuss the matter.

The counselor asked repeatedly about a convenient time, but Mr. Martinez seemed to avoid the answer and to give excuses. He had to work tomorrow, and could not make the appointment. The counselor stressed strongly how important the meeting was for the daughter's welfare and that several missed hours of work were unimportant in light of the seriousness of the situation. Mr. Martinez suggested the possibility of a home visit, but Mrs. B. said it was impractical. The father then indicated he could make an evening or even a weekend appointment, but the counselor informed him that school policy prohibited evening meetings and she did not work over the weekend. Finally, the counselor suggested that the wife could initially come alone, but Mr. Martinez remained silent. With great reluctance, however, the father agreed to attend with his wife.

The very next day, Mr. and Mrs. Martinez showed up with a brother-in-law (Elena's godfather) at the office. The counselor was clearly upset by the presence of a third party and told the Martinezes that she wished to only speak with the immediate family, and that having another person present would complicate the matter. Whatever they discussed was confidential. Because both parents appeared anxious, the counselor tried to make the situation more personal and casual by addressing both by their first names: Miguel and Esmeralda.

The following day Mrs. B. reported to the school principal the session went poorly with minimal cooperation from the parents. She reported "It was like pulling teeth, trying to get the Martinezes to say anything at all. They were quite guarded and did not seem to understand the seriousness of Elena's behavior."

REFLECTION AND DISCUSSION QUESTIONS

1. What are some possible cultural factors that might be influencing the reactions of the Martinezes?

2. How might socioeconomic factors be affecting the father's response to a request for a meeting?

3. Why do you think the Martinezes had the godfather attend?

4. What role might being an undocumented immigrant play in Mr. Martinez's reluctance to use school or public services?

4. Do you believe that the Martinezes were uninvolved and uncaring parents?

5. If you were a helping professional, when would you consider making home visits? Under what conditions?

IDENTIFYING MULTICULTURAL COUNSELING ISSUES

The interplay of cultural differences and counseling approaches in the case of Elena is both complex and difficult to resolve. They challenge counseling/mental health professionals to (a) understand the worldviews, cultural values, and life circumstances of their culturally diverse clients; (b) free themselves from the cultural conditioning of what they believe is correct therapeutic practice; (c) develop new but culturally sensitive methods of working with clients; and (d) play new roles in the helping process outside of conventional psychotherapy. Let us briefly outline some cultural, class, linguistic, and political issues raised in this case.

Egalitarian versus Patriarchal Roles

It is entirely possible that the incidents reported by the counselor, Mrs. B., meant something quite different in traditional Mexican American culture. In this case, Mrs. B. seems unaware of her value system of egalitarianism in the husband–wife relationship. The Martinezes' division of roles (husband is protector/provider while wife cares for the home/family) may be *patriarchal* and allows both to exercise influence and to make decisions. Breaking the role divisions (especially by the woman) is done only out of necessity. A wife would be remiss in publicly making a family decision (setting up an appointment time) without consulting or obtaining agreement from the husband. Mrs. Martinez's hesitation on the phone may be a reflection of the husband–wife role relationship rather than a lack of concern for the daughter.

The counselor's insistence in having Mrs. Martinez decide may actually be forcing her to violate appropriate role behaviors. Further, the therapist's attempt to be informal and to put the Martinezes at ease by greeting them by first names (Miguel and Esmeralda) as opposed to a more formal title (Mr. and Mrs. Martinez), may have been a therapeutic mistake. In traditional Latino and Asian families, such initial informality and familiarity may be considered a lack of respect for the man's role as head of the household.

Nuclear versus Extended Families

Mrs. B. may also have seriously undermined the Latino/a concept of the *extended family* by expressing negativism toward the godfather's attendance at the counseling session. Middle-class White Americans consider the family to be the nuclear unit (husband, wife, and biological children), while most people of color define the family unit as an extended one. A Mexican American child can acquire a godmother (*madrina*) and a godfather (*padrino*) through a baptismal ceremony. Unlike in most White American families, the role of godparents in Mexican culture is more than symbolic, as they can become coparents (*compadre*) and take an active part in raising the child. Indeed, the role of the godparents is usually linked to the moral, religious, and spiritual upbringing of the child. Who else would be more appropriate to attend the counseling session than the godfather? Not only is he a member of the family, but the charges against Elena deal with legal and moral/ethical issues. It is obvious that Mrs. B. did not view the godfather as part of the family or understand his role in Elena's moral/ethical upbringing.

Socioeconomic Class Issues

Mrs. B. seems oblivious to the economic impact that missing a couple of hours' work might have on the family. Again, she tended to equate Mr. Martinez's reluctance to take off work for the "welfare of her daughter" as evidence of the parents' disinterest in their child. Trivializing the missing of work reveals major *social class/work* differences that often exist between mental health professionals and those from situations of less affluence. Most professionals are able to take time off for dental appointments, teacher conferences, or other personal needs without loss of income. This indeed is a middle- or upper-class luxury generally unavailable to those who face economic hardships or cannot access a flexible work schedule. For the Martinez family, loss of even a few hours' wages has serious financial repercussions. Most blue-collar workers may not have the luxury or options of making up their work. How, for example, would an assembly-line worker make up lost time when the plant closes at the end of the day? In addition, the worker often does not miss just a few hours, but must take a half or full day off. In many work situations, getting a substitute worker for just a few hours is not practical. To entice replacement workers, the company must offer more than a few hours (full day). Thus Mr. Martinez may actually be losing an entire day's wages! His reluctance to miss work may actually represent *high concern* for the family rather than *lack of concern*.

Flexible Alternative Services

The case of Elena raises another important question: What obligation do educational and mental health services have toward offering flexible and culturally appropriate services to their communities? Mr. Martinez's desire for a "home visit" or evening/weekend meetings brings this question into perspective. Must communities of color always conform to system rules and regulations in order to obtain services? We are not arguing with the school policy itself—in some schools there are very legitimate reasons for not staying after school hours. What we are arguing for is the need to provide alternative services to communities that fit their lifestyles and unique situations. It seems that meeting the needs of the M. family might have entailed home visits or some other arrangement, or flexible scheduling. If the M. family was unable to travel to the therapist's office for a conference, what blocked Mrs. B. from considering a home visit? Many therapists feel disinclined, fearful, or uncomfortable with such an arrangement. Their training dictates that they should practice in their offices and clients should come to them.

Linguistic Bias

Mrs. B. seems unaware that linguistic factors may be influencing the verbal participation of the parents. The counselor has already noted the "heavy accent" and limited English proficiency of Mr. Martinez. Their lack of verbal participation in the session may be due to this factor. Language barriers often place culturally diverse clients at a disadvantage. The primary medium by which mental health professionals do their work is through verbalization (talk therapies) via Standard English. Clients who do not speak Standard English, possess a pronounced accent, or have limited command of English (such as the M. family) may be victimized. The need to understand the meaning of linguistic differences and language barriers in counseling and psychotherapy has never been greater. The changing demographics may mean that many of our clients are born outside of the United States and speak English as their second language. In many cultures, mental health concepts are not equivalent to those in the United States. For example, mental health concepts in English often do not translate into equivalent language in Spanish.

Immigration Status

Mr. Martinez is an undocumented immigrant. What does that mean? It means he lives in the shadows of society, in constant fear of deportation, creditors, and especially the police. It means he faces abuses, resentments, and discrimination that create continual stress in his life and those of the family. It means he hides from public view, distrusts official contact with public services, and fears the loss of social services to his family. Studies reveal that undocumented immigrants like Mr. Martinez are more likely to suffer from depression, anxiety and medical problems, but are less likely to seek help for fear of being "outed." Thus another factor contributing to his reluctance to attend a school parent-teacher conference may be related to his legal status as an undocumented immigrant, and not lack of caring and concern for his daughter.

GENERIC CHARACTERISTICS OF COUNSELING/THERAPY

All theories of counseling and psychotherapy are influenced by assumptions that theorists make regarding the goals for therapy, the methodology used to invoke change, and the definition of mental health and mental illness (Corey, 2013). Counseling and psychotherapy have traditionally been conceptualized in Western individualistic terms (Ivey, Ivey, Myers, & Sweeney, 2005). Whether the particular theory is psychodynamic, existential-humanistic, or cognitive behavioral in orientation, a number of multicultural specialists (Ponterotto, Utsey, & Pedersen, 2006; Ivey, Ivey, & Zalaquett, 2014) indicate that they share certain common components of White culture in their values and beliefs. Katz (1985) has described the components of White culture (see Table 7.1) that are reflected in the goals and processes of clinical work.

TABLE 7.1 Components of White Culture: Values and Beliefs	
Rugged Individualism	**Protestant Work Ethic**
Individual is primary unit	Working hard brings success
Individual has primary responsibility	**Progress and Future Orientation**
Independence and autonomy highly valued and rewarded	Plan for future
Individual can control environment	Delay gratification
Competition	Value continual improvement and progress
Winning is everything	**Emphasis on Scientific Method**
Win/lose dichotomy	Objective, rational, linear thinking
Action Orientation	Cause-and-effect relationships
Must master and control nature	Quantitative emphasis
Must always do something about a situation	**Status and Power**
Pragmatic/utilitarian view of life	Measured by economic possessions
Communication	Credentials, titles, and positions
Standard English	Believe "own" system
Written tradition	Believe better than other systems
Direct eye contact	Owning goods, space, property
Limited physical contact	**Family Structure**
Control of emotions	Nuclear family is the ideal social unit
Time	Male is breadwinner and the head of the household
Adherence to rigid time	Female is homemaker and subordinate to the husband
Time is viewed as a commodity	Patriarchal structure
Holidays	**Aesthetics**
Based on Christian religion	Music and art based on European cultures
Based on White history and male leaders	Women's beauty based on blonde, blue-eyed, thin, young
History	Men's attractiveness based on athletic ability, power, economic status
Based on European immigrants' experience in the United States	**Religion**
Romanticize war	Belief in Christianity
	No tolerance for deviation from single god concept

Source: From *The Counseling Psychologist* (p. 618) by J. Katz, 1985, Beverly Hills, CA: Sage. Copyright 1985 by Sage Publications, Inc. Reprinted by permission.

In the United States and in many other countries as well, psychotherapy and counseling are used mainly with middle- and upper-class segments of the population (Smith, 2010). These have often been referred to as the "generic characteristics" of counseling (see Table 7.2). As a result, culturally diverse clients do not share many of the values and characteristics seen in both the goals and the processes of therapy (American Psychological Association, Task Force on Socioeconomic Status, 2007; Reed & Smith, 2014). Schofield (1964) has noted that therapists tend to prefer clients who exhibit the *YAVIS syndrome*: young, attractive, verbal, intelligent, and successful. This preference tends to discriminate against people from different minority groups or those from lower socioeconomic classes. This situation led Sundberg (1981) to sarcastically point out that therapy is not for *QUOID* people (quiet, ugly, old, indigent, and dissimilar culturally). Table 7.3 summarizes these generic characteristics of counseling (culture, class, and linguistic), and compares them to four groups of color. As mentioned earlier, such a comparison can also be done for other groups that vary in gender, age, sexual orientation, ability/disability, and so on.

TABLE 7.2 Generic Characteristics of Counseling

Culture	Middle Class	Language
Standard English	Standard English	Standard English
Verbal communication	Verbal communication	Verbal communication
Individual centered	Adherence to time schedules (50-minute sessions)	
Verbal/emotional/behavioral expressiveness	Long-range goals	
Client-counselor communication		
Openness and intimacy		
Cause-effect orientation		
Clear distinction between physical and mental well-being		
Nuclear family		

TABLE 7.3 People of Color Group Variables

Culture	Lower Class	Language
	Asian Americans	
Asian language	Nonstandard English	Bilingual background
Family centered	Action oriented	
Restraint of feelings	Different time perspective	
Silence is respect	Immediate, short-range goals	

Advice seeking

Well-defined patterns of interaction (concrete structured)

Private versus public display (shame/disgrace/pride)

Physical and mental well-being defined differently

Extended family

African Americans		
Black language	Nonstandard English	Black language
Sense of "people-hood"	Action oriented	
Action oriented	Different time perspective	
Paranorm due to oppression	Immediate, short-range goals	
Importance placed on nonverbal behavior	Concrete, tangible, structured approach	
Extended family		
Latino/Hispanic Americans		
Spanish-speaking	Nonstandard English	Bilingual background
Group centered	Action oriented	
Temporal difference	Different time perspective	
Family orientation	Extended family	
Different pattern of communication	Immediate short-range goals	
Religious distinction between mind/body	Concrete, tangible, structured approach	
American Indians		
Tribal dialects	Nonstandard English	Bilingual background
Cooperative, not competitive individualism	Action oriented	
Present time orientation	Different time perspective	
Creative/experimental/intuitive/nonverbal	Immediate, short-range goals	
Satisfy present needs	Concrete, tangible, structured approach	
Use of folk or supernatural explanations		
Extended family		

Although an attempt has been made to clearly delineate three major variables that influence effective therapy, these are often inseparable from one another. For example, use of Standard English in counseling and therapy definitely places those individuals who do not speak English fluently at a disadvantage (Ngo-Metzger et al., 2003). However, cultural and class values that govern conversation conventions can also operate via language to cause serious misunderstandings. Furthermore, the fact that many African Americans, Latina/o Americans, and American Indians come from less affluent backgrounds often compounds class and culture variables. Thus it is often difficult to tell which variables are the most important impediments in therapy. Nevertheless, this distinction is valuable in conceptualizing barriers to effective multicultural counseling/therapy.

CULTURE-BOUND VALUES

Culture consists of all those things that people have learned to do, believe, value, and enjoy. It is the totality of the ideals, beliefs, skills, tools, customs, and institutions into which members of society are born (Ratts & Pedersen, 2014). Although being *bicultural* is a source of strength, the process of negotiating dual group membership may cause problems for many marginalized group members. The term *marginal person* was first coined by Stonequist (1937) and refers to a person's inability to form dual ethnic identification because of *bicultural* membership. Persons of color are placed under strong pressures to adopt the ways of the dominant culture. The cultural-deficit models tend to view culturally diverse groups as possessing dysfunctional values and belief systems that are often considered handicaps to be overcome and a source of shame. In essence, marginalized groups may be taught that to be different is to be deviant, pathological, or sick. Several culture-bound characteristics of therapy may be responsible for reinforcing negative beliefs.

Focus on the Individual

Most forms of counseling and psychotherapy tend to be *individual-centered* (i.e., they emphasize the "I-thou" relationship). Ivey et al. (2014) note that U.S. culture and society are based on the concept of *individualism* and that competition between individuals for status, recognition, achievement, and so forth, forms the basis for Western tradition. *Individualism*, autonomy, and the ability to become your own person are perceived as healthy and desirable goals. Pedersen and Pope (2010) note that not all cultures view *individualism* as a positive orientation; rather, it may be perceived in some cultures as a handicap to attaining enlightenment, one that may divert us from important spiritual goals. In many non-Western cultures, identity is not seen apart from the group orientation (*collectivism*). The notion of *atman* in India defines itself as participating in unity with all things and not being limited by the temporal world.

Many societies do not define the psychosocial unit of operation as the individual. In many cultures and subgroups, the psychosocial unit of operation tends to be the family, group, or collective society. In traditional Asian American culture, one's identity is defined within the family constellation. The greatest punitive measure to be taken out on an individual by the family is to be disowned. What this means, in essence, is that the person no longer has an identity. Although being disowned by a family in Western European culture is equally negative and punitive, it does not have the same connotations as in traditional Asian society. Although they may be disowned by a family, Westerners are always told that they have an individual identity as well. Likewise, many Hispanic individuals tend to see the unit of operation as residing within the family. African American psychologists (Parham, Ajamu, & White, 2011) also point out how the African view of the world encompasses the concept of "groupness."

Collectivism is often reflected in many aspects of behavior. Traditional Asian American and Hispanic elders, for example, tend to greet one another with the question, "How is your family today?" Contrast this with how most Americans tend to greet each other: "How are you today?" One emphasizes the family (group) perspective, while the other emphasizes the individual perspective. Likewise, affective expressions in therapy can also be strongly influenced by the particular orientation one takes. When individuals engage in wrongful behaviors in the United States, they are most likely to experience feelings of guilt. In societies that emphasize *collectivism*, however, the most dominant affective element to follow a wrongful behavior is shame, not guilt. Guilt is an individual affect, whereas shame appears to be a group one (it reflects on the family or group).

Verbal/Emotional/Behavioral Expressiveness

Many counselors and therapists tend to emphasize the fact that verbal/emotional/behavioral expressiveness is important in individuals. As therapists, we like our clients to be verbal, articulate, and able to express their thoughts and feelings clearly. Indeed, therapy is often referred to as talk therapy, indicating the importance placed on Standard English as the medium of expression. *Emotional expressiveness* is also valued, as we like individuals to be in touch with their feelings and to be able to verbalize their emotional reactions. We also value behavioral expressiveness and believe that it is important as well. We like individuals to be assertive, to stand up for their own rights, and to engage in activities that indicate they are not passive beings.

All these characteristics of therapy can place culturally diverse clients at a disadvantage. For example, Native Americans and Asian Americans tend not to value verbalizations in the same way as White Americans. In traditional Chinese culture, children have been taught not to speak until spoken to. Patterns of communication tend to be vertical, flowing from those of higher prestige and status to those of lower prestige and status. In a therapy situation, many Chinese clients, to show respect for a therapist who is older and wiser and who occupies a position of higher status, may respond with silence. Unfortunately, an unenlightened counselor or therapist may perceive this client as being inarticulate and less intelligent.

Emotional expressiveness in counseling and psychotherapy is frequently a highly desired goal. Yet many cultural groups value restraint of strong feelings. For example, traditional Latino/a and Asian cultures emphasize that maturity and wisdom are associated with one's ability to control emotions and feelings. This applies not only to public expressions of anger and frustration but also to public expressions of love and affection. Unfortunately, therapists unfamiliar with these cultural ramifications may perceive their clients in a very negative psychiatric light. Indeed, these clients are often described as inhibited, lacking in spontaneity, or repressed.

In therapy it has become increasingly popular to emphasize expressiveness in a behavioral sense. For example, one need only note the proliferation of cognitive-behavioral assertiveness training programs throughout the United States (Craske, 2010) and the number of self-help books that are being published in the popular mental health literature. This orientation fails to realize that there are cultural groups in which subtlety is a highly prized art. Yet doing things indirectly can be perceived by the mental health professional as evidence of passivity and a need for an individual to learn assertiveness skills. In their excellent review of assertiveness training, Wood and Mallinckrodt (1990) warn that therapists need to make certain that gaining such skills is a value shared by a client of color, and not imposed by therapists.

Insight

Another generic characteristic of counseling is the use of *insight* in both counseling and psychotherapy. This approach assumes that it is mentally beneficial for individuals to obtain *insight* or understanding into their underlying dynamics and motivations (Corey, 2013; Levenson, 2010). Educated in the tradition of psychoanalytic theory, many theorists tend to believe that clients who obtain better *insight* into themselves will be better adjusted. Although many behavioral schools of thought may not subscribe to this, most therapists use *insight* in their individual practice, either as a process of therapy or as an end product or goal (Antony & Roemer, 2011).

We need to realize that *insight* is not highly valued by many culturally diverse clients. There are major class differences as well (APA Task Force on Socioeconomic Status, 2007). People from lower socioeconomic classes frequently do not perceive *insight* as appropriate to their life situations and circumstances. Their concern may revolve around such questions as, "Where do I find a job?" "How do I feed my family?" and "How can I afford to take my sick daughter to a doctor?" When survival on a day-to-day basis is important, it seems inappropriate for the therapist to use insightful processes. After all, *insight* assumes that one has time to sit back, reflect, and contemplate motivations and behavior. For the individual who is concerned about making it through each day, this orientation proves counterproductive (Reed & Smith, 2014).

Likewise, many cultural groups do not value *insight*. In traditional Chinese society, psychology has little relevance. It must be noted, however, that a client who does not seem to work well in an *insight* approach may not be lacking in *insight* or psychological-mindedness. A person who does not value *insight* is not necessarily one who is incapable of *insight*. Simply put, many cultural groups do not value this method of self-exploration. It is interesting to note that many Asian elders believe that thinking too much about something can cause problems. Many older Chinese believe the road to mental health is to "avoid morbid thoughts." Advice from Asian elders to their children when they are frustrated, angry, depressed, or anxious is simply, "Don't think about it." Indeed, it is often believed that experiencing anger or depression is related to cognitive rumination. The traditional Asian way of handling these affective elements is to "keep busy and don't think about it."

Self-Disclosure (Openness and Intimacy)

Most forms of counseling and psychotherapy tend to value one's ability to self-disclose and to talk about the most intimate aspects of one's life. Indeed, self-disclosure has often been discussed as a primary characteristic of a healthy personality. Clients who do not self-disclose readily in counseling and psychotherapy are seen to possess negative features, i.e., being guarded, mistrustful, or paranoid.

There are two difficulties in this orientation toward self-disclosure: cultural and sociopolitical.

First, intimate revelations of personal or social problems may not be acceptable to Asian Americans because such admissions reflect not only on the individual but also on the whole family (Chang, McDonald, & O'Hara, 2014). Thus the family may exert strong pressures on the Asian American client not to reveal personal matters to strangers or outsiders. Similar conflicts have been reported for Hispanics (Torres-Rivera & Ratts, 2014) and American Indian clients (Thomason, 2014). A therapist who works with a client from a different cultural background may erroneously conclude that the person is repressed, inhibited, shy, or passive. All these traits are seen as undesirable by Western standards.

Related to this example is many health practitioners' belief in the desirability of self-disclosure. Self-disclosure refers to clients' willingness to tell therapists what they feel, believe, or think. Jourard (1964) suggests that mental health is related to one's openness in disclosing. Although this may be true, the parameters need clarification. As mentioned in Chapter 4, people of African descent are especially reluctant to disclose to White counselors because of hardships that they have experienced via racism (Ratts & Pedersen, 2014). African Americans initially perceive a White therapist more often as an agent of society who may use information against them, rather than as a person of good will. From the African American perspective, noncritical self-disclosure to others is not healthy.

The actual structure of the therapy situation may also work against intimate revelations. Among many American Indians and Hispanics, intimate aspects of life are shared only with close friends. Relative to White middle-class standards, deep friendships are developed only after prolonged contacts. Once friendships are formed, they tend to be lifelong in nature. In contrast, White Americans form relationships quickly, but the relationships do not necessarily persist over long periods of time. Counseling and therapy also seem to reflect these values. Clients talk about the most intimate aspects of their lives with a relative stranger once every week for a 50-minute session. To many culturally diverse groups who stress friendship as a precondition to self-disclosure, the counseling process seems utterly inappropriate and absurd. After all, how is it possible to develop a friendship with brief contacts once a week?

Scientific Empiricism

Counseling and psychotherapy in Western culture and society have been described as being highly linear, analytic, and verbal in their attempt to mimic the physical sciences. As indicated by Table 7.1, Western society tends to emphasize the so-called scientific method, which involves objective, rational, linear thinking. Likewise, we often see descriptions of therapists as objective, neutral, rational, and logical (Utsey, Walker, & Kwate, 2005). Therapists rely heavily on the use of linear problem solving, as well as on quantitative evaluation that includes psychodiagnostic tests, intelligence tests, personality inventories, and so forth. This cause–effect orientation emphasizes left-brain functioning. That is, theories of counseling and therapy are distinctly analytical, rational, and verbal, and they strongly stress the discovery of cause–effect relationships.

The emphasis on symbolic logic contrasts markedly with the philosophies of many cultures that value a more nonlinear, holistic, and harmonious approach to the world (Sue, 2015). For example, American Indian worldviews emphasize the harmonious aspects of the world, intuitive functioning, and a holistic approach—a worldview characterized by right-brain activities, minimizing analytical and reductionistic inquiries. Thus, when American Indians undergo therapy, the analytic approach may violate their basic philosophy of life (Garrett & Portman, 2011).

In the mental health fields, the most dominant way of asking and answering questions about the human condition tends to be the scientific method. The epitome of this approach is the *experiment*. In graduate schools we are often told that only through the experiment can we impute a cause–effect relationship. By identifying the independent and dependent variables and controlling for extraneous variables, we are able to test a cause–effect hypothesis. Although correlation studies, historical research, and other approaches may be of benefit, we are told that the experiment represents the epitome of our science. Other cultures, however, may value different ways of asking and answering questions about the human condition. We will explore this worldview in Chapter 10.

Distinctions Between Mental and Physical Functioning

Many American Indians, Asian Americans, African Americans, and Latinos hold different concepts of what constitutes mental health, mental illness, and adjustment. Among the Chinese, the concept of mental health or psychological well-being is not understood in the same way as it is in the Western context. Latino/a Americans do not make the same Western distinction between mental and physical health as do their White counterparts (Guzman & Carrasco, 2011). Thus nonphysical health problems are most likely to be referred to a physician, priest, or minister. Culturally diverse clients operating under this orientation may enter therapy expecting therapists to treat them in the same manner that doctors or priests do. Immediate solutions and concrete tangible forms of treatment (advice, confession, consolation, and medication) are expected.

Patterns of Communication

The cultural upbringing of many minorities dictates different patterns of communication that may place them at a disadvantage in therapy. Counseling, for example, initially demands that communication move from client to counselor. The client is expected to take the major responsibility for initiating conversation in the session, while the counselor plays a less active role.

However, American Indians, Asian Americans, and Latinos function under different cultural imperatives, which may make this difficult. These three groups may have been reared to respect elders and authority figures and not to speak until spoken to. Clearly defined roles of dominance and deference are established in the traditional family. Evidence indicates that Asians associate mental health with exercising will power, avoiding unpleasant thoughts, and occupying one's mind with positive thoughts. Therapy is seen as an authoritative process in which a good therapist is more direct and active and portrays a kind of father figure. A racial/ethnic minority client who is asked to initiate conversation may become uncomfortable and respond with only short phrases or statements. The therapist may be prone to interpret the behavior negatively, when in actuality it may be a sign of respect. We have much more to say about these communication style differences in the next chapter.

CLASS-BOUND VALUES

Social class and classism have been identified as two of the most overlooked topics in psychology and mental health practice (American Psychological Association, Task Force on Socioeconomic Status, 2007). Although many believe that the gap in income is closing, statistics suggest the opposite—income inequality is increasing. Those in the top 5% of income have enjoyed huge increases, whereas those in the bottom 40% are stagnant (American Psychological Association, Task Force on Socioeconomic Status, 2007). In the United States, 46 million Americans live in poverty; Blacks are three times more likely to live in poverty than Whites; the rate of poverty for Latinos is nearly 27%; for Asian/Pacific Islanders it is 11%; and for Whites it is 8% (Fouad & Chavez-Korell, 2014; Liu et al., 2004). These statistics clearly suggest that *social class* may be intimately linked to race because many racial/ethnic minority groups are disproportionately represented in the lower socioeconomic classes (Smith, 2010).

Impact of Poverty

Research indicates that lower socioeconomic class is related to higher incidence of depression (Lorant et al., 2003), lower sense of control (Chen, Matthews, & Boyce, 2002), poorer physical health (Gallo & Matthews, 2003), and exclusion from the mainstream of society (Reed & Smith, 2014). Mental health professionals are not often aware of additional stressors likely to confront clients who lack financial resources, nor do they fully appreciate how those stressors affect their clients' daily lives. For the therapist who comes from a middle- to upper-class background, it is often difficult to relate to the circumstances and hardships affecting the client who lives in poverty (cf. the case of Elena Martinez).

The phenomenon of poverty and its effects on individuals and institutions can be devastating (Liu, Hernandez, Mahmood, & Stinson, 2006). The individual's life is characterized by low wages, unemployment, underemployment, little property ownership, no savings, and lack of food reserves. Meeting even the most basic needs of food and shelter is in constant jeopardy. Pawning personal possessions and borrowing money at exorbitant interest rates leads only to greater debt. Feelings of helplessness, dependence, and inferiority develop easily under these circumstances. Therapists may unwittingly attribute attitudes that result from physical and environmental adversity to the cultural or individual traits of the person. Likewise, poverty may cause many parents to encourage children to seek employment at an early age. Delivering groceries, shining shoes, and hustling other sources of income may sap the energy of the schoolchild, leading to truancy and poor performance. Teachers and counselors may view such students as unmotivated and potential juvenile delinquents.

Therapeutic Class Bias

Considerable bias against people who are poor has been well documented (American Psychological Association, Task Force on Socioeconomic Status, 2007; Smith, 2013). It is clear to us that those who occupy the lower rungs of our society are the most likely to be oppressed and harmed. For example, clinicians perceive lower-social-class clients more unfavorably than upper-social-class clients (as having less education, being dysfunctional, and making poor progress in therapy). Research concerning the inferior and biased quality of treatment of lower-class clients is historically legend (American Psychological Association, Task Force on Socioeconomic Status, 2007). In the area of diagnosis, it has been found that an attribution of mental illness was more likely when the person's history suggested a lower rather than higher socioeconomic class origin (Liu et al., 2006). Many studies seem to demonstrate that clinicians given identical test protocols tend to make more negative prognostic statements and judgments of greater maladjustment when the individual was said to come from a lower- rather than a middle-class background.

In addition, the class-bound nature of mental health practice emphasizes the importance of assisting the client in self-direction through presenting the results of assessment instruments and through self-exploration via verbal interactions between client and therapist. However, the assumptions underlying these activities are permeated by middle-class values that do not suffice for those living in poverty. As early as the 1960s, Bernstein (1964) investigated the suitability of Standard English for the lower class in psychotherapy and concluded that it works to the detriment of those individuals. In an extensive historic research of services delivered to minorities and low socioeconomic clients, Lorion (1973) found that psychiatrists refer to therapy those persons who are most like themselves—White rather than non-White and from upper socioeconomic status. Lorion (1974) pointed out that the expectations of lower-class clients are often different from those of psychotherapists. For example, lower-class clients who are concerned with survival or making it through on a day-to-day basis expect advice and suggestions from the counselor.

Appointments made weeks in advance with short, weekly, 50-minute contacts are not consistent with the need to seek immediate solutions. Additionally, many lower-class people, through multiple experiences with public agencies, operate under what is called *minority standard time* (Schindler-Rainman, 1967). This is the tendency of poor people to have a low regard for punctuality. Poor people have learned that endless waits are associated with medical clinics, police stations, and government agencies. One usually waits hours for a 10- to 15-minute appointment. Arriving promptly does little good and can be a waste of valuable time. Therapists, however, rarely understand this aspect of life and are prone to see late arrival as a sign of indifference or hostility.

People from a lower socioeconomic status may also view *insight* and attempts to discover underlying intrapsychic problems as inappropriate. Many lower-class clients expect to receive advice or some form of concrete tangible treatment. When the therapist attempts to explore personality dynamics or to take a historical approach to the problem, the client often becomes confused, alienated, and frustrated. A harsh environment, where the future is uncertain and immediate needs must be met, makes long-range planning of little value. Many clients of lower socioeconomic status are unable to relate to the future orientation of therapy. To be able to sit and talk about things is perceived as a luxury of the middle and upper classes.

Because of the lower-class client's environment and past inexperience with therapy, the expectations of the individual may be quite different from those of the therapist, or even negative. The client's unfamiliarity with the therapy process may hinder success and cause the therapist to blame the client for the failure. Thus the client may be perceived as hostile and resistant. The results of this interaction may be a premature termination of therapy. Considerable evidence exists that clients from upper socioeconomic backgrounds have significantly more exploratory interviews with their therapists and that middle-class patients tend to remain in treatment longer than lower-class patients (Gottesfeld, 1995; Leong, Wagner, & Kim, 1995; Neighbors, Caldwell, Thompson, & Jackson, 1994). Furthermore, the now-classic study of Hollingshead and Redlich (1968) found that lower-class patients tend to have fewer ego-involving relationships and less intensive therapeutic relationships than do members of higher socioeconomic classes.

Poverty undoubtedly contributes to the mental health problems among racial/ethnic minority groups, and *social class* determines the type of treatment a minority client is likely to receive. In addition, as Atkinson, Morten, and Sue (1998, p. 64) conclude, "Ethnic minorities are less likely to earn incomes sufficient to pay for mental health treatment, less likely to have insurance, and more likely to qualify for public assistance than European Americans. Thus ethnic minorities often have to rely on public (government-sponsored) or nonprofit mental health services to obtain help with their psychological problems."

Working effectively with clients who are poor requires several major conditions. First, the therapist must spend time understanding his or her own biases and prejudices. Not confronting one's own classist attitudes can lead to a phenomenon called "White trashism." Manifestation of prejudicial or negative attitudes can be found in such descriptors as "trailer parkism," "hillbillyism," "uppity," "red-neck," and so on (Smith, 2013). These attitudes can affect the diagnosis and treatment of clients. Second, it becomes essential that counselors understand how poverty affects the lives of people who lack financial resources; behaviors associated with survival should not be pathologized. Third, counselors should consider that a more active approach in treatment, along with a taboo against information-giving activities, might be more appropriate than the passive, insight-oriented, and long-term models of therapy. Last, poverty and the economic disparities that are root causes affecting the mental health and quality of life of people in our society demand a social justice approach.

Several conclusions can be drawn from these findings: (a) low socioeconomic class presents stressors to people, especially those in poverty, and may seriously undermine the mental and physical health of clients; (b) a failure to understand the life circumstance of clients who lack financial resources, along with an unintentional class bias, may affect the ability of helping professionals to deliver appropriate mental health services; and (c) classism and its discriminating nature can make its appearance in the assessment, diagnosis, and treatment of lower socioeconomic clients.

LANGUAGE BARRIERS

Ker Moua, a Laotian refugee, suffered from a variety of ailments but was unable to communicate with her doctor. The medical staff enlisted the aid of 12-year-old Jue as the liaison between the doctor and the mother. Ker was diagnosed with a prolapsed uterus, the result of bearing 12 children. She took medication in the doses described by her son but became severely ill after two days. Fortunately, it was discovered that she was taking an incorrect dosage that could have caused lasting harm. The hospital staff realized that Jue had mistranslated the doctor's orders. When inquiries about the translation occurred, Jue said, "I don't know what a uterus is. The doctor tells me things I don't know how to say." (Burke, 2005, p. 5B)

Asking children to translate information concerning medical or legal problems is common in many communities with high immigrant and refugee populations but may have devastating consequences: (a) It can create stress and hurt the traditional parent–child relationship; (b) children lack the vocabulary and emotional maturity to serve as effective interpreters; (c) children may be placed in a situation where they are privy to confidential medical or psychiatric information about their relatives; and (d) they may be unfairly burdened with emotional responsibilities that only adults should carry (Coleman, 2003). In 2008, California Assembly Bill 775 was introduced to ban the use of children as interpreters. Further, the federal government has acknowledged that not providing adequate interpretation for client populations is a form of discrimination. The National Council on Interpreting in Health Care (2005) published national standards for interpreters of health care that address issues of cultural awareness and confidentiality.

These standards were based upon a number of important findings derived from focus groups of immigrants (Ngo-Metzger et al., 2003). First, nearly all immigrants interviewed expressed a preference for professional translators rather than family members. They wanted translators who were knowledgeable and respectful of their cultural customs. Second, using family members to interpret—especially children—was negatively received for fear of their inability to translate correctly. Third, discussing very personal or familial issues was often very uncomfortable (shame, guilt, and other emotional reactions) when a family member acted as the interpreter. Last, there was great concern that interpretation by a family member could be affected by the family dynamics or vice versa. Some general guidelines in selecting and working with interpreters are the following:

- Make sure that professional interpreters speak the same dialect. Monitor carefully whether the interpreter and client appear to have significant cultural or social differences.

- Establish a degree of familiarity with the interpreters; they should be understanding and comfortable with your therapeutic style. Use the same interpreter consistently with the same client.

- Be aware that the interpreter is not just an empty box in the therapeutic relationship. Rather than a two-person interaction in counseling, it is most likely a three-person alliance. Clients may initially develop a stronger relationship with the interpreter than with the counselor.

- Provide plenty of extra time in the counseling session.

- Ensure that the interpreter realizes the code of confidentiality.

- If you believe the interpreters are not fully translating and/or are interjecting their own beliefs, opinions, and assumptions, it is important to have a frank and open discussion about your observations.

- Be aware that interpreters may also experience intense emotions when traumatic events are discussed. Be alert for overidentification or countertransference. The therapist may need to work closely with the interpreter, allowing interpreters periodic debriefing sessions.

Clearly, use of Standard English in health care delivery may unfairly discriminate against those from a bilingual or lower socioeconomic background and result in devastating consequences (Ratts & Pedersen, 2014; Vedantam, 2005). This inequity occurs in our educational system and in the delivery of mental health services as well. Schwartz, Rodriguez, Santiago-Rivera, Arredondo, and Field (2010) indicate that psychologists are finding that they must interact with clients who may have English as a second language or who may not speak English at all. The lack of bilingual therapists and the requirement that the client communicate in English may limit the person's ability to progress in counseling and therapy. If bilingual individuals do not use their native tongue in therapy, many aspects of their emotional experience may not be available for treatment; they may be unable to use the wide complexity of language to describe their particular thoughts, feelings, and unique situations. Clients who are limited in English tend to feel like they are speaking as a child and choosing simple words to explain complex thoughts and feelings. If they were able to use their native tongue, they could easily explain themselves without the huge loss of emotional complexity and experience (Arredondo, Gallardo-Cooper, et al., 2014).

PATTERNS OF "AMERICAN" CULTURAL ASSUMPTIONS AND MULTICULTURAL FAMILY COUNSELING/THERAPY

Family systems theory may be equally culture bound, and this limitation may be manifested in marital or couple counseling, parent–child counseling, or work with more than one member of the family. *Family systems* therapy possesses several important characteristics (Corey, 2013; McGoldrick, Giordano, & Garcia-Preto, 2005):

- Highlights the importance of the family (versus the individual) as the unit of identity.

- Focuses on resolving concrete issues.

- Is concerned with family structure and dynamics.

- Assumes that these family structures and dynamics are historically passed on from one generation to another.

- Attempts to understand the communication and alliances via reframing.

- Places the therapist in an expert position.

Many of these qualities would be consistent with the worldviews of persons of color. The problem arises, however, in how these goals and strategies are translated into concepts of "the family" or what constitutes the "healthy" family. Some of the characteristics of healthy families may pose problems in therapy with various culturally diverse groups. They tend to be heavily loaded with value orientations that are incongruent with the value systems of many culturally diverse clients (McGoldrick et al., 2005):

- Allows and encourages expressing emotions freely and openly.

- Views each member as having a right to be his or her own unique self (individuate from the emotional field of the family).

- Strives for an equal division of labor among members of the family.

- Considers *egalitarian role* relationships between spouses desirable.

- Holds the *nuclear family* as the standard.

These orientations were first described by Kluckhohn and Strodtbeck (1961) as patterns of "American" values. Table 7.4 outlines the five major dimensions of White culture, and contrasts them with four major groups of color.

People–Nature Relationship

Traditional Western thinking believes in mastery and control over nature. As a result, most therapists operate from a framework that subscribes to the belief that problems are solvable and that both therapist and client must take an active part in solving problems via manipulation and control. Active intervention is stressed in controlling or changing the environment. As seen in Table 7.4, the four other ethnic groups view people as harmonious with nature.

TABLE 7.4 Cultural Value Preferences of Middle-Class White EuroAmericans and People of Color: A Comparative Summary

Area of Relationships	Middle-Class White Americans	Asian Americans	American Indians	Black Americans	Hispanic Americans
People to nature/ environment	Mastery over	Harmony with	Harmony with	Harmony with	Harmony with
Time orientation	Future	Past-present	Present	Present	Past-present
People relations	Individual	Collateral	Collateral	Collateral	Collateral
Preferred mode of activity	Doing	Doing	Being-in-becoming	Doing	Being-in-becoming
Nature of man	Good & bad	Good	Good	Good & bad	Good

Source: From *Family Therapy with Ethnic Minorities* (p. 232) by M. K. Ho, 1987, Newbury Park, CA: Sage. Copyright 1987 by Sage Publications. Reprinted by permission.

Confucian philosophy, for example, stresses a set of rules aimed at promoting loyalty, respect, and harmony among family members (Moodley & West, 2005). Harmony within the family and the environment leads to harmony within the self. Dependence on the family unit and acceptance of the environment seem to dictate differences in solving problems. Western culture advocates defining and attacking the problem directly. Asian cultures tend to accommodate or deal with problems through indirection. In child rearing, many Asians believe that it is better to avoid direct confrontation and to use deflection. A White family may deal with a child who has watched too many hours of TV by saying, "Why don't you turn the TV off and study?" To be more threatening, the parent might say, "You'll be grounded unless the TV goes off!" An Asian parent might respond by saying, "That looks like a boring program; I think your friend John must be doing his homework now" or "I think Father wants to watch his favorite program." Such an approach stems from the need to avoid conflict and to achieve balance and harmony among members of the family and the wider environment.

Thus it is apparent that U.S. values that call for us to dominate nature (i.e., conquer space, tame the wilderness, or harness nuclear energy) through control and manipulation of the universe are reflected in family counseling. *Family systems* counseling theories attempt to describe, explain, predict, and control family dynamics. The therapist actively attempts to understand what is going on in the family system (structural alliances and communication patterns), identify the problems (dysfunctional aspects of the dynamics), and attack them directly or indirectly through manipulation and control (therapeutic interventions). Ethnic minorities or subgroups that view people as harmonious with nature or believe that nature may overwhelm people ("acts of God") may find the therapist's mastery-over-nature approach inconsistent with or antagonistic to their worldview. Indeed, attempts to intervene actively in changing family patterns and relationships may be perceived as the problem because they may potentially unbalance the harmony that existed.

Time Dimension

How different societies, cultures, and people view time exerts a pervasive influence on their lives. U.S. society may be characterized as preoccupied with the future (Katz, 1985; Kluckhohn & Strodtbeck, 1961). Furthermore, our society seems very compulsive about time, in that we divide it into seconds, minutes, hours, days, weeks, months, and years. Time may be viewed as a commodity ("time is money" and "stop wasting time") in fixed and static categories rather than as a dynamic and flowing process. It has been pointed out that the United States' future orientation may be linked to other values as well: (a) stress on youth and achievement, in which the children are expected to "better their parents"; (b) controlling one's own destiny by future planning and saving for a rainy day; and (c) optimism and hope for a better future. The spirit of the nation may be embodied in an old General Electric slogan, "Progress is our most important product."

Table 7.4 reveals that both American Indians and Black Americans tend to value a present-time orientation, whereas Asian Americans and Hispanic Americans have a combination past–present focus. Historically, Asian societies have valued the past, as reflected in ancestor worship and the equating of age with wisdom and respectability. This contrasts with U.S. culture, in which youth is valued over the elderly and one's usefulness in life is believed to be over once one hits the retirement years. As compared to EuroAmerican middle-class norms, Latinos also exhibit a past–present time orientation. Strong hierarchical structures in the family, respect for elders and ancestors, and the value of *personalismo* all combine in this direction. American Indians also differ from their White counterparts in that they are very grounded in the here and now rather than the future. American Indian philosophy relies heavily on the belief that time is flowing, circular, and harmonious. Artificial division of time (schedules) is disruptive to the natural pattern. African Americans also value the present because of the spiritual quality of their existence and their history of victimization by racism. Several difficulties may occur when the counselor or therapist is unaware of the differences of time perspective (Hines & Boyd-Franklin, 2005).

First, if time differences exist between a family of color and the White Euro-American therapist, it will most likely be manifested in a difference in the pace of time: Both may sense things are going too slowly or too fast. An American Indian family who values being in the present and the immediate experiential reality of being may feel that the therapist lacks respect for them and is rushing them (Sutton & Broken Nose, 2005) while ignoring the quality of the personal relationship. On the other hand, the therapist may be dismayed by the "delays," "inefficiency," and lack of "commitment to change" among the family members. After all, time is precious, and the therapist has only limited time to impact upon the family. The result is frequently dissatisfaction among the parties, no establishment of rapport, misinterpretation of behaviors or situations, and probably discontinuation of future sessions.

Second, Inclan (1985) pointed out how confusions and misinterpretations can arise because Hispanics, particularly Puerto Ricans, mark time differently than do their U.S. White counterparts. The language of clock time in counseling (50-minute hour, rigid time schedule, once-a-week sessions) can conflict with minority perceptions of time (Garcia-Preto, 1996). The following dialogue between the therapist and Mrs. Rivera illustrates this point clearly:

> *"Mrs. Rivera, your next appointment is at 9:30 a.m. next Wednesday."*
>
> *"Good, it's convenient for me to come after I drop off the children at school."*
>
> Or *"Mrs. Rivera, your next appointment is for the whole family at 3:00 p.m. on Tuesday."*
>
> *"Very good. After the kids return from school we can come right in."* (Inclan, 1985, p. 328)

Since school starts at 8 a.m., the client is bound to show up very early, whereas in the second example, the client will most likely be late (school ends at 3 p.m.). In both cases, the counselor is likely to be inconvenienced, but worse yet is the negative interpretation that may be made of the client's motives (anxious, demanding, or pushy in the first case, while resistant, passive-aggressive, or irresponsible in the latter one). The counselor needs to be aware that many Hispanics may mark time by events rather than by the clock.

Relational Dimension

In general, the United States can be characterized as an achievement-oriented society, which is most strongly manifested in the prevailing Protestant work ethic. Basic to the ethic is the concept of *individualism:* (1) The individual is the psychosocial unit of operation; (2) the individual has primary responsibility for his or her own actions; (3) independence and autonomy are highly valued and rewarded; and (4) one should be internally directed and controlled. In many societies and groups within the United States, however, this value is not necessarily shared. Relationships in Japan and China are often described as being lineal, and identification with others is both wide and linked to the past (ancestor worship). Obeying the wishes of ancestors or deceased parents and perceiving your existence and identity as linked to the historical past are inseparable. Almost all racial/ethnic minority groups in the United States tend to be more collateral (collectivistic) in their relationships with people. In an individualistic orientation, the definition of the family tends to be linked to a biological necessity (*nuclear family*), whereas a collateral or lineal view encompasses various concepts of the *extended family*. Not understanding this distinction and the values inherent in these orientations may lead the family therapist to erroneous conclusions and decisions. Following is a case illustration of a young American Indian.

> *A young probationer was under court supervision and had strict orders to remain with responsible adults. His counselor became concerned because the youth appeared to ignore this order. The client moved around frequently and, according to the counselor, stayed overnight with several different young women. The counselor presented this case at a formal staff meeting, and fellow professionals stated their suspicion that the client was either a pusher or a pimp. The frustrating element to the counselor was that the young women knew each other and appeared to enjoy each other's company. Moreover, they were not ashamed to be seen together in public with the client. This behavior prompted the counselor to initiate violation proceedings. (Red Horse, Lewis, Feit, & Decker, 1981, p. 56)*

If an American Indian professional had not accidentally come upon this case, a revocation order initiated against the youngster would surely have caused irreparable alienation between the family and the social service agency. The counselor had failed to realize that the American Indian family network is structurally open and may include several households of relatives and friends along both vertical and horizontal lines. The young women were all first cousins to the client, and each was as a sister, with all the households representing different units of the family.

Likewise, African Americans have strong kinship bonds that may encompass both blood relatives and friends. Traditional African culture values the collective orientation over *individualism* (Franklin, 1988; Hines & Boyd-Franklin, 2005). This group identity has also been reinforced by what many African Americans describe as the sense of "peoplehood" developed as a result of the common experience of racism and discrimination. In a society that has historically attempted to destroy the Black family, near and distant relatives, neighbors, friends, and acquaintances have arisen in an *extended family* support network (Black, 1996). Thus, the Black family may appear quite different from the ideal *nuclear family*. The danger is that certain assumptions made by a White therapist may be totally without merit or may be translated in such a way as to alienate or damage the self-esteem of African Americans. For example, the absence of a father in the Black family does not necessarily mean that the children do not have a father figure. This function may be taken over by an uncle or male family friend.

We give one example here to illustrate that the moral evaluation of a behavior may depend on the value orientation of the cultural group: Because of their collective orientation, Puerto Ricans view obligations to the family as primary over all other relationships (Garcia-Preto, 2005). When a family member attains a position of power and influence, it is expected that he or she will favor the relatives over objective criteria. Businesses that are heavily weighted by family members, and appointments of family members in government positions, are not unusual in many countries. Failure to hire a family member may result in moral condemnation and family sanctions (Inclan, 1985). This is in marked contrast to what we ideally believe in the United States. Appointment of family members over objective criteria of individual achievement is condemned. It would appear that differences in the relationship dimension between the mental health provider and the minority family receiving services can cause great conflict. Although family therapy may be the treatment of choice for many minorities (over individual therapy), its values may again be antagonistic and detrimental to minorities. Family approaches that place heavy emphasis on *individualism* and freedom from the emotional field of the family may cause great harm. Our approach should be to identify how we might capitalize on collaterality to the benefit of minority families.

Activity Dimension

One of the primary characteristics of White U.S. cultural values and beliefs is an action (doing) orientation: (a) We must master and control nature; (b) we must always do things about a situation; and (c) we should take a pragmatic and utilitarian view of life. In counseling, we expect clients to master and control their own lives and environment, to take action to resolve their own problems, and to fight against bias and inaction. The doing mode is evident everywhere and is reflected in how White Americans identify themselves by what they *do* (occupations), how children are asked what they want to do when they grow up, and how a higher value is given to inventors over poets and to doctors of medicine over doctors of philosophy. An essay topic commonly given to schoolchildren returning to school in the fall is "What I did on my summer vacation."

It appears that both American Indians and Latinos/Hispanics prefer a being or being-in-becoming mode of activity. The American Indian concepts of self-determination and noninterference are examples. Value is placed on the spiritual quality of being, as manifested in self-containment, poise, and harmony with the universe. Value is placed on the attainment of inner fulfillment and an essential serenity of one's place in the universe. Because each person is fulfilling a purpose, no one should have the power to interfere or impose values. Often, those unfamiliar with Indian values perceive the person as stoic, aloof, passive, noncompetitive, or inactive. In working with families, the counselor role of active manipulator may clash with American Indian concepts of being-in-becoming (noninterference).

Likewise, Latino/Hispanic culture may be said to have a more here-and-now or being-in-becoming orientation. Like their American Indian counterparts, Hispanics believe that people are born with *dignidad* (dignity) and must be given *respeto* (respect). They are born with innate worth and importance; the inner soul and spirit are more important than the body. People cannot be held accountable for their lot in life (status, role, etc.) because they are born into this life state (Inclan, 1985). A certain degree of *fatalismo* (fatalism) is present, and life events may be viewed as inevitable (*Lo que Dios manda*, what God wills). Philosophically, it does not matter what people have in life or what position they occupy (farm laborer, public official, or attorney). Status is possessed by existing, and everyone is entitled to *respeto*.

Since this belief system deemphasizes material accomplishments as a measure of success, it is clearly at odds with EuroAmerican middle-class society. Although a doing-oriented family may define a family member's worth via achievement, a being orientation equates worth simply to belonging. Thus when clients complain that someone is not an effective family member, what do they mean? This needs to be clarified by the therapist. Is it a complaint that the family member is not performing and achieving (doing), or does it mean that the person is not respectful and accommodating to family structures and values (being)?

Ho (1987) describes both Asian Americans and African Americans as operating from the doing orientation. However, it appears that "doing" in these two groups is manifested differently than in the White American lifestyle. The active dimension in Asians is related not to individual achievement, but to achievement via conformity to family values and demands. Controlling one's own feelings, impulses, desires, and needs in order to fulfill responsibility to the family is strongly ingrained in Asian children. The doing orientation tends to be more ritualized in the roles of and responsibilities toward members of the family. African Americans also exercise considerable control (endure the pain and suffering of racism) in the face of adversity to minimize discrimination and to maximize success.

Nature of People Dimension

Middle-class EuroAmericans generally perceive the nature of people as neutral. Environmental influences, such as conditioning, family upbringing, and socialization, are believed to be dominant forces in determining the nature of the person. People are neither good nor bad but are a product of their environment. Although several minority groups may share features of this belief with Whites, there is a qualitative and quantitative difference that may affect family structure and dynamics. For example, Asian Americans and American Indians tend to emphasize the inherent goodness of people. We have already discussed the Native American concept of noninterference, which is based on the belief that people have an innate capacity to advance and grow (self-fulfillment) and that problematic behaviors are the result of environmental influences that thwart the opportunity to develop. Goodness will always triumph over evil if the person is left alone. Likewise, Asian philosophy (Buddhism and Confucianism) believes in people's innate goodness and prescribes role relationships that manifest the "good way of life." Central to Asian belief is the idea that the best healing source lies within the family (Daya, 2005; Walsh & Shapiro, 2006) and that seeking help from the outside (e.g., counseling and therapy) is nonproductive and against the dictates of Asian philosophy.

Latinos may be described as holding the view that human nature is both good and bad (mixed). Concepts of *dignidad* and *respeto* undergird the belief that people are born with positive qualities. Yet some Hispanics, such as Puerto Ricans, spend a great deal of time appealing to supernatural forces so that children may be blessed with a good human nature (Inclan, 1985). Thus, a child's "badness" may be accepted as destiny, so parents may be less inclined to seek help from educators or mental health professionals for such problems. The preferred mode of help may be religious consultations and ventilation to neighbors and friends who sympathize and understand the dilemmas (change means reaching the supernatural forces).

African Americans may also be characterized as having a mixed concept of people but in general they believe, like their White counterparts, that people are basically neutral. Environmental factors have a great influence on how people develop. This orientation is consistent with African American beliefs that racism, discrimination, oppression, and other external factors create problems for the individual. Emotional disorders and antisocial acts are caused by external forces (system variables) rather than by internal, intrapsychic, psychological forces. For example, high crime rates, poverty, and the current structure of the African American family are the result of historical and current oppression of Black people.

White Western concepts of genetic inferiority and pathology (African American people are born that way) hold little validity for the Black person.

OVERGENERALIZING AND STEREOTYPING

Although it is critical for therapists to have a basic understanding of the generic characteristics of counseling and psychotherapy and the culture-specific life values of different groups, overgeneralizing and stereotyping are ever-present dangers. For example, the listing of racial/ethnic minority group variables does not indicate that all persons coming from the same minority group will share all or even some of these traits. Generalizations are necessary for us; without them, we would become inefficient creatures. However, they are guidelines for our behaviors, to be tentatively applied in new situations, and they should be open to change and challenge. The information provided in the chapter tables should act as guidelines rather than absolutes. These generalizations should serve as the background from which the figure emerges.

IMPLICATIONS FOR CLINICAL PRACTICE

1. Become cognizant of the generic characteristics of counseling and psychotherapy: *culture-bound values*, *class-bound values*, and linguistic factors.

2. Know that we are increasingly becoming a multilingual nation and that the linguistic demands of clinical work may place minority populations at a disadvantage.

3. Consider the need to provide community counseling services that reach out to the minority population.

4. Realize that the problems and concerns of many groups of color are related to systemic and external forces rather than to internal psychological problems.

5. Know that our increasing diversity presents us with different cultural conceptions of the family. One definition cannot be seen as superior to another.

6. Realize that families cannot be understood apart from the cultural, social, and political dimensions of their functioning. The traditional definition of the *nuclear family* as consisting of heterosexual parents in a long-term marriage,

raising their biological children, and having the father as sole wage earner now refers to a statistical minority.

7. Be careful not to overgeneralize or stereotype. Knowing general group characteristics and guidelines is different from rigidly holding on to preconceived notions.

SUMMARY

Theories of counseling and psychotherapy are influenced by assumptions that theorists make regarding the goals for therapy, the method used to invoke change, and the definition of mental health and illness. Counseling and psychotherapy have traditionally been conceptualized in Western individualistic terms that may lead to premature termination of counseling and underutilization of mental health services by marginalized groups in our society. The *culture-bound values* that may prove antagonistic to those of diverse groups include the following: focus on the individual, verbal/emotional/behavioral expressiveness, *insight* orientation, self-disclosure, *scientific empiricism*, separation of mental and physical functioning, and pattern of communication.

In addition to this category, both *class-bound values* and linguistic factors may prove biased against culturally diverse groups. For the therapist who comes from a middle- to upper-class background, it is often difficult to relate to the circumstances and hardships affecting the client who lives in poverty. The phenomenon of poverty and its effects on individuals and institutions can be devastating. Use of Standard English in health care delivery may also unfairly discriminate against those from a bilingual or lower socioeconomic background and result in devastating consequences. The lack of bilingual therapists and the requirement that the client communicate in English may limit the person's ability to progress in counseling and therapy. If bilingual individuals do not use their native tongue in therapy, many aspects of their emotional experience may not be available for treatment.

Family systems theory, while seemingly consistent with the collectivistic orientation of many diverse groups, may be equally culture bound, as may be manifested in marital or couple counseling, parent–child counseling, or work with more than one member of the family. For example, the following Western beliefs and assumptions about healthy families may be incongruent with diverse groups:

(a) allow and encourage expressing emotions freely and openly, (b) view each family member as having a right to be his or her own unique self, (c) strive for an equal division of labor, (d) stress *egalitarian role* relationships, and (e) the *nuclear family* is the desirable standard. Especially useful for counselors to explore is the Kluckholn and Strodtbeck (1961) model of "American" cultural patterns and their manifestation in five dimensions: people–nature relationship, time orientation, relational focus, activity, and nature of people.

GLOSSARY TERMS

Activity dimension	Linguistic barriers
Biculturalism	Minority standard time
Class-bound values	Nature of people dimension
Collectivism	Nuclear families
Culture-bound values	Patriarchal roles
Egalitarian roles	QUOID
Emotional expressiveness	Relational dimension
Extended families	Scientific empiricism
Family systems	Self-disclosure
Individual-centered	Social class
Individualism	Time dimension
Insight	YAVIS syndrome

REFERENCES

American Psychological Association, Task Force on Socioeconomic Status. (2007). *Report of the APA Task Force on Socioeconomic Status.* Washington, DC: American Psychological Association.

Antony, M. M., & Roemer, L. (2011). *Behavior therapy.* Washington, DC: American Psychological Association.

Arredondo, P., Gallardo-Cooper, M., Delgado-Romero, E. A., & Zapata, A. L. (2014). *Culturally responsive counseling with Latinas/os.* Alexandria, VA: American Counseling Association.

Atkinson, D. R., Morten, G., & Sue, D. W. (1998). A minority identity development model. In D. R. Atkinson, G. Morten, & D. W. Sue (Eds.), *Counseling American minorities* (pp. 35–52). Dubuque, IA: W. C. Brown.

Bernstein, B. (1964). Elaborated and restricted codes: Their social origins and some consequences. *American Anthropologist, 66,* 55–69.

Black, L. (1996). Families of African origin: An overview. In M. McGoldrick, J. Giordano, & J. K. Pearce (Eds.), *Ethnicity and family therapy* (pp. 57–65). New York, NY: Guilford Press.

Burke, G. (2005, Oct. 24). Translating isn't kid stuff. *San Jose Mercury News,* p. 5B.

Chang, C. Y., McDonald, C. P., & O'Hara, C. (2014). Counseling clients from Asian and Pacific Island Heritages. In M. J. Ratts & P. B. Pedersen (Eds.), *Counseling for multiculturalism and social justice* (pp. 127–142). Alexandria, VA: American Counseling Association.

Chen, E., Matthews, K. A., & Boyce, W. T. (2002). Socioeconomic differences in children's health: How and why do these relationships change with age? *Psychological Bulletin, 128,* 295–329.

Coleman, J. (2003, April 2). Bill would ban using children as interpreters. *San Jose Mercury News,* p. A01.

Corey, G. (2013). *Theory and practice of counseling and psychotherapy* (9th ed.). Belmont, CA: Brooks/Cole.

Craske, M. G. (2010). *Cognitive-behavioral therapy.* Washington, DC: American Psychological Association.

Daya, R. (2005). Buddhist moments in psychotherapy. In R. Moodley & W. West (Eds.), *Integrating traditional healing practices into counseling and psychotherapy* (pp. 182–193). Thousand Oaks, CA: Sage.

Fouad, N. A., & Chavez-Korell, S. (2014). Considering social class and socioeconomic status in the context of multiple identities: An integrative clinical supervision approach. In C. A. Falender, E. P. Shafranske, & E. J. Falicov (Eds.), *Multiculturalism and diversity in clinical*

supervision (pp. 145–180). Washington, DC: American Psychological Association.

Franklin, J. H. (1988). A historical note on black families. In H. P. McAdoo (Ed.), *Black families* (pp. 3–14). Newbury Park, CA: Sage.

Gallo, L. C., & Matthews, K. A. (2003). Understanding the association between socioeconomic status and physical health: Do negative emotions play a role? *Psychological Bulletin, 129,* 10–51.

Garcia-Preto, N. (1996). Puerto Rican families. In M. McGoldrick, J. Giordano, & J. K. Pearce (Eds.), *Ethnicity and family therapy* (pp. 183–199). New York: Guilford Press.

Garcia-Preto, N. (2005). Puerto Rican families. In M. McGoldrick, J. Giordano, & N. Garcia-Preto (Eds.), *Ethnicity and family therapy* (2nd ed., pp. 242–255). New York, NY: Guilford Press.

Garrett, M. T., & Portman, T.A.A. (2011). *Counseling Native Americans.* Belmont, CA: Cengage.

Gottesfeld, H. (1995). Community context and the underutilization of mental health services by minority patients. *Psychological Reports, 76,* 207–210.

Guzman, M. R., & Carrasco, N. (2011). *Counseling Latino/a Americans.* Belmont, CA: Cengage.

Hines, P. M., & Boyd-Franklin, N. (2005). African American families. In M. McGoldrick, J. Giordano, & N. Garcia-Preto (Eds.), *Ethnicity and family therapy* (2nd ed., pp. 87–100). New York, NY: Guilford Press.

Ho, M. K. (1987). *Family therapy with ethnic minorities.* Newbury Park, CA: Sage.

Hollingshead, A. R., & Redlich, E. C. (1968). *Social class and mental health.* New York, NY: Wiley.

Inclan, J. (1985). Variations in value orientations in mental health work with Puerto Ricans. *Psychotherapy, 22,* 324–334.

Ivey, A. E., Ivey, M. B., & Zalaquett, C. P. (2014). *Intentional interviewing and counseling* (8th ed.). Belmont, CA: Brooks/Cole.

Ivey, A. E., Ivey, M., Myers, J., & Sweeney, T. (2005). *Developmental counseling and therapy.* Boston, MA: Lahaska.

Jourard, S. M. (1964). *The transparent self.* Princeton, NJ: Van Nostrand.

Katz, J. (1985). The sociopolitical nature of counseling. *Counseling Psychologist, 13,* 615–624.

Kluckhohn, F. R., & Strodtbeck, F. L. (1961). *Variations in value orientations.* Evanston, IL: Row, Patterson.

Leong, F.T.L., Wagner, N. S., & Kim, H. H. (1995). Group counseling expectations among Asian American students: The role of culture-specific factors. *Journal of Counseling Psychology, 42,* 217–222.

Levenson, H. (2010). *Brief dynamic therapy.* Washington, DC: American Psychological Association.

Liu, W. M., Ali, S. R., Soleck, G., Hopps, J., Dunston, K., & Pickett, T. (2004). Using social class in counseling psychology research. *Journal of Counseling Psychology, 51,* 3–18.

Liu, W. M., Hernandez, J., Mahmood, A., & Stinson, R. (2006). Linking poverty, classism, and racism in mental health: Overcoming barriers to multicultural competency. In M. G. Constantine & D. W. Sue (Eds.), *Addressing racism* (pp. 65–86). Hoboken, NJ: Wiley.

Lorant, V., Deliege, D., Eaton, W., Robert, A., Philippot, P., & Ansseau, M. (2003). Socioeconomic inequalities in depression: A meta-analysis. *American Journal of Epidemiology, 157,* 98–112.

Lorion, R. P. (1973). Socioeconomic status and treatment approaches reconsidered. *Psychological Bulletin, 79,* 263–280.

Lorion, R. P. (1974). Patient and therapist variables in the treatment of low-income patients. *Psychological Bulletin, 81,* 344–354.

McGoldrick, M., Giordano, J., & Garcia-Preto, N. (2005). *Ethnicity and family therapy.* New York, NY: Guilford Press.

Moodley, R., & West, W. (Eds.). (2005). *Integrating traditional healing practices into counseling and psychotherapy.* Thousand Oaks, CA: Sage.

National Council on Interpreting in Health Care. (2005). *National standards of practice for interpreters in health care.* Santa Rosa, CA: Author.

Neighbors, H. W., Caldwell, C. H., Thompson, E., & Jackson, J. S. (1994). Help-seeking behavior and unmet need. In S. Friedman (Ed.), *Disorders in African Americans* (pp. 26–39). New York, NY: Springer.

Ngo-Metzger, Q., Massagli, M. P., Clarridge, B. R., Manocchia, M., Davis, R. B., Iezzoni, L. I., & Phillips, R. S. (2003). Linguistic and cultural barriers to care: Perspectives of Chinese and Vietnamese immigrants. *Journal of General Internal Medicine, 18,* 44–52.

Parham, T. A., Ajamu, A., & White, J. L. (2011). *The psychology of Blacks: Centering our perspectives in the African consciousness.* Boston, MA: Prentice Hall.

Pedersen, P. B., & Pope, M. (2010). Inclusive cultural empathy for successful global leadership. *American Psychologist, 65,* 841–854.

Ponterotto, J. G., Utsey, S. O., & Pedersen, P. B. (2006). *Preventing prejudice: A guide for counselors, educators, and parents.* Thousand Oaks, CA: Sage.

Ratts, M. J., & Pedersen, P. B. (2014). *Counseling for multiculturalism and social justice.* Alexandria, VA: American Counseling Association.

Red Horse, J. G., Lewis, R., Felt, M., & Decker, J. (1981). Family structure and value orientation in American Indians. In R. H. Dana (Ed.), *Human services for cultural minorities.* Baltimore, MD: University Park Press.

Reed, R., & Smith, L. (2014). A social justice perspective on counseling and poverty. In M. J. Ratts & P. B. Pedersen (Eds.), *Counseling for multiculturalism and social justice* (pp. 259–273). Alexandria, VA: American Counseling Association.

Schindler-Rainman, E. (1967). The poor and the PTA. *PTA Magazine, 61*(8), 4–5.

Schofield, W. (1964). *Psychotherapy: The purchase of friendship.* Englewood Cliffs, NJ: Prentice Hall.

Schwartz, A., Rodriguez, M. M., Santiago-Rivera, A. L., Arredondo, P., & Field, L. D. (2010). Cultural and linguistic competence: Welcome challenges from successful diversification. *Professional Psychology: Research and Practice, 41,* 210–220.

Smith, L. (2010). *Psychology, poverty, and the end of social exclusion.* New York, NY: Teachers College Press.

Smith, L. (2013). Counseling and poverty. In D. W. Sue & D. Sue (Eds.), *Counseling the culturally diverse: Theory and practice* (6th ed., pp. 517–526). Hoboken, NJ: Wiley.

Stonequist, E. V. (1937). *The marginal man.* New York, NY: Scribner's.

Sue, D. W. (2015). Therapeutic harm and cultural oppression. *Counseling Psychologist.* doi: 0011000014565713.

Sundberg, N. D. (1981). Cross-cultural counseling and psychotherapy: A research overview. In A. J. Mansella & P. B. Pedersen (Eds.), *Crosscultural counseling and psychotherapy* (pp. 29–38). New York, NY: Pergamon Press.

Sutton, C. T., & Broken Nose, M. A. (2005). American Indian families: An overview. In M. McGoldrick, J. Giordano, & N. Garcia-Preto (Eds.), *Ethnicity and family therapy* (pp. 43–54). New York, NY: Guilford Press.

Thomason, T.C. (2014). Counseling Native Americans and social justice. In M. J. Ratts & P. B. Pedersen (Eds.), *Counseling for multiculturalism and social justice* (2nd ed. pp. 157–177). Alexandria, VA: American Counseling Association.

Torres-Rivera, E., & Ratts, M. J. (2014). Counseling Latino/as from a social justice perspective. In M. J. Ratts & P. B. Pedersen (Eds.), *Counseling for multiculturalism and social justice* (pp. 179–192). Alexandria, VA: American Counseling Association.

Utsey, S. O., Walker, R. L., & Kwate, N.O.A. (2005). Conducting quantitative research in a cultural context. In M. G. Constantine & D. W. Sue (Eds.), *Strategies for building multicultural competence in mental health and educational settings* (pp. 247–268). Hoboken, NJ: Wiley.

Vedantam, S. (2005, June 6). Patients' diversity is often discounted. *Washington Post,* p. A01.

Walsh, R., & Shapiro, S. L. (2006). The meeting of meditative disciplines and Western psychology. *American Psychologist, 61,* 227–239.

Wood, P. S., & Mallinckrodt, B. (1990). Culturally sensitive assertiveness training for ethnic minority clients. *Professional Psychology: Research & Practice, 21,* 5–11.

Communication Styles and Its Impact on Counseling and Psychotherapy

Chapter Objectives

1. Compare and contrast styles of communication between various racial/ethnic and other sociodemographic groups.

2. Define and recognize *nonverbal* communications and their cultural meanings.

3. Acquire knowledge and understandings of how counseling styles and roles may create barriers to effective multicultural counseling.

4. List several ways how *nonverbal communication* can (a) trigger off racial biases and fears, and (b) reflect our true beliefs and feelings.

5. Describe differences in how *proxemics, kinesics, paralanguage,* and *high-/low-context communications* are likely to affect communication,

6. Learn how different theories of counseling and psychotherapy can be distinguished by their communication or helping styles.

7. Explain the implications *communication styles* have for therapeutic intervention techniques.

I'M NOT CRAZY: THE CASE OF MR. CHANG

Mr. Henry Chang is a first-generation 85-year-old recently widowed Chinese-American gentleman who presented to his physician, Dr. Schulman, with complaints of poor digestion, loss of appetite, headaches, difficulty sleeping, and general malaise. His medical history is largely unremarkable, except for diagnoses of gastroesophageal reflex disease, a right knee replacement, and osteoarthritis. The patient's health problems were often exaggerated by his forgetfulness about regularly taking his medication. He informed Dr. Schulman that he used to be very socially active in his Church with many friends, but that things had changed and he no longer found joy in life. As a result, the physician requested a brief psychological evaluation as a means of ruling out any contributing mental health factors. The patient, however, failed to show twice for scheduled appointments with the psychologist.

Only with great urging from Dr. Schulman did Mr. Chang finally show for his third scheduled appointment. He was seen by a young White female psychologist, Dr. Martin, who reported great difficulty in establishing rapport with the client. Mr. Chang seemed uncooperative and guarded, and was somewhat reticent and reserved in the interview, offering minimal but polite responses to questions. According to Dr. Martin, he became very "defensive" when the topic of his mental state was discussed. Dr. Martin felt that the formality of the doctor-patient relationship might be creating a barrier between her and the client, so she tried to place Mr. Chang at ease with "small talk" about his family relationships, and by addressing him by his first name, "Henry." She tried to explore Mr. Chang's family relationships, the impact of the recent death of his wife, and his resistance to exploring his feelings. These she believed were responsible for his depression. Throughout the interview, Mr. Chang denied any emotional difficulties, stated he was not lonely or depressed, and became increasingly agitated and resistant to answering questions. Whenever Dr. Martin pressed him for feelings associated with his increasing age, death of his wife, and isolation, Mr. Chang seemed to withdraw more and more. When the session ended, the therapist recommended to Mr. Chang that he make another appointment, but he stated he would "think about it." In relating her impression to the treating physician, Dr. Martin described Mr. Chang as "obstinate," "inflexible," "passive-aggressive," and "resistant to psychological treatment." She concluded that Mr. Chang would not benefit from therapy, and that at his advanced years, it would be best to allow him to live the remainder of his life as he desired.

Although Mr. Chang never returned to see the psychologist, he did continue to show for his regular medical appointments. It was at one of these sessions that he confessed to Dr. Shulman about "feeling poorly," being constantly tired, and needing medication to address his stomach pain and improve his energy level. When asked about questions related to his mood, Mr. Chang admitted to feeling sad and hopeless, but denied being depressed. He did miss his wife and found their home too large to maintain. He noted that his arthritis and increased loss of balance made cooking his own meals and going to the bathroom at night difficult. He had fallen on two previous occasions when he

CASE STUDY

lost his balance in the bathtub. His two sons, who lived in different parts of the country, wanted him to move into an assisted living situation, but he had so far refused. His daughter, who was married with two younger children, had offered to have her father move into their spare room, but Mr. Chang said he did not want to burden her family.

Because Dr. Schulman did not feel comfortable giving advice to his patient, he again encouraged Mr. Chang to make an appointment with Dr. Martin and to discuss ways that might improve his outlook and to consider alternative living situations. At this suggestion, Mr. Chang loudly proclaimed that he was not "crazy", he would not see a "shrink," and denied any mental health problems. He stated that he preferred to speak with Dr. Schulman, who being an older man himself seemed to understand his situation better. Dr. Schulman, however, indicated he was not qualified to provide the type of assisted living advice required, and that his role was a medical one. Rather than refer Mr. Chang back to the psychologist, he recommended a social worker who could help "explore ways" in dealing with his current living situation. Dr. Schulman assured Mr. Chang that he would continue to be available for treating him medically. This reassurance seemed to elicit a positive response from Mr. Chang, who agreed to see the social worker.

The social worker, a woman close to Dr. Martin's age, explained her role at the clinic as a problem solver, reassured Mr. Chang that they would work together to address his living situation, and work closely with his physician to address health-related issues. She did not initially explore his emotive state, but confined her questions and comments toward practical matters related to Mr. Chang's medical problems, living situation, and ways to remember taking his medication, and showed an interest in how he spent his spare time. The social worker would often share her own thoughts and observations associated with her own aging parents, the physical changes they experienced, the loss of close friends and family, their feelings of frustration, and the emotional turmoil they underwent. Mr. Chang would listen intently, and seemed to enjoy providing insights about the social worker's parents. Indeed, at times, it appeared like the conversations about the social worker's elderly parents served as an indirect means of talking about Mr. Chang's own feelings of frustration, loneliness, and depression.

Throughout their interactions, the social worker always addressed her client as "Mr. Chang" and would present advice or suggestions tentatively. She would always ask Mr. Chang for his perspective, encouraged him to tell her whether her ideas seemed practical, and asked whether he had suggestions as well. She treated Mr. Chang with a great deal of respect and would often defer to him by asking for his advice, because as she put it, he was "older and wiser." This approach seemed to open the gateways to Mr. Chang's desire to talk and share his apprehensions, feelings, and family concerns, and he was no longer inflexible, guarded, and resistant. At their fourth session together, Mr. Chang took a major therapeutic step by admitting to thoughts of suicide, and said he was concerned that he was "going crazy."

Adapted from Carney & Sue (2014), pp. 253–256

CASE STUDY

REFLECTION AND DISCUSSION QUESTIONS

1. How do you make sense of Mr. Chang's adamant assertion that he was not "crazy" and would not see a "shrink"? If you were a therapist, how would you approach this task?

2. In what ways may race, gender and age affect the therapeutic relationship between Mr. Chang and Drs. Schulman and Martin and the social worker?

3. Mr. Chang seemed to respond poorly to Dr. Martin, but seemed to be more disclosing to both his personal physician and social worker. Why do you believe this to be the case?

This case illustrates how counseling styles and approaches must be adapted to meet the sociodemographic characteristics of a diverse clientele. Helping professionals unaware of culture, age, and gender differences may make inaccurate assessments and diagnoses, and offer inappropriate treatments. Dr. Martin seems unaware of how culture influences help-seeking behavior, the manner of symptom formation, and what constitutes culturally relevant helping among diverse groups. Let us briefly analyze the case of Mr. Chang to illustrate these points.

Flexible and Culturally Appropriate Counseling

The approach by Dr. Martin suggests that the actual process of counseling and psychotherapy may be antagonistic to the values held by culturally diverse clients. Mr. Chang's perceived resistance to counseling (*obstinate, inflexible, passive-aggressive,* and *resistant to psychological treatment*), and the therapist's use of potentially inappropriate counseling techniques (getting client to express feelings, informality in the therapeutic relationship) may prove to be a humiliating experience for the client. Ironically, the descriptors used by Dr. Martin to describe Mr. Chang's behavior in the session also conform to age-related stereotypes. Further, the therapist seems not to be aware of differences in *communication style* influenced by culture. As discussed in the last chapter, many cultures value subtlety and indirectness in discussing delicate matters. Discussion of personal and private matters is done indirectly rather than directly. In this case, Mr. Chang may be communicating his depression and loneliness by talking about somatic complaints as a means to an end. The social worker allowed Mr. Chang to "save face" by appearing to speak about physical/medical problems, and seeking his advice and outlook about her own aging parents. In actuality, however, both knew they were speaking about aging and emotional matters experienced by Mr. Chang.

Problem-Solving Approaches

Practical problem-solving approaches are often initially well received by clients of color and may serve as an entrée to discussing deeper psychological issues. But addressing these matters is important in itself. There are many clues in the case of Mr. Chang that point to concrete therapeutic goals in his life circumstance. First, it is important to address his current living situation. Ordinarily, an assisted living situation might ensure his safety (falls and emergency situations) and also provide him once again with a social support network (decrease isolation). Although he feels like a burden, most elderly Asian parents expect and prefer to spend their elderly years with family. This would have to be carefully explored with Mr. Chang and his daughter and sons. Second, lessening his social isolation, especially as he seems to have been a very socially active person in the past, would be a primary goal. Could his Church be enlisted to help in this regard? Would any of the congregants be able to help Mr. Chang once again be an active parishioner? What about senior centers? Third, family appears very important to Mr. Chang. Although his two sons and daughters live across the country, can they in some way alternate responsibility for visits or even invite their father to rotate staying with them for brief periods of time?

Cultural Expression of Mental Disorders

Culture and age have been found to influence how help is sought and how psychological distress is expressed in counseling. It is entirely possible that Mr. Chang's reluctance to talk about his feelings or see a psychologist/psychiatrist, and his focusing only upon somatic complaints, have age- and culture-related implications. Older adults, particularly those of the current 80+-year-old cohort, tend to have limited knowledge and understanding of mental health issues. Many of these individuals consider any mental health matter to be highly stigmatizing and may be limited in their ability to verbalize their issues and concerns in psychological terms. It is important to consider an Asian perspective associated with mental disorders as well. Restraint of strong feelings is a basic value that guides behavior, and is widely practiced; hence an unenlightened therapist might perceive the client as repressed, inhibited, or avoiding feelings. The therapist might not realize that asking Mr. Chang to talk about his feelings directly would violate a cultural norm.

Further, among traditional Asian groups, going for psychological help may bring shame and disgrace to the family ("being crazy"), and there are strong cultural sanctions against disclosure of family problems for fear that it would bring dishonor to everyone. Studies reveal that Asians and Asian Americans tend to underutilize counseling services, especially those associated with psychiatric problems. When Chinese do seek help, they are likely to present with a preponderance of somatic complaints or concrete problem-solving issues—not mental ones (Chang, McDonald, & O'Hara, 2014). For many Asian clients, physical complaints are viewed as less stigmatic than psychological ones and are more acceptable reasons to seek outside help.

Intersectionality of Age, Gender, and Race

It is important to note the contrasting styles of Dr. Martin and the social worker. The social worker seems to have been able to establish a better working relationship with Mr. Chang than the psychologist. Why? To address this question we need to look at both cultural factors that may influence the therapeutic relationship and sociodemographic differences between the provider and client. Three major differences are especially important in Asian culture: age, gender, and racial/cultural differences.

Mr. Chang is much older than Dr. Martin, he is a man in a relationship with a female therapist, and he is Chinese. In traditional Chinese culture, age is a powerful determinant of stature and influence. Younger individuals are expected to be respectful toward their elders, and to play the role of student who learns from the wiser person. Chinese culture is also patriarchal and values males over females as reflected in women's more subservient relationship to men. We are not advocating that these values be accepted by the therapist, but pointing out that age, gender, and race have a powerful effect on the working relationship. For Mr. Chang to be seen by a young, female White psychologist presents role reversals and interpersonal dilemmas that may strike at his pride and self-esteem. Dr. Martin does not appear to be aware of the cultural ramifications of her age, gender, and race upon Mr. Chang.

On the other hand, the social worker, who is equally young, female, and White, seems to have recognized these differences and altered her approach and strategy in working with Mr. Chang. One might surmise that Mr. Chang did not find Dr. Martin credible (her lack of cultural sensitivity), but respected the work of the social worker because she seemed to understand the cultural differences and responded accordingly. Unlike Dr. Martin, the social worker never used his first name but called him "Mr. Chang." In Asian culture, the more formal means of addressing an elder shows reverence. The social worker treated Mr. Chang in a manner that allowed him to feel respected and considered his knowledge and perceptions to be important and legitimate. She adroitly confined her initial work with him to very practical and applied matters related to his aging issues. For example, framing depression and other mental health problems as a physical illness and providing education related to its causes and treatment can be a helpful way of reducing stigma for older adults. Often, the concept of medical illness is more comfortable and familiar to elders, so education that frames the issue in terms of the physical causes and effects is often better received than more psychological explanations of symptoms.

Suicide Assessment

Finally, it is important to conduct a suicide assessment on Mr. Chang. Statistics support the fact that older adult males, age 85 and higher, are at higher risk for suicide than any other demographic group. There are of course racial/ethnic differences that a health provider would benefit from knowing. For example, older adult White males are three times more likely to commit suicide than their African American, Latino, and Hispanic counterparts. Evidence, however, indicates that the prevalence of suicide among older Asian Americans may be as high as that of older Whites (Carney & Sue, 2014). Regardless of race/ethnicity, however, suicide in the latter years must be a strong consideration for the health provider. It is important that a suicide lethality assessment be made in light of the many correlates of suicide found to be present with Mr. Chang: elderly male, recently widowed, feelings of hopelessness, lack of social support, and isolation from family. It is incumbent upon the mental health provider to be thoroughly knowledgeable and conversant with the correlates of suicide. Dr. Martin seems to be overlooking the warning signs associated with Mr. Chang's potential for suicide. For example, she seems to believe he is not a good candidate for "therapy" and that at his advanced age, he should be allowed to live as he desires. Behind this statement may lay a bias that is reflected in her work with older clients. One would wonder whether she would be equally cavalier if the client were a teenager.

The case of Mr. Chang illustrates the major focus of this chapter: understanding the need for culturally appropriate intervention skills, strategies, and roles. The importance of cultural flexibility in counseling and the need to approach counseling with culture-specific techniques such as how one addresses clients, activity level, mode of verbal intervention, focus and directness of conversations, tone of voice, content of remarks, and so forth are required understandings if the counselor is to meet the needs of the cultural background of diverse clients (Ratts & Pedersen, 2014).

COMMUNICATION STYLES

Effective helping depends on the counselor and the client being able to send and receive both verbal and nonverbal messages accurately and appropriately. It requires that the counselors not only *send* messages (make themselves understood) but also *receive* messages (attend to clients). The definition for effective counseling also includes *verbal* (content of what is said) and *nonverbal* (how something is said) elements. Most counselors seem more concerned with the *accuracy* of communication (getting to the heart of the matter) than with whether the communication is *appropriate*. The case of Mr. Chang illustrates how traditional Asian culture prizes a person's subtlety and indirectness in communication (Kim, 2011). In most cases, therapists have been trained to tune in to the content of what is said rather than to how something is said.

Communication style refers to those factors that go beyond the content of what is said. Communication specialists have historically found that only 30 to 40 percent of what is communicated conversationally is verbal (Ramsey & Birk, 1983; Singelis, 1994). What people say and do is usually qualified by other things that they say and do. A gesture, tone, inflection, posture, or degree of eye contact may enhance or negate the content of a message. *Communication styles* have a tremendous impact on our face-to-face encounters with others (Geva & Wiener, 2015). Whether our conversation proceeds in fits and starts, whether we interrupt one another continually or proceed smoothly, the topics we prefer to discuss or avoid, the depth of our involvement, the forms of interaction (e.g., ritual, repartee, argumentative, persuasive), and the channel we use to communicate (verbal–nonverbal versus nonverbal–verbal) are all aspects of *communication style*. Some refer to these factors as the *social rhythms* that underlie all our speech and actions. Communication styles are strongly correlated with race, culture, and ethnicity (Garrett & Portman, 2011; Ivey, Ivey & Zalaquett, 2014). Gender has been found to be a powerful determinant of *communication style* as well (Pearson, 1985; Robinson & Howard-Hamilton, 2000).

Reared in a EuroAmerican middle-class society, mental health professionals may assume that certain behaviors or rules of speaking are universal and possess the same meaning. This may create major problems for therapists and their culturally distinct clients. Since differences in *communication style* are most strongly manifested in *nonverbal communication*, this chapter concentrates on those aspects of communication that transcend the written or spoken word. First, we explore how race/culture may influence several areas of nonverbal behavior: (a) *proxemics*, (b) *kinesics*, (c) *paralanguage*, and (d) high-low context communication. Second, we briefly discuss the function and importance of nonverbal behavior as it relates to stereotypes and preconceived notions that we may have of diverse groups. Last, we propose a basic thesis that various racial minorities, such as Asian Americans, American Indians, African Americans, and Latino/Hispanic Americans, possess unique *communication styles* that may have major implications for mental health practice.

Nonverbal Communication

Although language, class, and cultural factors all interact to create problems in communication between culturally diverse clients and therapists, an oft neglected area is nonverbal behavior (Duran, 2006; Singelis, 1994). What people say can be either enhanced or negated by their nonverbals. When a man raises his voice, tightens his facial muscles, pounds the table violently, and proclaims, "Goddamn it, I'm not angry!" he is clearly contradicting the content of the communication. If we all share the same cultural and social upbringing, we may all arrive at the same conclusion. Interpreting nonverbals, however, is difficult for several reasons. First, the same nonverbal behavior on the part of an American Indian client may mean something quite different than if it were enacted by a White person (Locke & Bailey, 2014; Garrett & Portman, 2011). Second, nonverbals often occur outside our level of awareness but influence our evaluation and behavior. It is important to note that our discussion of nonverbal codes will not include all the possible areas, like olfaction (taste and smell), tactile cues, and artifactual communication (clothing, hairstyle, display of material things, etc.).

Proxemics

The study of *proxemics* refers to perception and use of personal and interpersonal space. Clear norms exist concerning the use of physical distance in social interactions. Edward Hall (1959) identified four interpersonal distance zones characteristic of U.S. culture: *intimate*, from contact to 1.5 ft.; *personal*, from 1.5 ft. to 4 ft.; *social*, from 4 ft. to 12 ft.; and *public* (lectures and speeches), greater than 12 ft.

In our society, individuals seem to grow more uncomfortable when others stand too close rather than too far away. This range of feelings and reactions associated with a violation of personal space includes flight, withdrawal, anger, and conflict (Pearson, 1985). On the other hand, we tend to allow closer proximity to people whom we like or feel interpersonal attraction toward. Some evidence exists that personal space can be reframed in terms of dominance and status. Those with greater status, prestige, and power may occupy more space (larger homes, cars, or offices).

However, different cultures dictate different distances in personal space. For Latin Americans, Africans, Black Americans, Indonesians, Arabs, South Americans, and French, conversing with a person dictates a much closer stance than is normally comfortable for EuroAmericans (Jensen, 1985; Nydell, 1996). A Latin American client's closeness may cause the therapist to back away. The client may interpret the therapist's behavior as aloofness, coldness, or a desire not to communicate. In some cross-cultural encounters, it may even be perceived as a sign of haughtiness and superiority. On the other hand, the therapist may misinterpret the client's behavior as an attempt to become inappropriately intimate, a sign of pushiness or aggressiveness. Both therapists and culturally diverse clients may benefit from understanding that their reactions and behaviors are attempts to create the spatial dimension to which they are culturally conditioned.

Research on *proxemics* leads to the inevitable conclusion that conversational distances are functions of the racial and cultural backgrounds of conversants (Mindess, 1999; Susman & Rosenfeld, 1982; Wolfgang, 1985). The factor of personal space has major implications for how furniture is arranged, where the seats are located, where you seat the client, and how far you sit from him or her. Latin Americans, for example, may not feel comfortable speaking to a person behind a desk. Many EuroAmericans, however, like to keep a desk between themselves and others. Some Eskimos may actually prefer to sit side by side rather than across from one another when talking about intimate aspects of their lives.

Kinesics

Whereas *proxemics* refers to personal space, *kinesics* is the term used to refer to bodily movements. It includes such things as facial expression, posture, characteristics of movement, gestures, and eye contact. Again, *kinesics* appears to be culturally conditioned. Many of our counseling assessments are based upon expressions on people's faces. We assume that facial cues express emotions and demonstrate the degree of responsiveness or involvement of the individual. For example, smiling is a type of expression in our society that is believed to indicate liking or positive affect. People attribute greater positive characteristics to others who smile; they are intelligent, have a good personality, and are pleasant (Singelis, 1994).

On the other hand, some Asians believe that smiling may suggest other meanings or even weakness. When Japanese smile and laugh, it does not necessarily mean happiness but may convey other meanings (e.g., embarrassment, discomfort, shyness). Among some Chinese and Japanese, restraint of strong feelings (anger, irritation, sadness, and love or happiness) is considered to be a sign of maturity and wisdom. Children learn that outward emotional displays (facial expressions, body movements, and verbal content) are discouraged except for extreme situations. Unenlightened counselors may assume that their Asian American client is lacking in feelings or is out of touch with them. More likely, the lack of facial expressions may be the basis of stereotypes, such as the statement that Asians are "inscrutable," "sneaky," "deceptive, " and "backstabbing."

A number of gestures and bodily movements have been found to have different meanings when the cultural context is considered (LaBarre, 1985). In the Sung Dynasty in China, sticking out the tongue was a gesture of mock terror and meant as ridicule; to the Ovimbundu of Africa, it means "You're a fool" (when coupled with bending the head forward); a protruding tongue in the Mayan statues of gods signifies wisdom; and in U.S. culture, it is generally considered to be a juvenile, quasi-obscene gesture of defiance, mockery, or contempt.

Head movements also have different meanings (Eakins & Eakins, 1985; Jensen, 1985). An educated Englishman may consider the lifting of the chin when conversing as a poised and polite gesture, but to EuroAmericans it may connote snobbery and arrogance ("turning up one's nose"). Whereas we shake our head from side to side to indicate "no," Mayan tribe members say "no" by jerking the head to the right. In Sri Lanka, one signals agreement by moving the head from side to side like a metronome (Singelis, 1994).

Most EuroAmericans perceive squatting (often done by children) as improper and childish. In other parts of the world, people have learned to rest by taking a squatting position. On the other hand, when we put our feet up on a desk, it is believed to signify a relaxed and informal attitude. Yet Latin Americans and Asians may perceive it as rudeness and arrogance, especially if the bottoms of the feet are shown to them.

Shaking hands is another gesture that varies from culture to culture and may have strong cultural/historical significance. Latin Americans tend to shake hands more vigorously, frequently, and for a longer period of time. Interestingly, most cultures use the right hand when shaking. Since most of the population of the world is right-handed, this may not be surprising. However, some researchers believe that shaking with the right hand may be a symbolic act of peace, as in older times it was the right hand that generally held the weapons. In some Muslim and Asian countries, touching anyone with the left hand may be considered an obscenity (the left hand aids in the process of elimination and is "unclean," whereas the right one is used for the intake of food and is "clean"). Offering something with the left hand to a Muslim may be an insult of the most serious type.

Eye contact is, perhaps, the nonverbal behavior most likely to be addressed by mental health providers. It is not unusual for us to hear someone say, "Notice that the husband avoided eye contact with the wife," or "Notice how the client averted his eyes when. . . ." Behind these observations is the belief that eye contact or lack of eye contact has diagnostic significance. We would agree with that premise but in most cases, counselors attribute negative traits to the avoidance of eye contact: shy, unassertive, sneaky, or depressed.

This lack of understanding has been played out in many different situations when Black–White interactions have occurred. In many cases it is not necessary for Blacks to look one another in the eye at all times to communicate. An African American may be actively involved in doing other things when engaged in a conversation. Many White therapists are prone to view the African American client as being sullen, resistant, or uncooperative. Smith (1981, p. 155) provides an excellent example of such a clash in communication styles:

> *For instance, one Black female student was sent to the office by her gymnasium teacher because the student was said to display insolent behavior. When the student was asked to give her version of the incident, she replied, "Mrs. X asked all of us to come over to the side of the pool so that she could show us how to do the backstroke. I went over with the rest of the girls. Then Mrs. X started yelling at me and said I wasn't paying attention to her because I wasn't looking directly at her. I told her I was paying attention to her (throughout the conversation, the student kept her head down, avoiding the principal's eyes), and then she said that she wanted me to face her and look her squarely in the eye like the rest of the girls [who were all White]. So I did. The next*

thing I knew she was telling me to get out of the pool, that she didn't like the way I was looking at her. So that's why I'm here."

As this example illustrates, African American styles of communication not only may be different from that of their White counterparts but also may lead to misinterpretations. Many Blacks do not nod their heads or say "uh-huh" to indicate they are listening (Hall, 1976; Kochman, 1981). Going through the motions of looking at the person and nodding the head is not necessary for many African Americans to indicate that they are listening (Hall, 1976). Statistics indicate that when White U.S. Americans listen to a speaker, they make eye contact with the speaker about 80 percent of the time. When speaking to others, however, they tend to look away (avoid eye contact) about 50 percent of the time. This is in marked contrast to many African Americans, who make greater eye contact when speaking and make infrequent eye contact when listening!

Paralanguage

The term *paralanguage* is used to refer to other vocal cues that individuals use to communicate. For example, loudness of voice, pauses, silences, hesitations, rate of speech, inflections, and the like all fall into this category. *Paralanguage* is very likely to be manifested forcefully in conversation conventions such as how we greet and address others and take turns in speaking. It can communicate a variety of different features about a person, such as age, gender, and emotional responses, as well as the race and sex of the speaker.

There are complex rules regarding when to speak or to yield to another person. For example, U.S. Americans frequently feel uncomfortable with a pause or silent stretch in the conversation, feeling obligated to fill it in with more talk. Silence is not always a sign for the listener to take up the conversation. While it may be viewed negatively by many, other cultures interpret the use of silence differently. The British and Arabs use silence for privacy, while the Russians, French, and Spanish read it as agreement among the parties (Hall, 1976). In Asian culture, silence is traditionally a sign of respect for elders. Furthermore, silence by many Chinese and Japanese is not a floor-yielding signal inviting others to pick up the conversation. Rather, it may indicate a desire to continue speaking after making a particular point. Often silence is a sign of politeness and respect rather than a lack of desire to continue speaking.

The amount of verbal expressiveness in the United States, relative to other cultures, is quite high. Most EuroAmericans encourage their children to enter freely into conversations, and teachers encourage students to ask many questions and state their thoughts and opinions. This has led many from other countries to observe that EuroAmerican youngsters are brash, immodest, rude, and disrespectful (Irvine & York, 1995; Jensen, 1985). Likewise, teachers of children of color may see reticence in speaking out as a sign of ignorance, lack of motivation, or ineffective teaching (Banks & Banks, 1993), when in reality the students may be showing proper respect (to ask questions is disrespectful because it implies that the teacher was unclear). American Indians, for example, have been taught that to speak out, ask questions, or even raise one's hand in class is immodest.

A mental health professional who is uncomfortable with silence or who misinterprets it may fill in the conversation and prevent the client from elaborating further. An even greater danger is to impute incorrect motives to the minority client's silence. One can readily see how therapy, which emphasizes talking, may place many minorities at a disadvantage.

Volume and intensity of speech in conversation are also influenced by cultural values. The overall loudness of speech displayed by many EuroAmerican visitors to foreign countries has earned them the reputation of being boisterous and shameless. In Asian countries, people tend to speak more softly and would interpret the loud volume of a U.S. visitor to be aggressiveness, loss of self-control, or anger. When compared to Arabs, however, people in the United States are soft-spoken. Many Arabs like to be bathed in sound, and the volume of their radios, DVDs, and televisions is quite loud. In some countries where such entertainment units are not plentiful, it is considered a polite and thoughtful act to allow neighbors to hear by keeping the volume high. We in the United States would view such behavior as being a thoughtless invasion of privacy.

A therapist or counselor working with clients would be well advised to be aware of possible cultural misinterpretations as a function of speech volume. Speaking loudly may not indicate anger and hostility, and speaking in a soft voice may not be a sign of weakness, shyness, or depression.

The directness of a conversation or the degree of frankness also varies considerably among various cultural groups. Observing the English in their parliamentary debates will drive this point home. The long heritage of open, direct, and frank confrontation leads to heckling of public speakers and quite blunt and sharp exchanges. Britons believe and feel that these are acceptable styles and may take no offense at being the object of such exchanges. However, U.S. citizens feel that such exchanges are impolite, abrasive, and irrational. Relative to Asians, EuroAmericans are seen as being too blunt and frank. Great care is taken by many

Asians not to hurt the feelings of or embarrass the other person. As a result, use of euphemisms and ambiguity is the norm.

Since many groups of color may value indirectness, the U.S. emphasis on "getting to the point" and "not beating around the bush" may alienate others. Asian Americans, American Indians, and some Latino/Hispanic Americans may see this behavior as immature, rude, and lacking in finesse. On the other hand, clients from different cultures may be negatively labeled as evasive and afraid to confront the problem.

REFLECTION AND DISCUSSION QUESTIONS

1. How can *proxemics* affect conversation distances and the use of personal space with culturally diverse clients in therapy?

2. When conversing with others, how aware are you of using your hands to talk, making eye contact, smiling or frowning, and other bodily movements?

3. Why is awareness of *kinesics* important in therapy?

4. Are you loud or soft-spoken? Do you speak quickly or slowly? When speaking to a person and a pause in the conversation occurs, are you comfortable or uncomfortable? Does silence bother you in counseling? How do you define a silent period: one second, two seconds, three seconds, or a minute? How may differences in *paralanguage* play out in the counseling session?

High-Low Context Communication

Edward Hall, author of such classics as *The Silent Language* (1959) and *The Hidden Dimension* (1969), is a well-known anthropologist who has proposed the concept of *high-* and *low-context* cultures (Hall, 1976). A *high context* (HC) communication or message is one that is anchored in the physical context (situation) or internalized in the person. Less reliance is placed on the explicit code or message content. An HC communication relies heavily on nonverbals and the group identification/understanding shared by those communicating. For example, a normal-stressed "no" by a U.S. American may be interpreted by an Arab as "yes." A real negation in Arab culture would be stressed much more emphatically.

In Filipino culture, a mild, hesitant "yes" is interpreted by those who understand as a "no" or a polite refusal. In traditional Asian society, many interactions are understandable only in light of *high-context* cues and situations. For example, to extend an invitation only once for dinner would be considered an affront because it implies that you are not sincere. One must extend an invitation several times, encouraging the invitee to accept. Arabs may also refuse an offer of food several times before giving in. However, most EuroAmericans believe that a host's offer can be politely refused with just a "no, thank you."

If we pay attention to only the explicit coded part of the message, we are likely to misunderstand the communication (Geva & Wiener, 2015). According to E. T. Hall (1976), *low-context* (LC) cultures place a greater reliance on the verbal part of the message. In addition, LC cultures have been associated with being more opportunistic, being more individual oriented than group oriented, and emphasizing rules of law and procedure.

It appears that the United States is an LC culture (although it is still higher than the Swiss, Germans, and Scandinavians in the amount of context required). China, perhaps, represents the other end of the continuum; its complex culture relies heavily on context. Asian Americans, African Americans, Hispanics, American Indians, and other minority groups in the United States also emphasize HC cues.

In contrast to LC communication, HC is faster, as well as more economical, efficient, and satisfying. Because it is so bound to the culture, it is slow to change and tends to be cohesive and unifying. LC communication does not unify but changes rapidly and easily.

Twins who have grown up together can and do communicate more economically (HC) than do two lawyers during a trial (LC). Bernstein's (1964) classic work in language analysis refers to restricted codes (HC) and elaborated codes (LC). Restricted codes are observed in families where words and sentences collapse and are shortened without loss of meaning. Elaborated codes, where many words are used to communicate the same content, are seen in classrooms, diplomacy, and law.

African American culture has been described as HC. For example, it is clear that many Blacks require fewer words than their White counterparts to communicate the same content (Irvine & York, 1995). An African American male who enters a room and spots an attractive woman may stoop slightly in her direction, smile, and tap the table twice while vocalizing a long drawn out "uh huh." What he has communicated would require many words from his White brother! The fact that African Americans may communicate more by HC cues has led many to characterize them as nonverbal, inarticulate, unintelligent, and so forth.

SOCIOPOLITICAL FACETS OF NONVERBAL COMMUNICATION

There is a common saying among African Americans: "If you really want to know what White folks are thinking and feeling, don't listen to what they say, but how they say it." In most cases, such a statement refers to the biases, stereotypes, and racist attitudes that Whites are believed to possess but consciously or unconsciously conceal.

Rightly or wrongly, many minority individuals through years of personal experience operate from three assumptions: The first assumption is that all Whites in this society are racist. Through their own cultural conditioning, they have been socialized into a culture that espouses the superiority of White culture over all others (Jones, 1997; Ridley, 2005; Sue, 2015). The second assumption is that most Whites find such a concept disturbing and will go to great lengths to deny that they are racist or biased. Some of this is done deliberately and with awareness, but in most cases one's racism is largely unconscious (Todd & Abrams, 2011). The last of these assumptions is that nonverbal behaviors are more accurate reflections of what a White person is thinking or feeling than what they say.

There is considerable evidence to suggest that these three assumptions held by various racial/ethnic minorities are indeed accurate (McIntosh, 1989; Ridley, 2005; Sue, 2010). Counselors and mental health practitioners need to be very cognizant of nonverbal cues from a number of different perspectives. In the last section we discussed how nonverbal behavior is culture bound and how the counselor or therapist cannot make universal interpretations about it. Likewise, nonverbal cues are important because they often (a) unconsciously reflect our biases and (b) trigger off stereotypes we have of other people.

Nonverbals as Reflections of Bias

Some time ago a TV program called *Candid Camera* was the rage in the United States. It operated from a unique premise, which involved creating very unusual situations for naive subjects who were then filmed as they reacted to them. One of these experiments involved interviewing housewives about their attitudes toward African American, Latino/Hispanic, and White teenagers. The intent was to select a group of women who by all standards appeared sincere in their beliefs that Blacks and Latinos were no more prone to violence than were their White counterparts. Unknown to them, they were filmed by a hidden camera as they left their homes to go shopping at the local supermarket.

The creator of the program had secretly arranged for an African American, a Latino, and a White youngster (dressed casually but nearly identically) to pass these women on the street. The experiment was counterbalanced; that is, the race of the youngster was randomly assigned as to which would approach the shopper first. What occurred was a powerful statement on unconscious racist attitudes and beliefs.

All the youngsters had been instructed to pass the shopper on the purse side of the street. If the woman was holding the purse in her right hand, the youngster would approach and pass on her right. If the purse was held with the left hand, the youngster would pass on her left. Studies of the film revealed consistent outcomes. Many women, when approached by the Black or the Latino youngster (approximately 15 feet away), would casually switch the purse from one arm to the other! This occurred infrequently with the White subject. Why?

The answer appears quite obvious to us. The women subjects who switched their purses were operating from biases, stereotypes, and preconceived notions about what minority youngsters are like: They are prone to crime, more likely to snatch a purse or rob, more likely to be juvenile delinquents, and more likely to engage in violence (Sue, 2010). The disturbing part of this experiment was that the selected subjects were, by all measures, sincere individuals who on a conscious level denied harboring racist attitudes or beliefs. They were not liars, nor were they deliberately deceiving the interviewer. They were normal, everyday people. They honestly believed that they did not possess these biases, yet when tested, their nonverbal behavior (purse switching) gave them away.

The power of *nonverbal communication* is that it tends to be least under conscious control. Studies support the conclusion that nonverbal cues operate primarily on an unaware level (DePaulo, 1992; Singelis, 1994), that they tend to be more spontaneous and more difficult to censor or falsify, and that they are more trusted than words. In our society, we have learned to use words (spoken or written) to mask or conceal our true thoughts and feelings. Note how our politicians and lawyers are able to address an issue without revealing much of what they think or believe.

Nonverbal behavior provides clues to conscious deceptions or unconscious bias (Utsey, Gernat, & Hammar, 2005). There is evidence that the accuracy of *nonverbal communication* varies with the part of the body used: Facial expression is more controllable than the hands, followed by the legs and the rest of the body (Hansen, Stevic, & Warner, 1982). The implications for multicultural counseling are obvious. Therapists who have not adequately dealt with their own biases and racist attitudes may unwittingly communicate them to culturally diverse clients. If counselors are unaware of their own biases, their nonverbals are most likely to reveal their true feelings. Studies suggest that women and persons of color are better readers of nonverbal cues than are White males (Hall, 1976; Jenkins, 1982). Much of this may be due to their HC orientation, but another reason may be *survival*. For an African American person to survive in a predominantly White society, he or she has to rely on nonverbal cues more often than verbal ones.

One of our male African American colleagues gives the example of how he must constantly be vigilant when traveling in an unknown part of the country. Just to stop at a roadside restaurant may be dangerous to his physical well-being. As a result, when entering a diner, he is quick to observe not only the reactions of the staff (waiter/waitress, cashier, cook, etc.) to his entrance but the reactions of the patrons as well. Do they stare at him? What type of facial expressions do they have? Do they fall silent? Does he get served immediately, or is there an inordinate delay? These nonverbal cues reveal much about the environment around him. He may choose to be himself or to play the role of a "humble" Black person who leaves quickly if the situation poses danger.

Interestingly, this very same colleague talks about tuning in to nonverbal cues as a means of *psychological survival*. He believes it is important for minorities to accurately read where people are coming from in order to prevent invalidation of the self. For example, a minority person driving through an unfamiliar part of the country may find him- or herself forced to stay at a motel overnight. Seeing a vacancy light flashing, the person may stop and knock on the manager's door. Upon opening the door and seeing the Black person, the White manager may show hesitation, stumble around in his or her verbalizations, and then apologize for having forgotten to turn off the vacancy light. The Black person is faced with the dilemma of deciding whether the White manager was telling the truth or is simply not willing to rent to a Black person.

Some of you might ask, "Why is it important for you to know? Why don't you simply find someplace else? After all, would you stay at a place where you were unwelcome?" Finding another place to stay might not be as important as the psychological well-being of the minority person. Racial/ethnic minorities have encountered too many situations in which double messages are given to them (microaggressions). For the African American to accept the simple statement, "I forgot to turn off the vacancy light," may be to deny one's own true feelings at being the victim of discrimination. This is especially true when the nonverbals (facial expression, anxiety in voice, and stammering) may reveal other reasons.

Too often, culturally diverse individuals are placed in situations where they are asked to deny their true feelings in order to perpetuate *White deception*. Statements that minorities are oversensitive (paranoid?) may represent a form of denial (Sue, Bucceri, Lin, Nadal, & Torino, 2007). Thus it is clear that racial/ethnic minorities are very tuned in to nonverbals. For therapists who have not adequately dealt with their own racism, clients of color will be quick to assess such biases. In many cases, clients of color may believe that the biases are too great to be overcome and will simply not continue in therapy. This is despite the good intentions of the White therapists who are not in touch with their own biases and assumptions about human behavior.

Nonverbals as Triggers to Biases and Fears

Often people assume that being an effective multicultural therapist is a straightforward process that involves the acquisition of knowledge about the various racial/ethnic groups. If we know that Asian Americans and African Americans have different patterns of eye contact and if we know that these patterns signify different things, then we should be able to eliminate biases and stereotypes that we possess. Were it so easy, we might have eradicated racism years ago. Although increasing our knowledge base about the lifestyles and experiences of marginalized groups is important, it is not a sufficient condition in itself. Our biased attitudes, beliefs, and feelings are deeply ingrained in our total being. Through years of conditioning they have acquired a strong irrational base, replete with emotional symbolism about each particular racial group. Simply opening a text and reading about African Americans and Latinos/Hispanics will not deal with our deep-seated fears and biases.

One of the major barriers to effective understanding is the common assumption that different cultural groups operate according to identical speech and communication conventions. In the United States, it is often assumed that distinctive racial, cultural, and linguistic features are deviant, inferior, or embarrassing (Kochman, 1981; Singelis, 1994; Stanback & Pearce, 1985). These value judgments then become tinged with beliefs that we hold about Black people: racial inferiority, being prone to violence and crime, quick to anger, and a threat to White folks. The *communication style* of Black people (manifested in nonverbals) can often trigger off these fears.

African American styles of communication are often high-key, animated, heated, interpersonal, and confrontational. Many emotions, affects, and feelings are generated (Hall, 1976; Shade & New, 1993; Weber, 1985). In a debate, African Americans tend to act as advocates of a position, and ideas are to be tested in the crucible of argument (Kochman, 1981). White middle-class styles, however, are characterized as being detached and objective, impersonal and nonchallenging. The person acts not as an *advocate* of the idea but as a *spokesperson* (truth resides in the idea). A discussion of issues should be devoid of affect because emotion and reason work against one another. One should talk things out in a logical fashion without getting personally involved. African Americans characterize their own style of communication as indicating that the person is sincere and honest, whereas EuroAmericans consider their own style to be reasoned and objective (Irvine & York, 1995). Many African Americans readily admit that they operate from a point of view and, as mentioned previously, are disinclined to believe that White folks do not. Smith (1981, p. 154) aptly describes the Black orientation in the following passage:

> *When one Black person talks privately with another, he or she might say: "Look, we don't have to jive each other or be like White folks; let's be honest with one another." These statements reflect the familiar Black saying that "talk is cheap," that actions speak louder than words, and that Whites beguile each other with words. . . . In contrast, the White mind symbolizes to many Black people deceit, verbal chicanery, and sterile intellectivity. For example, after long discourse with a White person, a Black individual might say: "I've heard what you've said, but what do you really mean?"*

Although African Americans may misinterpret White *communication styles*, it is more likely that Whites will misinterpret Black styles. The direction of the misunderstanding is generally linked to the activating of unconscious triggers or buttons about racist stereotypes and fears they represent. As we have repeatedly emphasized, one of the dominant stereotypes of African Americans in our society is that of the hostile, angry, prone-to-violence Black male. The more animated and affective communication style, closer conversing distance, prolonged eye contact when speaking, greater bodily movements, and tendency to test ideas in a confrontational/argumentative format lead many Whites to believe that their lives are in danger. It is not unusual for White mental health practitioners to describe their African American clients as being hostile and angry. We have also observed that some White trainees who work with Black clients respond nonverbally in such a manner as to indicate anxiety, discomfort, or fear (e.g., leaning away from their African American clients, tipping their chairs back, crossing their legs or arms). These are nonverbal distancing moves that may reflect the unconscious stereotypes that they hold of Black Americans. Although we would entertain the possibility that a Black client is angry, most occasions we have observed do not justify such a descriptor.

It appears that many EuroAmericans operate from the assumption that when an argument ensues, it may lead to a ventilation of anger with the outbreak of a subsequent fight. What many Whites fail to realize is that African Americans distinguish between an argument used to debate a difference of opinion and one that ventilates anger and hostility (DePaulo, 1992; Irvine & York, 1995; Kochman, 1981; Shade & New, 1993). In the former, the affect indicates sincerity and seriousness; there is a positive attitude toward the material; and the validity of ideas is challenged. In the latter, the affect is more passionate than sincere; there is a negative attitude toward the opponent; and the opponent is abused.

To understand African American styles of communication and to relate adequately to Black communication would require much study in the origins, functions, and manifestations of Black language (Jenkins, 1982). Weber (1985) believes that the historical and philosophical foundations of Black language have led to several verbal styles among Blacks. *Rapping* (not the White usage, rap session) was originally a dialogue between a man and a woman in which the intent was to win over the admiration of the woman. Imaginary statements, rhythmic speech, and creativity are aimed at getting the woman interested in hearing more of the rap. It has been likened to a mating call, an introduction of the male to the female, and a ritual expected by some African American women.

Another style of verbal banter is called *woofing*, which is an exchange of threats and challenges to fight. It may have derived from what African Americans refer to as *playing the dozens*, which is considered by many Blacks to be the highest form of verbal warfare and impromptu speaking (Jenkins, 1982; Kochman, 1981; Weber, 1985). To the outsider, it may appear cruel, harsh, and provocative. Yet to many in the Black community, it has historical and functional meanings.

The term *dozens* was used by slave owners to refer to Black people with disabilities. Because they were considered damaged goods, disabled Black people would often be sold at a discount rate with eleven other damaged slaves (making one dozen) (Weber, 1985). It was primarily a selling ploy in which *dozens* referred to the negative physical features. Often played in jest, the game requires an audience to act as judge and jury over the originality, creativity, and humor of the combatants. Here are three examples:

> *Say man, your girlfriend so ugly, she had to sneak up on a glass to get a drink of water. . . . Man, you so ugly, yo mamma had to put a sheet over your head so sleep could sneak up on you. (Weber, 1985, p. 248)*

A: Eat shit.

B: What should I do with your bones?

A: Build a cage for your mother.

B: At least I got one.

A: She is the least. (Labov, 1972, p. 321)

A: Got a match?

B: Yeah, my ass and your face or my farts and your breath. (Kochman, 1981, p. 54)

Woofing and *playing the dozens* seem to have very real functional value. First, they allow training in self-control and managing one's anger and hostility in the constant face of racism. In many situations, it would be considered dangerous by an African American to respond to taunts, threats, and insults. Second, *woofing* also allows a Black person to establish a hierarchy or pecking order without resorting to violence. Last, it can create an image of being fearless where one will gain respect.

This verbal and nonverbal style of communication can be a major aspect of Black interactions. Likewise, other minority groups have characteristic styles that may cause considerable difficulties for White counselors. One way of contrasting *communication style* differences may be in the overt activity dimension (the pacing/intensity) of *nonverbal communication*. Table 8.1 contrasts five different groups along this continuum. How these styles affect the therapist's perception and ability to work with culturally different clients is important for each and every one of us to consider.

TABLE 8.1 Communication Style Differences (Overt Activity Dimension—Nonverbal/Verbal)

American Indians	Asian Americans and Hispanics	Whites	Blacks
1. Speak softly/slower	1. Speak softly	1. Speak loud/fast to control listener	1. Speak with affect
2. Indirect gaze when listening or speaking	2. Avoidance of eye contact when listening or speaking to high-status persons	2. Greater eye contact when listening	2. Direct eye contact (prolonged) when speaking, but less when listening
3. Interject less; seldom offer encouraging communication	3. Similar rules	3. Head nods, nonverbal markers	3. Interrupt (turn taking) when can
4. Delayed auditory (silence)	4. Mild delay	4. Quick responding	4. Quicker responding
5. Manner of expression low-keyed, indirect	5. Low-keyed, indirect	5. Objective, task oriented	5. Affective, emotional, interpersonal

COUNSELING AND THERAPY AS COMMUNICATION STYLE

Throughout this text we have repeatedly emphasized that *different* theories of counseling and psychotherapy represent *different communication styles* (Ivey, Ivey, & Zalaquett, 2014). Just as race, culture, ethnicity, and gender may affect *communication styles*, there is considerable evidence that theoretical orientations in counseling will influence helping styles as well. When one watches Carl Rogers (Person-Centered Counseling) and Albert Ellis (Rational Emotive Behavior Therapy) conducting therapy, one is struck by how differently they interact with clients.

Differential Skills in Multicultural Counseling/Therapy

There is strong support for the belief that different cultural groups may be more receptive to certain counseling/*communication styles* because of cultural and sociopolitical factors (Choudhuri, Santiago-Rivera, & Garrett, 2012; Diller, 2011; West-Olatunji & Conwill, 2011). Indeed, the literature on multicultural counseling/therapy strongly suggests that American Indians, Asian Americans, Black Americans, and Hispanic Americans tend to prefer more active-directive forms of helping than nondirective ones (Brammer, 2012; Ratts & Pedersen, 2014). We briefly describe two of these group differences here to give the reader some idea of their implications.

Asian American clients who may value restraint of strong feelings and believe that intimate revelations are to be shared only with close friends may cause problems for the counselor who is oriented toward insight or feelings (a la Mr. Chang). It is entirely possible that such techniques as reflection of feelings, asking questions of a deeply personal nature, and making in-depth interpretations may be perceived as lacking in respect for the client's integrity (Locke & Bailey, 2014). Asian American clients may not initially value insight approaches. For example, some clients who come for vocational information may be perceived by counselors as needing help in finding out what motivates their actions and decisions. Requests for advice or information from the client are seen as indicative of deeper, more personal conflicts. Although this might be true in some cases, the blind application of techniques that clash with cultural values seriously places many Asian Americans in an uncomfortable and oppressed position (Chang et al., 2014).

Many years ago, Atkinson, Maruyama, and Matsui (1978) tested this hypothesis with a number of Asian American students. Two tape recordings of a contrived counseling session were prepared in which the client's responses were identical but the counselor's responses differed, being directive in one and nondirective in the other. Their findings indicated that counselors who use the directive approach were rated more credible and approachable than were those using the nondirective counseling approach. Asian Americans seem to prefer a logical, rational, structured counseling approach to an affective, reflective, and ambiguous one. Other researchers have drawn similar conclusions (Atkinson & Lowe, 1995; Leong, 1986; Lin, 2001).

In a classic and groundbreaking study, Berman (1979) found similar results with a Black population. The weakness of the previous study was its failure to compare equal responses with a White population. Berman's study compared the use of counseling skills between Black and White, male and female counselors. A videotape of culturally varied client vignettes was viewed by Black and White counselor trainees. They responded to the question, "What would you say to this person?" The data were scored and coded according to a microcounseling taxonomy that divided counseling skills into attending and influencing ones (Ivey, Ivey, & Zalaquett, 2014). The hypothesis made by the investigator was that Black and White counselors would give significantly different patterns of responses to their clients.

Data supported the hypothesis. Black males and females tended to use the more active expressive skills (directions, expression of content, and interpretation) with greater frequency than did their White counterparts. White males and females tended to use a higher percentage of attending skills. Berman concluded that the counselor's race/culture appears to be a major factor in his or her choice of skills, and that Black and White counselors appear to adhere to two distinctive styles of counseling. Berman also concluded that the more active styles of the Black counselor tend to include practical advice and allow for the interjection of a counselor's values and opinions.

The implications for therapy become glaringly apparent. Mental health training programs tend to emphasize the more passive attending skills. Therapists so trained may be ill equipped to work with culturally different clients who might find the active approach more relevant to their own needs and values (Parham, Ajamu, & White, 2011).

Implications for Multicultural Counseling/Therapy

Ivey's continuing contributions (Ivey, 1986; Ivey, D'Andrea, & Ivey, 2011; Ivey, Ivey, & Zalaquett, 2014) in the field of microcounseling, multicultural counseling, and developmental counseling seem central to our understanding of counseling/ *communication styles*. He believes that different theories are concerned with generating different sentences and constructs and that different cultures may also be expected to generate different sentences and constructs. Counseling and psychotherapy may be viewed as special types of temporary cultures (Ivey et al., 2011). When the counseling style of the counselor does not match the *communication style* of his or her culturally diverse clients, many difficulties may arise: premature termination of the session, inability to establish rapport, or cultural oppression of the client. Thus it becomes clear that effective multicultural counseling occurs when the counselor and the client are able to send and receive both verbal and nonverbal messages appropriately and accurately. When the counselor is able to engage in such activities, his or her credibility and attractiveness will be increased. *Communication styles* manifested in the clinical context may either enhance or negate the effectiveness of multicultural counseling. Several major implications for counseling can be discerned.

Therapeutic Practice

As practicing clinicians who work with a culturally diverse population, we need to move decisively in educating ourselves about the differential meanings of nonverbal behavior and the broader implications for *communication styles*. We need to realize that *proxemics*, *kinesics*, *paralanguage*, and high-low context factors are important elements of communication, that they may be highly culture bound, and that we should guard against possible misinterpretation in our assessment of clients. Likewise, it is important that we begin to become aware of and understand our own communication/helping style.

We believe that therapists must be able to shift their *therapeutic styles* to meet the developmental needs of clients. We contend further that effective mental health professionals are those who can also shift their helping styles to meet the cultural dimensions of their clients. Therapists of differing theoretical orientations will tend to use different skill patterns. These skill patterns may be antagonistic or inappropriate to the communication/helping styles of clients. In research cited earlier, it was clear that White counselors (by virtue of their cultural conditioning and training) tended to use the more passive attending and listening skills in counseling/therapy, whereas racial/ethnic minority populations appear more oriented toward an active influencing approach. There are several reasons why this may be the case.

First, we contend that the use of more directive, active, and influencing skills is more likely to provide personal information about where the therapist is coming from (self-disclosure). Giving advice or suggestions, interpreting, and telling the client how you, the counselor or therapist, feel are really acts of counselor self-disclosure. Although the use of attending or more nondirective skills may also include self-disclosure, it tends to use influencing skills only minimally. In multicultural counseling, the culturally diverse client is likely to approach the counselor with trepidation: "What makes you any different from all the Whites out there who have oppressed me?" "What makes you immune from inheriting the racial biases of your forebears?" "Before I open up to you [self-disclose], I want to know where you are coming from." "How open and honest are you about your own racism, and will it interfere with our relationship?" "Can you really understand what it's like to be Asian, Black, Hispanic, American Indian, or the like?" In other words, a culturally diverse client may not open up (self-disclose) until you, the helping professional, self-disclose first. Thus, to many minority clients, a therapist who expresses his or her thoughts and feelings may be better received in a counseling situation.

Second, the more positive response by people of color to the use of influencing skills appears to be related to diagnostic focus. Studies support the thesis that White therapists are more likely to focus their problem diagnosis in individual rather than societal terms. In a society where individualism prevails, it is not surprising to find that EuroAmerican counselors tend to view their clients' problems as residing within the individual rather than society. Thus the role of the therapist will be person-focused because the problem resides within the individual. Skills utilized will be individual-centered (attending), aimed at changing the person. Many marginalized groups accept the importance of individual contributions to the problem, but they also give great weight to systemic or societal factors that may adversely impact their lives. People of color who have been the victims of discrimination and oppression perceive that the problem resides externally to the person (societal forces). Active systems intervention is called for, and the most appropriate way to attack the environment (stressors) would be an active approach (Ratts & Pedersen, 2014). If the counselor shares this perception, he or she may take a more active role in the sessions, giving advice and suggestions, as well as teaching strategies (becoming a partner to the client).

Finally, although it would be ideal if we could effectively engage in the full range of therapeutic responses, such a wish may prove unrealistic. We cannot be all things to everyone; that is, there are personal limits to how much we can change our *communication styles* to match those of our clients. The difficulty in shifting styles may be a function of inadequate practice, inability to understand the other person's worldview, or personal biases or racist attitudes that have not been adequately resolved. In these cases, the counselor might consider several alternatives: (a) seek additional training/education, (b) seek consultation with a more experienced counselor, (c) refer the client to another therapist, and (d) become aware of personal *communication style* limitations and try to anticipate their possible impact on the culturally diverse client. Often, a therapist who recognizes the limitations of his or her helping style and knows how it will impact a culturally diverse client can take steps to minimize possible conflicts.

IMPLICATIONS FOR CLINICAL PRACTICE

1. Recognize that no one style of counseling or therapy will be appropriate for all populations and situations. A counselor or therapist who is able to engage in a variety of helping styles and roles is most likely to be effective in working with a diverse population.

2. Become knowledgeable about how race, culture, and gender affect *communication styles*.

3. Your clinical observation skills will be greatly enhanced if you sharpen your nonverbal powers of observation of clients.

4. Become aware of your own communication and helping styles. Know your social impact on others and anticipate how it affects your clients.

5. Try to obtain additional training and education on a variety of theoretical orientations and approaches in order to expand your helping styles.

6. Realize that we are *feeling, thinking, behaving, social, cultural, spiritual*, and *political* beings. Try to think holistically rather than in a reductionist manner when it comes to conceptualizing the human condition.

7. It is important for training programs to use an approach that calls for openness and flexibility both in conceptualizing the issues and in actual skill building. Develop and use helping strategies, techniques, and styles that consider not only individual characteristics, but cultural and racial factors as well.

SUMMARY

Counseling styles and approaches must be adapted to meet the sociodemographic characteristics of a diverse clientele. Helping professionals who are unaware of culture, age, and gender differences as they affect communication and helping styles may make inaccurate assessments, diagnoses, and treatments. They may assume that certain behaviors or rules of speaking are universal and possess the same meaning. *Communication style* refers to those factors that go beyond the content of what is said. Communication specialists have historically found that only 30 to 40 percent of what is communicated conversationally is verbal. A gesture, tone, inflection, posture, or degree of eye contact may enhance or negate the content of a message.

Differences in communication style are most strongly manifested in *nonverbal communication*, or those aspects of communication that transcend the written or spoken word. Race and culture may influence several areas of nonverbal behavior, leading to misunderstandings. *Nonverbal communication* includes the following dimensions: (a) *Proxemics* is the use of personal space between conversants. (b) *Kinesics* refers to bodily movements and includes facial expression, posture, characteristics of movement, gestures, and eye contact. (c) *Paralanguage* refers to vocal cues that individuals use to communicate, such as loudness of voice, pauses, silences, hesitations, rate of speech, and inflections. (d) *High-low context* communication refers to whether a person relies more on the context or the content to interpret the meaning of the message. Race, culture, ethnicity, and gender all influence how people communicate in these four dimensions.

Nonverbal cues are important because they often (a) unconsciously reflect our biases and (b) trigger off stereotypes we have of other people. Several important findings possess implications for work with diverse clients. First, *nonverbal communication* is least under conscious control. Second, it has been found that marginalized group members are better readers of nonverbal cues than their majority counterparts. Third, in multicultural counseling, an unenlightened mental health professional may unintentionally communicate his or her biases and fears to clients. Last, in working with Asian Americans, American Indians, African Americans, and Latino/Hispanic Americans, it is important to be cognizant of their unique *communication styles*, which have major implications for mental health practice.

GLOSSARY TERMS

Communication style	Nonverbals as triggers to bias
High-/low-context communication	Paralanguage
High-context cultures (HC)	Playing the dozens
Kinesics	Proxemics
Low-context cultures (LC)	Therapeutic style
Nonverbal communication	Verbal communication
Nonverbals as bias reflection	Woofing

REFERENCES

Atkinson, D. R., & Lowe, S. M. (1995). The role of ethnicity, cultural knowledge, and conventional techniques in counseling and psychotherapy. In J. G. Ponterotto, J. M. Casas, L. M. Suzuki, & C. M. Alexander (Eds.), *Handbook of multicultural counseling* (pp. 3–16). Thousand Oaks, CA: Sage.

Atkinson, D. R., Maruyama, M., & Matsui, S. (1978). The effects of counselor race and counseling approach on Asian Americans' perceptions of counselor credibility and utility. *Journal of Counseling Psychology, 25,* 76–83.

Banks, J. A., & Banks, C. A. (1993). *Multicultural education.* Boston, MA: Allyn & Bacon.

Berman, J. (1979). Counseling skills used by Black and White male and female counselors. *Journal of Counseling Psychology, 26,* 81–84.

Bernstein, B. (1964). Elaborated and restricted codes: Their social origins and some consequences. *American Anthropologist, 66,* 55–69.

Brammer, R. (2012). *Diversity in counseling.* Belmont, CA: Cengage.

Carney, K. O., & Sue, D. W. (2014). Clinical applications with older adults. In D. W. Sue, H. A. Neville, & M. E. Gallardo (Eds.), *Case studies in multicultural counseling and therapy* (pp. 247–265). Hoboken, NJ: Wiley.

Chang, C. Y., McDonald, C. P., & O'Hara, C. (2014). Counseling clients from Asian and Pacific Island Heritages. In M. J. Ratts & P. B. Pedersen (Eds.), *Counseling for multiculturalism and social justice* (pp. 127–142). Alexandria, VA: American Counseling Association.

Choudhuri, D. D., Santiago-Rivera, A. L., & Garrett, M. T. (2012). *Counseling and diversity.* Belmont, CA: Cengage.

DePaulo, B. M. (1992). Nonverbal behavior and self-presentation. *Psychological Bulletin, 111,* 203–243.

Diller, J. V. (2011). *Cultural diversity.* Belmont, CA: Cengage.

Duran, E. (2006). *Healing the soul wound.* New York, NY: Teachers College Press.

Eakins, B. W., & Eakins, R. G. (1985). Sex differences in nonverbal communication. In L. A. Samovar & R. E. Porter (Eds.), *Intercultural communication: A reader* (pp. 290–307). Belmont, CA: Wadsworth.

Garrett, M. T., & Portman, T.A.A. (2011). *Counseling Native Americans.* Belmont, CA: Cengage.

Geva, E., & Wiener, J. (2015). *Psychological assessment of culturally and linguistically diverse children and adolescents.* New York, NY: Springer.

Hall, E. T. (1959). *The silent language.* Greenwich, CT: Premier Books.

Hall, E. T. (1969). *The hidden dimension.* New York, NY: Anchor Press.

Hall, E. T. (1976). *Beyond culture.* New York, NY: Anchor Press.

Hansen, J. C., Stevic, R. R., & Warner, R. W. (1982). *Counseling: Theory and process.* Toronto, Canada: Allyn & Bacon.

Irvine, J. J., & York, D. E. (1995). Learning styles and culturally diverse students: A literature review. In J. A. Banks & C. A. McGee Banks (Eds.), *Handbook of research on multicultural education* (pp. 484–497). New York, NY: Macmillan.

Ivey, A. E. (1986). *Developmental therapy.* San Francisco, CA: Jossey-Bass.

Ivey, A. E., D'Andrea, M. J., & Ivey, M. B. (2011). *Theories of counseling and psychotherapy: A multicultural perspective.* Boston, MA: Allyn &Bacon.

Ivey, A. E., Ivey, M. B., & Zalaquett, C. P. (2014). *Intentional interviewing and counseling* (8th ed.). Belmont, CA: Brooks/Cole.

Jenkins, A. H. (1982). *The psychology of the Afro-American.* New York, NY: Pergamon Press.

Jensen, J. V. (1985). Perspective on nonverbal intercultural communication. In L. A. Samovar & R. E. Porter (Eds.), *Intercultural communication: A reader* (pp. 256–272). Belmont, CA: Wadsworth.

Jones, J. M. (1997). *Prejudice and racism* (2nd ed.). Washington, DC: McGraw-Hill.

Kim, B.S.K. (2011). *Counseling Asian Americans.* Belmont, CA: Cengage.

Kochman, T. (1981). *Black and White styles in conflict.* Chicago, IL: University of Chicago Press.

LaBarre, W. (1985). Paralinguistics, kinesics and cultural anthropology. In L. A. Samovar & R. E. Porter (Eds.), *Intercultural communication: A reader* (pp. 272–279). Belmont, CA: Wadsworth.

Labov, W. (1972). *Language in the inner city: Studies in the Black English vernacular.* Philadelphia, PA: University of Pennsylvania Press.

Leong, F.T.L. (1986). Counseling and psychotherapy with Asian-Americans: Review of literature. *Journal of Counseling Psychology, 33,* 196–206.

Lin, Y. (2001). The effects of counseling styles and stages on perceived counselor effectiveness from Taiwanese female university clients. *Asian Journal of Counselling, 8,* 35–60.

Locke, D. C., & Bailey, D. F. (2014). *Increasing multicultural understanding.* Thousand Oaks, CA: Sage.

McIntosh, P. (1989, July/August). White privilege: Unpacking the invisible knapsack. *Peace and Freedom,* pp. 8–10.

Mindess, A. (1999). *Reading between the signs.* Yarmouth, ME: Intercultural Press.

Nydell, M. K. (1996). *Understanding Arabs: A guide for Westerners.* Yarmouth, ME: Intercultural Press.

Parham, T. A., Ajamu, A., & White, J. L. (2011). *The psychology of Blacks. Centering our perspectives in the African consciousness.* Boston, MA: Prentice Hall.

Pearson, J. C. (1985). *Gender and communication.* Dubuque, IA: W. C. Brown.

Ramsey, S., & Birk, J. (1983). Preparation of North Americans for interaction with Japanese: Considerations of language and communication style. In D. Landis & R. W. Brislin (Eds.), *Handbook of intercultural training· Volume III* (pp. 227–259). New York, NY: Pergamon Press.

Ratts, M. J., & Pedersen, P. B. (Eds.) (2014). *Counseling for multiculturalism and social justice.* Alexandria, VA: American Counseling Association.

Ridley, C. R. (2005). *Overcoming unintentional racism in counseling and therapy* (2nd ed.). Thousand Oaks, CA: Sage.

Robinson, T. L., & Howard-Hamilton, M. F. (2000). *The convergence of race, ethnicity, and gender.* Columbus, OH: Merrill.

Shade, B. J., & New, C. A. (1993). Cultural influences on learning: Teaching implications. In J. A. Banks & C. A. McGee Banks (Eds.), *Multicultural education* (pp. 317–331). Boston, MA: Allyn & Bacon.

Singelis, T. (1994). Nonverbal communication in intercultural interactions. In R. W. Brislin & T. Yoshida (Eds.), *Improving intercultural interactions* (pp. 268–294). Thousand Oaks, CA: Sage.

Smith, E. J. (1981). Cultural and historical perspectives in counseling Blacks. In D. W. Sue (Ed.), *Counseling the culturally different: Theory and practice* (pp. 141–185). New York, NY: Wiley.

Stanback, M. H., & Pearce, W. B. (1985). Talking to "the man": Some communication strategies used by members of "subordinate" social groups. In L. A. Samovar & R. E. Porter (Eds.), *Intercultural communication: A reader* (pp. 236–253). Belmont, CA: Wadsworth.

Sue, D. W. (2010). *Microaggressions and marginality: Manifestations, dynamics, and impact.* Hoboken, NJ: Wiley.

Sue, D. W. (2015). *Race talk and the conspiracy of silence: Understanding and facilitating difficult dialogues on race.* Hoboken, NJ: Wiley.

Sue, D. W., Bucceri, J., Lin, A. I., Nadal, K. L., & Torino, G. C. (2007). Racial microaggressions and the Asian American experience. *Cultural Diversity and Ethnic Minority Psychology, 13,* 72–81.

Susman, N. M., & Rosenfeld, H. M. (1982). Influence of culture, language and sex on conversation distance. *Journal of Personality and Social Psychology, 42,* 66–74.

Todd, N. R., & Abrams, E. M. (2011). White dialectics: A new framework for theory, research and practice with White students. *Counseling Psychologist, 39,* 353–395.

Utsey, S. O., Gernat, C. A., & Hammar, L. (2005). Examining White counselor trainees' reactions to racial issues in counseling and supervision dyads. *Counseling Psychologist, 33,* 449–478.

Weber, S. N. (1985). The need to be: The sociocultural significance of Black language. In L. A. Samovar & R. E. Porter (Eds.), *Intercultural communication: A reader* (pp. 244–253). Belmont, CA: Wadsworth.

West-Olatunji, C. A., & Conwill, W. (2011). *Counseling African Americans.* Belmont, CA: Cengage.

Wolfgang, A. (1985). The function and importance of nonverbal behavior in intercultural counseling. In P. B. Pedersen (Ed.), *Handbook of cross-cultural counseling and therapy* (pp. 99–105). Westport, CT: Greenwood Press.

Multicultural Evidence-Based Practice

9

Chapter Objectives

1.   Become familiar with the role and importance of using research to determine what therapy treatment is best suited for diverse clients.

2.   Define *empirically supported treatments* (ESTs).

3.   Know the rationale for the development of *empirically supported relationships* (ESRs). Be able to describe the relationship variables that are considered to be research supported.

4.   Become aware of how evidence-based practice (EBP) and multicultural counseling are converging.

5.   Describe the modifications that need to be made in the counseling alliance (*empathy* and relationship building) to work with different ethnic groups.

6.   Describe how EBP differs from ESTs and ESRs. Be able to outline the advantages of focusing on client values and preferences.

7.   Describe similarities and differences between EBP and cultural competence.

8.   Become cognizant of the advantages and disadvantages of using "culturally adapted" forms of research-based psychotherapies.

Significant portions of this chapter are adapted from D. Sue and D. M. Sue (2008).

HAJIMI MATSUMOTO

Hajimi was a first-generation, 18-year-old, Japanese American male who lived most of his life in Japan before returning to the United States. He came to the university counseling center suffering from a severe social phobia. I was a White American female psychology intern being supervised by Dr. Katsumoto, a female Japanese American staff psychologist known for her work on multicultural psychology and cultural competence. I had seen the client, Hajimi, for approximately six sessions. Hajimi was an extremely shy young man who spoke in a barely audible voice, responded in short but polite statements, avoided eye contact, and sat facing my window rather than me. When I first met him, he would not shake my hand but simply nodded his head in acknowledgment. He fidgeted in his seat and seemed extremely uncomfortable in my presence. He described high anxiety in social or performance situations and was extremely nervous around women. He was afraid of being belittled by others, didn't know how to make "small talk," and constantly obsessed as to whether his personal hygiene (bad breath or body odor) might be offensive. Yet on none of his visits to my office did I detect any sort of strong or disagreeable odor.

Hajimi was referred to the counseling center by one of his professors after a particularly embarrassing and humiliating situation that occurred in the classroom: He "froze" in front of fellow students while doing a team oral presentation. Despite having detailed notes, he stammered, stuttered, and broke out in a profuse sweat that made it impossible to continue. When one of his female classmates on the team tried to offer support by placing her arm on his shoulder, Hajimi felt sure she could feel the perspiration on his shirt and panicked. He became embarrassed, broke away from her, quickly excused himself, and left the classroom. Apparently, these types of anxiety-provoking situations and encounters were very common in his life.

As all interns needed to take responsibility for making a client presentation at bimonthly case conference meetings, I chose to present my client, Hajimi. Case conferences are usually attended by staff psychologists, student interns, and the consulting psychiatrist. The psychiatrist, Dr. Machovitch, a White male at the medical school, was known for his psychodynamic orientation, whereas most of the psychologists at the center had either a multicultural or behavioral approach. After I had provided a detailed history of Hajimi including his symptoms and possible etiological factors, and offered a proposed treatment plan, a clear difference of opinion began to emerge between Drs. Machovitch and Katsumoto and another psychologist, Dr. Barnard. The three had quite a heated exchange, and I felt caught in the middle because they each recommended a different approach. Further, they all differed in their analysis and diagnosis of the problem.

Client Background:

Hajimi was the only son of a traditional Japanese couple who had wanted many more children but for unknown reasons could not conceive any others. All their hopes for

CASE STUDY

carrying on the family name resided in Hajimi. When Hajimi was first born, the parents were overjoyed to have a son, but as time wore on, the father became disappointed in his son's effeminate behavior, hypersensitivity, inability to control his emotions, and social-outcast role among classmates. The father belittled him, seemed to be ashamed to introduce Hajimi to friends, and isolated him from family gatherings. Whenever Hajimi would do something wrong and show remorse by crying, his father would say in Japanese, "Leave me, you offend me." The mother, who was more sympathetic to Hajimi's needs, nevertheless seldom intervened when her husband berated Hajimi almost on a daily basis. On one particularly angry encounter in which his father severely criticized him, Hajimi wept openly in front of his mother. His mother tried to console him by placing her arms around his shoulder and reassuring him that one day his father would be proud of him. Rather than being comforted, however, her actions seemed to cause further distress as he quickly ran to his bedroom and slammed the door.

Although Hajimi had done well academically in his early years, his grades began to suffer in college. Much of this was due to his severe social phobia, which affected his ability to speak up in classes and isolated him from fellow students and teachers. He was awkward and inept in social situations, became anxious around people, and would seldom speak. In his physical education classes, which required dancing with girls, he would panic and perspire freely. He felt embarrassed to touch the hands of his partner or to have them touch him for fear they would find his wet hands and clothes offensive. Hajimi often expressed his belief that he was not perfect enough. In school, he became increasingly obsessed with avoiding failure, playing it safe, and not making mistakes. Unfortunately, this approach had a negative impact on his academic work, as he would often take incompletes and withdraw from classes for fear that he was not doing well. He would frequently choose a college course on the basis of whether it offered a pass/no pass option. Hajimi admitted to an intense fear of failure and was aware that these choices allowed him to temporarily avoid poor grades. He knew that failing grades generated only greater criticism from his father.

THEORETICAL DIFFERENCES

The disagreement among the three therapists as to the diagnosis and treatment of Hajimi appeared tied to their theoretical orientations and/or their clinical experiences. Dr. Katsumoto stressed cultural factors, whereas Dr. Machovitch believed a psychodynamic approach was clearly indicated in work with Hajimi. The discussion was compounded by Dr. Barnard, a male psychologist with a strong cognitive-behavioral orientation who argued for a behavioral program of assertiveness training and systematic desensitization of his social phobia. The gist of their positions can be captured in the following snapshots of their arguments.

Dr. Katsumoto (Cultural Analysis):

Sociodemographic factors such as race, culture, and ethnicity are important in understanding Hajimi's difficulties. Many of the behaviors exhibited by him may be cultural dictates rather than pathology. For example, his behavior in the counseling session (lack of eye contact, low tone of voice, short but polite responses, and social distance) with the counselor may not be considered pathological in Japanese culture. Although I do believe he suffers from psychological problems, the diagnosis of social phobia may be inaccurate and lead to an inappropriate treatment plan. Even DSM-5 recognizes the existence of cultural syndromes, which are locality-specific patterns of aberrant behavior not linked to a specific DSM diagnosis. For example, in Japan and Korea, there is a condition called 'taijin kyofusho' that resembles a social phobia, which is accompanied by an intense fear that the person's body, its parts, or its functions displease or are offensive to people. It is often manifested in a fear that one's body odor may prove interpersonally repulsive. This psychological problem is actually listed in the Japanese manual of mental disorders. My suggestion would be to explore the possible adaptation of indigenous methods of treatment found effective in Japan. Although he is an American citizen, I believe he is more Japanese than Japanese American.

Dr. Machovitch (Psychodynamic Analysis):

Hajimi's social phobia is caused by a deep-seated underlying childhood conflict with his parents. The phobia is a symptom and symbolic of unresolved Oedipal feelings toward both parents that are reenacted in almost all his social relationships. His strong need for social approval from his father, his feelings of hostility toward him, and an intense fear of the father (fear of castration) make him uncomfortable and anxious around men and especially around authority figures. His unresolved oedipal relationship with his mother has impaired his ability to relate to members of the opposite sex and has contributed to his anxiety in developing intimacy with others. Note his intense feelings of anxiety around women and his overreaction to being touched by them.

As a female therapist [reference to me as the intern], you probably evoke this conflict as well. I believe that Hajimi, at crucial psychosexual stages, did not receive the love and care a child needs to develop into a healthy adult. He was neglected, rejected, and maternally/paternally isolated, a condition that symbolized all his social relationships. Because he felt unloved and worthless, Hajimi reenacts his pathological relationship with his parents in other social situations. Note, for example, the symbolic relationship between the father's repetitive declarations that Hajimi is 'offensive,' and Hajimi's fear that he will offend others; similar reactions to attempts by his mother and female classmate to comfort him; avoidance of being touched; and many other symbolic parallels. My suggestion is to deal with Hajimi's transference neurosis through an insight process so that he may be able to distinguish the pathological relationships of the past with the healthy ones he encounters now.

Dr. Barnard (Cognitive-Behavioral Analysis):

All of these explanations appear well and good, but the ultimate test of therapeutic effectiveness must be guided by the research literature. Work on empirically supported treatments

CASE STUDY

suggests that cognitive-behavioral approaches have been shown to be most effective in the treatment of phobias. Although culture is important and a psychodynamic explanation seems appealing, we should be ethically obligated to select the treatment based upon what research has shown works. Describing the client's problems in measurable and specific terms rather than abstract concepts will ultimately lead to a better treatment plan. For example, the roots of Hajimi's problems can be traced to his behavioral repertoire. Many of the behaviors he has learned are inappropriate, and his repertoire lacks useful, productive social skills. He has little practice in social relationships, lacks good role models, and has difficulty distinguishing between appropriate and inappropriate behaviors.

In addition, his constant belittlement by his father has probably created in his mind an irrational belief system that leads him to distort or misinterpret events: Others will reject him, he is worthless, and he will offend others. Much of this, no doubt, comes from the father's constant criticisms and belittlement. This leads Hajimi to believe that he is 'worthless' and will always be worthless. I believe that a program of assertiveness training, systematic desensitization, and relaxation exercises will help him immensely to develop social skills and to combat his high performance and interpersonal anxieties. Further, I would supplement his behavioral program with a cognitive treatment plan that (a) identifies irrational thinking and beliefs, (b) teaches him cognitive restructuring methods to combat them, and (c) replaces them with positive and more realistic self-appraisals. If you look at the research literature on treating social phobias, you cannot deny their effectiveness in treating this type of disorder.

REFLECTION AND DISCUSSION QUESTIONS

1. Before you continue reading, reflect upon what you believe to be the source of Hajimi's problems. What is causing him to be so anxious around people? What role do his parents play in the manifestation of his disorder?

2. How would you characterize your therapeutic orientation, and can you apply it to this case? Do your classmates and fellow peers offer different explanations? How would you work with Hajimi? Can you be specific in describing your treatment plan?

3. Are you knowledgeable about what research has shown about treating the type of disorder exhibited by Hajimi? How would you go about finding the information?

4. What role do you believe culture plays in Hajimi's problems?

The case of Hajimi and the three differing treatment perspectives raises important therapeutic issues that have literally spawned the movement toward evidence-based practice (EBP).

First, after careful assessment of the presenting problem and related factors, how do counselors decide on the most appropriate treatment for individuals from different ethnic groups? Indeed, this question is relevant to all groups regardless of race, culture, or ethnicity. Certainly, Drs. Katsumoto, Machovitch, and Barnard make important points, and their diagnosis, assessment, and treatment recommendations seem to make sense from their theoretical orientations. Because this text is about multicultural counseling, you might mistakenly assume that we will take the side of Dr. Katsumoto because she offers a perspective that we have emphasized throughout the text. As indicated in Chapter 2, however, it is entirely possible that all three perspectives may be right, but they may be limited in how they view the totality of the human condition. The cultural perspective views Hajimi as a cultural being, the psychodynamic perspective views him as a historical-developmental being, and the cognitive-behavioral approach views him as a behaving-and-thinking being (Ivey, Ivey, & Zalaquett, 2014). As we have emphasized throughout, we are all of these and more.

Second, historically therapeutic strategies used in treatment were often based on (a) the clinician's specific therapeutic orientation (à la Drs. Katsumoto, Machovitch, and Barnard), (b) ideas shared by "experts" in psychotherapy, or (c) "clinical intuition and experience" derived from years of work with clients. These approaches are problematic because there are countless "experts" and, at last count, some 400 schools of psychotherapy, each purporting that their techniques are valid (Corey, 2013); moreover, treatment is often implemented without questioning the relevance or appropriateness of a particular technique or approach for a specific client. Furthermore, reliance on clinical "intuition" to guide one's therapeutic approach can result in ineffective treatment. Thus it appears that the choice of a treatment plan is dictated by one's theoretical orientation, expert opinion, and/or clinical intuition. In other words, different mental health professionals may differ significantly from one another in how they conceptualize and treat a problem of the client. Given these points, who are we to believe and how do we resolve this problem?

Third, this question has propelled the field of mental health practice, including multicultural counseling/therapy, to consider the role of science and research in the treatment of mental disorders (Morales & Norcross, 2010). Of the three analyses given, Dr. Barnard brings up the issue of using the research literature to guide us in the choice of intervention techniques. Yet he offers a seemingly flawed culture-free or neutral interpretation of *empirically supported treatments* (ESTs), an issue we address shortly. Nevertheless, Dr. Barnard does raise very important questions for the field of multicultural counseling and therapy to consider. How important is it for counselors to be aware of and to utilize interventions that have research support? What interventions have been demonstrated in research to be effective for treating mental disorders? Has research on EBP been conducted on racial/ethnic minority groups, or is it simply for members of the majority culture (D. W. Sue, 2015)? To help answer these questions, we consider the evolution of ESTs, *empirically supported relationships* (ESRs), and EBP as they apply to diverse populations.

EVIDENCE-BASED PRACTICE (EBP) AND MULTICULTURALISM

The importance of EBP is becoming increasingly accepted in the field of multicultural counseling. Discussions of EBP originally focused on research-supported therapies for specific disorders, but the dialogue has now broadened to include clinical expertise, including "understanding the influence of individual and cultural differences on treatment" and the importance of considering client "characteristics, culture, and preferences in assessment, treatment plans, and therapeutic outcome" (American Psychological Association, Presidential Task Force on Evidence-Based Practice, 2006). In an article titled "Evidence-Based Practices with Ethnic Minorities: Strange Bedfellows No More," Morales and Norcross (2010) describe how multiculturalism and evidence-based treatment (EBT), two forces that were "inexorable" and "separate" are now converging and how they can complement each other. The authors state: "Multiculturalism without strong research risks becoming an empty political value, and EBT without cultural sensitivity risks irrelevancy" (p. 823).

Although the authors are optimistic about the convergence of these forces, there is still resistance to EBP among some individuals within the field of multicultural counseling (Wendt, Gone, & Nagata, 2015; D. W. Sue, 2015). As BigFoot and Schmidt (2010) note, "Historically, government and social service organization utilization of nonadapted or poorly adapted mental health treatments with diverse populations has led to widespread distrust and reluctance in such populations to seek mental health services" (p. 849). Conflicts often exist between the values espoused in conventional psychotherapy and the cultural values and beliefs of ethnic minorities (Lau, Fung, & Yung, 2010; Nagayama-Hall, 2001). As we have discussed in previous chapters, Western approaches to psychological treatment are often based on individualistic value systems instead of on the inter-dependent values found in many ethnic minority communities. Additionally, con-ventional therapies often ignore cultural influences, disregard spiritual and other healing processes, and pathologize the behavior and values of ethnic minorities and other diverse groups (S. Sue, Zane, Nagayama-Hall, & Berger, 2009).

It is apparent that conventional delivery of Western-based therapies may not be meeting the needs of many individuals from ethnic and other cultural minori-ties. These groups tend to underutilize mental health services (Thurston & Phares, 2008) and are more likely to attend fewer sessions or drop out of therapy sooner, compared with their White counterparts (Fortuna, Alegria, & Gao, 2010; Les-ter, Resick, Young-Xu, & Artz, 2010; Triffleman & Pole, 2010). Unfortunately, research on the effectiveness of empirically supported therapies for ethnic minori-ties is limited, as these groups are often not included or specifically identified in research investigations of particular treatments.

Although questions remain regarding the validity of evidence-based approaches for ethnic minority populations and other diverse populations (Bernal & Sáez-Santiago, 2006), we believe that EBPs offer an opportunity for infusing multicultural and diversity sensitivity into psychotherapy. In addition, all mental health professions (psychiatry, social work, clinical psychology, and counseling) now espouse the view that treatment should have a research base. Evidence-based interventions are increasingly promoted in social work (Bledsoe et al., 2007; Gibbs & Gambrill, 2002), school psychology (Kratochwill, 2002), clinical psychology (Deegear & Lawson, 2003), counseling (American Counseling Association, 2014; Chwalisz, 2001), and psychiatry.

In this chapter we will discuss the evolution of EBP, the integration of EST and ESR variables into multicultural counseling, and the relevance of enhancing cultural elements in therapy. We will also show how culturally sensitive strategies can become an important component of EBPs.

Empirically Supported Treatment (EST)

The concept of ESTs was popularized when the American Psychological Associa-tion began promoting the use of "validated" or research-supported treatments—specific treatments confirmed as effective for specific disorders. Not only were ESTs seen as an effective response to concerns about the use of unsupported tech-niques and psychotherapies, but they also address the issue of unintended harm that can result from ineffective or hazardous treatments (Lilienfeld, 2007; Wendt,

Gone & Nagata, 2015). ESTs typically involve a very specific treatment protocol for specific disorders. Because variability among therapists might produce error variance in research studies and because it is important for ESTs to be easily replicable as originally designed, ESTs are conducted using manuals.

According to the guidelines of the task force charged with defining and identifying ESTs (Chambless & Hollon, 1998), they must demonstrate (a) superiority to a placebo in two or more methodologically rigorous, controlled studies, (b) equivalence to a well-established treatment in several rigorous and independent controlled studies, usually randomized controlled trials, or (c) efficacy in a large series of single-case controlled designs (i.e., within-subjects designs that systematically compare the effects of a treatment with those of a control condition).

ESTs have been identified for anxiety, depressive, and stress-related disorders; obesity and eating disorders; severe mental conditions such as schizophrenia and bipolar disorder; substance abuse and dependence; childhood disorders; and borderline personality disorder. Several hundred different manualized treatments are listed as empirically supported (Chambless & Ollendick, 2001; Society of Clinical Psychology, 2011). (See Table 9.1 for a few examples of empirically supported therapies.)

TABLE 9.1 Examples of Empirically Supported Treatments (ESTs)	
"Well-Established" Treatments	"Probably Efficacious" Treatments
Cognitive-behavioral therapy for panic disorder	Cognitive therapy for obsessive-compulsive disorder (OCD)
Exposure/guided mastery for specific phobias	Exposure treatment for posttraumatic stress disorder (PTSD)
Cognitive therapy for depression	Brief dynamic therapy for depression
Cognitive-behavioral therapy for bulimia	Interpersonal therapy for bulimia
Cognitive-behavioral relapse prevention for cocaine dependence	Brief dynamic therapy for opiate dependence
Behavior therapy for headache	Reminiscence therapy for geriatrics patients
Behavioral marital therapy	Emotionally focused couples therapy

Source: Chambless & Hollon (1998).

Additionally, the American Psychological Association has developed a list of ESTs and practice guidelines for ethnic minorities (American Psychological Association, 1993); women and girls (American Psychological Association, 2007); older adults (American Psychological Association, 2014); and lesbian, gay, and bisexual clients (American Psychological Association, 2012). These guidelines can be consulted and modified, if necessary, in working with clients from these groups.

The rationale behind the establishment of ESTs is admirable; we believe that decisions regarding treatment approaches for particular issues or disorders should be based on research findings rather than on idiosyncratic, personal beliefs or sketchy theories. We owe it to our clients to provide them with treatment that has demonstrated efficacy. However, it is our contention that relying only on manualized treatment methods, albeit research-supported approaches, is insufficient with many clients and many mental health problems (D. W. Sue, 2015). Additionally, most ESTs have not been specifically demonstrated to be effective with ethnic minorities or other diverse populations. The shortcomings of the EST approach are summarized here:

- Owing to the focus on choosing treatment based on the specific disorder, contextual, cultural, and other environmental influences are not adequately considered (D. W. Sue, 2015).

- The validity of ESTs for minority group members is often questionable because these groups are not included in many clinical trials (Bernal & Sáez-Santiago, 2006; S. Sue et al., 2006).

- The importance of the therapist–client relationship is not adequately acknowledged. A number of studies have found that therapist effects contribute significantly to the outcome of psychotherapy. In many cases, these effects exceed those produced by specific techniques (Wampold, 2001).

- Too much emphasis is placed on randomized controlled trials versus other forms of research, such as qualitative research designs.

When treating clients with specific disorders, multicultural therapists have had the choice of ignoring ESTs or adapting them. Increasingly, there have been attempts to develop "*cultural adaptations*" of certain ESTs. For example, Organista (2000) made the following modifications to empirically supported cognitive-behavioral strategies when working with low-income Latinos suffering from depression:

1. *Engagement strategies*. Recognizing the importance of *personalismo* (the value of personal relationships), initial sessions are devoted to relationship building. Time is allotted for *presentaciones* (introductions), during which personal information is exchanged between counselor and client and issues that may affect ethnic minorities, such as acculturation difficulties, culture shock, and discrimination, are discussed.

2. *Activity schedules.* In the treatment of depression, a common recommendation is for clients to take some time off for themselves. This idea may run counter to the Latino/a value of connectedness and putting the needs of the family ahead of oneself. Therefore, instead of solitary activities, clients can choose social activities they find enjoyable, such as visiting neighbors, family outings, or taking children to the park. In recognizing the income status of clients, activities discussed are generally free or affordable.

3. *Assertiveness training.* Assertiveness is discussed within the context of Latino values. Culturally acceptable ways of expressing assertiveness, such as prefacing statements with *con todo respeto* (with all due respect) and *me permite expresar mis sentimientos?* (Is it okay if I express my feelings?) are discussed, as well as strategies for using assertion with spouses or higher-status individuals.

4. *Cognitive restructuring.* Rather than labeling thoughts that can reduce or increase depression as rational or irrational, the terms "helpful thoughts" and "unhelpful thoughts" are used. Recognizing the religious nature of many Latinos, the saying *Ayudate, que Dios te ayudara* (i.e., "God helps those who help themselves") is used to encourage follow-through with behavioral assignments.

This adapted approach, which maintains fidelity to both empirically supported techniques and cultural influences, has resulted in a lower dropout rate and better outcome for low-income Latino/a clients compared to nonmodified therapy. *Cultural adaptations* can include factors such as (a) matching language, racial or ethnic backgrounds of client and therapist; (b) incorporating cultural values in the specific treatment strategies; (c) utilizing cultural sayings or metaphors in treatment; and (d) considering the impact of environmental variables, such as acculturation conflicts, discrimination, and income status.

Culturally adapted ESTs have been successfully used with Latino/a and Haitian American adolescents (Duarte Velez, Guillermo, & Bonilla, 2010; Nicholas, Arntz, Hirsch, & Schmiedigen, 2011); Asian Americans experiencing phobias (Huey & Pan, 2006); Latino/a adults experiencing depression (Aguilera, Garza, & Munoz, 2010); American Indians suffering from trauma (BigFoot & Schmidt, 2010); African Americans recovering from substance abuse (Cunningham, Foster, & Warner, 2010); and Chinese immigrant families (Lau et al., 2010).

Horrell (2008) reviewed 12 studies on the effectiveness of cognitive-behavioral therapy for African, Asian, and Hispanic Americans experiencing a variety of psychological disorders; the majority of these studies involved some type of cultural modification. Although the results for African American clients were mixed, Asian and Hispanic American clients demonstrated significant treatment gains over those in placebo or wait-list control conditions. Overall, evidence is increasing that ESTs can be effective with ethnic minorities, particularly when the approach includes cultural adaptation.

A meta-analysis of studies involving the adaptation of ESTs to clients' cultural background revealed that adapted treatments for clients of color are moderately more effective than nonadapted treatments and that the most effective therapies were those that had the most *cultural adaptations* (Smith, Rodriguez, & Bernal, 2011). In a review of both published and unpublished studies of culturally adapted therapies, it was found that culturally adapted psychotherapy is more effective than nonadapted psychotherapy for ethnic minorities (Benish, Quintana, & Wampold, 2011).

Interestingly, these researchers believe that *cultural adaptations* are effective because most adapted therapies in their review allowed the therapist to explore the "illness myth" of the client (i.e., the client's explanation of his or her symptoms and beliefs about possible etiology, prognosis, and effective treatment). As the researchers conclude, "The superior outcomes resulting from myth adaptation indicate the importance of therapist inquiry and effort into understanding clients' beliefs about etiology, types of symptoms experienced, prediction of the course of illness, and consequences of the illness, as well as client opinion about what constitutes acceptable treatment"(Benish et al., 2011 p. 287). Even if a client's perspective regarding his or her symptoms is maladaptive, the process of listening and assessing client beliefs appears to enhance outcome. This approach seems also present in the "Cultural Formulation Outline Interview" advocated in *DSM-5* (American Psychiatric Association, 2013).

ESTs are useful in providing clinicians with information regarding which therapies are most effective with specific disorders. We should always be aware of experimentally supported techniques when working with client problems. However, the identification of treatments is only one step in a complex process; it is vital that we also consider contextual and cultural influences and therapist–client relationship factors in treatment outcome. This view (i.e., that contextual and therapist factors are also important in therapy outcome) allows the field to move beyond the traditional clinical framework in which an "objective" illness can be diagnosed and a specific cure recommended, to a greater understanding of the complexities involved in mental health issues and psychological disorders.

Implications

The applicability of many ESTs for many diverse groups has been insufficiently researched. Yet mental health practitioners are faced with the challenge of selecting effective interventions for their clients' mental health issues. For clients of color, we have the option of using a standard EST for the disorder, finding an EST (or adapted EST) with research demonstrating effectiveness for members of the client's ethnic group with the client's disorder (which is highly unlikely), or taking the time to develop and research a culture-specific EBT for the client's disorder. The latter would be inordinately difficult for most practitioners to accomplish. Additionally, culture-specific treatments may not be effective with people of color who are more acculturated. Thus, in choosing a treatment strategy, we believe that the best approach (given the current state of research) is for the counselor to select an intervention that is research based and subsequently adapt the approach for the individual client according to the client's individual characteristics, values, and preferences.

REFLECTION AND DISCUSSION QUESTIONS

1. What are your thoughts concerning the use of ESTs in your own practice? What reactions do you have about using research on therapeutic effectiveness to guide your work? Has your training exposed you to EBP? What challenges would you face trying to implement such an approach?

2. What would you need to know about ESTs and the cultural background of diverse clients in order to develop a culturally adapted therapeutic approach? Although it would be a massive undertaking, can you and your classmates discuss what specific steps need to be taken to culturally adapt an EST to African Americans, Asian Americans, and Latinos?

3. Do you believe that simply adapting ESTs to the cultural context of clients is sufficient in working with people of color?

Empirically Supported Relationships (ESRs)

Not everyone believes that *cultural adaptations* of *empirically supported treatments* are sufficient to deal with cultural differences, and some express concern that such adaptations result in the imposition of EuroAmerican norms on ethnic minorities.

As Gone (2009) argues, ESTs cannot be "adorned" with "a few beads here, some feathers there" (p. 760). Those critical of reliance on ESTs alone cite the multitude of other factors impacting treatment outcome, such as the therapeutic relationship, client values and beliefs, and the working alliance between client and therapist (DeAngelis, 2005; D. W. Sue, 2015). To remedy this shortcoming, the American Psychological Association Division 29 Psychotherapy Task Force was formed to review research and identify characteristics responsible for effective therapeutic relationships and to determine means of tailoring therapy to individual clients (Ackerman et al., 2001).

This focus provided the first opportunity for the inclusion of multicultural concerns within the evidence-based movement. It is widely agreed that the quality of the working relationship between the therapist and the client (i.e., the *therapeutic alliance*) is consistently related to treatment outcome (Castonguay, Goldfried, Wiser, Raue, & Hayes, 1996; Weinberger, 2002). This relationship may assume even greater significance for clients from diverse backgrounds (Davis, Ancis, & Ashby, 2015). In fact, difficulties in the *therapeutic alliance* may be a factor in the underutilization of mental health services and early termination of therapy seen with minority clients. After reviewing the research on therapist–client relationship variables as they relate to treatment outcome, the APA Division 29 Task Force reached these conclusions (Ackerman et al., 2001):

1. The therapeutic relationship makes substantial and consistent contributions to psychotherapy outcome, independent of the specific type of treatment.

2. The therapy relationship acts in concert with discrete interventions, client characteristics, and clinician qualities in determining treatment effectiveness.

3. Adapting or tailoring the therapy relationship to specific client needs and characteristics (in addition to diagnosis) enhances the effectiveness of treatment.

4. Practice and treatment guidelines should explicitly address therapist behaviors and qualities that promote a facilitative therapy relationship.

According to the APA Task Force, a number of relationship variables are considered "demonstratively effective" or "promising and probably effective" based on research findings (see Table 9.2). ESR variables include the development of a strong *therapeutic alliance*, a solid interpersonal bond (i.e., a collaborative, empathetic relationship based on *positive regard*, respect, warmth, and genuineness), and effective management of *countertransference*—all factors known to be critical for effective multicultural counseling. We elaborate on these relationship variables in the next few sections.

TABLE 9.2 Empirically Supported Relationship (ESR) Variables	
Demonstrably Effective	**Promising and Probably Effective**
Therapeutic alliance	Positive regard
Cohesion in group therapy	Congruence/genuineness
Empathy	Feedback
Goal consensus and collaboration	Repair of alliance ruptures
Customizing therapy	Self-disclosure
Management of countertransference	

Source: From Ackerman et al. (2001).

The Therapeutic Alliance

Research on *empirically supported relationships* has consistently identified the importance of a strong *therapeutic alliance*, which includes the core conditions of effective treatment described by Rogers (1957): *empathy*, respect, genuineness, and warmth. These dynamics typify a therapeutic relationship in which a client feels understood, safe, and encouraged to disclose intimate material. These characteristics transcend the therapist's therapeutic orientation or approach to treatment. The therapeutic relationship, or working alliance, is an important factor in effective treatment. Clients specifically asked about what contributed to the success of treatment often point to a sense of connection with their therapist. *Connectedness* has been described as having feelings of closeness with the therapist, working together in an enabling atmosphere, receiving support for change, and being provided an equality of status within the working relationship (Ribner & Knei-Paz, 2002). As we noted in Chapter 2, cultural humility may be a major aspect in the *therapeutic alliance* contributing to cultural competence (Hook, Davis, Owen, Worthington, & Utsey, 2013; Owen et al., 2014).

Similarly, clients report that therapist behaviors such as "openness to ideas, experiences, and feelings" or being "nonjudgmental and noncritical," "genuine," "warm," and "validating of experiences" are helpful in therapy (Curtis, Field, Knann-Kostman, & Mannix, 2004). A counselor's relationship skills and ability to develop a *therapeutic alliance* contribute significantly to satisfaction among clients of color (Constantine, 2002). Mulvaney-Day, Earl, Diaz-Linhart, and Alegria (2011) found that relationship variables with the therapist were particularly important for African American and Latino/a clients and concluded that "the basic yearning for authentic connection with a provider transcends racial categories" (p. 36). Thus the importance of feeling accepted by a therapist on an emotional and cognitive level seems to be a universal prerequisite for an effective *therapeutic alliance*.

Conceptualization of the *therapeutic alliance* often comprises three elements: (a) an emotional or interpersonal bond between the therapist and the client; (b) mutual agreement on appropriate goals, with an emphasis on changes valued by the client; and (c) intervention strategies or tasks that are viewed as important and relevant by both the client and the therapist (Garber, 2004). Defined in this manner, the *therapeutic alliance* exerts positive influences on outcome across different treatment modalities, accounting for a substantial proportion of outcome variance (Hojat et al., 2011; Zuroff & Blatt, 2006). In fact, the therapist–client relationship contributes as much as 30 percent to the variance in therapeutic outcome (Lambert & Barley, 2001).

We believe that the *therapeutic alliance* is of critical importance in the outcome of therapy for ethnic minority clients and will describe possible modifications that may help clinicians enhance this relationship. It is important to remember that there is no set formula or response that will ensure the formation of a strong *therapeutic alliance* with a particular client. In fact, counselors often need to demonstrate behavioral flexibility to achieve a good working relationship with clients; this may be particularly true when working with individuals from diverse populations.

In a qualitative study involving Black, Asian, Latino/a, and multiracial clients, most preferred an active counselor role, which was characterized by the counselor offering concrete suggestions, providing direct answers, challenging the client's thinking with thought-provoking questions, and providing psychoeducation regarding the therapy (Chang & Berk, 2009). Mulvaney-Day and colleagues (2011) found variability in the counseling relational style preferred by ethnic minority clients. A summary of the preferred relationship styles reported by the African American, Latino/a, and non-Latino White clients in their sample is presented in Table 9.3.

TABLE 9.3   Relational-Style Counselor Preferences of Ethnic Group Clients

Themes	African American Clients	Latino Clients	Non-Latino White Clients
Listening	Listen to who the client really is; recognize that clients are experts on themselves.	Listen in a way that communicates "paying attention."	Listen so that the client is comfortable enough to talk and express feelings.
Understanding	Understand beyond immediate impressions; understand hidden aspects of the client.	Understand feelings of client.	Understand complexity of client choices and circumstances.
Counselor Qualities	Counselor should "lower" self to client's level; egalitarian relationship.	Be authoritative, but connect first, then offer concrete advice and solutions.	Not judge because of social distance; maintain professional distance but be human.
Spending Time	Not listed as factor	Take time to connect deeply.	Allow time for feelings to emerge at their own pace.

Source: Mulvaney-Day et al. (2011).

Mental health practitioners need to be adaptable with their relationship skills in order to address the preferences and expectations of their clients. For example, many African American clients appear to value social interaction as opposed to problem-solving approaches, especially during initial sessions, whereas Latino/a clients seem to prefer a more interpersonal approach rather than clinical distance (Gloria & Peregoy, 1996; Kennedy, 2003). We have also seen earlier that many Asian American clients may prefer a problem-solving approach initially. However, these are broad generalizations, and counselors must test out the effectiveness of different relational skills with a particular client, assessing the impact of their interactions with the client and asking themselves questions such as "Does the client seem to be responding positively to my relational style?" and "Have I succeeded in developing a collaborative and supportive relationship with this client?" and modifying the approach when necessary. Although it is important not to react to clients in a stereotypic manner, it is important to continually be aware of cultural and societal issues that may affect the client. Asian, Black, Latino/a, and multiracial clients who were dissatisfied in cross-racial therapy complained about their therapist's lack of knowledge about racial identity development; the dynamics of power and privilege; the effects of racism, discrimination, and oppression due to their minority status (or multiple minority statuses); and cultural stigma associated with seeking help (Chang & Berk, 2009).

Cultural information is useful in providing general guidelines regarding an ethnic minority client's counseling-style preference or issues that need to be addressed in therapy. However, as a counselor develops a comprehensive understanding of each client's background, values, strengths, and concerns, it is essential that the counselor determine whether general cultural information "fits" the individual client. This ongoing "search for understanding" is important with respect to each of the following components of the *therapeutic alliance*.

Emotional or Interpersonal Bond

The formation of a bond between the therapist and the client is a very important aspect of the therapeutic relationship and is defined as a collaborative partnership based on *empathy*, *positive regard*, genuineness, respect, warmth, and self-disclosure. For an optimal outcome, the client must feel connected with, respected by, and understood by the therapist. In addition, the therapist must identify issues that may detract from the relationship, such as *countertransference* (i.e., reactions to the client based on the therapist's own personal issues). These qualities are described in detail below; their importance may vary according to the type of mental health issue being addressed and characteristics of the client (e.g., gender, socioeconomic status, ethnicity, cultural background).

The development of an *emotional bond* is enhanced by *collaboration*, a shared process in which a client's views are respected and his or her participation is encouraged in all phases of the therapy. An egalitarian stance and encouragement of sharing and *self-disclosure* facilitate the development of empathy (Dyche & Zayas, 2001) and reduce the power differential between therapist and client. The potential for a positive therapeutic outcome is increased when the client is "on board" regarding the definition of the problem, identification of goals, and choice of interventions. When differences exist between a client's view of a problem and the therapist's theoretical conceptualization, negative dynamics are likely to occur. Collaboration regarding definition of the problem reduces this possibility and is most effective when employed consistently throughout therapy.

Empathy

Empathy is known to significantly enhance the *therapeutic bond*. *Empathy* is defined as the ability to place oneself in the client's world, to feel or think from the client's perspective, or to be attuned to the client. *Empathy* allows therapists to form an *emotional bond* with clients, helping the clients to feel understood. It is not enough for the therapist to simply communicate this understanding; the client must perceive the responses from the therapist as empathetic. This is why it is vital for therapists to be aware of client receptivity by evaluating both verbal and nonverbal responses from the client ("How is the client responding to what I am saying?" "What are the client's verbal and bodily cues communicating?"). *Empathy* can be demonstrated in several different ways—having an emotional understanding or emotional connection with the client (*emotional empathy*) or understanding the client's predicament cognitively, whether on an individual, family, or societal level (*cognitive empathy*). Following is an illustration of emotional *empathy*:

A White male therapist in his late 20s is beginning therapy with a recently immigrated 39-year-old West Indian woman. The client expresses concern about her adolescent daughter, who she describes as behaving in an angry, hostile way toward her fiancé. The woman is well dressed and is somewhat abrupt, seeming to be impatient with the therapist. Though not a parent himself, the therapist recognizes the distress behind his client's sternness, and thinking of the struggles he had with his own father, he responds to the woman's obvious discomfort saying, "I imagine that must hurt you." This intuitive response from the therapist reduces the woman's embarrassment, and she pauses from the angry story of her daughter's ungratefulness to wipe a tear (Dyche & Zayas, 2001, p. 249).

Many counselors are trained to be very direct with emotional responses, using statements such as "You feel hurt" or "You sound hurt" in an effort to demonstrate *empathy*. The response "I imagine that must hurt you" would be rated a more intermediate response. Statements that are even less direct might include "Some people might feel hurt by that" or "If I was in the same situation, I would feel hurt." We have found that people differ in their reaction to the directness of *emotional empathy*, depending on such factors as the gender, ethnicity, or cultural background of the counselor or the client; the degree of comfort and *emotional bonding* with the therapist; and the specific issue involved.

For example, when working with Asian international students, we have found that although there are individual differences in preference, many prefer a less direct style of *emotional empathy*. However, some Asian international students are fine with direct *emotional empathy* (this is why the counselor must be flexible and test out different forms of *empathy* with clients rather than prejudging them because of membership in a specific group). In general, recognition of emotional issues through either indirect or direct *empathy* increases the client's feeling of being understood. Effective therapists continually evaluate client responses and thus are able to determine if the degree and style of *emotional empathy* being used is enhancing (or detracting) from the *emotional bond* between therapist and client.

Cognitive empathy involves the therapist's ability to understand the issues facing the client. For example, in the case just described, the therapist might explore the possibility that the daughter's anger is related to her immigration experiences by saying, "Sometimes moving to a new country can be difficult." The degree of directness can be varied by making the observation tentative by prefacing statements with "I wonder if. . .?" or "Is it possible that. . .?" *Cognitive empathy* can also be demonstrated by communicating an understanding of the client's worldview, including the influences of family issues or discriminatory experiences, such as racism, heterosexism, ageism, or sexism. By exploring or including broader societal elements such as these, a therapist is able to incorporate diversity or cross-cultural perspectives and potentially enhance understanding of the client's concerns.

Communicating an understanding of different worldviews and acknowledging the possibility of cultural influences can increase the therapist's credibility with the client. When working with diverse clients, we believe that *empathy* must include the ability to accept and be open to multiple perspectives of personal, societal, and cultural realities. This can be achieved by exploring the impact of cultural differences or diversity issues on client problems, goals, and solutions (Chung & Bernak, 2002; Dyche & Zayas, 2001).

Empathy may be difficult in multicultural counseling if counselors are unable to identify personal cultural blinders or values they may hold. For example, among counselors working with African American clients, those with color-blind racial attitudes (i.e., a belief that race is not a significant factor in determining one's chances in society) showed lower levels of *empathy* than those who were aware of the significance of racial factors (Burkard & Knox, 2004). Some research suggests that counselors' multicultural counseling competence (awareness of issues of race and discrimination, and knowledge of their social impact on clients) accounts for a large proportion of the variance in ratings of counselor competence, expertise, and trustworthiness made by clients of color (Constantine, 2002; Fuertes & Brobst, 2002).

In a study of gay and bisexual clients, a counselor's *universal–diversity orientation* (i.e., interest in diversity, contact with diverse groups, comfort with similarities and differences) was positively related to client ratings of the *therapeutic alliance*, whereas, surprisingly, similarities in sexual orientation between therapist and client were not. *Universal–diversity orientation* may facilitate therapy through affirmation and understanding of the issues that culturally diverse clients are facing (Stracuzzi, Mohr, & Fuertes, 2011).

In contrast, the *therapeutic alliance* can be adversely affected when ethnic minority clients perceive a therapist to be culturally insensitive or believe that the therapist is minimizing the importance of racial and cultural issues or pathologizing cultural values or communication styles (Constantine, 2007; D. W. Sue, Bucceri, Lin, Nadal, & Torino, 2007). This finding is likely true with other diverse groups who may endure heterosexism, ageism, religious intolerance, and/or prejudice against disability. Sensitivity to the possible impact of racial and societal issues can be made through statements such as the following:

- "How have experiences with discrimination or unfairness had an impact on the problems you are dealing with?"

- "Sometimes it's difficult to meet the societal demands of being a man (or a woman). How has this influenced your expression of emotions?"

- "Some people believe that family members should be involved in making decisions for individuals in the family. Is this true in your family?"

- "Being or feeling different can be related to messages we receive from our family, society, or religious institutions. Have you considered whether your feelings of isolation are related to messages you are getting from others?"

- "Families change over time. What are some of the standards or values you learned as a young child? I wonder if the conflicts in your family are related to differences in expectations between you and your parents."

These examples are stated in a very tentative manner. If a counselor has sufficient information, more direct statements of *cognitive empathy* can be made. We believe that the perception of and response to *empathy* varies from individual to individual. There are no set responses that will convey *empathy* and understanding to all clients. In general, therapists must learn to evaluate their use of both *cognitive* and *emotional empathy* to determine whether it is improving the *emotional bond* with the client and to make modifications, if needed, to enhance the client's perception of empathy within the relationship.

Positive Regard, Respect, Warmth, and Genuineness

The characteristics of *positive regard*, respect, warmth, and genuineness are important qualities in establishing an *emotional bond*. *Positive regard* is the demonstration by the therapist that he or she sees the strengths and positive aspects of the client, including appreciation for the values and differences displayed by the client. *Positive regard* is demonstrated when the counselor identifies and focuses on the strengths and assets of the individual rather than attending only to deficits or problems. This is especially important for members of ethnic minorities and other diverse groups whose behaviors are often pathologized. *Respect* is shown by being attentive and by demonstrating that you view the client as an important person. Behaviors such as asking clients how they would like to be addressed, showing that their comments and insights are valuable, and tailoring your interaction according to their needs or values are all ways of communicating respect. *Warmth* is the emotional feeling received by the client when the therapist conveys verbal and nonverbal signs of appreciation and acceptance. Smiling, the use of humor, or showing interest in the client can convey this feeling. *Genuineness* can be displayed in many different ways. It generally means a therapist is responding to a client openly and in a "real" manner, rather than responding in accordance with expected roles. These inter-personal attributes can strengthen the therapist–client alliance and increase the client's trust, cooperation, and motivation to participate in therapy.

Self-Disclosure

Although self-disclosure is considered to be a "promising and probably effective" technique (Ackerman et al., 2001), the topic of a therapist revealing personal thoughts or personal information remains controversial. In one study, brief or limited therapist self-disclosure in response to comparable self-disclosure by the client was associated with reductions in symptom distress and greater liking for the therapist (Barrett & Berman, 2001).

Counselor disclosure in cross-cultural situations (e.g., sharing reactions to clients' experiences of racism or oppression) may also enhance the *therapeutic alliance* (Burkard, Knox, Groen, Perez, & Hess, 2006; Cashwell, Shcherbakova, & Cash-well, 2003). Self-disclosures may show the therapist's human qualities and lead to the development of closer ties with the client. Research to determine the impact of therapist self-disclosure is difficult since it depends on many variables, such as the type of disclosure, its timing and frequency, and client characteristics. Although many clients report that therapist self-disclosure enhances the therapeutic relationship, some self-disclosures by a therapist (e.g., being wealthy or politically conservative) can actually interfere with the therapist–client relationship (Chang & Berk, 2009).

Some therapists feel that self-disclosure is not appropriate in therapy, and they either will not answer personal questions or will bounce the question back to the client. However, some clients who ask, "Has this ever happened to you?" may be doing so in an attempt to normalize their experience. Bouncing the question back to the client by saying, "Let's find out why you want to know this," can be perceived as patronizing rather than helpful (Hays, 2001). Should you make self-disclosures to a client? The answer is, "It depends." Sharing experiences or reactions can strengthen the *emotional bond* between therapist and client. However, such self-disclosure should be limited and aimed at helping the client with his or her issues. If the requests for self-disclosure become frequent or too personal, the therapist should explore with the client the reason for the inquiries.

Management of Countertransference

Appropriate management of *countertransference* can enhance the *therapeutic alliance*, as well as minimize ruptures in the therapeutic relationship. *Countertransference* involves the therapist's emotional reaction to the client based on the therapist's own set of attitudes, beliefs, values, or experiences. These emotional reactions, whether negative or positive, can bias a therapist's judgment when working with a client. For example, a therapist might exhibit negative reactions to a client owing to factors such as heterosexism, racism, or classism. Additionally, difficulty can occur when clients demonstrate values and perspectives similar to the therapist's own; such similarity may reduce therapist objectivity. Therapists sometimes over-identify with clients who are similar to them and subsequently underestimate the client's role in interpersonal difficulties. As we have seen in Chapter 3, this is most likely to happen in interracial/interethnic therapeutic relationships. These unconscious reactions can interfere with the formation of a healthy therapeutic *emotional bond* with the client. Because of the negative impact of *countertransference*, clinicians should examine their experiences, values, and beliefs when experiencing an emotional reaction to a client that is beyond what is expected from the therapy session.

A scientific frame of mind necessitates the examination of one's own values and beliefs in order to anticipate the impact of possible differences and similarities in worldviews on the *therapeutic alliance*. Multicultural therapists have been in the forefront of stressing the importance of acknowledging the influence of values, preferences, and worldviews on psychotherapy and the psychotherapist. It is important to be self-aware and recognize when personal needs or values are being activated in the therapeutic relationship and to not project our reactions onto clients (Brems, 2000).

Goal Consensus

An agreement on goals between the therapist and the client (i.e., *goal consensus*) is another important relationship variable. Unless the client agrees on what the goals should be, little progress will be made. As therapists, we too easily envision what the appropriate outcome should be when working with a client and become dismayed or discouraged when a client does not feel the same way or seems satisfied with more limited solutions. Goals should be determined in a collaborative manner with input from both client and therapist. Although it is very important to get the client's response in regard to the problem and goals, the therapist has the important task of clarifying client statements and providing tentative suggestions.

Clients often identify global goals, such as "wanting to improve self-esteem." The therapist's job is to help the client define the goal more specifically and to foster alternative ways of interpreting situations (Hilsenroth & Cromer, 2007). Concrete goals enhance the ability to measure progress in therapy. To obtain more specificity regarding a global goal, therapists can ask such questions as: "What does your low self-esteem prevent you from doing?" "How would your life be different if you had high self-esteem?" "What would you be able to do if you had more self-esteem?" or "How would you know if you are improving in self-esteem?" The answer to these questions, such as "being able to hold a job or ask for a raise," "feeling more comfortable in group situations," or "standing up for myself," can help identify aspects of self-esteem that are more concrete. Each of these responses can be used to define sub-goals. A client might be asked, "What are small steps that you can make that will show you are moving in the direction of higher self-esteem?"

Once goals are identified, the client and the therapist can work together to identify which strategies and techniques will be employed to help the client achieve the stated goals. In order for interventions to be useful, they need to make sense to the client. For ethnic minority clients, interventions may require "cultural adaptation," such as that described in the study by Huey and Pan (2006), in which the treatment of phobias was modified for Asian Americans by emphasizing the strategy of emotional control and maximizing a directive role for the therapist.

Although the selection of interventions depends upon the presenting problem and diagnosis, psychological interventions are most effective when they are consistent with client characteristics, including the client's culture and values (La Roche, Batista, & D'Angelo, 2011). It is also important that the client believe that the therapeutic approach will be helpful. In a study by Coombs, Coleman, and Jones (2002), clients who reported "understanding the therapy process" and "having positive expectations of the therapy" were more likely to improve.

Implications of Empirically Supported Relationships (ESRs)

The effectiveness of therapy is highly dependent on the quality of the relationship between the therapist and the client. This finding transcends racial and ethnic differences and contributes up to 30 percent of the variance in treatment outcome. It is evident that the relationship between the therapist and the client is critical. In many cases, when given a choice, clients would select a less effective treatment if it were provided by a caring, empathetic therapist. Ethnic minorities may differ in their relational styles preferences, so therapists should be flexible and evaluate the degree of fit between their relational style and that preferred by their client, and should vary their approach, if necessary, to improve the *therapeutic alliance*. As mentioned by Benish, Quintana, and Wampold (2011), exploring the "illness myth" of the client in regard to his or her beliefs regarding etiology, course, and treatment is highly important in the therapeutic relationship and can enhance collaborative identification of goals and interventions.

REFLECTION AND DISCUSSION QUESTIONS

1. What was your therapy training in regard to the formation of the *therapeutic alliance* with a client? Indicate how the relationship skills were discussed in relation to cross-cultural competence.

2. What is your experience in working with ethnic minorities or other diverse populations? Did they appear to require different relationship skills? Did you evaluate the effectiveness of your responses?

EVIDENCE-BASED PRACTICE (EBP) AND DIVERSITY ISSUES IN COUNSELING

The American Psychological Association's focus on *empirically supported relationships* (ESRs) provided an opening for counselors to address multicultural concerns within an evidence-based framework. However, the broader and more recent focus on evidence-based practice (EBP) has more formally introduced cultural sensitivity as an essential consideration in assessment, case conceptualization, and selection of interventions. Specifically, *EBP* refers to "the integration of the best available research with clinical expertise in the context of patient characteristics, culture, and preferences" (American Psychological Association, Presidential Task Force on Evidence-Based Practice, 2006, p. 273). (See Figure 9.1.)

FIGURE 9.1 Three Pillars of Evidence-Based Practice

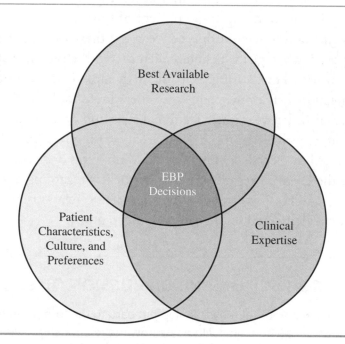

Source: Morales & Norcross (2010), p. 824.

Empirically based practice includes both evidence-based treatments and relationship variables but is broader and more comprehensive than a combination of the two. How does EBP differ from the EST and ESR frameworks?

First, the assumption underlying EBP is that the search for the "best research evidence" *begins* with a comprehensive understanding of the client's background and problem and goes on to consider which therapeutic approach is most likely to provide the best outcome. In other words, the selection of intervention occurs *only after* individual characteristics, such as cultural background, values, and preferences, are assessed. This allows for the individualizing of therapy with strong consideration given to client background and characteristics.

Second, unlike ESTs, which rely primarily on randomized controlled trials, EBP also accepts research evidence from qualitative studies, clinical observations, systematic case studies, and interventions delivered in naturalistic settings. This broadening of the definition of research allows mental health professionals greater latitude in deciding which therapy may be the best match for a particular client. For example, the National Registry of Evidence-based Programs and Practices (NREPP) provides specific information regarding treatments for substance abuse that consider the race and ethnicity of the participants, and treatments designed for certain ethnic groups, such as the American Indian Life Skills Development Program (Berke, Rozell, Hogan, Norcross, & Karpiak, 2011).

Third, the definition of clinical expertise within the EBP framework focuses not only on the quality of the therapeutic relationship and *therapeutic alliance* but also on skills essential for comprehensive assessment of the client's problem and strengths. Additionally, EBP considers clinical expertise involving factors such as knowledge about cultural differences; best practices in assessment, diagnosis, and case conceptualization; strategies for evaluating and selecting appropriate research-based treatments; and adapting selected treatments in a manner that respects the client's worldview, values, and preferences.

Fourth, EBP is based on an ongoing emphasis on client characteristics, culture, and preferences and the importance of working collaboratively with the client to develop goals and treatment strategies that are mutually agreeable. Identification of client variables includes (a) age and life stage, (b) sociocultural factors (e.g., gender, sexual orientation, ethnicity, disability), (c) environmental stressors (e.g., unemployment, recent life events, racism, health disparities), and (d) personal treatment preferences (i.e., treatment expectations, goals, and beliefs).

Because the *focus* is on the client and the consideration of cultural variables, EBP sets the stage for a multiculturally sensitive counseling relationship. The following illustration of how EBP and multicultural sensitivity can be integrated is based on the case of Anna, an American Indian female who developed PTSD following a sexual assault.

> *Anna is a 14-year-old American Indian female who was sexually abused by a 22-year-old male in her small community. Anna disclosed the abuse to her school counselor, who then reported the incident to tribal law enforcement. After word of the incident spread through the community, several individuals accused Anna of lying and then harassed her in an attempt to recant her allegation. Anna began isolating herself at home and stopped attending school. Anna*

> *became increasingly depressed and demonstrated symptoms consistent*
> *with PTSD. (BigFoot & Schmidt, 2010, p. 854)*

BigFoot and Schmidt (2010) were able to meld American Indian traditional healing processes and cultural teachings within an EBP framework. Aspects of this process included assessment of Anna's personal characteristics and preferences and the influence of culture on her reactions to the trauma. Following careful assessment, intervention strategies were selected based on assessment data, therapist expertise, research regarding effective treatments for posttraumatic stress, and cultural adaptation of the therapy selected. The steps involved the following:

- Research-supported treatments for childhood or adolescent trauma were identified. Trauma-focused cognitive-behavioral therapy (TF-CBT) was chosen because it was seen to complement many of the traditional healing practices used in Anna's tribe, including traditional beliefs about the relationship between emotions, beliefs, and behaviors. TF-CBT is a conjoint child and family psychotherapy that has been comprehensively evaluated and designated by the National Crime Victims Research and Treatment Center as having the highest level of research support as an "efficacious treatment" for childhood abuse and trauma.

  TF-CBT has been evaluated with Caucasian and African American children and adapted for American Indian/Alaska Native populations, Latinos, hearing-impaired individuals, immigrant Cambodians, and children of countries including Zambia, Uganda, South Africa, Pakistan, the Netherlands, Norway, Sweden, Germany, and Cambodia (National Child Traumatic Stress Network, 2008). The components of TF-CBT include a focus on reducing negative emotional and behavioral responses resulting from trauma and correcting trauma-related beliefs through gradual exposure to memories and emotional associations with the traumatic event. Relaxation training is used to reduce negative emotions. Parents are included in the treatment process as emotional support for the child; parents are provided with strategies for helping to manage their child's emotional reaction to the trauma.

- Client characteristics and values were identified through interviews with Anna and her family and by assessing their tribal and cultural identity. In Anna's case, both she and her family agreed that she had a strong American

Indian identity and valued traditional healing approaches. Thus it was decided that a culturally adapted TF-CBT would be the most appropriate. (If Anna and her family had expressed minimal tribal or American Indian cultural identification, standard TF-CBT might have been the treatment of choice.)

- *Cultural adaptations* of TF-CBT were developed. Because of cultural beliefs that trauma can bring about disharmony and result in distorted beliefs and unhealthy behaviors, traditional healing efforts focus on returning the individual to a state of harmony through teachings, ceremonies, and tribal practices, including a ritual called Honoring Children, Mending the Circle (HC-MC). The Circle represents the interconnectedness of spirituality and healing and the belief that all things have a spiritual nature; prayers, tribal practices, and rituals connect the physical and the spiritual worlds, bringing wellness and harmony. Additionally, adaptation of the affect management, relaxation, cognitive coping, and enhancing the parent–child relationship aspects of TF-CBT incorporated spiritual (saying prayers), relational (support from friends and family), mental (hearing messages of love and support), and physical (helping Anna reacquire physical balance) supports, thus increasing Anna's feelings of safety and security.

  Further adaptation involved the TF-CBT goal of extinguishing the fear response using a "trauma narrative" during which the child "revisits" the traumatic incident and is gradually exposed to threatening cues. In the adaptation, culturally accepted methods for telling the trauma story—including use of a journey stick, tribal dances, and storytelling procedure—were used to facilitate exposure. Relaxation techniques were also adapted by having Anna breathe deeply while focused on culturally relevant images, such as the "sway of wind swept grasses" or the movement of a woman's shawl during a ceremonial dance."

As BigFoot and Schmidt concluded, "the adaption of TF-CBT within an American Indian/Alaskan Native well-being framework can enhance healing through the blending of science and indigenous cultures. …The HC-MC adaptation seeks to honor what makes American Indians and Alaska Natives culturally unique through respecting beliefs, practices, and traditions within their families, communities, tribes, and villages that are inherently healing" (2010, p. 855).

REFLECTION AND DISCUSSION QUESTIONS

1. What is your reaction to EBP, especially as it applies to ethnic minorities and other diverse populations?

2. It is clear that using an EBP approach requires greater time and effort on the part of clinicians to develop a treatment plan. The implication is that counselors must do out-of-office education or consultation regarding what is available in the research literature that would help inform their practice. Is such an approach too time-consuming? Given that EBP research is exploding in the field, how would you keep current or informed as a practitioner?

IMPLICATIONS FOR CLINICAL PRACTICE

1. Realize that the early EST formulations inadequately addressed the needs of marginalized groups in our society, but have begun to incorporate cultural contexts in modifying evidence-based approaches. The standards used to determine ESTs and ESRs were often too rigid and ignored the cultural context in advocating for the role of science and research in the selection of therapeutic treatments and interventions.

2. Be aware that most mental health professionals have moved to the concept of EBP, (a) allowing for a broader array of means to determine the selection, process, and outcome of effective treatments and (b) integrating cultural factors and/or modifying approaches to fit the needs of diverse clients.

3. Know that *multicultural counseling* and EBP are "strange bedfellows no more" and that it is no longer adequate to devise a treatment plan solely on the basis of one's theoretical orientation, clinical intuition, or clinical expertise.

4. Be aware that EBP models focusing on client characteristics and evaluating the degree of fit between a therapeutic approach and an individual client have actually legitimized the outcry of those in the field of *multicultural counseling*— that it is essential to consider the cultural beliefs and values of the client and that relational counselor styles may need to vary according to an individual's cultural background.

5. Know that the integration of EBP and multiculturalism is resulting in an explosion of research. With the emphasis of the former on client characteristics, values, preference, and culture, EBP and multicultural therapy are becoming inextricably entwined, with each approach adding strengths to the other.

6. Understand that EBP can provide clinicians with information regarding which therapies are most effective with which specific disorders and which specific population. Thus, in choosing a treatment strategy, the best approach (given the current state of research) is for the counselor to select an intervention that is research based (if available) and subsequently adapt the approach for the individual client according to the client's individual characteristics, values, and preferences.

7. Know that culturally competent counseling and therapy is more than a technique-driven search for effective techniques and strategies. We now know that the *therapeutic alliance* or working relationship is crucial to therapeutic outcome.

8. Be prepared to modify your therapeutic style to be consistent with the cultural values, life styles, and needs of culturally diverse clients. Remember, respect, unconditional *positive regard*, warmth, and empathy are most effective in the *therapeutic alliance* when they are communicated in a culturally consistent manner.

9. Be aware that some research suggests that a counselor's *multicultural counseling* competence and humility (awareness of issues of race and discrimination and knowledge of their social impact on clients) accounts for a large proportion of the variance in ratings of counselor competence, expertise, and trustworthiness made by clients of color.

10. It is important to note that most approaches to counseling and therapy attempt to adapt the research findings of EBP to fit the unique cultural characteristics and needs of diverse populations. But what if we approach the challenge to develop culturally appropriate therapeutic techniques and relationships from an indigenous perspective first? This is a question we address in Chapter 10: *Non-Western Indigenous Methods of Healing.*

SUMMARY

The importance of evidence-based practice is becoming increasingly accepted in the field of *multicultural counseling*. Discussions of EBP originally focused on research-supported therapies for specific disorders, but the dialogue has now broadened to contain clinical expertise, including understanding the influence of individual and cultural differences on treatment and the importance of considering client characteristics and culture. Although optimism about the convergence of these forces is increasing, there is still resistance to EBP among some individuals within the field of *multicultural counseling*. The applicability of EBP for many diverse groups has been insufficiently researched, and the concept of "evidence" has historically been very narrow. Furthermore, the therapist–client relationship is not adequately acknowledged in the evidence-based treatment and empirically supported treatment formulations.

It is now widely agreed that the quality of the working relationship between the therapist and the client is consistently related to treatment outcome and has led to the formulation of *empirically supported relationships*. A number of relationship variables are considered effective based on research findings. ESR variables include the development of a strong *therapeutic alliance*, a solid interpersonal bond (i.e., a collaborative, empathetic relationship based on *positive regard*, respect, warmth, and genuineness), effective management of *countertransference*, and *goal consensus*—all factors known to be critical for effective *multicultural counseling*.

The assumption underlying EBP is that the best research evidence begins with a comprehensive understanding of the client's background and problem and goes on to consider which therapeutic approach is most likely to provide the best outcome. This allows for the individualizing of therapy with strong consideration given to client background and characteristics. It broadens the definition of research and allows mental health professionals greater latitude in deciding which therapy may be the best match for a particular client. EBP is based on an ongoing emphasis on client characteristics, culture, and preferences and the importance of working collaboratively with the client to develop goals and treatment strategies that are mutually agreeable. Because the focus is on the client and the consideration of cultural variables, EBP sets the stage for a multiculturally sensitive counseling relationship.

GLOSSARY TERMS

Cognitive empathy	Empathy
Countertransference	Empirically supported relationships
Cultural adaptations	Empirically supported treatments
Emotional bond	Evidence-based practices
Emotional empathy	Goal consensus

Multicultural counseling

Positive regard

Self-disclosure

Therapeutic alliance

Therapeutic bond

Universal–diversity orientation

REFERENCES

Ackerman, S. J., Benjamin, L. S., Beutler, L. E., Gelso, C. J., Goldfried, M. R., Hill, C., Lambert, M. J., Norcross, J. C., Orlinsky, D. E., & Rainer, J. (2001). Empirically supported therapy relationships: Conclusions and recommendations of the Division 29 Task Force. *Psychotherapy, 38*, 495–497.

Aguilera, A., Garza, M. J., & Munoz, R. F. (2010). Group cognitive-behavioral therapy for depression in Spanish: Culture-sensitive manualized treatment in practice. *Journal of Clinical Psychology: In Session, 66*, 857–867.

American Counseling Association. (2014). *Code of ethics.* Alexandria, VA: Author.

American Psychiatric Association. (2013). *Diagnostic and statistical manual of mental disorders* (5th ed.). Washington, DC: Author.

American Psychological Association. (1993). Guidelines for providers of psychological services to ethnic, linguistic, and culturally diverse populations. *American Psychologist, 48*, 45–48.

American Psychological Association. (2007). Guidelines for the psychological practice with girls and women. *American Psychologist, 62*, 949–979.

American Psychological Association (2014). Guidelines for psychological practice with older adults. *American Psychologist, 69*, 34–65.

American Psychological Association, Division 44/Committee on Lesbian, Gay, and Bisexual Concerns Joint Task Force on Guidelines for Psychotherapy with Lesbian, Gay, and Bisexual Clients. (2012). Guidelines for psychotherapy with lesbian, gay, and bisexual clients. *American Psychologist, 67*, 10–42.

American Psychological Association, Presidential Task Force on Evidence-Based Practice. (2006). Evidence-based practice in psychology. *American Psychologist, 61*, 271–285.

Barrett, M. S., & Berman, J. S. (2001). Is psychotherapy more effective when therapists disclose information about themselves? *Journal of Consulting and Clinical Psychology, 69*, 597–603.

Benish, S. G., Quintana, S., & Wampold, B. E. (2011). Culturally adapted psychotherapy and the legitimacy of myth: A direct-comparison meta-analysis. *Journal of Counseling Psychology, 58*, 279–289.

Berke, D. M., Rozell, C. A., Hogan, T. P., Norcross, J. C., & Karpiak, C. P. (2011). What clinical psychologists know about evidence-based practice: Familiarity with online resources and research methods. *Journal of Clinical Psychology, 67*, 329–339.

Bernal, G., & Sáez-Santiago, E. (2006). Culturally centered psychosocial interventions. *Journal of Community Psychology, 34*, 121–132.

BigFoot, D. S., & Schmidt, S. R. (2010). Honoring children, mending the circle: Cultural adaptation of trauma focused cognitive-behavioral therapy for American Indian and Alaska Native children. *Journal of Clinical Psychology: In Session, 66*, 847–856.

Bledsoe, S. E., Weissman, M. M., Mullen, E. J., Ponniah, K., Gameroff, M. J., Verdell, H., . . . Wichramaratne, P. (2007). Empirically supported psychotherapy in social work training programs: Does the definition of evidence matter? *Research on Social Work Practice, 17*, 449–455.

Brems, C. (2000). *Dealing with challenges in psychotherapy and counseling*. Belmont, CA: Brooks/Cole.

Burkard, A. W., & Knox, S. (2004). Effect of therapist color-blindness on empathy and attributions in cross-cultural counseling. *Journal of Counseling Psychology, 51*, 1–29.

Burkard, A. W., Knox, S., Groen, N., Perez, M., & Hess, S. (2006). European American therapist self-disclosure in cross-cultural counseling. *Journal of Counseling Psychology, 53*, 15–25.

Cashwell, C. S., Shcherbakova, J., & Cashwell, T. H. (2003). Effect of client and counselor ethnicity on preference for counselor disclosure. *Journal of Counseling and Development, 81*, 196–201.

Castonguay, L. G., Goldfried, M. R., Wiser, S., Raue, P. J., & Hayes, A. M. (1996). Predicting the effect of cognitive therapy for depression: A study of unique and common factors. *Journal of Consulting and Clinical Psychology, 64*, 497–504.

Chambless, D. L., & Hollon, S. (1998). Defining empirically supported therapies. *Journal of Consulting and Clinical Psychology, 66*, 7–18.

Chambless, D. L., & Ollendick, T. H. (2001). Empirically supported psychological interventions: Controversies and evidence. *Annual Review of Psychology, 52*, 685–716.

Chang, D. F., & Berk, A. (2009). Making cross-racial therapy work: A phenomenological study of clients' experiences of cross-racial therapy. *Journal of Counseling Psychology, 56*, 521–536.

Chung, R. C.-Y., & Bernak, F. (2002). The relationship of culture and empathy in cross-cultural counseling. *Journal of Counseling and Development, 80*, 154–159.

Chwalisz, K. (2001). A common factors revolution: Let's not "cut off our discipline's nose to spite its face." *Journal of Counseling Psychology, 48*, 262–267.

Constantine, M. G. (2002). Predictors of satisfaction with counseling: Racial and ethnic minority clients' attitudes toward counseling and ratings of their counselors' general and multicultural counseling competence. *Journal of Multicultural Counseling and Development, 30*(4), 210–215.

Constantine, M. G. (2007). Racial microaggressions against African American clients in a cross-racial counseling relationship. *Journal of Counseling Psychology, 54*, 1–16.

Coombs, M. M., Coleman, D., & Jones, E. E. (2002). Working with feelings: The importance of emotion in both cognitive-behavioral and interpersonal therapy in the NIMH Treatment of Depression Collaborative Research Program. *Psychotherapy: Theory/Research/Practice/Training, 39*, 233–244.

Corey, G. (2013). *Theory and practice of counseling and psychotherapy* (9th ed.). Belmont, CA: Brooks/Cole.

Cunningham, P. B., Foster, S. L., & Warner, S. E. (2010). Culturally relevant family-based treatment for adolescent delinquency and substance abuse: Understanding within-session processes. *Journal of Clinical Psychology: In Session, 66*, 830–846.

Curtis, R., Field, C., Knann-Kostman, I., & Mannix, K. (2004). What 75 psychoanalysts found helpful and hurtful in their own analysis. *Psychoanalytic Psychology, 21*, 183–202.

Davis, T. A., Ancis, J. R., & Ashby, J. S. (2015). Therapist effects, working alliance, and African American Women substance users. *Cultural Diversity and Ethnic Minority Psychology, 21*, 126–135.

DeAngelis, T. (2005). Shaping evidence-based practice. *Monitor on Psychology, 36*, 26–31.

Deegear, J., & Lawson, D. M. (2003). The utility of empirically supported treatments. *Professional Psychology: Research and Practice, 34*, 271–277.

Duarte-Velez, Y., Guillermo, B., & Bonilla, K. (2010). Culturally adapted cognitive-behavioral therapy: Integrating sexual, spiritual, and family identities in an evidence-based treatment of a depressed Latino adolescent. *Journal of Clinical Psychology: In Session, 66,* 895–906.

Dyche, L., & Zayas, L. H. (2001). Cross-cultural empathy and training the contemporary psychotherapist. *Clinical Social Work Journal, 29,* 245–258.

Fortuna, L. R., Alegria, M., & Gao, S. (2010). Retention in depression treatment among ethnic and racial minority groups in the United States. *Depression and Anxiety, 27,* 485–494.

Fuertes, J. N., & Brobst, K. (2002). Clients' ratings of counselor multicultural competency. *Cultural Diversity and Ethnic Minority Psychology, 8,* 214–223.

Garber, B. D. (2004). Therapist alienation: Foreseeing and forestalling third-party dynamics: Undermining psychotherapy with children of conflicted caregivers. *Professional Psychology: Research and Practice, 35,* 357–363.

Gibbs, L., & Gambrill, E. (2002). Evidence-based practice: Counterarguments to objections. *Research on Social Work Practice, 12,* 452–476.

Gloria, A. M., & Peregoy, J. J. (1996). Counseling Latino alcohol and other substance users/abusers. *Journal of Substance Abuse Treatment, 13,* 119–126.

Gone, J. P. (2009). A community-based treatment for Native American historical trauma: Prospects for evidence-based practice. *Journal of Consulting and Clinical Psychology, 12,* 751–762.

Hays, P. A. (2001). *Addressing cultural complexities in practice: A framework for clinicians and counselors.* Washington, DC: American Psychological Association.

Hilsenroth, M. J., & Cromer, T. D. (2007). Clinician interventions related to alliance during the initial interview and psychological assessment. *Psychotherapy: Theory, Research, Practice, Training, 44,* 205–218.

Hojat, M., Louis, D. Z., Markham, F. W., Wender, R., Rabinowitz, C., & Gonnella, J. S. (2011). Physicians' empathy and clinical outcomes for diabetic patients. *Academic Medicine, 86,* 359–364.

Hook, J. N., Davis, D. E., Owen, J., Worthington, E. L., & Utsey, S. O. (2013). Cultural humility: Measuring openness to culturally diverse clients. *Journal of Counseling Psychology, 60,* 353–366.

Horrell, S.C.V. (2008). Effectiveness of cognitive-behavioral therapy with adult ethnic minority clients: A review. *Professional Psychology: Research and Practice, 39,* 160–168.

Huey, S. J., & Pan, D. (2006). Culture-responsive one-session treatment for phobic Asian Americans: A pilot study. *Psychotherapy: Theory, Research, Practice, Training, 43,* 549–554.

Ivey, A. E., Ivey, M. B., & Zalaquett, C. P. (2014). *Intentional interviewing and counseling* (8th ed.). Belmont, CA: Brooks/Cole.

Kennedy, R. (2003). *Highlights of the American Psychiatric Association 55th Institute on Psychiatric Services.* Retrieved from http://www.medscape.com/viewarticle/471433

Kratochwill, T. R. (2002). Evidence-based interventions in school psychology: Thoughts on thoughtful commentary. *School Psychology Quarterly, 15,* 518–532.

Lambert, M. J., & Barley, D. E. (2001). Research summary on the therapeutic relationship and psychotherapy outcome. *Psychotherapy, 38,* 357–361.

LaRoche, M. J., Batista, C., & D'Angelo, E. (2011). A content analysis of guided imagery scripts: A strategy for the development of cultural adaptations. *Journal of Clinical Psychology, 67,* 45–57.

Lau, A. S., Fung, J. J., & Yung, V. (2010). Group parent training with immigrant Chinese families: Enhancing engagement and augmenting skills development. *Journal of Clinical Psychology: In Session, 66,* 880–894.

Lester, K., Resick, P. A., Young-Xu, Y., & Artz, C. (2010). Impact of race on early treatment termination and outcomes in posttraumatic stress disorder treatment. *Journal of Consulting and Clinical Psychology*, 78, 480–489.

Lilienfeld, S. O. (2007). Psychological treatments that cause harm. *Psychological Science*, 2, 53–70.

Morales, E., & Norcross, J. C. (2010). Evidence-based practices with ethnic minorities: Strange bedfellows no more. *Journal of Clinical Psychology: In Session*, 66, 821–829.

Mulvaney-Day, N. E., Earl, T. R., Diaz-Linhart, Y., & Alegria, M. (2011). Preferences for relational style with mental health clinicians: A qualitative comparison of African American, Latino and Non-Latino White patients. *Journal of Clinical Psychology*, 67, 31–44.

Nagayama-Hall, G. (2001). Psychotherapy research with ethnic minorities: Empirical, ethical, and conceptual issues. *Journal of Consulting and Clinical Psychology*, 69, 502–510.

National Child Traumatic Stress Network. (2008). *TF-CBT: Trauma focused cognitive behavioral therapy*. Retrieved from http://www.nctsnet.org/nctsn_assets/pdfs/promising_practices/TFCBT_General.pdf

Nicolas, G., Arntz, D. L., Hirsch, B., & Schmiedigen, A. (2011). Cultural adaptation of a group treatment for Haitian American adolescents. *Professional Psychology: Research and Practice*, 40, 378–384.

Organista, K. C. (2000). Latinos. In J. R. White & A. S. Freeman (Eds.), *Cognitive-behavioral group therapy: For specific problems and populations* (pp. 281–303). Washington, DC: American Psychological Association.

Owen, J., Jordan, T. A., Turner, D., Davis, D. E., Hook, J. N., & Leach, M. M. (2014). Therapists' multicultural orientation: Client perceptions of cultural humility, spiritual/religious commitment, and therapy outcomes. *Journal of Psychology and Theology*, 42, 91–98.

Ribner, D. S., & Knei-Paz, C. (2002). Client's view of a successful helping relationship. *Social Work*, 47, 379–387.

Rogers, C. R. (1957). The necessary and sufficient conditions of therapeutic personality change. *Journal of Consulting Psychology*, 21, 95–103.

Smith, T. B., Rodriguez, M. D., & Bernal, G. (2011). Culture. *Journal of Clinical Psychology: In Session*, 67, 166–175.

Society of Clinical Psychology (2011). *Psychological treatments*. Retrieved from http://bpd.about.com/gi/o.htm?zi=1/XJ&zTi=1&sdn=bpd&cdn=health&tm=6&f=00&tt=8&bt=1&bts=1&zu=http%3A//www.div12.org/PsychologicalTreatments/treatments.html

Stracuzzi, T. I., Mohr, J. J., & Fuertes, J. N. (2011). Gay and bisexual male clients' perceptions of counseling: The role of perceived sexual orientation similarity and counselor universal-diverse orientation. *Journal of Counseling Psychology*, 58, 299–309.

Sue, D., & Sue, D. M. (2008). *Foundations of counseling and psychotherapy: Evidence-based practices in a diverse society*. Hoboken, NJ: Wiley.

Sue, D. W. (2015). Therapeutic harm and cultural oppression. *Counseling Psychologist*. doi: 0011000014565713

Sue, D. W., Bucceri, J., Lin, A. I., Nadal, K. L., & Torino, G. C. (2007). Racial microaggressions and the Asian American experience. *Cultural Diversity and Ethnic Minority Psychology*, 13, 72–81.

Sue, S., Zane, N., Levant, R. F., Silverstein, L. B., Brown, L. S., & Olkin, R. (2006). How well do both evidence-based practices *and* treatment as usual satisfactorily address the various dimensions of diversity? In J. C. Norcross, L. F. Beutler, & R. F. Levant (Eds.), *Evidence-based practice in mental health: Debate and dialogue on the fundamental questions* (pp. 329–337). Washington, DC: American Psychological Association.

Sue, S., Zane, N., Nagayama-Hall, G. C., & Berger, L. K. (2009). The case for cultural competency in psychotherapeutic interventions. *Annual Review of Psychology, 60*, 525–548.

Thurston, I. B., & Phares, V. (2008). Mental health utilization among African American and Caucasian mothers and fathers. *Journal of Consulting and Clinical Psychology, 76*, 1058–1067.

Trifﬂeman, E. G., & Pole, N. (2010). Future directions in studies of trauma among ethnoracial and sexual minority samples: Commentary. *Journal of Consulting and Clinical Psychology, 78*, 490–497.

Wampold, B. E. (2001). *The great psychotherapy debate: Models, methods, and findings.* Mahwah, NJ: Erlbaum.

Weinberger, J. (2002). Short paper, large impact: Rosenzweig's influence on the common factor movement. *Journal of Psychotherapy Integration, 12*, 67–76.

Wendt, D. C., Gone, J. P., & Nagata, D. K. (2015). Potentially harmful therapy and multicultural counseling: Bridging two disciplinary discourses. *Counseling Psychologist, 43*, 334–358.

Zuroff, D. C., & Blatt, S. J. (2006). The therapeutic relationship in the brief treatment of depression: Contributions to clinical improvement and enhanced adaptive capacities. *Journal of Consulting and Clinical Psychology, 74*, 130–140.

Non-Western Indigenous Methods of Healing

Implications for Multicultural Counseling and Therapy

Chapter Objectives

1. Outline basic assumptions of *indigenous healing* and shamanism.

2. Explain shamanic explanations of illness.

3. Identify commonalities between what therapists and *shamans* do.

4. Describe how shamanism makes different assumptions from Western scientific approaches in mental health treatment.

5. Discuss the belief in altered states of consciousness or different planes of existence.

6. Explain how religion and *spirituality* affect the belief systems of indigenous groups.

7. Articulate your beliefs about the discomfort or comfort you would have in talking to clients about religion and *spirituality*.

8. Outline the argument for the role religion and *spirituality* play in counseling and therapy.

9. Discuss implications of non-Western indigenous beliefs and practices for work with diverse populations.

VANG XIONG

Vang Xiong is a former Hmong (Laotian) soldier who, with his wife and child, resettled in Chicago in 1980. The change from his familiar rural surroundings and farm life to an unfamiliar urban area must have produced a severe culture shock. In addition, Vang vividly remembers seeing people killed during his escape from Laos, and he expressed feelings of guilt about having to leave his brothers and sisters behind in that country. Five months after his arrival, the Xiong family moved into a conveniently located apartment, and that is when Vang's problems began.

Vang could not sleep the first night in the apartment, nor the second, nor the third. After three nights of very little sleep, Vang came to see his resettlement worker, a young bilingual Hmong man named Moua Lee. Vang told Moua that the first night he woke suddenly, short of breath, from a dream in which a cat was sitting on his chest. The second night, the room suddenly grew darker, and a figure like a large black dog came to his bed and sat on his chest. He could not push the dog off, and he grew quickly and dangerously short of breath. The third night, a tall, white-skinned female spirit came into his bedroom from the kitchen and lay on top of him. Her weight made it increasingly difficult for him to breathe; as he grew frantic and tried to call out, he could manage nothing but a whisper. He attempted to turn onto his side but found he was pinned down. After 15 minutes, the spirit left him, and he awoke, screaming. He was afraid to return to the apartment at night, afraid to fall asleep, and afraid he would die during the night, or that the spirit would make it so that he and his wife could never have another child. He told Moua that once, when he was 15, he had a similar attack; that several times, back in Laos, his elder brother had been visited by a similar spirit; and that his brother was subsequently unable to father children due to his wife's miscarriages and infertility. (Tobin & Friedman, 1983, p. 440)

> Moua Lee and mental health workers became very concerned in light of the high incidence of sudden death syndrome among Southeast Asian refugees. For some reason, the incidents of unexplained death, primarily among Hmong men, would occur within the first 2 years of residence in the United States. Autopsies produced no identifiable cause for the deaths. All the reports were the same: A person in apparently good health went to sleep and died without waking. Often the victim displayed labored breathing, screams, and frantic movements just before death. With this dire possibility evident for Vang, the mental health staff felt that they lacked the expertise for so complex and potentially dangerous a case. Conventional Western means of treatment for other Hmong clients had proved minimally effective. As a result, they decided to seek the services of Mrs. Thor, a 50-year-old Hmong woman who was widely respected in Chicago's Hmong community as a *shaman*. The description of the treatment follows.

CASE STUDY

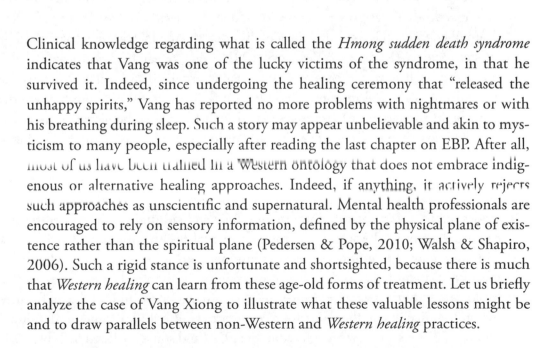

That evening, Vang Xiong was visited in his apartment by Mrs. Thor, who began by asking Vang to tell her what was wrong. She listened to his story, asked a few questions, and then told him she thought she could help. She gathered the Xiong family around the dining room table, upon which she placed some candles alongside many plates of food that Vang's wife had prepared. Mrs. Thor lit the candles and then began a chant that Vang and his wife knew was an attempt to communicate with spirits. Ten minutes or so after Mrs. Thor had begun chanting, she was so intensely involved in her work that Vang and his family felt free to talk to each other and to walk about the room without fear of distracting her. Approximately 1 hour after she had begun, Mrs. Thor completed her chanting, announcing that she knew what was wrong. . . .she had learned from her spirit that the figures in Vang's dreams who lay on his chest and made it so difficult for him to breathe were the souls of the apartment's previous tenants, who had apparently moved out so abruptly they had left their souls behind. Mrs. Thor constructed a cloak out of newspaper for Vang to wear. She then cut the cloak in two and burned the pieces, sending the spirits on their way with the smoke. She also had Vang crawl through a hoop, and then between two knives, telling him that these maneuvers would make it very hard for spirits to follow. Following these brief ceremonies, the food prepared by Vang's wife was enjoyed by all. The leftover meats were given in payment to Mrs. Thor, and she left, assuring Vang Xiong that his troubles with spirits were over. (Tobin & Friedman, 1983, p. 441)

Clinical knowledge regarding what is called the *Hmong sudden death syndrome* indicates that Vang was one of the lucky victims of the syndrome, in that he survived it. Indeed, since undergoing the healing ceremony that "released the unhappy spirits," Vang has reported no more problems with nightmares or with his breathing during sleep. Such a story may appear unbelievable and akin to mysticism to many people, especially after reading the last chapter on EBP. After all, most of us have been trained in a Western ontology that does not embrace indigenous or alternative healing approaches. Indeed, if anything, it actively rejects such approaches as unscientific and supernatural. Mental health professionals are encouraged to rely on sensory information, defined by the physical plane of existence rather than the spiritual plane (Pedersen & Pope, 2010; Walsh & Shapiro, 2006). Such a rigid stance is unfortunate and shortsighted, because there is much that *Western healing* can learn from these age-old forms of treatment. Let us briefly analyze the case of Vang Xiong to illustrate what these valuable lessons might be and to draw parallels between non-Western and *Western healing* practices.

LEGITIMACY OF CULTURAL SYNDROMES: NIGHTMARE DEATHS AND THE HMONG SUDDEN DEATH PHENOMENON

The symptoms experienced by Vang and the frighteningly high number of early Hmong refugees who have died these so-called "nightmare deaths" have baffled mental health workers for years. Indeed, researchers at the Federal Center for Disease Control and epidemiologists have studied it but remain mystified (D. Sue, D. W. Sue, D. M. Sue, & S. Sue, 2013; Tobin & Friedman, 1983). Such tales bring to mind anthropological literature describing voodoo deaths and *bangungut*, or Oriental nightmare death. What is clear, however, is that these deaths do not appear to have a primary biological basis and that psychological factors (primarily belief in the imminence of death, either by a curse, as in voodoo suggestion, or by some form of punishment and excessive stress) appear to be causative (Moodley, 2005).

Beliefs in spirits and spirit possession are not uncommon among many cultures, especially in Southeast Asia (American Psychiatric Association, 2013; Faiver, Ingersoll, O'Brien, & McNally, 2001). Such worldview differences pose problems for Western-trained mental health professionals, who may quickly dismiss these belief systems and impose their own explanations and treatments on culturally diverse clients. Working outside of the belief system of such clients may not have the desired therapeutic effect, and the risk of unintentional harm (in this case the potential death of Vang) is great (Wendt, Gone, & Nagata, 2015). That the sudden death phenomenon is a cultural form of disorder is being increasingly recognized by Western science (Kamarck & Jennings, 1991). Most researchers now acknowledge that attitudes, beliefs, and emotional states are intertwined and can have a powerful effect on physiological responses and physical well-being. Death from bradycardia (slowing of the heartbeat) seems correlated with feelings of helplessness, as in the case of Vang (when he couldn't get the cat, dog, or white-skinned spirit off his chest).

Beginning with the 4th and continuing into the 5th edition, the American Psychiatric Association's *Diagnostic and Statistical Manual of Mental Disorders* (*DSM-IV-TR* and *DSM-5*; American Psychiatric Association, 2000, 2013) has made initial strides in recognizing the importance of ethnic and cultural factors related to psychiatric diagnosis. The manual warns that mental health professionals who work with immigrant and ethnic minorities must take into account (a) the predominant means of manifesting disorders (e.g., possessing spirits, nerves, fatalism, inexplicable misfortune), (b) the perceived causes or explanatory models, and (c) the preferences for professional and indigenous sources of care. Cultural syndromes and cultural idioms of distress are now recognized in the *DSM* and some are listed in Table 10.1.

TABLE 10.1 Cultural Syndromes

Cultural syndromes are disorders specific to a cultural group or society but not easily given a *DSM* diagnosis. These illnesses or afflictions have local names, with distinct culturally sanctioned beliefs surrounding causation and treatment. Some of these are briefly described. Some taken from DSM-IV-TR are listed below.

Amok	This disorder was first reported in Malaysia but is found also in Laos, the Philippines, Polynesia, Papua New Guinea, and Puerto Rico, as well as among the Navajo. It is a dissociative episode preceded by introspective brooding and then an outburst of violent, aggressive, or homicidal behavior toward people and objects. Persecutory ideas, amnesia, and exhaustion signal a return to the premorbid state.
Ataque de nervios	This disorder is most clearly reported among Latinos from the Caribbean but is recognized in Latin American and Latin Mediterranean groups as well. It involves uncontrollable shouting, attacks of crying, trembling, verbal or physical aggression, and dissociative or seizure-like fainting episodes. The onset is associated with a stressful life event relating to family (e.g., death of a loved one, divorce, conflicts with children).
Brain fag	This disorder is usually experienced by high-school or university students in West Africa in response to academic stress. Students state that their brains are fatigued and that they have difficulties in concentrating, remembering, and thinking.
Ghost sickness	Observed among members of American Indian tribes, this disorder is a preoccupation with death and the deceased. It is sometimes associated with witchcraft and includes bad dreams, weakness, feelings of danger, loss of appetite, fainting, dizziness, anxiety, and a sense of suffocation.
Koro	This Malaysian term describes an episode of sudden and intense anxiety that the penis of the male or the vulva and nipples of the female will recede into the body and cause death. It can occur in epidemic proportions in local areas and has been reported in China, Thailand, and other South and East Asian countries.
Mal de ojo	Found primarily in Mediterranean cultures, this term refers to a Spanish phrase that means "evil eye." Children are especially at risk, and symptoms include fitful sleep, crying without apparent cause, diarrhea, vomiting, and fever.
Nervios	This disorder includes a range of symptoms associated with distress, somatic disturbance, and inability to function. Common symptoms include headaches, brain aches, sleep difficulties, nervousness, easy tearfulness, dizziness, and tingling sensations. It is a common idiom of distress among Latinos in the United States and Latin America.
Rootwork	This refers to cultural interpretations of illness ascribed to hexing, witchcraft, sorcery, or the evil influence of another person. Symptoms include generalized anxiety, gastrointestinal complaints, and fear of being poisoned or killed (voodoo death). Roots, spells, or hexes can be placed on people. It is believed that a cure can be manifested via a root doctor who removes the root. Such a belief can be found in the southern United States among both African American and European American populations and in Caribbean societies.
Shen-k'uei (Taiwan); Shenkui (China)	This is a Chinese-described disorder that involves anxiety and panic symptoms with somatic complaints. There is no identifiable physical cause. Sexual dysfunctions are common (premature ejaculation and impotence). The physical symptoms are attributed to excessive semen loss from frequent intercourse, masturbation, nocturnal emission, or passing of "white turbid urine" believed to contain semen. Excessive semen loss is feared and can be life threatening because it represents one's vital essence.

(continued)

| Susto | This disorder is associated with fright or soul loss and is a prevalent folk illness among some Latinos in the United States as well as inhabitants of Mexico, Central America, and South America. Susto is attributed to a frightening event that causes the soul to leave the body. Sickness and death may result. Healing is associated with rituals that call the soul back to the body and restore spiritual balance. |
| Zar | This term is used to describe spirits possessing an individual. Dissociative episodes, shouting, laughing, hitting the head against a wall, weeping, and other demonstrative symptoms are associated with it. It is found in Ethiopia, Somalia, Egypt, Sudan, Iran, and other North African and Middle Eastern societies. People may develop a long-term relationship with the spirit, and their behavior is not considered pathological. |

DSM-IV-TR (American Psychiatric Association, 2000).

In summary, it is very important for mental health professionals not only to become familiar with the cultural background of their clients but also to be knowledgeable about specific cultural syndromes. A primary danger from lack of cultural understanding is the tendency to overpathologize (overestimate the degree of pathology); the mental health professional would have been wrong in diagnosing Vang as a paranoid schizophrenic suffering from delusions and hallucinations. Most might have prescribed powerful antipsychotic medication or even institutionalization. The fact that he was cured so quickly indicates that such a diagnosis would have been erroneous. Interestingly, it is equally dangerous to underestimate the severity or complexity of a refugee's emotional condition.

Causation and Spirit Possession

Vang believed that his problems were related to an attack by undesirable spirits. His story in the following passage gives us some idea about beliefs associated with the fears.

VANG XIONG (CONTINUED)

The most recent attack in Chicago was not the first encounter my family and I have had with this type of spirit, a spirit we call Chia. My brother and I endured similar attacks about six years ago back in Laos. We are susceptible to such attacks because we didn't follow all of the mourning rituals we should have when our parents died. Because we didn't properly honor their memories, we have lost contact with their spirits, and thus we are left with no one to protect us from evil spirits. Without our parents' spirits to aid us, we will always be susceptible to spirit attacks. I had hoped flying so far in a plane to come to America would protect me, but it turns out spirits can follow even this far. (Tobin & Friedman, 1983, p. 444)

Western science remains skeptical of using supernatural explanations to explain phenomena and certainly does not consider the existence of spirits to be a scientifically sound belief. Yet belief in spirits and its parallel relationship to religious, philosophic, and scientific worldviews have existed in every known culture, including the United States (e.g., the witch hunts of Salem, Massachusetts). Among many Southeast Asian groups, it is not uncommon to posit the existence of good and evil spirits, to assume that they are intelligent beings, and to believe that they are able to affect the life circumstances of the living (Fadiman, 1997; E. Lee, 1996). Vang, for example, believed strongly that his problems were due to spirits who were unhappy with him and were punishing him. Interestingly, among the Hmong, good spirits often serve a protective function against evil spirits. Because Vang's parental spirits had deserted him, he believed he was more susceptible to the workings of evil forces. Many cultures believe that a cure can come about only through the aid of a *shaman* or a healer who can reach and communicate with the spirit world via divination skills.

Although mental health professionals may not believe in spirits, therapists are similar to the Hmong in their need to explain the troubling phenomena experienced by Vang and to construe meaning from them. Vang's sleep disturbances, nightmares, and fears can be seen as the result of emotional distress. From a Western perspective, his war experiences, flight, relocation, and survivor stress (not to mention the adjustment to a new country) have all contributed to combat fatigue (posttraumatic stress disorder, or PTSD) and survivor guilt (APA, 2013). Studies on hundreds of thousands of refugees from Southeast Asia suggest that they were severely traumatized during their flight for freedom (Mollica, Wyshak, & Lavelle, 1987). The most frequent diagnoses for this group were generally major affective disorder and PTSD. In addition to being a combat veteran, Vang is a disaster victim, a survivor of a holocaust that has seen perhaps 200,000 of the approximately 500,000 Hmong die. Vang's sleeplessness, breathing difficulties, paranoid belief that something attacked him in bed, and symptoms of anxiety and depression are the result of extreme trauma and stress. Tobin and Friedman (1983) believed that Vang also suffered from survivor's guilt and concluded:

> Applying some of the insights of the Holocaust literature to the plight of the Southeast Asian refugees, we can view Vang Xiong's emotional crisis (his breathing and sleeping disorder) as the result not so much of what he suffered as what he did not suffer, of what he was spared. . . . "Why should I live while others died?" So Vang Xiong,

> *through his symptoms, seemed to be saying, "Why should I sleep com-*
> *fortably here in America while the people I left behind suffer? How*
> *can I claim the right to breathe when so many of my relatives and*
> *countrymen breathe no more back in Laos?" (p. 443)*

Even though we might be able to recast Vang's problems in more acceptable psychological terminology, the effective multicultural helping professional requires knowledge of cultural relativism and respect for the belief system of culturally different clients (Eriksen, Jackson, Weld, & Lester, 2013). Respecting another's worldview does not mean that the helping professional needs to subscribe to it. Yet the counselor or therapist must be willing and ready to learn from indigenous models of healing and to function as a facilitator of indigenous support systems or *indigenous healing* systems.

The Shaman as Therapist: Commonalities

It is probably safe to conclude that every society and culture has individuals or groups designated as healers—those who comfort the ailing. Their duties involve not only physical ailments but also those related to psychological distress or behavioral deviance (Harner, 1990; Ross, 2014). Although every culture has multiple healers, the *shaman* in non-Western cultures is perhaps the most powerful of all because only he or she possesses the ultimate magico-religious powers that go beyond the senses (Eliade, 1972). Mrs. Thor was a well-known and respected *shaman* in the Hmong community of the Chicago area. Although her approach to treating Vang (incense, candle burning, newspaper, trance-like chanting, spirit diagnosis, and even her home visit) on the surface might resemble mysticism, there is much in her behavior that is similar to Western psychotherapy.

First, as we saw in Chapter 5, the healer's credibility is crucial to the effectiveness of therapy. In this case, Mrs. Thor had all the cultural credentials of a *shaman*; she was a specialist and professional with long years of training and experience dealing with similar cases. By reputation and behavior, she acted in a manner familiar to Vang and his family. More importantly, she shared their worldview as to the definition of the problem. Second, she showed compassion while maintaining a professional detachment, did not pity or make fun of Vang, avoided premature diagnosis or judgment, and listened to his story carefully. Third, like the Western therapist, she offered herself as the chief instrument of cure. She used her expertise and ability to get in touch with the hidden world of the spirits (in Western terms the unconscious?) and helped Vang to understand (become conscious of) the mysterious power of the spirits (unconscious) to effect a cure.

Because Vang believed in spirits, Mrs. Thor's interpretation that the nightmares and breathing difficulties were spiritual problems was intelligible, desired, and ultimately curative. It is important to note, however, that Vang also continued to receive treatment from the local mental health clinic in coming to grips with the deaths of others (his parents, fellow soldiers, and other family members).

In the case of Vang Xiong, non-Western and Western forms of healing were combined with one another for maximum effect. The presence of a mental health treatment facility that employed bilingual/bicultural practitioners, its vast experience with Southeast Asian immigrants, and its willingness to use indigenous healers provided Vang with a culturally appropriate form of treatment that probably saved his life. Not all immigrants, however, are so fortunate. Witness the following case of the Nguyen family.

THE NGUYEN FAMILY

Mr. and Mrs. Nguyen and their four children left Vietnam in a boat with 36 other people. Several days later, they were set upon by Thai pirates. The occupants were all robbed of their belongings; some were killed, including two of the Nguyens' children. Nearly all the women were raped repeatedly. The trauma of the event is still very much with the Nguyen family, who now reside in St. Paul, Minnesota. The event was most disturbing to Mr. Nguyen, who had watched two of his children drown and his wife being raped. The pirates had beaten him severely and tied him to the boat railing during the rampage. As a result of his experiences, he continued to suffer feelings of guilt, suppressed rage, and nightmares.

The Nguyen family came to the attention of the school and social service agencies because of suspected child abuse. Their oldest child, 12-year-old Phuoc, came to school one day with noticeable bruises on his back and down his spinal column. In addition, obvious scars from past injuries were observed on the child's upper and lower torso. His gym teacher had seen the bruises and scars and immediately reported them to the school counselor. The school nurse was contacted about the possibility of child abuse, and a conference was held with Phuoc. He denied that he had been hit by his parents and refused to remove his garments when requested to do so. Indeed, he became quite frightened and hysterical about taking off his shirt. Since there was still considerable doubt about whether this was a case of child abuse, the counselor decided to let the matter drop for the moment. Nevertheless, school personnel were alerted to this possibility.

Several weeks later, after 4 days of absence, Phuoc returned to school. The homeroom teacher noticed bruises on Phuoc's forehead and the bridge of his nose. When the incident was reported to the school office, the counselor immediately called Child Protective Services to report a suspected case of child abuse. Because of the heavy caseload experienced by Child Protective Services, a social worker was unable to visit the family until weeks later. The social worker, Mr. P., called the family and visited the home late on a Thursday afternoon. Mrs. Nguyen greeted Mr. P. upon his arrival. She appeared nervous, tense, and frightened. Her English was poor, and it was difficult to communicate with her. Since Mr. P. had specifically requested to see Mr. Nguyen as well, he inquired about his whereabouts. Mrs. Nguyen answered that he was not feeling well and was in the room downstairs. She said he was having "a bad day," had not been able to sleep last night, and was having flashbacks. In his present condition, he would not be helpful.

When Mr. P. asked about Phuoc's bruises, Mrs. Nguyen did not seem to understand what he was referring to. The social worker explained in detail the reason for his visit. Mrs. Nguyen explained that the scars were due to the beating given to her children by the Thai pirates. She became very emotional about the topic and broke into tears. Although this had some credibility, Mr. P. explained that there were fresh bruises on Phuoc's body as well. Mrs. Nguyen seemed confused, denied that there were new injuries, and denied that they would hurt Phuoc. The social worker pressed Mrs. Nguyen about the new injuries until she suddenly looked up and said, "*Thùôc Nam.*" It was obvious that Mrs. Nguyen now understood what Mr. P. was referring to. When asked to clarify what she meant by the phrase, Mrs. Nguyen pointed at several thin bamboo sticks and a bag of coins wrapped tightly in a white cloth. It looked like a blackjack! She then pointed downstairs in the direction of the husband's room. It was obvious from Mrs. Nguyen's gestures that her husband had used these to beat her son.

A Case of Child Abuse?

There are many similarities between the case of the Nguyen family and that of Vang Xiong. One of the most common experiences of refugees forced to flee their country is the extreme stressors that they experience. Constantly staring into the face of death was, unfortunately, all too common an experience. Seeing loved ones killed, tortured, and raped; being helpless to change or control such situations; living in temporary refugee or resettlement camps; leaving familiar surroundings; and encountering a strange and alien culture can only be described as multiple severe traumas.

It is highly likely that many Cambodian, Hmong/Laotian, and Vietnamese refugees suffer from serious PTSD and other forms of major affective disorders. Mr. and Mrs. Nguyen's behaviors (flashbacks, desire to isolate the self, emotional fluctuations, anxiety, and tenseness) might all be symptoms of PTSD. Accurate understanding of their life circumstances will prevent a tendency to overpathologize or underpathologize their symptoms. These symptoms, along with a reluctance to disclose to strangers and discomfort with the social worker, should be placed in the context of the stressors that they experienced and their cultural background. More important, as in the case of the Nguyen family, behaviors should not be interpreted to indicate guilt or a desire not to disclose the truth about child abuse.

Second, mental health professionals must consider potential linguistic and cultural barriers when working with refugees, especially when one lacks both experience and expertise. In this case, it is clear that the teacher, the school counselor, the school nurse, and even the social worker did not have sufficient understanding or experience in working with Southeast Asian refugees. For example, the social worker's failure to understand Vietnamese phrases and Mrs. Nguyen's limited English placed serious limitations on their ability to communicate accurately (Schwartz et al., 2010). The social worker might have avoided much of the misunderstanding if an interpreter had been present. In addition, the school personnel may have misinterpreted many culturally sanctioned forms of behavior on the part of the Vietnamese. Phuoc's reluctance to disrobe in front of strangers (the nurse) may have been prompted by cultural taboos rather than by attempts to hide the injuries. Traditional Asian culture dictates strongly that family matters are handled within the family. Many Asians believe that family affairs should not be discussed publicly, and especially not with strangers (Chang, McDonald, & O'Hara, 2014). Disrobing publicly and telling others about the scars or the trauma of the Thai pirates would not be done readily. Yet such knowledge is required by educators and social service agencies in order to make enlightened decisions.

Third, both school and social service personnel are obviously unenlightened about *indigenous healing* beliefs and practices. In the case of Vang Xiong, we saw how knowledge and understanding of cultural beliefs led to appropriate and helpful treatment. In the case of the Nguyen family, lack of understanding led to charges of child abuse. But is this really a case of child abuse? When Mrs. Nguyen said "*Thùôc Nam*," what was she referring to? What did the fresh bruises along Phuoc's spinal column, forehead, and bridge of the nose mean? And didn't Mrs. Nguyen admit that her husband used the bamboo sticks and bag of coins to "beat" Phuoc?

In Southeast Asia, traditional medicine derives from three sources: Western medicine (Thùôc Tay), Chinese or Northern medicine (Thùôc Bac), and Southern medicine (*Thùôc Nam*). Many forms of these treatments continue to exist among Asian Americans and are even more prevalent among the Vietnamese refugees who brought the treatments to the United States (Hong & Domokos-Cheng

Ham, 2001). *Thùôc Nam*, or traditional medicine, involves using natural fruits, herbs, plants, animals, and massage to heal the body. Massage treatment is the most common cause of misdiagnosis of child abuse because it leaves bruises on the body. Three common forms of massage treatment are *Băt Gió* ("catching the wind"), *Cao Gió* ("scratching the wind," or "coin treatment"), and *Giác Hoi* ("pressure massage," or "dry cup massage"). The latter involves steaming bamboo tubes so that the insides are low in pressure, applying them to a portion of the skin that has been cut, and sucking out "bad air" or "hot wind." *Cao Gió* involves rubbing the patient with a mentholated ointment and then using coins or spoons to strike or scrape lightly along the ribs and both sides of the neck and shoulders. *Băt Gió* involves using both thumbs to rub the temples and massaging toward the bridge of the nose at least 20 times. Fingers are used to pinch the bridge of the nose. All three treatments leave bruises on the parts of the body treated.

If the social worker could have understood Mrs. Nguyen, he would have known that Phuoc's 4-day absence from school was due to illness and that he was treated by his parents via traditional folk medicine. Massage treatments are a widespread custom practiced not only by Vietnamese but also by Cambodians, Laotians, and Chinese. These treatments are aimed at curing a host of physical ailments, such as colds, headaches, backaches, and fevers. In the mind of the practitioner, such treatments have nothing to do with child abuse. Yet the question still remains: Is it considered child abuse when traditional healing practices result in bruises? This is a very difficult question to answer because it raises a larger question: Can culture justify a practice, especially when it is harmful? Although unable to answer this second question directly (we encourage you to engage in dialogue about it), we point out that many medical practitioners in California do not consider it child abuse because (a) medical literature reveals no physical complications as a result of *Thùôc Nam*; (b) the intent is not to hurt the child but to help him or her; and (c) it is frequently used in conjunction with Western medicine. However, we would add that health professionals and educators have a responsibility to educate parents concerning the potential pitfalls of many folk remedies and indigenous forms of treatment.

THE PRINCIPLES OF INDIGENOUS HEALING

Ever since the beginning of human existence, all societies and cultural groups have developed not only their own explanations of abnormal behaviors but also their culture-specific ways of dealing with human problems and distress

(Gone, 2010; Solomon & Wane, 2005). Within the United States, counseling and psychotherapy are the predominant psychological healing methods. In other cultures, however, *indigenous healing* approaches continue to be widely used (Mpofu, 2011). Although there are similarities between EuroAmerican helping systems and the indigenous practices of many cultural groups, there are major dissimilarities as well. *Indigenous healing* can be defined as helping beliefs and practices that originate within the culture or society (Edwards, 2011). It is not transported from other regions, and it is designed for treating the inhabitants of the given group.

Western forms of counseling, for example, rely on sensory information defined by the physical plane of reality (Western science), whereas most indigenous methods rely on the spiritual plane of existence in seeking a cure. In keeping with the cultural encapsulation of our profession, *Western healing* has been slow to acknowledge and learn from these age-old forms of wisdom (Constantine, Myers, Kindaichi, & Moore, 2004; Gone, 2010). In its attempt to become culturally responsive, however, the mental health field must begin to put aside the biases of Western science, to acknowledge the existence of intrinsic help-giving networks, and to incorporate the legacy of ancient wisdom that may be contained in indigenous models of healing.

What is called the *universal shamanic tradition*, which encompasses the centuries-old recognition of healers (*shamans*) within a community, refers to people often called witches, witch doctors, wizards, medicine men or women, sorcerers, and magic men or women (E. Lee, 1996). These individuals are believed to possess the power to enter an altered state of consciousness and journey to other planes of existence beyond the physical world during their healing rituals (M.T. Garrett et al., 2011; Moodley, 2005). Such was the case of Mrs. Thor, a *shaman* who journeyed to the spirit world in order to find a cure for Vang.

Indigenous healing in non-Western countries found three approaches often used (C. C. Lee, Oh, & Mountcastle, 1992). First, there is heavy reliance on the use of communal, group, and family networks to shelter the disturbed individual (Saudi Arabia), to problem-solve in a group context (Nigeria), and to reconnect them with family or significant others (Korea). Second, spiritual and religious beliefs and traditions of the community are used in the healing process. Examples include reading verses from the Qur'an and using religious houses or churches. Third, use of *shamans* (called *piris* and *fakirs* in Pakistan and Sudan), who are perceived to be the keepers of timeless wisdom, constitutes the norm. In many cases, the person conducting a healing ceremony may be a respected elder of the community or a family member. Two representative *indigenous healing* approaches are exemplified in the Hawaiian *ho'oponopono* and the Native American *sweat lodge ceremony*.

Ho'oponopono

An excellent example that incorporates these approaches is the Native Hawaiian *ho'oponopono* healing ritual (Nishihara, 1978; Rezentes, 2006). Translated literally, the word means "a setting to right, to make right, to correct." In cultural context, *ho'oponopono* attempts to restore and maintain good relations among family members and between the family and the supernatural powers. It is a kind of family conference (family therapy) aimed at restoring good and healthy harmony in the family. Many Native Hawaiians consider it to be one of the soundest methods of restoring and maintaining good relations that any society has ever developed. Such a ceremonial activity usually occurs among members of the immediate family but may involve the extended family and even nonrelatives if they were involved in the *pilikia* (trouble). The process of healing consists of the following:

1. The *ho'oponopono* begins with *pule weke* (opening prayer) and ends with *pule ho'opau* (closing prayer). The pule creates the atmosphere for the healing and involves asking the family gods for guidance. These gods are not asked to intervene, but to grant wisdom, understanding, and honesty.

2. The ritual elicits *'oia'i'o* (truth telling), sanctioned by the gods, and makes compliance among participants a serious matter. The leader states the problem, prays for spiritual fusion among members, reaches out to resistant family members, and attempts to unify the group.

3. Once this occurs, the actual work begins through *mahiki*, a process of getting to the problems. Transgressions, obligations, righting the wrongs, and forgiveness are all aspects of *ho'oponopono*. The forgiving/releasing/severing of the wrongs, the hurts, and the conflicts produces a deep sense of resolution.

4. Following the closing prayer, the family participates in *pani*, the termination ritual in which food is offered to the gods and to the participants.

In general, we can see several principles of indigenous Hawaiian healing: (a) problems reside in relationships with people and spirits; (b) harmony and balance in the family and in nature are desirable; (c) healing must involve the entire group and not just an individual; (d) *spirituality*, prayer, and ritual are important aspects of healing; (e) the healing process comes from a respected elder of the family; and (f) the method of healing is indigenous to the culture (Rezentes, 2006).

Native American Sweat Lodge Ceremony

Another example of *indigenous healing* increasingly being employed by Western cultures in medicine, mental health, substance abuse, and correctional facilities is the Native American *sweat lodge ceremony* (sweat therapy) (M. T. Garrett & Portman, 2011; M. T. Garrett et al., 2011). Among Native Americans, the sweat lodge and the ensuing rituals are filled with cultural and spiritual symbolism and meaning. The sweat lodge itself is circular or oval and symbolizes the universe and/or womb from which life originates; the stone pit represents the power of the creator, and the stones (healing power of the earth) are heated by the sacred fire; the water used in the ceremony is essential for all life; the steam that rises when water is thrown on the stones represents both the prayers of the participants and ancient knowledge; and the sweat of the participants is part of the purification process. Consistent with most indigenous mandates, the *sweat lodge ceremony* is conducted under the following conditions as described by Garrett et al. (2011):

1. The lodge is constructed from materials garnered from Mother Earth. Permission is sought from the wood, bark, rocks, and other materials to participate in the sacred ritual. The reciprocity involved in requesting permission and giving thanks is part of the belief in the interrelationship of all things and the maintenance of balance and harmony.

2. A Fire Keeper has the responsibility of tending the sacred fire from which the stones will be heated.

3. Participants strip themselves of all clothing and jewelry and enter on their hands and knees to show respect for Mother Earth. They then sit in a sacred circle (hoop of life).

4. The ceremony begins in silence (true voice of the Creator); then invocation and thanks are given to the Great Spirit, Mother Earth, the four directions, spirits, and all relations in nature.

5. Water or an herbal mixture is then poured on the heated rocks, producing a purifying steam.

6. The ritualized cleansing of the body is meant to ensure harmony, balance, and wellness in the person. The participants purify themselves by joining with the powers of Mother Earth and the Universal Circle that connects living and nonliving beings.

7. Unlike most Western forms of healing, the *sweat lodge ceremony* takes place in the presence of a person's support network: the family, clan, and community. Not only does the ceremony cleanse the body, mind, and spirit, but it also brings together everyone to honor the energy of life.

As mentioned previously, sweat therapy has been increasingly adopted in Western society as a form of treatment. Its use, however, is based on other Western therapeutic rationales rather than that ascribed to Native Americans.

Those who study indigenous psychologies do not make an a priori assumption that one particular perspective is superior to another (Mikulas, 2006). The Western ontology of healing (counseling/therapy), however, does consider its methods to be more advanced and scientifically grounded than those found in many cultures. *Western healing* has traditionally operated from several assumptions: (a) reality consists of distinct and separate units or objects (therapist and client, observer and observed); (b) reality consists of what can be observed and measured via the five senses; (c) space and time are fixed and absolute constructs of reality; and (d) science operates from universal principles and is culture free (Highlen, 1996).

Although these guiding assumptions of Western science have contributed much to human knowledge and to the improvement of the human condition, most non-Western indigenous psychologies appear to operate from a different perspective. For example, many non-Western cultures do not separate the observer from the observed and believe that all life forms are interrelated with one another, including mother nature and the cosmos; that the nature of reality transcends the senses; that space and time are not fixed; and that much of reality is culture bound (Walsh & Shapiro, 2006). Let us briefly explore several of these parallel assumptions and see how they are manifested in *indigenous healing* practices.

Holistic Outlook, Interconnectedness, and Harmony

The concepts of separation, isolation, and individualism are hallmarks of the Euro-American worldview. On an individual basis, modern psychology takes a reductionist approach to describing the human condition (i.e., id, ego, and superego; belief, knowledge, and skills; cognitions, emotions, and behaviors). The search for cause and effect is linear and allows us to identify the independent variables, the dependent variables, and the effects of extraneous variables that we attempt to control. It is analytical and reductionist in character. The attempt to maintain objectivity, autonomy, and independence in understanding human behavior is also stressed. Such tenets have resulted in separation of the person from the group (valuing of individualism and uniqueness), science from *spirituality*, and man/woman from the universe.

Most non-Western indigenous forms of healing take a *holistic outlook* on well-being, in that they make minimal distinctions between physical and mental functioning and believe strongly in the unity of spirit, mind, and matter. The interrelatedness of life forms, the environment, and the cosmos is a given. As a result, the indigenous peoples of the world tend to conceptualize reality differently (Mpofu, 2011). The psychosocial unit of operation for many culturally diverse groups, for example, is not the individual but the group (collectivism). In many cultures, acting in an autonomous and independent manner is seen as the problem because it creates disharmony within the group.

Illness, distress, or problematic behaviors are seen as an imbalance in people relationships, a disharmony between the individual and his or her group, or a lack of synchrony with internal or external forces. Harmony and balance are the healer's goal. Among American Indians, for example, harmony with nature is symbolized by the circle, or hoop of life (M.T. Garrett & Portman, 2011; McCormick, 2005; Sutton & Broken Nose, 2005). Mind, body, spirit, and nature are seen as a single unified entity, with little separation between the realities of life, medicine, and religion. All forms of nature, not just the living, are to be revered because they reflect the creator or deity. Illness is seen as a break in the hoop of life, an imbalance, or a separation between the elements. Many indigenous beliefs come from a metaphysical tradition. They accept the interconnectedness of cosmic forces in the form of energy or subtle matter (less dense than the physical) that surrounds and penetrates the physical body and the world.

Both the ancient Chinese practice of acupuncture and chakras in Indian yoga philosophy involve the use of subtle matter to rebalance and heal the body and mind (Highlen, 1996). Chinese medical theory is concerned with the balance of yin (cold) and yang (hot) in the body, and it is believed that strong emotional states, as well as an imbalance in the type of foods eaten, may create illness (Pedersen & Pope, 2010; So, 2005). As we saw in the case of Phuoc Nguyen, treatment might involve eating specific types or combinations of foods or using massage treatment to suck out "bad" or "hot" air. Such concepts of illness and health can also be found in the Greek theory of balancing body fluids (blood, phlegm, black bile, and yellow bile) (Bankart, 1997).

The *Afrocentric perspective* also teaches that human beings are part of a holistic fabric—that they are interconnected and should be oriented toward collective rather than individual survival (Boyd-Franklin, 2010; Parham & Caldwell, 2015). The indigenous Japanese assumptions and practices of Naikan and Morita therapy attempt to move clients toward being more in tune with others and society, to move away from individualism, and to move toward interdependence, connectedness, and harmony with others (Bankart, 1997; Chen, 2005). Naikan therapy, which derives from Buddhist practice, requires clients to reflect on three aspects of human relationships: (a) what other people have done for them, (b) what they have done for others, and (c) how they cause difficulties to others (Walsh & Shapiro, 2006). The overall goal is to expand awareness of how much we receive from others, how much gratitude is due them, and how little we demonstrate such gratitude. This ultimately leads to a realization of the interdependence of the parts to the whole. Working for the good of the group ultimately benefits the individual.

Belief in Metaphysical Levels of Existence

Some time back two highly popular books—*Embraced by the Light* (Eadie, 1992) and *Saved by the Light* (Brinkley, 1994)—and several television specials described fascinating cases of near-death experiences. All had certain commonalities: The individuals who were near death felt like they were leaving their physical bodies, observed what was happening around them, saw a bright beckoning light, and journeyed to higher levels of existence. Although the popularity of such books and programs might indicate that the American public is inclined to believe in such phenomena, science has been unable to validate these personal accounts and remains skeptical of their existence. Yet many societies and non-Western cultures accept, as given, the existence of different levels or planes of consciousness, experience, or existence. They believe the means of understanding and ameliorating the causes of illness or problems of life are often found in a plane of reality separate from the physical world of existence.

Asian psychologies posit detailed descriptions of states of consciousness and outline developmental levels of *enlightenment* that extend beyond the concepts of Western psychology. Asian perspectives concentrate less on psychopathology and more on *enlightenment* and ideal mental health (Cashwell & Bartley, 2014; Pankhania, 2005). The normal state of consciousness in many ways is not considered optimal and may be seen as a "psychopathology of the average" (Maslow, 1968). Moving to higher states of consciousness has the effect of enhancing perceptual sensitivity and clarity, concentration, and sense of identity, as well as emotional, cognitive, and perceptual processes. Such movement, according to Asian philosophy, frees one from the negative pathogenic forces of life. Attaining *enlightenment* and liberation can be achieved through the classic practices of meditation and yoga.

Research findings indicate that yoga and meditation are the most widely used of all therapies (Walsh & Shapiro, 2006). They have been shown to reduce anxiety, specific phobias, and substance abuse (Kwee, 1990; Shapiro, 1982; West, 1987); to benefit those with medical problems by reducing blood pressure and aiding in the management of chronic pain (Kabat-Zinn, 1990); to enhance self-confidence, sense of control, marital satisfaction, and so on (Alexander, Rainforth, & Gelderloos, 1991); and to extend longevity (Alexander, Langer, Newman, Chandler, & Davies, 1989). Today, meditation and yoga in the United States have become accepted practices among millions, especially for relaxation and stress management. For practitioners of meditation and yoga, altered states of consciousness are unquestioned aspects of reality.

According to some cultures, nonordinary reality states allow some healers to access an invisible world surrounding the physical one. Puerto Ricans, for example, believe in *espiritismo* (spiritism), a world where spirits can have major impacts on the people residing in the physical world (Chavez, 2005). *Espiritistas*, or mediums, are culturally sanctioned indigenous healers who possess special faculties allowing them to intervene positively or negatively on behalf of their clients. Many cultures strongly believe that human destiny is often decided in the domain of the spirit world. Mental illness may be attributed to the activities of hostile spirits, often in reaction to transgressions of the victim or the victim's family (C. C. Lee, 1996; Mullavey-O'Byrne, 1994). As in the case of Mrs. Thor, *shamans*, mediums, or indigenous healers often enter these realities on behalf of their clients in order to seek answers, to enlist the help of the spirit world, or to aid in realigning the spiritual energy field that surrounds the body and extends throughout the universe.

Ancient Chinese methods of healing and the Hindu concept of chakras also acknowledge another reality that parallels the physical world. Accessing this world allows the healer to use these special energy centers to balance and heal the body and mind. Occasionally, the *shaman* may aid the helpee or novice to access that plane of reality so that he or she may find the solutions. The *vision quest*, in conjunction with the sweat lodge experience, is used by some American Indians as religious renewal or as a rite of passage (M.T. Garrett et al., 2011; Heinrich, Corbin, & Thomas, 1990; Smith, 2005). Underlying these uses is the human journey to another world of reality. The ceremony of the vision quest is intended to prepare the young man for the proper frame of mind; it includes rituals and sacred symbols, prayers to the Great Spirit, isolation, fasting, and personal reflection. Whether in a dream state or in full consciousness, another world of reality is said to reveal itself. Mantras, chants, meditation, and the taking of certain drugs (peyote) all have as their purpose a journey into another world of existence (Duran, 2006).

Spirituality in Life and the Cosmos

Native American Indians look on all things as having life, spiritual energy, and importance. A fundamental belief is that all things are connected. The universe consists of a balance among all of these things and a continuous flow of cycling of this energy. Native American Indians believe that we have a sacred relationship with the universe that is to be honored. All things are connected, all things have life, and all things are worthy of respect and reverence. *Spirituality* focuses on the harmony that comes from our connection with all parts of the universe—in which everything has a purpose and value exemplary of personhood, including plants (e.g., "tree people"), the land ("Mother Earth"), the winds ("the Four Powers"), "Father Sky," "Grandfather Sun," "Grandmother Moon," "The Red Thunder Boys." Spiritual being essentially requires only that we seek our place in the universe; everything else will follow in good time. Because everyone and everything was created with a specific purpose to fulfill, no one should have the power to interfere or to impose on others the best path to follow (J. T. Garrett & Garrett, 1994, p. 187).

The sacred Native American beliefs concerning *spirituality* are a truly alien concept to modern EuroAmerican thinking. The United States has had a long tradition in believing that one's religious beliefs should not enter into scientific or rational decisions (Duran, 2006). Incorporating religion in the rational decision-making process or in the conduct of therapy has generally been seen as unscientific and unprofessional. The schism between religion and science occurred centuries ago and has resulted in a split between science/psychology and religion (Fukuyama & Sevig, 1999). This is reflected in the oft-quoted phrase, "separation of Church and State." The separation has become a serious barrier to mainstream psychology's incorporation of indigenous forms of healing into mental health practice, especially when religion is confused with *spirituality*. Although people may not have a formal religion, indigenous helpers believe that *spirituality* is an intimate aspect of the human condition. Western psychology acknowledges the behavioral, cognitive, and affective realms, but it makes only passing reference to the spiritual realm of existence. Yet indigenous helpers believe that *spirituality* transcends time and space, mind and body, and our behaviors, thoughts, and feelings (C. C. Lee & Armstrong, 1995; Smith, 2005).

These contrasting worldviews are perhaps most clearly seen in definitions of "the good life" and in how our values are manifested in evaluating the worth of others. In the United States, for example, the pursuit of happiness is most often conceived to be manifested in material wealth and physical well-being, whereas other cultures value spiritual or intellectual goals. The worth of a person is anchored in the number of separate properties he or she owns and in his or her net worth and ability to acquire increasing wealth. Indeed, it is often assumed that such an accumulation of wealth is a sign of divine approval (Condon & Yousef, 1975). In cultures where spiritual goals are strong, people's worth is unrelated to material possessions but rather resides within individuals, emanates from their *spirituality*, and is a function of whether they live the "right life." People from capitalistic cultures often do not understand self-immolations and other acts of suicide in countries such as India. They are likely to make statements such as, "Life is not valued there" or, better yet, "Life is cheap." These statements indicate a lack of understanding about actions that arise from cultural forces rather than personal frustrations; they may be symbolic of a spiritual-valuing rather than a material-valuing orientation.

One does not have to look beyond the United States, however, to see such spiritual orientations; many racial/ethnic minority groups in this country are strongly spiritual. African Americans, Asian Americans, Latino/Hispanic Americans, and Native Americans all place strong emphasis on the interplay and interdependence of spiritual life and healthy functioning (Boyd-Franklin, 2010; M. T. Garrett & Portman, 2011). Puerto Ricans, for example, may sacrifice material satisfaction in favor of values pertaining to the spirit and the soul. The Lakota Sioux often say *Mitakuye Oyasin* at the end of a prayer or as a salutation. Translated, it means "to all my relations," which acknowledges the spiritual bond between the speaker and all people present and extends to forebears, the tribe, the family of man, and mother nature. It speaks to the philosophy that all life forces, Mother Earth, and the cosmos are sacred beings and that the spiritual is the thread that binds all together.

Likewise, a strong spiritual orientation has always been a major aspect of life in Africa, and this was also true during the slavery era in the United States.

> *Highly emotional religious services conducted during slavery were of great importance in dealing with oppression. Often signals as to the time and place of an escape were given then. Spirituals contained hidden messages and a language of resistance (e.g., "Wade in the Water" and "Steal Away"). Spirituals (e.g., "Nobody Knows the Trouble I've Seen") and the ecstatic celebrations of Christ's gift of salvation provided Black slaves with outlets for expressing feelings of pain, humiliation, and anger. (Hines & Boyd-Franklin, 1996, p. 74)*

The African American church has a strong influence over the lives of Black people and is often the hub of religious, social, economic, and political life (Boyd-Franklin, 2010). Religion is not separated from the daily functions of the church, as it acts as a complete support system for the African American family, with the minister, deacons, deaconesses, and church members operating as one big family. A strong sense of peoplehood is fostered via social activities, choirs, Sunday school, health-promotion classes, day care centers, tutoring programs, and counseling. To many African Americans the road to mental health and the prevention of mental illness lie in the health potentialities of their spiritual life.

Mental health professionals are becoming increasingly open to the potential benefits of *spirituality* as a means for coping with hopelessness, identity issues, and feelings of powerlessness (Eriksen et al., 2013). As an example of this movement, the Association for Counselor Education and Supervision (ACES) adopted a set of competencies related to *spirituality*. They define *spirituality* as:

> *the animating force in life, represented by such images as breath, wind, vigor, and courage. Spirituality is the infusion and drawing out of spirit in one's life. It is experienced as an active and passive process. Spirituality is also described as a capacity and tendency that is innate and unique to all persons. This spiritual tendency moves the individual towards knowledge, love, meaning, hope, transcendence, connectedness, and compassion. Spirituality includes one's capacity for creativity, growth, and the development of a values system. Spirituality encompasses the religious, spiritual, and transpersonal. (American Counseling Association, 1995, p. 30)*

Interestingly enough, it appears that many in the United States are experiencing a "spiritual hunger," or a strong need to reintegrate spiritual or religious themes into their lives (Gallup, 1995; Hage, 2004; Thoresen, 1998). For example, it appears that there is a marked discrepancy between what patients want from their doctors and what doctors supply. Often, patients want to talk about the spiritual aspects of their illness and treatment, but doctors are either unprepared or disinclined to do so (Eriksen et al., 2013). Likewise, most mental health professionals feel equally uncomfortable, disinclined, or unprepared to speak with their clients about religious or spiritual matters.

The relationship between *spirituality* and health is highly positive (Thoresen, 1998). Those with higher levels of *spirituality* have lower disease risk, fewer physical health problems, and higher levels of psychosocial functioning. It appears that people require faith as well as reason to be healthy and that psychology may profit from allowing the spirit to rejoin matters of the mind and body (Strawbridge, Cohen, Shema, & Kaplan, 1997).

In general, *indigenous healing* methods have much to offer to EuroAmerican forms of mental health practice. The contributions are valuable not only because multiple belief systems now exist in our society but also because counseling and psychotherapy have historically neglected the spiritual dimension of human existence. Our heavy reliance on science and on the reductionist approach to treating clients has made us view human beings and human behavior as composed of separate noninteracting parts (cognitive, behavioral, and affective). There has been a failure to recognize our spiritual being and to take a *holistic outlook* on life (Cashwell & Bartley, 2014). Indigenous models of healing remind us of these shortcomings and challenge us to look for answers in realms of existence beyond the physical world.

REFLECTION AND DISCUSSION QUESTIONS

1. What thoughts do you have about the role of spirituality and religion in psychology and mental health?

2. Should therapists avoid discussing these matters with clients and leave it to the clergy?

3. What are the possible positive and negative outcomes of doing so?

4. Would you feel comfortable talking about religion with your clients?

5. If you were in therapy, how important would it be to discuss your religious or spiritual beliefs?

6. Are you a religious person?

DANGERS AND BENEFITS OF SPIRITUALITY

Although we have discussed the important role that *indigenous healing* plays in many societies and cultures, there are downsides reflected in our historical past where an uncritical acceptance of religious belief systems may actually harm rather than heal or enlighten. Such was the case during a period known as the Middle Ages, when supernatural explanations of human behavior led to a total eclipse of science and resulted in the deaths of many innocent people, primarily those accused of being witches (women, the mentally ill, those with disfigurements, gypsies, and scientists who voiced beliefs that differed from the Church's doctrines). Early Christianity did little to promote science and in many ways actively discouraged it. The Church demanded uncompromising adherence to its tenets. Christian fervor brought with it the concepts of heresy and punishment; certain truths were deemed sacred, and those who challenged them were denounced as heretics. Scientific thought that was in conflict with Church doctrine, especially during the Middle Ages, was not tolerated.

The role of demons, witches, and possessions in explaining abnormal behavior has been part and parcel of many cultures and societies. There is good reason why Western science has viewed religion with skepticism. Until recently, the mental health profession has also been largely silent about the influence or importance of *spirituality* and religion in mental health. Thus, during therapy or work with clients, therapists have generally avoided discussing such topics. It has been found, for example, that many therapists (a) do not feel comfortable or competent in discussing spiritual or religious issues with their clients, (b) are concerned they will appear proselytizing or judgmental if they touch on such topics, (c) believe they may usurp the role of the clergy, and (d) may feel inauthentic addressing client concerns, especially if they are atheists or agnostics (Gonsiorek, Richards, Pargament, & McMinn, 2009; Knox, Catlin, Casper, & Schlosser, 2005).

Yet it has been found that greater than 80 percent of Americans say that religion is important in their lives, that in both medical and mental health care patients express a strong desire for providers to discuss spiritual and faith issues with them, and that persons of color believe that spiritual issues are intimately linked to their cultural identities (Gallup Organization, 2009, 2012). More compelling are findings that reveal a positive association between *spirituality*/religion and optimal health outcomes, longevity, and lower levels of anxiety, depression, suicide, and substance abuse (Cornah, 2006). Studies on the relationship of *spirituality* and health found that higher levels of *spirituality* were associated with lower disease risk, fewer physical health problems, and higher psychosocial functioning (Thoresen, 1998). On a therapeutic level, these findings provide a strong rationale for professionals in the field of counseling and psychology to incorporate *spirituality* into their research and practice.

Surveys support the inescapable conclusion that many in the United States are experiencing a spiritual hunger, or a strong need to reintegrate spiritual or religious themes into their lives (Hage, 2004). Many counseling/mental health professionals are becoming increasingly open to the potential benefits of *spirituality* in the treatment of clients. As part of that process, psychologists are making distinctions between *spirituality* and religion. *Spirituality* is an animating life force that is inclusive of religion and speaks to the thoughts, feelings, and behaviors related to a transcendent state. *Religion* is narrower, involving a specific doctrine and particular system of beliefs. *Spirituality* can be pursued outside a specific religion because it is transpersonal and includes one's capacity for creativity, growth, and love (Eriksen et al., 2013). Mental health professionals are increasingly recognizing that people are thinking, feeling, behaving, social, cultural, and spiritual beings and that the human condition is broad, complex, and holistic.

 ## IMPLICATIONS FOR CLINICAL PRACTICE

1. Do not invalidate the Indigenous belief systems of your culturally diverse client. Entertaining alternative realities does not mean that the counselor must subscribe to that belief system. It does mean, however, that the helping professional must avoid being judgmental.

2. Become knowledgeable about indigenous beliefs and healing practices. Counselors have a professional responsibility to become knowledgeable and conversant about the assumptions and practices of *indigenous healing* so that a process of desensitization and normalization can occur.

3. Avoid overpathologizing a culturally diverse client's problems. Therapists or counselors who are culturally unaware and who believe primarily in a universal psychology may often be culturally insensitive and inclined to see differences as deviance.

4. Avoid underpathologizing a culturally diverse client's problems. While being understanding of a client's cultural context, having knowledge of culture-bound syndromes, and being aware of cultural relativism are desirable, being oversensitive to these factors may predispose the therapist to minimize problems.

5. Be willing to consult with traditional healers or to make use of their services. Mental health professionals must be willing and able to form partnerships with indigenous healers or to develop community liaisons.

6. Recognize that *spirituality* is an intimate aspect of the human condition and a legitimate aspect of mental health work.

7. A counselor or therapist who does not feel comfortable dealing with the spiritual needs of clients or who believes in an artificial separation of the spirit (soul) from the everyday life of the culturally different client may not be providing the needed help.

8. Be willing to expand your definition of the helping role to community work and involvement. More than anything else, *indigenous healing* is community oriented and community focused.

SUMMARY

Since the beginning of human existence, all societies and cultural groups have developed their own explanations of abnormal behaviors and forms of healing. Within the United States, counseling and psychotherapy are the predominant psychological treatment methods. In other cultures, however, *indigenous healing* approaches continue to be widely used, and many people of color continue to be influenced by such beliefs and practices. In many societies the centuries-old recognition of healers (*shamans*) within a community refers to people often called witches, witch doctors, wizards, medicine men or women, sorcerers, and magic men or women. These individuals are believed to possess the power to enter an altered state of consciousness and journey to other planes of existence beyond the physical world during their healing rituals.

There are both similarities and differences between EuroAmerican helping systems and non-Western indigenous practices. *Shamans* share many common characteristics with Western therapists. In the eyes of clients, for example, both have high credibility, show compassion and a professional stance, share one another's worldviews, and offer themselves as the chief instruments for change. The differences, however, are great. Western forms of counseling rely on sensory information defined by the physical plane of reality (Western science), whereas most indigenous methods rely on the spiritual plane of existence in seeking a cure. *Indigenous healing* operates under three guiding principles: (a) *holistic outlook*, interconnectedness, and harmony; (b) belief in metaphysical levels of existence; and (c) *spirituality* in life and the cosmos. *Western healing* has been slow to acknowledge and learn from these age-old forms of wisdom. In its attempt to become culturally responsive, however, the mental health field must begin to put aside the biases of Western science, to acknowledge the existence of intrinsic help-giving networks, and to incorporate the legacy of ancient wisdom that may be contained in indigenous models of healing.

Such reconciliation may be found in the desire among many Americans for religious and spiritual integration. Studies show that an overwhelming number of Americans say that religion is important in their lives, that both medical and mental health care patients express a strong desire for providers to discuss spiritual and faith issues with them, and that persons of color believe that spiritual issues are intimately linked to their cultural identities.

GLOSSARY TERMS

Afrocentric perspective	Giác hoi
Băt Gió	Hmong Sudden Death Syndrome
Brain fag	Ho'oponopono
Cao Gió	Holistic outlook
Enlightenment	Indigenous healing
Espiritismo	Mahiki

'Oia'i'o or 'Oia'i'o	Sweat lodge ceremony
Pani	Thùôc nam
Pule weke	Universal shamanic tradition
Shaman	Western healing
Spirituality	

REFERENCES

Alexander, C., Langer, E., Newman, R., Chandler, H., & Davies, J. (1989). Transcendental meditation, mindfulness and longevity: An experimental study with the elderly. *Journal of Personality and Social Psychology, 57*, 950–964.

Alexander, C., Rainforth, M., & Gelderloos, P. (1991). Transcendental meditation, self-actualization and psychological health: A conceptual overview and statistical meta-analysis. *Journal of Social Behavior and Personality, 6*, 189–247.

American Counseling Association. (1995, December). Summit results in formation of spiritual competencies. *Counseling Today, 38*(6), 30.

American Psychiatric Association. (2000). *Diagnostic and statistical manual of mental disorders* (4th ed.). Text Revision. Washington, DC: Author.

American Psychiatric Association. (2013). *Diagnostic and statistical manual of mental disorders* (5th ed.). Washington, DC: Author.

Bankart, C. P. (1997). *Talking cures: A history of Western and Eastern psycho therapies.* Pacific Grove, CA: Brooks/Cole.

Boyd-Franklin, N. (2010). Incorporating spirituality and religion into the treatment of African American clients. *Counseling Psychologist, 38*, 976–1000.

Brinkley, D. (1994). *Saved by the light.* New York, NY: Villard Books.

Cashwell, C. S., & Bartley, J. L. (2014). Engaged spirituality: A heart for social justice. In M. J. Ratts & P. B. Pedersen (Eds.), *Counseling for multiculturalism and social justice* (pp. 275–288). Alexandria, VA: American Counseling Association.

Chang, C. Y., McDonald, C. P., & O'Hara, C. (2014). Counseling clients from Asian and Pacific Island heritages. In M. J. Ratts & P. B. Pedersen (Eds.), *Counseling for multiculturalism and social justice* (pp. 127–142). Alexandria, VA: American Counseling Association.

Chavez, L. G. (2005). Latin American healers and healing: Healing as a redefinition process. In R. Moodley & W. West (Eds.), *Integrating traditional healing practices into counseling and psychotherapy* (pp. 85–99). Thousand Oaks, CA: Sage.

Chen, C. P. (2005). Morita therapy: A philosophy of Yin/Yang coexistence. In R. Moodley & W. West (Eds.), *Integrating traditional healing practices into counseling and psychotherapy* (pp. 221–232). Thousand Oaks, CA: Sage.

Condon, J. C., & Yousef, F. (1975). *An introduction to intercultural communication.* New York, NY: Bobbs-Merrill.

Constantine, M. G., Myers, L. J., Kindaichi, M., & Moore, J. L. (2004). Exploring indigenous mental health practices: The roles of healers and helpers in promoting well-being in people of color. *Counseling and Values, 48*, 110–125.

Cornah, D. (2006). *The impact of spirituality on mental health: A review of the literature.* London, UK: Mental Health Foundation.

Duran, E. (2006). *Healing the soul wound.* New York, NY: Teachers College Press.

Eadie, B. J. (1992). *Embraced by the light.* Carson City, NV: Gold Leaf Press.

Edwards, S. D. (2011). A psychology of indigenous healing in southern Africa. *Journal of Psychology in Africa, 21,* 335–348.

Eliade, M. (1972). *Shamanism: Archaic techniques of ecstasy.* New York, NY: Pantheon.

Eriksen, K., Jackson, S. A., Weld, C., & Lester, S. (2013). Religion and spirituality. In G. McAuliffe & Associates (Eds.), *Culturally alert counseling* (2nd ed., pp. 453–503). Thousand Oaks, CA: Sage.

Fadiman, A. (1997). *The spirit catches you and you fall down.* New York, NY: Farrar, Straus & Giroux.

Faiver, C., Ingersoll, R. E., O'Brien, E., & McNally, C. (2001). *Explorations in counseling and spirituality.* Belmont, CA: Brooks/Cole.

Fukuyama, M. A., & Sevig, T. D. (1999). *Integrating spirituality into multicultural counseling.* Thousand Oaks, CA: Sage.

Gallup, G. (1995). *The Gallup poll: Public opinion 1995.* Wilmington, DE: Scholarly Resources.

Gallup Organization. (2009). *Religion.* Retrieved from http://www.gallup.com/poll/1690/Religion.aspx

Gallup Organization. (2012). *Religion.* Retrieved from http://www.gallup.com/poll1690/Religion.aspx

Garrett, J. T., & Garrett, M. W. (1994). The path of good medicine: Understanding and counseling Native American Indians. *Journal of Multicultural Counseling and Development, 22,* 134–144.

Garrett, M. T., & Portman, T.A.A. (2011). *Counseling Native Americans.* Belmont, CA: Cengage.

Garrett, M. T., Torres-Rivera, E., Brubaker, M., Portman, T.A.A., Brotherson, D., West-Olatunji, C., & Grayshield, L. (2011). Crying for a vision: The Native American sweat lodge ceremony as therapeutic intervention. *Journal of Counseling and Development, 89,* 318–325.

Gone, J. P. (2010). Psychotherapy and traditional healing for American Indians: Exploring the prospects for therapeutic integration. *Counseling Psychologist, 38,* 166–235.

Gonsiorek, J. C., Richards, P. S., Pargament, K. I., & McMinn, M. R. (2009). Ethical challenges and opportunities at the edge: Incorporating spirituality and religion into psychotherapy. *Professional Psychology: Research and Practice, 40,* 385–395.

Hage, S. M. (2004). A closer look at the role of spirituality in psychology training programs. *Professional Psychology: Research and Practice, 37,* 303–310.

Harner, M. (1990). *The way of the shaman.* San Francisco, CA: Harper & Row.

Heinrich, R. K., Corbin, J. L., & Thomas, K. R. (1990). Counseling Native Americans. *Journal of Counseling & Development, 69,* 128–133.

Highlen, P. S. (1996). MCT theory and implications for organizations/systems. In D. W. Sue, A. E. Ivey, & P. B. Pedersen (Eds.), *A theory of multicultural counseling and therapy* (pp. 65–85). Pacific Grove, CA: Brooks/Cole.

Hines, P. M., & Boyd-Franklin, N. (1996). African American families. In M. McGoldrick, J. Giodano, & J. K. Pearce (Eds.), *Ethnicity and family therapy* (pp. 66–84). New York, NY: Guilford Press.

Hong, G. K., & Domokos-Cheng Ham, M. (2001). *Psychotherapy and counseling with Asian American clients.* Thousand Oaks, CA: Sage.

Kabat-Zinn, J. (1990). *Full catastrophe living.* New York, NY: Delacorte.

Kamarck, T., & Jennings, J. R. (1991). Biobehavioral factors in sudden cardiac death. *Psychological Bulletin, 109,* 42–75.

Knox, S., Catlin, L., Casper, M., & Schlosser, L. Z. (2005). Addressing religion and spirituality in psychotherapy: Clients' perspectives. *Psychotherapy Research, 15,* 287–303.

Kwee, M. (1990). *Psychotherapy, meditation and health.* London, UK: East-West.

Lee, C. C. (1996). MCT theory and implications for indigenous healing. In D. W. Sue, A. E.

Ivey, & P. B. Pedersen (Eds.), *A theory of multicultural counseling and therapy* (pp. 86–98). Pacific Grove, CA: Brooks/Cole.

Lee, C. C., & Armstrong, K. L. (1995). Indigenous models of mental health intervention: Lessons from traditional healers. In J. G. Ponterotto, J. M. Casas, L. A. Suzuki, & C. M. Alexander (Eds.), *Handbook of multicultural counseling* (pp. 441–456). Thousand Oaks, CA: Sage.

Lee, C. C., Oh, M. Y., & Mountcastle, A. R. (1992). Indigenous models of helping in nonwestern countries: Implications for multicultural counseling. *Journal of Multicultural Counseling and Development, 20,* 1–10.

Lee, E. (1996). Chinese families. In M. McGoldrick, J. Geordano, & J. K. Pearce (Eds.), *Ethnicity and family therapy* (pp. 249–267). New York, NY: Guilford Press.

Maslow, A. H. (1968). *Toward a psychology of being.* Princeton, NJ: Van Nostrand.

McCormick, R. (2005). The healing path: What can counselors learn from aboriginal people about how to heal? In R. Moodley & W. West (Eds.), *Integrating traditional healing practices into counseling and psychotherapy* (pp. 293–304). Thousand Oaks, CA: Sage.

Mikulas, W. L. (2006). Integrating the world's psychologies. In L. T. Hoshmand (Ed.), *Culture, psychotherapy and counseling* (pp. 91–111). Thousand Oaks, CA: Sage.

Mollica, R. F., Wyshak, G., & Lavelle, J. (1987). The psychosocial impact of war trauma and torture on Southeast Asian refugees. *American Journal of Psychiatry, 144,* 1567–1572.

Moodley, R. (2005). Shamanic performances: Healing through magic and the supernatural. In R. Moodley & W. West (Eds.), *Integrating traditional healing practices into counseling and psychotherapy* (pp. 2–14). Thousand Oaks, CA: Sage.

Mpofu, E. (2011). *Counseling people of African ancestry.* Cambridge, MA: Cambridge University Press.

Mullavey-O'Byrne, C. (1994). Intercultural communication for health care professionals. In R. W. Brislin & T. Yoshida (Eds.), *Improving intercultural interactions* (pp. 171–196). Thousand Oaks, CA: Sage.

Nishihara, D. P. (1978). Culture, counseling, and ho'oponopono: An ancient model in a modern context. *Personnel and Guidance Journal, 56,* 562–566.

Pankhania, J. (2005). Yoga and its practice in psychological healing. In R. Moodley & W. West (Eds.), *Integrating traditional healing practices into counseling and psychotherapy* (pp. 246–256). Thousand Oaks, CA: Sage.

Parham, T. A., & Caldwell, L. D. (2015). Boundaries in the context of a collective community: An African-centered perspective. In B. Herlihy & G. Corey (Eds.), *Boundary issues in counseling* (pp. 96–100). Alexandria, VA: American Counseling Association.

Pedersen, P. B., & Pope, M. (2010). Inclusive cultural empathy for successful global leadership. *American Psychologist, 65,* 841–854.

Rezentes, W. C. III, (2006). Hawaiian psychology. In L. T. Hoshmand (Ed.), *Culture, psychotherapy and counseling* (pp. 113–133). Thousand Oaks, CA: Sage.

Ross, R. (2014). *Indigenous healing: Exploring traditional paths.* Toronto, Ontario: Penguin Group Canada.

Schwartz, S., Hoyte, J., James, T., Conoscenti, L., Johnson, R., & Liebschutz, J. (2010). Challenges to engaging Black male victims of community violence in healthcare research: Lessons learned from two studies. *Psychological Trauma: Theory, Research, Practice, and Policy, 2,* 54–62.

Shapiro, D. H. (1982). Overview: Clinical and physiological comparison of meditation with other self-control strategies. *American Journal of Psychiatry, 139,* 267–274.

Smith, D. P. (2005). The sweat lodge as psychotherapy. In R. Moodley & W. West (Eds.), *Integrating traditional healing practices into counseling and psychotherapy* (pp. 196–209). Thousand Oaks, CA: Sage.

So, J. K. (2005). Traditional and cultural healing among the Chinese. In R. Moodley & W. West (Eds.), *Integrating traditional healing practices into counseling and psychotherapy* (pp. 100–111). Thousand Oaks, CA: Sage.

Solomon, A., & Wane, J. N. (2005). Indigenous healers and healing in a modern world. In R. Moodley & W. West (Eds.), *Integrating traditional healing practices into counseling and psychotherapy* (pp. 52–60). Thousand Oaks, CA: Sage.

Strawbridge, W. J., Cohen, R. D., Shema, S. J., & Kaplan, G. A. (1997). Frequent attendance at religious services and mortality over 28 years. *American Journal of Public Health, 87,* 957–961.

Sue, D., Sue, D. W., Sue, D. M., & Sue, S. (2013). *Understanding abnormal behavior.* Belmont, CA: Cengage.

Sutton, C. T., & BrokenNose, M. A. (2005). American Indian families: An overview. In M. McGoldrick, J. Giordano, & N. Garcia-Preto (Eds.), *Ethnicity and family therapy* (pp. 43–54). New York, NY: Guilford Press.

Thoresen, C. E. (1998). Spirituality, health and science: The coming revival? In S. R. Roemer, S. R. Kurpius, & C. Carmin (Eds.), *The emerging role of counseling psychology in health care* (pp. 409–431). New York, NY: Norton.

Tobin, J. J., & Friedman, J. (1983). Spirits, shamans, and nightmare death: Survivor stress in a Hmong refugee. *American Journal of Orthopsychiatry, 53,* 439–448.

Walsh, R., & Shapiro, S. L. (2006). The meeting of meditative disciplines and Western psychology. *American Psychologist, 61,* 227–239.

Wendt, D. C., Gone, J. P., & Nagata, D. K. (2015). Potentially harmful therapy and multicultural counseling: Bridging two disciplinary discourses. *Counseling Psychologist, 43,* 334–358.

West, M. (1987). *The psychology of meditation.* Oxford, UK: Clarendon Press.

PART IV

Racial/Cultural Identity Development in Multicultural Counseling and Therapy

Racial/Cultural Identity Development in People of Color

Counseling Implications

Chapter Objectives

1. Learn the important factors that are influential in the development of racial/cultural identity in people of color.

2. Become familiar with racial identity development in various groups of color.

3. Describe how sociopolitical forces influence the identity development of people of color.

4. Define the developmental levels of racial consciousness and describe how they affect the attitudes, beliefs, and behaviors toward oneself, toward members of one's own group, and toward majority group members.

5. Become knowledgeable about how the racial consciousness of people of color impacts the counseling/therapy situation

6. Describe the various common characteristics of clients at each of the following levels of identity formation: conformity, dissonance, *resistance and immersion*, *introspection*, and *integrative awareness*.

7. Discuss the therapeutic challenges likely to confront a counselor or therapist working with clients at each of the five levels of identity development.

SANSEI (THIRD-GENERATION) JAPANESE AMERICAN FEMALE

CASE STUDY

For nearly all my life I have never seriously attempted to dissect my feelings and attitudes about being a Japanese American woman. Aborted attempts were made, but they were never brought to fruition, because it was unbearably painful. Having been born and raised in Arizona, I had no Asian friends. I suspect that given an opportunity to make some, I would have avoided them anyway. That is because I didn't want to have anything to do with being Japanese American. Most of the Japanese images I saw were negative. Japanese women were ugly; they had "cucumber legs," flat yellow faces, small slanty eyes, flat chests, and were stunted in growth. The men were short and stocky, sneaky and slimy, clumsy, inept, "wimpy looking," and sexually emasculated. I wanted to be tall, slender, large eyes, full lips, and elegant looking; I wasn't going to be typical Oriental!. . .

At Cal [University of California, Berkeley], I've been forced to deal with my Yellow-White identity. There are so many "yellows" here that I can't believe it. I've come to realize that many White prejudices are deeply ingrained in me; so much so that they are unconscious. . . .To accept myself as a total person, I also have to accept my Asian identity as well. But what is it? I just don't know. Are they the images given me through the filter of White America, or are they the values and desires of my parents?

Yesterday, I had a rude awakening. For the first time in my life I went on a date with a Filipino boy. I guess I shouldn't call him a "boy," as my ethnic studies teacher says it is derogatory toward Asians and Blacks. I only agreed to go because he seemed different from the other "Orientals" on campus. (I guess I shouldn't use that word either.) He's president of his Asian fraternity, very athletic and outgoing. . . .When he asked me, I figured, "Why not?" It'll be a good experience to see what it's like to date an Asian boy. Will he be like White guys who will try to seduce me, or will he be too afraid to make any move when it comes to sex?. . .We went to San Francisco's Fisherman's Wharf for lunch. We were seated and our orders were taken before two other White women. They were, however, served first. This was painfully apparent to us, but I wanted to pretend that it was just a mix-up. My friend, however, was less forgiving and made a public fuss with the waiter. Still, it took an inordinate amount of time for us to get our lunches, and the filets were overcooked (purposely?). My date made a very public scene by placing a tip on the table, and then returning to retrieve it. I was both embarrassed but proud of his actions.

This incident and others made me realize several things. For all my life I have attempted to fit into White society. I have tried to convince myself that I was different, that I was like all my other White classmates, and that prejudice and discrimination didn't exist for me. I wonder how I could have been so oblivious to prejudice and racism. I now realize that I cannot escape from my ethnic heritage and from the way people see me. Yet I don't know how to go about resolving many of my feelings and conflicts. While I like my newly found Filipino "male" friend (he is sexy), I continue to have difficulty seeing myself married to anyone other than a White man. (Excerpts from a Sansei student class journal)

RACIAL AWAKENING

Oriental, Asian, or White?

This Sansei (third-generation) Japanese American female is experiencing a *racial awakening* that has strong implications for her racial/cultural identity development. Her previous belief systems concerning White Americans and Asian Americans are being challenged by social reality and the experiences of being a "visible racial/ethnic minority." First, a major theme involving societal portrayals of Asian Americans is clearly expressed in the student's beliefs about racial/cultural characteristics: She describes the Asian American male and female in highly unflattering terms. She seems to have internalized these beliefs and to be using White standards to judge Asian Americans as being desirable or undesirable. For this student, the process of incorporating these standards has not only attitudinal but behavioral consequences as well. In Arizona, she would not have considered making Asian American friends even if the opportunity presented itself. In her mind, she was not a "typical Oriental"; she disowned or felt ashamed of her ethnic heritage, and she even concludes that she would not consider marrying anyone but a White male.

Denial Breakdown

Second, her denial that she is an Asian American is beginning to crumble. Being immersed in the student body on a campus in which there are many fellow Asian Americans in attendance forces her to explore ethnic identity issues—a process she has been able to avoid while living in a predominantly White area. In the past, when she encountered prejudice or discrimination, she had been able to deny it or to rationalize it away. The differential treatment she received at a restaurant and her male friend's labeling it as "discrimination" makes such a conclusion inescapable. The shattering of illusions is manifest in her realization that (a) despite her efforts to "fit in," it is not enough to gain social acceptance among many White Americans; (b) she cannot escape her racial/cultural heritage; and (c) she has been brainwashed into believing that one group is superior over another.

The Internal Struggle for Identity

Third, the student's internal struggle to cast off the cultural conditioning of her past and the attempts to define her ethnic identity are both painful and conflicting. We have clear evidence of the internal turmoil she is undergoing when she (a) refers to her "Yellow-White" identity; (b) writes about the negative images of Asian American males but winds up dating one; (c) uses the terms "Oriental" and "boy" (in reference to her Asian male friend) but acknowledges their derogatory racist nature; (d) describes Asian men as "sexually emasculated" but sees her Filipino date as "athletic," "outgoing," and "sexy"; (e) expresses embarrassment at confronting the waiter about discrimination but feels proud of her Asian male friend for doing so; and (f) states that she finds him attractive but could never consider marrying anyone but a White man. Understanding the process by which racial/cultural identity develops in persons of color is crucial for effective multicultural counseling/therapy.

Locus of the Problem

Fourth, it is clear that the Japanese American female is a victim of ethnocentric monoculturalism. As we mentioned previously, the problem being experienced by the student does not reside in her but in our society. It resides in a society that portrays racial/ethnic characteristics as inferior, primitive, deviant, pathological, or undesirable. The resulting damage strikes at the self-esteem and self/group identity of many culturally different individuals in our society; many, like this student, may come to believe that their racial/cultural heritage or characteristics are burdens to be changed or overcome. Understanding racial/cultural identity development and its relationship to therapeutic practice are the goals of this chapter.

RACIAL/CULTURAL IDENTITY DEVELOPMENT MODELS

The historic work on racial/cultural identity development among minority groups has led to major breakthroughs in the field of multicultural counseling/therapy (Atkinson, Morten, & Sue, 1998; Cross, 1971, 1995; Cross, Smith, & Payne, 2002; Helms, 1984, 1995; Horse, 2001; J. Kim, 1981; Ruiz, 1990). Most would agree that Asian Americans, African Americans, Latino/Hispanic Americans, and American Indians have distinct cultural heritages that make each different from the other. Yet such cultural distinctions can lead to a monolithic view of minority group attitudes and behaviors. The erroneous belief that all Asians are the same, all Blacks are the same, all Latinas/os are the same, or all American Indians are the same has led to numerous therapeutic problems.

First, therapists may often respond to culturally diverse clients in a very stereotypic manner and fail to recognize within-group or individual differences. For example, research indicates that Asian American clients seem to prefer and benefit most from a highly structured and directive approach, rather than an insight/feeling-oriented one (Hong & Domokos-Cheng Ham, 2001; B.S.K. Kim, 2011; Sandhu, Leung, & Tang, 2003). Although such approaches may generally be effective, they are often blindly applied without regard for possible differences in client attitudes, beliefs, and behaviors. Likewise, conflicting findings in the literature regarding whether people of color prefer therapists of their own race seem to be a function of our failure to make such distinctions. Preference for a racially or ethnically similar therapist may really be a function of the cultural/racial identity of the individual (within-group differences) rather than of race or ethnicity per se.

Second, the strength of racial/cultural identity models lies in their potential diagnostic value. Premature termination rates among clients of color may be attributed to the inappropriateness of transactions that occur between the helping professionals and culturally diverse clients. Research suggests that reactions to counseling, the counseling process, and counselors are influenced by cultural/racial identity and are not simply linked to minority group membership. The high failure-to-return rate of many clients seems to be intimately connected to the mental health professional's inability to assess the cultural identity of clients accurately (Ivey, D'Andrea, & Ivey, 2011).

A third important contribution derived from racial identity models is their acknowledgment of sociopolitical influences in shaping identity (à la the Sansei student). Early models of racial identity development all incorporated the effects of racism and prejudice (oppression) upon the identity transformation of their victims. Vontress (1971), for instance, theorized that African Americans moved through decreasing levels of dependence on White society to emerging identification with Black culture and society (Colored, Negro, and Black). Other similar models for African Americans have been proposed (Cross, 1971; Jackson, 1975; Thomas, 1970, 1971). The fact that other marginalized groups, such as Asian Americans (J. Kim, 2012; S. Sue & Sue, 1971), Latinas/os (Ferdman & Gallegos, 2012), Native Americans (Horse, 2012), women (Downing & Roush, 1985; McNamara & Rickard, 1989), lesbians/gays (Cass, 1979), and individuals with disabilities (Olkin, 1999), have similar processes may indicate experiential validity for such models as they relate to various oppressed groups.

Black Identity Development Models

Early attempts to define a process of minority identity transformation came primarily through the works of Black social scientists and educators (Cross, 1971; Jackson, 1975; Thomas, 1971. Although there are several *Black identity development models*, the Cross model of psychological *nigrescence* (the process of becoming Black) is perhaps the most influential and well documented (Cross, 1971, 1991, 1995). The original Cross model was developed during the civil rights movement and delineates a five-stage process in which Blacks in the United States move from a White frame of reference to a positive Black frame of reference: *preencounter, encounter, immersion-emersion, internalization, and internalization-commitment.*

- The *preencounter* stage is characterized by African Americans' consciously or unconsciously devaluing their own Blackness and concurrently valuing White values and ways. There is a strong desire to assimilate and acculturate into White society. Blacks at this stage evidence self-hate, low self-esteem, and poor mental health (Vandiver, 2001).

- In the *encounter* stage, a two-step process begins to occur. First, the individual encounters a profound crisis or event that challenges his or her previous mode of thinking and behaving; second, the Black person begins to reinterpret the world, resulting in a shift in worldviews. Cross points out how the slaying of Martin Luther King Jr. was such a significant experience for many African Americans. More recently, the shooting of Michael Brown in Ferguson, Missouri, and the choking death of Eric Gardner in New York in 2014 are examples of such events. The person experiences both guilt and anger over being brainwashed by White society.

- In the third stage, *immersion-emersion*, the person withdraws from the dominant culture and becomes immersed in African American culture. Black pride begins to develop, but *internalization* of positive attitudes toward one's own Blackness is minimal. In the emersion phase, feelings of guilt and anger begin to dissipate with an increasing sense of pride.

- The next stage, *internalization*, is characterized by inner security, as conflicts between the old and new identities are resolved. Global anti-White feelings subside as the person becomes more flexible, more tolerant, and more bicultural/multicultural.

• The last stage, *internalization-commitment*, speaks to the commitment that such individuals have toward social change, social justice, and civil rights. It is expressed not only in words but also in actions that reflect the essence of their lives.

Cross's original model makes a major assumption: The evolution from the *preencounter* stage to the *internalization* stage reflects a movement from psychological dysfunction to psychological health (Vandiver, 2001).

Confronted with evidence that these stages may mask multiple racial identities, questioning his original assumption that all Blacks at the preencounter stage possess self-hatred and low self-esteem, and aware of the complex issues related to *race salience*, Cross (1991) revised his theory of *nigrescence* in his book *Shades of Black*. His changes, which are based on a critical review of the literature on Black racial identity, have increased the model's explanatory powers and promise high predictive validity (Vandiver, Fhagen-Smith, Cokley, Cross, & Worrell, 2001; Worrell, Cross, & Vandiver, 2001). In essence, the revised model contains nearly all the features from the earlier formulation, but it differs in several significant ways.

First, Cross introduces the concept of *race salience*, the degree to which race is an important and integral part of a person's approach to life. The Black person may function with "race" consciousness playing either a large role in his or her identity or a minimal one. In addition, salience for Blackness can possess positive (pro-Black) or negative (anti-Black) valence. Instead of using the term "pro-White" in describing the *preencounter* stage, Cross now uses the term *race salience*. Originally, Cross believed that the rejection of Blackness and the acceptance of an American perspective were indicative of only one identity, characterized by self-hate and low self-esteem. His current model now describes two identities: (a) *preencounter assimilation* and (b) *preencounter* anti-Black. The former has low salience for race and a neutral valence toward Blackness, whereas the latter describes individuals who hate Blacks and hate being Black (high negative salience). In other words, it is possible for a Black person at the *preencounter* stage who experiences the salience of race as very minor and whose identity is oriented toward an "American" perspective not to be filled with self-hate or low self-esteem.

The sense of low self-esteem, however, is linked to the *preencounter* anti-Black orientation. According to Cross, such a psychological perspective is the result of miseducation and self-hatred. The miseducation is the result of the negative images of Blacks portrayed in the mass media; among neighbors, friends, and relatives; and in the educational literature (Blacks are unintelligent, criminal, lazy, and prone to violence). The result is an incorporation of such negative images into the personal identity of the Black person. Interestingly, the female Sansei student described earlier in this chapter, though Japanese American, would seem to possess many of the features of Cross's *preencounter* anti-Black identity.

Second, the *immersion-emersion* stage once described one fused identity (anti-White/pro-Black) but is now divided into two additional ones: anti-White alone and anti-Black alone. While Cross speaks about two separate identities, it appears that there are three possible combinations: anti-White, pro-Black, and an anti-White/pro-Black combination.

Third, Cross has collapsed the fourth and fifth stages (internalization and *internalization-commitment*) into one: *internalization*. He observed that minimal differences existed between the two stages except in the characteristic of "sustained interest and commitment." This last stage is characterized by Black self-acceptance and can be manifested in three types of identity: (a) Black nationalist (high Black positive *race salience*), (b) biculturalist (Blackness and fused sense of American-ness), and (c) multiculturalist (multiple identity formation, including race, gender, sexual orientation, etc.).

Although Cross's model has been revised significantly and the newer version is more sophisticated, his original 1971 *nigrescence* theory continues to dominate the racial identity landscape. Unfortunately, this has created much confusion among researchers and practitioners. We encourage readers to familiarize themselves with his most recent formulation (Cross, 1991, 1995).

Asian American Identity Development Models

Asian American identity development models have not advanced as far as those relating to Black identity. One of the earliest heuristic "type" models was developed by S. Sue and Sue (1971) to explain what they saw as clinical differences among Chinese American students treated at the University of California, Berkeley, Counseling Center: (a) *traditionalist*—a person who internalizes conventional Chinese customs and values, resists acculturation forces, and believes in the "old ways"; (b) *marginal person*—a person who attempts to assimilate and acculturate into White society, rejects traditional Chinese ways, internalizes society's negativism toward minority groups, and may develop racial self-hatred (à la the Sansei student); and (c) *Asian American*—a person who is in the process of forming a positive identity, who is ethnically and politically aware, and who becomes increasingly bicultural.

Other similar models have been proposed for other groups such as Japanese Americans (Kitano, 1982).

These early type models suffered from several shortcomings (Lee, 1991). First, they failed to provide a clear rationale for why an individual develops one ethnic identity type over another. Although they were useful in describing characteristics of the type, they represented static entities rather than a dynamic process of identity development. Second, the early proposals seem too simplistic to account for the complexity of racial identity development. Third, these models were too population specific, in that they described only one Asian American ethnic group (Chinese American or Japanese American), and one wonders whether they are equally applicable to Korean Americans, Filipino Americans, Vietnamese Americans, and so on. Last, with the exception of a few empirical studies (Lee, 1991; D. W. Sue & Frank, 1973), testing of these typologies is seriously lacking.

In response to these criticisms, theorists have begun to move toward the development of stage/process models of Asian American identity development (J. Kim, 1981; Lee, 1991; Sodowsky, Kwan, & Pannu, 1995). Such models view identity formation as occurring in stages, evolving from less healthy to more healthy identities. With each stage there exists a constellation of traits and characteristics associated with racial/ethnic identity. These models also attempt to explain the conditions or situations that might retard, enhance, or impel the individual forward.

After a thorough review of the literature, J. Kim (1981) used a qualitative narrative approach with third-generation Japanese American women to posit a progressive and sequential stage model of Asian American identity development: (a) ethnic awareness, (b) White identification, (c) awakening to social political consciousness, (d) redirection to Asian American consciousness, and (e) incorporation. Her model integrates the influence of acculturation, exposure to cultural differences, environmental negativism to racial differences, personal methods of handling race related conflicts, and the effects of group or social movements on the Asian American individual.

1. The *ethnic awareness* stage begins around the age of three to four, when the child's family members serve as the significant ethnic group model. Positive or neutral attitudes toward one's own ethnic origin are formed, depending on the amount of ethnic exposure conveyed by the caretakers.

2. The *White identification* stage begins when children enter school, where peers and the surroundings become powerful forces in conveying racial prejudice

that negatively impacts their self-esteem and identity. The realization of "differentness" from such interactions leads to self-blame and a desire to escape racial heritage by identifying with White society.

3. The *awakening to social political consciousness* stage means the adoption of a new perspective, often correlated with increased political awareness. J. Kim (1981) believed that significant political events such as the civil rights and women's movements often precipitate this new awakening. The primary result is an abandoning of identification with White society and a consequent understanding of oppression and oppressed groups.

4. The *redirection* stage means a reconnection or renewed connection with one's Asian American heritage and culture. This is often followed by the realization that White oppression is the culprit for the negative experiences of youth. Anger against White racism may become a defining theme, with concomitant increases of Asian American self-pride and group pride.

5. The *incorporation* stage represents the highest form of identity evolution. It encompasses the development of a positive and comfortable identity as Asian American and consequent respect for other cultural/racial heritages. Identification with a stance for or against White culture is no longer an important issue.

Latino/ Hispanic American Identity Development Models

Although a number of ethnic identity development models have been formulated to account for Latino/a identity (Bernal & Knight, 1993; Casas & Pytluk, 1995; Szapocznik, Santisteban, Kurtines, Hervis, & Spencer, 1982), the one most similar to those of African Americans and Asian Americans was proposed by Ruiz (1990). His model was formulated from a clinical perspective via case studies of Chicano/Latino subjects. Ruiz made several underlying assumptions. First, he believed in a culture-specific explanation of identity for Chicano, Mexican American, and Latina/o clients. Although models of the development of other ethnic groups or the more general models were helpful, they lacked the specificity of referring to Latina/o cultures. Second, the marginal status of Latinos is highly correlated with maladjustment. Third, negative experiences of forced assimilation are considered destructive to an individual. Fourth, having pride in one's cultural heritage and ethnic identity is positively correlated with mental health. Last, pride in one's ethnicity affords the Hispanic greater freedom to choose freely. These beliefs underlie Ruiz's five-stage model.

1. *Causal stage:* During this period messages or injunctions from the environment or significant others ignore, negate, or denigrate the ethnic heritage of the person. Affirmation about one's ethnic identity is lacking, and the person may experience traumatic or humiliating experiences related to ethnicity. There is a failure to identify with Latina/o culture.

2. *Cognitive stage:* As a result of negative/distorted messages, three erroneous belief systems about Chicano/Latina/o heritage become incorporated into mental sets: (a) Ethnic group membership is associated with poverty and prejudice; (b) assimilation to White society is the only means of escape; and (c) assimilation is the only possible road to success.

3. *Consequence stage:* Fragmentation of ethnic identity becomes very noticeable and evident. The person feels ashamed and is embarrassed by ethnic markers, such as name, accent, skin color, cultural customs, and so on. The unwanted self-image leads to estrangement and rejection of one's Chicano/Latina/o heritage.

4. *Working-through stage:* Two major dynamics distinguish this stage. First, the person becomes increasingly unable to cope with the psychological distress of ethnic identity conflict. Second, the person can no longer be a "pretender" by identifying with an alien ethnic identity. The person is propelled to reclaim and reintegrate disowned ethnic identity fragments. Ethnic consciousness increases.

5. *Successful resolution stage:* This last stage is exemplified by greater acceptance of one's culture and ethnicity. There is an improvement in self esteem and a sense that ethnic identity represents a positive and success-promoting resource.

The Ruiz model has a subjective reality that is missing in many of the empirically based models. This is expected, since it was formulated based on the study of a clinical population. It has the added advantage of suggesting intervention focus and direction for each of the stages. For example, the focus of counseling in the causal stage is disaffirming and restructuring of the injunctions; for the cognitive stage, it is the use of cognitive strategies attacking faulty beliefs; for the consequence stage, it is reintegration of ethnic identity fragments in a positive manner; for the working-through stage, ethnocultural identification issues are important; and for the successful resolution stage, the promotion of a positive identity becomes important.

A RACIAL/CULTURAL IDENTITY DEVELOPMENT MODEL

In the past several decades, Asian Americans, Latinas/os, and American Indians have experienced sociopolitical identity transformations so that a *Third World consciousness* has emerged, with the awareness of cultural oppression as the common unifying force. As a result of studying these models and integrating them with their own clinical observations, Atkinson et al. (1998) proposed a five-stage Minority Identity Development model (MID) in an attempt to pull out common features that cut across the population-specific proposals. D. W. Sue and Sue (1990, 1999) later elaborated on the MID, renaming it the Racial/Cultural Identity Development model (R/CID), to (a) encompass a broader population, and (b) avoid the disempowering term "minority." As discussed shortly, this model may be applied to White identity development as well.

The *R/CID model* proposed here is not a comprehensive theory of personality, but rather a conceptual framework to aid therapists in understanding their culturally diverse clients' attitudes and behaviors. Five levels of development that oppressed people experience as they struggle to understand themselves in terms of their own culture, the dominant culture, and the oppressive relationship between the two cultures are described: *conformity, dissonance, resistance and immersion, introspection,* and *integrative awareness.* At each level of identity there are four corresponding beliefs and attitudes, the understanding of which may help therapists better understand their clients. These attitudes/beliefs are an integral part of identity, and are manifest in how a person views (a) the self, (b) others of the same minority, (c) others of another minority, and (d) majority individuals. Table 11.1 outlines the *R/CID model* and the interaction of phases with the attitudes and beliefs.

Conformity Phase

Similar to individuals in the *preencounter* stage (Cross, 1991), persons of color are distinguished by their unequivocal preference for dominant cultural values over those of their own culture. White Americans in the United States represent their reference group, and the identification set is quite strong. Lifestyles, value systems, and cultural/physical characteristics that most resemble those of White society

TABLE 11.1   The Racial/Cultural Identity Development Model

Phases of Minority Development Model	Attitude Toward Self	Attitude Toward Others of the Same Group	Attitude Toward Others of a Different Marginalized Group	Attitude Toward Dominant Group
Stage 1—Conformity	Self-depreciating or neutral due to low race salience	Group-depreciating or neutral due to low race salience	Discriminatory or neutral	Group-appreciating
Stage 2—Dissonance	Conflict between self-depreciating and group-appreciating	Conflict between group-depreciating views of minority hierarchy and feelings of shared experience	Conflict between dominant-held and group-depreciating	Conflict between group-appreciating and group-depreciating
Stage 3—Resistance and immersion	Self-appreciating	Group-appreciating experiences and feelings of culturocentrism	Conflict between feelings of empathy for other minority	Group-depreciating
Stage 4—Introspection	Concern with basis of self-appreciation	Concern with nature of unequivocal appreciation	Concern with ethnocentric basis for judging others	Concern with the basis of group depreciation
Stage 5—Integrative awareness	Self-appreciating	Group-appreciating	Group-appreciating	Selective appreciation

Source: From D. R. Atkinson, G. Morten, and D. W. Sue, *Counseling American minorities: A cross cultural perspective,* 5th ed. Copyright © 1998 McGraw-Hill, Boston, MA. All rights reserved. Reprinted by permission.

are highly valued, whereas those most associated with their own group of color may be viewed with disdain or may hold low salience for the person. We agree with Cross that individuals at this stage can be oriented toward a pro-American identity without subsequent disdain or negativism toward their own group. Thus, it is possible for a Chinese American to feel positive about U.S. culture, values, and traditions without evidencing disdain for Chinese culture or feeling negatively about oneself (absence of self-hate). Nevertheless, we believe that such individuals represent a small proportion of persons of color at this stage. Research on their numbers, on how they have handled the social-psychological dynamics of majority-minority relations, on how they have dealt with their marginalized status, and on how they fit into the models (progression issues) needs to be conducted.

We believe that the *conformity* phase continues to be most characterized by individuals who have bought into majority societal definitions about their marginalized status in society. Because the *conformity* phase represents, perhaps, the most damning indictment of White racism and because it has such a profound negative impact on persons of color, understanding its sociopolitical dynamics is of utmost importance for the helping professional. Those in the *conformity* phase are really victims of larger social-psychological forces operating in our society. The key issue here is the dominant–subordinate relationship between two different cultures (Atkinson et al., 1998; Freire, 1970). It is reasonable to believe that members of one cultural group tend to adjust themselves to the group possessing the greater prestige and power in order to avoid feelings of inferiority. Yet it is exactly this act that creates ambivalence in the individual. The pressures for assimilation and acculturation (melting-pot theory) are strong, creating possible culture conflicts. These individuals are victims of *ethnocentric monoculturalism*: (a) belief in the superiority of one group's cultural heritage—its language, traditions, arts-crafts, and ways of behaving (White) over all others; (b) belief in the inferiority of all other lifestyles (non-White); and (c) the power to impose such standards onto the less powerful group.

Internalized racism has been the term used to describe the process by which persons of color absorb the racist messages that are omnipresent in our society and internalize them (Kohli, 2013; Pyke, 2010). Constantly bombarded on all sides by reminders that Whites and their way of life are superior and that all other lifestyles are inferior, many begin to wonder whether they themselves are somehow inadequate, whether members of their own group are not to blame, and whether subordination and segregation are not justified. Clark and Clark (1947) first brought this to the attention of social scientists by stating that racism may contribute to a sense of confused self-identity among Black children. In a study of racial awareness and preference among Black and White children, they found that (a) Black children preferred playing with a White doll over a Black one, (b) the Black doll was perceived as being "bad," and (c) approximately one-third, when asked to pick the doll that looked like them, picked the White one.

It is unfortunate that the inferior status of people of color is constantly reinforced and perpetuated by the mass media through television, movies, newspapers, radio, books, and magazines. This contributes to widespread stereotypes that tend to trap them: Blacks are superstitious, childlike, ignorant, fun loving, dangerous, and criminal; Hispanics are dirty, sneaky, and criminal; Asian Americans are sneaky, sly, cunning, and passive; Indians are primitive savages. Such portrayals cause widespread harm to the self-esteem of minorities who may incorporate them. The incorporation of the larger society's standards may lead group members to react negatively toward their own racial and cultural heritage. They may become ashamed of who they are, reject their own group identification, and attempt to identify with the desirable "good" White minority. In the *Autobiography of Malcolm X* (Haley, 1966), Malcolm X relates how he tried desperately to appear as White as possible. He went to painful lengths to straighten and dye his hair so that he would appear more like White males. It is evident that many marginalized group members do come to accept White standards as a means of measuring physical attractiveness, attractiveness of personality, and social relationships. Such an orientation may lead to the phenomenon of *internalized racism* or racial self-hatred, in which people dislike themselves for being Asian, Black, Hispanic, or Native American. People at the *conformity* stage seem to possess the following characteristics:

1. *Attitudes and beliefs toward the self* (self-depreciating attitudes and beliefs): Physical and cultural characteristics identified with one's own racial/cultural group are perceived negatively, as something to be avoided, denied, or changed. Physical characteristics (black skin color, "slant-shaped eyes" of Asians), traditional modes of dress and appearance, and behavioral characteristics associated with the minority group are a source of shame. There may be attempts to mimic what is perceived as White mannerisms, speech patterns, dress, and goals. Low internal self-esteem is characteristic of the person.

2. *Attitudes and beliefs toward members of the same group* (group-depreciating attitudes and beliefs): Majority cultural beliefs and attitudes about the minority group are also held by the person in this stage. These individuals may have internalized the majority of White stereotypes about their group. In the case of Hispanics, for example, the person may believe that members of his or her own group have high rates of unemployment because "they are lazy, uneducated, and unintelligent." Little thought or validity is given to other viewpoints, such as unemployment's being a function of job discrimination, prejudice, racism, unequal opportunities, and inferior education. Because persons in the *conformity* stage find it psychologically painful to identify with these negative traits, they divorce themselves from their own group. The denial mechanism most commonly used is, "I'm not like them, I've made it on my own; I'm the exception."

3. *Attitudes and beliefs toward members of different marginalized groups* (discriminatory): Because the conformity-stage person most likely strives for identification with White society, the individual shares similar dominant attitudes and beliefs not only toward his or her own group but toward other marginalized groups as well. Groups most similar to White cultural groups are viewed more favorably, whereas those most different are viewed less favorably.

For example, Asian Americans may be viewed more favorably than African Americans or Latino/Hispanic Americans in some situations. Although stratification probably exists, we caution readers that such a ranking is fraught with hazards and potential political consequences. Such distinctions often manifest themselves in debates over which group is more oppressed and which group has done better than the others. Such debates are counterproductive when used to (a) negate another group's experience of oppression, (b) foster an erroneous belief that hard work alone will result in success in a democratic society, (c) shortchange a marginalized group (i.e., Asian Americans) from receiving the necessary resources in our society, and (d) pit one marginalized group against another (divide and conquer) by holding up one group as an example to others.

4. *Attitudes and beliefs toward members of the dominant group* (group-appreciating attitude and beliefs): This stage is characterized by a belief that White cultural, social, and institutional standards are superior. Members of the dominant group are admired, respected, and emulated. White people are believed to possess superior intelligence. Some individuals may go to great lengths to appear White. Consider again the example from the *Autobiography of Malcolm X*, in which the main character would straighten his hair and primarily date White women. Reports that Asian women have undergone surgery to reshape their eyes to conform to White female standards of beauty may typify this dynamic.

Dissonance Phase

No matter how much one attempts to deny his or her own racial/cultural heritage, an individual will encounter information or experiences that are inconsistent with culturally held beliefs, attitudes, and values. An Asian American who believes that Asians are inhibited, passive, inarticulate, and poor in people relationships may encounter an Asian person who seems to break all these stereotypes (e.g., the Sansei student). A Latina/o who feels ashamed of his or her cultural upbringing may encounter another Latina/o who seems proud of his or her cultural heritage. An African American who believes that race problems are due to laziness, untrustworthiness, or personal inadequacies of his or her own group may suddenly encounter racism on a personal level. Denial begins to break down, which leads to a questioning and challenging of the attitudes/beliefs of the *conformity* stage. This was clearly what happened when the Sansei student encountered discrimination at the restaurant.

In all probability, movement into the *dissonance* stage is a gradual process. Its very definition indicates that the individual is in conflict between disparate pieces of information or experiences that challenge his or her current self-concept. People generally move into this stage slowly, but a traumatic event may propel some individuals to move into *dissonance* at a much more rapid pace. Cross (1971) stated that a monumental event such as the assassination of a major leader like Martin Luther King Jr. can often push people quickly into the ensuing stage.

1. *Attitudes and beliefs toward the self* (conflict between self-depreciating and self-appreciating attitudes and beliefs): There is now a growing sense of personal awareness that racism does exist, that not all aspects of their own culture or majority culture are good or bad, and that one cannot escape one's cultural heritage. For the first time the person begins to entertain the possibility of positive attributes in their own group's culture and, with it, a sense of pride in self. Feelings of shame and pride are mixed in the individual, and a sense of conflict develops. This conflict is most likely to be brought to the forefront quickly when other members of the group may express positive feelings toward the person: "We like you because you are Asian [or Black, American Indian, or Latino]." At this stage, an important personal question is being asked: "Why should I feel ashamed of who and what I am?"

2. *Attitudes and beliefs toward members of the same group* (conflict between group-depreciating and group-appreciating attitudes and beliefs): Dominant-held views of their own group's strengths and weaknesses begin to be questioned as new, contradictory information is received. Certain aspects of their culture begin to have appeal. For example, a Latino who values individualism may marry, have children, and then suddenly realize how Latina/o cultural values that hold the family as the psychosocial unit possess positive features. Or a person may find certain members of his or her group to be very attractive as friends, colleagues, lovers, and so forth.

3. *Attitudes and beliefs toward members of a different marginalized group* (conflict between dominant-held views of minority hierarchy and feelings of shared experience): Stereotypes associated with other marginalized groups are questioned, and a growing sense of comradeship with other oppressed groups is felt. It is important to keep in mind, however, that little psychic energy is associated with resolving conflicts with other marginalized groups. Almost all energies are expended toward resolving conflicts toward the self, one's own group, and the dominant group.

4. *Attitudes and beliefs toward members of the dominant group* (conflict between group-appreciating and group-depreciating attitudes): The person experiences a growing awareness that not all cultural values of the dominant group are beneficial. This is especially true when the person experiences personal discrimination. Growing suspicion and some distrust of certain members of the dominant group develop.

Resistance and Immersion Phase

The primary orientation of individuals in this phase is the tendency to endorse minority-held views completely and to reject values of the dominant society and culture. Desire to eliminate oppression becomes an important motivation of the individual's behavior. During the *resistance and immersion* stage, the three most active types of affective feelings are *guilt, shame,* and *anger.* There are considerable feelings of guilt and shame that in the past the individual has sold out his or her own racial and cultural group. The feelings of guilt and shame extend to the perception that during this past "sellout," one has been a contributor to and participant in the oppression of one's own group and other marginalized groups. This is coupled with a strong sense of anger at the oppression, and feelings of having been brainwashed by forces in White society. Anger is directed outwardly in a very strong way toward oppression and racism. Movement into this stage seems to occur for two reasons. First, a resolution of the conflicts and confusions of the previous stage allows greater understanding of social forces (racism, oppression, and discrimination) and one's own role as a victim. Second, a personal questioning of why people should feel ashamed of themselves develops. The answer to this question evokes feelings of guilt, shame, and anger.

1. *Attitudes and beliefs toward the self* (self-appreciating attitudes and beliefs): The individual at this stage is oriented toward self-discovery of one's own history and culture. There is an active seeking out of information and artifacts that enhance that person's sense of identity and worth. Cultural and racial characteristics that once elicited feelings of shame and disgust become symbols of pride and honor. The individual moves into this stage primarily because he or she asks the question, "Why should I be ashamed of who and what I am?" The original low self-esteem engendered by widespread prejudice and racism that was most characteristic of the *conformity* stage is now actively challenged in order to raise self-esteem. Phrases such as "Black is beautiful" represent a symbolic relabeling of identity for many Blacks. Racial

self-hatred begins to be actively rejected in favor of the other extreme: unbridled racial pride.

2. *Attitudes and beliefs toward members of the same group* (group-appreciating attitudes and beliefs): The individual experiences a strong sense of identification with and commitment to his or her group as enhancing information about the group is acquired. There is a feeling of connectedness with other members of the racial and cultural group, and a strengthening of the new identity begins to occur. Members of one's group are admired, respected, and often viewed now as the new reference group or ideal. Cultural values of the group are accepted without question. As indicated, the pendulum swings drastically from original identification with White ways to identification in an unquestioning manner with the group's ways. Persons in this phase are likely to restrict their interactions as much as possible to members of their own group.

3. *Attitudes and beliefs toward members of a different marginalized group* (conflict between feelings of empathy for other marginalized group experiences and feelings of culturocentrism): Although members at this stage experience a growing sense of comradeship with persons from other socially devalued groups, a strong culturocentrism develops as well. Alliances with other groups tend to be transitory and based on short-term goals or some global shared view of oppression. There is less of an attempt to reach out and understand other racial-cultural groups and their values and ways, and more of a superficial surface feeling of political need. Alliances generally are based on convenience factors or are formed for political reasons, such as combining together as a large group to confront an enemy perceived to be larger.

4. *Attitudes and beliefs toward members of the dominant group* (group depreciating attitudes and beliefs): The individual is likely to perceive the dominant society and culture as an oppressor and as the group most responsible for the current plight of minorities in the United States. Characterized by both withdrawal from the dominant culture and immersion in one's cultural heritage, this stage also gives rise to considerable anger and hostility directed toward White society. There is a feeling of distrust and dislike for all members of the dominant group in an almost global anti-White demonstration and feeling. White people, for example, are not to be trusted because they are the oppressors or enemies. In extreme form, members may advocate complete destruction of the institutions and structures that have been characteristic of White society.

Introspection Phase

Several factors seem to work in unison to move the individual from the *resistance and immersion* phase into the *introspection* phase. First, the individual begins to discover that this level of intensity of feelings (anger directed toward White society) is psychologically draining and does not permit one to really devote more crucial energies to understanding oneself or one's own racial-cultural group. The *resistance and immersion* phase tends to be a reaction against the dominant culture and is not proactive in allowing the individual to use all energies to discover who or what he or she is. Self-definition in the previous stage tends to be reactive (against White racism), and now a need for positive self-definition in a proactive sense emerges.

Second, the individual experiences feelings of discontent and discomfort with group views that may be quite rigid in the *resistance and immersion* phase. Often, in order to please the group, the individual is asked to submerge individual autonomy and individual thought in favor of the group good. Many group views may now be seen as conflicting with individual ones. A Latina/o individual who may form a deep relationship with a White person may experience considerable pressure from his or her culturally similar peers to break off the relationship because that White person is the "enemy." However, the personal experiences of the individual may, in fact, not support this group view.

It is important to note that some clinicians often confuse certain characteristics of the introspective stage with parts of the *conformity* stage. A person in the introspective stage who speaks against the decisions of his or her group may often appear similar to the conformity-stage person. The dynamics are quite different, however. While the conformity-stage person is motivated by global racial self-hatred, the introspective person has no such global negativism directed at his or her own group.

1. *Attitudes and beliefs toward the self* (concern with basis of self-appreciating attitudes and beliefs): Although the person originally, in the *conformity* phase, held predominant majority group views and notions to the detriment of his or her own group, the person now feels that he or she has too rigidly held onto the group views and notions in order to submerge personal autonomy. The conflict now becomes quite great between responsibility and allegiance to one's own group and notions of personal independence and autonomy. The person begins to spend more and more time and energy trying to sort out these aspects of self-identity and begins increasingly to demand individual autonomy.

2. *Attitudes and beliefs toward members of the same group* (concern with the unequivocal nature of group appreciation): Although attitudes of identification are continued from the preceding *resistance and immersion* stage, concern begins to build up regarding the issue of group-usurped individuality. Increasingly, the individual may see his or her own group taking positions that might be considered quite extreme. In addition, there is now increasing resentment over how one's group may attempt to pressure or influence the individual into making decisions that may be inconsistent with the person's values, beliefs, and outlooks. Indeed, it is not unusual for a minority group to make it clear to individual members that if they do not agree with the group, they are against it. A common ploy used to hold members in line is exemplified in questions such as "How Asian are you?" and "How Black are you?"

3. *Attitudes and beliefs toward members of a different marginalized group* (concern with the ethnocentric basis for judging others): There is now greater uneasiness with culturocentrism, and an attempt is made to reach out to other groups to find out what types of oppression they experience and how this has been handled. Although similarities are important, there is now a movement toward understanding potential differences in oppression that other groups might have experienced.

4. *Attitudes and beliefs toward members of the dominant group* (concern with the basis of group depreciation): The individual experiences conflict between attitudes of complete distrust for the dominant society and culture and attitudes of selective trust and distrust according to the dominant individual's demonstrated behaviors and attitudes. Conflict is most likely to occur here because the person begins to recognize that there are many elements in U.S. American culture that are highly functional and desirable, yet feels confusion about how to incorporate these elements into one's own culture. Would acceptance of certain White cultural values make the person a sellout to his or her own race? There is a lowering of intense feelings of anger and distrust toward the dominant group and a continued attempt to discern elements that are acceptable.

Integrative Awareness Phase

Persons in this stage have developed an inner sense of security and now can own and appreciate unique aspects of their culture as well as those of U.S. culture. One's own culture is not necessarily in conflict with White dominant cultural ways. Conflicts and discomforts experienced in the previous stage become resolved, allowing greater individual control and flexibility. There is now the belief that there are acceptable and unacceptable aspects in all cultures and that it is very important for the person to be able to examine and to accept or reject those aspects of a culture that are not seen as desirable. At the *integrative awareness* stage, the person has a strong commitment and desire to eliminate all forms of oppression.

1. *Attitudes and beliefs toward the self* (self-appreciating attitudes and beliefs): The individual develops a positive self-image and experiences a strong sense of self-worth and confidence. Not only is there an integrated self-concept that involves racial pride in identity and culture, but the person develops a high sense of autonomy. Indeed, the client becomes bicultural or multicultural without a sense of having "sold out one's integrity." In other words, the person begins to perceive his or her self as an autonomous individual who is unique (individual level of identity), a member of one's own racial-cultural group (group level of identity), a member of a larger society, and a member of the human race (universal level of identity).

2. *Attitudes and beliefs toward members of same group* (group-appreciating attitudes and beliefs): The individual experiences a strong sense of pride in the group without having to accept group values unequivocally. There is no longer the conflict over disagreeing with group goals and values. Strong feelings of empathy with the group experience are coupled with awareness that each member of the group is also an individual. In addition, tolerant and empathic attitudes are likely to be expressed toward members of one's own group who may be functioning in a less adaptive manner to racism and oppression.

3. *Attitudes and beliefs toward members of a different marginalized group* (group-appreciating attitudes): There is now literally a reaching out toward different oppressed groups in order to understand their cultural values and ways of life. There is a strong belief that the more one understands other cultural values and beliefs, the greater is the likelihood of understanding among the various ethnic groups. Support for all oppressed people, regardless of similarity to the individual's minority group, tends to be emphasized.

4. *Attitudes and beliefs toward members of the dominant group* (attitudes and beliefs of selective appreciation): The individual experiences selective trust and liking for and from members of the dominant group who seek to eliminate oppressive activities of the group. The individual also experiences openness to the

constructive elements of the dominant culture. The emphasis here tends to be on the fact that White racism is a sickness in society and that White people are also victims who are in need of help.

COUNSELING IMPLICATIONS OF THE R/CID MODEL

Let us first point out some broad general clinical implications of the *R/CID model* before discussing specific meanings within each of the phases. First, an understanding of cultural identity development should sensitize therapists and counselors to the role that oppression plays in an individual's development. In many respects, it should make us aware that our role as helping professionals should extend beyond the office and should include dealing with the many manifestations of racism. Although individual therapy is needed, combating the forces of racism means a proactive approach for both the therapist and the client. For the helping professional, social justice advocacy and systems intervention are often the answers. For culturally diverse clients, it means the need to understand, control, and direct those forces in society that negate the process of positive identity. Thus a wider sociocultural approach to therapy is mandatory.

Second, the model will aid counselors in recognizing differences between members of the same minority group with respect to their cultural identity. It serves as a useful assessment and diagnostic tool for therapists to gain a greater understanding of their culturally diverse clients. In many cases, an accurate delineation of the dynamics and characteristics of the phases may result in better prescriptive treatment. Counselors who are familiar with the sequence of identity development are better able to plan intervention strategies that are most effective for culturally diverse clients. For example, a client experiencing feelings of isolation and alienation in the *conformity* phase may require an approach different from the one he or she would require in the introspection phase.

Third, the model allows helping professionals to realize the potentially changing and developmental nature of cultural identity among clients. If the goal of multicultural counseling/therapy is to move a client toward the *integrative awareness* stage, then the therapist is able to anticipate the sequence of feelings, beliefs, attitudes, and behaviors likely to arise. Acting as a guide and providing an understandable end point will allow the client to understand more quickly and work through issues related to his or her own identity. We now turn our attention to the *R/CID model* and its implications for the counseling process.

Conformity Phase: Counseling Implications

For the vast majority of those in the *conformity* phase, several therapeutic implications can be derived. First, persons of color are most likely to prefer a White counselor or therapist over those from other groups. This flows logically from the belief that Whites are more competent and capable than are members of their own race. Such a racial preference can be manifested in the client's reaction to a counselor of color via negativism, resistance, or open hostility. In some instances, the client may even request a change in counselor (preferably to someone White). Likewise, the *conformity* individual who is seen by a White therapist may be quite pleased about it. In many cases, the client, in identifying with White culture, may be overly dependent on the White therapist. Attempts to please, appease, and seek approval from the helping professional may be quite prevalent.

Second, most *conformity* individuals will find that attempts to explore issues of race, racism, or cultural identity or to focus upon feelings are very threatening. Clients in this stage generally prefer a task-oriented, problem-solving approach because an exploration of identity may eventually touch upon feelings of low self-esteem, dissatisfaction with personal appearance, vague anxieties, and racial self-hatred, and may challenge the client's self-deception that he or she is not like the other members of his or her own race.

Whether you are White or a counselor of color working with a *conformity* individual, the general goal may be the same. There is an obligation to help the client sort out conflicts related to racial/cultural identity through some process of reeducation. Somewhere in the course of counseling or therapy, issues of cultural racism, majority–minority group relations, racial self-hatred, and racial cultural identity need to be dealt with in an integrated fashion. We are not suggesting a lecture or a solely cognitive approach, to which clients at this stage may be quite intellectually receptive, but exercising good clinical skills that take into account the client's socioemotional state and readiness to deal with feelings. Only in this manner will the client be able to distinguish the difference between positive attempts to adopt certain values of the dominant society and a negative rejection of one's own cultural value (an ability characteristic of the *integrative awareness* stage).

Although the goals for the White and counselor of color are the same, the way a therapist works toward them may be different. For example, a counselor of color will likely have to deal with hostility from the racially and culturally similar client. As we saw in Chapter 3, a therapist of color working with a client of his or her own race or any person of color may symbolize all that the client is trying to reject. Because therapy stresses the building of a coalition, establishment of rapport, and to some degree a mutual identification, the process may be especially threatening. The opposite may be true of work with a White counselor. The client of color may be overeager to identify with the White professional in order to seek approval.

Rather than being detrimental to multicultural counseling/therapy, these two processes can be used quite effectively and productively. If the therapist of color can aid the client in working through his or her feelings of antagonism and if the majority therapist can aid the client in working through his or her need to overidentify, then the client will be moved closer to awareness and away from self-deception. In the former case, the therapist can take a nonjudgmental stance toward the client and provide a positive person of color role model. In the latter, the White therapist needs to model positive attitudes toward cultural diversity. Both need to guard against unknowingly reinforcing the client's self-denial and rejection.

Dissonance Phase: Counseling Implications

As individuals become more aware of inconsistencies between dominant-held views and those of their own group, a sense of *dissonance* develops. Preoccupation and questions concerning self, identity, and self-esteem are most likely brought in for therapy. More culturally aware than their *conformity* counterparts, *dissonance* clients may prefer a counselor or therapist who possesses good knowledge of the client's cultural group, although there may still be a preference for a White helper. However, the fact that minority helping professionals are generally more knowledgeable of the client's cultural group may serve to heighten the conflicting beliefs and feelings of this stage. Since the client is so receptive toward self-exploration, the therapist can capitalize on this orientation in helping the client come to grips with his or her identity conflicts.

Resistance and Immersion Phase: Counseling Implications

Clients at this stage are likely to view their psychological problems as products of oppression and racism. They may believe that only issues of racism are legitimate areas to explore in therapy. Furthermore, openness or self-disclosure to therapists not of one's own group is dangerous because White counselors or therapists are "enemies" and members of the oppressing group.

Clients in the *resistance and immersion* stage believe that society is to blame for their present dilemma and actively challenge the establishment. They are openly suspicious of institutions such as mental health services because they view them as agents of the establishment. Very few of the more ethnically conscious and militant minorities will use mental health services because of its identification with the status quo. When they do, they are usually suspicious and hostile toward the helping professional. A therapist working with a client at this stage of development needs to realize several important things.

First, he or she will be viewed by the client as a symbol of the oppressive society. If you become defensive and personalize the attacks, you will lose effectiveness in working with the client. It is important not to be intimidated or afraid of the anger that is likely to be expressed; often, it is not personal and is quite legitimate. White guilt and defensiveness can serve only to hinder effective multicultural counseling/therapy. It is not unusual for clients at this stage to make sweeping negative generalizations about White Americans. The White therapist who takes a nondefensive posture will be better able to help the client explore the basis of his or her racial tirades.

In general, clients at this stage prefer a therapist of their own race. However, the fact that you share the same race or culture as your client will not insulate you from the attacks. Again, as outlined in Chapter 3, therapists of color working with a same-race client at the stage of resistance can encounter unique challenges. For example, an African American client may perceive the Black counselor as a sellout of his or her own race, or as an Uncle Tom. Indeed, the anger and hostility directed at the therapist may be even more intense than that directed at a White one.

Second, realize that clients in this stage will constantly test you. In earlier chapters we described how minority clients will pose challenges to therapists in order to test their trustworthiness (sincerity, openness, and nondefensiveness) and expertise (competencies). Because of the active nature of client challenges, therapy sessions may become quite dynamic. Many therapists find that this stage is frequently the most difficult to deal with because counselor self-disclosure is often necessary for establishing credibility.

Third, individuals at this phase are especially receptive to approaches that are more action-oriented and aimed at external change (challenging racism). Also, group approaches with persons experiencing similar racial/cultural issues are well received. It is important that the therapist be willing to help the culturally different client explore new ways of relating to both minority and White persons.

Introspection Phase: Counseling Implications

Clients at the *introspection* phase may continue to prefer a counselor of their own race, but they are also receptive to help from therapists of other cultures as long as the therapists understand their clients' worldview. Ironically, clients at this stage may, on the surface, appear similar to *conformity* persons. *Introspection* clients are in conflict between their need to identify with their own group and their need to exercise greater personal freedom. Exercising personal autonomy may occasionally mean going against the wishes or desires of their own group. This is often perceived by marginalized members and their group as a rejection of their own cultural heritage. This is not unlike *conformity* persons, who also reject their racial/cultural heritage. The dynamics within the two groups, however, are quite dissimilar. It is very important for therapists to distinguish the differences. The *conformity* person moves away from his or her own group because of perceived negative qualities associated with it. The *introspection* person wants to move away on certain issues but perceives the group positively. Again, self-exploration approaches aimed at helping the client integrate and incorporate a new sense of identity are important. Believing in the functional values of White American society does not necessarily mean that a person is selling out or going against his or her own group.

Integrative Awareness Phase: Counseling Implications

Clients at this stage have acquired an inner sense of security around their self-identity. They have pride in their racial/cultural heritage but can exercise a desired level of personal freedom and autonomy. Other cultures and races are appreciated, and there is a development toward becoming more multicultural in perspective. Although discrimination and oppression remain a powerful part of their existence, persons at the *integrative awareness* phase possess greater psychological resources to deal with these problems. Being action- or systems-oriented, clients respond positively to the designing and implementation of strategies aimed at community and societal change. Preferences for therapists are based not on race, but on the ability to share, understand, and accept their worldview. In other words, attitudinal similarity between therapist and client is a more important dimension than membership-group similarity.

VALUE OF R/CID FRAMEWORK

The R/CID framework is a useful heuristic tool for counselors who work with culturally diverse populations. The model reminds therapists of several important clinical imperatives: (a) Within-group differences are very important to acknowledge in clients of color because not all members of a racial/cultural group are the same. Depending on their levels of racial consciousness, the attitudes, beliefs, and orientations of clients of color may be quite different from one another. (b) A culturally competent counselor needs to be cognizant of and to understand how sociopolitical factors influence and shape identity. Identity development is not solely due to cultural differences but to how the differences are perceived in our society. (c) The model alerts clinicians working with clients of color to certain likely challenges associated with each stage or level of racial/cultural consciousness. Not only may it serve as a useful diagnostic tool, but it provides suggestions of what may be the most appropriate treatment intervention. (d) Other socially marginalized or devalued groups undergo similar identity processes. For example, formulations for women, LGBT groups, those with disabilities, and so forth, can now be found in the psychological literature. Mental health professionals hoping to work with these specific populations would be well served to become familiar with these models as well.

One important aspect relatively untouched in the clinical and research literature is the racial identity development of helping professionals. We have spent considerable time describing the identity development of people of color from the perspective of clients. We have, however, in Chapter 3 indicated that the level of racial consciousness of the minority therapist may impact that of the client of color. In the next chapter we address the issue of White identity development and discuss how it may impact clients of color. But it is equally important for counselors of color to consider their own racial consciousness and how it may interact with a client from their own group. We present several questions for you to consider in the following reflection and discussion questions.

REFLECTION AND DISCUSSION QUESTIONS

1. What types of conflict and/or challenge confront a therapist of color at the *conformity* stage when working with a client of color at the *resistance and immersion* stage? How would they perceive one another? How may they respond to one another? What therapeutic issues are likely to arise? What needs to be done in order for the therapist to be helpful?

2. Can you discuss other stage combinations and their implications for therapists and clients of color working with one another?

3. Does a counselor of color have to be at the *integrative awareness* stage to be helpful to clients of color?

Research on racial/cultural identity development has slowed considerably since the 1990s (Ponterotto & Mallinckrodt, 2007; Yoon, 2011), and little change in the models presented in this chapter has occurred. In some respects, this reflects the widespread acceptance of the importance of identity development and how much it has become a part of the social-psychological and mental health landscape (Wijeyesinghe & Jackson, 2012). On the other hand, this slowing of research also reflects the considerable confusion about the theory and measurement of racial/cultural identity. Indeed, a special issue of the *Journal of Counseling Psychology* in 2007 (Cokley, 2007; Helms, 2007) discussed in detail the conceptual and methodological challenges confronting the field. Although many measures have been developed in an attempt to assess and/or test the conceptual models, most have proven limited because of the sometimes nuanced aspects of measurement. It is clear that we have encountered an impasse that can be broken only through the development of more sophisticated and better measures of racial and ethnic identity.

 IMPLICATIONS FOR CLINICAL PRACTICE

1. Be aware that the *R/CID model* should not be viewed as a global personality theory with specific identifiable phases that serve as fixed categories. The process of cultural identity development is dynamic, not static.

2. Do not fall victim to stereotyping in using these models. Most clients of color may evidence a dominant characteristic, but there are mixtures from other stages as well.

3. Know that identity development models are conceptual aids and that human development is much more complex.

4. Know that a number of issues and questions still exist. Is cultural identity development primarily a linear process? Do individuals always start at the beginning of these stages? Is it possible to skip stages? Can people regress?

5. Be careful of the implied value judgments given in almost all development models. They assume that some cultural resolutions are healthier than others. For example, the *R/CID model* obviously does hold the *integrative awareness* stage as a higher form of healthy functioning.

6. Be aware that racial/cultural identity development models seriously lack an adequate integration of gender, class, sexual orientation, and other sociodemographic group identities.

7. Know that a great deal of evidence is mounting that suggests that although identity may sequentially move through identifiable stages, affective, attitudinal, cognitive, and behavioral components of identity may not move in a uniform manner. It is entirely possible that the emotions and affective elements associated with certain stages do not have a corresponding one-to-one behavioral impact.

8. Begin to look more closely at the possible therapist and client stage combinations. As mentioned earlier, therapeutic processes and outcomes are often the function of the identity stage of both therapist and client. White identity development of the therapist can either enhance or retard effective therapy.

SUMMARY

In the past several decades, work on racial/cultural identity development among marginalized groups has led to major breakthroughs in the field of multicultural counseling/therapy. Racial identity development models have proven helpful in many respects. First, they reveal major within-group differences that occur depending on one's level of identity. Second, research suggests that reactions to counseling, the counseling process, and counselors are influenced by cultural/racial identity and are not simply linked to minority group membership. Third, they clarify the impact of sociopolitical forces in shaping racial identity. And fourth, identity development models that discuss the oppressor–oppressed relationship seem equally applicable to other marginalized groups, such as women, lesbians/gays, and individuals with disabilities.

The *R/CID model* proposed is a conceptual framework to aid therapists in understanding their culturally diverse clients' attitudes and behaviors. Five levels of development that oppressed people experience as they struggle to understand themselves in terms of their own culture, the dominant culture, and the oppressive relationship between the two cultures are described: *conformity, dissonance, resistance and immersion, introspection,* and *integrative awareness.* At each level of identity, four corresponding beliefs and attitudes, the understanding of which may help therapists better understand their clients, are discussed. These attitudes/beliefs are an integral part of identity, and are manifest in how a person views (a) the self, (b) others of the same minority, (c) others of another minority, and (d) majority individuals.

Each specific level of racial identity offers unique challenges for the counselor. Clients in the *conformity* phase are dealing with *internalized racism* and may not respond well to therapists of color; dissonance clients are dealing with racial inconsistencies in their previous belief systems; *resistance and immersion* clients are likely to reveal strong anger about racism; *introspection* clients struggle with group loyalties and self-autonomy; and *integrative awareness* clients are self-secure and motivated toward multicultural integration. A culturally competent counselor needs to be cognizant of and to understand how sociopolitical factors influence and shape identity. Identity development is not solely due to cultural differences but to how the differences are perceived in our society.

GLOSSARY TERMS

Active commitment

Asian American identity development models

Black identity development models

Conformity

Dissonance

Encounter

Identity synthesis

Immersion-emersion

Integrative awareness

Internalization

Internalization-commitment

Internalized racism

Introspection

Latino/Hispanic American identity development models

Marginal person

Nigrescence

Preencounter

R/CID model

Race salience

Racial awakening

Redirection

Resistance and immersion

Traditionalist

REFERENCES

Atkinson, D. R., Morten, G., & Sue, D. W. (1998). *Counseling American minorities* (5th ed.). Boston, MA: McGraw-Hill.

Bernal, M. E., & Knight, G. P. (1993). *Ethnic identity: Formation and transmission among Hispanics and other minorities.* Albany, NY: State University of New York Press.

Casas, J. M., & Pytluk, S. D. (1995). Hispanic identity development. In J. G. Ponterotto, J. M. Casas, L. A. Suzuki, & C. M. Alexander (Eds.), *Handbook of multicultural counseling* (pp. 155–180). Thousand Oaks, CA: Sage.

Cass, V. C. (1979). Homosexual identity formation: A theoretical model. *Journal of Homosexuality, 4,* 219–235.

Clark, K. B., & Clark, M. K. (1947). Racial identification and preference in Negro children. In T. M. Newcomb & E. L. Hartley (Eds.), *Readings in social psychology* (pp. 169–178). New York, NY: Holt, Reinhart & Winston.

Cokley, K. (2007). Critical issues in the measurement of ethnic and racial identity: A referendum on the state of the field. *Journal of Counseling Psychology, 54,* 224–239.

Cross, W. E. (1971). The Negro-to-Black conversion experience: Towards a psychology of Black liberation. *Black World, 30,* 13–27.

Cross, W. E. (1991). *Shades of Black: Diversity in African American identity.* Philadelphia, PA: Temple University Press.

Cross, W. E. (1995). The psychology of Nigrescence: Revising the Cross model. In J. G. Ponterotto, J. M. Casas, L. A. Suzuki, & C. M. Alexander (Eds.), *Handbook of multicultural counseling* (pp. 93–122). Thousand Oaks, CA: Sage.

Cross, W. E., Smith, L., & Payne, Y. (2002). Black identity. In P. B. Pedersen, J. G. Draguns, W. J. Lonner, & J. E. Trimble (Eds.), *Counseling across cultures* (pp. 93–108). Thousand Oaks, CA: Sage.

Downing, N. E., & Roush, K. L. (1985). From passive acceptance to active commitment: A model of feminist identity development for women. *Counseling Psychologist, 13,* 695–709.

Ferdman, B. M., & Gallegos, P. I. (2012). Latina and Latino ethnoracial identity orientations. In C. Wijeyesinghe & B. W. Jackson (Eds.), *New perspectives on racial identity: A theoretical and practical anthology* (pp. 51–80). New York, NY: New York University Press.

Freire, P. (1970). *Cultural action for freedom.* Cambridge, MA: Harvard Educational Review Press.

Haley, A. (1966). *The autobiography of Malcolm X.* New York, NY: Grove Press.

Helms, J. E. (1984). Toward a theoretical explanation of the effects of race on counseling: A Black and White model. *Counseling Psychologist, 12,* 153–165.

Helms, J. E. (1995). An update of Helms's White and people of color racial identity models. In J. G. Ponterotto, J. M. Casas, L. A. Suzuki, & C. M. Alexander (Eds.), *Handbook of multicultural counseling* (pp. 181–191). Thousand Oaks, CA: Sage.

Helms, J. E. (2007). Some better practices for measuring racial and ethnic identity constructs. *Journal of Counseling Psychology, 54*(3), 235–246.

Hong, G. K., & Domokos-Cheng Ham, M. (2001). *Psychotherapy and counseling with Asian American clients.* Thousand Oaks, CA: Sage.

Horse, P. G. (2001). Reflections on American Indian identity. In C. Wijeyesinghe & B. W. Jackson (Eds.), *New perspectives on racial identity: A theoretical and practical anthology* (pp. 91–107). New York, NY: New York University Press.

Horse, P. G. (2012). Twenty-first century Native American consciousness. In C. Wijeyesinghe & B. W. Jackson (Eds.), *New perspectives on racial identity: Integrating emerging frameworks* (2nd ed., pp 108–120). New York, NY: New York University Press.

Ivey, A. E., D'Andrea, M. J., & Ivey, M. B. (2011). *Theories of counseling and psychotherapy: A multicultural perspective.* Boston, MA: Allyn & Bacon.

Jackson, B. (1975). Black identity development. *Journal of Educational Diversity, 2,* 19–25.

Kim, B.S.K. (2011). *Counseling Asian Americans.* Belmont, CA: Cengage.

Kim, J. (1981). *The process of Asian American identity development: A study of Japanese-American women's perceptions of their struggle to achieve personal identities as Americans of Asian ancestry.* Dissertation Abstracts International, *42,* 155 1A. (University Microfilms No. 81–18080).

Kim, J. (2012). Asian American identity development theory. In C. Wijeyesinghe & B. W. Jackson (Eds.), *New perspectives on racial identity: A theoretical and practical anthology* (pp. 138–160). New York, NY: New York University Press.

Kitano, H.H.L. (1982). Mental health in the Japanese American community. In E. E. Jones & S. J. Korchin (Eds.), *Minority mental health* (pp. 149–164). New York, NY: Praeger.

Kohli, R. (2013). *Race, ethnicity and education.* London, UK: Rutledge.

Lee, F. Y. (1991). *The relationship of ethnic identity to social support, self-esteem, psychological distress, and help seeking behavior among Asian American college students.* Unpublished doctoral dissertation, University of Illinois, Urbana-Champaign.

McNamara, K., & Rickard, K. M. (1989). Feminist identity development: Implications for feminist therapy with women. *Journal of Counseling and Development, 68,* 184–193.

Olkin, R. (1999). *What psychotherapists should know about disability.* New York, NY: Guilford Press.

Ponterotto, J. G., & Mallinckrodt, B. (2007). Introduction to the special issue on racial and ethnic identity in counseling psychology: Conceptual and methodological challenges and proposed solutions. *Journal of Counseling Psychology, 54,* 210–223.

Pyke, D. D. (2010). What is internalized racial oppression and why don't we study it? Acknowledging racism's hidden injuries. *Sociological Perspectives, 53,* 551–572.

Ruiz, A. S. (1990). Ethnic identity: Crisis and resolution. *Journal of Multicultural Counseling and Development, 18,* 29–40.

Sandhu, D. S., Leung, A. S., & Tang, M. (2003). Counseling approaches with Asian Americans and Pacific Islander Americans. In F. D. Harper & J. McFadden (Eds.), *Culture and counseling* (pp. 99–114). Boston, MA: Allyn & Bacon.

Sodowsky, G. R., Kwan, K. K., & Pannu, R. (1995). Ethnic identity of Asians in the United States. In J. G. Ponterotto, J. M. Casas, L. A. Suzuki, & C. M. Alexander (Eds.), *Handbook of multicultural counseling* (pp. 123–154). Thousand Oaks, CA: Sage.

Sue, D. W., & Frank, A. C. (1973). A topological approach to the study of Chinese- and Japanese-American college males. *Journal of Social Issues, 29,* 129–148.

Sue, D. W., & Sue, D. (1990). *Counseling the culturally different: Theory and practice.* New York, NY: Wiley.

Sue, D. W., & Sue, D. (1999). *Counseling the culturally different: Theory and practice* (3rd ed.). New York, NY: Wiley.

Sue, S., & Sue, D. W. (1971). Chinese-American personality and mental health. *Amerasian Journal, 1,* 36–49.

Szapocznik, J., Santisteban, D., Kurtines, W. M., Hervis, O. E., & Spencer, F. (1982). Life enhancements counseling: A psychosocial model of services for Cuban elders. In E. E. Jones & S. J. Korchin (Eds.), *Minority mental health* (pp. 296–329). New York, NY: Praeger.

Thomas, C. W. (1970). Different strokes for different folks. *Psychology Today, 4*, 49–53, 80.

Thomas, C. W. (1971). *Boys no more.* Beverly Hills, CA: Glencoe Press.

Vandiver, B. J. (2001). Psychological nigrescence revisited: Introduction and overview. *Journal of Multicultural Counseling and Development, 29*, 165–173.

Vandiver, B. J., Fhagen-Smith, P. E., Cokley, K. O., Cross, W. E., & Worrell, F. C. (2001). Cross's nigrescence model: From theory to scale to theory. *Journal of Multicultural Counseling and Development, 29*, 174–200.

Vontress, C. E. (1971). Racial differences: Impediments to rapport. *Journal of Counseling Psychology, 18*, 7–13.

Wijeyesinghe, C., & Jackson, B. W. (Eds.).(2012). *New perspectives on racial identity development: Integrating emerging frameworks* (2nd ed.). New York, NY: New York University Press.

Worrell, F. C., Cross, W. E., & Vandiver, B. J. (2001). Nigrescence theory: Current status and challenges for the future. *Journal of Multicultural Counseling and Development, 29*, 201–211.

Yoon, E. (2011). Measuring ethnic identity in the ethnic identity scale and the multigroup ethnic identity measure—revised. *Cultural Diversity and Ethnic Minority Psychology, 17*, 144–155.

White Racial Identity Development

Counseling Implications

Chapter Objectives

1. Acquire understanding of what it means to be White. Be able to discern differences between how Whites and people of color see the meaning of *"Whiteness."*

2. Analyze resistance by White Americans to identifying themselves as "White."

3. Learn the meaning of nested or embedded emotions experienced by Whites as they come to accept their *Whiteness*.

4. Define *White privilege*.

5. Understand how *Whiteness* advantages Whites and disadvantages people of color.

6. Describe and discuss the various developmental levels of *White racial identity development*.

7. Learn how the level of White racial consciousness may affect the counseling process.

8. Understand how *White racial identity development* may influence the definition of normality-abnormality, assessment, diagnosis, and treatment of culturally diverse clients.

9.   Learn what a White person needs to do in order to develop a *nonracist* and *antiracist White identity*.

10. Learn what White helping professionals need to do in order to prevent their *Whiteness* from negatively impacting clients of color.

As a person of color, I have often wondered how White people identify themselves as racial/cultural beings. At times, I noted that White trainees often seemed to believe race was confined to persons of color and did not apply to them. To explore this phenomenon more deeply, I asked people in downtown San Francisco "What does it mean to be White?" These were some of the responses I received (Sue, 2003, pp. 115–117).

42-Year-Old White Male Businessperson

Q: What does it mean to be White?

A: Frankly, I don't know what you're talking about!

Q: Aren't you White?

A: Yes, but I come from Italian heritage. I'm Italian, not White.

Q: Well then, what does it mean to be Italian?

A: Pasta, good food, love of wine (obviously agitated). This is getting ridiculous!

26-Year-Old White Female College Student

Q: What does it mean to be White?

A: Is this a trick question? . . . I've never thought about it. . . Well, I know that lots of Black people see us as being prejudiced and all that stuff. I wish people would just forget about race differences and see one another as human beings. People are people and we should all be proud to be Americans.

34-Year-Old White Female Stockbroker

Q: What does it mean to be White?

A: I don't know (laughing), I've never thought about it.

Q: Are you White?

A: Yes, I suppose so (seems very amused).

Q: Why haven't you thought about it?

A: Because it's not important to me.

Q: Why not?

A: It doesn't enter into my mind because it doesn't affect my life. Besides, we are all individuals. Color isn't important.

39-Year-Old Black Male Salesperson

Q: What does it mean to be White?

A: Is this a school exercise or something? Never expected someone to ask me that question in the middle of the city. Do you want the politically correct answer or what I really think?

Q: Can you tell me what you really think?

A: You won't quit, will you (laughing)? If you're White, you're right. If you're Black, step back.

Q: What does that mean?

A: White folks are always thinking they know all the answers. A Black man's word is worth less than a White man's. When White customers come into our dealership and see me standing next to the cars, I become invisible to them. Actually, they may see me as a well-dressed janitor (laughs), or actively avoid me. They will search out a White salesman. Or, when I explain something to a customer, they always check out the information with my White colleagues. They don't trust me. When I mention this to our manager, who is White, he tells me I'm oversensitive and being paranoid. That's what being White means. It means having the authority or power to tell me what's really happening even though I know it's not. Being White means you can fool yourself into thinking that you're not prejudiced, when you are. That's what it means to be White. (Sue, 2003, pp. 118–119).

REFLECTION AND DISCUSSION QUESTIONS

1. Is this a fair or unfair question?

2. Can you discern any common responses among the three given by White pedestrians? In what ways do they differ?

3. How do Whites view themselves as racial/cultural beings?

4. What seems to prevent these three individuals from viewing themselves as White?

5. If asked what it means to be White, would people of color also find difficulty answering the question? Why or why not?

6. How does the Black salesman's response differ from his White counterparts?

7. Which perception is the most accurate? Why?

Research on *Whiteness*, *White privilege*, and *White racial identity development* point to one of the greatest barriers to racial understanding for White Americans: *the invisibility of their Whiteness* (Bell, 2003; Helms, 1990; Spanierman, Poteat, Beer, & Armstrong, 2006; Tatum, 1992; Todd & Abrams, 2011). Just as ethnocentric monoculturalism and implicit bias achieve their oppressive powers through invisibility, so too does *Whiteness* (Boysen, 2010; Sue, 2004). During racial interactions or conversations, many Whites appear oblivious to the meaning of their *Whiteness*, how it intrudes and disadvantages people of color, and how it affects the way they perceive the world (Bell, 2002; Sue, 2013).

It appears that the denial and mystification of *Whiteness* for White EuroAmericans are related to two underlying factors. First, most people seldom think about the air that surrounds them and about how it provides an essential life-giving ingredient, oxygen. We take it for granted because it appears plentiful; only when we are deprived of it does it suddenly become frighteningly apparent. *Whiteness* is transparent precisely because of its everyday occurrence—its institutionalized normative features in our culture—and because Whites are taught to think of their lives as morally neutral, average, and ideal (Sue, 2004). To people of color, however, *Whiteness* is not invisible because it may not fit their normative qualities (e.g., values, lifestyles, experiential reality). Persons of color find White culture quite visible because even though it is nurturing to White EuroAmericans, it may invalidate the lifestyles of multicultural populations.

Second, EuroAmericans often deny that they are White, seem angered by being labeled as such, and often become very defensive (e.g., saying, "I'm not White; I'm Irish," "You're stereotyping, because we're all different," or "There isn't anything like a White race"). In many respects, these statements have validity. Nonetheless, many White Americans would be hard pressed to describe their Irish, Italian, German, or Norwegian heritage in any but the most superficial manner. One of the reasons is related to the processes of assimilation and acculturation. Although there are many ethnic groups, being White allows for assimilation. While persons of color are told to assimilate and acculturate, the assumption is that there exists a receptive society. People of color are told in no uncertain terms that they are allowed only limited access to the fruits of our society.

Third, the accuracy of whether *Whiteness* defines a race is largely irrelevant. What is more relevant is that *Whiteness* is associated with unearned privilege—advantages conferred on White Americans but not on persons of color. It is our contention that much of the denial associated with being White is related to the denial of *White privilege*, which is unmasked by this Black salesman when asked "What does it mean to be White?"

The response given by the Black salesman is markedly different from those of the other three responders by its specificity, clarity, and perspective. In essence, he believes being White means (a) having the power to define reality, (b) possessing unconscious stereotypes that people of color are less competent and capable, (c) deceiving the self that one is not prejudiced, and (d) being oblivious to how *Whiteness* disadvantages people of color and advantages White people. This worldview is in marked contrast to the White respondents who would rather not think about their *Whiteness*, are uncomfortable or react negatively to being labeled "White," deny its importance in affecting their lives, and seem to believe that they are unjustifiably accused of being bigoted by virtue of being White. Strangely enough, "*whiteness*" is most visible when it is denied, evokes puzzlement or negative reactions, and equated with normalcy. Few people of color react negatively when asked what it means to be Black, Asian American, Latino or a member of their race. Most could readily inform the questioner about what it means to be a person of color.

UNDERSTANDING THE DYNAMICS OF WHITENESS

Our analysis of the responses from both Whites and the person of color leads us to the inevitable conclusion that part of the problem of race relations (and by inference multicultural counseling and therapy) lies in the different worldviews of both groups. It goes without saying that the racial reality of Whites is radically different from that of people of color (Sue, 2010). Which group, however, has the more accurate assessment related to this topic? The answer seems to be contained in the following series of questions: If you want to understand oppression, should you ask the oppressor or the oppressed? If you want to learn about sexism, do you ask men or women? If you want to understand homophobia, do you ask straights or gays? If you want to learn about racism, do you ask Whites or persons of color? It appears that the most accurate assessment of bias comes not from those who enjoy the privilege of power, but from those who are most disempowered (Hanna, Talley, & Guindon, 2000; Sue, 2015). Taking this position, the following conclusions are made about the dynamics of *Whiteness*.

First, it is clear that most Whites perceive themselves as unbiased individuals who do not harbor racist thoughts and feelings; they see themselves as working toward social justice and possessing a conscious desire to better the life circumstances of those less fortunate than they. Although these are admirable qualities, this self-image serves as a major barrier to recognizing and taking responsibility for admitting and dealing with one's own prejudices and biases. To admit to being racist, sexist, or homophobic requires people to recognize that the self-images they hold so dear are based on false notions of the self.

Second, being a White person in this society means chronic exposure to ethnocentric monoculturalism as manifested in *White supremacy* (Hays, 2014). It is difficult, if not impossible, for anyone to avoid inheriting the racial biases, prejudices, misinformation, deficit portrayals, and stereotypes of their forebears (Cokley, 2006). To believe that one is somehow immune from inheriting such aspects of *White supremacy* is to be naive or to engage in self-deception. Such a statement is not intended to assail the integrity of Whites but to suggest that they also have been victimized. It is clear to us that no one was born wanting to be racist, sexist, or homophobic. Misinformation is not acquired by free choice but is imposed upon White people through a painful process of cultural conditioning (Gallardo & Ivey, 2014). In general, lacking awareness of their biases and preconceived notions, counselors may function in a therapeutically ineffective manner.

Third, if White helping professionals are ever able to become effective multicultural counselors or therapists, they must free themselves from the cultural conditioning of their past and move toward the development of a *nonracist White identity*. Unfortunately, many White EuroAmericans seldom consider what it means to be White in our society. Such a question is vexing to them because they seldom think of race as belonging to them—nor of the privileges that come their way by virtue of their white skin (Toporek & Worthington, 2014). Katz (1985) points out a major barrier blocking the process of White EuroAmericans investigating their own cultural identity and worldview:

> *Because White culture is the dominant cultural norm in the United States, it acts as an invisible veil that limits many people from seeing it as a cultural system. . . .Often, it is easier for many Whites to identify and acknowledge the different cultures of minorities than accept their own racial identity. . . .The difficulty of accepting such a view is that White culture is omnipresent. It is so interwoven in the fabric of everyday living that Whites cannot step outside and see their beliefs, values, and behaviors as creating a distinct cultural group. (pp. 616–617)*

As we witnessed in Chapter 6, the invisible veil allows for racial, gender, and sexual orientation microaggressions to be delivered outside the level of awareness of perpetrators. Ridley (1995) asserts that this invisible veil can be unintentionally manifested in therapy with harmful consequences to clients of color:

> *Unintentional behavior is perhaps the most insidious form of racism. Unintentional racists are unaware of the harmful consequences of their behavior. They may be well-intentioned, and on the surface, their behavior may appear to be responsible. Because individuals, groups, or institutions that engage in unintentional racism do not wish to do harm, it is difficult to get them to see themselves as racists. They are more likely to deny their racism. (p. 38)*

The conclusion drawn from this understanding is that White counselors and therapists may be unintentional racists: (a) They are unaware of their biases, prejudices, and discriminatory behaviors; (b) they often perceive themselves as moral, good, and decent human beings and find it difficult to see themselves as racist; (c) they do not have a sense of what their *Whiteness* means to them; and (d) their therapeutic approaches to multicultural populations are likely to be more harmful (unintentionally) than helpful. These conclusions are often difficult for White helping professionals to accept because of the defensiveness and feelings of blame they are likely to engender. Nonetheless, we ask White therapists and students not be turned off by the message and lessons of this chapter. We ask you to reread Chapter 1 where we discussed the emotive reactions likely to impede learning. And, we ask you to continue your multicultural journey in this chapter as we explore the question, "What does it mean to be White?"

MODELS OF WHITE RACIAL IDENTITY DEVELOPMENT

A number of multicultural experts in the field have begun to emphasize the need for White therapists to deal with their concepts of *Whiteness* and to examine their own racism (Gallardo & Ivey, 2014; Ponterotto, Utsey, & Pedersen, 2006; Todd & Abrams, 2011). These specialists point out that while racial/cultural identity development for minority groups proves beneficial in our work as therapists, more attention should be devoted toward the White therapist's racial identity. Since the majority of therapists and trainees are White middle-class individuals, it would appear that White identity development and its implication for multicultural counseling/therapy would be important aspects to consider, both in the actual practice of clinical work and in professional training.

For example, research has found that the level of White racial identity awareness is predictive of racism and internal interpersonal characteristics (Miville, Darlington, Whitlock, & Mulligan, 2005; Perry, Dovidio, Murphy, & van Ryn, 2015; Pope-Davis & Ottavi, 1994; Spanierman, Todd, & Anderson, 2009; Vinson & Neimeyer, 2000, 2003; Wang et al., 2003): (a) the less aware subjects were of their White identity, the more likely they were to exhibit increased levels of racism; (b) the higher the level of White identity development, the greater the reported multicultural counseling competence, more positive opinions toward minority groups, and better therapeutic alliances; (c) higher levels of mature interpersonal relationships and a better sense of personal well-being were associated with higher levels of White identity consciousness; and (d) as a group, women were more likely than men to exhibit higher levels of White consciousness and were less likely to be racially biased.

It was suggested that this last finding was correlated with women's greater experiences with discrimination and prejudice. Evidence also exists that multicultural counseling/therapy competence is correlated with White racial identity attitudes

(Neville, Awad, Brooks, Flores, & Bluemel, 2013). Other research suggests that a relationship exists between a White EuroAmerican therapist's racial identity and his or her readiness for training in multicultural awareness, knowledge, and skills (Falender, Shafranske, & Falicov, 2014; Utsey, Gernat, & Hammar, 2005). Since developing multicultural sensitivity is a long-term developmental task, the work of many researchers has gradually converged toward a conceptualization of the stages/levels/statuses of consciousness of racial/ethnic identity development for White EuroAmericans. A number of these models describe the salience of identity for establishing relationships between the White therapist and the culturally different client, and some have now linked stages of identity with stages for appropriate training.

The Hardiman White Racial Identity Development Model

One of the earliest integrative attempts at formulating a *White racial identity development* model is that of Rita Hardiman (1982). Intrigued with why certain White Americans exhibit a much more nonracist identity than do other White Americans, Hardiman studied the autobiographies of individuals who had attained a high level of racial consciousness. This led her to identify five White developmental stages: (a) naiveté—lack of social consciousness, (b) acceptance, (c) resistance, (d) redefinition, and (e) internalization.

1. The *naiveté stage* (lack of social consciousness) is characteristic of early childhood, when we are born into this world innocent, open, and unaware of racism and the importance of race. Curiosity and spontaneity in relating to race and racial differences tend to be the norm. A young White child who has almost no personal contact with African Americans, for example, may see a Black man in a supermarket and loudly comment on the darkness of his skin. In general, awareness and the meaning of race, racial differences, bias, and prejudice are either absent or minimal. The negative reactions of parents, relatives, friends, and peers toward issues of race, however, begin to convey mixed signals to the child. This is reinforced by the educational system and mass media, which instill racial biases in the child and propel him or her into the acceptance stage.

2. The *acceptance stage* is marked by a conscious belief in the democratic ideal—that everyone has an equal opportunity to succeed in a free society and that those who fail must bear the responsibility for their failure. White Euro-Americans become the social reference group, and the socialization process

consistently instills messages of White superiority and minority inferiority into the child. The underemployment, unemployment, and undereducation of marginalized groups in our society are seen as support for the belief that non-White groups are lesser than Whites. Because everyone has an equal opportunity to succeed, the lack of success of minority groups is seen as evidence of some negative personal or group characteristic. Victim blaming is strong, as the existence of oppression, discrimination, and racism is denied. Hardiman believes that although the naiveté stage is brief in duration, the acceptance stage can last a lifetime.

3. In the *resistance stage*, the individual begins to challenge assumptions of White superiority and the denial of racism and discrimination. The White person's denial system begins to crumble because of a monumental event or a series of events that not only challenge but also shatter the individual's denial system. A White person may, for example, make friends with a coworker of color and discover that the images he or she has of "these people" are untrue. The person may have witnessed clear incidents of unfair discrimination toward persons of color and may now begin to question assumptions regarding racial inferiority. In any case, the racial realities of life in the United States can no longer be denied. The person becomes conscious of being White, is aware that he or she harbors racist attitudes, and begins to see the pervasiveness of oppression in our society. Feelings of anger, pain, hurt, rage, and frustration are present. In many cases, the White person may develop a negative reaction toward his or her own group or culture. Although those at this stage may romanticize people of color, they cannot interact confidently with them because they fear that they will make racist mistakes. This discomfort is best exemplified in a passage by Sara Winter (1977, p. 1):

> *We avoid Black people because their presence brings painful questions to mind. Is it OK to talk about watermelons or mention "black coffee"? Should we use Black slang and tell racial jokes? How about talking about our experiences in Harlem, or mentioning our Black lovers? Should we conceal the fact that our mother still employs a Black cleaning lady?. . .We're embarrassedly aware of trying to do our best but to "act natural" at the same time. No wonder we're more comfortable in all-White situations where these dilemmas don't arise.*

4. In the *redefinition stage*, asking the painful question of who one is in relation to one's racial heritage, honestly confronting one's biases and prejudices, and accepting responsibility for one's *Whiteness* are the culminating characteristics. New ways of defining one's social group and one's membership in that group become important. The intense soul-searching is most evident in Winter's 1977 personal journey as she writes,

> *In this sense we Whites are the victims of racism. Our victimization is different from that of Blacks, but it is real. We have been programmed into the oppressor roles we play, without our informed consent in the process. Our unawareness is part of the programming: None of us could tolerate the oppressor position, if we lived with a day-to-day emotional awareness of the pain inflicted on other humans through the instrument of our behavior. . . . We Whites benefit in concrete ways, year in and year out, from the present racial arrangements. All my life in White neighborhoods, White schools, White jobs, and dealing with White police (to name only a few), I have experienced advantages that are systematically not available to Black people. It does not make sense for me to blame myself for the advantages that have come my way by virtue of my* Whiteness. *But absolving myself from guilt does not imply forgetting about racial injustice or taking it lightly (as my guilt pushes me to do). (p. 2)*

There is realization that *Whiteness* has been defined in opposition to people of color—namely, by standards of *White supremacy*. By being able to step out of this racist paradigm and redefine what her *Whiteness* meant to her, Winter is able to add meaning to developing a nonracist identity. She no longer denies being White, honestly confronts her racism, and understands the concept of *White privilege*.

5. The *internalization stage* is the result of forming a new social and personal identity. With the greater comfort in understanding oneself and the development of a *nonracist White identity* come a commitment to social action as well. The individual accepts responsibility for effecting personal and social change without always relying on persons of color to lead the way. As Winter 1977 explains,

> *To end racism, Whites have to pay attention to it and continue to pay attention. Since avoidance is such a basic dynamic of racism,*

paying attention will not happen naturally. We Whites must learn how to hold racism realities in our attention. We must learn to take responsibility for this process ourselves, without waiting for Blacks' actions to remind us that the problem exists, and without depending on Black people to reassure us and forgive us for our racist sins. In my experience, the process is painful but it is a relief to shed the fears, stereotypes, immobilizing guilt we didn't want in the first place. (p. 2)

The Helms White Racial Identity Development Model

Working independently of Hardiman, Janet Helms (1984, 1990, 1994, 1995) created perhaps the most elaborate and sophisticated White racial identity model in the field. Not only has her model led to the development of an assessment instrument to measure White racial identity, but it also has been scrutinized empirically (Carter, 1990; Helms & Carter, 1990) and has generated much research and debate in the psychological literature. Like Hardiman (1982), Helms assumes that racism is an intimate and central part of being a White American. To her, developing a healthy White identity requires movement through two phases: (a) abandonment of racism and (b) defining a *nonracist White identity* (Helms, 2015).

Six specific racial identity statuses are distributed equally in the two phases: contact, disintegration, reintegration, pseudo-independence, immersion/emersion, and autonomy. Originally, Helms used the term *stages* to refer to the six; but because of certain conceptual ambiguities and the controversy that ensued, she has abandoned its usage.

1. *Contact status:* People in this status are oblivious to and unaware of racism, believe that everyone has an equal chance for success, lack an understanding of prejudice and discrimination, have minimal experiences with persons of color, and may profess to be color-blind. Such statements as "People are people," "I don't notice a person's race at all," and "You don't act Black" are examples. Although there is an attempt to minimize the importance or influence of race, there is on both a conscious and an unconscious level a definite dichotomy between persons of color and Whites regarding stereotypes and the superior/inferior dimensions of the races. Because of obliviousness and compartmentalization, it is possible for two diametrically opposed belief systems to coexist: (a) Uncritical acceptance of White supremacist notions

relegates minorities into the inferior category with all the racial stereotypes, and (b) there is a belief that racial and cultural differences are unimportant. This allows Whites to avoid perceiving themselves as dominant group members or as having biases and prejudices. Such an orientation is aptly stated by Peggy McIntosh (1989) in her own White racial awakening:

> *My schooling gave me no training in seeing myself as an oppressor, as an unfairly advantaged person, or as a participant in a damaged culture. I was taught to see myself as an individual whose moral state depended on her individual moral will. . . . Whites are taught to think of their lives as morally neutral, normative, and average, and also ideal, so that when we work to benefit others, this is seen as work which will allow "them" to be more like "us." (p. 8)*

2. *Disintegration status:* Although in the previous status the individual does not recognize the polarities of democratic principles of equality and the unequal treatment of minority groups, such obliviousness may eventually break down. The White person becomes conflicted over irresolvable racial moral dilemmas that are frequently perceived as polar opposites: believing one is nonracist, yet not wanting one's son or daughter to marry a minority group member; believing that all men are created equal, even though society treats people of color as second-class citizens; and not acknowledging that oppression exists and then witnessing it (e.g., the killing of Michael Brown and Eric Garner in 2014). Conflicts between loyalty to one's group and humanistic ideals may manifest themselves in various ways. The person becomes increasingly conscious of his or her *Whiteness* and may experience dissonance and conflict, resulting in feelings of guilt, depression, helplessness, or anxiety. Statements such as "My grandfather is really prejudiced, but I try not to be" and "I'm personally not against interracial marriages, but I worry about the children" are representative of personal struggles occurring in the White person.

    Although a healthy resolution might be to confront the myth of meritocracy realistically, the breakdown of the denial system is painful and anxiety provoking. Attempts at resolution, according to Helms, may involve (a) avoiding contact with persons of color, (b) not thinking about race, and (c) seeking reassurance from others that racism is not the fault of Whites.

3. *Reintegration status:* This status can best be characterized as a regression in which the pendulum swings back to the most basic beliefs of White superiority and minority inferiority. In their attempts to resolve the dissonance created from the previous process, there is a retreat to the dominant ideology associated with race and one's own socioracial group identity. This ego status results in idealizing the White EuroAmerican group and the positives of White culture and society; there is a consequent negation and intolerance of minority groups. In general, a firmer and more conscious belief in White racial superiority is present. Racial/ethnic minorities are blamed for their own problems.

> *I'm an Italian grandmother. No one gave us welfare or a helping hand when we came over [immigrated]. My father worked day and night to provide us with a decent living and to put all of us through school. These Negroes are always complaining about prejudice and hardships. Big deal! Why don't they stop whining and find a job? They're not the only ones who were discriminated against, you know. You don't think our family wasn't? We never let that stop us. In America everyone can make it if they are willing to work hard. I see these Black welfare mothers waiting in line for food stamps and free handouts. You can't convince me they're starving. Look at how overweight most of them are. . . . Laziness—that's what I see. (Quoted from a workshop participant)*

4. *Pseudo-independence status:* This status initiates the second phase of Helms's model, which involves defining a *nonracist White identity*. As in the Hardiman model, a person is likely to be propelled into this phase because of a painful or insightful encounter or event that jars the person from the reintegration status. The awareness of visible racial/ethnic minorities, the unfairness of their treatment, and a discomfort with their racist White identity may lead individuals to identify with the plight of persons of color. However, the well-intentioned White person at this status may suffer from several problematic dynamics: (a) Although intending to be socially conscious and helpful to minority groups, the White individual may unknowingly perpetuate racism by helping minorities adjust to the prevailing White standards; and (b) identifying with minority individuals is based on how similar they are to him or her, and the primary mechanism used to understand racial issues is intellectual and conceptual.

5. *Immersion/emersion status:* If the person is reinforced to continue a personal exploration of him- or herself as a racial being, questions become focused on what it means to be White. Helms states that the person searches for an understanding of the personal meaning of racism and the ways in which one benefits from *White privilege.* There is an increasing willingness to confront one's own biases, to redefine *Whiteness,* and to become more active in directly combating racism and oppression. This status is different from the previous one in two major ways: It is marked by (a) a shift in focus from trying to change people of color to changing the self and other Whites and (b) an increasing experiential and affective understanding that was lacking in the previous status. The ability to achieve this affective/experiential upheaval leads to a euphoria, or even a feeling of rebirth, and is a necessary condition to developing a new, *nonracist White identity.* Winter (1977) states,

> Let me explain this healing process in more detail. We must unearth all the words and memories we generally try not to think about, but which are inside us all the time: "nigger," "Uncle Tom," "jungle bunny," "Oreo," lynching, cattle prods, castrations, rapists, "black pussy," and black men with their huge penises, and hundreds more. (I shudder as I write.) We need to review three different kinds of material: (1) All our personal memories connected with blackness and black people, including everything we can recall hearing or reading; (2) all the racist images and stereotypes we've ever heard, particularly the grossest and most hurtful ones; (3) any race-related things we ourselves said, did, or omitted doing which we feel bad about today.
>
> . . . Most whites begin with a good deal of amnesia. Eventually the memories crowd in, especially when several people pool recollections. Emotional release is a vital part of the process. Experiencing feelings seems to allow further recollections to come. I need persistent encouragement from my companions to continue. (p. 3)

6. *Autonomy status:* Increasing awareness of one's own *Whiteness,* reduced feelings of guilt, acceptance of one's role in perpetuating racism, and renewed determination to abandon White entitlement lead to an autonomy status. The person is knowledgeable about racial, ethnic, and cultural differences; values the diversity; and is no longer fearful, intimidated, or uncomfortable with the experiential reality of race. Development of a *nonracist White identity*

becomes increasingly strong. Indeed, the person feels comfortable with his or her *nonracist White identity*, does not personalize attacks on *White supremacy*, and can explore the issues of racism and personal responsibility without defensiveness. A person in this status "walks the talk" and actively values and seeks out interracial experiences.

Helms's model is by far the most widely cited, researched, and applied of all the White racial identity formulations. Part of its attractiveness and value is the derivation of "defenses," "protective strategies," or what Helms (1995) formally labels *information-processing strategies* (IPSs), which White people use to avoid or assuage anxiety and discomfort around the issue of race. Table 12.1 lists examples of IPS statements likely to be made by White people in each of the six *ego statuses*. Understanding these strategic reactions is important for White American identity development, for understanding the barriers that must be overcome in order to move to another status, and for potentially developing effective training or clinical strategies.

TABLE 12.1   White Racial Identity Ego Statuses and Information-Processing Strategies

1. *Contact status:* Satisfaction with racial status quo, obliviousness to racism and one's participation in it. If racial factors influence life decisions, they do so in a simplistic fashion. Information-processing strategy. IPS: Obliviousness.

    Example: "I'm a White woman. When my grandfather came to this country, he was discriminated against, too. But he didn't blame Black people for his misfortunes. He educated himself and got a job. That's what Blacks ought to do. If White callers [to a radio station] spent as much time complaining about racial discrimination as your Black callers do, we'd never have accomplished what we have. You all should just ignore it" (quoted from a workshop participant).

2. *Disintegration status:* Disorientation and anxiety provoked by irresolvable racial moral dilemmas that force one to choose between own-group loyalty and humanism. May be stymied by life situations that arouse racial dilemmas. IPS: Suppression and ambivalence.

    Example: "I myself tried to set a nonracist example [for other Whites] by speaking up when someone said something blatantly prejudiced—how to do this without alienating people so that they would no longer take me seriously was always tricky—and by my friendships with Mexicans and Blacks who were actually the people with whom I felt most comfortable" (Blauner, 1993, p. 8).

3. *Reintegration status:* Idealization of one's sociocracial group, denigration and intolerance of other groups. Racial factors may strongly influence life decisions. IPS: Selective perception and negative out-group distortion.

    Example: "So what if my great-grandfather owned slaves. He didn't mistreat them; and besides, I wasn't even here then. I never owned slaves. So I don't know why Blacks expect me to feel guilty for something that happened before I was born. Nowadays, reverse racism hurts Whites more than slavery hurts Blacks. At least they got three square [meals] a day. But my brother can't even get a job with the police department because they have to hire less-qualified Blacks. That [expletive] happens to Whites all the time" (quoted from a workshop participant).

4. *Pseudo-independence status:* Intellectualized commitment to one's own socioracial group and deceptive tolerance of other groups. May make life decisions to "help other racial groups." IPS: Reshaping reality and selective perception.

   Example: "Was I the only person left in America who believed that the sexual mingling of the races was a good thing, that it would erase cultural barriers and leave us all a lovely shade of tan?...Racial blending is inevitable. At the very least, it may be the only solution to our dilemmas of race" (Allen, 1994, p. C4).

5. *Immersion/emersion status:* Search for an understanding of the personal meaning of racism and the ways by which one benefits and a redefinition of Whiteness. Life choices may incorporate racial activism. IPS: Hypervigilance and reshaping.

   Example: "It's true that I personally did not participate in the horror of slavery, and I don't even know whether my ancestors owned slaves. But I know that because I am White, I continue to benefit from a racist system that stems from the slavery era. I believe that if White people are ever going to understand our role in perpetuating racism, then we must begin to ask ourselves some hard questions and be willing to consider our role in maintaining a hurtful system. Then we must try to do something to change it" (quoted from a workshop participant).

6. *Autonomy status:* Informed positive socioracial group commitment, use of internal standards for self-definition, capacity to relinquish the privileges of racism. May avoid life options that require participation in racial oppression. IPS: Flexibility and complexity.

   Example: "I live in an integrated [Black-White] neighborhood, and I read Black literature and popular magazines. So I understand that the media presents a very stereotypic view of Black culture. I believe that if more of us White people made more than a superficial effort to obtain accurate information about racial groups other than our own, then we could help make this country a better place for all peoples" (quoted from a workshop participant).

Source: Helms, 1995, p. 185.

The Helms model, however, is not without its detractors. In an article critical of the Helms model and of most "stage" models of *White racial identity development*, Rowe, Bennett, and Atkinson (1994) raised some serious objections.

First, they claim that Helms's model is erroneously based on racial/ethnic minority identity development models (discussed in the previous chapter). Because minority identity development occurs in the face of stereotyping and oppression, it may not apply to White identity, which does not occur under the same conditions.

Second, they believe that too much emphasis is placed on the development of White attitudes toward minorities and that not enough is placed on the development of White attitudes toward themselves and their own identity.

Third, they claim that there is a conceptual inaccuracy in putting forth the model as developmental via stages (linear) and that the progression from less to more healthy seems to be based on the author's ethics.

Last, Rowe (2006) attacks the Helms model of *White racial identity development* because it is based upon the White Racial Identity Attitude Scale (Helms & Carter, 1990), which he labels as "pseudoscience" because he asserts that the psychometric properties are not supported by the empirical literature. It is important to note that the critique of the Helms (1984) model has not been left unanswered. In subsequent writings, Helms (1994) has disclaimed the Rowe et al. (1994, 1995) characterization of her model and has attempted to clarify her position. The continuing debate has proven beneficial in adding greater clarity to the issues of *White racial identity development* and has resulted in increased research.

THE PROCESS OF WHITE RACIAL IDENTITY DEVELOPMENT: A DESCRIPTIVE MODEL

Although there are differences in the models, it appears important for Whites to view their developmental history in order to gain a sense of their past, present, and future as they struggle with racial identity development. In our work with White trainees and clinicians, we have observed some very important changes through which they seem to move as they work toward multicultural competence (Sue, 2011). We have been impressed with how Whites seem to go through parallel racial/cultural identity transformations. This is especially true if we accept the fact that Whites are as much victims of societal forces (i.e., they are socialized into racist attitudes and beliefs) as are their counterparts (Sue, 2003). No child is born wanting to be a racist! Yet White people do benefit from the dominant–subordinate relationship in our society. It is this factor that Whites need to confront in an open and honest manner.

Using the formulation of our past work (Sue & Sue, 1990), we propose a seven-step process that integrates many characteristics from the other formulations. Furthermore, we make some basic assumptions with respect to those models:

1. Racism is an integral part of U.S. life, and it permeates all aspects of our culture and institutions (ethnocentric monoculturalism).

2. Whites are socialized into the society and therefore inherit all the biases; stereotypes; and racist attitudes, beliefs, and behaviors of the larger society.

3. How Whites perceive themselves as racial beings follows an identifiable sequence that can occur in a linear or nonlinear fashion.

4. The status of *White racial identity development* in any multicultural encounter affects the process and outcome of interracial relationships.

5. The most desirable outcome is one in which the White person not only accepts his or her *Whiteness* but also defines it in a nonracist and antiracist manner.

Seven-Step Process

The seven phases of *white racial identity development* and their implications for White Americans are described in the following. We encourage Whites to use this information to explore themselves as racial/cultural beings and to think about their implications for work with culturally diverse clients.

1. *Naiveté phase:* This phase is relatively neutral with respect to racial/cultural differences. Its length is brief and is marked by a naive curiosity about race. As mentioned previously, racial awareness and burgeoning social meanings are absent or minimal, and the young child is generally innocent, open, and spontaneous regarding racial differences. Between the ages of three and five, however, the young White child begins to associate positive ethnocentric meanings to his or her own group and negative ones to others. The child is bombarded by misinformation through the educational channels, mass media, and significant others in his or her life, and a sense of the superiority of *Whiteness* and the inferiority of all other groups and their heritage is instilled. The following passage describes one of the insidious processes of socialization that leads to propelling the child into the conformity stage.

> *It was a late summer afternoon. A group of White neighborhood mothers, obviously friends, had brought their four- and five-year-olds to the local McDonald's for a snack and to play on the swings and slides provided by the restaurant. They were all seated at a table watching their sons and daughters run about the play area. In one corner of the yard sat a small Black child pushing a red truck along the grass. One of the White girls from the group approached the Black boy and they started a conversation. During that instant, the mother of the girl exchanged quick glances with the other mothers, who nodded knowingly. She quickly rose from the table, walked over to the two, spoke to her daughter, and gently pulled her away to join her previous playmates. Within minutes, however, the girl again approached the Black boy and both began to play with the truck. At that point, all the mothers rose from the table and loudly exclaimed to their children, "It's time to go now!" (Taken from Sue, 2003, pp. 89–90)*

2. *Conformity phase:* The White person's attitudes and beliefs in this phase are very ethnocentric. There is minimal awareness of the self as a racial being and a strong belief in the universality of values and norms governing behavior. The

White person possesses limited accurate knowledge of other ethnic groups, but he or she is likely to rely on social stereotypes as the main source of information. Consciously or unconsciously, the White person believes that White culture is the most highly developed and that all others are primitive or inferior. The *conformity phase* is marked by contradictory and often compartmentalized attitudes, beliefs, and behaviors. A person may believe simultaneously that he or she is not racist but that minority inferiority justifies discriminatory and inferior treatment, and that minority persons are different and deviant but that "people are people" and differences are unimportant. As with their marginalized counterparts at this phase, the primary mechanism operating here is one of denial and compartmentalization. For example, many Whites deny that they belong to a race that allows them to avoid personal responsibility for perpetuating a racist system. Like a fish in water, Whites either have difficulty seeing or are unable to see the invisible veil of cultural assumptions, biases, and prejudices that guide their perceptions and actions. They tend to believe that White EuroAmerican culture is superior and that other cultures are primitive, inferior, less developed, or lower on the scale of evolution.

It is important to note that many Whites in this phase of development are unaware of these beliefs and operate as if they are universally shared by others. They believe that differences are unimportant and that "people are people," "we are all the same under the skin," "we should treat everyone the same," "problems wouldn't exist if minorities would only assimilate," and discrimination and prejudice are something that others do. The helping professional with this perspective professes color-blindness, views counseling/therapy theories as universally applicable, and does not question their relevance to other culturally different groups. The primary mechanism used in encapsulation is denial—denial that people are different, denial that discrimination exists, and denial of one's own prejudices. Instead, the locus of the problem is seen to reside in marginalized groups. Socially devalued groups would not encounter problems if they would only assimilate and acculturate (melting pot), value education, or work harder.

3. *Dissonance phase:* Movement into the *dissonance phase* occurs when the White person is forced to deal with the inconsistencies that have been compartmentalized or encounters information/experiences at odds with denial. In most cases, individuals are forced to acknowledge *Whiteness* at some level, to examine their own cultural values, and to see the conflict between upholding

humanistic nonracist values and their contradictory behavior. For example, a person who may consciously believe that all people are created equal and that he or she treats everyone the same suddenly experiences reservations about having African Americans move next door or having one's son or daughter involved in an interracial relationship. These more personal experiences bring the individual face-to-face with his or her own prejudices and biases. In this situation, thoughts that "I am not prejudiced," "I treat everyone the same regardless of race, creed, or color," and "I do not discriminate" collide with the denial system. Additionally, some major event (e.g., the assassination of Martin Luther King Jr.) may force the person to realize that racism is alive and well in the United States.

The increasing realization that one is biased and that EuroAmerican society does play a part in oppressing minority groups is an unpleasant one. Dissonance may result in feelings of guilt, shame, anger, and depression. Rationalizations may be used to exonerate one's own inactivity in combating perceived injustice or personal feelings of prejudice; for example, "I'm only one person—what can I do?" or "Everyone is prejudiced, even minorities." As these conflicts ensue, the White person may retreat into the protective confines of White culture (encapsulation of the *conformity phase*) or move progressively toward insight and revelation (*resistance and immersion phase*).

Whether a person regresses is related to the strength of positive forces pushing the individual forward (support for challenging racism) and negative forces pushing the person backward (fear of some loss) (Sue, 2011; Todd & Abrams, 2011). For example, challenging the prevailing beliefs of the times may mean risking ostracism from White relatives, friends, neighbors, and colleagues. Regardless of the choice, there are many uncomfortable feelings of guilt, shame, anger, and depression related to the realization of inconsistencies in one's belief systems. Guilt and shame are most likely related to the recognition of the White person's role in perpetuating racism in the past. Guilt may also result from the person's being afraid to speak out on the issues or to take responsibility for his or her part in a current situation. For example, the person may witness an act of racism, hear a racist comment, or be given preferential treatment over a minority person but decide not to say anything for fear of violating racist White norms. Many White people rationalize their behaviors by believing that they are powerless to make changes. Additionally, there is a tendency to retreat into White culture. If, however, others (which may include some family and friends) are more accepting, forward movement is more likely.

4. *Resistance and immersion phase:* The White person who progresses to this phase will begin to question and challenge his or her own racism. For the first time, the person begins to realize what racism is all about, and his or her eyes are suddenly open. Racism is seen everywhere (e.g., advertising, television, educational materials, interpersonal interactions). This phase of development is marked by a major questioning of one's own racism and that of others in society. In addition, increasing awareness of how racism operates and its pervasiveness in U.S. culture and institutions is the major hallmark of this level. It is as if the person awakens to the realities of oppression; sees how educational materials, the mass media, advertising, and other elements portray and perpetuate stereotypes; and recognizes how being White grants certain advantages denied to various minority groups.

There is likely to be considerable anger at family and friends, institutions, and larger societal values, which are seen as having sold him or her a false bill of goods (democratic ideals) that were never practiced. Guilt is also felt for having been a part of the oppressive system. Strangely enough, the person is likely to undergo a form of racial self-hatred at this phase. Negative feelings about being White are present, and the accompanying feelings of guilt, shame, and anger toward oneself and other Whites may develop. The White liberal syndrome may develop and be manifested in two complementary styles: the paternalistic protector role or the overidentification with another minority group (Helms, 1984; Ponterotto, 1988). In the former, the White person may devote his or her energies in an almost paternalistic attempt to protect minorities from abuse. In the latter, the person may actually want to identify with a particular minority group (e.g., Asian, Black) in order to escape his or her own *Whiteness.* The White person will soon discover, however, that these roles are not appreciated by minority groups and will experience rejection. Again, the person may resolve this dilemma by moving back into the protective confines of White culture (*conformity phase*), again experience conflict (dissonance), or move directly to the *introspective phase.*

5. *Introspective phase:* This phase is most likely a compromise of having swung from an extreme of unconditional acceptance of White identity to a rejection of *Whiteness.* It is a state of relative quiescence, introspection, and reformulation of what it means to be White. The person realizes and no longer denies that he or she has participated in oppression and benefited from *White privilege* or that racism is an integral part of U.S. society. However, individuals

at this phase become less motivated by guilt and defensiveness, accept their *Whiteness*, and seek to redefine their own identity and that of their social group. This acceptance, however, does not mean a less active role in combating oppression. The process may involve addressing the questions, "What does it mean to be White?" "Who am I in relation to my *Whiteness*?" and "Who am I as a racial/cultural being?"

The feelings or affective elements may be existential in nature and involve feelings of disconnectedness, isolation, confusion, and loss. In other words, the person knows that he or she will never fully understand the minority experience but feels disconnected from the EuroAmerican group as well. In some ways, the *introspective phase* is similar in dynamics to the *dissonance phase*, in that both represent a transition from one perspective to another. The process used to answer the previous questions and to deal with the ensuing feelings may involve a searching, observing, and questioning attitude. Answers to these questions involve dialoging and observing one's own social group and actively creating and experiencing interactions with various minority group members as well.

6. *Integrative awareness phase:* Reaching this level of development is most characterized as (a) understanding the self as a racial/cultural being, (b) being aware of sociopolitical influences regarding racism, (c) appreciating racial/cultural diversity, and (d) becoming more committed toward eradicating oppression. A nonracist White EuroAmerican identity is formed, emerges, and becomes internalized. The person values multiculturalism, is comfortable around members of culturally different groups, and feels a strong connectedness with members of many groups. Most important, perhaps, is the inner sense of security and strength that needs to develop and that is needed to function in a society that is only marginally accepting of integrative, aware White persons.

7. *Commitment to antiracist action phase:* Someone once stated that the ultimate *White privilege* is the ability to acknowledge it but do nothing about it. This phase is most characterized by social action. There is likely to be a consequent change in behavior and an increased commitment toward eradicating oppression. Seeing "wrong" and actively working to "right" it requires moral fortitude and direct action. Objecting to racist jokes; trying to educate family, friends, neighbors, and coworkers about racial issues; and taking direct action

to eradicate racism in the schools and workplace and in social policy (often in direct conflict with other Whites) are examples of actions taken by individuals who achieve this status. Movement into this phase can be a lonely journey for Whites because they are oftentimes isolated by family, friends, and colleagues who do not understand their changed worldview. Strong pressures in society to not rock the boat, threats by family members that they will be disowned, avoidance by colleagues, threats of being labeled a troublemaker or not being promoted at work are all possible pressures for the White person to move back to an earlier phase of development. To maintain a nonracist identity requires Whites to become increasingly immunized to social pressures for conformance and to begin forming alliances with persons of color or other liberated Whites who become a second family to them. As can be seen, the struggle against individual, institutional, and societal racism is a monumental task in this society.

DEVELOPING A NONRACIST AND ANTIRACIST WHITE IDENTITY

I sometimes visualize the ongoing cycle of racism as a moving walkway at the airport. Active racist behavior is equivalent to walking fast on the conveyor belt. The person engaged in active racist behavior has identified with the ideology of White supremacy *and is moving with it. Passive racist behavior is equivalent to standing still on the walkway. No overt effort is being made, but the conveyor belt moves the bystanders along to the same destination as those who are actively walking. Some of the bystanders may feel the motion of the conveyor belt, see the active racists ahead of them, and choose to turn around, unwilling to go to the same destination as the White supremacists. But unless they are walking actively in the opposite direction at a speed faster than the conveyor belt — unless they are actively antiracist — they will find themselves carried along with the others. (Tatum, 1997, pp 11–12)*

What does this metaphor of racism tell about the difference between active and passive racism? What is the "destination" of the walkway? If it represents our society, can you describe what that destination looks like? What does the conveyor belt symbolize? Are you on the conveyor belt? Which direction are you traveling? Do you even feel the movement of the belt? What would it take for you to reverse directions? More importantly, how can you stop the movement of the conveyor belt? What changes would need to occur for you at the individual level to reverse directions? What changes would need to happen at the institutional and societal levels to stop or reverse the direction of the conveyor belt?

As repeatedly emphasized in earlier chapters, *White supremacy* must be seen through a larger prism of individual, institutional, and societal racism. All these elements conspire in such a manner as to avoid making the "invisible" visible, and thus directly or indirectly discourage honest racial dialogue and self-exploration. Let us briefly return to the "walkway" metaphor provided by Tatum (1997) in her classic book, *Why Are All the Black Kids Sitting Together in the Cafeteria?*

First, the walkway metaphor is a strong and powerful statement of the continuous and insidious nature of racism; it is ever-present, dynamic, and oftentimes invisible as it takes us on a journey to White supremacist notions, attitudes, beliefs, and behaviors. The visible actions of White supremacists moving quickly on the belt represent the overt racism that we're aware of; these forms we consciously condemn. The conveyor belt represents the invisible forces of society or the biased institutional policies, practices, and structures that control our everyday lives. From the moment of birth, we are placed on the conveyor belt, culturally conditioned, and socialized to believe that we are headed in "the right direction." For many White people, the movement of the belt is barely noticeable, and its movement remains hidden from conscious awareness. This allows White people to remain naïve and innocent about the harm their inaction imparts on people of color.

Second, as indicated by Tatum (1997), one need not be actively racist in order to be racist. The pace by which one walks with the flow of the conveyor belt determines the degree to which one consciously or unconsciously harbors White supremacist notions: (a) "active racists" who are aware and deliberate in beliefs and actions move quickly, (b) those slowly strolling may be unintentional racists, unaware of their biases and the direction they are taking, and (c) "passive racists" may choose not to walk at all. Despite choosing not to walk in the direction of the walkway, passive racists are, nevertheless, being moved in a direction that allows for racism to thrive. On a personal level, despite beliefs of justice, equity, and fairness, inaction on the walkway ultimately means that these individuals are also responsible for the oppression of others.

Third, most people of color are desperately trying to move or run in the opposite direction. The voices of people of color are filled with attempts to make well-intentioned Whites aware of the direction they are taking and aware of the harm they are inflicting on people of color. But they are hindered by many obstacles; well-intentioned White Americans who tell them they are going the wrong way and don't believe them; institutional policies and practices that put obstacles in their retreating path (institutional racism); and punishment from society for "not obeying the traffic rules"—a one-way street of bias and bigotry.

Fourth, despite limited success in battling the constant forces of racism, people of color are also slowly but surely being swept in a dangerous direction that has multiple implications for their psychological health, physical well-being, and standard of living. Walking at a fast pace or running in the opposite direction are never-ending activities that are exhausting and energy depleting for people of color. Worse yet, they are being trampled by the large numbers of well-intentioned White Americans moving in the opposite direction. Giving up or ultimately being swept to the end of the walkway means a life of oppression and subordination.

Last, the questions being posed to trainees are challenging. How do we motivate White Americans to (a) notice the subtle movement of the walkway (making the invisible visible), (b) discern the ominous direction it is taking (White racial supremacy), (c) take action by moving in the opposite direction (antiracism), and (d) stop the conveyor belt and/or reverse its direction (institutional and societal change)?

As indicated in the *White racial identity development* sections, becoming *nonracist* means soul searching, individual change, and working on the self; becoming *antiracist*, however, means taking personal action to end external racism that exists systemically and in the action of others. The invisibility of *White privilege* and *Whiteness* allow for denying the pain and suffering experienced by people of color, but more importantly, it absolves White Americans of personal responsibility for perpetuating injustice, and allows them to remain passive and inactive.

Principles of Prejudice Reduction

Although *White racial identity development* models tell us much about the characteristics most likely to be exhibited by individuals as they progress through these phases, they are very weak in giving guidance about how to develop a *nonracist White identity* (Helms, 2015). Possible answers seem to lie in the social-psychological literature about the basic principles or conditions needed to reduce prejudice through intergroup contact first formulated by Gordon Allport (1954) in his classic book *The Nature of Prejudice*. His work has been refined and expanded by other researchers and scholars (Aboud, 1988; Amir, 1969; Cook, 1962; Gaertner,

Rust, Dovidio, Bachman, & Anastasio, 1994; Jones, 1997). Sue (2003) has summarized these findings into the basic principles of prejudice reduction: (1) having intimate and close contact with others, (2) cooperation rather than competition on common tasks, (3) sharing mutual goals, (4) exchanging accurate information rather than stereotypes, (5) sharing an equal status relationship, (6) support for prejudice reduction by authorities and leaders, and (7) feeling a sense of connection and belonging with one another. To this we might add the contributions of *White racial identity development* theorists, who have indicated the importance of understanding oneself as a racial/cultural being. It has been found, for example, that a person's level of White racial awareness is predictive of his or her level of racism (Pope-Davis & Ottavi, 1994; Wang et al., 2003); the less aware that participants in research projects were of their White racial identity, the more likely they exhibited increased levels of racism.

The seven basic principles outlined above arose primarily through studies of how to reduce intergroup conflict and hostility, but several seem consistent with reducing personal prejudice through experiential learning and the acquisition of accurate information about other groups. Translating these principles into roles and activities for personal development has come from recommendations put forth by the American Psychological Association, Presidential Task Force on Preventing Discrimination and Promoting Diversity (2012), from the President's Initiative on Race (1998, 1999), from educators and trainers (Ponterotto et al., 2006; Young & Davis-Russell, 2002), and from studies on difficult racial dialogues (Sue, Lin, Torino, Capodilupo, & Rivera, 2009; Sue, Rivera, Capodilupo, Lin, & Torino, 2010).

Sue (2003) outlines five basic learning situations and activities, or principles, most likely to enhance change in developing a *nonracist White identity*.

Principle 1: Learn about People of Color from Sources within the Group

- You must experience and learn from as many sources as possible (not just the media or what your neighbor may say) in order to check out the validity of your assumptions and understanding.

- If you want to understand racism, White people may not be the most insightful or accurate sources. Acquiring information from persons of color allows you to understand the thoughts, hopes, fears, and aspirations from the perspective of people of color. It also acts as a counterbalance to the worldview expressed by White society about minority groups.

Principle 2: Learn from Healthy and Strong People of the Culture

- A balanced picture of racial/ethnic groups requires that you spend time with healthy and strong people of that culture. The mass media and our educational texts (written from the perspectives of EuroAmericans) frequently portray minority groups as uncivilized or pathological, or as criminals or delinquents.

- You must make an effort to fight such negative conditioning and ask yourself what are the desirable aspects of the culture, the history, and the people. This can come about only if you have contact with healthy representatives of that group.

- Since you seldom spend much intimate time with persons of color, you are likely to believe the societal projection of minorities as being law breakers and unintelligent, prone to violence, unmotivated, and uninterested in relating to the larger society.

- Frequent minority-owned businesses, and get to know the proprietors.

- Attend services at a variety of churches, synagogues, temples, and other places of worship to learn about different faiths and to meet religious leaders.

- Invite colleagues, coworkers, neighbors, or students of color to your home for dinner or a holiday.

- Live in an integrated or culturally diverse neighborhood, and attend neighborhood organizational meetings and attend/throw block parties.

- Form a community organization on valuing diversity, and invite local artists, authors, entertainers, politicians, and leaders of color to address your group.

- Attend street fairs, educational forums, and events put on by the community.

Principle 3: Learn from Experiential Reality

- Although listening to readings, attending theater, and going to museums are helpful to increase understanding, you must supplement your factual understanding with the experiential reality of the groups you hope to understand. These experiences, however, must be something carefully planned to be successful.

- It may be helpful to identify a cultural guide: someone from the culture who is willing to help you understand his or her group; someone willing to introduce you to new experiences; someone willing to help you process your thoughts, feelings, and behaviors. This allows you to more easily obtain valid information on issues of race and racism.

Principle 4: Learn from Constant Vigilance of Your Biases and Fears

- Your life must become a "have to" in being constantly vigilant to manifestations of bias in both yourself and the people around you.

- Learn how to ask sensitive racial questions of your minority friends, associates, and acquaintances. Persons subjected to racism seldom get a chance to talk about it with a nondefensive and nonguilty person from the majority group.

- Most minority individuals are more than willing to respond, to enlighten, and to share *if they sense that your questions and concerns are sincere and motivated by a desire to learn and serve the group.*

Principle 5: Learn from Being Committed to Personal Action against Racism

- Dealing with racism means a personal commitment to action. It means interrupting other White Americans when they make racist remarks, tell racist jokes, or engage in racist actions, even if this is embarrassing or frightening.

- It means noticing the possibility for direct action against bias and discrimination in your everyday life: in the family, at work, and in the community.

- It means taking initiative to make sure that minority candidates are fairly considered in your place of employment, advocating to your children's teachers to include multicultural material in the curriculum, volunteering in community organizations to have them consider multicultural issues, and contributing to and working for campaigns of political candidates who will advocate for social justice.

- The journey to developing a White nonracist identity is not an easy path to travel. Remember, racial identity and cultural competence are intimately linked to one another. Becoming a culturally competent helping professional involves more than "book learning"; it requires both experiential learning and taking personal action. Are you ready for the challenge?

REFLECTION AND DISCUSSION QUESTIONS

1. Do these suggestions and strategies make sense to you? Are there others that come to mind?

2. What would make it difficult for you to personally implement these suggestions? What barriers stand in the way? For example, what would make it difficult for you to interrupt a stranger or even a family member when a racist or sexist joke is made?

3. Have you ever been in a situation where you were the only White person in an activity or event full of Black, Asian, or Latino/a people? What feelings did you have? How did you think? Were you uncomfortable or fearful?

4. What would you need in the way of support or personal moral courage to move toward developing a White nonracist identity?

 ## IMPLICATIONS FOR CLINICAL PRACTICE

1. Ultimately, the effectiveness of White therapists is related to their ability to overcome sociocultural conditioning and to make their *Whiteness* visible.

2. Accept the fact that racism is a basic and integral part of U.S. life and permeates all aspects of our culture and institutions. Know that as a White person you are not immune.

3. Understand that the level of *White racial identity development* in a cross-cultural encounter (e.g., working with minorities, responding to multicultural training) affects the process and outcome of an interracial relationship (including counseling/therapy).

4. Work on accepting your own *Whiteness*, but define it in a nondefensive, nonracist, and antiracist manner.

5. Spend time with healthy and strong people from another culture or racial group.

6. Know that becoming culturally aware and competent comes through lived experience and reality.

7. Attend cultural events, meetings, and activities led by minority communities. This allows you to hear from church leaders, to attend community celebrations, and to participate in open forums so that you may sense the strengths of the community, observe leadership in action, personalize your understanding, and develop new social relationships.

8. When around persons of color, pay attention to feelings, thoughts, and assumptions that you have when race-related situations present themselves.

9. Dealing with racism means a personal commitment to action.

SUMMARY

"What does it mean to be White?" is often an uncomfortable and perplexing question for White Americans. Exploring the basis of this discomfort and its meaning is important for cultural competence in mental health practice. Being a White person in this society means chronic exposure to ethnocentric monoculturalism as manifested in *White supremacy*. Research suggests that it is nearly impossible for anyone to avoid inheriting the racial biases, prejudices, misinformation, deficit portrayals, and stereotypes of their forebears. If White helping professionals are ever able to become effective multicultural counselors or therapists, they must free themselves from the cultural conditioning of their past and move toward the development of a nonracist and *antiracist White identity*.

White racial identity development models have been found to be helpful in describing how majority group members go through a process of racial awakening that has direct meaning to multicultural counseling. Two of the influential models are those presented by Rita Hardiman and Janet Helms. It has been found that the level of White racial identity awareness is predictive of racism and internal and interpersonal characteristics. The less aware subjects studied were of their White identity, the more likely they were to exhibit higher levels of racism, while the greater their White identity development, the greater their levels of multicultural counseling competence, the higher their positive opinions toward diverse groups, and the better their ability to form therapeutic alliances with clients of color.

A descriptive model of *White racial identity development* identifies a seven-phase process by which Whites become increasingly aware of themselves as racial/cultural beings: (1) naiveté, (2) conformity, (3) dissonance, (4) resistance and immersion, (5) introspective, (6) integrative awareness, and (7) commitment to antiracist action. Becoming *nonracist* means soul searching, individual change, and working on the self; becoming *antiracist*, however, means taking personal action to end external racism that exists systemically and in the actions of others. Five basic principles are provided to facilitate racial/cultural awareness. Learn (1) from the groups you hope to understand, (2) from healthy and strong people of the culture, (3) from experiential reality, (4) from constant vigilance of fears and biases, and (5) from being committed to anti-bias action.

GLOSSARY TERMS

Antiracist white identity

Commitment to antiracist action phase

Conformity phase

Dissonance phase

Ego statuses

Hardiman White racial identity development

Helms White racial identity development

Information processing strategies

Integrative awareness phase

Introspective phase

Naiveté phase

Nonracist white identity

Resistance and immersion phase

Unintentional racism

White privilege

White racial identity development

White racial identity development descriptive model

White supremacy

Whiteness

REFERENCES

Aboud, F. E. (1988). *Children and prejudice.* Cambridge, MA: Basil Blackwell.

Allen, A. (1994, May 29). Black unlike me: Confessions of a white man confused by racial etiquette. *Washington Post*, p. C1.

Allport, G. W. (1954). *The nature of prejudice.* Reading, MA: Addison-Wesley.

American Psychological Association, Presidential Task Force on Preventing Discrimination and Promoting Diversity. (2012). *Dual pathways to a better America: Preventing discrimination and* promoting diversity. Washington, DC: American Psychological Association.

Amir, Y. (1969). Contact hypothesis in ethnic relations. *Psychological Bulletin, 71*, 319–342.

Bell, L. A. (2002). Sincere fictions: The pedagogical challenges of preparing White teachers for multicultural classrooms. *Equity and Excellence in Education, 35*, 236–244.

Bell, L. A. (2003). Telling tales: What stories can teach us about racism. *Race, Ethnicity and Education, 6*, 3–28.

Blauner, B. (1993). But things are much worse for the negro people: Race and radicalism in my life and work. In J. H. Stanfield II (Ed.), *A history of race relations research: First-generation recollections* (pp. 1–36). Newbury Park, CA: Sage.

Boysen, G. A. (2010). Integrating implicit bias into counselor education. *Counselor Education and Supervision, 49,* 210–226.

Carter, R. T. (1990). The relationship between racism and racial identity among White Americans: An exploratory investigation. *Journal of Counseling and Development, 69,* 46–50.

Cokley, K. (2006). The impact of racialized schools and racist (mis)education on African American students' academic identity. In M. G. Constantine & D. W. Sue (Eds.), *Addressing Racism* (pp. 127–144). Hoboken, NJ: Wiley.

Cook, S. W. (1962). The systematic study of socially significant events: A strategy for social research. *Journal of Social Issues, 18,* 66–84.

Falender, C. A., Shafranske, E. P., & Falicov, E. J. (2014). *Multiculturalism and diversity in clinical supervision.* Washington, DC: American Psychological Association.

Gaertner, S. L., Rust, M. C., Dovidio, J. F., Bachman, B. A., & Anastasio, P. A. (1994). The contact hypothesis: The role of common ingroup identity on reducing intergroup bias. *Small Group Research, 25,* 224–249.

Gallardo, M. E., & Ivey, A. (2014). What I see could be me. In M. E. Gallardo (Ed.), *Developing cultural humility* (pp. 223–263.). Thousand Oaks, CA: Sage

Hanna, F. J., Talley, W. B., & Guindon, M. H. (2000). The power of perception: Toward a model of cultural oppression and liberation. *Journal of Counseling and Development, 78,* 430–446.

Hardiman, R. (1982). *White identity development: A process oriented model for describing the racial consciousness of White Americans.* (Doctoral dissertation). *Dissertation Abstracts International,* *43,* 104A. (University Microfilms No. 82–10330).

Hays, P. A. (2014). Finding a place in the multicultural revolution. In M. E. Gallardo (Ed.), *Developing cultural humility* (pp. 49–59). Thousand Oaks, CA: Sage.

Helms, J. E. (1984). Toward a theoretical explanation of the effects of race on counseling: A Black and White model. *Counseling Psychologist, 12,* 153–165.

Helms, J. E. (1990). *Black and White racial identity: Theory, research, and practice.* Westport, CT: Greenwood Press.

Helms, J. E. (1994). How multiculturalism obscures racial factors in the therapy process: Comment on Ridley et al. (1994), Sodowsky et al. (1994), Ottavi et al. (1994), and Thompson et al. (1994). *Journal of Counseling Psychology, 41,* 162–165.

Helms, J. E. (1995). An update of Helms's White and people of color racial identity models. In J. G. Ponterotto, J. M. Casas, L. A. Suzuki, & C. M. Alexander (Eds.), *Handbook of multicultural counseling* (pp. 181–191). Thousand Oaks, CA: Sage.

Helms, J. E. (2015). Taking action against racism in a post-racism era: The origins and almost demise of an idea. *Counseling Psychologist, 43,* 138–145.

Helms, J. E., & Carter, R. T. (1990). Development of the White racial identity attitude inventory. In J. E. Helms (Ed.), *Black and White racial identity: Theory, research, and practice* (pp. 67–80). Westport, CT: Greenwood Press.

Jones, J. M. (1997). *Prejudice and racism* (2nd ed.). Washington, DC: McGraw-Hill.

Katz, J. (1985). The sociopolitical nature of counseling. *Counseling Psychologist, 13,* 615–624.

McIntosh, P. (1989, July/August). White privilege: Unpacking the invisible knapsack. *Peace and Freedom,* pp. 8–10.

Miville, M. L., Darlington, P., Whitlock, B., & Mulligan, T. (2005). Integrating identities: The relationship of racial, gender, and ego identities among White college students. *Journal of College Student Development, 46*, 157–175.

Neville, H. A., Awad, G. H., Brooks, J. E., Flores, M. P., and Bluemel, J. (2013). Color-blind racial ideology: Theory, training, and measurement implications in psychology. *American Psychologist, 68*, 455–466.

Perry, S. P., Dovidio, J. F., Murphy, M. C., & van Ryn, M. (2015). The joint effect of bias awareness and self-reported prejudice on intergroup anxiety and intentions for intergroup contact. *Cultural Diversity and Ethnic Minority Psychology, 21*, 89–96.

Ponterotto, J. G. (1988). Racial consciousness development among White counselors' trainees: A stage model. *Journal of Multicultural Counseling and Development, 16*, 146–156.

Ponterotto, J. G., Utsey, S. O., & Pedersen, P. B. (2006). *Preventing prejudice: A guide for counselors, educators, and parents.* Thousand Oaks, CA: Sage.

Pope-Davis, D. B., & Ottavi, T. M. (1994). Examining the association between self-reported multicultural counseling competencies and demographic and educational variables among counselors. *Journal of Counseling and Development, 72*, 651–654.

President's Initiative on Race. (1998). *One America in the twenty-first century.* Washington, DC: U.S. Government Printing Office.

President's Initiative on Race. (1999). *Pathways to one America in the 21st century.* Washington, DC: U.S. Government Printing Office.

Ridley, C. R. (1995). *Overcoming unintentional racism in counseling and therapy.* Thousand Oaks, CA: Sage.

Rowe, W. (2006). White racial identity: Science, faith and pseudoscience. *Journal of Multicultural Counseling and Development. 34*, 235–243.

Rowe, W., Bennett, S., & Atkinson, D. R. (1994). White racial identity models: A critique and alternative proposal. *Counseling Psychologist, 22*, 120–146.

Spanierman, L. B., Poteat, V. V., Beer, A. M., & Armstrong, P. I. (2006). Psychosocial costs of racism to Whites: Exploring patterns through cluster analysis. *Journal of Counseling Psychology, 53*, 434–441.

Spanierman, L. B., Todd, N. R., & Anderson, C. J. (2009). Psychosocial costs of racism to Whites: Understanding patterns among university students. *Journal of Counseling Psychology, 56*, 239–252.

Sue, D. W. (2003). *Overcoming our racism: The journey to liberation.* San Francisco, CA: Jossey-Bass.

Sue, D. W. (2004). Whiteness and ethnocentric monoculturalism: Making the invisible visible. *American Psychologist, 59*, 761–769.

Sue, D. W. (2010). *Microaggressions in everyday life: Race, gender, and sexual orientation.* Hoboken, NJ: Wiley.

Sue, D. W. (2011). The challenge of White dialectics: Making the "invisible" visible. *Counseling Psychologist, 39*, 414–423.

Sue, D. W. (2013). Race talk: The psychology of racial dialogues. *American Psychologist, 68*, 663–672.

Sue, D. W. (2015). *Race talk and the conspiracy of silence: Understanding and facilitating difficult dialogues on race.* Hoboken, NJ: Wiley.

Sue, D. W., Lin, A. I., Torino, G. C., Capodilupo, C. M., & Rivera, D. P. (2009). Racial microaggressions and difficult dialogues on race in the classroom. *Cultural Diversity and Ethnic Minority Psychology, 15*, 183–190.

Sue, D. W., Rivera, D. P., Capodilupo, C. M., Lin, A. I., & Torino, G. C. (2010). Racial dialogues and White trainee fears: Implications for education and training. *Cultural Diversity and Ethnic Minority Psychology, 16*, 206–214.

Sue, D. W., & Sue, D. (1990). *Counseling the culturally different: Theory and practice.* New York, NY: Wiley.

Tatum, B. D. (1992). Talking about race, learning about racism: The application of racial identity development theory in the classroom. *Harvard Educational Review, 62,* 1–24.

Tatum, B. D. (1997). *Why are all the Black kids sitting together in the cafeteria?* New York, NY: Basic Books.

Todd, N. R., & Abrams, E. M. (2011). White dialectics: A new framework for theory, research and practice with White students. *Counseling Psychologist, 39,* 353–395.

Toporek, R. L., & Worthington, R. L. (2014). Integrating service learning and difficult dialogues pedagogy to advance social justice training. *Counseling Psychologist, 46,* 919–945.

Utsey, S. O., Gernat, C. A., & Hammar, L. (2005). Examining white counselor trainees' reactions to racial issues in counseling and supervision dyads. *Counseling Psychologist, 33,* 449–478.

Vinson, T., & Neimeyer, G. J. (2000). The relationship between racial identity development and multicultural counseling competence. *Journal of Multicultural Counseling and Development, 28,* 177–192.

Vinson, T., & Neimeyer, G. J. (2003). The relationship between racial identity development and multicultural counseling competence: A second look. *Journal of Multicultural Counseling and Development, 31,* 262–277.

Wang, Y., Davidson, M. M., Yakushko, O. F., Savoy, H. B., Tan, J. A., & Bleier, J. K. (2003). The scale of ethnocultural empathy: Development, validation, and reliability. *Journal of Counseling Psychology, 50,* 221–234.

Winter, S. (1977). Rooting out racism. *Issues in Radical Therapy, 17,* 24–30.

Young, G., & Davis-Russell, E. (2002). The vicissitudes of cultural competence: Dealing with difficult classroom dialogue. In E. Davis-Russell (Ed.), *The California School of Professional Psychology handbook of multicultural education, research, intervention, and training* (pp. 37–53). San Francisco, CA: Jossey-Bass.

SECTION TWO

Multicultural Counseling and Specific Populations

While Section One addressed common principles, practices, and issues of multicultural counseling and therapy that are often applicable across groups, this section is divided into four parts that recognize the unique challenges and group differences between socially marginalized groups in our society. Section Two was created for several reasons.

1. First, we recognize that while issues of culture-conflict, prejudice, and discrimination occur to almost all socially devalued groups in our society, the history of each group and the challenges that confront it are unique. The specific challenges confronting people of color, for example, may differ substantially from those that confront women, people who live in poverty, and religious minorities.

2. Second is the recognition that the terms *multiculturalism*, *diversity*, and *multicultural counseling competence* are broad terms that include race, gender, social class, religious orientation, sexual orientation, and many other sociodemographic classifications in our society. To not acknowledge this fact is to render certain groups invisible, thereby invalidating their existence as unique.

3. Third, numerous instructors continue to find the coverage of specific populations helpful to their students. The extensive coverage in Section Two allows instructors freedom to use all of the chapters in this section or to selectively choose those that fit their course requirements.

4. Last, but equally important, is our guideline on applying an open and flexible assessment process that avoids stereotypical and rigid therapeutic applications while using the information in the population-specific chapters (see Part V). Section Two contains the following four parts:

- Part V: Understanding Specific Populations

- Part VI: Counseling Marginalized Racial/Ethnic Group Populations

- Part VII: Counseling and Special Circumstances Involving Ethnic Populations

- Part VIII: Counseling and Special Circumstances Involving Other Multicultural Populations

PART V

Understanding Specific Populations

Culturally Competent Assessment

David Sue and Diane M. Sue

Chapter Objectives

1. Understand the many variables that influence assessment, diagnosis, and case conceptualization.

2. Develop awareness of the dangers of stereotyping and the importance of appreciating the individuality of each client.

3. Learn how cultural competence prevents diagnostic errors.

4. Understand contextual and *collaborative assessment*.

5. Understand *DSM-5* cultural formulations.

6. Learn how to infuse cultural competence into standard clinical assessments.

Significant portions of this chapter are adapted from D. Sue & D. M. Sue (2008), *Foundations of counseling and psychotherapy: Evidence-based practices in a diverse society.* Hoboken, NJ: Wiley.

"Bias is a very real issue," said Francis Lu, a psychiatrist at the University of California at San Francisco. "We don't talk about it—it's upsetting. We see ourselves as unbiased and rational and scientific.". . .Psychiatrist Heather Hall, a colleague of Lu's, said she had to correct the diagnoses of about 40 minorities over a two-year period. . . Advocates for cultural competence say both clinicians and patients are unwilling to acknowledge that race might matter: "In a cross-cultural situation, race or ethnicity is the white elephant in the room," said Lillian Comas-Diaz. (Vedantam, 2005, p. 1)

Accurate assessment, diagnosis, and case conceptualization, key prerequisites to the provision of appropriate treatment, are dependent upon the characteristics, values, and worldviews of both the therapist and the client (American Psychological Association, Presidential Task Force on Evidence-Based Practice, 2006). Most clinicians recognize that client variables, such as socioeconomic status, gender, and racial or cultural background, can significantly affect assessment, diagnosis, and conceptualization. However, we often forget that as clinicians we are not "objective" observers of our clients. Instead, we each have our own set of beliefs, values, and theoretical assumptions. To reduce error, a mental health professional must be aware of potential biases that can affect clinical judgment, including the influence of *stereotypes* (i.e., generalizations based on limited or inaccurate information). Unfortunately, our current methods of assessment and diagnosis often do not adequately consider these factors, especially with respect to therapist variables. Additionally, many of our instruments and processes for assessment and diagnosis do not address client variables in a meaningful manner.

If we are to follow best-practice guidelines and the ethical standards of our profession, we must consider broad background factors, including the worldview of each client. How can this be accomplished? First and foremost, it is critical that we operate from the awareness that a thorough understanding of our clients' beliefs, expectations, and experiences is an essential aspect of the assessment and case conceptualization process. We believe that *culturally competent assessment* occurs through a combination of evidence-based guidelines for assessment and a cultural competency framework.

In this chapter we will cover (a) the impact of therapist variables on assessment and diagnosis, emphasizing the dangers of stereotyping; (b) ways in which culturally competent practices can reduce diagnostic errors; (c) contextual and *collaborative assessment*; and (d) ideas for infusing cultural competence into standard intake and assessment procedures. Careful consideration of these factors when using evidence-based guidelines to conduct assessment will ensure that clinicians form an accurate and complete picture of the problems and issues facing each client. We will demonstrate how *culturally competent assessment* should be conducted—in a manner that considers the unique background, values, and beliefs of each client. We hope that as you proceed through the final chapters of this book—chapters describing general characteristics and special challenges faced by various oppressed populations—you will remember that we are providing this information so you will have some knowledge of the specific research and the sociopolitical and cultural factors that *might* be pertinent to a client or family from the population being discussed. However, it is critical that when counseling diverse clientele you actively work to avoid succumbing to *stereotypes* (i.e., basing your opinions of the client on limited information or prior assumptions). Instead, your task is to develop an in-depth understanding of each client, taking into consideration the individual's unique personal background and worldview. By doing this, you will be in a position to develop an individually tailored treatment plan that effectively addresses presenting problems in a culturally sensitive manner.

THERAPIST VARIABLES AFFECTING DIAGNOSIS

Assessment is best conceptualized as a two-way street, influenced by both client and therapist variables. Because humans filter observations through their own set of values and beliefs, we begin our discussion by focusing on therapist self-assessment.

> *A treatment team observing a clinical interview erupted in laughter when the foreign-born psychiatric resident attempted to find out what caused or precipitated the client's problem. In poor and halting English, the resident asked, "How brought you to the hospital?" The patient responded, "I came by car." (Chambliss, 2000, pp. 186)*

Later, during the case conference, the psychiatric resident attributed the patient's response to concrete thinking, a characteristic sometimes displayed by people with schizophrenia. The rest of the treatment team, however, believed the response was due to a poorly worded question. This example illustrates what can occur when therapists focus solely on the client without considering the impact of therapist variables. Personal characteristics, attitudes, and beliefs can (and do) influence how assessment is conducted and what is assessed, as well as interpretations of clinical data. Counselors and other mental health professionals are often unaware of how strongly personal beliefs can affect clinical judgment.

In one study, 108 psychotherapists read an intake report involving a male client whose sexuality was revealed through references to his previous and present partners; all clinical data were identical with the exception of references to sexual orientation. Details suggesting heterosexual or same-sex orientation had little impact on clinical ratings; however, therapists given data suggesting the client was bisexual were more likely to "detect" emotional disturbance. The researchers concluded that these differing diagnostic perceptions were the result of *stereotypes* of bisexual men being "confused and conflicted" (Mohr, Weiner, Chopp, & Wong, 2009).

In conducting *culturally competent assessment*, we must not only be aware of the influence of *stereotypes* but also be alert for common diagnostic errors such as the following:

- *Confirmatory strategy:* Searching for evidence or information that supports one's hypothesis and ignoring data that are inconsistent with this perspective. When working with clients, mental health professionals might search for information that confirms beliefs based on their worldviews or theoretical orientation (Osmo & Rosen, 2002). In a similar manner, our views or *stereotypes* of the characteristics and values of ethnic and other diverse groups can act as blinders when working with clients from these groups. Counselors can combat this type of error by working cooperatively with clients to understand and interpret the presenting problem. Diagnostic accuracy is increased when clinicians test any hypotheses they formulate with the client. When determining whether these possible interpretations resonate with the client, it is critical that the therapist be open to both confirmatory and disconfirmatory information.

- *Attribution error:* The therapist places an undue emphasis on internal causes regarding a client's problem. For example, a therapist might interpret a problem as stemming from a personal characteristic of the client rather than considering environmental or sociocultural explanations such as poverty, discrimination, or oppression. Attribution error can be reduced by performing a thorough assessment that includes consideration of sociocultural and environmental factors and testing hypotheses regarding extrapsychic (i.e., residing outside the person) as well as intrapsychic (residing within the person) influences.

- *Judgmental heuristics:* Commonly used quick-decision rules. These can be problematic because they short-circuit our ability to engage in self-correction. For example, if we quickly identify our client as "defensive" or "overreactive," these characterizations will reduce our attempt to gather additional or contradictory information. In one study (Stewart, 2004), 300 clinicians received identical vignettes regarding hypothetical clients, with the only difference being the clients' stated birth order. Birth order influenced the judgment of the clinicians, including the expected prognosis for the client, even though there is little research support for personality differences associated with birth order. These kinds of beliefs or spontaneous associations occur automatically and need to be identified and addressed. Therapists can reduce this tendency by acknowledging the existence of *judgmental heuristics*, questioning the basis for quick decisions, assessing additional factors, and evaluating the accuracy of opinions about clients.

- *Diagnostic overshadowing:* The client's problem receives inadequate treatment because attention is diverted to a more salient characteristic. For example, individuals who are gay or lesbian can have a number of psychological issues that have nothing to do with their sexual orientation. In *diagnostic overshadowing*, a therapist might perceive the presenting problem as related to conflicts over sexual orientation and fail to address other critical issues. Other salient characteristics are race, religious affiliation, and visible disabilities.

We must be aware of our beliefs and values as we work with clients and their specific presenting problems. We are all susceptible to making errors in clinical judgment during assessment; therefore it is important to adopt a tentative stance and test out our observations. Those who remember that errors in judgment are possible can reduce their effect by using a self-corrective model. In the next section, for example, we discuss why it is important to consider whether the current focus on cultural competence may, in fact, be creating new sources of errors—errors resulting from applying cultural information in a stereotypic, "one size fits all" manner.

CULTURAL COMPETENCE AND PREVENTING DIAGNOSTIC ERRORS

> *Regina, a mixed-race (Asian/White) student felt that her therapist had "this kind of book-learned. . .image of some kind of immigrant family, instead of. . .an emotional understanding of what it's like to be Asian in [specific small city, in the intermountain West]." (Chang & Berk, 2009, p. 527)*

"You shouldn't expect a lot of African American clients to be in touch with their feelings and do some real intrapsychic work. Sometimes you have to be more directive and problem-focused in dealing with Black people." (Constantine & Sue, 2007, p. 146)

Given the growing multicultural nature of the United States population, all mental health organizations now promote cultural competence and the ability to work effectively with multicultural clients. However, is it possible that this focus on cultural differences is creating unintended consequences? Is the emphasis on understanding cultural factors leading to problems such as stereotyping or the blind application of cultural information? The two previous examples illustrate the problems that can occur when general cultural information is applied to clients without assessing for individual differences. Surprisingly, in the second case, the speaker was a supervisor giving *stereotype*-based advice to her supervisee.

Multicultural awareness can, in fact, lead to *diagnostic overshadowing* if a clinician's attention to race or other diversity characteristics results in neglect of important aspects of the client (Vontress & Jackson, 2004). This tendency is increased in workshops and classes that focus primarily on the memorization of cultural information (Kissinger, 2014). As clinicians working with diverse populations, we need to consider all aspects of each client's life and not automatically assume that presenting problems are based on racial or diversity issues. In fact, it would be irresponsible for a clinician to focus on a client's diversity or environmental stressors when there are other significant concerns (Weinrach & Thomas, 2004).

Some mental health professionals have argued that the emphasis on culture and the development of culture-specific approaches have led to fragmentation, confusion, and controversy in the field of counseling and psychotherapy. Diversity training has been accused of producing "professionally sanctioned stereotyping," in which the therapist gives primary consideration to cultural attributes rather than focusing on understanding the uniqueness and life circumstances of the individual client (Freitag, Ottens, & Gross, 1999; D. W. Sue & D. Sue, 2013). Although it is important to understand group-specific differences, it is equally critical that we avoid a "cookbook" approach, in which the characteristics of different groups are memorized and applied to all clients who belong to a specific group (Lee, 2006).

Do guidelines for increasing cultural competence (e.g., increasing knowledge about different cultural groups and developing multicultural clinical skills) contribute to assessment errors, such as confirmatory bias, *diagnostic overshadowing*, or stereotyping? These errors certainly can happen and are most likely to occur when clinicians fail to use self-correcting strategies or fail to consider the individuality of each client. It is our belief that effective *culturally competent assessment* can, in fact, minimize the dangers of stereotyping or placing inordinate weight on race or other diversity issues.

Cultural competence is defined in different ways. We will use the definition focusing on the following three components: (a) self-awareness (i.e., self-reflection and awareness of one's values and biases); (b) knowledge of culturally diverse groups (e.g., marginalized status, characteristics, strengths, norms, and values); and (c) specific clinical skills, including the ability to generate a wide variety of verbal and nonverbal helping responses, form a *therapeutic alliance*, and intervene at the individual, group, institutional, and societal levels. We believe that appropriate use of these aspects of cultural competence can prevent diagnostic and treatment errors due to inaccurate assumptions and *stereotypes*.

Cultural Competence: Self-Awareness

Self-awareness is important with respect to both cultural competency and evidence-based practice. Therapists may be unaware that *stereotypes* are affecting their views and/or responses to clients or that differences between themselves and their clients are affecting the therapeutic process. For example, studies have found that mental health professionals may pathologize clients who display nontraditional gender role behavior (Seem & Johnson, 1998) and may rate female clients as less competent than males (Danzinger & Welfel, 2000).

Such judgments (or inferential errors) constitute deviations from cultural competence and the evidence-based practice model of self-reflection and awareness regarding the impact of one's values and beliefs. Identifying one's biases or taking the time to self-reflect can help reduce such errors. Questions such as "Which of my identities allow me to experience privilege?" "Which identities expose me to oppression?" and "How do I feel about these experiences?" can help clinicians reflect on how their own backgrounds and experiences have shaped their worldviews (Singh & Chun, 2010, p. 36).

Further, we need to develop an awareness of our assessment processes and identify our values, theoretical orientation, and beliefs about different groups whose social, cultural, or ethnic backgrounds differ from our own. We might ask such questions as "Do I hold assumptions about gender roles, sexual orientation, older individuals, political philosophy, or 'healthy' family structure that may influence my clinical judgment?" "Do I hold certain *stereotypes* or impressions of the client or the cultural groups to which the client belongs?" Such self-assessment is a necessary step in working with clients who differ from us and is an important component of counselor competence (Ridley, Mollen, & Kelly, 2011).

Cultural Competence: Knowledge

The knowledge component of cultural competence involves the awareness of different worldviews (e.g., that the majority of cultures in the world have a collectivistic and interdependent orientation; that the structure of some families is hierarchical in nature). Such knowledge is crucial in working with ethnic minority populations. In our special-population chapters, you will encounter descriptions such as the following:

- African American families often show adaptability in family roles, strong kinship bonds, and a strong religious orientation.

- American Indian/Native American and Alaska Native families are often structured with the extended family as the basic family unit; children are frequently raised by aunts, uncles, and grandparents who live in separate households.

- Asian American families are often hierarchical and patriarchal in structure, with males typically having higher status than females.

- Latina/o American families tend to strongly value family unity (*familismo*). The extended family can include not only relatives but also godparents and close friends.

This type of cultural knowledge is useful in helping counselors understand family patterns commonly seen among different ethnic minority populations; such information can be particularly helpful when patterns differ from the family and relationship structure typical of White American families. However, these descriptions are "modal" cultural characteristics and may or may not be applicable to a particular client. Knowledge also involves the awareness that significant within-group differences can exist—individuals can vary, for example, in degree of acculturation, level of identification with cultural values, and unique personal experiences.

Cultural information should not be applied rigidly; it is necessary to determine the degree of fit between general cultural information and the individual client in front of us. Gone (2009), for example, points out that it is not enough to know that a client is American Indian; you need to ask, "What kind of Indian are you?" In other words, you need to learn what tribe the client is affiliated with (if any), the nature of connection with the tribe, and, if the client is closely connected, the particular values and practices of the tribal culture. Among ethnic minorities, within- and between-group differences are quite large—some individuals and families are quite acculturated, while others retain a more traditional cultural orientation. Cultural differences, such as the degree of assimilation, socioeconomic background, family experiences, and educational level, affect each individual in a unique manner.

Knowledge of cultural values associated with specific groups can help us generate hypotheses about the manner in which a client (or family members) might view a disorder. However, the accuracy of such cultural hypotheses must be assessed for each client. Thus it is critical that we communicate with the client in order to confirm or disconfirm any hypotheses generated from our cultural "knowledge." In our opinion, the cultural competence component of "knowledge" requires not only that we be open to the worldview of others, but that we take care to remember that every client has a unique life story.

Cultural Competence: Multicultural Skills

The multicultural skills component of cultural competence requires that counselors effectively apply a variety of helping skills when forming a *therapeutic alliance*. As discussed in our chapter on evidence-based practice, it is important to individualize the choice of helping skills and avoid a blind application of techniques to all situations and all populations. Our manner of developing an effective therapeutic bond will differ from individual to individual and may differ from ethnic group to ethnic group. It is important to individualize relationship skills and to consistently evaluate the effectiveness of our verbal and nonverbal interactions with the client.

Research-based information regarding ethnic minorities (e.g., African Americans prefer an egalitarian therapeutic relationship; Asian Americans prefer a more formal relationship and concrete suggestions from the counselor; Latina/o Americans do better with a more personal relationship with the counselor; American Indians/Native American and Alaska Natives prefer a relaxed, client-centered listening style) can alert counselors to possible variations in therapeutic style that may enhance therapeutic progress. However, the applicability of the information needs to be evaluated for each client. The therapist's task is to help clients identify strategies for dealing with problems within cultural constraints and to develop the skills to negotiate cultural differences with the larger society. To achieve this, the counselor must sometimes be willing to adopt a variety of helping modes, such as advisor, consultant, and advocate.

In summary, errors in assessment can occur because of biases, mistakes in thinking, and *stereotypes* held by the clinician. In the past, assessment practices focused only on the client; potential counselor biases or inaccurate assumptions were not taken into consideration. It is now clear that effective assessment requires that therapist characteristics also be considered. Do cultural competency guidelines contribute to *stereotypes*? Some mental health practitioners believe that this is the case. However, we would argue precisely the opposite. If used appropriately, cultural competency and evidence-based practice guidelines that focus on awareness of one's values and biases, appropriate use of cultural knowledge, and the value of understanding the unique background and experience of each client help *prevent* stereotyping.

CONTEXTUAL AND COLLABORATIVE ASSESSMENT

Self-awareness is an important first step in reducing errors in multicultural assessment. However, this is only one part of the equation. Only through close collaboration with the client can we accurately identify the specific issues involved in the presenting problem and eliminate the blind application of cultural knowledge. This is best accomplished with a *collaborative approach* in which clients are given opportunities to share their beliefs, perspectives, and expectations, as well as their explanations of problems. If a client's belief about the presenting problem differs from that of the therapist, treatment based only on the therapist's views is likely to be ineffective. Here we will share some approaches a therapist might use to introduce the assessment and case conceptualization process in a way that facilitates dialogue and a collaborative relationship.

> *What we are going to do today is gather information about you and the problem that brings you in for counseling. In doing so, I'll need your help. In therapy we'll work together to decide what concerns to address and what solutions you feel comfortable with. Some of the questions I ask may seem very personal, but they are necessary to get a clear picture of what may be going on in your life. As I mentioned before, everything that we discuss is confidential, with the exceptions that we already went over. I will also ask about your family and other relationships and about your values and beliefs, since they might be related to your concerns or might help us decide the best strategies to use in therapy. Sometimes our difficulties are not just due to personal*

issues but are also due to expectations from our parents, friends, or society. The questions I'll be asking will help us put together a more complete picture of what might be happening with you and what might be causing the symptoms you came here to address. When we get to that point, we can talk together to see if my ideas about what might be going on seem to be on the right track. If there are any important issues I don't bring up, please be sure to let me know. Do you have any questions before we begin?

Assessment and diagnosis are critical elements in the process of devising a treatment plan. An introduction such as the one just presented helps set the stage for a collaborative and contextual intake interview. Clients are informed that family, environmental, and social-cultural influences will be explored. Many clinical assessments and interviews do not consider these factors and, therefore, must be modified. To remedy this shortcoming, we stress the importance of both the *collaborative approach*, in which the client and the therapist work together to construct an accurate definition of the problem, and the *contextual viewpoint*, which acknowledges that both the client and the therapist are embedded in systems such as family, work, and culture. These perspectives are gaining support within various mental health professions. For example, ethical principles regarding informed consent about therapy emphasize the need to give clients the information necessary to make sound decisions and, thus, be collaborators in the therapy process (Behnke, 2004).

The importance of collaboration was also stressed in the report of the President's New Freedom Commission on Mental Health (2003), in which clients are described as "consumers" and "partners" in the planning, selection, and evaluation of services. As we have already discussed, contextualism is also important: recognizing that both therapist and client operate from their own experiences and worldviews. Just as clients may have socialization experiences or experiences with prejudice or discrimination that play a role in their presenting concerns, therapists may hold worldviews or have had experiences that influence their perceptions of the client or the client's issues.

Karen Seeley (2004) is a mental health practitioner who describes herself as a "White, middle-class North American therapist." She recognized that she differed from ethnic minority clients in terms of culture, nationality, race, and personal history and that these differences could inhibit communication in therapy and produce inaccurate assessment. She was also aware that the therapeutic techniques developed for "mainstream Westerners" may be inappropriate in multicultural situations. Hence she strives to use cultural knowledge not as an end in itself, but as a starting point from which to investigate each client's particular cultural formation and identity. Seeley demonstrates many of the qualities of cultural competence, starting with self-awareness, as illustrated in her work with clients. The following case studies are taken from her work.

DIANE (AS DESCRIBED IN SEELEY, 2004)

CASE STUDY

Diane sought treatment when she began to feel emotionally destabilized by the psychological problems of an acquaintance. She worked off campus as the assistant manager of a bookstore and one of her employees had developed a severe eating disorder. Diane had become increasingly distressed as she witnessed the employee's deterioration. In addition, she began to experience a loss of appetite and became convinced that she, too, was developing an eating disorder. In the intake interview, Diane did not present significant anorexic symptoms. At first glance, she seemed to need help differentiating herself from others. During the second session, Diane expressed even greater emotional distress because her employee had announced that she would be leaving her job to receive treatment for anorexia. Diane shared that she felt responsible for her employee's condition and explained how she had tried very hard to get her to eat. She felt a great sense of failure when she was unable to do so. In conceptualizing the case, Seeley needed to determine why her client was so distressed and so involved in the employee's struggles with anorexia. Were Diane's symptoms the result of obsessive tendencies or were they possibly related to unhealthy identity and boundary aspects of her relationship with her employee? In other words, was the presenting problem an internal (i.e., intrapsychic) phenomenon? Because Diane was an immigrant raised in Samoa, Seeley wanted to entertain the possibility of cultural factors in Diane's behavior and emotional distress.

Seeley conducted an *ethnographic inquiry*, asking Diane about work relationships in Samoa, especially between supervisors and employees. Diane explained how the work relationship was "like a family" and how supervisors assume responsibility for the well-being of their employees. When asked how she viewed the relationship with her current employee in Samoan terms, she compared it to a "mother-daughter" relationship. In addition, Diane explained how eating and food are a very important part of social relationships in Samoa, describing how a good host is responsible for making sure that everyone eats and has enough to eat.

With this additional information, Seeley hypothesized that Diane's feelings of "excessive responsibility" were probably the result of cultural influences rather than obsessive tendencies or boundary issues. When Seeley presented this hypothesis to Diane, she agreed that this could be the cause of her distress about the employee's welfare. After discovering the roots of her symptoms, Diane began an exploration of the differences in expectations in employer–employee relationships in the United States compared to Samoa. This process helped Diane reduce her feelings of responsibility and distress, with a resultant reduction in depressive symptoms. Seeley's use of a cultural inquiry allowed her to conceptualize the problem accurately. We believe this case demonstrates a highly effective use of cultural competency guidelines.

Collaborative Conceptualization Model

ERICA

Erica is a biracial (North American father and Korean mother) college student who was raised in Korea. She sought counseling to relieve feelings of loneliness and anxiety at the university. Erica speaks unaccented fluent English and considers herself bicultural. When asked to describe her background and her current problem, she was reluctant to give much information. The counselor entertained the possibility that cultural constraints might be involved in Erica's difficulty to talk about mental health issues and inquired about how she would describe her problems in a Korean setting. Erica responded that in Korea people did not convey their problems to others; it would be considered selfish and self-centered. With Erica's help, the problem was conceptualized as a conflict between Korean norms and values and those of the United States. Erica's roommates believed she was too "passive and meek" and encouraged her to be more assertive. Erica explained that in Korea people were "tuned into" her needs, so she did not need to directly verbalize them. Erika began to realize that her social anxiety and loneliness were related to differing cultural expectations and concluded that she would need to learn new ways of communicating. (Seeley, 2004)

CASE STUDY

The preceding example illustrates the importance of *collaborative assessment* and the value of obtaining clients' input regarding social and cultural elements that may be associated with their presenting problems. Gambrill (2005) identifies ways in which therapists can enhance the accuracy and effectiveness of assessment, conceptualization, and treatment planning. First, as we have emphasized previously, therapists need to be aware of the impact that their own values, worldviews, and beliefs have on their practice. Similarly, clients' unique characteristics, values, and circumstances should always be considered. Additionally, clients should be encouraged to actively participate in the assessment and conceptualization process. In other words, case conceptualization, as well as assessment, is best done in a collaborative manner in which therapist self-awareness, client involvement, and the scientific method are all utilized. With this approach, the therapist and the client can choose intervention strategies that involve the integration of high-quality research, clinical expertise, and client input.

Principles of Collaborative Conceptualization

Collaborative conceptualization (modified from Spengler, Strohmer, Dixon, & Shivy, 1995, to include client involvement) consists of the following steps:

1. *Use both clinician skill and client perspective to understand the problem.* Clinical expertise is essential in assessment, developing hypotheses, eliciting client participation, and guiding conceptualization. Therapists bring experience, knowledge, and clinical skill to this process; clients bring an understanding of their own background and their perspective on the problem. Therapists should be aware of their own values, biases, preferences, and theoretical assumptions and how these factors might influence their work with clients.

2. *Collaborate and jointly define the problem.* Within this framework, the clinician and the client, either jointly or independently, formulate conceptualizations of the problem. A joint process generally leads to more accurate conceptualization. In cases where definitions of the problem differ, these differences are discussed, and the agreed-upon aspects of the problem can receive primary focus. In some cases, the therapist can reframe the client's conceptualization in a manner that results in mutual agreement.

3. *Jointly formulate a hypothesis regarding the cause of the problem.* The therapist can tentatively address possibilities concerning what is causing or maintaining the problem with questions such as "Could the problems you are having with your children be due to the values that they are being exposed to?" "Are you trying too hard to be accepted by society and denying your own identity?" "You mentioned before that you get really down on yourself when you feel you aren't living up to your parents' expectations. Do you think that might have anything to do with how you've been feeling lately?" or "I remember you saying that it's been hard to be so far away from others who share your religious background. Do you think that has anything to do with your depression?" When perceptions or explanations of the problem differ, these differences can be acknowledged and an attempt made to identify and focus on similarities.

4. *Jointly develop ways to confirm or disconfirm the hypothesis on the problem, continuing to consider alternative hypotheses.* The therapist might say, "If your

depression is due, in part, to a lack of activity, how would we determine if this is the case?" or "How can we figure out if your parents' wanting you to get all A's in college is part of what is going on?" or "What else might be involved in your feeling depressed?"

5. *Test out the hypothesis using both the client and the therapist as evaluators.* The therapist might ask, "You explored the positive aspects of your identity. Did that reduce your depressive feelings?" or "You mentioned you felt more depressed this week when you were thinking how you were not as good as other people. Do you think that these critical thoughts might be contributing to your depression?" or "It sounds like you were really feeling down after you talked to your parents this week and shared that you had gotten a B on your calculus exam. What do you think that might mean in terms of what is going on with your depression?"

6. *If the conceptualization appears to be valid, develop a treatment plan.* The therapist might say, "You mentioned you felt better when you spent some time with friends this week. It sounds to me like you confirmed your hypothesis that being alone increases your depression. You also noticed that you tend to spend less time thinking negative thoughts about yourself when you're around others. Let's talk about how that important information can be used when we decide how to best treat your depression."

7 *If the hypothesis is not borne out, therapist and client collect additional data and formulate new, testable hypotheses.* The therapist might say, "It's good we checked out that idea that there is a connection between your negative thoughts and being home alone. You mentioned that when you went out walking, you started thinking about the times you've been rejected and your depression seemed to get even worse. Can I ask you to share some of the thoughts that were going through your head when you were walking?"

We believe it is of critical importance to go through a collaborative process such as this; therapist and client can adopt a scientific framework as they work to conceptualize the problem and then have an equal voice in evaluating the problem definition. Unless there is substantial agreement on the definition of a problem, therapeutic progress is likely to be less than optimal.

There is a movement away from relying on "practitioners' ideology" or preferences for treatment options to interventions that have received research support (Edmond, Megivern, Williams, Rochman, & Howard, 2006). As mentioned in our discussion of evidence-based practice in Chapter 9, we believe that intervention strategies should align with facilitating qualities possessed by therapists (empathy, warmth, and genuineness), client characteristics (motivation, personality, and support systems), and research-based therapeutic techniques. Interventions should not be rigidly applied but instead should be modified according to client characteristics and feedback. Consensus between therapist and client regarding the course of therapy strengthens the therapeutic relationship. In addition, using a *collaborative approach* allows clients to develop confidence that the therapist understands their issues and is using methods that are likely to achieve desired goals. Thus collaboration improves treatment outcome by enhancing clients' hope and optimism.

INFUSING CULTURAL COMPETENCE INTO STANDARD CLINICAL ASSESSMENTS

Many interview forms and diagnostic systems place little emphasis on collaboration or contextualism. Instead, the traditional medical model is usually followed and diagnosis is primarily made through the identification of symptoms, without attempts to validate impressions or determine the meaning of the symptoms for the client. In this approach, problems are seen to reside in the individual, with little attention given to family, community, or environmental influences.

The fifth edition of the *Diagnostic and Statistical Manual of Mental Disorders* (*DSM-5*) (American Psychiatric Association, 2013) acknowledges the importance of cultural influences on diagnoses such as culture-related and gender-related issues for each mental disorder. For effective assessment, determining the cultural context of the illness is "essential." The "Outline for Cultural Formulation" includes an overall cultural assessment that takes into account the cultural identity of the individual; cultural conceptualizations of distress, psychosocial stressors, and cultural features of vulnerability and resilience; and cultural differences between the individual and the clinician. *DSM-5* also contains a Cultural Formulation Interview (CFI) comprising sixteen questions "that clinicians may use to obtain information during a mental health assessment about the impact of culture on key aspects of an individual's clinical presentation and care" (American Psychiatric Association, 2013, p. 750). Similar mental health cultural assessment forms are also available online (Transcultural Mental Health Centre, 2015). Although *DSM-5* has expanded the emphasis on the importance of cultural factors in assessment, most standard intake forms only provide cursory assessment of cultural influences.

Therapists who recognize and value the importance of a collaborative and contextual approach may decide to make modifications in standard assessment intake forms. We will suggest ways in which consideration of cultural and environmental factors can be included in or added to standard intake interviews.

Culturally Sensitive Intake Interviews

Nearly everyone in the mental health field conducts diagnostic intake interviews during the first sessions. Typically, the client is informed that the assessment session is not a therapy session but rather a time to gather information in order get to know the client and more fully understand the client's concerns. The specific relationship-building skills previously addressed with respect to evidence-based practice (in Chapter 9) are extremely important in the context of assessment as well as therapy. For example, it is important that the clinician ask questions and respond to answers in a supportive and empathetic manner.

Intake forms generally include questions concerning client demographic information, the presenting problem, history of the problem, previous therapy, psychosocial history, educational and occupational experiences, family and social supports, medical and medication history, and risk assessment. Many standard intake questions are focused primarily on the individual, with little consideration of situational, family, sociocultural, or environmental issues. We realize that it is difficult to modify standard intake forms used by clinics and other mental health agencies, but consideration can be given to these contextual factors when gathering data or making a diagnosis. Common areas of inquiry found in standard diagnostic evaluations and the rationale for each area are presented below (Rivas-Vazquez, Blais, Rey, & Rivas-Vazquez, 2001), together with suggestions for specific contextual queries that can be used to supplement the standard interview for ethnic minorities and other diverse populations.

- *Identifying information.* Asking about the reason for seeking counseling allows the therapist to gain an immediate sense of the client and his or her reason for seeking therapy. Other information gathered includes age, gender, ethnicity, marital status, and referral source. It is also important to inquire about cultural groups to which the client feels connected. Clinicians should also consider whether other areas of diversity, such as religion, sexual orientation, age, gender, or disability, are important in understanding the client or any of the difficulties the client is facing. For ethnic minorities or immigrants, clinicians can inquire about the degree of acculturation or adherence to traditional values. When relevant, ask about the primary language used in the home or the degree of language proficiency of the client or family members. Determine whether an interpreter is needed. (It is important not to rely on family members to translate when assessing clinical matters.)

- *Presenting problem.* To understand the source of distress in the client's own words, obtain his or her perception of the problem and assess the degree of insight the client has regarding the problem and the chronicity of the problem. Some questions clinicians can consider include: What is the client's explanation for his or her symptoms? Does it involve somatic, spiritual, or culture-specific causes? Among all groups potentially affected by disadvantage, prejudice, or oppression, does the client's own explanation involve internalized causes (e.g., internalized heterosexism among gay males or lesbians or self-blame in a victim of a sexual assault) rather than external, social, or cultural factors? What does the client perceive are possible solutions to the problem?

- *History of the presenting problem.* To assist with diagnostic formulation, it is helpful to have a chronological account of and perceived reasons for the problem. It is also important to determine levels of functioning prior to the problem and since it developed and to explore social and environmental influences. When did the present problem first occur, and what was going on when this happened? Has the client had similar problems before? How was the client functioning before the problem occurred? What changes have happened since the advent of the problem? Are there any family issues, value conflicts, or societal issues involving such factors as gender, ability, class, ethnicity, or sexual orientation that may be related to the problem?

- *Psychosocial history.* Clinicians can benefit from understanding the client's perceptions of past and current functioning in different areas of living, as well as early socialization and life experiences, including expectations, values, and beliefs from the family that may play a role in the presenting problem. How does the client describe his or her level of social, academic, or family functioning during childhood and adolescence? Were there any traumas during this period? Were there any past social experiences or problems with the family or community that may be related to the current problem? McAuliffe and Eriksen (1999) describe some questions that can be used, when appropriate, to assess social background, values, and beliefs: "How has your gender role or social class influenced your expectations and life plans?" "Do religious or spiritual beliefs play a role in your life?" "How would you describe your ethnic heritage; how has it affected your life?" "Within your family, what was considered to be appropriate behavior in childhood and adolescence, and as an adult?" "How does your family respond to differences in beliefs about gender, acculturation, and other diversity issues?" "What changes would you make in the way your family functions?"

- *Abuse history.* Despite the potential importance of determining if the client is facing any harmful or dangerous situations, many mental health professionals do not routinely inquire about abuse histories, even in populations known to be at increased risk of abuse. In one study, even when the intake form included a section on abuse, less than one-third of those conducting intake interviews inquired about this topic (Young, Read, Barker-Collo, & Harrison, 2001). It is extremely important to address this issue since background information such as a history of sexual or physical abuse can have important implications for diagnosis, treatment, and safety planning. The following questions involve domestic violence for women (Stevens, 2003, p. 6) but can and should be expanded for use with other groups, including men and older adults:

    Have you ever been touched in a way that made you feel uncomfortable?
    Have you ever been forced or pressured to have sex?
    Do you feel you have control over your social and sexual relationships?
    Have you ever been threatened by a (caretaker, relative, partner)?
    Have you ever been hit, punched, or beaten by a (caretaker, relative, or partner)?
    Do you feel safe where you live?
    Have you ever been scared to go home? Are you scared now?

    If during the intake process a client discloses a history of having been abused and there are no current safety issues, the therapist can briefly and empathetically respond to the disclosure and return to the issue at a later time in the conceptualization or therapy process. Of course, developing a safety plan and obtaining social and law enforcement support may be necessary when a client discloses current abuse issues.

- *Strengths.* It is important to identify culturally relevant strengths, such as pride in one's identity or culture, religious or spiritual beliefs, cultural knowledge and living skills (e.g., hunting, fishing, folk medicine), family and community supports, and resiliency in dealing with discrimination and prejudice (Hays, 2009). The focus on strengths often helps put a problem in context and defines support systems or positive individual or cultural characteristics that can be activated in the treatment process. This is especially important for ethnic group members and individuals of diverse populations subjected to negative *stereotypes*. What are some attributes they are proud of? How have they successfully handled problems in the past? What are some strengths of the client's family or community? What are sources of pride, such as school or work performance, parenting, or connection with the community? How can these strengths be used as part of the treatment plan? Using one's strengths has been found to lower depression and increase happiness (Gander, Proyer, Ruch, & Wyss, 2013).

- *Medical history.* It is important to determine whether there are medical or physical conditions or limitations that may be related to the psychological problem and important to consider when planning treatment. Is the client currently taking any medications, or using herbal substances or other forms of folk medicine? Has the client had any major illnesses or physical problems that might have affected his or her psychological state? How does the client perceive these conditions? Is the client engaging in appropriate self-care? If there is some type of physical limitation or disability, how has this influenced daily living? How have family members, friends, or society responded to this condition?

- *Substance abuse history.* Although substance use can affect diagnosis and treatment, this potential concern is often underemphasized in clinical assessment. Because substance-use issues are common, it is important to ask about drug and alcohol use. What is the client's current and past use of alcohol, prescription medications, and illegal substances, including age of use, duration, and intensity? If the client drinks alcohol, how much is consumed? Do the client or family members have concerns about the client's substance use? Has drinking or other substance use ever affected the social or occupational functioning of the client? What are the alcohol- and substance-use patterns of family members and close friends?

- *Risk of harm to self or others.* Even if clients do not share information about suicidal or violent thoughts, it is important to consider the potential for self-harm or harm to others. What is the client's current emotional state? Are there strong feelings of anger, hopelessness, or depression? Is the client expressing intent to harm him- or herself? Does there appear to be the potential to harm others? Have there been previous situations involving dangerous thoughts or behaviors? Asking a client a simple question such as "How likely is it that you will hurt yourself?" may yield accurate self-predictions of future self-harm. (Peterson, Skeem, & Manchak, 2011)

Diversity Focused Assessment

Diversity considerations can easily be infused into the intake process. Such questions can help the therapist understand the client's perspective on various issues. Questions that might provide a more comprehensive account of the client's perspective include (Dowdy, 2000):

- *"How can I help you?"* This addresses the reason for the visit and client expectations regarding therapy. Clients can have different ideas of what they want to achieve. Unclear or divergent expectations between client and therapist can hamper therapy.

- *"What do you think is causing your problem?"* This helps the therapist to understand the client's perception of the factors involved. In some cases, the client will not have an answer or may present an implausible explanation. The task of the therapist is to help the client examine different areas that might relate to the problem, including interpersonal, social, and cultural influences. However, one must be careful not to impose an "explanation" on the client.

- *"Why do you think this is happening to you?"* This question taps into the issue of causality and possible spiritual or cultural explanations for the problem. Some may believe the problem is due to fate or is a punishment for "bad behavior." If this question does not elicit a direct answer or if you want to obtain a broader perspective, you can inquire, "What does your mother (husband, family members, friends) believe is happening to you?"

- *"What have you done to treat this condition?"* *"Where else have you sought treatment?"* These questions can lead to a discussion of previous interventions, the possible use of home remedies, and the client's evaluation of the usefulness of these treatments. Responses can also provide information about previous providers of treatment and the client's perceptions of prior treatment.

- *"How has this condition affected your life?"* This question helps identify individual, interpersonal, health, and social issues related to the concern. Again, if the response is limited, the clinician can inquire about each of these specific areas.

IMPLICATIONS FOR CLINICAL PRACTICE

Although there is increased focus on cultural competence in assessment, difficulties in effective implementation of culturally competent practices are prevalent. Hansen et al. (2006) conducted a random sample survey of 149 clinicians regarding the importance of multicultural competencies and, more importantly, whether they practiced these recommendations. Although the participants rated competencies such as "using DSM cultural formulations," "preparing a cultural formulation," "using racially/ethnically sensitive data-gathering techniques," and "evaluating one's own multicultural competence" as very important, they were much less likely to actually use these competencies in their practice.

What accounts for this discrepancy between the ratings of importance of multicultural competencies and the actual use of recommended practices? We believe that a contributing factor is the continued reliance on counseling and psychotherapy practices that were developed without consideration of diversity issues or the impact of therapist qualities on assessment and conceptualization. Many intake interviews and clinical assessments continue to reflect the view that a disorder resides in the individual. Until assessment questionnaires systematically include specific questions such as those discussed in this chapter, cultural competency will receive only lip service.

Knowledge of cultural variables and sociopolitical influences affecting members of different groups can sensitize therapists to *possible* cultural, social, or environmental influences on individual clients. As you read the remaining chapters in this text, which deal with a variety of specific populations, we hope you do not see the information as an end in itself, but rather as a means to assist you to create hypotheses when working collaboratively with clients in the assessment and conceptualization process. As we advise repeatedly throughout the chapters, it is important not to stereotype clients or overgeneralize based on the information presented. Inappropriate reliance on cultural information can lead to misdiagnosis and mistaken treatment recommendations such as seeking treatment with a folk healer. Such problems can be minimized by combining cultural and traditional psychiatric or psychological assessments (Paniagua, 2013).

In the following chapters on diverse populations, we present various characteristics, and strengths of each population, specific challenges of working with them, and implications of these factors for clinical practice. It is our hope that you will refer back to this chapter for guidance as you strive to implement culturally competent practices with clients from these specific populations.

SUMMARY

Accurate assessment, diagnosis, and case conceptualization are essential for the provision of culturally appropriate treatment. Most clinicians recognize that socio-economic status, gender, and racial/cultural background play an important role. Counselors often forget that their own beliefs, values, theoretical assumptions, and other biases can affect clinical judgment. Contextual and *collaborative assessment*, which infuses cultural factors into standard intake and assessment procedures and takes into consideration the client's unique personal and cultural background, can reduce diagnostic errors.

Assessment is influenced by both client and therapist variables. Clinicians should be aware of the influence of *stereotypes*, and remain alert for common diagnostic errors. Such errors include (a) *confirmatory strategy*—searching only for evidence or information supporting one's hypothesis; (b) *attribution errors*—holding a different perspective on the problem from that of the client; (c) *judgmental heuristics*—using quick-decision labels or automatic associations; and (d) *diagnostic overshadowing*—minimizing the client's actual problem by attending primarily to other salient characteristics such as age, ethnicity, or sexual orientation as causal factors. We are all susceptible to making errors and it is important to adopt a tentative stance and test out our observations.

Culturally competent assessment involves self-awareness, knowledge of culturally diverse groups, specific clinical skills, and the ability to intervene at the individual, group, institutional, and societal levels. This process works best with a contextual and *collaborative approach*, acknowledging that both the client and the therapist are embedded in systems such as family, work, and culture, and working with the client to develop an accurate definition of the problem, the appropriate goals, and effective interventions. Steps involved with *collaborative assessment* include (a) using both clinician skill and client perspective to understand the problem; (b) jointly defining the problem; (c) working together to formulate and evaluate a hypothesis on the cause of the problem; (d) confirming or disconfirming the hypothesis; and (e) developing a treatment plan.

Standard clinical assessment forms need to account for the cultural identity of the individual, cultural conceptualizations of distress and appropriate treatment, psychosocial stressors, and any cultural differences between the individual and the clinician. These diversity considerations can easily be infused into the intake process.

GLOSSARY TERMS

Attribution errors	Culturally sensitive intake interviews
Collaborative approach	Diagnostic overshadowing
Collaborative assessment	Ethnographic inquiry
Collaborative conceptualization	Judgmental heuristics
Confirmatory strategy	Stereotypes
Contextual viewpoint	Therapeutic alliance
Culturally competent assessment	

REFERENCES

American Psychiatric Association. (2013). *Diagnostic and statistical manual of mental disorders* (5th ed.). Arlington, VA: Author.

American Psychological Association, Presidential Task Force on Evidence-Based Practice. (2006). Evidence-based practice in psychology. *American Psychologist, 61,* 271–285.

Behnke, S. (2004). Informed consent and APA's new ethics code: Enhancing client autonomy, improving client care. *Monitor on Psychology, 35,* 80–81.

Chambliss, C. H. (2000). *Psychotherapy and managed care: Reconciling research and reality.* Boston, MA: Allyn & Bacon.

Chang, D. F., & Berk, A. (2009). Making cross-racial therapy work: A phenomenological study of clients' experiences of cross-racial therapy. *Journal of Counseling Psychology, 56,* 521–536.

Constantine, M. G., & Sue, D. W. (2007). Perceptions of racial microaggressions among Black supervisees in cross-racial dyads. *Journal of Counseling Psychology, 54,* 142–153.

Danzinger, P. R., & Welfel, E. R. (2000). Age, gender and health bias in counselors: An empirical analysis. *Journal of Mental Health Counseling, 22,* 135–149.

Dowdy, K. G. (2000). The culturally sensitive medical interview. *Journal of the American Academy of Physicians Assistants, 13,* 91–104.

Edmond, T., Megivern, D., Williams, C., Rochman, E., & Howard, M. (2006). Integrating evidence based practice and social work field education. *Journal of Social Work Education, 42,* 377–396.

Freitag, R., Ottens, A., & Gross, C. (1999). Deriving multicultural themes from bibliotherapeutic literature: A neglected resource. *Counselor Education & Supervision, 39,* 120–133.

Gambrill, E. (2005). *Critical thinking in clinical practice.* Hoboken, NJ: Wiley.

Gander, F., Proyer, R. T., Ruch, W., & Wyss, T. (2013). Strength-based positive interventions: Further evidence for their potential in enhancing well-being and alleviating depression. *Journal of Happiness Studies, 14,* 1241–1259.

Gone, J. P. (2009). A community-based treatment for Native American historical trauma: Prospects for evidence-based practice. *Journal of Consulting and Clinical Psychology, 17,* 751–762.

Hansen, N. D., Randazzo, K. V., Schwartz, A., Marshall, M., Kalis, D., Frazier, R., Burke, C., . . . & Novig, G. (2006). Do we practice what we preach? An exploratory survey of multicultural psychotherapy competencies. *Professional Psychology: Research and Practice, 37,* 66–74.

Hays, P. A. (2009). Integrating evidence-based practice, cognitive-behavior therapy, and multicultural therapy: Ten steps for culturally competent practice. *Professional Psychology: Research and Practice, 40*, 354–360.

Kissinger, D. (2014). *Sharing the burden of intercultural stress.* Retrieved from http://www .psychiatrictimes.com/cultural-psychiatry /sharing-burden-intercultural-stress

Lee, C. C. (2006). Ethical issues in multicultural counseling. In B. Herlihy & G. Corey (Eds.), *ACA ethical standards casebook* (6th ed.). Alexandria, VA: American Counseling Association.

McAuliffe, G. J., & Eriksen, K. P. (1999). Toward a constructivist and developmental identity for the counseling profession: The context-phase-stage style model. *Journal of Counseling and Development, 77*, 267–280.

Mohr, J. J., Weiner, J. L., Chopp, R. M., & Wong, S. J. (2009). Effects of client bisexuality on clinical judgment: When is bias most likely to occur? *Journal of Counseling Psychology, 56*, 164–175.

Osmo, R., & Rosen, A. (2002). Social workers' strategies for treatment hypothesis testing. *Social Work Research, 26*, 9–18.

Paniagua, F. A. (2013). Culture-bound syndromes, cultural variations, and psychopathology. In F. A. Paniagua & A.-M. Yamada (Eds.), *Handbook of multicultural mental health: Assessment and treatment of diverse populations* (2nd ed., pp. 25–48). San Diego, CA: Academic Press

Peterson, J., Skeem, J., & Manchak, S. (2011). If you want to know, consider asking. How likely is it that patients will hurt themselves in the future? *Psychological Assessment, 23*, 626–634.

President's New Freedom Commission on Mental Health. (2003). *Achieving the promise: Transforming mental health care in America. Final report.* DHHS Pub. No. SMA-03–3832. Rockville, MD: Author.

Ridley, C. R., Mollen, D., & Kelly, S. M. (2011). Beyond microskills: Toward a model of counseling competence. *Counseling Psychologist, 39*, 825–864.

Rivas-Vazquez, R. A., Blais, M. A., Rey, G. J., & Rivas-Vazquez, A. A. (2001). A brief reminder about documenting the psychological consultation. *Professional Psychology: Research and Practice, 32*, 194–199.

Seeley, K. M. (2004). Short-term intercultural psychotherapy: Ethnographic. *Social Work, 49*, 121–131.

Seem, S. R., & Johnson, E. (1998). Gender bias among counseling trainees: A study of case conceptualization. *Counselor Education and Supervision, 37*, 257–268.

Singh, A. A., & Chun, K.S.Y. (2010). From "margins to the center": Moving towards a resilience based model of supervision with queer people of color. *Training and Education in Professional Psychology, 4*, 36–46.

Spengler, P. M., Strohmer, D. C., Dixon, D. N., & Shivy, V. A. (1995). A scientist-practitioner model of psychological assessment: Implications for training, practice, and research. *Counseling Psychologist, 23*, 506–534.

Stevens, L. (2003, November 20). Improving screening of women for violence: Basic guidelines for physicians. Retrieved from http:// www.medscape.org/viewarticle/464417.

Stewart, A. E. (2004). Can knowledge of client birth order bias clinical judgment? *Journal of Counseling and Development, 82*, 167–176.

Sue, D., & Sue, D. M. (2008). *Foundations of counseling and psychotherapy: Evidence-based practices in a diverse society.* Hoboken, NJ: Wiley.

Sue, D.W., & Sue, D. (2013). *Counseling the culturally diverse: Theory and practice.* Hobboken, NJ: Wiley.

Transcultural Mental Health Centre. (2015). *Assessment guidelines and tools.* Retrieved from http:// www.dhi.health.nsw.gov.au/Transcultural-Mental-Health-Centre/Programs-and-

Campaigns/GPs/Cultural-Resource-Kit/Assessment-Guidelines-and-Tools/default.aspx

Vedantam, S. (2005, June 6). Patients' diversity is often discounted. *Washington Post*, p. A01.

Vontress, C. E., & Jackson, M. L. (2004). Reactions to the multicultural counseling competencies debate. *Journal of Mental Health Counseling, 26,* 74–80.

Weinrach, S. G., & Thomas, K. R. (2004). The AMCD multicultural counseling competencies: A critically-flawed initiative. *Journal of Mental Health Counseling, 26,* 81–93.

Young, M., Read, J., Barker-Collo, S., & Harrison, R. (2001). Evaluating and overcoming barriers to taking abuse histories. *Professional Psychology: Research and Practice, 32,* 407–414.

PART VI

Counseling Marginalized Racial/ Ethnic Group Populations

Counseling African Americans

Eric Garner was approached by police officers for selling "loosies" or unpackaged cigarettes, a minor offence in Staten Island. When he argued with the officers, one deputy used a headlock to subdue him and other police officers kneeled on this back as he lay face down handcuffed. He complained about not being able to breathe at least 11 times. The coroner ruled his death a "homicide" due to compression of the neck and chest. (Allen, 2015)

A Justice Department civil rights investigation of the Ferguson Police Department and the city's municipal court after the shooting death of Michael Brown concluded that both agencies had engaged in discriminatory practices against African Americans as evidenced by "targeting them disproportionately for traffic stops, use of force, and jail sentences." (Perez, 2015)

In a study of women scientists working in the fields of science, technology, engineering, and math, nearly half of African American women scientists had experienced being mistakenly identified as custodial or administrative staff as compared to one-third of white women scientists. African American women attributed the incidents as because of their race while white women believed that it was because of their gender. (Williams, Phillips, & Hall, 2014)

The confederate flag has been removed from the state capitol ground after the killing of nine congregants of the Emanuel African Methodist Episcopal Church. As Governor Haley stated, "While the flag for many South Carolinians stands for noble traditions of history, heritage and ancestry, for many others it's a deeply offensive symbol of a brutally oppressive past." (Associated Press, 2015) [Confederate symbols are also being removed in other states.]

The African American population was 41.7 million in 2013, representing 13% of the total population. The poverty rate for African Americans remains nearly twice as high as that of all households (25.8% versus 14.3%) (U.S. Census Bureau, 2013, 2014), and the unemployment rate is over twice that of White Americans (9.5% versus 4.6%) (U.S. Department of Labor, 2015). Approximately 23% of African American adults do not have a high school diploma (Fry, 2010). Of African American males, 38% are experiencing greater downward mobility out of the middle class compared with the 21% of White males (Acs, 2011). Further, infant mortality for Blacks is over twice that of Whites (Centers for Disease Control, 2013), and the lifespan of African Americans is 5 to 6 years shorter than that of White Americans. Although African Americans are only 13% of the U.S. population, 40% of those incarcerated are Black while Whites who make up 64% of the population account for only 39% of those in prison (Hagler, 2015). African American women are also more likely to be arrested than Latinas or White women (Brame, Bushway, Paternoster, & Turner, 2014).

Although these statistics are grim, much of the literature is based on the economically disadvantaged rather than on other segments of the African American population (Holmes & Morin, 2006). This focus on those living in poverty masks the great diversity that exists among African Americans and the significant variance in socioeconomic status, educational level, cultural identity, family structure, and reactions to *racism*. For example, 38% of African American households are middle income and 12% are upper income, compared with 44% and 26% of White households respectively (Parlapiano, Gebeloff, & Carter, 2015). Many middle- and upper-class African Americans embrace the values of the dominant society, believe that advances can be made through hard work, feel that race has a relative rather than a pervasive influence on their lives, and take pride in their heritage. As Hugh Price, former president of the National Urban League, observed, "This country is filled with highly successful Black men who are leading balanced, stable, productive lives working all over the labor market" (Holmes & Morin, 2006, p. 1). However, even among this group of successful African American men earning $75,000 a year or more, six in ten reported being victims of *racism* and having someone close to them murdered or incarcerated.

CHARACTERISTICS AND STRENGTHS

In the following sections, we consider the characteristics, values, and strengths of African Americans and their implications in treatment. The African American population is becoming increasingly heterogeneous in terms of ethnic and *racial identity*, social class, educational level, and political orientation, so it is important to remember that the following are generalizations; their applicability needs to be assessed for each client.

Ethnic and Racial Identity

Many scholars believe that minorities go through a sequential process of *racial identity* development. For many African Americans, the process involves a transformation from a non-Afrocentric identity to one that is *Afrocentric* (although some African Americans consistently embrace a Black identity through early socialization). The Cross (1991, 1995) model, as described in Chapter 11, identifies the stages of preencounter, encounter, immersion-emersion, and internalization. These stages are associated with differences in perspective regarding the self and relationships with others, beginning with the acceptance of White standards and deprecation of Black culture and culminating in an appreciation of both Black culture and aspects of the White culture. The current stage of an individual's *racial identity* affects awareness of and willingness to discuss racial issues or *racism* (Forsyth, Hall & Carter, 2015).

Implications

African Americans who are at the preencounter level are less likely to report racial discrimination, whereas those in the immersion stage tend to be least satisfied with societal conditions. African Americans with the greatest internalization of Black *racial identity* report the highest self-esteem (Pierre & Mahalik, 2005). African American preferences for counselor ethnicity are often related to their current stage of *racial identity*. Parham and Helms (1981) found that African Americans at the preencounter stage preferred a White counselor, whereas those in later stages preferred an African American counselor. In a study involving 128 Black college students, over 75 percent had no preference regarding the race of the counselor for issues such as depression, anxiety, drug or alcohol problems, meeting new people, overcoming loneliness, and dealing with anger. However, 50 percent indicated preference for a Black counselor for racial issues and problems with personal relationships. Elevated *cultural mistrust* and strong internalized *Afrocentric* attitudes were associated with a stronger preference for a Black counselor (Townes, Chavez-Korell, & Cunningham, 2009).

Often, the most important counselor characteristic for African Americans is the cultural sensitivity of the counselor. Culturally sensitive counselors (those who acknowledge the possibility that race or culture might play a role in a client's problem) are seen as more competent than culture-blind counselors (those who do not assess for environmental issues such as *prejudice*) (Want, Parham, Baker, & Sherman, 2004). Among a group of working-class African American clients, the degree of therapeutic alliance with White counselors was affected not only by the client's stage of *racial identity* but also by similarities in gender, age, attitudes, and beliefs. Additionally, clients facing issues related to parenting, drug use, or anxiety looked for therapists with understanding of these specific issues (Ward, 2005).

Family Structure

Although about 44% of African American households are headed by married couples, many African American families are headed by single parents (Vespa, Lewis, & Kreider, 2013). Black children are significantly less likely than other children to be living with two married parents (44% versus 84% for Asian children, 64% for Hispanic children, and 75% for White children) (Child Trends, 2010). In 2008, 72% of all births to Black women were outside of marriage, compared with 29% for non-Hispanic White women (Black Demographics. com, 2011). The African American family is often described as matriarchal; among lower-class African American families, 63% are headed by women versus 33% of all U.S. households (Taylor, Larsen-Rife, Conger, Widaman, & Cutrona, 2010). Given the varied structure of African American families, it is important to take into account *kinship bonds* with *extended family* and friends, as illustrated in the following case study.

JOHNNY

A mother, Mrs. J., brought her 13-year-old son Johnny in for counseling due to recent behavioral problems at home and in school. After asking, "Who is living in the home?" the therapist learned that Johnny lived with his mom, a stepfather, and five brothers and sisters. Also, the mother's sister, Mary, and three children had been staying with the family while their apartment was repaired. The mother also had a daughter living with an aunt in another state. The aunt was helping the daughter raise her child. When asked, "Who helps you out?" Mrs. J. responded that her mother sometimes helps watch the children but that, more frequently, a neighbor (who has children of a similar age) watches the younger children when Mrs. J. works during school hours.

Further questioning revealed that Johnny's problem developed soon after his aunt and cousins moved in. Before this, Johnny had been his mother's primary helper and took charge of the children until the stepfather returned home from work. The changes in the family structure that occurred when the sister and her children arrived were stressful for Johnny. Family treatment included Mrs. J. and her children, the stepfather, Mary and her children, and Mrs. J.'s mother. Pressures on Johnny were

CASE STUDY

discussed, and alternatives were considered. Mrs. J.'s mother agreed to invite Mary and her children to come live with her temporarily. To deal with these additional disruptions in the family, follow-up meetings focused on clarifying roles in the family system. Johnny once again assumed the role of helping his mother and stepfather watch the younger children. Within a period of months, his behavioral problems at home and school disappeared.

Implications

Because of the possibility of extended or nontraditional family arrangements, questions should be directed toward clarifying who is living in the home and who helps with childcare. Therapists should work to strengthen and increase functionality of the existing family structure rather than attempt to change it. One of the strengths of the African American family is that men, women, and children are allowed to adopt multiple roles within the family. For example, as in the case of Johnny, older children might adopt a caretaking role, and friends or grandparents might help raise children. In such cases, therapy might focus on enhancing the working alliance among caregivers (Muroff, 2007).

A counselor's reaction to a client's family structure may be affected by a Eurocentric, nuclear-family orientation. Similarly, many assessment forms and evaluation processes are based on a middle-class EuroAmerican perspective of what constitutes a family. For family therapy to be successful, counselors must first identify their own set of beliefs and values regarding appropriate roles and communication patterns within a family and take care not to impose these beliefs on other families. Similarly, it is helpful to move away from a deficit model to an asset or strengths perspective when evaluating families (Rockymore, 2008). For example, a supportive parenting style that includes warmth, communication, and consistent discipline appears to be protective against drug use by African American youth (Gibbons et al., 2010). However, physical discipline or critical comments, unless unduly harsh, should not necessarily be viewed negatively; each situation should be assessed individually. Culturally sensitive parent education programs designed for African Americans focus on different types of discipline, single parenting, and strategies for dealing with culture conflicts and responding to *racism*. In working with economically disadvantaged African American families, the counselor may need to assume various roles, including advocate, case manager, problem solver, and facilitating mentor, and to help the family navigate community systems, including the educational or judicial system.

Spiritual and Religious Values

D.

D. is a 42-year-old African American woman recently divorced after 20 years of marriage and raising two children with little support from her ex-husband. She presented with depressive-like symptoms—feelings of loneliness, lack of energy, lack of appetite, and crying spells. . . Although part of the treatment focused on traditional psychological interventions, such as cognitive restructuring, expression of feelings, and changing behaviors, D.'s treatment also included participation in two church-related programs, including the women's ministry, a program that provides social and emotional support. Treatment also included participation in "The Mother to Son Program," a program targeting single mothers parenting African American boys. This program provides support for mothers and mentoring relationships for their sons. (Queener & Martin, 2001, p. 120)

CASE STUDY

Spirituality and religion play an important role in many African American families; church participation provides comfort, economic support, and opportunities for self-expression, leadership, and community involvement. Over 75% of African Americans state that religion is very important to them and rely on religious and spiritual communities to deal with mental health issues (Avent & Cashwell, 2015). Among a sample of low-income African American children, those whose parents regularly attended church had fewer problems (Christian & Barbarin, 2001). Support systems connected with the church (including friends and club involvement) were found to promote resilience in African American undergraduates exposed to racial microaggressions (Watkins, Labarrie, & Appio, 2010). The African American church often functions as a religious, social, and political hub, facilitating social events that serve to foster a sense of "peoplehood" (Boyd Franklin, 2010).

Implications

Spiritual beliefs are important to many African Americans and serve as a protective factor in response to stressors. If a client is heavily involved in church activities or has strong religious beliefs, the counselor might consider enlisting church leaders to help the client (or family) deal with social and economic stressors or conflicts involving the family, school, or community. Church personnel are often aware of the family dynamics and living conditions of parishioners. In addition, churches often sponsor parenting programs or activities that enrich family life.

CASE STUDY

Educational Characteristics

JACKIE

Jackie, a 10-year-old African American female, came in with her mother presenting with anger problems, low mood, suicidal thoughts, and family discord. She had always been a stellar student, but her grades had begun to fall from straight As to Bs and Cs. Jackie notes that "she is not smart enough to keep up with the other kids." (Muroff, 2007, p. 131)

African American parents, acutely aware of obstacles produced by *racism* and economic conditions, often encourage their children to develop career and educational goals at an early age. In one study of 1,225 school-aged African American males (6th to 10th graders), 62% aspired to go to college, similar to rates for White male students. Black males with plans to attend college frequently reported positive feelings about their school and teachers (Toldson, Braithwaite, & Rentie, 2009). The gap in educational attainment between African American and White children is gradually narrowing. In 2013, over 90% of African Americans vs 94% of White Americans had completed high school, although only 20% had a bachelor's degree or higher compared to 40% of Whites (Child Trends, 2014).

The educational environment is often negative for African American youth. They are two to five times more likely to be suspended from school and often receive harsher consequences than their White peers (Rudd, 2014). School personnel often hold stereotypes of African American parents as being neglectful or incompetent and blame children's problems on a lack of parental support for schooling. As one teacher stated, "The parents are the problem! They [the African American children] have absolutely no social skills, such as not knowing how to walk, sit in a chair, . . .it's cultural" (Harry et al., 2005, p. 105); but when these researchers visited the homes of parents who were criticized, they often observed parental love, effective parenting skills, and family support for education.

Implications

Factors associated with school failure, especially in African American males, must be identified and system-level intervention strategies applied. Traditional educational practices often do not meet the needs of diverse populations. For example, many African American youths display an animated, persuasive, and confrontational communication style, while schools often have norms of quiet conformity;

teacher-focused instruction; and individualized, competitive activities. White teachers may perceive the typical communication patterns, physical movement, and walking style of African American youth as aggressive or noncompliant (Monroe, 2005). It is important for educators to recognize culturally based behaviors that are not intended to be disruptive. If teachers are not sensitive to these cultural differences, they may respond inappropriately to minority group members. Students often learn best when curricula and classroom styles are modified taking cultural factors into consideration.

African American Youth

CASE STUDY

LEAJAY HARPER

LeaJay Harper says she was a typically rebellious teenager raised by a single mother. She left home at 17 and lived on the streets, surviving on stale donated bread and sleeping on church porches. When she was 18, she was arrested for stealing a $10 bag of McDonald's food. "I was hungry," she said. She went to jail. (Mulady, 2011, p. 1)

For many urban African American adolescents, life is complicated by problems of poverty, illiteracy, and *racism*. African American youth are more likely to be victims of violence, such as stabbings or shootings, but are reluctant to report these incidents because of fear of the police or of being accused of "snitching" (Schwartz et al., 2010). Most African American youth feel strongly that race is still a factor in how people are judged (Pew Research Center, 2010). In fact, White undergraduate females are more likely to overestimate the age of African American youth offenders and believe them to have greater culpability for crimes than White or Latina/o juvenile offenders (Goff et al., 2014). Even young African American children are well aware of stereotypes regarding the occupational status of African Americans. In one study, they identified service jobs as those performed by "only Black people" and high-status jobs as those performed by White Americans (Bigler & Averhart, 2003).

Issues presented in counseling may differ to some extent between boys and girls. Although African American adolescent girls display higher self-confidence, lower levels of substance use, and more positive body images than other groups of adolescent girls (Belgrave, Chase-Vaughn, Gray, Addison, &

Cherry, 2000), they often encounter sexism as well as *racism*. While striving to succeed in relationships and careers, African American adolescent girls not only are burdened by living in a male-dominated society but also undergo the stressors associated with being African American or living in poverty (Talley-rand, 2010). Acute awareness of issues of *racism* and sexism is reflected in the following comment:

> *Well, in this time I think it's really hard to be an African American woman. . .we are what you call a double negative; we are Black and we are a woman and it's really hard. . .society sees African American females as always getting pregnant and all that kind of thing and being on welfare. (Shorter-Gooden & Washington, 1996, p. 469)*

In interviews with African American adolescent girls, Shorter-Gooden and Washington (1996) found that the struggle over *racial identity* was a more salient factor than gender identity in establishing self-definition. These adolescents believed that they had to be strong and were determined to overcome obstacles resulting from societal misperceptions involving Blackness. About half were raised by single mothers, and most indicated the importance of the mother–daughter relationship. Careers were important to two thirds of the group, and most reported that their parents had instilled strong motivation to succeed academically.

Unfortunately, there is a growing trend toward incarceration of African American girls and young women. They are the fastest-growing incarcerated group of young people in the United States. In California, the arrest rate is 49 per 1,000 for Black girls, compared with 9 per 1,000 for White girls and 15 per 1,000 for Latinas (Pfeffer, 2011). In general, the crimes committed are not violent and are frequently associated with poverty, homelessness, and maltreatment within the home. Further, zero tolerance policies in schools disproportionately affect African American girls, who may be disciplined for talking back, interpersonal conflict, or truancy. LeaJay Harper, quoted at the beginning of this section, was arrested a second time for stealing pajamas and underwear for her young daughter. Instead of jail time, she was sent to a six-month treatment program and now runs the Young Mothers United Program at the Center for Young Women's Development in San Francisco, helping other African American girls and young women who are at risk of losing their children because of arrests for similar nonviolent offenses (Mulady, 2011).

Implications

African American youth often do not come to counseling willingly. They may be referred by social agencies or brought in by family members. Because of this, lack of interest in counseling may be an issue, as seen in the following case.

MICHAEL

Michael is a 19-year-old African American male brought to counseling by his aunt, Gloria, with whom he has lived for the past 2 years. Gloria is concerned about Michael's future. . .Although Michael graduated from high school and is employed part-time at a fast-food restaurant, he is frustrated with this work and confused about his future. He believes that Black men "don't get a fair shake" in life and is discouraged about his prospects about getting ahead. . .Michael's aunt. . .is concerned that Michael's peers are involved in gangs and illegal activities. She thinks the rap music he listens to is beginning to fill his head with hate and anger. . .Michael's major issues center around a need to develop a positive identity as an African American man and discover his place in the world. (Frame & Williams, 1996, p. 22)

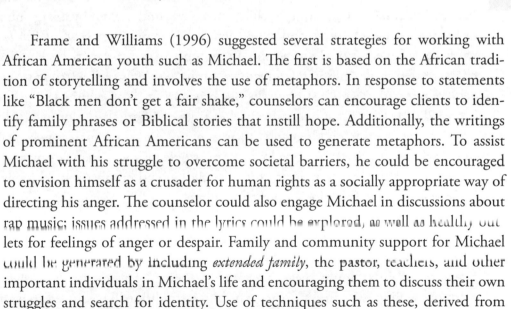

CASE STUDY

Frame and Williams (1996) suggested several strategies for working with African American youth such as Michael. The first is based on the African tradition of storytelling and involves the use of metaphors. In response to statements like "Black men don't get a fair shake," counselors can encourage clients to identify family phrases or Biblical stories that instill hope. Additionally, the writings of prominent African Americans can be used to generate metaphors. To assist Michael with his struggle to overcome societal barriers, he could be encouraged to envision himself as a crusader for human rights as a socially appropriate way of directing his anger. The counselor could also engage Michael in discussions about rap music; issues addressed in the lyrics could be explored, as well as healthy outlets for feelings of anger or despair. Family and community support for Michael could be generated by including *extended family*, the pastor, teachers, and other important individuals in Michael's life and encouraging them to discuss their own struggles and search for identity. Use of techniques such as these, derived from African American experiences, can lead to personal empowerment.

In counseling African American girls, issues involving *racial identity* and conflict should be explored. Counselors can help African American girls and women counteract negative images associated with being Black and being female. Enhancing internal strength by developing pride and dignity in Black womanhood can serve as a buffer to *racism* and sexism and can prevent the incorporation of negative images into their own belief systems (Owens, Stewart & Bryant, 2011).

Cultural Strengths

Protective factors and strengths among African Americans include positive ethnic identity or racial pride; resourcefulness and coping skills to deal with societal issues; familial, extended kin, and community support systems; flexible family roles; achievement orientation; and spiritual beliefs and practices (Kaslow et al., 2010; LaTaillade, 2006). Family and religious protective factors have been hypothesized to account for findings that African Americans have lower levels of heavy and binge drinking than any other ethnic group, with the exception of Asian Americans (Substance Abuse and Mental Health Services Administration, 2013). Additionally, African American adolescents have low rates of substance use compared to Whites and other ethnic groups (Johnston, O'Malley, Miech, Bachman, & Schulenberg, 2014).

The African American family structure has many advantages. Among families headed by females, the rearing of children is often undertaken by a large number of relatives, older children, and close friends. For many, the *extended family* network provides emotional and economic support. African American families are characterized by flexibility in family roles, strong *kinship bonds*, a strong work and achievement ethic, and a strong religious orientation (McCollum, 1997; Rockymore, 2008). Kinship support diminishes risks of internalizing or externalizing problem behaviors in children and can ameliorate conditions such as poor parenting (Taylor et al., 2010). Among low-income single mothers, many displayed substantial parenting involvement with their children and emphasized achievement, self-respect, and racial pride with their children.

Despite the challenges of *racism* and *prejudice*, many African American families have been able to instill positive self-esteem in their children by means of role flexibility. African American men and women value behaviors such as assertiveness; within a family, males are more accepting of women's work roles and are more willing to share in the responsibilities traditionally assigned to women. Many women demonstrate a "Strong Black Woman" image that includes pride in *racial identity*, self-reliance, and capability in handling challenges—all while nurturing the family. Although self-efficacy can be a strength, excessive investment in meeting the expectations of such a role can lead to emotional suppression and difficulty expressing vulnerability or distress (Harrington, Crowther, & Shipherd, 2010).

SPECIFIC CHALLENGES

In the following sections we consider challenges often faced by African Americans and consider their implications in treatment.

Racism and Discrimination

Racism and discrimination are significant concerns within the African American community. As President Obama observed during his eulogy for Rev. Clementa Pinckney and eight of his congregants who were shot to death by a White supremacist, racial bias can be evident or may occur without realization such as "the subtle impulse to call Johnny back for a job interview—but not Jamal" (Moser, 2015). A study by Bertrand and Mullainathan (2004) did find that résumés with either African American or White sounding names (Lakisha and Jamal versus Emily and Greg) sent to help wanted ads received a differential response. The "White" names received 50% more calls for interviews.

African Americans perceive both subtle and direct forms of *racism* in the United States. Whereas about half of Whites believe Blacks have equal societal opportunities, 81% of Blacks believe more change is necessary (Pew Research Center, 2010). Due to the deaths of unarmed Black men at the hands of the police, 57% of Americans believe that racial relationships are a cause for concern (Dann, 2014a). A Black Lives Matter movement arose to take a stand against police brutality and the anti-Black *racism* in society. In response to the tragedy involving Sandra Bland, whose stop for changing lanes without signaling resulted in a sequence of events that ended with her death, U.S. Attorney General Loretta Lynch remarked, "I think that it highlights the concern of many in the Black community that a routine stop for many of the members of the Black community is not handled with the same professionalism and courtesy that other people may get from the police" (Glum, 2015). The Black Lives Matter movement points out that Black people are singled out and "intentionally left powerless at the hands of the state . . . and are deprived of basic human rights and dignity" (Black Lives Matter, 2015). This movement is gaining strength nationally and challenges instances of *racism* against African Americans.

However, there is a large racial gap between Blacks and Whites in their views about the police and their actions. While 70% of Whites believe that the police treat both races equally, only 28% of Blacks have the same belief (Dann, 2014b). Many African Americans believe that racial profiling occurs frequently. In situations involving suspected racial profiling, Black men often report thinking,

"Maybe I am being treated this way because I am Black," and needing to decide, "Do I protest it or just take it?" (Fausset & Huffstutter, 2009, p. 1).

Consciously or unconsciously, many people associate African Americans with crime and favor harsher punishments for African Americans. In research studies Whites, when primed to think about crime, focused their attention on Black rather than White faces and were more likely to identify blurry images as weapons when exposed to Black faces. When Whites read descriptions of a juvenile offender convicted of rape, harsher sentences were supported when he was described as Black (Weir, 2014). In a study involving African American defendants who were convicted of killing White victims, Eberhardt and colleagues (2006) found that defendants with darker skin and broader noses were twice as likely to receive the death penalty compared to African Americans who looked less stereotypically black. Similarly, Viglione, Hannon, and DeFina (2011) found that African American women with lighter skin received shorter sentences than women with darker skin who committed similar crimes.

Youth with an incarcerated parent have increased risk of poverty, school failure, emotional distress, criminal activity, and drug use. This effect can further exacerbate the cycle of racial inequality, substance abuse, and imprisonment (Roettger, Swisher, Kuhl, & Chavez, 2011). The experience of perceived racial discrimination is associated with decreased levels of self-esteem and life satisfaction and increased depressive symptoms in African American and Caribbean Black youth (Seaton, Caldwell, Sellers, & Jackson, 2011). Some African American adolescents report drug use as a way of coping with feelings of anger in reaction to racial discrimination (Gibbons et al., 2010).

African American parents differ in the ways in which they address *racism* with their children. Some address *racism* and *prejudice* directly and help their children to develop a strong Black identity, whereas others consider race to be of minor importance, ignore the topic of race, and focus on human values or discuss the issue only if brought up by their children. *Racial socialization* can help buffer the negative effects of *racism* and discrimination (Lee & Ahn, 2013). Neal-Barnett (1997) found that ignoring racial issues in socialization leaves children vulnerable to anxiety when African American peers accused them of "acting White." In homes where race is not discussed, children have fewer opportunities to develop coping strategies when faced with discrimination. Similarly, protective factors for African American youth include parental focus on increasing positive feelings about self and enhancing a sense of pride in one's culture (Belgrave et al., 2000). Messages of cultural pride from parents is associated with the

FIGURE 14.1 The Interaction of Four Sets of Factors in the Jones Model

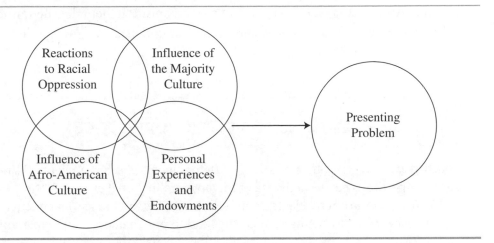

Source: From "Psychological Functioning in Black Presenting Americans: A Conceptual Guide for Use in Psychotherapy," by A. C. Jones, 1985, *Psychotherapy, 22,* p. 367. Copyright 1985 by *Psychotherapy.* Reprinted by permission of the Editor, *Psychotherapy.*

development of positive ethnic identity, self-esteem, and socioemotional competence in African American children (Rodriguez, McKay, & Bannon, 2008). Therapists may decide to discuss the positive benefits of *racial socialization* with African American parents.

Implications

Since the mental health environment is a microcosm of the larger society, mental health professionals need to identify their own racial attitudes and be ready to address mistrust from African American clients concerned about being viewed through the lens of a stereotype (Jordan, Lovett, & Sweeton, 2012). Therapists should carefully assess both the problems confronting a client and the client's response to the problem situation, including the way he or she usually deals with *racism.*

Jones (1985) described four interactive factors that should be considered in working with African American clients (see Figure 14.1). The first factor is racial oppression. Most African Americans have faced *racism*, and the possibility that this factor plays a role in the presenting problem should be examined. Other interactive factors described by Jones include the possible influence of African American culture and traditions on the client's behavior, the degree to which the client has adopted majority culture values, and the personal experiences of the individual. Individual experiences with racial oppression can vary significantly among African Americans. The task of the therapist is to help the client understand the effects of such experiences and allow the understanding to guide conscious, growth-producing choices.

IMPLICATIONS FOR CLINICAL PRACTICE

The first therapy sessions are crucial in determining whether a client will return. African Americans have a high rate of therapy termination (Fortuna, Alegria, & Gao, 2010). Termination often reflects a counselor's inability to establish an effective therapeutic alliance. African American clients tend to prefer an egalitarian relationship, so it is critically important to answer questions, explain the counseling and assessment process, and enlist the client's assistance in determining goals and treatment strategies. Prior experiences may render issues of trust very important. The counselor can deal with these issues by discussing them directly and by being open, authentic, and empathetic. Clients often make a decision regarding continuation of therapy based on their personal evaluation of the counselor. As one African American client stated, "I am assessing to see if that person [counselor] is willing to go that extra mile and speak my language and talk about my Blackness" (Ward, 2005, p. 475). Counselors may need to have a broader role and more flexible style, including being more direct, serving in an educative function, and helping the client deal with agencies or with issues involving health and employment. Although the order of these elements can be modified and some can be omitted, these steps may be helpful to the counselor and the client:

1. *Understand that power and privilege can affect counseling.* During the first session, it may be beneficial to bring up the reaction of the client to working with a counselor of a different ethnic background. (Although African Americans show a same-race preference, being culturally competent is an even more important factor.) A statement such as, "Sometimes clients feel uncomfortable working with a counselor of a different race. Would this be a problem for you?" Be open if the client discusses any experiences with *racism* or discrimination.

2. *Recognize that there is great diversity among African Americans.* Assess the clients' values and preferences by identifying their expectations and worldview and what they believe counseling entails. Explore their feelings about counseling. Determine how they view the problem and possible solutions.

3. *If clients are there involuntarily, discuss how counseling can be made useful for them.* Explain your relationship with the referring agency and the limits of confidentiality.

4. *Assess the positive assets of the client,* such as personal strengths, family (including relatives and nonrelated friends), community resources, and church.

5. *Help the client define goals and appropriate means of attaining them.* Assess ways in which the client, family members, and friends have handled similar problems successfully.

6. *Establish an egalitarian relationship.* Many African Americans are comfortable establishing a close personal connection with the counselor. This may be accomplished by self-disclosure. If the client appears hostile or aloof, discussing some noncounseling topics may be useful.

7. *After the therapeutic alliance has been formed, collaboratively determine interventions.* Consider culturally adapted evidence-based therapies that have been found to be effective with African Americans. Problem-solving and time-limited approaches may be most acceptable. Analysis of the client's *racial identity* and family structure can be helpful in deciding if alternative treatment modes and approaches might be beneficial.

8. *Determine any external factors that might be related to the presenting problem.* Determine whether and how the client has responded to discrimination and *racism*, both in unhealthy and healthy ways. Do not dismiss issues of *racism* as "just an excuse"; instead, help the client address issues of discrimination and identify productive means of dealing with such problems.

9. *Examine issues around racial identity,* taking into account that many clients at the preencounter stage will not believe that race is an important factor. For some, increased African American identification will be an important factor in establishing a positive self-identity. In these cases, elements of African/African American culture can be incorporated in counseling through readings, movies, music, and discussions of prominent African Americans.

SUMMARY

African Americans represent approximately 13 percent of the U.S. population. On nearly all measures of education, employment, earnings, and psychological and physical health, they experience a standard of living much below their White counterparts. Individual, institutional, and cultural *racism* account for many of these disparities. The life experience of African Americans affects the manifestation of mental disorders, and the therapeutic process. To work effectively with African American clients, therapists must be knowledgeable of their characteristics and strengths. Ethnic and *racial identity*, family structure, spiritual and religious values, education characteristics, and the experiences of Black youths all suggest important dimensions to consider in counseling African Americans. An important aspect of cultural competency with African Americans is the recognition of protective factors and the strengths that have allowed them to survive in an intolerant society. Nine clinical implications for counselor practice are identified.

GLOSSARY TERMS

Afrocentric

Cultural mistrust

Extended family

Healthy cultural paranoia

Kinship bonds

Prejudice

Racial identity

Racial socialization

Racism

Spirituality

REFERENCES

Acs, G. (2011). *Waking up from the American dream.* Retrieved from http://www.pewtrusts.org/uploadedFiles/wwwpewtrustsorg/Reports/Economic_Mobility/Pew_PollProject_Final_SP.pdf

Allen, T. J. (2015). *Why Eric Garner couldn't breathe.* Retrieved from http://inthesetimes.com/article/17518/why_eric_garner_couldnt_breathe

Associated Press. (2015, July 6). *"I felt disgusted": South Carolina governor explains how the "pure hate" of the Charleston church massacre turned her against the Confederate flag.* Retrieved from http://www.dailymail.co.uk/news/article-3150347/I-felt-disgusted-South-Carolina-governor-explains-pure-hate-Charleston-church-massacre-turned-against-Confederate-flag.html#ixzz3f87bo7nl

Avent, J. R., & Cashwell, C. S. (2015). *The Black church: Theology and implications for counseling African Americans.* Retrieved from http://tpcjournal.nbcc.org/the-black-church-theology-and-implications-for-counseling-african-americans/

Belgrave, F. Z., Chase-Vaughn, G., Gray, F., Addison, J. D., & Cherry, V. R. (2000). The effectiveness of a culture- and gender-specific intervention for increasing resiliency among African American preadolescent females. *Journal of Black Psychology, 26,* 133–147.

Bertrand, M., & Mullainathan, S. (2004). Are Emily and Greg more employable than Lakisha and Jamal? A field experiment on labor. *The American Economic Review, 94,* 991–1013.

Bigler, R. S., & Averhart, C. J. (2003). Race and the workforce: Occupational status, aspirations, and stereotyping among African

American children. *Developmental Psychology,* *39,* 572–580.

Black Demographics.com. (2011). *African American population.* Retrieved from http://www.blackdemographics.com/population.html

Black Lives Matter. (2015). *Black Lives Matter. This is not a moment, but a movement.* Retrieved from http://blacklivesmatter.com/about/

Boyd-Franklin, N. (2010). Incorporating spirituality and religion into the treatment of African American clients. *Counseling Psychologist, 38,* 976–1000.

Brame, R., Bushway, S. D., Paternoster, R., & Turner, M. G. (2014). Demographic patterns of cumulative arrest prevalence by ages 18 and 23. *Crime & Delinquency, 60,* 471–486.

Centers for Disease Control and Prevention. (2013). *Infant mortality statistics from the 2010 period linked birth/infant death data set.* Retrieved from http://www.cdc.gov/nchs/data/nvsr/nvsr62/nvsr62_08.pdf

Child Trends. (2010). *Family structure.* Retrieved from www.childtrendsdatabank.org/?q=node/231

Child Trends. (2014). *Educational attainment.* Retrieved from http://www.childtrends.org/?indicators=educational-attainment

Christian, M. D., & Barbarin, O. A. (2001). Cultural resources and psychological adjustment of African American children: Effects of spirituality and racial attribution. *Journal of Black Psychology, 27,* 43–63.

Cross, W. E. (1991). *Shades of Black: Diversity in African American identity.* Philadelphia, PA: Temple University Press.

Cross, W. E. (1995). The psychology of Nigrescence: Revising the Cross model. In J. G. Ponterotto, J. M. Casas, L. A. Suzuki, & C. M. Alexander (Eds.), *Handbook of multicultural counseling* (pp. 93–122). Thousand Oaks, CA: Sage.

Dann, C. (2014a). *Poll: 57 Percent of Americans say race relations in U.S. are bad.* Retrieved from http://www.nbcnews.com/politics/first-read/poll-57-percent-americans-say-race-relations-u-s-are-n269491

Dann, C. (2014b). *Poll: Huge racial gap in confidence in local cops.* Retrieved from http://www.nbcnews.com/politics/first-read/poll-huge-racial-gap-confidence-local-cops-n200151

Eberhardt, J., Davies, P., Purdie-Vaughns, V., & Johnson, S. (2006). Looking deathworthy: Perceived Stereotypicality of Black defendants predicts capital-sentencing outcomes. *Psychological Science, 17,* 383–386.

Fausset, R., & Huffstutter, P. J. (2009). *Black males' fear of racial profiling very real, regardless of class.* Retrieved from http://www.latimes.com/news/nationworld/nation/la-na-racial-profiling25-2009jul25, 0, 7041188.story

Forsyth, J. M., Hall, S., & Carter, R. T. (2015). Racial identity among African Americans and Black West Indian Americans. *Professional Psychology: Research and Practice.* Advance online publication. http://dx.doi.org/10.1037/a0038076

Fortuna, L. R., Alegria, M., & Gao, S. (2010). Retention in depression treatment among ethnic and racial minority groups in the United States. *Depression and Anxiety, 27,* 485–494.

Frame, M. W., & Williams, C. B. (1996). Counseling African Americans: Integrating spirituality in therapy. *Counseling and Values, 41,* 16–28.

Fry, R. (2010). *Hispanics, high school dropouts and the GED.* Retrieved from http://pewhispanic.org/reports/report.php?ReportID=122

Gibbons, F. X., Etcheverry, P. E., Stock, M. L., Gerrard, M., Weng, C.-Y., & O'Hara, R. E. (2010). Exploring the link between racial discrimination and substance use: What mediates? What buffers? *Journal of Personality and Social Psychology, 99,* 785–801.

Glum, J. (2015). *U.S. Attorney General Loretta Lynch says Sandra Bland's death highlights Black community's concerns about police.* Retrieved from http://www.ibtimes.com/loretta-lynch-says-sandra-blands-death-highlights-black-communitys-concerns-about-2024943

Goff, P. A., Jackson, M. C., Di Leone, B. A., Culotta, C. M., & DiTomasso, N. A. (2014). The essence of innocence: Consequences of dehumanizing Black children. *Journal of Personality and Social Psychology, 106*, 526–545.

Hagler, J. (2015). *8 facts you should know about the criminal justice system and people of color.* Retrieved from https://www.americanprogress .org/issues/race/news/2015/05/28/113436 /8-facts-you-should-know-about-the-criminal-justice-system-and-people-of-color/

Harrington, E. F., Crowther, J. H., & Shipherd, J. C. (2010). Trauma, binge eating, and the "strong Black woman." *Journal of Consulting and Clinical Psychology, 78*, 469–479.

Harry, B., Klingner, J.K., & Hart, J. (2005). African American families under fire: Ethnographic views of family strengths. *Remedial and Special Education, 26*, 101–112.

Holmes, S. A., & Morin, R. (2006, June 3). *Black men torn between promise and doubt.* Retrieved from http://www.msnbc.nsn.com/id/print/1 /displaymode/1098

Johnston, L. D., O'Malley, P. M., Miech, R. A., Bachman, J. G., & Schulenberg, J. E. (2014). *Monitoring the future national results on drug use: 1975–2013: Overview, key findings on adolescent drug use.* Ann Arbor, MI: Institute for Social Research, University of Michigan.

Jones, A. C. (1985). Psychological functioning in Black Americans: A conceptual guide for use in psychotherapy. *Psychotherapy, 22*, 363–369.

Jordan, A. H., Lovett, B. J., & Sweeton, J. L. (2012). The social psychology of Black-White interracial interactions: Implications for culturally competent clinical practice. *Journal of Multicultural Counseling and Development, 40*, 132–143.

Kaslow, N. J., Leiner, A. S., Reviere, S., Jackson, E., Bethea, K., & Thompson, M. P. (2010). Suicidal, abused African American women's response to a culturally informed intervention. *Journal of Consulting and Clinical Psychology, 78*, 449–458.

LaTaillade, J. J. (2006). Considerations for treatment of African American couple relationships. *Journal of Cognitive Psychotherapy: An International Quarterly, 20*, 341–354.

Lee, D., & Ahn, S. (2013). The relation of racial identity, ethnic identity, and racial socialization to discrimination–distress: A meta-analysis of Black Americans. *Journal of Counseling Psychology, 60*, 1–14.

McCollum, V.J.C. (1997). Evolution of the African American family personality: Considerations for family therapy. *Journal of Multicultural Counseling and Development, 25*, 219–229.

Monroe, C. R. (2005). Why are "bad boys" always Black? Causes of disproportionality in school discipline and recommendations for change. *Clearing House, 79*, 45–50.

Moser, W. (2015). *Finding the "Jamal" in Barack Obama's immediately famous eulogy.* Retrieved from http://www.chicagomag.com/city-life /July-2015/Finding-the-Jamal-in-Barack -Obamas-Immediately-Famous-Eulogy/

Mulady, K. (2011). *Behind bars: For African-American girls acting out is a crime.* Retrieved from http://www.equalvoiceforfamilies.org/?p=430

Muroff, J. (2007). Cultural diversity and cognitive behavior therapy. In T. Ronen & A. Freeman (Eds.), *Cognitive behavior therapy in clinical social work practice* (pp. 109–146). New York, NY: Springer.

Neal-Barnett, A. (1997). *Young children and racism.* Retrieved from http://webshare.northseattle. edu/fam180/topics/anti-bias/yngchildracism. html

Owens, D., Stewart, T. A., & Bryant, R. M. (2011). Urban African American high school female adolescents' perceptions, attitudes, and experiences with professional school counselors: A pilot study. *Georgia School Counselors Association Journal, 18*, 34–41.

Parham, T. A., & Helms, J. E. (1981). The influence of Black students' racial attitudes on preferences for counselor's race. *Journal of Counseling Psychology, 28*, 250–257.

Parlapiano, A., Gebeloff, R., & Carter, S. (2015). The shrinking American middle class. Retrieved from http://www.nytimes.com /interactive/2015/01/25/upshot/shrinking -middle-class.html?abt=0002&abg=0

Perez, E. (2015). *Justice report finds systematic discrimination against African Americans in Ferguson.* Retrieved from http://www.cnn .com/2015/03/03/politics/justice-report -ferguson-discrimination/

Pew Research Center. (2010). *A year after Obama's election: Blacks upbeat about Black progress, prospects.* Retrieved from http://pewresearch.org/ pubs/1459/year-after-obama-election-black- public-opinion

Pfeffer, R. (2011). *Growing incarceration of young African-American women a cause for concern.* Retrieved from http://oaklandlocal .com/posts/2011/05/growing-incarceration- young-african-american-women-cause-concern

Pierre, M. R., & Mahilik, J. R. (2005). Examining African self-consciousness and Black racial identity as predictors of Black men's psychological well-being. *Cultural Diversity and Ethnic Minority Psychology, 11,* 28–40.

Queener, J. E., & Martin, J. K. (2001). Providing culturally relevant mental health services: Collaboration between psychology and the African American church. *Journal of Black Psychology, 27,* 112–122.

Rockymore, M. (2008). *A practice guide for working with African American families in the child welfare system: The role of the caseworker in identifying, developing and supporting strengths in African American families involved in child protection services.* (DHS-4702-ENG 8–06). St. Paul, MN: Minnesota Department of Human Services, Child Safety and Permanency Division.

Rodriguez, J., McKay, M. M., & Bannon, W. M. (2008). The role of racial socialization in relation to parenting practices and youth behavior: An exploratory analysis. *Social Work in Mental Health, 6,* 30–54.

Roettger, M. E., Swisher, R. R., Kuhl, D. C., & Chavez, J. (2011). Paternal incarceration and trajectories of marijuana and other illegal drug use from adolescence into young adulthood: Evidence from longitudinal panels of males and females in the United States. *Addiction, 106,* 121–132.

Rudd, T. (2014). *Racial disproportionality in school discipline.* Retrieved from http:// kirwaninstitute.osu.edu/racial-disproportionality -in-school-discipline-implicit-bias-is-heavily -implicated/

Schwartz, S., Hoyte, J., James, T., Conoscenti, L., Johnson, R., & Liebschutz, J. (2010). Challenges to engaging Black male victims of community violence in healthcare research: Lessons learned from two studies. *Psychological Trauma: Theory, Research, Practice, and Policy, 2,* 54–62.

Seaton, E. K., Caldwell, C. H., Sellers, R. M., & Jackson, J. S. (2011). An intersectional approach for understanding perceived discrimination and psychological well-being among African American and Caribbean Black youth. *Developmental Psychology, 46,* 1372–1379.

Shorter-Gooden, K., & Washington, N. C. (1996). Young, Black, and female: The challenge of weaving an identity. *Journal of Adolescence, 19,* 465–475.

Substance Abuse and Mental Health Services Administration. (2013). *Results from the 2012 National Survey on Drug Use and Health: Summary of national findings.* (NSDUH Series H 46, HHS Publication No. SMA 13–4795.) Rockville, MD: Author.

Talleyrand, R. M. (2010). Eating disorders in African American girls: Implications for counselors. *Journal of Counseling and Development, 88,* 319–324.

Taylor, Z. E., Larsen-Rife, D., Conger, R. D., Widaman, K. F., & Cutrona, C. E. (2010). Life stress, maternal optimism, and adolescent competence in single mother, African American families. *Journal of Family Counseling, 24,* 468–477.

Toldson, I. A., Braithwaite, R. L., & Rentie, R. J. (2009). Promoting college aspirations among school-aged Black American males. *Diversity in Higher Education, 7*, 117–137.

Townes, D. L., Chavez-Korell, S., & Cunningham, N. J. (2009). Reexamining the relationships between racial identity, cultural mistrust, help-seeking attitudes, and preference for a Black counselor. *Journal of Counseling Psychology, 56*, 330–336.

U.S. Census Bureau (2013). *Poverty rates for selected detailed race and Hispanic groups by state and place: 2007–2011.* Retrieved from http://www.census.gov/prod/2013pubs/acsbr11–17.pdf

U.S. Census Bureau (2014). *People quickfacts.* Retrieved from http://quickfacts.census.gov/qfd/states/00000.html

U.S. Department of Labor. (2015). *Employment status of the civilian population by race, sex, and age.* Retrieved from http://www.bls.gov/news.release/empsit.t02.htm

Vespa, J., Lewis, J. M., & Kreider, R. M. (2013). *America's families and living arrangements: 2012.* Retrieved from http://www.census.gov/hhes/families/data/cps2012F.html

Viglione, J., Hannon, L., & DeFina, R. (2011). The impact of light skin on prison time for Black female offenders. *Social Science Journal, 48*, 250–258.

Want, V., Parham, T. A., Baker, R. C., & Sherman, M. (2004). African American students' ratings of Caucasian and African American counselors varying in racial consciousness. *Cultural Diversity and Ethnic Minority Psychology, 10*, 123–136.

Ward, E. C. (2005). Keeping it real: A grounded theory study of African American clients engaging in counseling at a community mental health agency. *Journal of Counseling Psychology, 52*(4), 471–481.

Watkins, N. L., Labarrie, T. L., & Appio, L. M. (2010). Black undergraduates' experiences with perceived racial microaggressions in predominately White colleges and universities. In D. W. Sue (Ed.), *Microaggressions and marginality* (pp. 25–51). Hoboken, NJ: Wiley.

Weir, K. (2014). Injustice, in black and white. *Monitor on Psychology, 45*, 14–15.

Williams, J. C., Phillips, K. W., & Hall, E. V. (2014). *Double jeopardy: Gender bias against women of color in science.* Retrieved from http://www.toolsforchangeinstem.org/tools/double-jeopardy-report

Counseling American Indians/ Native Americans[*] and Alaska Natives

---

[*]American Indian and Native American are used interchangeably in this chapter.

Of the 175 Indian languages once spoken in the United States, only about 20 are still passed on to younger generations. James Jackson, Jr., remembers his experience in a boarding school when a teacher grabbed him when he was speaking his native language and threatened to wash out his mouth with soap: "That's where we lost it [our language]." (Brooke, 1998)

In 2010, the University of North Dakota agreed to retire the fighting Sioux name and logo to comply with a ban from the NCAA (National Collegiate Athletic Association). Do the Native-themed mascots or logos impact the psychological well-being of American Indians? The American Psychological Association (2005) believes such symbols and imagery undermine respectful and accurate images of the American Indians' culture.

In 2014, the city of Eureka, California, drafted an apology to the Wiyot tribe for the 1860 massacre on Indian Island, during which 200 sleeping Wiyot, including women and children, were slaughtered. The City Council removed the apology part of the letter for fear of opening itself up to liability and substituted language acknowledging that the Wiyot people had been massacred but not stating who was responsible. (Lee, 2015)

American Indians/Alaska Natives form a highly heterogeneous group composed of 566 distinct *tribes*, some consisting of only four or five members (Bureau of Indian Affairs, 2014). The American Indian and Alaska Native population was 3.8 million, representing 1.2% of the total U.S. population (U.S. Census Bureau, 2014). An additional 1.81 million Americans report having Indian roots. About 34% of American Indians live on *reservations*, whereas 57% reside in metropolitan areas (Bureau of Indian Affairs, 2011). Fewer American Indians are high school graduates than the general U.S. population (71% versus 80%). American Indians have the highest national poverty rate, 27%, with income only 69% of the mean income of all households (Macartney, Bishaw, & Fontenot, 2013). American Indians differ in their degree of *acculturation*. Although most do not live on *reservations* or with their *tribes*, many are returning because of casino jobs or a more nurturing environment. One man who returned described his need for a more "friendly place, friendly face, and friendly greetings" (Shukovsky, 2001, p. A1).

What constitutes an Indian is often an area of controversy. The U.S. Census depends on self-report of racial identity. Congress has formulated a legal definition: An individual must have an Indian blood quantum of at least 25% to be considered an Indian. This definition has caused problems both within and outside the Indian community. Some *tribes* have developed their own criteria and specify either tribal enrollment or blood quantum levels. Tribal definitions typically allow inclusion of the 60% of American Indians who have mixed heritage, including Black, White, and Latino/a backgrounds (Trimble, Fleming, Beauvais, & Jumper-Thurman, 1996).

Because American Indian/Native American and Alaska Natives (AI/AN) comprise such a small percentage of the U.S. population, they are relatively "invisible," which makes information about them susceptible to stereotypes. This is one of the reasons many oppose the use of Indian-themed mascots and logos. American Indians want the ability to define themselves and are aware of the harmful effects of stereotyped portrayals (Jacobs, 2014). American Indian high school and college students who viewed these types of images reported higher levels of depression, lower self-esteem, and decreased feelings of community worth (Fryberg, Markus, Oyserman, & Stone, 2008). In examining online responses to this controversy, Steinfeldt et al. (2010) found hostile attitudes from non-Indian respondents who did not appear to understand the issues involved: "If the nickname is taken away, we should take away Indian educational programming and funding" and "We are being victimized by reverse racism and PC society."

Health statistics reveal significant concerns. The death rate by any cause is nearly 50% higher for AI/AN persons than for White individuals (Espey et al., 2014). The alcoholism mortality rate is over twice as high for Indians as for the U.S. population as a whole (Centers for Disease Control and Prevention, 2008). AI/AN individuals have death rates for unintentional injuries due to motor vehicle traffic crashes, poisoning, and falls that are 1.4 to 3 times higher than among Whites (Murphy et al., 2014). Injuries and violence account for 75% of all deaths for American Indian/Native American and Alaska Native Americans between the ages of 1 and 19. These populations also suffer disproportionately from depression, anxiety, and substance abuse (Office of Minority Health, 2012). Among Native American women at a private care facility in New Mexico, 21% reported mood disorders, 47% had an anxiety disorder, and 14% had alcohol dependence or abuse issues. These rates are 2 to 2.5 times higher than found in the general population (Duran et al., 2004).

CHARACTERISTICS AND STRENGTHS

In the following sections we discuss the characteristics, values, and strengths of American Indian/Native Alaska populations and consider their implications in treatment. Remember that these are generalizations and that their applicability needs to be assessed for particular clients and their families.

Tribal Social Structure

For the many American Indians, living both on and off *reservations*, the *tribe* is of fundamental importance. The *tribe* and the *reservation*, an interdependent system, provide Native Americans with a sense of belonging and security. Tribal connections are significant because individuals see themselves as an extension of their *tribe*. Status is achieved, and rewards gained, by adherence to tribal structure. Indians judge themselves in terms of whether their behaviors are of benefit to the *tribe*. Personal accomplishments are honored and supported if they serve to benefit the *tribe*.

Implications

Interventions and decision-making with American Indian/Native American and Alaska Native individuals should take into account the importance placed on tribal relationships. In a study of 401 American Indian/Native American youth (half tribal-based and half urban-based), urban-based youth were more likely to identify personal, familial, and environmental strengths than were tribal-based youth, whereas the latter identified more tribal strengths (Stiffman et al., 2007). The *tribe* is very important for many Indians, even those who do not reside on the *reservation*. Many use the word *here* to describe the *reservation* and the word *there* to describe everything that is outside. The *reservation* is a place to conduct ceremonies and social events and to maintain cultural identity. Indians who leave the *reservation* to seek greater opportunities sometimes report losing their sense of personal identity (Lone-Knapp, 2000).

Family Structure

It is difficult to describe "the Indian family." It varies from the matriarchal structures seen in the Navajo, where women govern the family, to patriarchal structures, in which men are the primary authority figures. Some generalizations can be made, however. A high fertility rate, out-of-wedlock births, and strong roles for women are commonly seen. For most *tribes*, the *extended family* is the basic unit. Children are often partially raised by relatives such as aunts, uncles, and grandparents, who live in separate households (Garrett, 2006).

Implications

The concept of the *extended family* is often misunderstood by those in the majority culture who operate under the concept of the nuclear family. Misinterpretations are possible if a counselor believes that parents should raise and be responsible for their own children. The *extended family* often includes distant relatives and even friends. It is not unusual for children to stay in multiple households. In work with children, counselors should determine the roles of various family members, so that interventions can include appropriate individuals. The emphasis on collectivism is strong. If the goals or techniques of therapy lead to discord within the family or *tribe*, they will not be effective. Interventions may need to include the input of family, relatives, friends, elders, or tribal leaders.

Cultural and Spiritual Values

Because of the great diversity and variation among American Indians/Native Americans, it is difficult to describe a set of values that encompasses all groups. However, certain generalizations can be made regarding common values (Garrett & Portman, 2011; Jumper-Reeves, Dustman, Harthun, Kulis, & Brown, 2014).

1. *Sharing.* Honor and respect are gained by *sharing* and giving, in contrast with the dominant U.S. culture, where status is gained by the accumulation of material goods.

    Implications. Once enough money is earned, youth and adults may stop working and spend time and energy in ceremonial activities. The accumulation of wealth is not a high priority but is a means to enjoy the present. Interventions targeting alcohol or drug use should take into consideration the emphasis on *sharing*.

2. *Cooperation.* Having a harmonious relationship is important and the *tribe* and the family take precedence over the individual. The children are often sensitive to the opinions and attitudes of their peers and may actively avoid disagreements or contradictions. Most do not like to be singled out and made to perform in school unless the whole group benefits.

Implications: Instead of going to work or school, children or adults may prioritize assisting a family member needing help. Children may be seen as unmotivated in school because of their reluctance to compete with peers.

3. *Noninterference.* It is important not to interfere with others and observe rather than react impulsively. Rights of others are respected. This belief in noninterference extends to parenting style.

   Implications: Culture significantly shapes parent–child relationships. American Indians/Native Americans are more indulgent and less punitive than parents from other ethnic groups (BigFoot & Funderburk, 2010). EuroAmerican parenting styles may conflict with American Indian values. One culturally sensitive parent education program developed for this population included (a) use of the oral tradition of storytelling to teach lessons to children; (b) understanding the spiritual nature of child rearing and the spiritual value of children; and (c) use of the *extended family* in child rearing. The eight-session program included social time for parents and children before each session, including storytelling and a potluck meal. The program applied traditional teaching methods, such as nurturing, use of nature to teach lessons, and use of harmony as a guiding principle for family life (Gorman & Balter, 1997).

4. *Time orientation.* There is a greater focus on the present than on the future. Ideas of punctuality or planning for the future may be unimportant. Life is to be lived in the here and now.

   Implications: Tasks may be approached from a logical perspective rather than according to deadlines. In contrast, the U.S. majority culture values delay of gratification and planning for future goals. In working with these issues, the counselor should acknowledge such value differences and help the individual or family develop strategies to negotiate value conflicts.

5. *Spirituality.* The spirit, mind, and body are all interconnected. Illness involves disharmony between these elements. Positive emotions can be curative; healing can take place through events such as talking to an old friend on the phone or watching children play (Garrett & Wilbur, 1999).

   Implications: Traditional curative approaches attempt to restore spirit–mind–body harmony. The *sweat lodge* and *vision quest* are often used to reestablish connections between the mind, body, and spirit. To treat a problem successfully, all of these elements may need to be considered and addressed.

Counselors can help clients identify factors involved in disharmony; determine curative events, behaviors, and feelings; and use client-generated solutions to create balance.

6. *Nonverbal communication.* Learning occurs by listening rather than talking. Families tend to ask few direct questions. Direct eye contact with an elder may be seen as a sign of disrespect.

   Implications: Differences in *nonverbal communication* can lead to misunderstandings. For example, lack of eye contact or direct communication may be viewed as a sign of disrespect. It is important to determine whether specific behaviors are due to cultural values or are actual problems.

Cultural Strengths

American Indian/Native American and Alaska Native populations had to endure extermination and assimilation efforts and were able to do so because of cultural values and strengths such as *spirituality*; respect for traditional values and ceremonies; *extended family* networks; allegiance to the family, community, and *tribe*; wisdom of the elders; respect for the environment and the land; connection to the past, adaptability, and the promotion of such themes as belonging, mastery, independence, and generosity (APA, 2014; Gilgun, 2002). The values of listening and observing rather than reacting can enhance communication and decrease conflict. Spiritual and traditional practices also act as a protective factor (Garroutte et al., 2003). The respect shown for the environment and the interconnection between humans and the environment is something that can be emulated by all cultures. Additionally, the focus on the present is increasingly recognized as an asset, particularly among those who incorporate mindfulness activities into clinical practice (Chiesa & Serretti, 2011).

SPECIFIC CHALLENGES

In the following sections we describe the challenges often faced by American Indian/Native American populations and consider their implications in treatment.

Historical and Sociopolitical Background

In North America, wars and diseases that resulted from contact with Europeans decimated the American Indian/Native American population; by the end of the

18th century, only about 10% of the original population remained. Additionally, the *tribes* suffered massive loss of their land. Their experience in America is not comparable to that of any other ethnic group. In contrast to immigrants, who arrived with few resources and struggled to gain equality, American Indians/ Native Americans originally had resources. However, their land and status were severely eroded by imperial, colonial, and then federal and state policies (Johnson et al., 1995). For years, extermination and seizure of lands seemed to be the primary governmental policy toward Indians.

In the 1830s, more than 125,000 people from different *tribes* were forced from their homes in many different states to a *reservation* in Oklahoma. The move was traumatic for their families and, in many cases, disrupted their cultural traditions. Assaults against their culture also occurred in the form of attempts to "civilize" them. Children were removed from their families and placed in English-speaking boarding schools. They were not allowed to speak their own language and were forced to spend 8 continuous years away from their families and *tribes*. Children were also removed from their homes and placed with non-Indian families until the Indian Child Welfare Act of 1978 prohibited these practices (Choney, Berryhill-Paapke, & Robbins, 1995; Johnson et al., 1995). However, during the 1998 congressional hearings regarding possible amendments to the Indian Child Welfare Act, statistics were cited indicating that over 90% of American Indian children were still being placed by state courts and child welfare workers into non-Indian homes (*Congressional Record*, 1997). Although amendments to the original act dramatically reduced this type of placement, the National Indian Child Welfare Association (2014) and other advocacy organizations recently asked the Department of Justice to investigate Indian Child Welfare Act violations.

These disruptive events had a tremendous negative impact on family and tribal cohesion and prevented the transmission of cultural values from parents to children. Some professionals believe that the experiences of colonization, coercive assimilation experiences in boarding schools, and the widespread loss of indigenous languages and customs may result in "historical trauma" in which the distress and dysfunction experienced by an individual can be passed down intergenerationally (Gone, 2014). Individuals may have unresolved grief—"soul wounds"—that lead to behavioral dysfunction and substance abuse. The following case study illustrates some of the disruptions caused by a boarding school experience.

MARY

Mary was born on the *reservation*. She was sent away to school when she was 12 and did not return to the *reservation* until she was 20. By the time she returned, her mother had died from pneumonia. She didn't remember her father, the medicine man of the *tribe*, very well. Shortly after she returned, she became pregnant by a non-Indian man she met at a bar. Mary's father . . . looked forward to teaching and leaving to his grandson, John, the ways of the medicine man . . . . John felt his grandfather was out of step with the 20th century . . . . Mary . . . could not validate the grandfather's way of life . . . [because] she remembered having difficulty fitting in when she returned to the *reservation* . . . . In response to the growing distance between her father and her son, she became more and more depressed and began to drink heavily. (Sage, 1997, p. 48)

CASE STUDY

In the past, the *tribe*, through the *extended family*, was responsible for the education and training of children. The sense of tribal identity developed through this tradition was significantly eroded by governmental policies. In addition, even recent history is full of broken treaties, the seizure or misuse of Indian land, and battles led by local or federal officials to remove or severely limit fishing and hunting rights. Thus American Indians/Native Americans are often suspicious of the motives of the majority culture; many expect that they will not be treated fairly by non-Indians (Cruz & Spence, 2005).

Implications

When working with children and families, it is important to consider the historical sociopolitical relationship between American Indians/Native Americans and the local, state, and federal government. The counselor should understand not only the national history of oppression but also local issues and specific tribal history.

The historic disruption of families resulting in the Indian Child Welfare Act has important implications for how American Indians/Native Americans might view child protective services or respond to runaway youth. Currently, decisions regarding the placement of their children are held in tribal courts. Testimony from expert witnesses familiar with the specific tribal or cultural group must be obtained before children can be removed from their homes. Additionally, if children are removed from their parents, residence with *extended family* members, other tribal members, or other American Indian/Native American families is given primary consideration.

Educational Concerns

There is a high rate of school failure among American Indian/Native American and Alaska Native populations (Whitesell, Mitchell, Spicer, & the Voices of Indian Teen Project Team, 2009) and they have the lowest postsecondary gradua-tion rate of any minority group (National Center for Education Statistics, 2013). In fact, the educational achievement gap of American Indian/Native American and Alaska Native youth with White youth has widened in recent years (Edu-cation Trust, 2013). The children appear to do well during the first few years of school. However, by the fourth grade, a pattern of academic decline and truancy develops; a significant drop in achievement motivation often occurs in middle school. Although some have argued that traditional cultural values and beliefs are incompatible with those of the educational system, there is increasing support for the view that perceived barriers to mobility are the culprit for reduced academic performance. In other words, academic success is not perceived as leading to rewards or success. Some contend that once children realize their "Indianness," achievement motivation drops (Wood & Clay, 1996). In addition, many youth see that jobs are available in casinos or on the *reservation*, so they do not see the value in pursuing a "White man's education." Many never finish high school. Only 13% have a bachelor's degree, versus 28% of the U.S. population (Ogun-wole, Drewery, & Rios-Vargas, 2012). Such educational gaps are believed to per-petuate the cycle of poverty and reduced opportunities and may contribute to the high suicide rate among American Indian adolescents (Keane, Dick, Bechtold, & Manson, 1996).

Implications

The blame for school failure has generally been placed on the individual rather than on the school environment. However, many youths who leave school report feeling "pushed out" and express mistrust of teachers who represent the same White community that has historically exerted control over the economic, social, and religious lives of Indians (Deyhle & Swisher, 1999). At a systems level, pos-itive changes could occur if public schools and institutions of higher education (a) recognized the sociocultural history of American Indians/Native Americans and acknowledged their perceptions of schools as a potentially hostile environ-ment and (b) increased efforts to accommodate some of the social and cultural differences of the students, including adapting curricula to reflect these students' cultural background (Reyhner, 2002). The perceived lack of reward for academic achievement also needs to be addressed. Schools must help students bridge the two worlds of American Indian/Native American and White cultures. Some *tribes* have given up on the public school system and have developed their own learning centers and community colleges.

The AlterNative Education Program was created to interest American Indians/Native Americans in postsecondary education. It recruits indigenous students and alumni at Columbia University to travel to *reservations* in New Mexico and teach high school–aged youth about their identity and past. The program covers areas such as oppression, stereotypes, and colonialism; focuses on identity building; and encourages higher education. Responses from the participants have been quite positive and have resulted in increased interest in college enrollment (Aronowitz, 2014).

Acculturation Conflicts

> When I attended the university, that's the first time I saw a pow-wow. . . .It's only now [that] I start learning my culture.

> I don't know the meaning of the symbols of our culture. Instead, I know the symbols of the Catholic faith. (Gone, 2009, p. 757)

Not only do Indian children and adolescents face the same developmental issues as other youth, but they also may experience conflict over exposure to two very different cultures, a factor that may result in failure to develop a positive self-image or strong ethnic identity (Garrett & Portman, 2011). Many youth are caught between the expectations of their parents to maintain traditional values and the necessity to adapt to the majority culture (Rieckmann, Wadsworth, & Deyhle, 2004). In one study of adolescents, the most serious problems identified involved ethnic identity, family relationships, grades, and concerns about the future. One-third of the girls surveyed reported feeling they did not want to live (Bee-Gates, Howard-Pitney, LaFromboise, & Rowe, 1996).

Many Indians are acculturated and hold the values of the larger society. The degree to which a client identifies with the native culture or is acculturated to U.S. culture should always be considered. Garrett and Pichette (2000) have formulated five levels of cultural orientation:

1. *Traditional.* The individual may speak little English and practice traditional tribal customs and methods of worship.

2. *Marginal.* The individual may be bilingual but has lost touch with his or her cultural heritage, yet is not fully accepted in mainstream society.

3. *Bicultural.* The person is conversant with both sets of values and can communicate in a variety of contexts.

4. *Assimilated.* The individual embraces only the mainstream culture's values, behaviors, and expectations.

5. *Pantraditional.* The individual has been exposed to and adopted mainstream values but is making a conscious effort to return to the "old ways."

Implications

Counselors need to discuss the client's tribal affiliation (if any), languages spoken, self-identity, and residential background, and find out whether there is a current relationship to a *tribe* or tribal culture (Garrett & Pichette, 2000). The types of problems and the therapeutic process and goals appropriate for someone living on a rural *reservation* may be very different from those appropriate for an urbanized Indian who retains few traditional beliefs. Individuals with a traditional orientation may be unfamiliar with expectations of the dominant culture and may want to develop the skills and resources to deal with mainstream society. In contrast, assimilated or marginal American Indians may want to examine self-identity conflicts and may face issues such as (a) lack of pride in or denial of their heritage, (b) pressure to adopt majority cultural values, (c) guilt over not knowing or participating in the cultural customs or events, (d) negative views regarding their group, and (e) a lack of an extended support or belief system. It may be healthiest to have a bicultural orientation which allows the individual to live in both worlds. This perspective appears to confer strength and resiliency in American Indians (Flynn, Olson & Yellig, 2014).

The client's level of *acculturation* should also be a factor that guides the therapist's selection of therapeutic interventions. For example, acculturated and bicultural American Indians/Native Americans have found success with all components of cognitive behavior therapy (CBT), whereas those who are traditionally oriented are responsive to the short-term focus, activity schedule, and homework assignments in CBT but have difficulty with the underlying theoretical assumptions regarding the association between thoughts and emotional symptoms (Jackson, Schmutzer, Wenzel, & Tyler, 2006). In these cases, modified explanations for CBT may be useful.

Alcohol and Substance Abuse

> *D1 talked about lack of things to do on the reservation and how it related to substance abuse: That's all there is to do. There's really not much going on, especially on the reservation, but to drink and get high. I mean from what I've seen before, that's all you really have to look forward to is getting high or getting drunk (Myhra & Wieling, 2014, p. 306).*

Substance abuse is one of the greatest problems faced by American Indian/ Native American and Alaska Native populations. Many youth begin substance use at an early age, use multiple substances, and maintain high levels of use during adolescence (Boyd-Ball, Véronneau, Dishion, & Kavanagh, 2014). Although rates of alcohol use vary across *tribes* and regions, American Indians/Native American and Alaska Natives have the highest weekly alcohol consumption of any ethnic group (Chartier & Caetano, 2010). Thus alcoholism is a significant concern for many *tribes* (Spillane, Cyders, & Maurelli, 2012). However, it must be remembered that there is variability in alcohol-use patterns between specific subgroups; for example, Southwest Indians, especially females, have low rates of alcohol consumption (Chartier & Caetano, 2010).

A variety of explanations have been put forth for the high levels of alcohol abuse. Although drinking alcoholic beverages may initially have been incorporated into cultural practices as an activity of *sharing*, giving, and togetherness (Swinomish Tribal Mental Health Project, 1991), heavy alcohol use is associated with other factors, such as feelings of powerlessness (Taylor, 2000). Substance abuse is also related to low self-esteem, cultural identity conflicts, lack of positive role models, childhood maltreatment, social pressure to use substances, hopelessness about life, and a breakdown in the family (Whitesell, Beals, Crow, Mitchell, & Novins, 2012)).

Implications

Successful drug treatment programs have incorporated appropriate cultural elements. Because peers often support substance use, prevention and interventions should involve not only the individual but also the community and family, including siblings, cousins, and friends (Boyd-Ball, Véronneau, Dishion, & Kavanagh, 2014). One tribal community reduced their alcoholism rate from 95% to 5% in 10 years by revitalizing traditional culture and taking a strong community stance against alcohol abuse (Thomason, 2000). Many *tribes* have developed similar programs to deal with alcohol- and drug-abuse issues. Programs have the greatest chance of breaking the cycle of substance abuse when they incorporate cultural strengths, evidence-based strategies, and traditional tribal practices such as talking circles and ceremonies (Jumper-Reeves et al., 2014).

Domestic Violence

The rate of domestic violence, along with physical and sexual assault, is quite high in many native communities. Statistics indicate that American Indian/Native American and Alaska Native women experience domestic violence and physical assault at much higher rates than women of other ethnicities (Peters, Straits, & Gauthier, 2015). Native women often experience sexual and physical abuse early in life; abuse is especially high among lesbian and bisexual women (D'Oro, 2010). The high incidence of domestic violence may result from changes in traditional roles for men and women, as well as substance abuse and stressors associated with social and economic marginalization. There is an intergenerational pattern of violence in many families in which individuals who witnessed family or domestic violence become aggressive with their own partners (Myhra & Wieling, 2014). Thus the cycle of violence is perpetuated.

Implications

During counseling, it may be difficult to determine whether domestic violence is occurring within a family or couple. Native American women who are abused may remain silent because of cultural barriers, a high level of distrust of White-dominated agencies, fear of familial alienation, and the historical failure of state and tribal agencies to protect women from domestic crimes (Wahab & Olson, 2004). Jurisdictional struggles between state and tribal authorities can also result in a lack of help for women. Many *tribes* acknowledge the problem of family violence and have developed community-based domestic violence interventions using strategies from the Indian cultural perspective (Hamby, 2000). When working with a domestic-violence issue with an Native American woman, tribal issues, tribal programs, and family support options should be identified.

Suicide

At the Montana Indian Reservation, sixteen-year-old Franci Jackson considered hanging herself with a rope when she felt she couldn't take any more bullying at school. But then she changed her mind. "I thought of my mom and dad and how much they love me. And if I leave, what would they do without me? But most kids don't think," she said in tears. Six American Indian students living in her area had killed themselves in the previous year with another 20 attempting suicide. (Associated Press, 2011)

Suicide rates have reached epidemic proportions among American Indian/Native American and Alaskan Natives. For individuals between the ages of 15 and 34 years, the suicide rate is about 250 percent higher than the general population and is the second leading cause of death among those aged 15 to 34 years (Centers for Disease Control and Prevention, 2013). Adolescence through early adulthood is the time of greatest risk for suicide, especially among males (Middlebrook, LeMaster, Beals, Novins, & Manson, 2001). American Indian/Native American and Alaska Native youth have twice the rate of attempted and completed suicide as other youth (D'Oro, 2011). Among a sample of 122 middle-school children living on a North Plains *reservation*, 20 percent had made a nonfatal suicide attempt and of this group, nearly half had attempted suicide two or more times (LaFromboise, Medoff, Harris, & Lee, 2007). Death rates from suicide are highest among AI/NA/AN populations in Alaska and in the northern plain states (Herne, Bartholomew, & Weahkee, 2014). The high incidence of suicide is associated with alcohol abuse, poverty, boredom, family breakdown, and disconnection from their culture and community (Gray & McCullagh, 2014).

Implications

There are many societal and economic issues facing American Indians/Native Americans and Alaska Natives. For those who live on a *reservation* or identify with a *tribe*, community activities sometimes focus on reducing suicidal ideation and promoting resilience in youth. Effective programs need to be culturally consistent. For example, many Indians believe that mental health issues are due to unbalanced spiritual relationships (Limb & Hodge, 2010). In traditional belief systems, there is not only a seen world but also an unseen world. Events that disrupt the unseen world disturb the harmony in the seen world. Therefore, if intervention focuses only on the seen world, change will likely not occur (Cruz & Spence, 2005).

A promising culturally tailored suicide intervention program was implemented by LaFromboise and Howard-Pitney (1995) at the request of the Zuni Tribal High School. Scores on a suicide probability measure indicated that 81%

of the students were in the moderate-to-severe risk range. Of the participants, 18% reported having attempted suicide, and 40% reported knowing of a relative or friend who had committed suicide. The program included role-playing, building self-esteem, identifying emotions and stressors, recognizing and eliminating negative thoughts or emotions, receiving information on suicide and intervention strategies, and setting personal and community goals. The program was effective in reducing feelings of hopelessness and suicidal probability ratings. Intervention programs may need to be developed based on the needs of individual *tribes*. For example, although among the Pueblo suicidal ideation was associated with the suicidal behavior of friends, for adolescents from Northern Plain *tribes* the most significant factors were low self-esteem and depression (LaFromboise, 2006).

 IMPLICATIONS FOR CLINICAL PRACTICE

1. Explore the client's ethnic identity, tribal affiliation, and adherence to cultural values. Also, discuss family members' association with a *tribe* or *reservation* and the importance of rituals or ceremonies in healing. In addition, determine the appropriateness of a mind-body-spirit emphasis. Keep in mind that many American Indians adhere completely to mainstream values, whereas others, especially those living on or near *reservations*, are more likely to hold traditional values (Peters et al., 2015).

2. Understand the extensive history of oppression and social injustice experienced by American Indians and learn about local issues associated with the client's *tribe* or *reservation*.

3. Learn about the client using a client-centered listening style, and gradually determine when it is appropriate to use more structure and questions. Try not to hurry the individual. Allow sufficient time for clients to finish statements and thoughts. Be aware that some clients may prefer brief interventions (Flynn et al., 2014).

4. Assess the problem from the perspective of the individual, family, *extended family*, and, if appropriate, the tribal community; attempt to determine the role of cultural and experiential factors and if they have seen a traditional healer.

5. If necessary, address basic needs such as problems involving food, shelter, childcare, and employment. Identify possible resources, such as Indian Health Services or tribal programs.

6. Be alert for problems such as domestic violence, substance abuse, depression, and suicidality.

7. Identify possible environmental contributors to problems, such as racism, discrimination, poverty, and *acculturation* conflicts; consider how knowledge of these factors can help reduce self-blame.

8. Help children and adolescents determine whether cultural values or an unreceptive environment contribute to their problem. Strategize different ways of dealing with these conflicts. For some, strengthening their sense of cultural identity can be helpful.

9. Help determine concrete goals that incorporate cultural, family, *extended family*, and community perspectives.

10. Determine whether child-rearing practices are consistent with traditional methods and how they may conflict with mainstream methods.

11. In family interventions, identify *extended family* members, determine their roles, and request their assistance when appropriate.

12. Generate possible solutions with the client and consider the possible consequences of change from individual, family, and community perspectives. When appropriate, include strategies that may involve cultural elements and that focus on holistic factors (mind, body, spirit).

SUMMARY

American Indian/Native American and Alaska Natives comprise such a small percentage of the U.S. population that they are relatively "invisible." Life-expectancy and mental/physical health problems, however, are among the worst for this population. Their experience in America is not comparable to that of any other ethnic group. In contrast to immigrants, who arrived with few resources and struggled to gain equality, they originally had resources, which were severely eroded or destroyed by imperial, colonial, and federal and state policies. Alcohol and substance abuse, domestic violence, and suicide are among the most problematic disorders facing this population. In work with AI/NA/AN, counselors need to understand how the values of *sharing, cooperation, noninterference*, time orientation, *spirituality*, and *nonverbal communication* are relevant to mental health practice. Twelve clinical implications for counselor practice are identified.

GLOSSARY TERMS

Acculturation

Cooperation

Extended family

Noninterference

Nonverbal communication

Reservation

Sharing

Spirituality

Sweat lodge

Tribe

Vision quest

REFERENCES

American Psychiatric Association. (2014). *Mental health disparities: American Indians and Alaska Natives.* Retrieved from http://www.psychiatry.org/home/search-results?k=Mental%20health%20disparities:%20American%20Indians%20and%20Alaska%20Natives

American Psychological Association. (2005). *APA resolution recommending the immediate retirement of American Indian mascots, symbols, images, and personalities by schools, colleges, universities, athletic teams, and organizations.* Retrieved from http://www.apa.org/about/governance/council/policy/mascots.pdf

Aronowitz, N. W. (2014). *Proud heritage: Mentors teach Native students about their pasts.* Retrieved from http://www.nbcnews.com/news/education/proud-heritage-mentors-teach-native-students-about-their-pasts-n184271

Associated Press. (2011). *Senate hearing in Montana examines Indian suicides.* Retrieved from http://ndnnews.com/2011/08/senate-hearing-in-mont-examines-indian-suicides/

Bee-Gates, D., Howard-Pitney, B., LaFromboise, T., & Rowe, W. (1996). Help-seeking behavior of Native American Indian high school students. *Professional Psychology: Research and Practice, 27,* 495–499.

BigFoot, D. S., & Funderburk, B. W. (2010). *Honoring children, making relatives: Indigenous traditional parenting practices compatible with evidence-based treatment.* Retrieved from http://www.apa.org/pi/oema/resources/communique/2010/08/indigenous-parenting.aspx

Boyd-Ball, A. J., Véronneau, M. H., Dishion, T. J. & Kavanagh, K. (2014). Monitoring and peer influences as predictors of increases in alcohol use among American Indian youth. *Prevention Science, 15,* 526–535.

Brooke, J. (1998, April 9). Indians strive to save their languages. *New York Times,* p. 1.

Bureau of Indian Affairs. (2011). *What we do.* Retrieved from http://www.bia.gov/WhatWeDo/index.htm

Bureau of Indian Affairs. (2014). *Indian entities recognized and eligible to receive services from the United States Bureau of Indian Affairs.* Retrieved from http://www.bia.gov/cs/groups/xofa/documents/text/indian_entities_2014–01–29.pdf

Centers for Disease Control and Prevention. (2008). *Alcohol-attributable deaths and years of potential life lost among American Indians and Alaska Natives—United States, 2001–2005.* Retrieved from http://www.cdc.gov/mmwr/preview/mmwrhtml/mm5734a3.htm

Centers for Disease Control and Prevention. (2013). *Web-Based Injury Statistics Query and Reporting System (WISQARS). Fatal injury reports.* Atlanta, GA: National Center for Injury Prevention and Control. Retrieved from http://www.cdc.gov/injury/wisqars/index.html

Chartier, K., & Caetano, R. (2010). *Ethnicity and health disparities in alcohol research.* Retrieved from http://findarticles.com/p/articles/mi_m0 CXH/is_1–2_33/ai_n55302113/

Chiesa, A., & Serretti, A. (2011). Mindfulness based cognitive therapy for psychiatric disorders: A systematic review and meta-analysis. *Psychiatry Research, 87,* 441–453.

Choney, S. K., Berryhill-Paapke, E., & Robbins, R. R. (1995). The acculturation of American Indians: Developing frameworks for research and practice. In J. G. Ponterotto, J. M. Casas, L. A. Suzuki, & C. M. Alexander (Eds.), *Handbook of multicultural counseling* (pp. 73–92). Thousand Oaks, CA: Sage.

Congressional Record. (1997). *Indian Child Welfare Act Amendments of 1997—Hon. George Miller.* Washington, DC: Author.

Cruz, C. M., & Spence, J. (2005). *Oregon tribal evidence based and cultural best practices.* Retrieved from www.oregon.gov/OHA/mentalhealth/ebp/tribal-ebp-report.pdf

D'Oro, R. (2010). Stemming Native Americans' suicide rates. *Seattle Times,* p. A11.

D'Oro, R. (2011). *Suicide rate remains high in Alaska, especially among Natives.* Retrieved from http://www.adn.com/2011/01/12/1645956/report-says-suicide-remains-an.html

Deyhle, D., & Swisher, K. (1999). Research in American Indian and Alaska Native education: From assimilation to self-determination. *Review of Research in Education, 22,* 113–194.

Duran, B., Sanders, M., Skipper, B., Waitzkin, H., Malcoe, L. H., Paine, S., & Yager, J. (2004). Prevalence and correlates of mental disorders among Native American women in primary care. *American Journal of Public Health, 94,* 71–77.

Education Trust. (2013). *The state of education of Native students.* Retrieved from http://edtrust.org/resource/the-state-of-education-for-native-students/

Espey, D. K., Jim, M. A., Cobb, N., Bartholomew, M., Becker, T., Haverkamp, D., & Plescia, M. (2014). Leading causes of death and all-cause mortality in American Indians and Alaska Natives. *American Journal of Public Health, 104,* S303–S311.

Flynn, S. V., Olson, S. D., & Yellig, A. D. (2014). American Indian acculturation: Tribal lands to predominately White postsecondary settings. *Journal of Counseling and Development, 92,* 280–293.

Fryberg, S. A., Markus, H. R., Oyserman, D., & Stone, J. M. (2008). Of warrior chiefs and Indian princesses: The psychological consequences of American Indian mascots. *Basic and Applied Social Psychology, 30,* 208–218.

Garrett, M. T. (2006). When Eagle speaks: Counseling Native Americans. In C. C. Lee (Ed.), *Multicultural issues in counseling: New approaches to diversity* (pp. 25–53). Alexandria, VA: American Counseling Association.

Garrett, M. T., & Pichette, E. F. (2000). Red as an apple: Native American acculturation and counseling with or without reservation. *Journal of Counseling and Development, 78,* 3–13.

Garrett, M. T., & Portman, T.A.A. (2011). *Counseling Native Americans.* Belmont, CA: Cengage.

Garrett, M. T., & Wilbur, M. P. (1999). Does the worm live in the ground? Reflections on Native American spirituality. *Journal of Multicultural Counseling & Development, 27,* 193–207.

Garroutte, E. M., Goldberg, J., Beals, J., Herrell, R., Manson, S. M., & AI-SUPERPFP Team. (2003). Spirituality and attempted suicide among American Indians. *Social Science & Medicine, 56,* 1571–1579.

Gilgun, J. F. (2002). Completing the circle: American Indian medicine wheels and the promotion of resilience of children and youth in care. *Journal of Human Behavior in the Social Environment, 6,* 65–84.

Gone, J. P. (2009). A community-based treatment for Native American historical trauma: Prospects for evidence-based practice. *Journal of Consulting and Clinical Psychology, 17,* 751–762.

Gone, J. P. (2014). Reconsidering American Indian historical trauma: Lessons from an early Gros Ventre war narrative. *Transcultural Psychiatry, 51,* 387–406.

Gorman, J. C., & Balter, L. (1997). Culturally sensitive parent education: A critical review of quantitative research. *Review of Educational Research, 67,* 339–369.

Gray, J. S., & McCullagh, J. A. (2014). Suicide in Indian country: The continuing epidemic in rural Native American communities. *Journal of Rural Mental Health, 38,* 79–86.

Hamby, S. L. (2000). The importance of community in a feminist analysis of domestic violence among American Indians. *American Journal of Community Psychology, 28,* 649–669.

Herne, M. A., Bartholomew, M. L., & Weahkee, R. L. (2014). Suicide mortality among American Indians and Alaska Natives, 1999–2009. *American Journal of Public Health, 104,* S336–S342.

Jackson, L. C., Schmutzer, P. A., Wenzel, A., & Tyler, J. D. (2006). Applicability of cognitive-behavioral therapy with American Indian individuals. *Psychotherapy: Theory, Research, Practice, Training, 43,* 506–517.

Jacobs, M. R. (2014). Race, place, and biography at play: Contextualizing American Indian viewpoints on Indian mascots. *Journal of Sport & Social Issues, 38,* 322–345.

Johnson, K. W., Anderson, N. B., Bastida, E., Kramer, B. J., Williams, D., & Wong, M. (1995). Macrosocial and environmental influences on minority health. *Health Psychology, 14,* 601–612.

Jumper-Reeves, L., Dustman, P. A., Harthun, M. L., Kulis, S., & Brown, E. F. (2014). American Indian cultures: How CBPR illuminated intertribal cultural elements fundamental to an adaptation effort. *Prevention Science, 15,* 547–556.

Keane, E. M., Dick, R. W., Bechtold, D. W., & Manson, S. M. (1996). Predictive and concurrent validity of the Suicide Ideation Questionnaire among American Indian adolescents. *Journal of Abnormal Child Psychology, 24,* 735–747.

LaFromboise, T. D. (2006). American Indian youth suicide prevention. *Prevention Researcher, 13,* 16–18.

LaFromboise, T. D., & Howard-Pitney, B. (1995). The Zuni life skills development curriculum. *Journal of Counseling Psychology, 42,* 479–486.

LaFromboise, T. D., Medoff, L., Harris, A., & Lee, C. C. (2007). Psychological and cultural correlates of suicidal ideation among American Indian early adolescents on a Northern Plains reservation. *Research in Human Behavior, 41,* 119–143.

Lee, T. H. (2015). *7 apologies made to American Indians.* Retrieved from http://indiancountry todaymedianetwork.com/2015/07/01/7 -apologies-made-american-indians-160914

Limb, G. E., & Hodge, D. R. (2010). Helping child welfare workers improve cultural competence by utilizing spiritual genograms with Native American families and children. *Children and Youth Services Review, 32,* 239–245.

Lone-Knapp, F. (2000). Rez talk: How reservation residents describe themselves. *American Indian Quarterly, 24,* 635–640.

Macartney, S., Bishaw, A., & Fontenot, K. (2013). *Poverty rates for selected detailed race and Hispanic groups by state and place: 2007–2011.* Retrieved from www.census.gov/prod/.../acsbr 11–17.pdf

Middlebrook, D. L., LeMaster, P. L., Beals, J., Novins, D. K., & Manson, S. M. (2001).

Suicide prevention in American Indian and Alaska Native communities: A critical review of programs. *Suicide and Life-Threatening Behavior, 31,* 132–149.

Murphy, T., Pokhrel, P., Worthington, A., Billie, H., Sewell, M., & Bill, N. (2014). Unintentional injury mortality among American Indians and Alaska Natives in the United States, 1990–2009. *American Journal of Public Health, 104*(S3), 470–480.

Myhra, L. L., & Wieling, E. (2014). Psychological trauma among American Indian families: A two-generation study. *Journal of Loss and Trauma: International Perspectives on Stress & Coping, 19,* 289–313.

National Center for Education Statistics. (2013). *Public school graduates and dropouts from the common core of data: School year 2009–2010.* Retrieved from http://nces.ed.gov /pubs2013/2013309rev.pdf

National Indian Child Welfare Association. (2014). *Letter asking the Justice Department to investigate ICWA violations.* Retrieved from http://narfnews.blogspot.com/2014/02 /native-american-rights-fund-calls-for.html

Office of Minority Health. (2012). *Mental health and American Indians/Alaska Natives.* Retrieved from http://minorityhealth.hhs.gov/omh/browse .aspx?lvl=4&lvlID=39

Ogunwole, S. U., Drewery Jr., M. P., & Rios-Vargas, M. (2012). *The population with a bachelor's degree or higher by race and Hispanic origin: 2006–2010.* Retrieved from http:// www.census.gov/library/publications/2012 /acs/acsbr10–19.html

Peters, W.M.K., Straits, K.J.E., & Gauthier, P. E. (2015). Psychological practice with Native women. In C. Zerbe Enns, J. Rice, & R. L. Nutt (Eds.), *Psychological practice with women: Guidelines, diversity, empowerment.* Psychology of Women book series (pp. 191–224). Washington, DC: American Psychological Association.

Reyhner, J. (2002). *American Indian/Native American and Alaska Native education: An overview.* Retrieved from http://jan.ucc.nau.edu/~jar /AIE/Ind_Ed.html

Rieckmann, T. R., Wadsworth, M. E., & Deyhle, D. (2004). Cultural identity, explanatory style, and depression in Navajo adolescents. *Cultural Diversity and Ethnic Minority Psychology, 10,* 365–382.

Sage, G. P. (1997). Counseling American Indian adults. In C. C. Lee (Ed.), *Multicultural issues in counseling* (2nd ed., pp. 35–52). Alexandria, VA: American Counseling Association.

Shukovsky, P. (2001, March 29). "Urban Indians" are going home. *Seattle Post-Intelligencer,* pp. A1–A13.

Spillane, N. S., Cyders, M. A., & Maurelli, K. (2012). Negative urgency, problem drinking and negative alcohol expectancies among members from one First Nation: A moderated-mediation model. *Addictive Behaviors, 37,* 1285–1288.

Steinfeldt, J. A., Foltz, B. D., Kaladow, J., Carlson, T. N., Pagano, L. A., Benton, E., & Steinfeldt, M. C. (2010). Racism in the electronic age: Role of online forums in expressing racial attitudes about American Indians. *Cultural Diversity and Ethnic Minority Psychology, 16,* 362–371.

Stiffman, A. R., Brown, E., Freedenthal, S., House, L., Ostmann, E., & Yu, M. S. (2007). American Indian youth: Personal, familial, and environmental strengths. *Journal of Child and Family Studies, 16,* 331–346.

Swinomish Tribal Mental Health Project. (1991). *A gathering of wisdoms.* LaConner, WA: Swinomish Tribal Community.

Taylor, M. J. (2000). The influence of self-efficacy on alcohol use among American Indians. *Cultural Diversity and Ethnic Minority Psychology, 6,* 152–167.

Thomason, T. C. (2000). Issues in the treatment of Native Americans with alcohol problems.

Journal of Multicultural Counseling and Development, 28, 243–252.

Trimble, J. E., Fleming, C. M., Beauvais, F., & Jumper-Thurman, P. (1996). Essential cultural and social strategies for counseling Native American Indians. In P. B. Pedersen, J. G. Draguns, W. J. Lonner, & J. E. Trimble (Eds.), *Counseling across cultures* (4th ed., pp. 177–209). Thousand Oaks, CA: Sage.

U.S. Census Bureau. (2014). *Facts for features: American Indian and Alaska Native heritage month: November 2014.* Retrieved from http://www.census.gov/newsroom/facts-for -features/2014/cb14-ff26.html

Wahab, S., & Olson, L. (2004). Intimate partner violence and sexual assault in Native American communities. *Trauma, Violence, & Abuse, 5,* 353–366.

Whitesell, N. R., Beals, J., Crow, C. B., Mitchell, C. M., & Novins, D. K. (2012). Epidemiology and etiology of substance use among American Indians and Alaska Natives: Risk, protection, and implications for prevention. *American Journal of Drug and Alcohol Abuse, 38,* 376–382.

Whitesell, N. R., Mitchell, C. M., Spicer, P., & the Voices of Indian Teens Project Team. (2009). A longitudinal study of self-esteem, cultural identity, and academic success among American Indian adolescents. *Cultural Diversity and Ethnic Minority Psychology, 15,* 38–50.

Wood, P. B., & Clay, W. C. (1996). Perceived structural barriers and academic performance among American Indian high school students. *Youth and Society, 28,* 40–46.

16

Counseling Asian Americans and Pacific Islanders

> *Among traditionally oriented Chinese Americans, depression is described with terms such as discomfort, pain, dizziness, or other physical symptoms, rather than as feelings of sadness. Many feel that a diagnosis of depression is "morally unacceptable." (Kleinman, 2004)*

> *Asian parents hold dearly to the centuries-old culture of shame and honor so that when they arrive to the United States, it often gets passed down to the next generation. So much so that if their children need help for issues related to low self-esteem, depression, anxiety, or any personal struggles, they can be seen as tarnishing the family's prestige. (Louie, 2014a)*

> *Calling Asian Indians the new "model minority" isn't a compliment. It's an attempt to fit them into a box for political purposes. . . The phase "model minority" inherently pits one minority group against others . . . After all, if one community is the "model, " then the others are problematic and less desirable. (Srivastava, 2009, p. 1)*

The Asian American population is growing rapidly and, as of 2013, was close to 18 million, representing 5.3% of the total population. Native Hawaiian and other Pacific Islanders number 1.2 million and comprise 0.4% of the total population (U.S. Census Bureau, 2015). The largest Asian groups in the United States include

(Pew Research Center, 2013)

- over 4 million Chinese,

- 3.4 million Filipinos,

- 3.2 million Asian Indians,

- 1.7 million Vietnamese,

- 1.6 million Koreans, and

- 1.3 million Japanese.

Nearly three-quarters of Asian American adults were born abroad and about two-thirds speak a language other than English at home; approximately half do not speak English "very well." Between-group differences within the Asian American population are quite large, since the population is composed of at least

40 distinct subgroups that differ in language, religion, and values. Counselors should not assume that Asian Americans are all the same. Individuals diverge on variables such as ethnicity, culture, migration and relocation experiences, degree of *assimilation* or *acculturation*, identification with the home country, facility in their native language and in English, family composition, educational background, religion, and sexual orientation (Nadal et al., 2012).

CHARACTERISTICS AND STRENGTHS

In the following section, we present some of the cultural values, behavioral characteristics, and expectations that Asian Americans might have about therapy and consider the implications of these factors in treatment. The level of accuracy of these group generalizations for each individual client or family must be determined by the therapist.

Asian Americans: A Success Story?

The contemporary image of Asian Americans is that of a highly successful minority that has "made it" in society. Indeed, a close analysis of census data (U.S. Census Bureau, 2011a) seems to support this contention. Of those over the age of 25, over half of Asian/Pacific Islanders have a bachelor's degree, versus 30% of their White counterparts; 20% have an advanced degree, compared with 10% of Whites (U.S. Census Bureau, 2011b). Words such as *intelligent, hardworking, enterprising,* and *disciplined* are frequently applied to this population (Lim, 2014). The median income of Asian American families was $66,000 as compared with $49,800 for the U.S. population as a whole (Pew Research Center, 2013).

However, a closer analysis of the status of Asian Americans reveals a somewhat different story. First, in terms of economics, references to the higher median income of Asian Americans do not take into account (a) the higher percentage of Asian American families having more than one wage earner, (b) between-group differences in education and income, and (c) a higher prevalence of poverty despite the higher median income (12.5% for Asian Americans and 15.1% for Pacific Islanders, versus 9.4% for non-Hispanic Whites) (U.S. Census Bureau, 2010). Rates of poverty are particularly high among Hmong, Guamanian, Indonesian, and Cambodian immigrants (Ramakrishnan & Ahmad, 2014).

Second, in the area of education, Asian Americans show a disparate picture of extraordinarily high educational attainment among a few and a large, undereducated mass. Among the Hmong, only 40% have completed high school. Fewer than 14% of Tongan, Cambodian, Laotian, and Hmong adults and only 18% of Pacific Islanders have a bachelor's degree (Aronowitz, 2014). When averaged out, this bimodal distribution indicates how misleading statistics can be.

Third, there is now widespread recognition that Chinatowns, Manilatowns, and Japantowns in San Francisco and New York represent ghetto areas with prevalent unemployment, poverty, health problems, and juvenile delinquency. People outside these communities seldom see the deplorable social conditions that exist behind the bright neon lights, restaurants, and quaint shops.

Fourth, although Asian Americans underutilize mental health services, it is unclear if this is due to low rates of socioemotional difficulties or cultural values inhibiting self-referral (Zane & Ku, 2014). It is possible that a large portion of the mental illness, adjustment problems, and juvenile delinquency among Asians is hidden. The discrepancy between official and real rates of adjustment difficulties may be due to cultural factors, such as the shame and disgrace associated with admitting to emotional problems, the handling of problems within the family rather than relying on outside resources, and the manner of symptom formation, such as a low prevalence of acting-out disorders.

Fifth, Asian Americans have been exposed to discrimination and racism throughout history and continue to face anti-Asian sentiments. Even fourth- and fifth-generation Asian Americans are sometimes identified as "foreign" (Tsuda, 2014). In a survey of Chinese Americans, 58% reported being subjected to verbal harassment such as being made fun of, called names, or threatened; disrespectful or unfair treatment; unfairness in career advancement; stereotyping; and physical harassment (Larson, 2009). Perceived racial discrimination is associated with higher psychological distress, anxiety, depression, and suicidal ideation (Hwang & Goto, 2009).

It is important for those who work with Asian Americans to look behind the success myth and to understand the historical and current experiences of Asians in America. The matter is even more pressing for counselors when we realize that Asian Americans underutilize counseling and other mental health facilities. The approach of this chapter is twofold. First, we attempt to indicate how the interplay of social and cultural forces has served to shape and define the lifestyle of recent immigrants/refugees and American-born Asians. Second, we explore how an understanding of Asian American values and social experiences suggests a need for modifications in counseling and psychotherapeutic practices when working with some members of this population.

Collectivistic Orientation

> *I was born and raised in Korea and came to the United States in 1968. . .I must move back to Seoul to take care of my aging mother. I am a man of Asian values (filial piety), and my children are young college graduates of American values (career advancement and development). (Choi, 1999, p. 7)*

Instead of promoting individual needs and personal identity, Asian families tend to have a family and group orientation. Children are expected to strive for family goals and not engage in behaviors that might bring dishonor to the family. Parents believe they should have influence on their children's career choices (Pew Research Center, 2013). Asian American parents tend to show little interest in children's viewpoints regarding family matters. Instead, the emphasis is on adherence to "correct" values, family harmony, and adapting to the needs of family members, especially elders (P. H. Chen, 2009). Asian American adolescents are often expected to assist, support, and respect their families even when exposed to a society that emphasizes adolescent autonomy and independence (Fuligni et al., 1999).

Whereas EuroAmerican parents rated being "self-directed" as the most important attribute in children's social competence, Japanese American parents chose "behaves well" (O'Reilly, Tokuno, & Ebata, 1986). Chinese American parents also believed that politeness and calmness are important childhood characteristics (Jose, Huntsinger, & Liaw, 2004). Asian American families do differ, however, in the degree to which they place individual needs over family needs. For example, in the case just given, the client accepted the fact that his adult children would not return home to stay with his wife (their mother) while he was in Korea taking care of his mother. Although he decries American society, in which individualism prevails over collectivism, he acknowledges that his children have honored the family by being successful and that they define family obligations in a different manner.

Implications

Because of a possible *collectivistic orientation*, it is important to consider the family and community context during assessment and problem definition. A therapist should be open to different family orientations and to avoid automatically considering interdependence as a sign of enmeshment. After doing a client-centered analysis of the problem, counselors can ask, "How does your family see the problem?" For traditionally oriented Asian Americans, a focus on individual client needs and wishes may run counter to the values of *collectivism*. Goals and treatment approaches may need to include a family focus (e.g., "How important is it for you to consult your family before deciding how to deal with the problem?" and "How would achieving your goals affect you, your family, friends, and social community?"). Questions such as these allow the therapist to assess the degree of *collectivism* in the family. Acculturated Asian Americans with an individualistic orientation can often benefit from traditional counseling approaches, but family issues should also be considered, since *acculturation* conflicts are common.

Hierarchical Relationships

Traditional Asian American families tend to be hierarchical and patriarchal in structure, with males and older individuals occupying a higher status (Kim, 2011). Communication flows downward from parents to children; children are expected to defer to their elders as a matter of obligation and duty (A. Lau, Fung, & Yung, 2010). Sons are expected to carry on the family name and tradition. Even when they marry, their primary allegiance is to the parents. Between-group differences do exist. Japanese Americans are the most acculturated. The majority are third- or fourth-generation Americans. Filipino American families tend to be more egalitarian, whereas Korean, Southeast Asian, and Chinese American families tend to be more patriarchal and traditional in orientation (Blair & Qian, 1998). Modern Chinese societies are moving toward more egalitarian relationships between husband and wife and between parents and children (E. W.-C. Chen, 2009).

Implications

Clients should be aware that Asian Americans may respond to the counselor as an authority figure, be reluctant to express true feelings and concerns, and say what they think the mental health professional wants to hear (Son & Ellis, 2013). In family therapy, it is important to determine the family structure and communication pattern. Does it appear to be egalitarian or hierarchical? If the structure is not clear, addressing the father first and then the mother may be most productive.

If English is a problem, use an interpreter. Having children interpret for the parents can be counterproductive because it upsets the hierarchical structure. For very traditionally oriented families, having communication between family members directed to the therapist may be more congruent with cultural values than having family members address one another. It is also important to assess possible status changes within the family. It is not uncommon among Asian immigrants for women to retain their occupational status while men are either underemployed or unemployed. Such loss of male status may result in family conflict, particularly if males attempt to maintain their status by becoming even more authoritarian. In such cases, it may be helpful to cast societal factors as the problem that needs to be addressed.

Parenting Styles

Amy Chua, author of the book Battle Hymn of the Tiger Mom, *raised a storm of criticism when she described her child-rearing strategies, including banning sleepovers, play dates, watching TV, or playing computer games and considering any grade less than an "A" as unacceptable. Her children are required to complete all of their school work and must practice their musical instruments three hours each day. (One daughter, Sophia, played at Carnegie Hall at age 14 and the other daughter, Lulu, is a gifted violinist.) (Corrigan, 2011)*

Asian American parenting styles tend to be more authoritarian and directive than those in EuroAmerican families (Kim, 2011), although a relaxed style is often used with children younger than the age of 6 or 7 (Jose et al., 2004). For example, Chinese parenting is based on the concepts of *chiao shun* (to train) and *guan* (to govern and to love) (Russell, Crockett & Chao, 2010). Shame, the induction of guilt, and love withdrawal are often used to control and train the children (J. S. Lau, Fung, Wang, & Kang, 2009). Problem behavior in children is viewed as a lack of discipline. While praise is frequently used in the majority culture to reinforce desired behaviors, many Asian families consider instruction to be the main parenting strategy (Paiva, 2008). As one parent stated, "I don't understand why I should reward things they should already be doing. Studying hard is a normal responsibility. Listening to parents is a must. Why should they feel proud when they are merely meeting a basic obligation?" (A. S. Lau et al., 2010, p. 887). Criticism rather than praise is believed to be effective in changing behaviors. However, differences in parenting style between Asian American groups have been found. Japanese and Filipino American families tend to have the most egalitarian relationships, whereas Korean, Chinese, and Southeast Asian Americans are more authoritarian (Blair & Qian, 1998).

Implications

Egalitarian or Western-style parent-effectiveness training strategies may run counter to traditional child-rearing patterns. Traditional Asian American families exposed to Western techniques or styles may feel that their parenting skills are being criticized. Instead of attempting to establish egalitarian relationships, the therapist can focus on identifying different aspects of parenting, such as teaching and modeling. The therapist can help refocus on the more positive aspects of Asian child-rearing strategies, framing the change as helping the children with problems rather than altering traditional parenting. It is also important to commiserate with parents regarding the difficulties they encounter raising children in a society with different cultural standards (A. S. Lau, 2012).

Emotionality

Patients may not be willing to discuss their moods or psychological states because of fears of social stigma and shame. In many Asian cultures, mental illness is stigmatizing; it reflects poorly on family lineage and can influence others' beliefs about the suitability of an individual for marriage. (Louie, 2014b)

Strong emotional displays, especially in public, are considered signs of immaturity or lack of self-control; control of emotions is considered a sign of strength (Kim, 2011). Thus, in many Asian families, there is generally less open display of emotions. Instead, care and concern are shown by attending to the physical needs of family members. Fathers frequently maintain an authoritative and distant role and are not generally emotionally demonstrative or involved with children. Their role is to provide for the economic and physical needs of the family. Mothers are more responsive to the children but use less nurturance and more verbal and physical punishment than do EuroAmerican mothers (Kelly & Tseng, 1992). However, mothers are expected to meet the emotional needs of the children and often serve as the intermediary between the father and the children. When the children are exposed to more open displays of emotions from Western society, they may begin to question the comparative lack of emotion displayed by their parents.

Implications

Counseling techniques that focus directly on emotions may be uncomfortable and produce shame for traditional Asian Americans. Emotional behavior can be recognized in a more indirect manner. For example, if a client shows discomfort, the therapist could respond by saying either "You look uncomfortable" or "This situation would make someone uncomfortable." In both cases, the discomfort would be recognized. We have found that many Asian Americans are more responsive to the second, more indirect acknowledgment of emotions. Feelings of shame or embarrassment may interfere with self-disclosure and need to be addressed in counseling. The process may be facilitated by affirming that the sharing of personal information, although it may be uncomfortable, is a natural process in therapy (Zane & Ku, 2014). It is also helpful to focus on behaviors more than emotions and to identify how family members are meeting each other's needs. Among traditional Asian American couples, care and concern may be demonstrated by taking care of the physical needs of the partner rather than by verbally expressing concern. Western therapies that emphasize verbal and emotional expressiveness may not be appropriate in work with traditional Asian couples or families.

Holistic View on Mind and Body

A female Asian American client described her symptoms, including dizziness, loss of appetite, an inability to complete household chores, and insomnia. She asked the therapist if her problem could be due to "nerves." The therapist suspected depression, since her symptoms included many of the physical manifestations of the disorder. She asked the client if she felt depressed and sad. At this point, the client paused and looked confused. She finally stated that she feels very ill and that these physical problems are making her sad. Her perspective was that it is natural to feel sad when sick. When the therapist followed up by asking if there was a family history of depression, the client displayed even more discomfort and defensiveness. Although the client never directly contradicted the therapist, she never returned. (Tsui & Schultz, 1985)

Because the mind and body are considered inseparable, Asian Americans may express emotional difficulties through *somatic complaints* (Grover & Ghosh, 2014). Physical complaints are a common and culturally accepted means of expressing psychological and emotional stress. It is believed that physical problems cause emotional disturbances and that symptoms will disappear once the physical illness is treated. Instead of mentioning anxiety or depression, Asian clients often mention headaches, fatigue, restlessness, and disturbances in sleep and appetite (Wong, Tran, Kim, Kerne, & Calfa, 2010). Even psychotic patients typically focus on *somatic complaints* and seek treatment for these physical ailments (Nguyen, 1985).

Implications

Treat *somatic complaints* as real problems. Inquire about medications or other treatments that are being used to treat the symptoms. To address possible psychological factors, counselors can ask questions such as, "Dealing with headaches and dizziness can be quite troublesome; how are these affecting your mood or relationships with others?" This approach both legitimizes the physical complaints and allows an indirect way to assess psychosocial factors. It is beneficial to develop an approach that deals with both *somatic complaints* and the consequences of being "ill."

Academic and Occupational Goal Orientation

> *I want to write. I have to write. . . This is not the choice my parents would make, and surely not the choice they would wish me to make. . .I must not let it deter my progress or shut down my dreams, my purpose. (Ying, Coombs, & Lee, 1999, p. 357)*

There is great pressure for children to succeed academically and to have a successful career, since both are indicative of a successful upbringing. As a group, Asian Americans perform better academically than do their EuroAmerican counterparts. Although Asian American students have high levels of academic achievement, they also have more fear of academic failure and spend twice as much time each week studying as their non-Asian peers (Eaton & Dembo, 1997). Their achievement often comes with a price. Asian American adolescents report feeling isolated, depressed, and anxious, and report little praise for their accomplishments from their parents (Lorenzo, Pakiz, Reinherz, & Frost, 1995). Asian American parents often have specific career goals in mind for their children (generally in technical fields or the hard sciences). Because choice of vocation may reflect parental expectations rather than personal talent, Asian college students are sometimes uncertain about realistic career options (Lucas & Berkel, 2005). Deviations from either academic excellence or "appropriate" career choices can produce conflict with family members.

Implications

Counselors can inquire about and discuss conflicts between parental academic or career goals and the client's strengths, interests, and desires. When working with parents, counselors can encourage the recognition of all positive behaviors and contributions made by their children, rather than just academic performance. For career or occupational conflicts, counselors can acknowledge the importance parents place on their children achieving success, while indicating that there are many career options that can be considered. Differences of opinion can be presented as a culture conflict. The counselor can help the client brainstorm ways to present other possibilities to the parents. Because Asian American students often lack clarity regarding vocational interests, they may need additional career counseling assistance (Lucas & Berkel, 2005).

Cultural Strengths

Asian Americans' cultural values can provide resiliency and strength. The family orientation allows members to achieve honor by demonstrating respect for parents and elders and supporting siblings in their endeavors. These customs produce a collective support system that can shield the individual and family from sources of stress. Because the achievements and success of an individual are considered a source of pride for the family rather than the individual, group harmony is primary. Enculturation or identification with one's racial and ethnic background can serve as a buffer against prejudice, discrimination, and family conflicts (Hwang, Woods, & Fujimoto, 2010; Kim, 2011). For Korean American adolescents, ethnic identity pride is positively related to self-esteem, especially when there is strong parental support (Chang, Han, Lee, & Qin, 2015).

Pacific Islanders have faced a history of colonization and oppression. Despite these challenges and obstacles, cultural strengths such as collectivity, harmony in family relationships, and respect for elders have been an important source of resilience. Pacific Islanders can rely on the community and family during times of stress (Vakalahi, 2009). Korean American college students were found to have strong cognitive flexibility. In dealing with conflicts with parents, these individuals used creative means to prevent or resolve problems in a way that accommodated traditional cultural expectations and their own personal needs (Ahn, Kim, & Park, 2009).

SPECIFIC CHALLENGES

In the following sections we describe the challenges often faced by Asian Americans and consider their implications in treatment.

Racial Identity Issues

> *White privilege was a concept I was unaware of, even though it was intricately woven into the fabric of my life. If someone had asked me then, I would probably have said that I have not experienced racism, and I did not feel oppressed in any way. This is not to say I had not experienced racism. I just never thought of those encounters as racism because, most of the times, they were subtle. I reacted to racial micro-aggressions with confusion, fear, and frustration, although I never understood my emotions. (Lo, 2010, p. 26)*

As Asian Americans are progressively exposed to the standards, norms, and values of the wider U.S. society, the result is increasing *assimilation* and *acculturation*. Bombarded on all sides by peers, schools, and the mass media, which uphold Western standards, Asian Americans are frequently placed in situations of extreme culture conflict and experience distress regarding their behavioral and physical differences (Kim, 2011). Asian American college women report lower self-esteem and less satisfaction with their racially defined features than do their Caucasian counterparts (Mintz & Kashubeck, 1999). C.-R. Lee (1995) described his experiences as "straddling two worlds and at home in neither" and tells how he felt alienated from both American and Korean cultures. As with other adolescents, those of Asian American descent also struggle with the question of "Who am I?" In the case above, Lo talks about the struggles encountered during his racial identity development. Individuals undergoing *acculturation* conflicts may respond in one of the following ways (Huang, 1994):

1. *Assimilation.* Seeking to become part of the dominant society to the exclusion of one's own cultural group

2. *Separation or enculturation.* Identifying exclusively with the Asian culture

3. *Integration/biculturalism.* Retaining many Asian values while simultaneously learning the necessary skills and values for adaptation to the dominant culture

4. *Marginalization.* Perceiving one's own culture as negative but feeling inept at adapting to the majority culture

Implications

Although identity issues can be a problem for some Asian Americans, others believe that ethnic identity is not salient or important. Assessing the ethnic self-identity of clients is important because it can affect how we conceptualize the presenting problems and how we choose the techniques to be used in therapy. Those who adhere to Asian values have a more negative view toward seeking counseling (Kim, 2007). Acculturated Asian American college students hold beliefs similar to those of counselors, whereas less acculturated students do not (Mallinckrodt, Shigeoka, & Suzuki, 2005). Assimilated Asian clients are generally receptive to Western styles of counseling and may not want reminders of their ethnicity. Traditionally identified Asians are more likely to be recent immigrants who retain strong cultural values and are more responsive to a culturally adapted counseling approach. Bicultural Asian Americans adhere to some traditional values, while also incorporating many Western values. Being bicultural is associated with resilience in facing stressful situations (Sirikantraporn, 2013). Programs that help Asian American youth develop social awareness about ethnic identity issues and societal imbalance in power are associated with increased pride, self-efficacy, racial and ethnic esteem, and increased interest in contributing to societal change in its participants (Suyemoto, Day, & Schwartz, 2015).

Acculturation Conflicts

Children of Asian descent who are exposed to different cultural standards often attribute their psychological distress to their parents' backgrounds and different values. The issue of not quite fitting in with their peers yet being considered "too Americanized" by their parents is common. Parent–child conflicts are among the most common presenting problems for Asian American college students seeking counseling (R. M. Lee, Su, & Yoshida, 2005) and are often related to dating and marriage issues (Ahn, Kim, & Park, 2009). Chinese immigrant mothers report a larger *acculturation* gap with sons than with daughters (Buki, Ma, Strom, & Strom, 2003). The larger the *acculturation* gap between parents and children, the greater the number of family problems. Parents may complain, "My children have lost their cultural heritage" (Hwang et al., 2010). The inability to resolve differences in *acculturation* results in misunderstandings, miscommunication, and conflict (R. M. Lee, Choe, Kim, & Ngo, 2000). Parents may feel at a loss in terms of how to deal with their children. Some respond by becoming more rigid.

Implications

To prevent negative interpersonal exchanges between parents and their children, therapists can reframe problems as resulting from *acculturation* conflicts. In this way, both the parents and their children can discuss cultural standards and the expectations from larger society. Although family therapy would seem to be the ideal medium in which to deal with problems for Asian Americans, certain difficulties exist. Most therapy models are based on EuroAmerican perspectives of egalitarian relationships and require verbal and emotional expressiveness. Some models assume that a problem in a family member is reflective of dysfunction between family members. In addition, the use of direct communication between child and parents, confrontational strategies, or nonverbal techniques such as "sculpting" may be an affront to the parents.

Assess the structure of the Asian American family. Is it hierarchical or more egalitarian? What is their perception of healthy family functioning? How are decisions made in the family? How are family members showing respect for each other and contributing to the family? Focus on the positive aspects of the family and reframe conflicts to reduce confrontation. Expand systems theory to include societal factors such as prejudice, discrimination, poverty, and conflicting cultural values. Issues revolving around the pressures of being an Asian American family in this society need to be investigated. Describe the session as a solution-oriented one and explain that family problems are not uncommon. As much as possible, allow sensitive communications between family members to come through the therapist. The therapist can function as a culture broker in helping the family negotiate conflicts with the larger society.

Expectations Regarding Counseling

Because psychotherapy may be a foreign concept for some Asian Americans, it is important to carefully explain the nature of the assessment and treatment process and the necessity of obtaining personal information and insight into family dynamics. Asian American clients may expect concrete goals and strategies focused on solutions. Even acculturated Asian American college students prefer counselors to serve as direct helpers offering advice, consultation, and the facilitation of family and community support systems (Atkinson, Kim, & Caldwell, 1998). Mental health professionals must be careful not to impose techniques or strategies. Counselors often believe that they should adopt an authoritarian or highly directive stance with Asian American clients. What many Asian American clients expect is that the counselor take an active role in structuring the session and outlining expectations for client participation in the counseling process. It can be helpful for the therapist to accept the role of being the expert regarding therapy, while the client is given the role of expert regarding his or her life. In this way, clients can assist the therapist by facilitating understanding of key issues and possible means of approaching the problem (S.W.-H. Chen & Davenport, 2005).

Implications

Carefully describe the client's role in the therapy process, indicating that problems can be individual, relational, environmental, or a combination of these and that you will perform an assessment of each of these areas. Introduce the concept of *co-construction*—that effective counseling involves the client and the counselor working together to identify problems and solutions. The therapist might explain, "In counseling we try to understand the problem as it affects you, your family, friends, and community, so I will ask you questions about these different areas. With your help we will also consider possible solutions that you can try out." *Co-construction* reduces the chance that the therapist will impose his or her worldview on the client.

The counselor should direct therapy sessions but should ensure full participation from clients in developing goals and intervention strategies. Suggestions can be given and different options presented for consideration by the client. Clients can also be encouraged to suggest their own solutions and then select the option that they believe will be the most useful in dealing with the problem. The opportunity for Asian American clients to try interventions on their own promotes the cultural value of self-sufficiency. The consequences for any actions taken should be considered, not only for the individual client, but also for the family. The client's perspective is also important in determining what needs to be done if cultural or family issues are involved.

Therapy should be time limited, should focus on concrete resolution of problems, and should deal with the present or immediate future. Cognitive-behavioral and other solution-focused strategies are useful in working with Asian Americans (S.W.-H. Chen & Davenport, 2005). However, as with other Eurocentric approaches, these approaches may need to be altered because the focus is on the individual, whereas the unit of treatment for Asian Americans may actually be the family, community, or society. Cognitive-behavioral approaches can be modified to incorporate a *collectivistic* rather than an individualistic perspective. For example, assertiveness training can be altered for Asian clients by first considering possible cultural and social factors that may affect assertiveness (e.g., minority status or personal values such as modesty). Then the therapist and client can identify situations where assertiveness might be functional, such as in class or when seeking employment, while recognizing other situations where a traditional cultural style might be more appropriate (e.g., with parents or other elders). Additionally, possible cultural or societal influences that affect social anxiety or assertiveness can be discussed. Finally, the client can practice role-playing to increase assertiveness in specific situations. This concrete alteration of a cognitive-behavioral approach considers cultural factors and allows clients to establish self-efficacy.

Racism and Discrimination

Katie also said she had not been "exposed to racism, personally," defining racism as making fun of or discriminating against others because one feels superior . . . "except for those annoying little people that walk around the street and walk by me and go, 'ching, chong, ching' or whatever." (Suyemoto, Day, & Schwartz, 2015, p. 130)

Asian Americans continue to face issues of racism and discrimination (Hwang & Goto, 2009). However, some Asian American youth, such as Katie in the previous example, lack awareness of or minimize discriminatory behavior toward them, describing racial jokes and teasing as unintentional or "just for fun." Exposure to racism or discrimination does affect mental health. In a sample of 444 Chinese American adolescents, it was found that discrimination in early adolescence was related to depression, alienation, and lower academic performance in middle adolescence (Brenner & Kim, 2009). Experience with discrimination in foreign-born and Asian American–born college students was not only related to depression but also to intergenerational conflicts, especially with the mother, probably because she is the one whom family members interact primarily with to navigate social problems (Chang, Chen, & Cha, 2015). Southeast Asian refugees who experienced racial discrimination reported high rates of depression (Noh, Beiser, Kaspar, Hou, & Rummens, 1999).

Implications

A therapist must assess the effects of possible environmental factors, such as racism, on mental health issues in Asian Americans and help ensure that clients not internalize issues based on discriminatory practices. Instead, the focus should be on how to deal with racism and on possible efforts to change the environment. If a problem occurs in school, the therapist can help assess the school's social receptivity to Asian students. The same can be done with discriminatory practices at the client's place of employment. Intervention may have to occur at a systems level, with the therapist serving in the role of advocate for the client.

 ## IMPLICATIONS FOR CLINICAL PRACTICE

[A] one-size-fits-all approach to clinical work with Asian Americans is potentially problematic. Instead, it is important for clinicians to identify within-group differences among their Asian American clients based on their mental illness, lay beliefs, and level of enculturation. (Wong et al., 2010, p. 328)

There is a range of acceptable practices in working with Asian American clients. Qualities such as attitudinal similarity between the counselor and the Asian American client and agreement on the cause and treatment of a disorder are more important than racial match in promoting counselor credibility and a strong therapeutic alliance (Meyer, Zane, & Cho, 2011). Asian Americans view counselors who demonstrate multicultural competence by addressing the cultural beliefs of clients as more competent (Wang & Kim, 2010). Helping Asian American clients formulate culturally acceptable strategies can improve their problem-solving abilities and facilitate the development of skills for successful interactions within the larger society, including balancing conflicting values. Many of the counseling skills learned in current mental health programs, such as cognitive behavioral therapies, can be effective, especially if modifications are made for less acculturated clients (W.-Y. Lau, Chan, Li, & Au, 2010). Considerations in working with Asian American clients include the following:

1. Be aware of cultural differences between the therapist and the client in the areas of counseling, appropriate goals, and process. Use strategies appropriate to the *collectivistic*, hierarchical, and patriarchal orientation of Asian Americans, when needed.

2. Build rapport by discussing confidentiality and explaining the client role, including the process of co-constructing the problem definition and solutions.

3. Identify and incorporate the client's beliefs about the etiology and appropriate treatment regarding the disorder.

4. Assess not just from an individual perspective but include family, community, and societal influences on the problem. Obtain the worldview, degree of *acculturation*, and ethnic identity of the Asian American client.

5. Conduct a positive assets search. What strengths, skills, problem-solving abilities, and social supports are available to the individual or family? How have problems been successfully solved in the past?

6. Consider or reframe the problem, when possible, as one involving issues of culture conflict or *acculturation*.

7. Determine whether *somatic complaints* are involved, and assess their influence on mood and relationships. Discuss somatic as well as psychological issues.

8. Take an active role, but allow Asian Americans to choose and evaluate suggested interventions. Asian Americans may prefer an immediate resolution to a problem rather than in-depth exploration.

9. Use problem-focused, time-limited approaches that have been modified to incorporate possible cultural factors.

10. Self-disclosure regarding strategies the counselor has used in the past to solve problems similar to those faced by the client can be helpful.

11. With family therapy, the therapist should be aware that Western-based theories and techniques may not be appropriate for Asian families. Determine the structure and communication patterns among the members. It may be helpful to address the father first and to initially have statements by family members directed to the therapist. Focus on positive aspects of parenting, such as modeling and teaching.

12. In couples counseling, assess for societal or *acculturation* conflicts, and determine the couple's perspective on what an improved relationship would look like. Problems often occur when there are differences in *acculturation* between the partners. Determine the ways that caring, support, or affection is shown, including providing for economic needs.

13. With Asian children and adolescents, common problems involve *acculturation* conflicts with parents, feeling guilty or stressed over poor academic performance, negative self-image or identity issues, and struggles between interdependence and independence.

14. Consider the need to act as an advocate or to engage in systems-level intervention in cases of institutional racism or discrimination.

SUMMARY

Asian Americans/Pacific Islanders are nearly 6% of the population, but are composed of 40 distinct subgroups, each with its own language, religion, and customs. The counselor should not assume that they are all the same. Asian Americans are often seen as a *"model minority"*; the myth has masked the historical and continuing prejudice and discrimination directed toward them. Counselors working with Asian American/Pacific Islanders must be cognizant of major cultural differences such as *collectivism, hierarchical relationships,* parenting styles, *emotionality,* holistic orientation, and academic/occupational goal orientations that contrast with EuroAmerican characteristics. A failure to acknowledge these differences may lead to inappropriate and ineffective treatments. Further, it is important to understand and work with the strengths of the group, and be knowledgeable about racial identity development, *acculturation* conflicts, and the different expectations Asian Americans may have of counseling. Fourteen clinical implications for counselor practice are identified.

GLOSSARY TERMS

Acculturation	Hierarchical relationships
Assimilation	Integration/biculturalism
Co-construction	Model minority
Collectivistic orientation	Saving face
Emotionality	Somatic complaints

REFERENCES

Ahn, A. J., Kim, B.S.K., & Park, Y. S. (2009). Asian cultural values gap, cognitive flexibility, coping strategies, and parent-child conflicts among Korean Americans. *Asian American Journal of Psychology, S*(1), 1, 29–44.

Aronowitz, N. W. (2014). *Proud heritage: Mentors teach Native students about their pasts.* Retrieved from http://www.nbcnews.com/news/education/proud-heritage-mentors-teach-native-students-about-their-pasts-n184271

Atkinson, D. R., Kim, B.S.K., & Caldwell, R. (1998). Ratings of helper roles by multicultural psychologists and Asian American students: Initial support for the three-dimensional model of multicultural counseling. *Journal of Counseling Psychology, 45,* 414–423.

Blair, S. L., & Qian, Z. (1998). Family and Asian students' educational performance. *Journal of Family Issues, 19,* 355–374.

Brenner, A. D., & Kim, S. Y. (2009). Experiences of discrimination among Chinese American adolescents and the consequences for socio-emotional and academic development. *Developmental Psychology, 45,* 1682–1694.

Buki, L. P., Ma, T.-C., Strom, R. D., & Strom, S. K. (2003). Chinese immigrant mothers of adolescents: Self-perceptions of acculturation effects on parenting. *Cultural Diversity and Ethnic Minority Psychology, 9,* 127–140.

Chang, H.-L., Chen, S.-P., & Cha, C. H. (2015). Perceived discrimination, intergenerational family conflicts, and depressive symptoms in foreign-born and U.S.-born Asian American emerging adults. *Asian American Journal of Psychology, 6,* 107–116.

Chang, T.-F., Han, E.-J., Lee, J.-S., & Qin, D. B. (2015). Korean American adolescent ethnic-identity pride and psychological adjustment: Moderating effects of parental support and school environment. *Asian American Journal of Psychology, 6,* 190–199.

Chen, E. W.-C. (2009). Chinese Americans. In E. W.-C. Chen and G. J. Yoo, *Encyclopedia of Asian American issues today* (vol. 1, pp. 222–223). Westport, CT: Greenwood.

Chen, P.-H. (2009). A counseling model for Self-relation coordination for Chinese clients with interpersonal conflicts. *Counseling Psychologist, 37,* 987–1009.

Chen, S. W.-H., & Davenport, D. S. (2005). Cognitive-behavioral therapy with Chinese American clients: Cautions and modifications. *Psychotherapy: Theory, Research, Practice, Training, 42,* 101–110.

Choi, Y. H. (1999, September 7). Commentary: Asian values meet Western realities. *Los Angeles Times,* p. 7.

Corrigan, M. (2011). *Tiger mothers: Raising children the Chinese way.* Retrieved from http://www.npr.org/2011/01/11/132833376/tiger-mothers-raising-children

Eaton, M. J., & Dembo, M. H. (1997). Differences in the motivational beliefs of Asian Americans. *Journal of Educational Psychology, 89,* 433–440.

Fuligni, A. J., Burton, L., Marshall, S., Perez-Febles, A., Yarrington, J., Kirsh, L. B., & Merriwether-DeVries, C. (1999). Attitudes toward family obligations among American adolescents with Asian, Latin American, and European backgrounds. *Child Development, 70,* 1030–1044.

Grover, S., & Ghosh, A. (2014). Somatic symptom and related disorders in Asians and Asian Americans. *Asian Journal of Psychiatry, 7,* 77–79.

Huang, L. N. (1994). An integrative approach to clinical assessment and intervention with Asian-American adolescents. *Journal of Clinical Child Psychology, 23,* 21–31.

Hwang, W.-C., & Goto, S. (2009). The impact of perceived racial discrimination on the mental health of Asian American and Latino college students. *Asian American Journal of Psychology, S*(1), 15–28.

Hwang, W.-C., Woods, J. J., & Fujimoto, K. (2010). Acculturative family distancing (AFD) and depression in Chinese American families. *Journal of Consulting and Clinical Psychology, 78,* 655–667.

Jose, P. E., Huntsinger, P. R., & Liaw, L. (2004). Parental values and practices relevant to young children's social development in Taiwan and the United States. *Journal of Cross-Cultural Psychology, 31,* 677–702.

Kelly, M., & Tseng, H. (1992). Cultural differences in childrearing: A comparison of immigrant Chinese and Caucasian American mothers. *Journal of Cross-Cultural Psychology, 23,* 444–455.

Kim, B.S.K. (2007). Adherence to Asian and European American cultural values and attitudes toward seeking professional psychological help among Asian American students. *Journal of Counseling Psychology, 54,* 474–480.

Kim, B.S.K. (2011). *Counseling Asian Americans.* Belmont, CA: Cengage.

Kleinman, A. (2004). Culture and depression. *New England Journal of Medicine, 351,* 951–953.

Larson, J. L. (2009). *2009 national survey: Public attitudes toward Chinese and Asian Americans.* Retrieved from http://committee100 .typepad.com/committee_of_100_newslett /survey_pressclips

Lau, A. S. (2012). Reflections on adapting parent training for Chinese immigrants: Blind alleys, thoroughfares, and test drives. In G. Bernal & M. M. Domenech Rodriguez (Eds.), *Cultural adaptations: Tools for evidence-based practice with diverse populations* (pp. 133–156). Washington, DC: American Psychological Association.

Lau, A. S., Fung, J. J., & Yung, V. (2010). Group parent training with immigrant Chinese families: Enhancing engagement and augmenting skills development. *Journal of Clinical Psychology: In Session, 66,* 880–894.

Lau, J. S., Fung, J., Wang, S.-W., & Kang, S.-M. (2009). Explaining elevated social anxiety among Asian Americans: Emotional attunement and a cultural double bind. *Cultural Diversity and Ethnic Minority Psychology, 15,* 77–85.

Lau, W.-Y., Chan, C. K.-Y., Li, J. C.-H., & Au, T. K. F. (2010). Effectiveness of group cognitive-behavioral treatment for childhood anxiety in community clinics. *Behaviour Research and Therapy, 48,* 1067–1077.

Lee, C.-R. (1995) *Native speaker.* New York, NY. Berkley.

Lee, R. M., Choe, J., Kim, G., & Ngo, V. (2000). Construction of the Asian American Family Conflicts Scale. *Journal of Counseling Psychology, 47,* 211–222.

Lee, R. M., Su, J., & Yoshida, E. (2005). Coping with intergenerational family conflict among Asian American college students. *Journal of Counseling Psychology, 52,* 389–399.

Lim, B. N. (2014). *I am not a model minority.* Retrieved from http://www.thecrimson.com /article/2014/2/13/harvard-model-minority/

Lo, H.-W. (2010). My racial identity development and supervision: A self-reflection. *Training and Education in Professional Psychology, 4,* 26–28.

Lorenzo, M. K., Pakiz, B., Reinherz, H. Z., & Frost, A. (1995). Emotional and behavioral problems of Asian American adolescents: A comparative study. *Child and Adolescent Social Work Journal, 12,* 197–212.

Louie, S. (2014a). *Asian shame and honor: A cultural conundrum and case study.* Retrieved from https://www.psychologytoday .com/blog/minority-report/201406/asian -shame-and-honor

Louie, S. (2014b). *Honor and suicide.* Retrieved from https://www.psychologytoday .com/blog/minority-report/201406/asian -honor-and-suicide

Lucas, M. S., & Berkel, L. A. (2005). Counseling needs of students who seek help at a university counseling center: A closer look at gender and multicultural issues. *Journal of College Student Development, 46,* 251–266.

Mallinckrodt, B., Shigeoka, S., & Suzuki, L. A. (2005). Asian and Pacific Island American students' acculturation and etiology beliefs about typical counseling presenting problems. *Cultural Diversity and Ethnic Minority Psychology, 11,* 227–238.

Meyer, O., Zane, N., & Cho, Y. I. (2011). Understanding the psychological processes of the racial match effect in Asian Americans. *Journal of Counseling Psychology, 58,* 335–345. Retrieved from http://www.ncbi.nlm.nih.gov /pubmed/21574698

Mintz, L. B., & Kashubeck, S. (1999). Body image and disordered eating among Asian American and Caucasian college students: An examination of race and gender differences. *Psychology of Women Quarterly, 23,* 781–796.

Nadal, K. L., Escobar, K. M., Prado, G., David, E.J.R., & Haynes, K. (2012). Racial microaggressions and the Filipino American experience: Recommendations for counseling and development. *Journal of Multicultural Counseling and Development, 40,* 156–173.

Nguyen, S. D. (1985). Mental health services for refugees and immigrants in Canada. In T. C. Owen (Ed.), *Southeast Asian mental health: Treatment, prevention, services, training, and research* (pp. 261–282). Washington, DC: National Institute of Mental Health.

Noh, S., Beiser, M., Kaspar, V., Hou, F., & Rummens, J. (1999). Perceived racial discrimination, depression, and coping: A study of Southeast Asian refugees in Canada. *Journal of Health and Social Behavior, 40,* 193–207.

O'Reilly, J. P., Tokuno, K. A., & Ebata, A. T. (1986). Cultural differences between Americans of Japanese and European ancestry in parental valuing of social competence. *Journal of Comparative Family Studies, 17,* 87–97.

Paiva, N. D. (2008). South Asian parents' constructions of praising their children. *Clinical Child Psychology and Psychiatry, 13,* 191–207.

Pew Research Center. (2013). *The rise of Asian Americans.* Retrieved from http://www/pewsocialtrends.org/2012/06/the-rise-of-asian-americans/2/

Ramakrishnan, K., & Ahmad, F. Z. (2014). *Income and poverty.* Retrieved from https://cdn.americanprogress.org/wp-content/.../AAPI-IncomePoverty.pdf.

Russell, S. T., Crockett, L. J., & Chao, R. (Eds.) (2010). *Asian American parenting and parent-adolescent relationships.* New York, NY: Springer.

Sirikantraporn, S. (2013). Biculturalism as a protective factor: An exploratory study on resilience and the bicultural level of acculturation among Southeast Asian American youth who have witnessed domestic violence. *Asian American Journal of Psychology, 4,* 109–115.

Son, E., & Ellis, M. V. (2013). A cross-cultural comparison of clinical supervision in South Korea and the United States. *Psychotherapy, 50,* 189–205.

Srivastava, S. (2009). *Nobody's model minority.* Retrieved from http://theroot.com/Home/Nobody'sModelMinority

Suyemoto, K. L., Day, S. C., & Schwartz, S. (2015). Exploring effects of social justice youth programming on racial and ethnic identities and activism for Asian American youth. *Asian American Journal of Psychology, 6,* 125–135.

Tsuda, T. (2014). "I'm American, not Japanese!": The struggle for racial citizenship among later-generation Japanese Americans. *Ethnic and Racial Studies, 37,* 405–424.

Tsui, P., & Schultz, G. L. (1985). Failure of rapport: When psychotherapeutic engagement fails in the treatment of Asian clients. *American Journal of Orthopsychiatry, 55,* 561–569.

U.S. Census Bureau. (2010). *Facts for features: Asian American heritage month.* Retrieved from http://www.census.gov/newsroom/releases/archives/facts_for_features_special_editions/cb10-ff07.html

U.S. Census Bureau. (2011a). *Age and sex composition: 2010.* Retrieved from http://www.census.gov/prod/cen2010/briefs/c2010br-03.pdf

U.S. Census Bureau. (2011b). *Hispanic heritage month.* Retrieved from http://www.census.gov/newsroom/releases/archives/facts_for_features_special_editions/cb11-ff18.html

U.S. Census Bureau. (2015). *People quickfacts.* Retrieved from http://quickfacts.census.gov/qfd/states/00000.html

Vakalahi, H.F.O. (2009). Pacific Islander American students: Caught between a rock and a hard place? *Children and Youth Services Review, 31,* 1258–1263.

Wang, S., & Kim, B.S.K. (2010). Therapist multicultural competence, Asian American participants' cultural values, and counseling process. *Journal of Counseling Psychology, 57,* 394–401.

Wong, Y. J., Tran, K. K., Kim, S.-H., Kerne, V.V.H., & Calfa, N. A. (2010). Asian Americans' lay beliefs about depression and professional help seeking. *Journal of Clinical Psychology, 66*, 317–332.

Ying, Y.-W., Coombs, M., & Lee, P. A. (1999). Family intergenerational relationship of Asian American adolescents. *Cultural Diversity and Ethnic Minority Psychology, 5*, 350–363.

Zane, N., & Ku, H. (2014). Effects of ethnic match, gender match, acculturation, cultural identity, and face concern on self-disclosure in counseling for Asian Americans. *Asian American Journal of Psychology, 5*, 66–74.

Counseling Latinas/os

Diane M. Sue and David Sue

Chapter Objectives

1. Learn the demographics and characteristics of Latinas/os.

2. Identify counseling implications of the information provided for Latinas/os.

3. Provide examples of strengths that are associated with Latinas/os.

4. Know the special challenges faced by Latinas/os.

5. Understand how the implications for clinical practice can guide assessment and therapy with Latinas/os.

Nearly a quarter of Americans say Hispanics face a lot of discrimination in society today, making them the racial/ethnic group the public sees as most often subjected to discrimination. (Pew Research Center, 2010a)

It was sometimes hard to adjust. When I went outside, I was in America but inside my house, it was Mexico. My father was the leader of the house. It wasn't that way for some of my American friends. (Middleton, Arrendondo, & D'Andrea, 2000, p. 24)

Even the most patriotic of us Mexican-Americans has a couple of members in our family who are here illegally. We also think there is nothing wrong with them being here illegally because we know they're just trying to build a better life for themselves. . . illegal immigrant isn't some random statistic that conservative pundits always seem to bitch about stealing lucrative 'merican' jobs like picking strawberries and working as dishwasher at Denny's (Felix, 2014).

In this chapter, we use the term *Latinas/os* in reference to individuals living in the United States with ancestry from Mexico, Puerto Rico, Cuba, the Dominican Republic, and Central or South American Spanish-speaking countries. However, people vary in preference for the terms used for self-identification. For example, more than half of the *Latina/o* youth (ages 16 to 25) in one sample self-identified first by their family's country of origin (i.e., Mexican, Cuban), while approximately 20% self-identified as "Hispanic" or "*Latina/o*," and 24% self-identified as "American." Among youth who are third-generation or higher, about half chose "American" as their first term of self-description (Pew Research Center, 2009). The U.S. Census uses the term *Hispanic* as an ethnic descriptor rather than the term *Latina/o*.

Throughout Latin America, the immigration of European, African, and Asian populations and subsequent mixture with indigenous groups has resulted in a wide range of phenotypes. Thus the physical traits of Latinas/os vary greatly and include characteristics of indigenous groups, Africans, Asians, and fair-skinned Europeans. Latinas/os are currently the largest minority group in the United States, comprising 17.1% of the total U.S. population (U.S. Census Bureau, 2015). Because of immigration patterns and high birthrates (one in four infants born in the United States is *Latina/o*), more than half of the growth in the total U.S. population between 2000 and 2010 resulted from increases in this population.

According to the U.S. Census Bureau (2014), there are 54.6 million *Latina/o* Americans, of whom 64% are of Mexican origin, 9.4% are from Puerto Rico or of Puerto Rican descent, 3.7% have Cuban ancestry, and 16% originate from Central and South America.

Approximately 37% of Latinas/os are immigrants, including the 11% of foreign-born individuals who have become U.S. citizens. However, approximately one-fourth of the *Latina/o* adults are undocumented immigrants; about two-thirds of all undocumented immigrants are from Mexico (Marrero, 2011). It is not surprising that nearly half of all *Latina/o* American adults express concern that they, a family member, or a close friend will be deported (Lopez, Taylor, Funk, & Gonzalez-Barrera, 2013). Those who are undocumented occupy the lowest rung of the labor pool and are often taken advantage of because they have no legal status.

Although *Latina/o* groups share many characteristics, there are many between-group and within-group differences. Many are strongly oriented toward their ethnic group, whereas others are quite acculturated to mainstream values. About three-fourths of U.S.-born Latinas/os are third-generation or higher, with many descended from the large wave of Latin Americans who began immigrating in the 1960s. In certain states and cities, they make up a substantial percentage of the population. Mexican Americans are the dominant *Latina/o* group in metropolitan areas throughout the United States. Most Puerto Ricans reside in the Northeast, and most Cubans live in Florida (Lopez & Dockterman, 2011). Median wealth of White households is more than 10 times that of *Latina/o* households (Pew Research Center, 2014b). Members of this group have high unemployment, are overrepresented among the poor, and often live in substandard housing. Many hold semiskilled or unskilled occupations (U.S. Census Bureau, 2010b).

CHARACTERISTICS AND STRENGTHS

In the following sections we describe the characteristics, values, and strengths of *Latina/o* individuals and consider their implications in treatment. These are generalizations and their applicability needs to be assessed for each client or family.

Cultural Values and Characteristics

The development and maintenance of interpersonal relationships are central to the *Latina/o* culture (Kuhlberg, Pena, & Zayas, 2010). There is typically deep respect and affection among a large network of family and friends. Family unity, respect, and tradition (*familismo*) are an important aspect of life. Cooperation among family members is stressed. For many, the *extended family* includes not only relatives but also close friends and godparents. Each member of the family has a role: mother (self-denial), father (responsibility), children (obedience), grandparents (wisdom), and godparents (resourcefulness) (Lopez-Baez, 2006).

Implications

Familismo refers not only to family cohesiveness and interdependence but also to loyalty and placing the needs of close friends and family members before personal needs (Baumann, Kuhlberg, & Zayas, 2010). Counselors can inquire about clients' connectedness with extended and nuclear family members and the value placed on *familismo*. Because of these strong familial and social relationships, Latinas/os often wait until resources from *extended family* and close friends are exhausted before seeking help. Even in cases of severe mental illness, many delay obtaining assistance (Kouyoumdjian, Zamboanga, & Hansen, 2003).

Although there are many positive features of the *extended family*, emotional involvement and obligations with numerous family and friends can function as a source of stress, particularly when decisions are made that affect the individual negatively (Aguilera, Garza, & Muñoz, 2010). Problem definition may need to incorporate the perspectives of both nuclear and *extended family* members, and solutions may need to bridge cultural expectations and societal demands. Additionally, family responsibilities sometimes take precedence over outside concerns, such as school attendance or work obligations. For example, older children may be kept home to care for ill siblings, attend family functions, or work (Headden, 1997). Under these circumstances, problematic behaviors (i.e., absenteeism) can be addressed by framing them as a conflict between cultural and societal expectations.

Family Structure

Latinas/os often live in households having five or more members (U.S. Census Bureau, 2010a). Traditional oriented families are hierarchical in form, with special authority given to parents, older family members, and males. Within the family, sex roles are clearly delineated. The father is typically the primary authority figure (Lopez-Baez, 2006). Children are expected to be obedient and are typically not involved in family decisions; parents may expect adolescents to work to help meet family financial obligations (Lefkowitz, Romo, Corona, Au, & Sigman, 2000).

Parents reciprocate by providing for children through young adulthood and even after marriage. This type of reciprocal relationship is a lifelong expectation. Older children are expected to care for and protect their younger siblings; older sisters often function as surrogate mothers. Also, in traditionally oriented marriages, emphasis is placed on social activities involving *extended family* and friends rather than on activities as a couple (Negy & Woods, 1992).

Implications

Assessment of family structure should consider the family hierarchy and the ways that decisions are made within the family unit. Conflicts among family members often involve differences in *acculturation* and conflicting views of roles and expectations for family members, as well as clashes between cultural values and mainstream societal expectations (Baumann et al., 2010). In less acculturated families, counselors may find success by helping family members reframe these issues as responses to *acculturation* stress; they can then negotiate conflicting cultural norms and values. Counselors can help clients consider ways in which they can demonstrate their allegiance to the family without significantly compromising their own *acculturation*. One such approach is demonstrated in the following case:

> During family therapy, a Puerto Rican mother indicated to her son, "You don't care for me anymore. You used to come by every Sunday and bring the children. You used to respect me and teach your children respect. Now you go out and work, you say, always doing this or that. I don't know what spirit [que diablo] has taken over you." (Inclan, 1985, p. 332)

In response, the son explained that he was sacrificing and working hard because he wanted to be a successful provider and someone of whom his children could be proud. The son has adopted future oriented, mainstream U.S. values, stressing hard work and individual achievement. The mother was disappointed because she believed her son should spend time with her, encourage the family to gather together, and prioritize the family over individual desires. This clash in values was at the root of the problem.

In working with this family, the therapist provided alternative ways of viewing the conflict. He explained how our views are shaped by the values that we hold. He asked the mother about her socialization and early childhood values. The son expressed how difficult it was to lose his parents' respect but also his belief that he needed to work hard and focus on the future in order to succeed in the United States. The therapist pointed out that different adaptive styles may be necessary for different situations and that what "works best" may be dependent on the social context. Both mother and son acknowledged that they demonstrate love and affection in different ways. As a result of the sessions, mother and son better understood the nature of their conflicts and were able to improve their relationship.

Gender Role Expectations

Latinas/os often experience conflicts over gender roles. In traditional culture, men are expected to be strong, dominant, and the provider for the family (*machismo*), whereas women are expected to be nurturing, modest, virtuous, submissive to the male, and self-sacrificing (*marianismo*) (Deardorff et al., 2013). As head of the family, the father expects family members to be obedient. Individuals with greater ethnic identity are more likely to subscribe to traditional male and female roles. Areas of possible gender role conflict for males (especially among immigrants) include the following (Avila & Avila, 1995; Constantine, Gloria, & Baron, 2006):

1. *Lack of confidence in areas of authority. Latino* men may lack confidence interacting with agencies and individuals outside of the family; this can result in feelings of inadequacy and concern about diminished authority, especially if the wife or children are more fluent in English.

2. *Feelings of isolation and depression because of the need to be strong.* Talking about concerns or stressors may be seen as a sign of weakness. This difficulty discussing feelings can produce isolation and anger or depression.

3. *Conflicts over the need to be consistent in his role.* As ambiguity and stress increase, there may be more rigid adherence to traditional roles.

For women, conflicts may involve (a) expectations associated with traditional roles, (b) anxiety or depression over not being able to live up to these standards, and (c) inability to express feelings of anger (Lopez-Baez, 2006). Latina immigrants are often socialized to feel inferior and to expect suffering or martyrdom. With greater exposure to the dominant culture, such views may be questioned. Certain roles may change more than others. Some women may be very modern in their views regarding education and employment but remain traditional in the area of sexual behavior and personal relationships. Others remain very traditional in all areas. Cultural differences between partners are associated with strained marital relationships while couples with cultural similarity have a more positive marital experience (Cruz et al., 2014).

Implications

Therapists should explore the client's degree of adherence to traditional gender norms, as well as the gender role views among family members. It is important to consider the potential impact of *acculturation* on marital relationships, particularly when women function independently in the work setting or when dealing with schools and other agencies. For both men and women, role conflict is likely to occur if the man is unemployed, if the woman is employed, or both.

When dealing with gender role conflicts, counselors who believe in equal relationships must be careful not to impose their views on clients. Instead, if a Latina client desires greater independence, the counselor can help her consider the consequences of change, including potential problems within her family and community, and work toward this goal within a cultural framework. It is helpful to frame conflicts in gender roles as an external issue involving differing expectations between cultural and mainstream values and to encourage problem solving to deal with the different sets of expectations.

Spiritual and Religious Values

> *Mrs. Lopez, age 70, and her 30-year-old daughter sought counseling because they had a very conflictual relationship. . . . The mother was not accustomed to a counseling format. . . .At a pivotal point in one session, she found talking about emotional themes overwhelming and embarrassing. . . .In order to reengage her, the counselor asked what resources she used when she and her daughter quarreled. She. . .prayed to Our Lady of Guadalupe. (Zuniga, 1997, p. 149)*

The therapist subsequently employed a culturally adapted strategy of having Mrs. Lopez use prayer and spiritual guidance to understand her daughter and to find solutions to their conflicts. This use of a cultural perspective allowed the sessions to continue. Religion (often, but not always, Catholicism) is important to many Latinas/os, although less so among younger individuals (Pew Research Center, 2014a). Prayers requesting guidance from patron saints can be a source of comfort in times of stress. Latinas/os often believe that life's misfortunes are inevitable and feel resigned to their fate (*fatalismo*). Consequently, they may take a seemingly passive approach to problems and lack experience assertively addressing challenges. Also, some *Latina/o* groups believe that evil spirits cause mental health problems and rely on indigenous healing practices.

Implications

During assessment, it is important to consider religious or spiritual beliefs and to explore the spiritual meanings of presenting problems. If there is a strong belief in fatalism, instead of attempting to change this view, the therapist can acknowledge this attitude and help the individual or family determine the most adaptive response to the situation. A therapist might say, "Given that the situation is unchangeable, how can you and your family deal with this?" with the aim of helping the client develop problem-solving skills within certain parameters. The strong reliance on religion can be a resource (e.g., evoking God's support through prayer to facilitate problem solving). Fatalism can be countered by stressing *"Ayudate, que Dios te ayudara,"* which is the equivalent of "God helps those who help themselves" (Organista, 2000). Indigenous healing practices can also be incorporated into the therapeutic process.

Educational Characteristics

> *Peer pressure to drop out can be nearly overwhelming in the Latina/o community, as DeAnza Montoya, a pretty Santa Fe teen, can attest. In her neighborhood, it was considered "Anglo" and "nerdy" to do well in school. . . "In school they make you feel like a dumb Mexican," she says, adding that such slights only bring Latinas/os closer together. (Headden, 1997, p. 64)*

Many *Latina/o* students do not fare well in the public school system and have a high likelihood of dropping out of school; this is particularly true among first-generation (immigrant) youth and those who are third-generation or higher (Pew Research Center, 2009). Approximately 41% of adults do not have a regular high school diploma, including 52% of those who are foreign-born. Additionally, the vast majority (90%) of youth who drop out of high school never attain a General Educational Development (GED) credential and thus are not eligible to attend college or vocational programs or to enter the military (Fry, 2010).

A number of problems contribute to the high dropout rate of *Latina/o* students. Educational difficulties may be related to limited English proficiency.

Spanish is the primary language spoken in over half of the households; others speak Spanish on a more limited basis. Although most second-generation Latinas/os are bilingual (exposed to Spanish in the home and to English in school), their command of both English and Spanish may be marginal. The high pregnancy rate for Latina girls also contributes to school dropout rates. Although teen pregnancy among 15- to 19-year-old Latinas is decreasing, the birth rate (70 live births per 1,000 women in this age group) is significantly higher than for other groups (Hamilton, Martin, & Ventura, 2009). In some schools there is peer pressure against "acting White" or doing well academically. Higher grades in *Latina/o* youth are associated with a decrease in peer popularity and could explain underperformance in schools (Fryer, 2006).

However, there are some grounds for optimism about education. Many Latina/o youth value education and are optimistic about the future and performing better in school (Pew Research Center, 2009). In 2013, 79% completed high school which is an all-time high and the dropout rate has gone down to 14% in 2013 as compared to 32% in 2000. College attendance is also increasing among Latina/o young people: 18% were in college in 2013 versus 12% in 2009. Although there is improvement, Latina/o young adults continue to lag substantially behind White youth in obtaining a bachelor's degree (9% versus 69%) (Fry, 2014).

Implications

Although teachers often attempt to accommodate Latina/o cultural learning styles and adapt lessons for students with limited English skills, the move against bilingual education and the rapid immersion of Spanish-speaking students in English can exacerbate academic difficulties. Many immigrant parents do not realize they have the right to question school decisions. Difficulty communicating with Spanish-speaking parents compounds the problem. Some parents are unable to attend conferences because of work requirements, and this may be interpreted as a lack of caring about the child's education. To engage parents, conferences can be scheduled at flexible hours and interpreters be made available. Face-to-face communication or other personal contact is more successful than written material (even if written in Spanish) since many parents have limited literacy skills. Trust develops slowly, and it is important to identify and support the family's strengths rather than focusing on its shortcomings (Espinosa, 1997). Altering instructional strategies to fit cultural values (i.e., cooperation) is also important. Latina/o students often have high educational expectations but don't know how to apply for financial assistance and are unaware of university application procedures.

Providing information regarding resources and help through this process can increase the chances for a college education (Gonzalez, Stein, Shannonhouse, & Prinstein, 2012).

Cultural Strengths

> *Cinthya grew up in poverty. She is now attending Columbia University working on her public health degree. Asked how she persevered against the odds, Cinthya speaks with emotion and credits her success to her family. "It's my parents," she said. "They have sacrificed so much to give us the opportunity to go to school, to grow." (New Journalism on Latina/o Children, 2010, p. 1)*

Most Latina/o children grow up in two-parent families, often supported by a strong kinship system. *Familismo* and the related sense of connectedness and loyalty among immediate and *extended family* can be a source of significant social and emotional support for individuals and families (Kuhlberg et al., 2010). Traditional Latina/o values place a great deal of emphasis on creating a harmonious atmosphere and accord within the family system. *Personalismo* refers to a personalized communication style that is characterized by interactions that are respectful, interdependent, and cooperative. *Simpatico* refers to the relational style displayed by many Latinas/os—a style emphasizing social harmony and a gracious, hospitable, and personable atmosphere (Holloway, Waldrip, & Ickes, 2009). Cultural identity and values can serve as a protective asset against stress by promoting a sense of belonging (Ai, Aisenberg, Weiss, & Salazar, 2014) while a strong system of spiritual and religious beliefs can be nurtured as a source of strength when dealing with personal or family issues.

SPECIFIC CHALLENGES

In the following sections we consider challenges often faced by *Latina/o* individuals and reflect on their implications in treatment.

Stigma Associated with Mental Illness

Depressive symptoms are common among Latinas, with 53% reporting moderate to severe symptoms versus 37% of White women (Diaz-Martinez, Interian, & Waters, 2010). Mexican American males and Puerto Ricans of both genders have high rates of weekly alcohol consumption and binge-drinking; additionally, alcoholism among these groups is more likely to be chronic (Chartier & Caetano, 2010). Statistics such as these confirm the need for mental health support. However, the cultural stigma associated with mental illness, including fear that psychiatric medications can cause addiction, results in reluctance to seek treatment. Latina/o immigrants are also more likely than members of the majority culture to fear embarrassment or social discrimination from family, friends, and employers if they acknowledge psychological distress, and are more likely to express psychological distress via somatic symptoms.

"When *Latino* think of mental illness, they just think one thing: *loco*," says Clara Morato, whose son, Rafaelo, was diagnosed with bipolar disorder at age 18 (Dichoso, 2010, p. 1). *Machismo* may also be a barrier to seeking treatment, owing to concerns about lost time from work (Vega, Rodriguez, & Ang, 2010). Additionally, Latinas/os underutilize resources for their children. Although most young children are citizens, one or both parents may be undocumented and, therefore, reluctant to seek assistance (Capps, Fix, Ost, Reardon-Anderson, & Passel, 2005). Many Latinas/os are afraid to sign up for programs such as the Affordable Care Act over concern that their undocumented family members will get discovered, and deported. This results in the inability to pay for mental health treatment (Dembosky, 2014).

Implications

Clinicians can anticipate and help counteract the stigma associated with mental illness by taking the time to build rapport and provide psychoeducation about therapeutic approaches (Vega et al., 2010). Comas-Diaz (2010), a Puerto Rican multicultural therapist, advocates exploring the client's heritage, history of cultural translocation, and views about counseling early in therapy and encourages a flexible therapeutic approach that might include roles functioning as that of an healer, advisor, coach, teacher, guide, advocate, consultant, and mentor. Developing a culturally relevant therapeutic alliance, providing psychoeducation about how treatment is conducted and how goals are developed in a collaborative manner, and using a flexible, culture-centered approach can help clients overcome their fear of the stigma associated with seeking help and their reluctance to participate openly in treatment.

Acculturation Conflicts

As with many ethnic minority groups, Latinas/os are frequently faced with societal values distinctly different from their own. Additionally, the severing of ties to family and friends, the loss of supportive resources, language inadequacy, unemployment, and culture conflict all function as stressors for recent immigrants. Some maintain their traditional orientation, whereas others assimilate and exchange their native cultural practices and values for those of the host culture. Differences in *acculturation* between family members can produce stress within the family unit as seen in the following case:

> *Juan, a 46-year-old Latino, was born in Mexico and has lived in the United States for 10 years. He works as a cook, has been married for over 20 years, and has five children. Juan has frequent conflicts with his wife and children, believing that they want freedom from him and that they have become too "Americanized." He strongly believes in the cultural values of* familismo *(family connectedness),* machismo *(being head of the family, with responsibility for providing for the family), and* respecto *(respect) from his children. As husband and father, he believes that he should set the rules in the family and that his wife and children should respect his rules. Juan often feels stressed, angry, hopeless, and depressed and has had suicidal thoughts and thoughts of hurting his wife. When angry, he resorts to threats and physical violence. (Santiago-Rivera et al., 2008)*

Juan's therapist recognized that traditional cognitive behavior therapy (an evidence-based treatment for depression) might not adequately address the environmental stressors, *acculturation* conflicts, and feeling of isolation and powerlessness Juan was experiencing. Instead, the therapist modified another evidence-based treatment (behavioral activation therapy). He encouraged Juan to participate in free or low-cost activities (e.g., socializing with and attending church services with his wife and children), thus enhancing family relationships and building social networks within the community. Differences between Juan's upbringing in Mexico and the American culture faced by his children were also discussed in therapy, increasing Juan's understanding of issues faced by his wife and children. At the end of therapy, Juan was no longer depressed and reported improved relationships with his wife and children (Santiago-Rivera et al., 2008).

Those who either completely reject or accept the values of the host culture appear to experience greater stress than those who partially accept them (Miville, Koonce, Darlington, & Whitlock, 2000). Miranda and Umhoefer (1998a, 1998b) found that both highly and minimally acculturated Mexican Americans score high on social dysfunction, alcohol consumption, and acculturative stress.

They concluded that a *bicultural orientation* (i.e., maintaining some components of the native culture while incorporating practices and beliefs of the host culture) may be the "healthiest" resolution for *acculturation*; those with *bicultural* values are able to accept and negotiate aspects of both cultures. Some of the issues involved in *acculturation* conflict are evident in the following case:

> *A Latino teenager, Mike, was having difficulty knowing "who he was" or what group he belonged with. His parents had given him an Anglo name to ensure his success in American society. They only spoke to him in English because they were fearful that he might have an accent. During his childhood, he felt estranged from his relatives because his grandparents, aunts, and uncles could speak only Spanish. At school, he did not fit in with his non-Latino peers, but also felt different from the Mexican American students who would ask him why he was unable to speak Spanish. Mike's confusion over his ethnic identity resulted in significant distress. (Avila & Avila, 1995)*

During their early teen years, Latina/o children begin to have questions about their identity and question whether they should adhere to mainstream or traditional values. The representation of Latinas/os on English-language channels often involves characters who behave criminally or are violent. The mixed heritage of many Latina/o Americans raises additional identity questions. Should those of Mexican heritage call themselves "Mexican," "American," "Mexican American," "Chicano," "Latina/o," or "Hispanic"? What about those with indigenous, Asian, or African ancestry? An ethnic identity provides a sense of belonging and group membership. Many *Latina/o* youngsters undergo the process of searching for an identity. This struggle in combination with acculturative stresses may contribute to problems such as substance abuse, aggressive behavior, delinquency, low self-esteem, and an increased risk for suicide (Smokowski, Rose, & Bacallao, 2010). Retention of one's culture may be related to positive mental health. Mexican American students who maintained their ethnic identity and heritage had higher levels of self-esteem and life satisfaction. Cultural retention may help prevent problem behaviors (Navarro, Ojeda, Schwartz, Piña-Watson, & Luna, 2014).

Implications

The client's degree of *acculturation* has important implications for treatment, especially during initial therapy sessions, and can influence both perceptions of and responses to counseling. For example, individuals with minimal *acculturation* may have difficulty being open and self-disclosing or discussing their issues in depth and may believe that counseling will take only one session (Dittmann, 2005). *Acculturation* can be assessed by inquiring about the client's background, generational status, residential history, reasons for immigration, primary language, religious orientation and strength of religious beliefs, extent of support from *extended family*, and other factors related to *acculturation*. The therapist needs to determine the client's degree of adherence both to traditional values and to those of the majority culture. Second-generation Latina/o Americans are often marginal in both native and majority cultures. They are often bilingual (exposed to Spanish at home and English at school) but frequently have less-than-optimal use of either language. The therapeutic alliance can be enhanced by beginning the counseling relationship in a more formal manner and working to build trust before beginning comprehensive exploration of the presenting problem or extensive interviewing regarding sensitive topics.

Ethnic identity issues should be recognized and incorporated during assessment and treatment of youth and adults. Conflicts between mainstream values and ethnic group values can be discussed, and clients can help brainstorm methods for bridging these differences. It should be stressed that ethnic identity is part of the normal development process. In many cases, a *bicultural* perspective may be the most functional, since such a perspective does not involve the wholesale rejection of either culture.

Counselors should also inquire about potential *acculturation* conflicts, including their impact on client symptoms or family conflicts. Although values such as *familismo* can be a source of strength for youth, distress may feel unbearable when there is parent–child discord (Hernandez, Garcia, & Flynn, 2010). Identification with core cultural values appears to serve as a protective factor against risky behavior such as substance abuse and to serve as a source of strength for children and adolescents (Dettlaff & Johnson, 2011). Counselors can help youth explore and retain their cultural values and ethnic identity to bolster self-esteem and life satisfaction (Ai et al., 2014).

Research attempting to identify the risk factors accounting for the high incidence of suicide attempts among Latinas, particularly among girls whose mothers place high value on *familismo*, suggests that although *familismo* can be a protective factor with respect to emotional and behavioral health, conflicts that result from adolescent strivings for autonomy and resultant parent–child discord can be a risk factor, particularly for those accustomed to close parent–child relationships and harmony in the family unit (Kuhlberg et al., 2010). Adolescents may question family obligations and parental rules and desire input into decisions. Such behavior may be viewed as disrespectful by parents and *extended family*.

Females may feel overprotected by parents and question their rules or expectations, such as staying at home to care for others and being monitored on dates or forbidden to date; such *acculturation* conflict may be particularly distressing to girls, since gender socialization for females emphasizes their role in maintaining harmonious relationships. Mother–daughter conflicts are exacerbated when the family orientation is traditional and the daughter has a high mainstream cultural involvement (Derlan, Umaña-Taylor, Toomey, Updegraff, & Jahromi, 2015). Both *biculturalism* and *familismo* are related to higher self-esteem and greater flexibility in negotiating both cultures among *Latina/o* adolescents (Smokowski et al., 2010). Effective interventions for parent–child conflict include enhancing *bicultural* understanding and promoting adaptive interpersonal behaviors (e.g., improved communication, increased parental affection, and emotional connection) (Kuhlberg et al., 2010).

Racism and Discrimination

> *Arizona state law allows the state superintendent of Public Education to disallow any ethnic studies class that "promotes resentment towards a race or class of people. . .(or) advocates ethnic solidarity instead of treatment of pupils as individuals." (Martinez & Gutierrez, 2010, p. 1)*

> *Because of anti-immigration rhetoric, Latinas/os are now seen as the ethnic group suffering from the most discrimination. Almost 80 percent of Latinas/os believe that there is "a lot" or "some" discrimination against their group. (Pew Research Center, 2010b)*

Stressors such as racism and discrimination can lead to emotional difficulties, particularly when combined with *acculturation* conflicts. Legislators in Arizona and Alabama recently enacted some of the broadest measures against undocumented immigrants in U.S. history. Such recent legislation includes making it a crime for noncitizens to be without documents (i.e., a visa or immigration forms) authorizing their presence in the United States and requiring law enforcement officers and other officials (including school personnel) to verify immigration status. These laws (supported by the majority of U.S. citizens) have been heavily criticized for promoting racial profiling.

Additionally, Arizona has implemented a state law banning any ethnic studies classes that "advocate ethnic solidarity instead of treatment of pupils as individuals" and not allowing instructors with "heavy accents" to teach English classes (Martinez & Gutierrez, 2010; Navarrette, 2011). Latina/o adolescents are particularly vulnerable to the effects of *acculturation* conflict and societal racism. Perceived discrimination among Mexican American adolescents increased psychological distress and such behaviors as drug use, fights, and sexual promiscuity (Flores, Tschann, Dimas, Pasch, & deGroat, 2010). Many youth attempt to deal with family distress, discrimination, and feelings of hopelessness by involvement in gang activities (Baca & Koss-Chioino, 1997).

Implications

Clinicians must assess not only intrapsychic issues but also the degree to which external conditions are involved in mental health issues. Thus it is important to be sensitive to sociopolitical issues (e.g., anti-immigrant sentiments) and client experiences with disenfranchisement and discrimination. For example, highly educated Latinas/os report demoralizing situations in which their academic success is questioned or they are assumed to be less qualified than they actually are (Rivera, Forquer, & Rangel, 2010). Additionally, many clients may be dealing with issues related to unemployment and poverty, including stressful interactions with bureaucracies (Vasquez, 1997).

Careful assessment of the source of emotional distress is necessary before appropriate action can be taken. This should be done early in the treatment process, as illustrated by the case of a migrant worker in his mid-50s who was fearful of leaving his home because he heard threatening voices. In working with him, Ruiz (1981) initiated an analysis of possible external causes, suggesting that the client undergo a complete physical examination, with special attention to exposure to pesticides and other agricultural chemicals that might result in mental symptoms. Additionally, interviews revealed that the client was quite anxious owing to fears of deportation, suspiciousness of outside authorities, and recent encounters with creditors.

Linguistic Issues

Considerable evidence suggests that assessment results can be influenced by linguistic differences or misunderstandings. Assessments should always be conducted in the primary language of the client and interpreted within a sociocultural context.

Implications

It is essential that clinicians consider the validity of tests for Latina/o clients and the influence of cultural or social factors as well as language barriers, discrimination, immigration stress, and poverty. Because of the lack of bilingual counselors, problems in diagnosis can occur with clients who are not proficient in English. For example, Marcos (1973) reported that Mexican American clients were considered to have greater psychopathology when interviewed in English than when interviewed in Spanish. However, interpreters themselves may present difficulties in the counseling process, such as distortions in communication.

IMPLICATIONS FOR CLINICAL PRACTICE

Several writers (Bean, Perry, & Bedell, 2001; Paniagua, 1994; Velasquez et al., 1997) have made suggestions about initial counseling sessions with Latina/o clients.

1. Assess the *acculturation* level of the client and family members and modify your interactions and assessment accordingly.

2. It is important to engage in a respectful, warm, and mutual introduction with the client. Less acculturated clients may expect a more formal relationship and see the counselor as an authority figure. Paniagua (1994) recommends interviewing the father for a few minutes during the beginning of the first session, showing recognition of the father's authority and sensitivity to cultural factors in counseling.

3. Determine whether a translator is needed. Be careful not to interpret slow speech or long silences as indicators of depression or cognitive dysfunction. The client may be struggling with English communication skills.

4. Give a brief description of what counseling is and the role of each participant. Such information is particularly important for less acculturated clients, who may expect to meet for only one or two sessions or expect to have medication prescribed.

5. Explain the notion of confidentiality. Even immigrants with legal status have inquired about whether the information shared during counseling would "end up in the hands of the Border Patrol or other immigration authorities" (Velasquez et al., 1997, p. 112). Immigrant families may also be uncertain about the limits of confidentiality, especially as it applies to child abuse or neglect issues. Physical discipline is used in some families. Parents may be fearful about how their child-rearing practices will be perceived.

6. Have clients state in their own words the problem or problems as they see them. Determine the possible influence of religious or spiritual beliefs. Use paraphrasing to summarize and clarify the problem.

7. Consider whether there are cultural or societal aspects to the problem. What are the impacts of racism, poverty, and acculturative stress on the problem?

8. Determine the positive assets and resources available to the client and his or her family. Have they, other family members, or friends successfully dealt with similar problems?

9. Help the client prioritize the problems and decide on the goals and expectations for therapy.

10. Discuss possible negative consequences of achieving the indicated goals for the individual and the family.

11. Discuss the possible participation of family members in therapy. Within the family, determine the hierarchical structure, as well as the degree of *acculturation* of the different members.

12. Assess possible problems from external sources, such as the need for food, shelter, or employment, or stressful interactions with agencies. Provide necessary assistance in developing and maintaining environmental supports.

13. Explain the treatment to be used, why it was selected, and how it will help achieve the goals (culturally adapted evidence-based therapies should be considered). Consistently evaluate the client's or family's response to the therapeutic approach you have chosen.

14. With the client's input, determine a mutually agreeable length of treatment. It is better to offer time-limited, solution-based therapies.

15. Remember that *personalismo* is a basic cultural value for many Latinas/os. Although initial meetings may be quite formal, once trust has developed, clients often develop a close personal bond with the counselor, may treat the counselor as a close friend or family member, and may give gifts or extend invitations to family functions. These behaviors are culturally based and not evidence of dependency or a lack of boundaries.

16. When there are *acculturation* conflicts, have clients identify external demands rather than merely focusing on intrapsychic or relational issues.

SUMMARY

The term "Latina/o" refers to a diverse group of people whose country of origin includes Mexico, Puerto Rico, Cuba, and other Spanish-speaking countries. As with other groups of color, their standard of living is far below that of their White counterparts and they have been subjected to continual racism and bias. Understanding major differences in family structure (*familismo*), gender role expectations (*machismo* and *marianismo*), spiritual and religious values, educational characteristics, and cultural strengths of this group is important for culturally competent practice. Counselors must anticipate specific challenges they face such as mental illness stigma, *acculturation* conflicts, linguistic issues, and racism/discrimination. Sixteen clinical implications for counselor practice are identified.

GLOSSARY TERMS

Acculturation

Bicultural orientation

Extended family

Familismo

Fatalismo

Latina/o Americans

Machismo

Marianismo

Personalismo

Respecto

Simpatico

REFERENCES

Aguilera, A., Garza, M. J., & Muñoz, R. F. (2010). Group cognitive-behavioral therapy for depression in Spanish: Culture-sensitive manualized treatment in practice. *Journal of Clinical Psychology: In Session, 66*, 857–867.

Ai, A. L., Aisenberg, E., Weiss, S. I., & Salazar, D. (2014). Racial/ethnic identity and subjective physical and mental health of Latino Americans: An asset within? *American Journal of Community Psychology, 53*, 173–184.

Avila, D. L., & Avila, A. L. (1995). Mexican Americans. In N. A. Vacc, S. B. DeVaney, & J. Wittmer (Eds.), *Experiencing and counseling multicultural and diverse populations* (3rd ed., pp. 119–146). Bristol, PA: Accelerated Development.

Baca, L. M., & Koss-Chioino, J. D. (1997). Development of a culturally responsive group counseling model for Mexican American adolescents. *Journal of Multicultural Counseling and Development, 25*, 130–141.

Baumann, A. A., Kuhlberg, J. A., & Zayas, L. H. (2010). Familism, mother-daughter mutuality, and suicide attempts of adolescent Latinas. *Journal of Family Psychology, 24*, 616–624.

Bean, R. A., Perry, B. J., & Bedell, T. M. (2001). Developing culturally competent marriage and family therapists: Guidelines for working with

Hispanic families. *Journal of Marital and Family Therapy, 27*, 43–54.

Capps, R., Fix, M., Ost, J., Reardon-Anderson, J., & Passel, J. S. (2005). The health and well-being of young children of immigrants. *Immigrant families and workers: Facts and perspectives.* Washington, DC: Urban Institute.

Chartier, K., & Caetano, R. (2010). *Ethnicity and health disparities in alcohol research.* Retrieved from http://findarticles.com/p/articles/mi_m0CXH/is_1–2_33/ai_n55302113/

Comas-Diaz, L. (2010). On being a Latina healer: Voice, conscience and identity. *Psychotherapy Theory, Research, Practice, Training, 47*, 162–168.

Constantine, M. G., Gloria, A. M., & Baron, A. (2006). Counseling Mexican American college students. In C. C. Lee (Ed.), *Multicultural issues in counseling* (3rd ed., pp. 207–222). Alexandria, VA: American Counseling Association.

Cruz, R. A., Gonzales, N. A., Corona, M., King, K. M., Cauce, A. M., Robins, R. W. . . & Conger, R. D. (2014). Cultural dynamics and marital relationship quality in Mexican-origin families. *Journal of Family Psychology, 28*(4), 844–854.

Deardorff, J., Cham, H., Gonzales, N. A., White, R. M., Tein, J. Y., Wong, J. J., & Roosa, M. W. (2013). Pubertal timing and Mexican-origin girls' internalizing and externalizing symptoms: The influence of harsh parenting. *Developmental Psychology, 49*, 1790–1804.

Dembosky, A. (2014). *Latinos still reluctant to sign up for Obamacare.* Retrieved from http://www.marketplace.org/topics/health-care/latinos-still-reluctant-sign-obamacare

Derlan, C. L., Umaña-Taylor, A. J., Toomey, R. B., Updegraff, K. A., & Jahromi, L. B. (2015). Person–environment fit: Everyday conflict and coparenting conflict in Mexican-origin teen mother families. *Cultural Diversity and Ethnic Minority Psychology, 21*, 136–145.

Dettlaff, A. J., & Johnson, M. A. (2011). Child maltreatment dynamics among immigrant and U.S.-born Latino children: Findings from the National Survey of Child and Adolescent Well-Being (NSCAW). *Children and Youth Services Review, 33*, 936–944.

Diaz-Martinez, A. M., Interian, A., & Waters, D. M. (2010). The integration of CBT, multicultural and feminist psychotherapies with Latinas. *Journal of Psychotherapy Integration, 20*, 312–326.

Dichoso, S. (2010). *Stigma haunts mentally ill Latinos.* Retrieved from http://www.cnn.com/2010/HEALTH/11/15/latino.health.stigma/index.html

Dittmann, M. (2005). Homing in on Mexican Americans' mental health access. *Monitor on Psychology, 36*, 70–72.

Espinosa, P. (1997). School involvement and Hispanic parents. *Prevention Researcher, 5*, 5–6.

Felix, R. (2014). *4 things only Mexican-Americans will understand.* Retrieved from http://thoughtcatalog.com/raul-felix/2014/06/4-things-only-mexican-americans-will-understand/

Flores, E., Tschann, J. M., Dimas, J. M., Pasch, L. A., & deGroat, C. L. (2010). Perceived racial/ethnic discrimination, posttraumatic stress symptoms, and health risk behaviors among Mexican American adolescents. *Journal of Counseling Psychology, 57*, 264–273.

Fry, R. (2010). *Hispanics, high school dropouts and the GED.* Retrieved from http://pewhispanic.org/reports/report.php?ReportID=122

Fry, R. (2014). *U.S. high school dropout rate reaches record low, driven by improvements among Hispanics, blacks.* Retrieved from http://www.pewresearch.org/fact-tank/2014/10/02/u-s-high-school-dropout-rate-reaches-record-low-driven-by-improvements-among-hispanics-blacks/

Fryer, R. G. (2006). *"Acting White:" The social price paid by the best and brightest minority students.*

Retrieved from: http://educationnext.org/acting white/

Gonzalez, L. M., Stein, G. L., Shannonhouse, L. R., & Prinstein, M. J. (2012). Latina/o adolescents in an emerging immigrant community: A qualitative exploration of their future goals. *Journal for Social Action in Counseling and Psychology*, *4*, 83–102.

Hamilton, B. E., Martin, J. A., & Ventura, S. J. (2009). Births: Preliminary data for 2009. *National Vital Statistics Reports*, 59(3). Hyattsville, MD: National Center for Health Statistics.

Headden, S. (1997). The Hispanic dropout mystery. *U.S. News & World Report*, *123*, 64–65.

Hernandez, B., Garcia, J.I.R., & Flynn, M. (2010). The role of familism in the relation between parent-child discord and psychological distress among emerging adults of Mexican descent. *Journal of Family Psychology*, *24*, 105–114.

Holloway, R. A., Waldrip, A. M., & Ickes, W. (2009). Evidence that a simpatico self-schema accounts for differences in the self-concepts and social behavior of Latinos versus Whites (and Blacks). *Journal of Personality and Social Psychology*, *96*, 1012–1028.

Inclan, J. (1985). Variations in value orientations in mental health work with Puerto Ricans. *Psychotherapy*, *22*, 324–334.

Kouyoumdjian, H., Zamboanga, B. L., & Hansen, D. J. (2003). Barriers to community mental health services for Latinos: Treatment considerations. *Clinical Psychology: Science and Practice*, *10*, 394–422.

Kuhlberg, J. A., Pena, J. B., & Zayas, L. H. (2010). Familism, parent-adolescent conflict, self-esteem, internalizing behaviors and suicide attempts among adolescent Latinas. *Child Psychiatry and Human Development*, *41*, 425–440.

Lefkowitz, E. S., Romo, L.F.L., Corona, R., Au, T. K.-F., & Sigman, M. (2000). How Latino American and European American adolescents discuss conflicts, sexuality, and AIDS with their mothers. *Developmental Psychology*, *36*, 315–325.

Lopez, M. H., & Dockterman, D. (2011). *U.S. Hispanic country of origin counts for nation, top 30 metropolitan areas*. Retrieved from http://pewhispanic.org/reports/report.php?ReportID=142

Lopez, M. H., Taylor, P., Funk, C., & Gonzalez-Barrera, A. (2013). *On immigration policy, deportation relief seen as more important than citizenship*. Retrieved from http://www.pewhispanic.org/2013/12/19/on-immigration-policy-deportation-relief-seen-as-more-important-than-citizenship/

Lopez-Baez, S. I. (2006). Counseling Latinas: Culturally responsive interventions. In C. C. Lee (Ed.), *Multicultural issues in counseling* (3rd ed., pp. 187–194). Alexandria, VA: American Counseling Association.

Marcos, L. R. (1973). The language barrier in evaluating Spanish-American patients. *Archives of General Psychiatry*, *29*, 655–659.

Marrero, P. (2011, August 8). Migración mexicana permanece estable. *La Opinion*. Retrieved from http://www.impre.com/laraza/noticias/2011/8/3/migracion-mexicana-permanece-e-266040-2.html

Martinez, M., & Gutierrez, T. (2010). *Tucson teachers sue Arizona over new "anti-Hispanic" school law*. Retrieved from http://www.cnn.com/2010/US/10/19/arizona.ethnic.studies.lawsuit/?hpt=T2

Middleton, R., Arredondo, P., & D'Andrea, M. (2000, December). The impact of Spanish-speaking newcomers in Alabama towns. *Counseling Today*, p. 24.

Miranda, A. O., & Umhoefer, D. L. (1998a). Acculturation, language use, and demographic variables as predictors of the career self-efficacy of Latino career counseling clients. *Journal of Multicultural Counseling and Development*, *26*, 39–51.

Miranda, A. O., & Umhoefer, D. L. (1998b). Depression and social interest differences between Latinos in dissimilar acculturation stages. *Journal of Mental Health Counseling, 20,* 159–171.

Miville, M. L., Koonce, D., Darlington, P., & Whitlock, B. (2000). Exploring the relationship between racial/cultural identity and ego identity among African Americans and Mexican Americans. *Journal of Multicultural Counseling and Development, 28,* 208–224.

Negy, C., & Woods, D. J. (1992). The importance of acculturation in understanding research with Hispanic-Americans. *Hispanic Journal of Behavioral Sciences, 14,* 224–247.

Navarrete, R. Jr. (2011). *Brewer's "birther" veto was the right call.* Retrieved from http://www.cnn.com/2011/OPINION/04/20/navarette.brewer.birther/_1_birther-bill-brewer-arizona-secretary?_s=PM:OPINION

Navarro, R. L., Ojeda, L., Schwartz, S. J., Piña-Watson, B., & Luna, L. L. (2014). Cultural self, personal self: Links with life satisfaction among Mexican American college students. *Journal of Latina/o Psychology, 2,* 1–20.

New Journalism on Latina/o Children. (2010). *The cultural strengths of Latino families.* Retrieved from http://www.ewa.org/site/DocServer/NJLC_CulturalStrengths_WEB.pdf?docID=641

Organista, K. C. (2000). Latinos. In J. R. White & A. S. Freeman (Eds.), *Cognitive-behavioral group therapy: For specific problems and populations* (pp. 281–303). Washington, DC: American Psychological Association.

Paniagua, F. A. (1994). *Assessing and treating culturally diverse clients.* Thousand Oaks, CA: Sage.

Pew Research Center. (2009). *Between two worlds: How young Latinas/os come of age in America.* Retrieved from http://pewresearch.org/pubs/1438/young-Latina/oLatinas/os-coming-of-age-in-america

Pew Research Center. (2010a). *Hispanics: Targets of discrimination.* Retrieved from http://www.pewresearch.org/daily-number/hispanics-targets-of-discrimination/

Pew Research Center. (2010b). *Obama's ratings little affected by recent turmoil.* Retrieved from http://people-press.org/2010/06/24/section-3-opinions-about-immigration

Pew Research Center (2014a). *The shifting religious identity of Latinas/os in the United States.* Retrieved from http://www.pewforum.org/2014/05/07/the-shifting-religious-identity-of-Latina/oLatinas/os-in-the-united-states/

Pew Research Center (2014b). *Wealth inequality has widened along racial, ethnic lines since end of Great Recession.* Retrieved from http://www.pewresearch.org/fact-tank/2014/12/12/racial-wealth-gaps-great-recession/

Rivera, D. P., Forquer, E. E., & Rangel, R. (2010). Microaggressions and the life experience of Latina/o Americans. In D. W. Sue (Ed.), *Microaggressions and marginality* (pp. 59–83). Hoboken, NJ: Wiley.

Ruiz, A. (1981). Cultural and historical perspectives in counseling Hispanics. In D. W. Sue (Ed.), *Counseling the culturally different: Theory & practice* (pp. 186–215). New York, NY: Wiley.

Santiago-Rivera, A., Kanter, J., Benson, G., Derose, T., Illes, R., & Reyes, W. (2008). Behavioral activation as an alternative treatment approach for Latinas/os with depression. *Psychotherapy: Theory, Research, Practice, Training, 45,* 173–185.

Smokowski, P. R., Rose, R. A., & Bacallao, M. (2010). Influence of risk factors and cultural assets on Latina/o adolescents' trajectories of self-esteem and internalizing symptoms. *Child Psychiatry and Human Development, 41,* 133–155.

U.S. Census Bureau. (2010a). *America's families and living arrangements: 2010.* Retrieved from http://www.census.gov/population/www /socdemo/hh-fam/cps2010.html

U.S. Census Bureau. (2010b). *20th anniversary of Americans with Disabilities Act: July 26.* Retrieved from http://www.census.gov/news room/releases/archives/facts_for_features _special_editions/cb10-ff13.html

U.S. Census Bureau. (2011). *Hispanic heritage month.* Retrieved from http://www.census .gov/newsroom/releases/archives/facts_for _features_special_editions/cb11-ff18.html

U.S. Census Bureau. (2014). *Facts for features: Hispanic heritage month 2014.* Retrieved from http://www.census.gov/newsroom/facts -for-features/2014/cb14-ff22.html

U.S. Census Bureau. (2015). *State and county quickfacts.* Retrieved from http://quickfacts .census.gov/qfd/states/00000.html

Vasquez, J. A. (1997). Distinctive traits of Hispanic students. *Prevention Researcher, 5,* 1–4.

Vega, W. A., Rodriguez, M. A., & Ang, A. (2010). Addressing stigma of depression in Latina/o primary care patients. *General Hospital Psychiatry, 32,* 182–191.

Velasquez, R. J., Gonzales, M., Butcher, J. N., Castillo-Canez, I., Apodaca, J. X., & Chavira, D. (1997). Use of the MMPI-2 with Chicanos: Strategies for counselors. *Journal of Multicultural Counseling and Development, 25,* 107–120.

Zuniga, M. E. (1997). Counseling Mexican American seniors: An overview. *Journal of Multicultural Counseling and Development, 25,* 142–155.

18

Counseling Multiracial Individuals

Why is President Obama generally considered to be black? It is true he is black, but he is also equally white, since his father was black and his mother was white. Despite this, Barack Obama is almost exclusively described as being black. Why? (Desmond-Harris, 2015)

When people try to get to know you, it's as if you're being demeaned to some sub-human creature. You always feel pressured to explain your ethnicity . . . you just feel like some wax model in a museum exhibit. People gaze upon you either in wonder or confusion. Their reactions are predictably insensitive and inconsiderate. "Um, what are you?" they ask, overwhelmed with curiosity. (Howard, 2013)

Hector is a 16-year-old boy whose mother is European American and whose father immigrated to the United States from Mexico. Hector was referred for counseling because he was acting out in school and making frequent racist remarks. He appeared to be White and openly claimed only his White identity . . . He frequently joked about "Mexicans." Hector admitted that although he knew he made racist remarks, he did not like strangers to make derogatory comments about Mexicans or Mexican Americans. (McDowell et al., 2005, p. 408)

People of mixed-race heritage are often ignored, neglected, and considered nonexistent in educational materials, media portrayals, and psychological literature (Bailey, 2013). *Multiracial* individuals are also faced with the "What are you?" question. For years, *multiracial* individuals have fought for the right to identify themselves as belonging to more than one racial group. Our society, however, is one that tends to force people to choose one racial identity over another. Hector, described above, received counseling, which helped him understand the source of his ambivalence about his Mexican heritage. He admitted making jokes before someone else could do so at his expense. One *multiracial* psychology intern (Japanese mother and Irish father) working in a Black community was asked by his supervisor how his clients felt about working with a "White" psychologist. When the supervisor noticed the confusion on the intern's face he stated, "I know you are Asian but you look White" (Murphy-Shigematsu, 2010). The intern considered the supervisor's reaction to him to be a microaggression and felt it interfered with their working relationship.

Such dynamics can lead to major psychological and social stressors in the area of identity formation. The *multiracial* person often has feelings of existing between the margins of two or more cultures, as well as a sense of discrepancy between one's own self-identity and that imposed by others. Unfortunately, mental health professionals often receive little training in working with *multiracial* clients who are distressed or confused by having *monoracial* categories imposed upon them (Gillem, Lincoln, & English, 2007). In fact, counselors may have conscious and unconscious attitudes, biases, and stereotypes similar to those of the layperson regarding race mixing (*miscegenation*) and "racial contamination." Attitudes against interracial marriage continue to exist. In a poll, 46% of Mississippi Republicans thought that interracial marriage should be illegal (Webster, 2011).

In more ways than one, the 2000 U.S. Census set in motion a complex psychological and political debate when for the first time it allowed people to check more than one box for their racial identities and to be counted as *multiracial* (Nittle, 2011). Proponents of the change have argued that it is unfair to force *multiracial* people to choose only one identity because such practices (1) create alienation and identity confusion, (2) deny racial realities, (3) undermine pride in being *multiracial*, and (4) ignore important personal information (e.g., medical advantages of knowing one's racial heritage).

Custom, history, and prejudices, however, continue to affect perceptions of those who are *multiracial*. Additionally, many civil rights organizations, including the National Association for the Advancement of Colored People (NAACP), believe that *multiracial* categorization will dilute the strength of their constituencies, and because census numbers on race and ethnicity figure into sociopolitical calculations involving antidiscrimination laws, dispersal of funds for minority programs may be adversely affected. Caught in the struggle—often with significant social and emotional consequences—are persons of mixed racial heritage.

CHARACTERISTICS AND STRENGTHS

In the following sections we consider the characteristics of *multiracialism* in the United States, its history, strengths of *multiracial* individuals, and implications for treatment. These are generalizations and their applicability needs to be assessed for each client or family.

Multiracialism in the United States

Mental health professionals can increase their understanding of *multiracialism* and related issues by increasing awareness of facts such as the following (Frey, 2014; U.S. Census Bureau, 2010):

- The *biracial* baby boom in the United States started in 1967, when the last laws against race mixing (anti-*miscegenation*) were repealed. As a result, there was a rapid increase in interracial marriage and a subsequent rise in the number of *multiracial* children in the United States. About 15% of recent marriages now involve partners from different racial or ethnic backgrounds. From 2008 to 2010, new *multiracial* marriages most commonly involved American Indians/Alaska Natives (over 80%), Asians (46%), Hispanics (43%), African Americans (28%), and Whites (18%) (Frey, 2014).

- It is estimated that *multiracial* people make up 2.4% of the national population, or more than 7.5 million people. However, *multiracial* ethnicity is probably much more common among those who are Latina/o. The census does not count Hispanic as a race, so people who see themselves as a mix of Hispanic and another race may end up marking only one race and not be counted as two or more races in the census (Alpert, 2013). The percentage of *multiracial* people is as high as 6.9% if one takes into account the racial background of people's parents' and grandparents (Pew Research Center, 2015).

- Census figures also underestimate the *multiracial* population since many *multiracial* individuals choose to self-identify with only one race. One-third of U.S. Latinas/os admit having a mixed racial background but only 13% select two or more races on census forms (Gonzales-Barrera, 2015). In addition, 30% to 70% of African Americans are *multiracial* by multigenerational history, as are the vast majority of Latinas/os, Filipinos, American Indians, and Native Hawaiians.

Implications

These statistics raise major questions regarding the *monoracial* versus *multiracial* climate of our society. For example, why are the offspring of a Black–White union considered Black by our society? Why not White? Why is it easy for us to accept the notion that children of certain mixed couples (e.g., Asian/White, Native American/White) are *multiracial* but that other combinations that involve African Americans are not? Why do some people of mixed-race heritage choose to identify themselves with only one race? Are certain interracial relationships more acceptable than others? Why? What accounts for the fact that Asian American women and Latinas are more likely than their male counterparts to marry outside of their ethnic group?

Mental health professionals who work with *multiracial* clients need to understand the implications of these questions if they are to be effective in their work with racially mixed clients. They need to examine their own attitudes toward interracial couples and *multiracial* children. In our journey to understand the implications of the issues confronting *multiracial* individuals, we concentrate on several themes that have been identified as important in working with this population.

The "One Drop of Blood" Rule

Alvin Poussaint, an African American Harvard psychiatrist, stood before a packed audience and posed a pointed question to them: "Do you know how powerful Black blood is?" After an awkward silence, he answered, "It is so powerful that one tiny drop will contaminate the entire bloodstream of a White person!" What Poussaint was referring to is called *hypodescent*, or the *"One Drop Rule*," a class-based social system that maintains the myth of *monoracialism* by assigning the person of mixed racial heritage to the least desirable racial status. This system was further institutionalized by an 1894 Supreme Court decision (Plessy v. Ferguson) that determined that a person who was seven-eighths White and one-eighth Black and "maintained that he did not look Negro" was nonetheless to be classified as Negro (Davis, 1991).

In essence, the *hypodescent* concept stemmed from a variety of self-serving motives. Initially, it was an attempt by White European immigrants to maintain racial purity and superiority by passing laws against interracial marriages (anti-*miscegenation* laws), primarily directed at Blacks and Native Americans. As early as the 1660s, laws were passed making it a crime for "Negro slaves" to marry "free-born English women" (Wehrly, Kenney, & Kenney, 1999). *Hypodescent* thinking and laws not only maintained racial purity but also generated additional property for slave owners. Africans were purchased as slave laborers; the more slaves an owner possessed, the greater his wealth and access to free labor. Thus, economically, it was beneficial to classify offspring of a Black–White union as "Negro" because it increased owners' wealth. Also, the prevalent beliefs of the time were that "Negroes and Indians" were subhuman creatures, uncivilized, lower in intellect, and impulsively childlike. One drop of Black blood in a person would make him or her contaminated and Black.

The rule of *hypodescent* applies to other racial/ethnic minority groups as well, but it appears to predominate with African Americans. Although groups of color are often averse to discussing social desirability differences between them, conventional wisdom and some data suggest that African Americans are often considered less desirable than their Asian American counterparts (L. A. Jackson et al., 1996), although Asian Americans are still considered significantly less desirable than Whites. It also appears that the sex of a minority group member affects how he or she is perceived by society. For example, images of Asian American women are much more favorable (e.g., petite, exotic, and sexually pleasing) than those of their male counterparts (e.g., passive, inhibited, and unattractive; D. Sue, 2005).

These biases help explain why interracial marriages between Asian Americans and European Americans occur more frequently than marriages between Blacks and Whites and why mixed-race children of the former union are more likely to be considered *multiracial*, whereas those of the latter are more likely to be considered Black (Jackman, Wagner, & Johnson, 2001). These double standards not only lead to hard feelings and resentments between African Americans and Asian Americans but also create friction among men and women within the Asian American population as well as in other racial minority groups. It is important to understand that such antagonism between racial/ethnic minority groups and between the sexes of a group originate from these biased sociopolitical processes. The true cause is society's ongoing and differential acceptance and stereotyping of minority groups.

Implications

> . . . *I was frequently annoyed, and to some degree felt personal discomfort, that strangers assumed I was White when that was only part of how I viewed myself. (Brown & Brown, 2014, p. 603)*

Many *multiracial* individuals find that society imposes a racial identity upon them. Such identities are often influenced not only by their phenotype and racial heritage, but also by the societal status associated with their particular background (Moss & Davis, 2008). In fact, individuals of mixed-racial heritage are generally considered to have "lower status" compared to European Americans. *Multiracial* children, when asked their heritage, have been found to answer one way internally and another way to the questioner (Cross, 1991). The external answer may be an attempt to fit in, to not violate the expectations of the interrogator, or to take the path of least resistance.

For example, answering that one is *biracial* is often not satisfactory to the questioner and is likely to result in further probing. Unable to identify their conflicts and feelings about being *multiracial* and about the frequent questions about their identity, children often settle for the answer most likely to end the questions, responding by giving the "most acceptable" *monoracial* identity. However, such answers often result in internal disharmony, a false sense of self, social marginality, and guilt (McDowell et al., 2005). These factors may be responsible for the finding that *multiracial* youth have higher rates of depressive symptoms compared to their *monoracial* counterparts (Fisher, Reynolds, Hsu, Barnes, & Tyler, 2014).

Multiracial Strengths

Although a multicultural identity can result in challenges, many cite advantages, such as having access to and support from several cultural communities (Sanchez et al., 2009). *Multiracial* individuals who have multiple racial identity integration appear to have higher levels of psychological adjustment (K.F. Jackson, Yoo, Guevarra, & Harrington, 2012). Other advantages include the ability to see issues from a variety of perspectives (Cheng & Lee, 2009). Those who have an integrated multiple racial identity have lower stress levels and feelings of alienation than individuals who are in conflict about their racial identity (Binning, Unzueta, Huo, & Molina, 2009). When adolescents were asked what they perceived were advantages to being *multiracial*, they mentioned three things in particular: having greater opportunities for international travel, being comfortable with people from different racial backgrounds, and being intriguing to others (Bosquet & Sarinana, 2014).

In the present day there is much greater acceptance of interracial marriage, especially among young adults (Pew Research Center, 2015). *Multiracial* individuals are quite visible on television, in movies, and in advertising. Support groups have arisen. For example, Michelle Lopez-Mullin, president of the *Multiracial* and Biracial Student Association, has one parent who is Chinese and Peruvian and one who is White and American Indian and finds pride in her identity (Saulny, 2011). Instead of feeling marginalized, many *multiracial* individuals possess enhanced cultural competence and feel comfortable in more than one cultural setting. They may be able to "borrow from their various racial backgrounds, culling out strengths specific to these cultures, and using them to support their well-being" (Pedrotti, Edwards, & Lopez, 2008, p. 199). And, as in the case of Michelle Lopez-Mullin, pride may develop through membership in different cultural groups. In a recent survey, about 60% of *multiracial* individuals are proud of the mixed race heritage and believe their background has made them more open to other cultures (Pew Research Center, 2015).

SPECIFIC CHALLENGES

In the following sections we consider challenges often faced by *multiracial* populations and consider their implications for treatment. Remember that these are generalizations and that their applicability needs to be assessed for each client.

Racial/Ethnic Ambiguity: "What Are You?"

> *My sister and I are half black, a quarter white, and a quarter Indian with British accents, and everyone we meet seems eager to immediately "place" us into neat boxes. It's human nature to be curious about people's backgrounds, and trying to solve the "puzzle" of a* multiracial *person is understandably interesting. But being the puzzle that people want to solve isn't always great. (Bahadur, 2015)*

Racial/ethnic ambiguity occurs when people are not easily able to distinguish the *monoracial* category of the *multiracial* individual from phenotypic characteristics. Phenotypic traits play a major role in how people perceive others. If African American traits are apparent, the *One Drop Rule* will automatically classify the person as Black, regardless of the answer of the *multiracial* individual; the questioner might think, "She says she's mixed, but she is really Black" (Bean & Lee, 2009). For *multiracial* individuals with ambiguous features, the "What are you?" question becomes a constant dilemma.

The "What are you?" question requires the individual to justify his or her existence in a world rigidly built on the concepts of racial purity and *monoracialism*. This is reinforced by a *multiracial* person's attempt to answer such a question by discerning the motives of the interrogator: "Why is the person asking?" "Does it really matter?" "Are they really interested in the answer, or am I going to violate their expectations?" "Do they see me as an oddity?" If the person answers "American," this will only lead to further inquiry. If the answer is "mixed," the interrogator will query further: "What ethnicity are you?" If the answer is "part White and Black," other questions follow: "Who are your parents?" "Which is Black?" "Why did they marry?" The *multiracial* person begins to feel picked apart and fragmented by such questioning about his or her racial background (Root, 1990). The problem with giving an answer is that it is often "not good enough."

The communication from our society is quite clear: "There is something different about you." We cannot stress enough the frequency with which *multiracial* persons face a barrage of questions about their racial identities, from childhood to adulthood (Houston, 1997). The inquisition can result in invalidation, conflicting loyalties to the racial/ethnic identities of parents, internal trauma, and confused identity development.

Implications

Multiracial children often feel quite isolated and may find little support, even from their parents. This is especially true for *monoracial* parents, who themselves are not *multiracial*. How, for example, does a White mother married to a Black husband raise her child? White? Black? Mixed? Parents of interracial marriages may fail to understand the challenges encountered by their children, gloss over differences, or raise the child as if he or she were *monoracial*. The child may, therefore, lack role models and feel even greater loneliness. Even being a *multiracial* parent may not result in greater empathy for or understanding of the unique challenges faced by *multiracial* children, especially if the parents (themselves victims of a *monoracial* system) have not adequately resolved their own identity conflicts. Therapists can help interracial couples prepare their children for questions about their racial heritage. Children are more likely to develop positive *multiracial* identities if the parents have modeled strong ethnic identities (Stepney, Sanchez, & Handy, 2015).

Existing between the Margins

> *Kayci Baldwin remembers how her Black father and White mother were concerned about other children accepting her. After some initial struggles regarding her racial identity, Kayci now actively embraces her multicultural identity and is involved with a nationwide multicultural teen group. (Associated Press, 2009)*

Root (1990) asserted that mixed race people begin life as "marginal individuals" because society refuses to view the races as equal and because their ethnic identities are ambiguous. They are often viewed as fractionated people—composed of fractions of each race, culture, or ethnicity in their heritage. A person who is Asian, White European, and African may not be completely accepted by any of these groups. *Multiracial* people may encounter prejudice and discrimination not only from the dominant group but also from secondary ethnic groups (Sanchez, Shih, & Garcia, 2009). Physical appearance may strongly influence a person's sense of group belonging and racial self-identification (AhnAllen, Suyemoto, & Carter, 2006). Racial identity is also often influenced by environmental factors, such as where one grows up (i.e., in an integrated neighborhood versus in an ethnic community).

Although being *multiracial* does not itself lead to emotional problems, societal reaction to race mixture can introduce stressors. Issues of racial identity and racial discrimination among *multiracial* adolescents have been associated with substance abuse and other problem behaviors (Choi, Harachi, Gillmore, & Catalano, 2006). However, many young mixed-race adults are rejecting the traditional color definitions and adopting a more fluid sense of identity (Saulny, 2011).

In Chapter 11 we spent considerable time discussing racial/cultural identity development among minority group members. Criticisms leveled at these theories include the following: (a) they were developed from a *monoracial* perspective rather than a *multiracial* one; (b) they falsely assume that *multiracial* individuals will be accepted by their parent culture or cultures; and (c) their linear nature is inadequate to describe the complexity of the many possible *multiracial* resolutions (Kerwin & Ponterotto, 1995; Root, 1996). The experiences and attitudes of *multiracial* individuals differ significantly depending on the races that make up their background and how the world sees them. For example, *multiracial* adults with an African American background have experiences, attitudes, and interactions that are closely aligned to the Black community while *biracial* White and Asian individuals are more likely to feel more connected to Whites rather than Asians. *Biracial* adults who are White and American Indian have only weak ties to their Native American background and most say they have a lot in common with Whites (Pew Research Center, 2015).

Compounding the difficulty with the application of *monoracial* identity theory to *multiracial* individuals is that 61% of those with a mixed racial background do not consider themselves to be "*multiracial*." Reasons why individuals do not identify as *multiracial* include (respondents could have more than one reason):

- They look like one race (47%); this was the reason given by President Obama.

- They were raised as one race (47%).

- They closely identify with a single race (39%).

- They never knew the family member or ancestor who was a different race (34%).

In addition, 21% of mixed-race Americans reported receiving pressure from family, friends, or society to identify as a single race. Another problem for ethnic identity theories is that the identity for many *multiracial* individuals is fluid. About 30% of *multiracial* adults indicate that the way they viewed their race has changed over time. Some who first thought of themselves as only one race now consider themselves *multiracial,* and others who thought of themselves as *multiracial* now view themselves as one race (Pew Research Center, 2015). These factors raise questions about the applicability of *monoracial* identity theories to *multiracial* Americans.

Many *multiracial* individuals confront the process of resolving marginality and developing a healthy identity throughout their lives. Root (1998) describes four possible healthy resolutions of marginality.

1. The *multiracial* individual accepts the identity assigned by society. For example, the child of a Black–Japanese union is likely to be considered Black by friends, peers, and family. Root believes that this can be a positive choice if the person is satisfied with the identity, receives family support, and is active rather than passive in evidencing the identity. The individual in this situation, however, may have a very fluid identity that changes radically in different situations. If the person, for example, travels or moves to another community or region of the country, the assigned racial identity may become Japanese or even mixed.

2. The person may choose to resolve marginality through *identification with both groups.* "I think a lot of us are chameleons. We can sit in a group of White people and feel different, but still fit in. . . . But we can turn around and sit in a group of Black people, even though we are not Black in the same way" (Miville, Constantine, Baysden, & So-Lloyd, 2005, p. 512). In this case, the person is able to shift from one identity (White American) when with one group to another identity (African American) when with a different group. This method of adaptation is healthy as long as individuals view the ability to move in two worlds as positive, do not lose their sense of self-integrity, and can relate well to positive aspects of both identities and cultures.

3. The person may decide to *choose a single racial identity* in an active manner. Although it may appear similar to the first option, it differs in two ways: (1) It is the individual, not society, who makes the choice of racial group identity, and (2) the identity is less prone to shifting when the situational context changes. Actively choosing a single racial identity can be a positive option when the individual does not deny his or her other racial heritage and when

the group with whom the individual chooses to identify does not marginalize the person.

4. Identification with a *mixed-race heritage* or *multiracial identity* is another option. "I think it [being multiracial] has made me expertly cued to cultural cues. Kind of as an observer, I'm always trying to learn, 'ok, what's going on here, how does one act here, and what are the cultural norms'" (Suyemoto, 2004, p. 216). In fact, bicultural/*biracial* or multicultural/*multiracial* identification rather than identifying with only one race is increasing in frequency (Brunsma, 2005; Suzuki-Crumly & Hyers, 2004). A multicultural identity allows equal valuing of all aspects of one's racial/cultural heritage, the ability to relate to both groups, and feelings of being well integrated.

Implications

In therapy with *multiracial* individuals, identity issues sometimes come to the surface. The type of conflict and resolution may differ depending on gender, the type of composition of the *multiracial* combination, and other group identity factors, such as socioeconomic status, age, and sexual orientation. Also, identities may shift, with the degree of fluidity displayed depending on the situational context. It is also possible as suggested by Root that there may be more than one resolution to identity developed that can lead to healthy adjustment. However, it should not be assumed that racial identity issues are the source of a client's problem. If feelings of marginality are producing distress, positive resolution can occur with any of the choices discussed. Therapists should be aware that a growing number of *multiracial* individuals are choosing "*multiracial*" as their ethnic identity. This choice should not be considered pathological and interpreted as confusion or an inability to commit to an integrated identity (Suyemoto, 2004).

Intermarriage, Stereotypes, and Myths

In 2010, 15% of all new marriages in the United States were between spouses of a different race or ethnicity, which is more than double the percentage in 1980 (6.7%). Of these marriages, 9% of Whites, 17% of African Americans, 26% of Latinas/os, and 28% of Asian were with people of a different racial group. Of African American males 24% married outside their race compared to 9% of females. Gender patterns of Asian Americans went in the other direction with 36% of Asian females marrying outside of their race versus 17% of Asian males. Gender differences were not found in intermarriage rates among White and Hispanic newlyweds. Over a third of Americans indicate that a family member or close relative is married to someone of a different race and two-thirds of Americans said it would be fine if a family member or close relative marries someone of a different race. However, 28% of Americans believe that intermarriage was unacceptable (Wang, 2012).

That intermarriage is not acceptable to many is illustrated by the reaction to a Cheerios ad on television involving a mixed racial girl with a White mother and an African American father. So many racist reactions were posted on *YouTube* in response to the ad that the comments section was disabled (Stump, 2013). There is considerable evidence that myths and stereotypes associated with *multiracial* individuals and interracial couples have involved attempts to prevent the mixing of races through stigmatizing such mixture (Wehrly et al., 1999). African Americans, especially males, are often stereotyped as possessing "primitive sexuality" and as being "passionate, potent, and sexually virile" (Frankenberg, 1993). History is replete with incidents reflecting society's hostility and antagonism toward African Americans.

Unfortunately, sociopsychological research on this topic has often perpetuated and reinforced inaccurate beliefs about race mixing and mixed-race people. Even now, some individuals still view interracial relationships as an oddity. When an interracial couple is asked "So how did the two of you meet?" the inquiry may not be due to pure curiosity but may instead reflect the question: "How did you two end up together?" (Goff, 2014). Early research and writings on the characteristics and dynamics of interracial relationships and marriages focused primarily on negative attributes. It was believed that individuals who chose to marry outside their racial group were somehow deficient, lacked self-esteem, or harbored feelings of inferiority (Beigel, 1966), that they were rebelling against parental authority (Saxton, 1968), or that they were experiencing mental health issues (Brayboy, 1966). Stereotypes have fluctuated depending on the race and the gender of each partner. A White person who violated social norms against interracial marriages might be described as experimenting with the "exotic," attempting to express a liberal view, possessing low self-esteem, or being a social/occupational failure unable to attract a member of his or her own race (Rosenblatt, Karis, & Powell, 1995). Members of a minority group in mixed-race relationships were often seen as trying to elevate themselves socially, economically, and psychologically.

Discrimination and Racism

Multiracial individuals have also been subjected to instances of racism and discrimination. About 55% have been exposed to racial slurs or jokes. The degree of reported exposure varied according to the specific races that were part of the individual's racial background. Although 40% of mixed-race adults with an African American background said they were unfairly stopped by police, only 15% of White and American Indian adults, and 6% of *biracial* White and Asian individuals reported the same experience. A similar pattern was found for other forms of racial discrimination. In fact, the exposure to racism and discrimination of mixed-race adults was similar to that reported by single-race individuals of a specific race. *Biracial* individuals with an African American background reported the same level of discrimination as single-race African Americans while mixed-race adults with an Asian background reported discrimination at the same level as single-race Asians (Pew Research Center, 2015).

Implications

In general, early myths about mixed marriages implied that these unions were the result of unhealthy motives by the partners and that *multiracial* offspring were doomed to suffer deficiencies and pathologies. These assumptions, and the early studies of mixed-race individuals, were problematic. First, if partners in mixed marriages and their *multiracial* offspring experienced identity issues, conflicts, and psychological problems, it is likely that these difficulties were the result of an intolerant and hostile society. In other words, they would have resulted from bias, discrimination, and racism rather than from anything inherent in the marriage or the "unhealthy" qualities of those involved. Second, we already know that research is influenced by and reflects societal views. It seems likely, therefore, that early researchers most likely asked questions and designed studies with a focus on identifying pathology rather than the healthy and functional traits of the group. Third, in the case of interracial relationships, current research now suggests that these marriages are based on the same ingredients as other marriages: love, companionship, and compatible interests and values (Rosenblatt et al., 1995).

Negative views of mixed marriages also contribute to the racism and discrimination that *multiracial* individuals are exposed to. It is important to understand that research has identified beneficial sociopsychological traits associated with a *multiracial* heritage, including an increased sense of uniqueness, greater variety in one's life, greater tolerance and understanding of people, a greater ability to deal with racism and to interact and build alliances with diverse people and groups (Sanchez et al., 2009; Saulny, 2011).

A Multiracial Bill of Rights

> *Countless numbers of times I have fragmented and fractionalized myself in order to make the other more comfortable in deciphering my behavior, my words, my loyalties, my choice of friends, my appearance, my parents, and so on. And given my multiethnic history, it was hard to keep track of all the fractions, to make them add up to one whole. It took me over 30 years to realize that fragmenting myself seldom served a purpose other than to preserve the delusions this country has created around race. Reciting the fractions to the other was the ultimate act of buying into the mechanics of racism in this country. (Root, 1996, pp. 4–5)*

These words were written by Maria Root, a leading psychologist in the field of *multiracial* identity and development, who expressed concerns about the way in which society has historically relegated *multiracial* persons to deviant status or ignored their existence because they do not fit into a *monoracial* classification. In her personal and professional journey, Root (1996) developed a Bill of Rights for Racially Mixed People that asserts the right of *multiracial* individuals not to justify their existence or ethnic legitimacy, the right to self-identity rather than assume the identity expected by others, and the right to identify with more than one group of people.

Implications

Root's assertions has major implications for mental health providers because it challenges our notions of a *monoracial* classification system, reorients our thoughts about the many myths of *multiracial* persons, makes us aware of the systemic construction and rationalizations of race, warns us about the dangers of fractionating identities, and advocates freedom of choice for the *multiracial* individual.

IMPLICATIONS FOR CLINICAL PRACTICE

Although *monoracial* minority group members experience many of the issues faced by *multiracial* individuals, the latter, in addition to dealing with racism, are likely to experience unique stressors related to their multiple racial/ethnic identities. For example, most *monoracial* minorities find their own groups receptive and supportive of them. *Multiracial* individuals may be placed in the awkward situation of not being fully accepted by any group. Likewise, *monoracial* minority group children can expect psychological and emotional support from their parents—the parents share common experiences with their children, can act as mentors, and relate to the experiences their children encounter with respect to minority status. However, *multiracial* children are likely to have *monoracial* parents who do not understand the challenges facing their children (Townsend, Markus, & Bergsieker, 2009). Common problems for *multiracial* youth and adults include communication difficulties with their parents about racial identity issues, reactions of peers and society to their identity, and pressure to assume a *monoracial* identity (Jolivette & Gutierrez-Mock, 2008). Here are twelve guidelines for working with *multiracial* clients:

1. Become aware of your own stereotypes and preconceptions regarding interracial relationships and marriages. When you see a racially mixed couple, do you pay extra attention to them? What thoughts and images do you have? Awareness of your own biases will help you avoid imposing them upon your clients.

2. When working with *multiracial* clients, avoid stereotyping. As with interracial relationships, cultural conditioning creates beliefs about racially mixed people. In general, these images are based on mistaken convictions that may deny the mixed-race heritage of the person and his or her uniqueness.

3. It is important to see *multiracial* people in a holistic fashion rather than as fractions of a person. This means being cautious about the "What are you?" question. It is important to emphasize the positive qualities of the total person rather than seeing the person as parts.

4. Remember that being a *multiracial* person often means coping with marginality and isolation resulting from external factors related to prejudice. Hence mixed-race persons often experience forced-choice situations and strong feelings of loneliness, rejection, anger, and guilt/shame from not fully integrating all aspects of their racial heritage. These feelings are often submerged and hidden because there is no one in whom they can confide or who understands. As mentioned earlier, mixed-race children often come from homes with *monoracial* parents.

5. Be willing to discuss the client's racial/cultural identity. Since mixed-race people have historically been portrayed as possessing deficiencies, stress their positive attributes and the advantages of being *multiracial* and multicultural.

6. Identify the strengths associated with a multicultural identity and the resources available to the client rather than focusing only on challenges.

7. With mixed-race clients, emphasize the freedom to choose one's identity. There is no one identity suitable for everyone. The racial identity models discussed in this chapter all have limitations, and it is important to note that identities are often changing and fluid rather than fixed.

8. Take an active psychoeducational approach. *Multiracial* individuals are often subjected to an inflexible *monoracial* system that stereotypes and fits them into rigid categories. Oftentimes, children may learn to internalize the stereotypes and accept an identity imposed upon them. Somewhere in the counseling process, clients can be helped to understand the forces of oppression and racism, and the counselor can empower clients to take an active part in formulating their identities.

9. Recognize that family counseling may be especially valuable in working with mixed-race clients, especially if they are children. Frequently, parents (especially those who are *monoracial*) are unaware of the unique conflicts related to their child's *multiracial* journey. Interracial couples should also be assessed to see if differing cultural values and expectations may be impacting their children in a negative manner. Parents can be taught to empower their children, convey positive aspects of being *multiracial*, and help them integrate a healthy identity.

10. When working with *multiracial* clients, ensure that you possess basic knowledge of the history and issues related to *hypodescent* thinking (the *One Drop Rule*), ambiguity (the "What are you?" question), and marginality. The knowledge cannot be superficial but must entail a historical, political, social, and psychological understanding of the treatment of race, racism, and *monoracialism* in this society. In essence, these four dynamics form the context within which the *multiracial* individual operates on a continuing basis.

11. Remember that many multicultural individuals are proud of their identity or have resolved their identity in a healthy manner and that their *multiracial* identity is not a factor in their presenting problem.

12. Educational institutions should provide support services for *multiracial* students, and opportunities to increase awareness and understanding of *multiracial* issues in the curriculum (Ingram, Chaudhary, & Jones, 2014).

SUMMARY

Multiracial people are often ignored, neglected, and considered nonexistent in educational materials, media portrayals, and psychological literature. *Multiracial* individuals are faced with "What are you?" questions because society and even groups of color see race as *monoracial.* They may feel they are existing between the margins of two or more cultures, and sense a discrepancy between their own self-identity and that imposed by others. Mental health professionals often receive little training in working with *multiracial* clients who are distressed or confused by having *monoracial* categories imposed upon them. To work effectively with *multiracial* individuals, the therapist must understand *multiracial* identity development; the unique challenges of existing on the margins; the stereotypes and myths associated with being *multiracial*; and concepts such as "*hypodescent.*" Many mixed-race individuals do not identify as being *multiracial,* and for others, identity may shift over time. There are different routes to a healthy *multiracial* identity. Twelve clinical implications for counselor practice are identified.

GLOSSARY TERMS

Biracial

Biracial/Multiracial identity development

Hypodescent

Miscegenation

Monoracial

Multiracial

One Drop Rule

Racial/ethnic ambiguity

REFERENCES

AhnAllen, J. M., Suyemoto, K. L., & Carter, A. S. (2006). Relationship between physical appearance, sense of belonging and exclusion, and racial/ethnic self-identification among multiracial Japanese European Americans. *Cultural Diversity and Ethnic Minority Psychology, 12,* 673–686.

Alpert, E. (2013). *More Americans consider themselves multiracial.* Retrieved from http://articles.latimes.com/2013/jun/12/local/la-me-multiracial-growth-20130613

Associated Press. (2009, May 28). *Multiracial America is fastest growing group.* Retrieved from http://www.msnbc.msn.com/id/30986649/ns/us_news-life/t/multiracial-america-fastest-growing-group/#.TyvltsUS2Ag

Bahadur, N. (2015). *19 things multiracial women want you to know.* Retrieved from http://www.huffingtonpost.com/2015/06/09/multiracial-women_n_7520140.html

Bailey, E. J. (2013). *The new face of America: How the emerging multiracial, multiethnic majority is changing the United States*. Santa Barbara, CA: ABC-CLIO.

Bean, F. D., & Lee, J. (2009). Multiraciality and the dynamics of race relations in the United States. *Journal of Social Issues, 65,* 205–219.

Beigel, H. G. (1966). Problems and motives in interracial relationships. *Journal of Sex Research, 2,* 185–205.

Binning, K. R., Unzueta, M. M., Huo, Y. J., & Molina, L. E. (2009). The interpretation of multiracial status and its relation to social engagement and psychological well-being. *Journal of Social Issues, 65,* 35–49.

Bosquet, S., & Sarinana, S.A.L. (2014). *Perceived advantages of multiraciality among multiracial adolescents*. Washington, DC: American Psychological Association.

Brayboy, T. L. (1966). Interracial sexuality as an expression of neurotic conflict. *Journal of Sex Research, 2,* 179–184.

Brown, C., & Brown, B. (2014). On passing (or not): Developing under multicultural heritages. *Journal of the American Academy of Child & Adolescent Psychiatry, 53,* 603–605.

Brunsma, D. L. (2005). Interracial families and racial identity of mixed-race children: Evidence from the early childhood longitudinal study. *Social Forces, 84,* 1131–1157.

Cheng, C., & Lee, F. (2009). Multiracial identity integration: Perceptions of conflict and distance among multiracial individuals. *Journal of Social Issues, 65,* 51 68.

Choi, Y. H., Harachi, T. W., Gillmore, M. R., & Catalano, R. F. (2006). Are multiracial adolescents at greater risk? Comparisons of rates, patterns, and correlates of substance use and violence between monoracial and multiracial adolescents. *American Journal of Orthopsychiatry, 76,* 86–97.

Cross, W. E. (1991). *Shades of black: Diversity in African American identity*. Philadelphia, PA: Temple University Press.

Davis, J. F. (1991). *Who is Black?: One nation's definition*. University Park, PA: Pennsylvania State University Press.

Davis, L. E., & Gelsomino, J. (1994). As assessment of practitioner cross-racial treatment experiences. *Social Work, 39,* 116–123.

Desmond-Harris, J. (2015). *Study illuminates why multiracial Americans almost never call themselves White*. Retrieved from http://www.vox.com/2015/6/15/8768515/biracial-multiracial-identity-white

Fisher, S., Reynolds, J. L., Hsu, W.-Wen., Barnes, J., & Tyler, K. (2014). Examining multiracial youth in context: Ethnic identity development and mental health outcomes. *Journal of Youth and Adolescence, 43,* 1688–1699.

Frankenberg, R. (1993). *Euro-American women: Race matters*. Minneapolis, MN: University of Minnesota Press.

Frey, S. (2014). *Programs target crucial summer before college*. Retrieved from http://edsource.org/2014/programs-target-crucial-summer-before-college/66896#.VN4rvy4sDoa

Gillem, A. R., Lincoln, S. K., & English, K. (2007). Biracial populations. In M. G. Constantine (Ed.), *Clinical practice with people of color* (pp. 104–124). New York, NY: Teachers College Press.

Goff, R. (2014). *The ongoing stigma of interracial dating*. Retrieved from http://www.thedailybeast.com/articles/2014/09/15/the-ongoing-stigma-of-interracial-dating.html

Gonzalez-Barrera, A. (2015). "Mestizo" and "Mulatto": Mixed-race identities among U.S. Hispanics. Retrieved from http://www.pewresearch.org/fact-rank/2015/07/10/mestizo-and-mulatto-mixed-race-identities-unique-to hispanics/

Houston, H. R. (1997). "Between two cultures": A testimony. *Amerasia Journal, 23,* 149–154.

Howard, S. (2013). *The invisible child: What it's like being multiracial in America*. Retrieved from http://dlmagazine.org/2013/10/invisible-child-multiracial-america/

Ingram, P., Chaudhary, A. K., & Jones, W. T. (2014). How do biracial students interact with others on the college campus? *College Student Journal, 48*, 297–311.

Jackman, C. F., Wagner, W. G., & Johnson, J. T. (2001). The Attitudes Toward Multiracial Children Scale. *Journal of Black Studies, 27*, 86–99.

Jackson, K. F., Yoo, H. C., Guevarra, R. Jr., & Harrington, B. A. (2012). Role of identity integration on the relationship between perceived racial discrimination and psychological adjustment of multiracial people. *Journal of Counseling Psychology, 59*, 240–250.

Jackson, L. A., Hodge, C. N., Gerard, D. A., Ingram, J. M., Ervin, K. S., & Sheppard, L. A. (1996). Cognition, affect and behavior in the prediction of group attitudes. *Personality and Social Psychology Bulletin, 22*, 306–316.

Jolivette, A., & Gutierrez-Mock, J. (2008). *A report on the health and wellness of multiracial youth in the Bay Area.* Funded by the K. & F. Baxter Foundation, RIMI Program, and the National Center on Minority Health and Health Disparities.

Kerwin, C., & Ponterotto, J. G. (1995). Biracial identity development: Theory and research. In J. Ponterotto, J. M. Casas, L. A. Suzuki, & C. M. Alexander (Eds.), *Handbook of multicultural counseling* (pp. 199–217). Newbury Park, CA: Sage.

McDowell, T., Ingoglia, L., Serizawa, T., Holland, C., Dashiell, J. W. Jr., & Stevens, C. (2005). Raising multicultural awareness in family therapy through critical conversations. *Journal of Marital and Family Therapy, 31*, 399–412.

Miville, M. L., Constantine, M. G., Baysden, M. F., & So-Lloyd, G. (2005). Chameleon changes: An exploration of racial identity themes of multiracial people. *Journal of Counseling Psychology, 52*, 507–516.

Moss, R. C., & Davis, D. (2008). Counseling biracial students: A review of issues and interventions. *Journal of Multicultural Counseling and Development, 36*, 219–230.

Murphy-Shigematsu, S. (2010). Microaggressions by supervisors of color. *Training and Education in Professional Psychology, 4*, 16–18.

Nittle, N. K. (2011). *Five myths about multiracial people in the U.S.* Retrieved from http://racerelations.about.com/od/understandingrac1/a/Five-Myths-About-Multiracial-People-In-The-U-S.htm

Pedrotti, J. T., Edwards, L. M., & Lopez, S. J. (2008). Working with multicultural clients in therapy: Bridging theory, research, and practice. *Professional Psychology: Research and Practice, 39*, 192–201.

Pew Research Center (2015). *Multiracial in America: Proud, diverse and growing in numbers.* Washington, DC: Author.

Root, M.P.P. (1990). Resolving "other" status: Identity development of biracial individuals. In L. S. Brown & M.P.P. Root (Eds.), *Diversity and complexity in feminist therapy* (pp. 185–205). New York, NY: Haworth Press.

Root, M.P.P. (Ed.). (1996). *The multiracial experience.* Thousand Oaks, CA: Sage.

Root, M.P.P. (1998). Facilitating psychotherapy with Asian American clients. In D. R. Atkinson, G. Morten, & D. W. Sue (Eds.), *Counseling American minorities: A cross-cultural perspective* (pp. 214–234). Boston, MA: McGraw-Hill.

Rosenblatt, P. C., Karis, T. A., & Powell, R. D. (1995). *Multiracial couples.* Thousand Oaks, CA: Sage.

Sanchez, D. T., Shih, M., & Garcia, J. A. (2009). Juggling multiple racial identities: Malleable racial identification and psychological well-being. *Cultural Diversity and Ethnic Minority Psychology, 15*, 243–254.

Saulny, S. (2011). *Black? White? Asian? More young Americans choose all of the above.* Retrieved from http://www.amren.com/mtnews/archives/2011/01/black_white_asi.php

Saxton, L. (1968). *The individual, marriage, and the family.* Belmont, CA: Wadsworth.

Stepney, C. T., Sanchez, D. T., & Handy, P. E. (2015). Perceptions of parents' ethnic identities and the personal ethnic-identity and racial attitudes of biracial adults. *Cultural Diversity and Ethnic Minority Psychology, 21*, 65–75

Stump, S. (2013). *"Angry over what?" Kids react to mixed-race Cheerios ad in new video.* Retrieved from http://www.today.com/news/angry-over-what-kids-react-mixed-race-cheerios-ad-new-6C10658002

Sue, D. (2005). Asian American masculinity and therapy: The concept of masculinity in Asian American males. In G. R. Brooks & G. E. Good (Eds.), *The new handbook of psychotherapy and counseling with men: A comprehensive guide to settings, problems, and treatment approaches* (pp. 357–368). Hoboken, NJ: Wiley.

Sue, S., & Sue, D. W. (1971). Chinese-American personality and mental health. *Amerasian Journal, 1*, 36–49.

Suyemoto, K. L. (2004). Racial/ethnic identities and related attributed experiences of multiracial Japanese European Americans. *Journal of Multicultural Counseling and Development, 32*, 206–221.

Suzuki-Crumly, J., & Hyers, L. L. (2004). The relationship among ethnic identity, psychological well-being, and intergroup competence: An investigation of two biracial groups. *Cultural Diversity and Ethnic Minority Psychology, 10*, 137–150.

Townsend, S.S.M., Markus, H. R., & Bergsieker, H. B. (2009). My choice, your categories: The denial of multiracial identities. *Journal of Social Issues, 65*, 185–204.

U.S. Census Bureau. (2010). *United States profile.* Retrieved from http://www.census.gov

Wang, W. (2012). *The rise of intermarriage.* Retrieved from http://www.pewsocialtrends.org/2012/02/16/the-rise-of-intermarriage/

Webster, S. C. (2011). *Shock poll: 46% of Mississippi Republicans think interracial marriage should be illegal.* Retrieved from http://www.rawstory.com/rs/2011/04/07/shock-poll-46-of-mississippi-republicans-think-interracial-marriage-should-be-illegal

Wehrly, B., Kenney, K. R., & Kenney, M. E. (1999). *Counseling multiracial families.* Thousand Oaks, CA: Sage.

PART VII

Counseling and Special Circumstances Involving Ethnic Populations

Counseling Arab Americans and Muslim Americans

Chapter Objectives

1. Learn the demographics and characteristics of Arab Americans and *Muslim* Americans.

2. Understand the differences between these two populations

3. Identify counseling implications of the information provided for Arab Americans and *Muslim* Americans.

4. Provide examples of strengths that are associated with Arab and *Muslim* Americans.

5. Know the special challenges faced by Arab Americans and *Muslim* Americans.

6. Understand how the implications for clinical practice can guide assessment and therapy with Arab Americans and *Muslim* Americans.

Democrats were forced to defend their appointment of Rep. Andre Carson of Indiana, a Muslim, *to the House Intelligence Committee after anti-Muslim protests erupted on Twitter and other social media with complaints that exposing American secrets to Carson could be dangerous. (Associated Press, 2015)*

Teenagers were asked to identify what role in a movie or on television people from various ethnic backgrounds would most likely play. For Arab Americans, the roles selected were that of a terrorist or a convenience store clerk. This result was obtained even though the study predated the September 11, 2001, terrorist attacks. (Zogby, 2001a)

"Nice to see a movie where the Arabs are portrayed for who they really are—vermin scum intent on destroying us," said one Twitter post in response to the movie American Sniper.

Nineteen year old Yusor Mohammed, a Muslim, *felt like a "proud and blessed" American who fit in. "That's the beautiful thing here, is it doesn't matter where you come from . . . But here we're all one." She, her 23-year-old husband Deah Shaddy Barakat, and her 19-year-old sister Razan Mohammad Abu-Salha were later shot to death by an angry neighbor (Botelho & Davis, 2015).*

More than 1000 Muslims *formed a human shield around Oslo's synagogue on Saturday, offering symbolic protection for the city's Jewish community and condemning an attack on a synagogue in neighbouring Denmark last weekend. Chanting "No to anti-Semitism, no to Islamophobia," Norway's* Muslims *formed what they called a ring of peace a week after Omar Abdel Hamid El-Hussein, a Danish-born son of Palestinian immigrants, killed two people at a synagogue. (Reuters, 2015)*

CHARACTERISTICS AND STRENGTHS

In the following sections we discuss the characteristics, values, and strengths of Arab and *Muslim* Americans and consider their implications in treatment. Remember that these are generalizations and their applicability needs to be assessed for each client.

Arab Americans

Arabs are individuals who originate from countries located in the Middle East and North Africa and whose primary language is Arabic. *Arabs* began immigrating to the United States in the late 1800s. Arab Americans, descending from about 20 different countries, are heterogeneous in terms of race, religion, and political ideology. The majority of Arab Americans are native-born U.S. citizens.

Arab Americans can have African, Asian, or European ancestry. Approximately 56% of Arab Americans trace their ancestry to Lebanon, while 14% are from Syria, 11% from Egypt, 9% from Palestine, 4% from Jordan, 2% from Iraq, and 4% from other countries (El-Badry, 2006). Although the populations of Arabic-speaking countries include large numbers of *Muslims*, only about one-quarter of Arab Americans are *Muslims* (Jackson & Nassar-McMillan, 2006).

Because of categorization systems used in the U.S. Census, it is difficult to determine the precise size of the Arab American population. The U.S. Census estimates that there are 1.8 million Arab Americans. However, the Arab American Institute believes the U.S. Census severely underestimates the number in the group and that there are actually 3,665,789 Arab Americans, with 94% living in metropolitan areas such as Los Angeles, Detroit, New York, Chicago, and Washington, D.C. (Arab American Institute, 2012).

The majority of Arab American immigrants arrived in two major waves (Nassar-McMillan & Hakim-Larson, 2003; Suleiman, 1999). The first lasted from 1875 to World War II and primarily involved Arab Christians from Lebanon and Syria who immigrated for economic reasons. The second wave began after World War II and included Palestinians, Iraqis, and Syrians, who left in order to escape the Arab-Israeli conflicts and civil war. This latter group included larger numbers of *Muslims*. The aftermath of the September 11 attacks initially reduced Arab immigration. However, it has once again increased, and more than 40,000 immigrants from *Muslim* countries such as Egypt, Pakistan, and Morocco, were admitted to the United States in 2005 (Elliott, 2006).

In comparison with the U.S. population as a whole, Arab Americans are more likely to be married (61% versus 54%), male (57% versus 49%), young, and highly educated (46% have bachelor's degree versus 28% of the total adult population) (Arab American Institute, 2011). Sixty-nine percent indicate they speak a language other than English at home, but 65% speak English "very well." The majority work as executives, professionals, and office and sales staff. Forty-two percent work in management positions. Arab American income is higher than the national median income ($59,012 versus $52,029) (Arab American Institute, 2011). However, the poverty rate is also higher (17% versus 12%; U.S. Census Bureau, 2005). Arab Americans participate in a variety of religions. More than 33% are Roman Catholic, 25% are Muslim, 18% are Eastern Orthodox, 10% are Protestant, and 13% report other religion or no affiliation (Arab American Institute, 2003).

Muslim Americans

It is estimated that about 2 to 3 million *Muslims*—followers of *Islam*—are living in the United States. The *Qur'an*, the Islamic holy book, is considered to be the literal word of God. *Islam* is one of the fastest growing religions in the United States, with approximately one-fourth of U.S. *Muslims* being converts to the faith (U.S. Department of State, 2002). Within *Islam*, there are two major sects—*Sunni* and *Shiite*. The *Sunnis* are the larger group, accounting for about 90% of *Muslims* worldwide. The remaining 10% are *Shiites*. Most *Muslims* in America are *Sunni*, whereas those in Iraq, Bahrain, Lebanon, and Iran are mainly *Shiite*.

Although many conflate *Muslims* with *Arabs*, most *Muslims* do not descend from Arabic-speaking countries. While there are about 1 billion *Muslims* worldwide, only about 200 million are Arab (Amri, 2010). The global Muslim population will increase by about 35% and reach 2.2 billion by 2020 or about 26.4% of the world's projected population. It is increasing at twice the rate of the non-Muslim population. The percentage of Muslims currently found in different regions of the world comprise Asia-Pasific (62.1%), Middle East–North Africa (19.9%), Sub-Saharan Africa (15%), Europe (2.7%), and Americas (0.3%) (Pew Research Center, 2011a).

Over a third of Muslim Americans were born in the U.S. and although there is a large percentage of Muslims who are immigrants, about 81% are citizens of the U.S. including 70% of those born outside the U.S.—a higher citizenship rate than in other immigrant groups.

First-generation *Muslim* Americans come from a wide range of countries around the world. About 41% are immigrants from the Middle East or North Africa, while about 26% come from South Asian nations including Pakistan (14%), Bangladesh (5%), and India (3%). Others came to the United States from sub-Saharan Africa (11%), European countries (7%), Iran (5%), or other countries (9%). In the United States, 30% of *Muslim* Americans report their race as White, 23% Black, 21% Asian, 6% Hispanic, and 9% other or mixed race (Pew Research Center, 2011b). The Muslim American population is much younger than the non-Muslim population—59% of adult Muslims are between the ages of 18 and 39 versus 40% of other adults in the U.S.

Muslim Americans have liberal attitudes on a number of current political issues. In general, they are highly religious and about half think of themselves first as *Muslim* and then American. This is similar to Christians, of whom about 46% think of themselves as Christian first and then American. *Muslim* Americans appear to be highly integrated into American society and they are largely content with their lives (Pew Research Center, 2011a).

Cultural and Religious Values

The lives of *Muslims* are governed by *Islamic* laws derived from the *Qur'an*, which deals with social issues, family life, economics and business, sexuality, and other aspects of life. The name of their religion means "submission to God." Adherence to *Islam* is demonstrated by individual accountability and a declaration of faith ("There is no god but God and *Muhammad* is his messenger"). *Muslims* engage in the ritual of prayer five times a day and annually fast during daylight hours throughout the holy month of *Ramadan*—a time for inner reflection, devotion to God, and spiritual renewal. Almsgiving and a pilgrimage to Mecca are additional signs of devotion (Nobles & Sciarra, 2000). Some *Muslim* women, particularly those of Arab descent, wear traditional clothing because of the *Islamic* teachings of modesty.

Family Structure and Values

Family structure and values of Arab Americans and *Muslim* Americans differ widely, depending on the specific country of origin and acculturation level. An Arab American engineer living in San Francisco made the following observation: "American values are, by and large, very consistent with *Islamic* values, with a focus on family, faith, hard work, and an obligation to better self and society" (U.S. Department of State, 2002, p. 1).

Some generalizations can be made about the values of Arab Americans. Hospitality is considered an important aspect of interpersonal interactions (Nobles & Sciarra, 2000). Family obligations and interdependence among members are very important. This group orientation can result in pressure for conformity and high expectations for children. Parents expect to remain part of their children's lives for as long as possible. In traditional Arab American families, there is a strong sense of a community and an identity that revolves around culture and God. The family structure tends to be patriarchal, with the men being the authority and head of the family. Women are responsible for raising the children and instilling cultural values in the offspring. In general, boys are advised by older males, and girls are advised by older females. The maintenance of traditional gender roles has resulted in lower employment levels for even highly educated Arab women (Al Harahsheh, 2011).

Arab culture tends to be collectivistic, hence the success or failure of an individual reflects on the entire family. This personal responsibility for social behavior sometimes leads to stress and anxiety. Arab college students appear to have higher than expected rates of social anxiety, which may result from internalized norms of social responsibility for their conduct (Iancu et al., 2011). Personal problems are often disclosed only to close family or friends. Opposite-sex discussions with other than a family member may be problematic (Jackson & Nassar-McMillan, 2006). Seeking treatment for emotional problems may be considered shameful, so outside help is likely to be sought only as a last resort.

In traditionally oriented *Muslim* families, the oldest son is prepared to become the head of the extended family. Family roles are complementary, with men serving as providers and head of the family and women maintaining the home and rearing children. Mothers are likely to behave affectionately toward their children, whereas fathers may be aloof, generating both fear and respect (Dwairy, 2008). Many *Muslim* women avoid physical contact with nonrelated males, such as shaking hands or hugging (Tummala-Narra & Claudius, 2013). However, wide variations exist. Some *Muslim* American women shake hands with men, support gay marriage, and consider themselves devout even though they do not wear a Hijab or head covering (Lawrence, 2014). Contrary to public opinion, U.S. women who have converted to *Islam* do not consider themselves to be "brainwashed" or having forfeited their "free will" (Aleccia, 2013).

Implications

Counselors should be aware that traditional Arab American and *Muslim* families tend to be hierarchical, with men considered to be the head of the family. Although Western media often portray women as powerless victims of emotional and physical abuse, in most Arab and *Muslim* families, women are treated with honor and respect (Ibrahim & Dykeman, 2011). Problems can occur with acculturation conflicts involving the struggle between adhering to traditional familial patterns (culturally collective support) and seeking individual fulfillment.

Cultural Strengths

Arab Americans and *Muslim* Americans tend to be collectivistic rather than individualistic in orientation. Family and community supports can be protective factors in dealing with prejudice and discrimination from the larger society. Family resources can be brought to bear on personal issues and problems. Newer immigrants receive support and acceptance within Arab communities. Arab Americans have high levels of educational and economic success, partially due to their ability to acculturate and assimilate quickly (Nassar-McMillan, 2011). Similarly, being part of a religious community can provide guidance in dealing with problems and issues. Being a *Muslim* provides not only religious beliefs but also a code of behavior that encompasses cultural, racial, gender, and familial considerations.

SPECIFIC CHALLENGES

In the following sections we discuss the challenges often faced by Arab Americans and *Muslim* Americans and consider their implications in treatment.

Stereotypes, Racism, and Discrimination

> *During the Texas Muslim Capitol Day, Texas Rep. Molly White, R-Belton, commented to the anti-Islam protestors who were gathering, saying: "I did leave an Israeli flag on the reception desk in my office with instructions to staff to ask representatives from the* Muslim *community to renounce Islamic terrorist groups and publicly announce allegiance to America and our laws." (McGaughy, 2015)*

> *When an Indian American, Nina Davuluri, won the Miss America crown, social media responses included: "Congratulations Al-Qaeda. Our Miss America is one of you," "So miss america is a terrorist," and "How the f—k does a foreigner win miss America? She is a Arab! #Idiots" (Golgowski, 2013).*

> *Rita Zaweidah, the co-founder of the Arab American Community Coalition of Washington State explains, "When somebody is picked up or arrested or they've done something, they don't just mention that it is a male that was picked up. It's a* Muslim *male. You never see them saying a Christian male or an Irish male or an English male or female or whatever else. But for some reason when it's anything regarding the Middle East, the religion is the first word somewhere in that sentence." (Zaki, 2011)*

In recent years, *Muslims* and "Arab-appearing" individuals have been subjected to increased discrimination and attacks. Although Arab Americans and *Muslims* have always encountered prejudice and discrimination, negative behavior directed toward these groups accelerated following the September 11, 2001, attacks, the Boston marathon bombings in 2013, and the murders of political cartoonists at the offices of the Charlie Hebdo magazine in France in 2015. Hate crimes against *Muslims* are now second only to those perpetrated against Jewish Americans (Federal Bureau of Investigation, 2010).

Arabs, Arab Americans, and *Muslims* are often stereotyped in movies as sheiks, barbarians, or terrorists (Nassar-McMillan, Lambert, & Hakim-Larson, 2011). As was mentioned in the poll of teenagers at the beginning of the chapter, *Arabs* are frequently associated with terrorism. *Arabs* are so commonly stereotyped as being violent or terrorists that, in one study, individuals who played a terrorist-themed video game showed an increase in negative attitudes toward *Arabs*—even though the game involved Russian characters. This finding clearly demonstrates a "strong associative link" between *Arabs* and terrorism (Saleem & Craig, 2013).

Further, *Islam* has been portrayed as a violent religion. In fact, in 2006, Pope Benedict XVI created a storm of protests from the *Muslim* world when he read a quote from a 14th-century emperor: "Show me just what *Muhammad* brought that was new, and there you will find only evil and inhuman, such as his command to spread by the sword the faith he preached." The pope later professed "total and profound respect for all *Muslims*" and said he was trying to make the point that religion and violence do not go together. Nonetheless, followers of *Islam* were deeply hurt by his statement.

Americans falsely conflate Arab and *Muslim* communities, assuming that most Arab Americans are *Muslim*, when less than a third are, and that most American *Muslims* are Arab, when less than a quarter are (Wisniewski, 2014). Thus, because Americans often confuse *Arabs* and *Muslims*, negative press regarding one group or the other produces a negative reaction against both. Further, these groups often become targets when a violent event involving an Arab or *Muslim* occurs, either in the United States or abroad. A familiar chain of events may occur for the Arab American and *Muslim* American communities: feelings of shock and grief, followed by a fear of reprisal and the dread of becoming a target, and then learning that an Arab American or *Muslim* American totally unconnected to the original event has been victimized by a hate crime. This is a chain of events that Arab American and *Muslim* Americans "know all too well" (Haq, 2013).

The terrorist attacks on September 11, 2001, and the Boston Marathon bombings both had a profound impact on how Arab Americans and *Muslim* Americans were viewed in the United States. After these terrorists acts, hate crimes increased, with thousands of Arab American and *Muslim* American males subjected to deportation hearings, airline passenger profiling, vandalism, physical violence, and increased discrimination (Haq, 2013; Moradi & Hasan, 2004). Many Arab American and *Muslim* Americans became cautious about qualities that might draw attention to themselves, such as their dress or their names. Some women who previously wore headscarves discontinued the practice or stayed inside their homes. The vast majority of Arab Americans and *Muslim* Americans were angered, upset, and dismayed by the terrorist attacks, as were all Americans, and many supported retaliation against the countries supporting the terrorist attacks (Zogby, 2001b). At the same time, they were aware of the increased negative response by the public to *Muslims* or those of Arab descent.

Unfortunately, many of their fears regarding discrimination were realized. In a report covering incidents involving Arab Americans occurring between September 11, 2001, and October 11, 2002 (American-Arab Anti-Discrimination Committee, 2003), the following facts were reported:

- More than 700 violent incidents were directed at Arab Americans or those perceived to be Arab Americans or *Muslims* during the first 9 weeks after the September 11 attacks.

- More than 800 cases of employment discrimination against Arab Americans occurred.

- More than 80 cases of illegal or discriminatory removal from aircrafts after boarding occurred (removal based on perceived ethnicity).

- Thousands of Arab men were required to submit to a "voluntary interview" by government officials.

- Numerous instances of denial of services and housing occurred.

Behavioral changes resulted from the scrutiny given to Arab Americans and *Muslims*. A *Muslim* American woman stopped giving to *Muslim* charities, assuming that authorities were monitoring donations. An Imam (leader of prayer at a *mosque*) in Sacramento shaved part of his beard. Among *Muslim* Americans who worship at a *mosque*, nearly 100% reported being called a profane name in public, being profiled at airports, or having been visited by authorities. Because of the harassment and resulting fear, some stopped attending prayer services (Sahagun, 2006). *Muslim* American women face added stressors since their traditional garments are clearly identifiable (Winerman, 2006). Although more than a decade has passed since the September 11 attacks, Arab Americans and *Muslim* Americans remain wary. Their concerns may be warranted. Results from a recent poll indicated that 36% of Americans believe that *Muslims* are too extreme in their religious beliefs and 28% believe that *Muslims* are sympathetic to Al Qaeda terrorists (Newport, 2011).

In reality, the vast majority of *Muslim* Americans reject extremism and express concern over its rise both in the United States and in other countries. Nearly half express the opinion that *Muslim* leaders have not done enough in speaking out against Islamic extremists. They believe the biggest problems *Muslim* Americans face include discrimination and prejudice, being viewed as terrorists, being called offensive names, and being singled out or profiled by police and security officials (Pew Research Center, 2011b). *Muslim* groups started a "Respond with Love" campaign to raise funds to help rebuild the six predominantly Black churches that were damaged by fire during a two-week period in 2015 and to "stand against hate." Regardless of the cause of the fires, the group wanted to demonstrate with "our African American brothers and sisters" a stand against "institutionalized racism and racist violence" (Bever, 2015).

Americans' attitudes towards *Arabs* and *Muslims* are becoming progressively more negative, with Republicans and senior citizens reporting the strongest unfavorable views. The favorable opinion of *Muslims* dropped from 35% in 2010 to 27% in 2014 and for *Arabs* from 43% to 32%. Further, 42% of Americans support law enforcement profiling of Arab Americans and *Muslim* Americans (Wisniewski, 2014). American politicians have also expressed negative reactions to *Muslim* Americans. For example, in a letter to his constituents, U.S. Congressman Virgil Goode wrote, "I fear that in the next century we will have many more *Muslims* in the United States if we do not adopt the strict immigration policies that I believe are necessary to preserve the values and beliefs traditional to the United States of America" (Frommer, 2006, p. 1). Goode wrote this letter in response to a request made by a newly elected *Muslim* congressman to use the *Qur'an* during his swearing-in ceremony. More recently, Governor Jindal of Louisiana has warned of an *Islamic* "invasion" that will impose Sharia law on unsuspecting Americans. "If they want to come here and they want to set up their own culture and values, that's not immigration. That's really invasion, if you're honest about it" (Weber, 2015).

Implications

Because many Americans have negative views of *Muslims* and Arab Americans, mental health professionals should examine their own attitudes toward these groups.

- Have you been influenced by the negative stereotypes of individuals from these groups? Would you feel less safe during air travel with Arab-looking passengers or if you noticed a fellow passenger carrying a *Qur'an*? What would your reaction be if a client came in wearing traditional clothing?

- It is important to realize that Arab Americans, especially those who appear to be from an Arab country or who are *Muslims*, are bombarded by negative stereotypes, prejudice, and discrimination.

- Mental health professionals should ask about discriminatory actions directed toward clients and be willing to explore these experiences and help seek solutions.

- Therapists should be informed regarding antidiscrimination policies, provide clients with information about recourses for discriminatory actions, and support client efforts to challenge discrimination. If clients are encountering job or housing discrimination, the therapist can discuss their legal rights and assist them in taking appropriate actions, such as reporting hate crimes to the police.

- The website for the American-Arab Anti-Discrimination Committee (ADC) offers legal resources and information on addressing discrimination in these and other areas.

Acculturation Conflicts

A 14-year-old Middle Eastern Muslim boy was suspended from school for the use of alcohol and skipping school. He had been receiving good grades and had no previous behavioral problems. His problems stemmed from acculturation conflicts and the stigma associated with the 9/11 terrorist attacks. (Measham, Guzder, Rousseau, & Nadeau, 2010)

Elkugia, who was born in Libya, was voted homecoming queen for her high school. While playing basketball for her high school team, she wears a headscarf, a long jersey, and athletic pants instead of shorts. Her clothing reflects her Muslim faith and is a "form of modesty." (Iwasaki, 2006)

As with many groups that face discrimination and prejudice, some Arab Americans and *Muslim* Americans do not acknowledge their religion or ethnic background and have changed their names to be more "American sounding." Although some Arab Americans are bicultural and accept both their Arab and American identities (Nobles & Sciarra, 2000), others try to hide their religious and ethnic identities by wearing American-style clothing. Many have completely assimilated, especially those from the first wave of Arab American immigration, who were primarily Christian. Recent immigrants are more likely to maintain their traditional identity and live in ethnic communities and are more likely to be *Muslim* and practice their religion in an open fashion (Amri, 2010). Some women in this group may wear the *hijab*, or head scarf, as a sign of modesty. Traditionally oriented Arab and *Muslim* Americans may avoid certain aspects of American society, preferring to maintain contact with individuals from their own religious group or country of origin. The September 11 attacks appeared to strengthen the ethnic identity of many Arab Americans, with 88% of those polled after the attacks responding that they were proud of their heritage and 84% indicating that their ethnic heritage is important in defining their identity. More than 80% said that securing Palestinian rights is personally important to them (Zogby, 2001b).

Implications

Because culture, values, and religion can differ significantly within the Arab and *Muslim* American communities, therapists need to determine the background and beliefs of each client or family, rather than responding in a stereotypical manner. Some individuals may be highly acculturated or assimilated, whereas others may adhere strongly to traditional cultural and religious standards; this is especially true for Arab Americans who are *Muslims*. Generational acculturation conflicts are common, with children acculturating more quickly than parents. This may be especially problematic for traditionally oriented Arab Americans who adhere to a hierarchical family structure in which the children are expected to "behave appropriately."

IMPLICATIONS FOR CLINICAL PRACTICE

Arab Americans are a very diverse group in terms of religion, culture, country of origin, and degree of acculturation. There is similar diversity within the *Muslim* community. Recent *Muslim* immigrants are likely to adhere more strictly to Islamic principles, whereas those who have lived in the United States for much of their lives are more likely to have a moderate perspective (Ibrahim & Dykeman, 2011). In general, non-Arab Americans and non-Muslims possess little knowledge about these groups and have often been exposed to misinformation. Because of this, many individuals view the actions of extremist *Islamic* groups as representing the view of *Muslims* and Arab Americans. As mental health workers, we need to understand Arab culture and *Muslim* beliefs.

The following are recommendations for working with Arab American and *Muslim* clients (Amri, 2010; Ibrahim & Dykeman, 2011):

1. Identify your attitudes about Arab Americans and *Muslims*.

2. Recognize that many face discrimination and violence because of their Arab background or their religious beliefs.

3. Be ready to help those who have been discriminated against in seeking legal recourse.

4. Cross-gender counselor pairing may be problematic with Arab or *Muslim* clients. Inquire if gender of the therapist is a factor to be considered.

5. Recognize that Arab Americans and *Muslim* Americans are diverse groups. Recent immigrants are more likely to hold stronger traditional values and beliefs. Collaborate with each client or family to gain an understanding of their lifestyle and beliefs, including their religion and the importance of religion in their lives. Religion may not be a factor in the presenting problem

6. Determine the structure of the family through questions and observation. With traditional families, try addressing the husband or male first. Traditional families may appear highly interdependent, a common cultural characteristic. Determine if acculturation conflicts are producing stress within the family.

7. Be careful of self-disclosures that may be interpreted as weakness. Positive self-disclosures may enhance the therapeutic alliance.

8. In traditionally oriented Arab Americans families, there may be reluctance to share family issues or to express negative feelings with a therapist.

9. There may be greater acceptance to holistic approaches that incorporate family members and the religious or social community, especially with clients who hold traditional values.

10. Be open to exploring spiritual beliefs and the use of prayer or fasting to reduce distress. Alternative explanations and expressions of psychological distress should be accepted without the imposition of a Western worldview. Counselors should be open to talking about religion and drawing on religious coping strategies. *Islam* encourages self-responsibility in actions and encourages alternatives to negative thoughts. Identifying the client's views regarding *Islam* may be useful in adapting therapy (Ebrahimi, Neshatdoost, Mousavi, Asadollahi, & Nasiri, 2013; Meer & Mir, 2014).

11. Cognitive-behavioral strategies may be productive for *Muslims* if distressing thoughts are modified in accordance with *Islamic* beliefs (Khodayarifard & McClenon, 2011).

SUMMARY

Arab Americans are descendants from countries located in the Middle East and North Africa and are heterogeneous in terms of race, religion, and political ideology. The majority of Arab Americans are native-born U.S. citizens. *Muslims* are followers of *Islam*, one of the fastest growing religions in the United States. Most *Muslims* do not descend from Arabic-speaking countries. Effective work with these populations require knowledge of cultural and religious dictates, especially *Islamic* laws derived from the *Qur'an* which deals with social issues, family life, economics and business, sexuality, and other aspects of life. Collectivism, hierarchical family structure, and patriarchy are important cultural differences. The increase of prejudice and discrimination toward these groups accelerated following the September 11, 2001, terrorist attacks. Hate crimes against *Muslims* are now second only to those perpetrated against Jewish Americans. Eleven clinical implications for counselor practice are identified.

GLOSSARY TERMS

Arabs	Mosques
Islam	Muhammad

Muslim religion

Qur'an

Ramadan

Shiite

Sunni

REFERENCES

Al Harahsheh, S. (2011). *Sons, daughters, and Arab-American family dynamics: Does a child's gender matter?* Retrieved from http://digital commons.wayne.edu/oa_dissertations/366

Aleccia, J. (2013). *Not "brainwashed": American women who converted to Islam speak out.* Retrieved from http://usnews.nbcnews.com/_news/2013/04/26/17897741-not-brainwashed-american-women-who-converted-to-islam-speak-out

American-Arab Anti-Discrimination Committee. (2003). *Report on hate crimes and discrimination against Arab Americans.* Retrieved from http://www.adc.org/hate_crimes.htm

Amri, S. (2010). *Counseling Arab and Middle Eastern population: Perspectives from an Arab-American counselor.* Retrieved from http://www.counseling.org/handouts/2010/596.pdf

Arab American Institute. (2003). *Religious affiliations of Arab Americans.* Retrieved from http://www.aaiusa.org

Arab American Institute. (2011). *Arab American demographics.* Retrieved from http://www.aaiusa.org/pages/demographics/

Arab American Institute. (2012). *National Arab American demographics.* Retrieved from http://www.aaiusa.org/pages/demographics/

Associated Press. (2015). Democrats defend naming Muslim to House Intelligence panel. Retrieved from http://news.yahoo.com/democrats-defend-naming-muslim-house-intelligence-panel-173656959—politics.html

Bever, L. (2015). *Muslim charities raise nearly $45K to rebuild burned-down black churches.* Retrieved from http://www.chicagotribune.com/news/nationworld/ct-muslim-charities-help-black-churches-arson-20150711-story.html

Botelho, G., & Davis, R. (2015). *N.C. Muslim shooting victim said she felt blessed to be an American.* Retrieved from http://www.cnn.com/2015/02/13/us/chapel-hill-shooting/

Dwairy, M. (2008). Counseling Arab and Muslim clients. In P. B. Pedersen, J. G. Draguns, W. J. Lonner, & J. E. Trimble (Eds.), *Counseling across cultures* (6th ed., pp. 147–160). Thousand Oaks, CA: Sage.

Ebrahimi, A., Neshatdoost, H. T., Mousavi, S. G., Asadollahi, G. A., & Nasiri, H. (2013). Controlled randomized clinical trial of spiritually integrated psychotherapy, cognitive-behavioral therapy and medication intervention on depressive symptoms and dysfunctional attitudes in patients with dysthymic disorder. *Advanced Biomedical Research, 2,* 1–7.

El-Badry, S. (2006). *Arab American demographics.* Retrieved from http://www.allied-media-com/Arab-American/Arab%20american%

Elliott, A. (2006, September 10). Muslim immigration has bounced back. *Seattle Times,* p. A18.

Federal Bureau of Investigation. (2010). *Hate crime statistics, 2009.* Retrieved from http://www2.fbi.gov/ucr/hc2009/index.html

Frommer, F. J. (2006, December 20). *Congressman criticized for Muslim letter.* Retrieved from http://seattlepi.newsource.com/national/1133AP_Ellison_Qur'an.html

Golgowski, N. (2013). *Miss America crowns first winner of Indian descent, and critics slam her as Arab terrorist.* Retrieved from http://www.today.com/style/new-miss-americas-heritage-evokes-racist-comments-twitter-8C11167234

Haq, H. (2013). *Boston bombing: US Muslims react with fear, frustration, and new resolve*. Retrieved from http://www.csmonitor.com/USA/Society/2013/0425/Boston-bombing-US-Muslims-react-with-fear-frustration-and-new-resolve

Iancu, I., Sarel, A., Avital, A., Abdo, B., Joubran, S., & Ram, E. (2011). Shyness and social phobia in Israeli Jewish vs Arab students. *Comprehensive Psychiatry, 52*, 708–714.

Ibrahim, F. A., & Dykeman, C. (2011). Counseling Muslim Americans: Cultural and spiritual assessments. *Journal of Counseling and Development, 89*, 387–396.

Iwasaki, J. (2006, December 19). *The best of both worlds*. Retrieved from http://seattlepi.nwsource.com/printer2/index.asp?ploc=t&ref

Jackson, M. L., & Nassar-McMillan, S. (2006). Counseling Arab Americans. In C. C. Lee (Ed.), *Multicultural issues in counseling: New approaches to diversity* (3rd ed., pp. 235–247). Alexandria, VA: American Counseling Association.

Khodayarifard, M., & McClenon, J. (2011). Family therapy in Iran: A case study of obsessive-compulsive disorder. *Journal of Multicultural Counseling and Development, 39*, 78–89.

Lawrence, L. (2014). *Islam, the American way*. Retrieved from http://www.csmonitor.com/USA/Society/2014/0216/Islam-the-American-way

McGaughy, L. (2015). *Texas Muslim Capitol Day marred by anti-Islam protesters*. Retrieved from http://www.chron.com/news/politics/texas/article/Texas-Muslim-Capitol-Day-marred-by-anti-Islam-6048881.php

Measham, T., Guzder, J., Rousseau, C. M., & Nadeau, L. (2010). Cultural considerations in child and adolescent psychiatry. *Cross-Cultural Psychiatry, 27*, 1–5.

Meer, S., & Mir, G. (2014). Muslims and depression: The role of religious beliefs in therapy. *Journal of Integrative Psychology and Therapeutics*. Retrieved from http://www.hoajonline.com/journals/pdf/2054–4723–2–2.pdf

Moradi, B., & Hasan, N. T. (2004). Arab American persons' reported experiences of discrimination and mental health: The mediating role of personal control. *Journal of Counseling Psychology, 51*, 418–428.

Nassar-McMillan, S. C. (2011). *Counseling & Diversity: Counseling Arab Americans*. Belmont, CA: Brooks/Cole.

Nassar-McMillan, S. C., & Hakim-Larson, J. (2003). Counseling considerations among Arab Americans. *Journal of Counseling and Development, 81*, 150–158.

Nassar-McMillan, S. C., Lambert, R. G., & Hakim-Larson, J. (2011). Discrimination history, backlash fear, and ethnic identity among Arab Americans: Post-9/11 snapshots. *Journal of Multicultural Counseling and Development, 39*, 38–47.

Newport, F. (2011). *For first time, majority of Americans favor legal gay marriage*. Retrieved from http://gallup.com/poll/147662/First-Time-Majority-Americans-Favor-Legal-Gay-Marriage.asp

Nobles, A. Y., & Sciarra, D. T. (2000). Cultural determinants in the treatment of Arab Americans: A primer for mainstream therapists. *American Journal of Orthopsychiatry, 70*, 182–191.

Pew Research Center. (2011a). *The future of the global Muslim population*. Retrieved from http://stage.pewforum.org/uploadedFiles/Topics/Religious_Affiliation/Muslim/Future-GlobalMuslimPopulation-WebPDF-Feb10.pdf

Pew Research Center. (2011b). *Muslim Americans: No signs of growth in alienation or support for extremism*. Retrieved from http://www.pewforum.org/2011/08/30/muslim-americans-no-signs-of-growth-in-alienation-or-support-for-extremism/

Reuters. (2015). *Norway's Muslims form protective human ring around synagogue*. Retrieved from http://www.msn.com/en-us/news/world/norways-muslims-form-protective-human-ring-around-synagogue/ar-BBhOP6n?srcref=rss

Sahagun, L. (2006, September 8). A post-9/11 identity shift. *Seattle Post-Intelligencer*, pp. A1, 22.

Saleem, M., & Craig, A. (2013). Arabs as terrorists: Effects of stereotypes within violent contexts on attitudes, perceptions, and affect. *Psychology of Violence, 3*, 84–99

Suleiman, M. W. (1999). *The Arab immigrant experience*. Philadelphia, PA: Temple University Press.

Tummala-Narra, P., & Claudius, M. (2013). A qualitative examination of Muslim graduate international students' experiences in the United States. *International Perspectives in Psychology: Research, Practice, Consultation, 2*, 132–147.

U.S. Census Bureau (2005). *We the people of Arab Ancestry in the United States*. Retrieved from https://www.census.gov/prod/.../censr-21.pdf

U.S. Department of State. (2002). *Muslim life in America*. Retrieved from http://usinfo.state.gov/products/pubs/muslimlife

Weber, P. (2015). *If Bobby Jindal wants to preach forced American assimilation, he should visit Brooklyn*. Retrieved from http://theweek.com/articles/536168/bobby-jindal-wants-preach-forced-american-assimilation-should-visit-brooklyn

Winerman, L. (2006). Reaching out to Muslim and Arab Americans. *APA Monitor, 37*, 54.

Wisniewski, M. (2014). *American opinion of Arabs, Muslims is getting worse—poll*. Retrieved from http://af.reuters.com/article/worldNews/idAFKBN0FY1ZK20140729?pageNumber=2&virtualBrandChannel=0&sp=true

Zaki, M. (2011). *Life for Arab and Muslim Americans a decade after 9/11*. Retrieved from http://www.kuow.org/program.php?id=24539

Zogby, J. J. (2001a, March). *National survey: American teen-agers and stereotyping*. Retrieved from http://www.niaf.org/research/report_zogby.asp

Zogby, J. J. (2001b, October). *Arab American attitudes and the September 11 attacks*. Retrieved from http://www.aaiusa.org/PDF/attitudes.pdf

Counseling Immigrants and Refugees

Chapter Objectives

1. Learn the demographics and characteristics of *immigrants* and *refugees*.

2. Identify counseling implications of the information provided for *immigrants* and *refugees*.

3. Provide examples of strengths that are associated with *immigrants* and *refugees*.

4. Know the special challenges faced by *immigrants* and *refugees*.

5. Understand how the implications for clinical practice can guide assessment and therapy with *immigrants* and *refugees*.

Alexis Molina was just 10 years old when his mother was abruptly cut out of his life and his carefree childhood unraveled overnight. Gone were the egg-and-sausage tortillas that greeted him when he came home from school, the walks in the park, the hugs at night when she tucked him into bed. Today the sweet-faced boy of 11 spends his time worrying about why his father cries so much, and why his mom can't come home. (Oneil, 2012)

Abrahim Mosavi, a national of Iran and resident of the United States for more than three decades, applied to naturalize in 2000. Although he is eligible to become a citizen, he has waited thirteen years for a final decision on his application. "No one can tell me why I should have to wait so long," said Mr. Mosavi. (ACLU, 2013)

When Mexico sends its people, they're not sending their best . . . They're sending people that have lots of problems, and they're bringing those problems with us. They're bringing drugs. They're bringing crime. They're rapists. And some, I assume, are good people." (Statement by Donald Trump; Tani, 2015)

The foreign-born population in the United States (including *undocumented immigrants*) was 41.3 million in July 2013; nearly one out of every six adults living in the United States is foreign born (Zeigler & Camarota, 2014). Approximately 12 million are from Mexico, 10.5 million from South and East Asia, 4 million from the Caribbean, 3.2 million from Central America, 3 million from South America, 1.6 million from the Middle East, and about 7.5 million from other countries. Mexican *immigrants* comprised about 28% of all U.S. *immigrants* and Asians are currently the fastest-growing group of *immigrants* in the United States (Pew Research Center, 2014).

About 11.4 million *immigrants* are unauthorized, having entered the United States without inspection or overstayed their temporary stay; approximately 60% of *undocumented immigrants* have been here for more than a decade (Baker & Rytina, 2013). Of the unauthorized *immigrants* in the United States, an estimated 5,850,000 are from Mexico, 1,700,000 from Central America, 1,400,000 from Asia, 600,000 from Europe and Canada, 550,000 from the Caribbean, 400,000 from the Middle East or Africa, and 190,000 from South America (Pew Research Center, 2014).

The reasons for *migration* include escape from poverty, seeking a higher quality of life, and political unrest (Negy, Schwartz, & Reig-Ferrer, 2009). Many *immigrants*, particularly those from undeveloped countries and those who are undocumented, earn extremely low wages. Approximately 23% of *immigrants* and their U.S.-born children live in poverty (Camarota, 2012). About 60% of farm workers, who help pick billions of dollars of agricultural products, are undocumented *immigrants*. Nearly 25% of workers who butcher meat, poultry, and fish are undocumented, including many women. Most *undocumented immigrants* subsist on poverty-level wages and are exposed to exploitation and abuse in the workplace. A high percentage of women working in these food industries are subject to sexual abuse (Southern Poverty Law Center, 2010).

Recently there has been a surge of unaccompanied immigrant children, primarily from Central American countries such as Guatemala, Honduras, or El Salvador; many of these children have come to the United States to escape the escalating gang violence in their home countries. Young children and teens are forced to join gangs and, if they refuse, they and their families are subjected to violent retribution from the gangs. While border patrol agents can quickly deport children from Mexico, those from Central American countries are given full court proceedings (Lind, 2014). This is creating a backlog of immigration cases. Other countries, such as Mexico, Panama, Nicaragua, and Belize, are also inundated with Central Americans seeking *asylum* (Restrepo & Garcia, 2014).

There is a wide range of educational levels among *immigrants*, with about one-third having a college degree. *Immigrants* make up nearly 28% of physicians, 31% of computer programmers, and 47% of medical scientists. Nearly 75% of the foreign-born with college degrees are Asian or White and 17% are of Latino origin (Ji & Batalova, 2012). Asians are the most highly educated *immigrants* in U.S. history, with more than 60% having at least a bachelor's degree (Pew Research Center, 2014). In contrast, 33% of U.S. adult *immigrants* have not completed high school (compared with 12.5% of the total adult population). Among the *immigrant* secondary school population, the high school dropout rate was 21% in 2009, rates significantly higher than the national average. Although *immigrants* comprise 10% of high school students, they account for 27% of high school dropouts (Child Trends, 2014). In general, children of *immigrant* families have high rates of poverty (35%), and almost half are uninsured (Wight Chau, & Aratani, 2011).

According to the Department of Homeland Security, only about 39% of *undocumented immigrants* arrived after the year 2000. Most *undocumented immigrants* are well integrated into society and many have children born in the United

States—children whose dominant language is English and who have never visited their parents' homeland. Having established their lives in the United States and having children who only know life in the United States is a powerful reason for these *immigrants* to want to remain in the country. The work of these *undocumented immigrants* is indispensable in areas such as agriculture, construction, and childcare, and in the restaurant and hotel industry (Marrero, 2011).

Despite the belief that *immigrants* are dangerous or a drain on society, they are no more likely to use social services and are less likely to commit crimes than native-born Americans. Although incidents such as the shooting of a young woman in San Francisco in 2015 by an undocumented Mexican raise fears about crime regarding this population, studies have found that *immigrants* have a much lower rate of crime and are less likely to be behind bars than native-born individuals. The findings apply "for both legal *immigrants* and the unauthorized regardless of their country of origin or level of education" (Ewing, Martínez, & Rumbaut, 2015). Fear regarding *immigrants*, especially those who are undocumented, may be a product of negative stereotyping or inordinate attention to the criminal acts of a few. Also, the belief that unauthorized *immigrants* are a financial burden on society ignores the fact that they pay billions of dollars in taxes each year, and nearly half of the adults who have been in the United States for more than 10 years are homeowners (CAP Immigration Team, 2014).

CHARACTERISTICS AND STRENGTHS

In the following sections we describe the historical, sociopolitical, cultural, and gender characteristics of *immigrants*, implications for treatment, and the strengths often seen among those who emigrate. Remember that these are generalizations and their applicability needs to be assessed for each client.

Historical and Sociopolitical Factors

> *Latino students have started vanishing from Alabama public schools in the wake of a court ruling that upheld the state's tough new law cracking down on illegal immigration. . . .Several districts with large immigrant enrollments. . .reported a sudden exodus of children from Latino families, some of whom told officials they would leave the state to avoid trouble with the law, which requires schools to check students' immigration status. (Reeves, 2011, p. 1)*

Historically, many U.S. immigration policies and laws have been unfair and exclusionary. Until 1952, only White persons were allowed to become *naturalized citizens*. With the Immigration Act of 1965, people from any nation were finally allowed to apply for citizenship. In part, the U.S. civil rights movement facilitated this change. Even now, however, under a little-known federal program, the "Controlled Application Review and Resolution Program" (CARRP), the government excludes many applicants for citizenship or work visas from Arab, Middle Eastern, Muslim, and South Asian communities by delaying and denying their applications. According to the ACLU (2013), it does so by "relying on extraordinarily overbroad criteria that treat religious practices, national origin, and innocuous associations and activities as national security concerns." Thus individuals from these countries and religious backgrounds do not appear to have the same opportunities as other *immigrant* groups to work or to gain citizenship in the United States.

There is an ongoing political struggle over *immigrants*, especially those who are undocumented. In 2012, President Obama took executive action authorizing DACA, Deferred Action for Childhood Arrivals, which provided temporary deportation protection for more than 500,000 unauthorized young *immigrants* and allowed them to apply for work permits; these young adults, called "dreamers," were brought to the U.S. illegally as children. In November 2014, Obama extended DACA to provide deportation relief and work permit eligibility for another 4.7 million *undocumented immigrants* who have lived in the United States for at least five years and whose children are citizens or legal permanent residents. These actions could provide deportation protection for about 5.5 million *undocumented immigrants,* while about 6 million others would not qualify for temporary deportation relief under these programs (Lind, 2015).

In response to President Obama's executive orders authorizing this temporary deportation relief, in January 2015 the U.S. House passed a bill with amendments to defund these programs. Further, a U.S. District Court injunction issued in February 2015 delayed implementation of Obama's executive order extending DACA. It is evident that the battle over immigration and deportation relief will continue in various political and judicial arenas.

Additionally, some states have passed laws that target *immigrants*. In some states, election officials at polling places are allowed to make inquiries of registered voters who appear to be *immigrants* (e.g., "Are you a native or a *naturalized citizen*? Where were you born? What official documentation do you possess to prove your citizenship"?). The voters are then required to provide documentation and to declare, under oath, that they are the person named in the documentation. Going even further, Arizona enacted legislation that made it a crime for noncitizens to be in Arizona without official documents authorizing their presence in the United States; further, law enforcement officers must verify immigration status when lawfully stopping, detaining, or arresting someone they believe might be in the United States illegally. This law has been criticized as a form of "racial profiling." Additionally, new laws in Arizona have banned instructors with "heavy accents" from teaching English classes (Martinez & Gutierrez, 2010; Navarrette, 2011).

These laws and actions are likely to continue to provoke fear and unease within *immigrant* communities, as well as decrease the likelihood of *immigrants* reporting crimes or abuse. In response to recently implemented state laws requiring schools to inquire about the immigration status of students, federal officials have stated that school districts must "ensure that any required documents would not unlawfully bar or discourage a student who is undocumented or whose parents are undocumented from enrolling in or attending school." In other words, immigration status should not play a role in establishing residency within a school district (Khadaroo, 2014).

Many citizens are opposed to the number of *immigrants* entering the United States and the idea of providing a path to citizenship for *illegal immigrants*. The argument is often made that *undocumented immigrants* violated the law by not following immigration policy and that they are a drain on the social system. Those on the other side of the debate counter that businesses have benefited from and continue to rely on the work provided by undocumented workers, many of whom have lived in the United States for decades, paying taxes and contributing to their communities. Seventy-two percent of the public and 83% of Latinos surveyed indicate that they would support a policy allowing "foreigners who have jobs but who are staying illegally in the United States the opportunity to eventually become legal American citizens if they pay a fine, any back taxes, pass a security background check, and take other required steps" (Hart Research Associates, 2014).

Cultural and Acculturation Issues

Immigrants face the overwhelming task of learning about the workings of U.S. society. *Immigrants* need to negotiate the educational system, acquire language proficiency, and seek employment. They must adjust and adapt to new cultural customs within a completely different society and navigate the mixed reception they receive from U.S. citizens. Placed in unfamiliar settings, adjusting to climactic differences, and lacking community and social support, many experience severe culture shock (Bemak & Chung, 2014). Feelings of isolation, loneliness, disorientation, helplessness, anxiety, and depression often characterize the immigration experience. The only sources of comfort and support may be a small circle of relatives or friends, who also may be adjusting to a different way of life.

In families in which the degree of acculturation varies, the exposure to different values, attitudes, and behavioral expectations can result in acculturation-based problems. In *immigrant* families, children and adolescents attend school and more quickly acculturate and adapt to U.S. culture, whereas the parents and older family members tend to adhere to traditional cultural values. Children may believe that their parents are unable to offer advice or help with social problems. Parents may begin to feel that the children are abandoning them and their cultural background. Parent–child acculturation discrepancies can lead to a sense of alienation between family members. *Immigrant* families may seek therapy when parent–child communication difficulties lead to intergenerational conflicts or produce psychological symptoms in the child (American Psychological Association, Presidential Task Force on Immigration, 2013).

Implications

Counselors often need to take on multiple roles with clients who are recent *immigrants*, including educator (providing information on services and education about their rights and responsibilities) and advocate (helping negotiate the institutional structures of the health care, education, and employment systems). In addition to traditional mental health services, psychoeducational approaches are often required to assist *immigrants* to acquire (1) education and training for themselves and their children; (2) knowledge of employment opportunities, job search skills, and the ability to manage financial demands; (3) language proficiency to ensure success in U.S. society; and (4) strategies to manage family relationship conflicts.

To effectively assist *immigrants*, it is important to understand the life circumstances of immigrant groups, to have liaisons within the *immigrant* community, and to be familiar with community resources aimed at helping *immigrants* adjust to a new world. When addressing family problems around acculturation issues, it is often helpful to cast the exposure to different values and expectations as the source of acculturation conflicts and help family members problem-solve methods of dealing with differing cultural expectations.

Gender Issues and Domestic Violence

Many *immigrants* come from countries in which there are gender inequities and spousal abuse; women may be reluctant to seek help because of self-blame, concern for the children, or lack of knowledge about abuse protection laws (Ting & Panchanadeswaran, 2009). Fear of reporting partner abuse may also be influenced by economic dependence or fear of retaliation (Quiroga & Flores-Ortiz, 2000). Further, many *immigrant* women have been socialized to sacrifice their own personal needs for the good of their husbands and children. Such training leads to ignoring or denying their own distress and prioritizing family needs (Ro, 2002).

Male *immigrants* may face the loss of status and develop a sense of powerlessness. They may have lost their assigned roles within the family and society as a whole and may be unemployed or underemployed. Because women often find it easier to gain employment, the resulting changes in the balance of power may increase the risk of domestic violence as men attempt to reestablish their authority and power (Bemak & Chung, 2014).

Implications

As with other cases involving family violence, the following steps are recommended:

- Assess the lethality of the situation. If there is a high degree of danger, develop a safety plan. The woman should know where she and her children can stay if she needs to leave home. The therapist should help identify shelters or other resources available for the particular *immigrant* group to which the woman belongs.

- If the degree of violence is nonlethal and the woman does not want to leave the home, provide psychoeducational information on abusive relationships, the cycle of violence, and legal recourse. Give crisis numbers or other contact information to use if the violence escalates.

- Convey an understanding of both the cultural and situational obstacles the client faces. Recognize that some women may define their role as the one who protects and cares for everyone's welfare. Forming a strong therapeutic relationship is especially important if no support is available from other family members or friends.

- Attempt to expand support systems for the client, especially within the client's community. Support groups and services are now available for a number of different *immigrant* groups.

Cultural Strengths

The attributes from the various ethnic and cultural groups to which *immigrants* belong strengthen the diversity of our nation. *Immigrants* have made positive social, political, and cultural contributions to U.S. society for many generations. *Immigrants* often demonstrate significant loyalty to the United States as their chosen homeland and have brought with them both ingenuity and a strong work ethic. They have a "high level of engagement" in the labor market and generally have good psychological and physical health (American Psychological Association, Presidential Task Force on Immigration, 2013).

Many *immigrants* are from countries with a collectivistic orientation; they often serve as role models of interdependence and cooperation with multiple extended family and community supports. *Immigrants* are often supportive of each other and promote group identification and acceptance of differences. These kinds of supports can help ameliorate stressors involved in living in a new culture, especially a society that stresses the individual.

SPECIFIC CHALLENGES

In the following sections we consider challenges faced by *immigrant* individuals and consider their implications for treatment. Remember that these are generalizations and that their applicability needs to be assessed for each client.

Prejudice and Discrimination

> *Refugees who are forced to leave their countries because of persecution or war, are often described in negative terms such as "waves" of refugees that threaten to flood the country, "sponges off the welfare system," "criminals," "lacking in morals," "cockroaches" or "parasites."*
> *(Hamilton, Medianu, & Esses, 2013, p. 94)*

The September 11, 2001, terrorist attacks had a dramatic impact on attitudes toward *immigrants* and *refugees*. The resulting emphasis on preventing the entry of terrorists into the United States resulted in not only Arab or Muslim Americans being viewed with suspicion, but also anyone who "appears foreign." *Immigrants* became regarded as possible terrorists. Following the trauma of September 11, the movement toward legalization of *undocumented immigrants* slowed, and there was a dramatic decline in admission of *refugees* (Patrick, 2004). Events such as the Boston Marathon bombing, other terrorists attacks, and even films such as *American Sniper*, in which Iraqis are referred to as "ragheads" and "savages," have resulted in increased animosity to Arabs, Middle Easterners, and Muslims (Associated Press, 2015). The anti-immigration nativism movement, promoting the position that only U.S. "natives" (understood to be people of European descent) belong in the United States, is receiving greater support (Nassir, 2014). Similarly, the English-only movement, viewed by many *immigrants* and others as being exclusionary, is strengthening.

Although *immigrants* already use less than half of available health care resources as compared with the average U.S. citizen (National Immigration Law Center, 2006), the climate of fear has led to even further decreases in the utilization of medical or government services by *immigrants*. Although *immigrants'* children born in the United States are citizens, many undocumented parents harbor great fear and anxiety about their own immigration status or that of close family members. Citizens with undocumented family members are hesitant to sign up for insurance under the Affordable Care Act because of concern that the information required during the application process might result in the deportation of their spouses, siblings, or other relatives (Karlamangla & Terhune, 2014). Other *immigrants*, even those who are permanent legal residents, are afraid that seeking assistance might suggest an inability to live here independently and increase the chances of deportation or not being granted citizenship.

Implications

Mental health professionals should be aware that *immigrant* clients or their families may see the therapist as an arm of government. The therapist should also be aware of the rights or exclusions associated with *immigrant* status (Bernstein, 2006):

- Hospitals are required to provide emergency care to anyone in need, including *undocumented immigrants*. Other treatments depend on local laws. Information regarding other *immigrant* issues can be obtained from the National Immigration Law Center.

- Free community clinics exist that will treat individuals regardless of immigration status.

- *Immigrants* can ask health care providers for interpreter services.

- Most documented *immigrants* are not eligible to receive Medicaid, food stamps, or social security benefits during their first five years in the United States or longer, regardless of how much they have paid in taxes.

- *Undocumented immigrants* face tremendous difficulties when seeking a higher education. The imposition of out-of-state tuition fees effectively keeps them out of college in most of the United States. In support of higher education for these students, 18 states currently have provisions allowing for in-state tuition rates for undocumented students and 5 states (California, Minnesota, New Mexico, Texas, and Washington) allow undocumented students to receive state financial aid. Three states (Arizona, Georgia, and Indiana) prohibit in-state tuition rates for undocumented students, and two (Alabama and South Carolina) prohibit them from enrolling at any public postsecondary institution (National Conference of State Legislatures, 2015).

- Many advocacy agencies now encourage *immigrant* parents to have a detailed plan in place in case they are deported, including granting power of attorney to someone who can take custody of their children (Oneil, 2012).

Barriers to Seeking Treatment

Multiple barriers exist for *immigrants* in their utilization of social and mental health services. As mentioned earlier, *immigrants* utilize health care services much less than U.S. citizens. Mental health providers need to understand how cultural, linguistic, and informational barriers can affect *immigrants*.

In a survey of health care providers, several barriers to accessing services were identified:

- *Communication difficulties due to language differences.* More than half of the providers identified language barriers as the major source of difficulty in providing service. These barriers affect critical areas, such as obtaining accurate information during assessment. The providers also mentioned that it is difficult to obtain interpreter services, especially given the diversity of dialects within some ethnic groups (Weisman et al., 2005).

- *Lack of knowledge of mainstream service delivery.* Many *immigrants* lack knowledge about how the health care system operates in the United States. Extra time is required when providers try to explain clinic practices and paperwork. Often, apparent noncompliance in following through with recommendations is due to poor understanding of services.

- *Cultural factors.* Many *immigrant* groups are hesitant to speak about "family issues" or issues of personal concern because of the cultural importance of privacy (Chung & Bemak, 2007). Women who were abused by their husbands or who have been sexually assaulted may not talk about these issues because of cultural norms and shame, as well as fear of deportation. A stigma exists for many *immigrants* around seeking help for mental health problems and there may be fear that mental health issues will be blamed on the family.

- *Lack of resources.* Many *immigrant* families are living in poverty and may lack transportation to go to the service location. In addition, they may not have time to attend sessions, due to inflexible work schedules or the economic necessity of working as many hours as possible.

Linguistic and Communication Issues

If *immigrants* are not fluent in English, the use of *interpreters* may be necessary. Many therapists and *interpreters* are not aware of the dynamics involved when another individual is involved in the therapy relationship. Most *interpreters* receive little or no training in working with distressed or traumatized individuals, and they may experience uncontrollable feelings of emotional distress when hearing traumatic stories, especially when their backgrounds are similar to those of the clients (Miller, Zoe, Pazdirek, Caruth, & Lopez, 2005). For example, one interpreter discovered that in order to protect herself from distressing feelings as she was interpreting for traumatized clients, she became dismissive and casual when describing the violent events brought up by the clients. In another case, a therapist observed, "I had one interpreter start shaking. It was too much for her. . . She just became incredibly upset and angry" (Miller et al., 2005, p. 34).

Therapists also report developing reactions to *interpreters*. Some think of the *interpreters* as "translation machines," whose interpersonal qualities are unimportant. Eventually, however, therapists realize that *interpreters* form part of a three-person alliance. Initially, clients may develop a stronger attachment to the interpreter than to the therapist. Because of this, therapists need to deal with feelings of "being left out" and to accept that their relationships with these clients might develop in a slower fashion. Therapists may also choose to use *interpreters* as important cultural resources by obtaining the interpreter's thoughts about issues discussed in sessions. In general, therapists are appreciative of *interpreters* and do not perceive any long-term negative effects on therapeutic progress. Sometimes, however, *interpreters* interject their own opinions, intervene directly with clients, or question interventions because they do not understand the therapeutic approach (Miller et al., 2005).

Implications

Both therapists and *interpreters* benefit from knowledge of best practices such as the following (Searight & Searight, 2009; Yakushko, 2010):

- *Interpreters* should receive brief training in specific mental disorders and the interventions employed in therapy, particularly treatment of trauma, grief, and loss.

- Because traumatic experiences discussed in therapy can affect *interpreters*, therapists should discuss self-care strategies for the interpreter, as well as ways of dealing with exposure to traumatic reports.

- Clients do not regard *interpreters* as translation machines. Therefore, *interpreters* should be trained in the relationship skills that are needed in therapy. In the triadic relationship, interpersonal skills such as empathy and congruence are necessary.

- Therapists should also receive training on how to work effectively with *interpreters* and become conversant with different models of interpreting. Some prefer simultaneous translation, whereas others prefer delayed translation.

Therapists should be aware that, in many cases, the therapeutic alliance may form first with the interpreter. Many therapists who have worked with *interpreters* understand that for non-English-speaking clients, *interpreters* are the bridge between the therapist and the client and are critical in assessment and the provision of therapy.

Counseling Refugees

> *Deng fled the civil war in Sudan and has been in the United States for the past 2 years. He is 28 years old and spent 4 years in a refugee camp before coming to the United States. He describes fleeing burning villages outside of Darfur and seeing many people from his own family and community slaughtered, raped, and beaten. He remembers running and hiding, being near starvation, drinking muddy water, avoiding crocodiles and once a lion, and being alarmed when bombs dropped nearby. . . He wonders what happened to his family and friends and feels guilty for having escaped. (Chung & Bemak, 2007, p. 133)*

Deng's escape from Sudan and the trauma he experienced are not uncommon for *refugees*. The United States provides refugee status to persons who have been persecuted or have a well-founded fear of persecution. In 2013, the 69,909 persons admitted to the United States as *refugees* were primarily from four countries: Iraq (27.9%), Burma (23.3%), Bhutan (13.1%), and Somalia (10%). Additionally, 25,199 individuals from China (34%), Egypt (14%), Ethiopia (3.5%), Nepal (3.4%), and Syria (3.2%) were granted *asylum* (Martin & Yankay, 2014). In contrast to other *immigrants*, who voluntarily left their country of origin, *refugees* are individuals who flee their country in order to escape persecution due to race, religion, nationality, political opinion, or membership in a particular social group. *Asylees*, individuals who meet the criteria for refugee status, are physically present in the United States or at a point of entry when granted permission to reside in the United States. Any alien present in the United States or arriving at a port of entry may seek *asylum*. Individuals granted *asylum* are authorized to work in the United States. In addition, an asylee is eligible for certain public benefits including employment assistance, a social security card, and social services. Similar to *refugees*, *asylum* seekers have been uprooted from their countries of origin, often after suffering years of persecution or torture directed toward themselves, their family and friends, or even their entire community. Predetermined allotments for specific geographical locations limit the number of *refugees* and asylees accepted by the U.S. government; these limits change from year to year.

What characterizes the life experience of many *refugees* is their pre-*migration* trauma, which is often life-threatening in nature. The impact of trauma is likely to be exacerbated by the challenges of adjustment to a new world. Being displaced from their country of origin, *refugees* often express concern about adapting to a new culture and country. Losing their cultural identity is also a worry. Lacking a support or community group, *refugees* often feel estranged and isolated. Many report feelings of homesickness and concerns over the breakup of their family and the loss of community ties. There are often worries about the future, difficulties communicating in English, and unemployment.

Refugees want their children to learn their native language and to maintain family and cultural traditions. Many refugee parents are also especially concerned about the Americanization of their children, given the U.S. societal emphasis on openness and individuality. Parents may worry about the academic and social adjustment of their children and what they perceive to be a lack of discipline in American society. Because of the limitations on available employment, many have inflexible, low-wage jobs that prevent them from adequately supervising their children (Weine et al., 2006).

Effects of Past Persecution, Torture, or Trauma

Post-traumatic stress disorder (PTSD) and elevated rates of mood and anxiety disorders are frequent in this population (Nickerson, Bryant, Silove, & Steel, 2011), including nightmares and symptoms involving dissociation, intrusive thoughts, and hypervigilance (Chung & Bemak, 2007). It is important to note, however, that the vast majority of *refugees* are able to make a healthy transition to life in the United States. Although many of the challenges faced by *refugees* are similar to those encountered by *immigrants*, differences do exist. In general, *refugees* are under more stress compared to *immigrants*. Most *immigrants* had time to prepare for their move to the United States, whereas for most *refugees* the escape was sudden and traumatic. Family members are often left behind. With the exception of women and female immigrants, who often have experienced military, hunger, and sexual assault, *refugees* have typically been exposed to more trauma than other *immigrants* (Bemak & Chung, 2014).

The pre-*migration* experiences of many *refugees* include the atrocities of war, torture and killing, sexual assault, incarceration, and a continuing threat of death. For example, Central American *refugees* from El Salvador, Guatemala, Nicaragua, and Honduras report violent experiences, such as witnessing beatings and killings, fearing for their own lives or that of family members, being injured, or being victims of sexual assault. These Central American *refugees* reported feelings of isolation and exhibited high levels of mistrust with service providers (Asner-Self & Marotta, 2005). *Refugees* often experience emotional reactions related to the destruction of their family and social networks, sometimes as a result of genocide. Many report that memories of war intrude into their daily lives.

Implications

To see loved ones raped, beaten, and killed can have lasting, long-term consequences. It may be difficult to share such traumatic experiences with a therapist. In order to have a strong therapeutic relationship with traumatized *refugees*, it is especially important to establish trust and to recognize that the disclosure of traumatic experiences takes time. Questions not related to violence, exposure to weapons, or other stressful incidents might allow for greater comfort in revealing traumatic experiences and reduce feelings of fear, shame, or humiliation later (Asner-Self & Marotta, 2005).

It is important to consider the cultural perspective of *refugees* concerning mental and physical disorders to determine how their views might be different from those of the dominant culture. For example, in some countries, women victimized by sexual assault are shunned and considered unfit for marriage. In addition, many *immigrants* take a somatic view of psychological disorders and see mental disorders as resulting from physical problems. If a client brings up somatic symptoms, the therapist can work first with these complaints. Also, because there may be a lack of understanding of *PTSD* symptoms, therapists can help clients understand why they occur. Symptoms can be framed as normal reactions to trauma that anyone in their situation might develop. Therapists can reassure clients that the symptoms can be treated and are not signs that they are "going crazy."

Safety Issues and Coping with Loss

Refugees often come from politically unstable situations. In such cases, issues of safety are salient and must be addressed. In the process of requesting refugee status, some clients may have faced the adversarial experience of having to prove that they were persecuted. Because of this, they may be reluctant to relate their experiences or seem fearful that they will not be believed.

The loss of friends, family, and status is very troubling to *refugees*. They often feel guilty about leaving other family members behind and may go through a bereavement process. Many will not be able to resume their previous level of occupational and social functioning. It is important to identify their perceptions about what is lost.

Implications

Therapists should discuss confidentiality and the reason for assessment early in the intake process. Based on negative experiences with governmental powers in their homeland, *refugees* may be concerned about providing information or may be worried that information shared will be used against them. Also, since problem behaviors or mental difficulties may be seen as a source of shame for the individual or the family, knowing that the information obtained will be confidential may offer some relief. It is helpful to acknowledge the difficulty involved in sharing private information, with reassurance that it is necessary in order to develop the best solutions. To explore the possibility that cultural constraints exist, the counselor might also state something like the following: "Sometimes people in counseling believe that family issues should stay in the family. How do you feel about this belief?"

To understand the loss experienced by *refugees*, it may be beneficial to obtain a *migration* narrative as part of the assessment. This provides an understanding of the individual's social and occupational life prior to leaving his or her country of origin. Information regarding family life, friends, and activities can be gathered by asking questions such as, "How would you describe your daily life in your country of origin? What did you like and dislike about your country? What was family life like? What kind of job or family roles did you have? What was your community like?" Therapists can also inquire about experiences with transition from their homeland and any traumas associated with this process. "What happened before, during, and after you left your country? What differences do you see between living in your country and living in America? What do you see as advantages and disadvantages of living in either country?" It is important to understand experiences with resettlement camps and find out whether family members were separated. In addition, therapists should inquire about clients' experiences with prejudice and discrimination in their homeland and since arriving in the United States. This process gives a clearer picture of the perceived losses and experiences of *refugees* (Weisman et al., 2005).

IMPLICATIONS FOR CLINICAL PRACTICE

Many *immigrants* hold cultural belief systems that are collectivistic. In contrast to the individualistic Western worldview, they may consider interpersonal relationships and social networks to be of paramount importance. Mental health systems that value independence over interdependence, separate mental functioning from physical functioning, attribute causation as internally located, and seek to explain events from a Western empiricist approach can be at odds with the cultural belief systems of *immigrants* and *refugees*. Counselors may inadvertently impose their belief systems on these clients and communicate a disrespect for their worldview. Counselors should perform a self-assessment with respect to their own attitudes by asking themselves questions such as "How do I feel about *immigrants* and *refugees* coming to our country?" "What are my feelings about *undocumented immigrants*?" (Villalba, 2009). It is important for therapists to consider the following (Bemak & Chung, 2014; Burnett & Thompson, 2005):

1. Remember that *immigrants* and *refugees* face multiple stressors, including the stress of moving to and living in another country; learning another language; and negotiating new social, economic, political, educational, and social systems. It is often a confusing and frightening experience. Mental health providers who understand the complexities of this situation can do much to reassure clients by demystifying the process.

2. Be aware that the client may have day-to-day stressors, such as limited resources, a need for permanent shelter, lack of employment, or frustrating interactions with agencies. Allow time to understand and to provide support related to these immediate needs, or help the client locate resources related to specific needs.

3. Do not assume that the client has an understanding of mental health services or counseling. Give a description of what counseling is and the roles of therapist and client.

4. Inquire about clients' beliefs regarding the cause of their difficulties, listening for sociopolitical, cultural, religious, or spiritual interpretations. Understanding and validating clients' conceptualizations of presenting problems within their cultural matrix is an important aspect of providing culturally relevant services.

5. Allow time for clients to share their backgrounds, their pre-*migration* stories, and changes in their lives since immigrating.

6. Clearly describe the symptoms of mental disorders, outline various psychother-apeutic approaches, and explain how chosen strategies will help the client make desired changes. Modify evidence-based therapies to include cultural beliefs.

7. Cultural adaptations include condensation of treatment sessions, review of con-cepts covered, and modifications of materials such as the inclusion of visual aids and of culturally relevant metaphors, values, and proverbs (Ramos & Alegría, 2014).

8. Keep current regarding what is happening at the local, state, and federal level relative to immigration and refugee issues, particularly the tone of the debate. As our review indicates, sociopolitical conditions and public policy can have either positive or detrimental effects on their life experiences.

9. Families may be impacted by poverty, fear of immigration raids, parents working multiple jobs, and a lack of an extended family network. In addition, acculturation conflicts can occur. In some families, children have learned to threaten parents with dialing 911 when physically disciplined (Leidy, Guerra, & Toro, 2010).

10. Mental health providers should consider offering services within the *immigrant* community rather than outside of it. These services should be made culturally relevant and partially staffed by members from the *immigrant* community.

11. Help *undocumented immigrants* have a plan in place for dealing with possible deportation of family members and to secure advocacy resources that are avail-able to them.

12. In the course of assessment and diagnosis of mental disorders, take into account environmental factors, language barriers, and potential exposure to discrimination and hostility. When necessary, use skilled and knowledgeable interpreters.

13. Be knowledgeable about refugee experiences and psychological strategies commonly used to cope with stress. Understand that symptom manifestations may include post-traumatic stress and other mental disorders that arise from experiences of war, imprisonment, persecution, rape, and torture. Symptoms might involve nightmares, avoidance, hopelessness, or negative beliefs about the self and others.

14. Develop your own system of self-care to decrease the effects of intense work with clients with traumatic histories.

SUMMARY

Immigrants come to this country to escape poverty or political unrest, and to seek a better life. Despite the belief that *immigrants* are dangerous or a drain on society, they are no more likely to use social services and to commit crimes than native-born Americans. Nevertheless, many citizens are opposed to the number of *immigrants* entering the United States, and are against providing a path to citizenship for those who are undocumented. *Refugees* are those forced to leave their countries in order to escape persecution due to race, religion, nationality, political opinion, or membership in a particular social group. In addition to facing major cultural differences and coping with a new environment, both groups have been subjected to individual, institutional, and societal prejudice and discrimination. Clinicians need to be attuned to linguistic and communication issues, pre-*migration* trauma, and post-traumatic stress for *refugees*. Fourteen clinical implications for counselor practice are identified.

GLOSSARY TERMS

Asylum

Bilingualism

"Illegal" immigrants

Immigrant

Interpreters

Migration

Naturalized citizens

Post-traumatic stress disorder (PTSD)

Refugees

Survivor's guilt

Undocumented immigrants

REFERENCES

ACLU. (2013). *Muslims need not apply.* Retrieved from http://www.lccr.com/newsroom/new-report-exposes-covert-u-s-government-immigration-program-unlawfully-prevents-many-muslim-applicants-becoming-citizens-lawful-immigrants/

American Psychological Association, Presidential Task Force on Immigration. (2013). *Crossroads: The psychology of immigration in the new century.* Washington, DC: American Psychological Association.

Asner-Self, K. K., & Marotta, S. A. (2005). Developmental indices among Central American immigrants exposed to war-related trauma: Clinical implications for counselors. *Journal of Counseling and Development, 83,* 163–172.

Associated Press. (2015). *"American Sniper" can fight anti-Arab speech, says civil rights group.* Retrieved from http://pagesix.com /2015/01/29/american-sniper-can-fight-anti -arab-speech-says-civil-rights-group/

Baker, B., & Rytina, N. (2013). *Estimates of the unauthorized immigrant population residing in the United States.* Washington, DC: U.S. Department of Homeland Security, Office of Immigration Statistics.

Bemak, F., & Chung, R.C.-Y. (2014). Immigrants and refugees. In F.T.L. Leong, L. Comas-Diaz, G. C. Nagayama Hall, V. C. McLoyd, & J. E. Trimble (Eds.), *APA handbook of multicultural psychology, Vol. 1: Theory and research* (pp. 503–517). Washington, DC: American Psychological Association.

Bernstein, N. (2006, March 3). Recourse grows slim for immigrants who fall ill. *New York Times*, p. A14.

Burnett, A., & Thompson, K. (2005). Enhancing the psychosocial well-being of asylum seekers and refugees. In K. H. Barrett & W. H. George (Eds.), *Race, culture, psychology, and law* (pp. 205–224). Thousand Oaks, CA: Sage.

Camarota, S. A. (2012). *Immigrants in the United States, 2010: A profile of America's foreign-born population.* Retrieved from http://cis.org/2012-profile-of-americas -foreign-born-population

CAP Immigration Team. (2014). *The facts on immigration today.* Retrieved from https://www.americanprogress.org/issues /immigration/report/2014/10/23/59040 /the-facts-on-immigration-today-3/

Child Trends. (2014). *High school dropout rates.* Retrieved from http://www.childtrends.org /?indicators=high-school-dropout-rates

Chung, R.C.Y., & Bemak, F. (2007). In M. G. Constantine (Ed.), *Clinical practice with people of color* (pp. 125–142). New York, NY: Teachers College Press.

Ewing, W. A., Martinez, D. E., & Rumbaut, R. G. (2015). *The criminalization of immigration in the United States.* Retrieved from

http://immigrationpolicy.org/special-reports /criminalization-immigration-united-states

Hamilton, L. K., Medianu, S., & Esses, V. M. (2013). Towards an immigration as a defining feature of the twenty-first century. In A. G. deZavala & A. Cichocka (Eds.), *Social psychology of social problems* (pp. 82–113). New York, NY: Palgrave Macmillan.

Hart Research Associates. (2014). NBC News/ Wall Street Journal survey. Retrieved from http://www.online.wsj.com/public/resources /documents/WSJNBCpoll09092014.pdf

Ji, Q., & Batalova, J. (2012). *College-educated immigrants in the United States.* Retrieved from http://www.migrationpolicy.org/article /college-educated-immigrants-united-states

Karlamangla, S., & Terhune, C. (2014). *Many Latinos shun Obamacare for fear of getting relatives deported.* Retrieved from http://www.msn.com /en-us/news/us/many-latinos-shun-obamacare -for-fear-of-getting-relatives-deported /ar-AA7nfNF

Khadaroo, S. T. (2014). *Illegal immigration: Feds tell schools what they can and can't do.* Retrieved from http://www.csmonitor.com/USA/Politics /2014/0508/Illegal-immigration-Feds-tell -schools-what-they-can-and-can-t-do

Leidy, M. S., Guerra, N. G., & Toro, R. I. (2010). Positive parenting, family cohesion, and child social competence among immigrant Latino families. *Journal of Family Psychology, 24,* 252–260.

Lind, D. (2014). *14 facts that help explain America's child migrant crisis.* Retrieved from http://www.vox.com/2014/6/16/5813406 /explain-child-migrant-crisis-central-america -unaccompanied-children-immigrants-daca

Lind, D. (2015). *Mitch McConnell might have figured out how to prevent a DHS shutdown.* Retrieved from http://www.vox.com/ 2015/2/23/8094849/dhs-shutdown-mcconnell

Marrero, P. (2011, August 8). Migración mexicana permanece estable. *La Opinion.* Retrieved from http://www.impre.com/laraza/noticias/2011/8/3/migracion-mexicana-permanece-e-266040–2.html

Martin, D. C., & Yankay, J. E. (2014). *Refugees and asylees: 2013.* Retrieved from http://www.dhs.gov/publication/refugees-and-asylees-2013

Martinez, M., & Gutierrez, T. (2010). *Tucson teachers sue Arizona over new "anti-Hispanic" school law.* Retrieved from http://www.cnn.com/2010/US/10/19/arizona.ethnic.studies.lawsuit/?hpt=T2

Miller, K. E., Zoe, L. M., Pazdirek, L., Caruth, M., & Lopez, D. (2005). The role of interpreters in psychotherapy with refugees: An exploratory study. *American Journal of Orthopsychiatry, 75,* 27–39.

Nassir, A. (2014). *Nativism in America today.* Retrieved from http://hubpages.com/hub/Nativism-in-America-Today

National Conference of State Legislatures. (2015). *Undocumented student tuition: Overview.* Retrieved from http://www.ncsl.org/research/education/undocumented-student-tuition-overview.aspx

National Immigration Law Center. (2006). *Fact about immigrants' low use of health services and public benefits.* Retrieved from http://www.nilc.org

Navarrette, R. Jr. (2011). *Brewer's "birther" veto was the right call.* Retrieved from http://www.cnn.com/2011/OPINION/04/20/navarette.brewer.birther/_1_birther-bill-brewer-arizona-secretary?_s=P-M:OPINION

Negy, C., Schwartz, S., & Reig-Ferrer, A. (2009). Violated expectations and acculturative stress among U.S. Hispanic immigrants. *Cultural Diversity and Ethnic Minority Psychology, 15,* 255–264.

Nickerson, A., Bryant, R. A., Silove, D., & Steel, Z. (2011). A critical review of psychological treatments of posttraumatic stress disorder in refugees. *Clinical Psychology Review, 31,* 399–417.

Oneil, A. (2012). *Parents deported, what happens to US-born kids?* Retrieved from http://news.yahoo.com/parents-deported-happens-us-born-kids-160817545—finance.html

Patrick, E. (2004). *The U.S. refugee resettlement program.* Retrieved from http://www.migrationinformation.org/USFocus/print.cfm?ID=229

Pew Research Center. (2014). *Unauthorized immigrant population trends for states, birth countries and regions.* Retrieved from http://www.pewhispanic.org/2014/12/11/unauthorized-trends/

Quiroga, S. S., & Flores-Ortiz, Y. G. (2000). Barriers to health care for abused Latina and Asian immigrant women. *Journal of Health Care for the Poor and Underserved, 11,* 33–44.

Ramos, Z., & Alegría, M. (2014). Cultural adaptation and health literacy refinement of a brief depression intervention for Latinos in a low-resource setting. *Cultural Diversity & Ethnic Minority Psychology, 20,* 293–301.

Reeves, J. (2011). *Alabama immigration law cutting Latinos in schools.* Retrieved from http://www.sfgate.com/cgi-bin/article.cgi?f=/c/a/2011/09/30/MNVJ1LBST8.DTL

Restrepo, D., & Garcia, A. (2014). *The surge of unaccompanied children from Central America.* Retrieved from http://www.bespacific.com/surge-unaccompanied-children-central-america/

Ro, M. (2002). Moving forward: Addressing the health of Asian American and Pacific Islander women. *American Journal of Public Health, 92,* 516–519.

Searight, H. R., & Searight, B. K. (2009). Working with foreign language interpreters: Recommendations for psychological practice. *Professional Psychology: Research and Practice, 40,* 444–451.

Southern Poverty Law Center. (2010). *Injustice on our plates: Immigrant women in the U.S. food industry.* Retrieved from http://www.splcenter.org/sites/default/files/downloads/publication/Injustice_on_Our_Plates.pdf

Tani, M. (2015). *Donald Trump just got into a heated exchange with Don Lemon over his comments about immigrants.* Retrieved from http://www.businessinsider.com/donald-trump-defends-mexican-immigrant-comments-2015–7

Ting, L., & Panchanadeswaran, S. (2009). Barriers to help-seeking among immigrant African American women survivors of partner abuse: Listening to women's own voices. *Journal of Aggression, Maltreatment & Trauma, 18,* 817–838.

Villalba, J. A. (2009). Addressing immigrant and refugee issues in multicultural counselor education. *Journal of Professional Counseling: Practice, Theory, and Research, 37,* 1–10.

Weine, S., Feetham, S., Kulauzovic, Y., Knafl, K., Besic, S., Klebic, A., & Pavkovic, I. (2006). A family beliefs framework for socially and culturally specific preventive interventions with refugee youth and families. *American Journal of Orthopsychiatry, 76,* 1–9.

Weisman, A., Feldman, G., Gruman, C., Rosenberg, R., Chamorro, R., & Belozersky, I. (2005). Improving mental health services for Latino and Asian immigrant elders. *Professional Psychology: Research and Practice, 36,* 642–648.

Wight, V. R., Chau, M., & Aratani, Y. (2011). *Who are America's poor children?* Retrieved from: http://www.nccp.org/publications/pub_1001.html

Yakushko, O. (2010). Clinical work with limited English proficiency clients: A phenomenological exploration. *Professional Psychology: Research and Practice, 41,* 449–455.

Zeigler, K., & Camarota, S. A. (2014). *U.S. immigrant population record 41.3 million in 2013.* Washington, DC: Center for Immigration Studies.

Counseling Jewish Americans

Chapter Objectives

1. Learn the demographics and characteristics of Jewish Americans.

2. Identify counseling implications of the information provided for Jewish Americans.

3. Provide examples of strengths that are associated with Jewish Americans.

4. Know the special challenges faced by Jewish Americans.

5. Understand how the implications for clinical practice can guide assessment and therapy with Jewish Americans.

"Congress, the White House and Hollywood, Wall Street, are owned by the Zionists. . . Everybody is in the pocket of the Israeli lobbies, which are funded by wealthy supporters, including those from Hollywood. Same thing with the financial markets." Quote from Helen Thomas, former member of the White House press corps (Weiss, 2013).

Thirty percent believe that American Jews are more loyal to Israel than to America, and 26 percent believe that Jews are responsible for the death of Christ. Nineteen percent of Americans believe Jews have too much power in the business world. One out of five African Americans and more than a third of foreign-born Hispanics hold anti-Semitic beliefs. (Anti-Defamation League, 2013)

Because of conflicts in the Middle East, anti-Semitic incidents in New York City jumped 35% from 2013 to 2014, with violent assaults more than doubling. (Jamieson, 2014)

Anti-Semitism *appears to be rearing its head across Europe yet again. The perpetrators of the recent terror attacks in Paris and Copenhagen both targeted Jews . . . Reports of anti-Semitic incidents have risen in the U.K. as well as in France, where the most European Jews live. (Looft, 2015)*

Jewish Americans include (a) people who practice *Judaism* and have a Jewish ethnic background, (b) people who have converted to *Judaism* but do not have Jewish parents, and (c) individuals with a Jewish ethnic background who do not practice *Judaism* but still maintain their cultural identity and connection to their Jewish descent (Schlosser, 2006). Although most Jewish Americans do not follow all Jewish religious traditions (only 40% indicate that religion plays a major role in their lives), many retain strong Jewish connections by celebrating the major holy days of *Yom Kippur*, Hanukkah, and Passover. Also, some regularly attend *synagogue* services and follow the tradition of keeping kosher homes (food rules and preparation that adheres to religious dietary guidelines) (Younis, 2009). Although Jewish individuals have experienced centuries of discrimination both within the United States and throughout the world, they have received little attention in the multicultural literature.

In the United States, approximately, 4.2 million individuals are Jewish by religion, while another 1.1 million are secular or cultural Jews, who say that they have no religion but consider themselves to be Jewish (Pew Research Center, 2013). These individuals form the largest Jewish community in the world outside of Israel (where there is a Jewish population of 7.8 million); there are also large Jewish populations in Canada and Argentina. The earliest Jews to arrive in the United States immigrated from Spain and Portugal. The second group of Jewish immigrants emigrated from Germany and Eastern Europe because of persecution and/or for economic reasons.

By World War I, 250,000 German-speaking Jews had arrived in America. Eastern European Jews came to America as a result of overpopulation, poverty, and persecution. Between 1880 and 1942, more than 2 million Jews from Russia, Austria, Hungary, and Romania entered the United States and constituted the largest group of Jews in the United States (Zollman, 2006). Because of their historical and political background, Jewish Americans are among the most liberal political groups in America, with about 70% supporting the Democratic Party. In general, Jews describe themselves politically as "liberal" or "very liberal." However, one subgroup, the Orthodox Jews, are not as liberal, with half describing themselves as political conservative and supporting the Republican Party (Pew Research Center, 2013).

Since 1990, the Jewish population in the United States has decreased from 5.5 million to 4.2 million. According to the Pew Research Center (2013), this population decline is due to aging (many are older than age 65, and younger individuals are more likely to identify themselves as having no religion), falling birth rate, intermarriage (over one-third of Jewish individuals who intermarry do not raise their children to be Jewish), and assimilation. Approximately 52% of Jewish women between the ages of 30 to 34 have not had any children, compared with 27% of all American women; the fertility rate of Jewish women is below that needed to maintain the population (Berkofsky, 2006). Adherence to Jewish traditions has also declined over time. In terms of religiosity, two-thirds of Jews do not belong to a *synagogue*, about a quarter do not believe in God, and one-third celebrate Christmas (Goldstein, 2013).

Approximately 85% of Jewish Americans were born in the United States, and almost all are native English speakers. Some speak Hebrew, Yiddish, or the language of their country of origin. Most of those born outside the United States are from the former Soviet Union. Jews are a highly educated group, with 62% of those 18 and older possessing at least a bachelor's degree, versus 22.4% of non-Jews. Their income level and household wealth is much higher than that of the total population (Chua & Rubenfeld, 2014). Most Jewish individuals consider themselves to be a minority group and indicate that their heritage is "very" or "somewhat" important to them. About half report "strong emotional ties" to Israel. Jewish Americans were in the forefront of the civil rights movement in the 1960s. In fact, half of the White Freedom Riders and civil rights attorneys involved in the movement were Jewish Americans. Jewish Americans are well represented in all aspects of American society in terms of business, education, politics, entertainment, and the arts.

CHARACTERISTICS AND STRENGTHS

In the following sections we consider the characteristics, values, and strengths of individuals who are Jewish, and consider their implications in treatment. Remember that these are generalizations and their applicability needs to be assessed for particular clients and their families.

Spiritual and Religious Values

Judaism, with its belief in an omnipotent God who created humankind, was one of the earliest monotheistic religions. According to *Judaism*, God established a covenant with the Jewish people and revealed his commandments to them in the *Torah*, the holy book. The most important commandments are the Ten Commandments. Individuals who wish to convert to *Judaism* go through the process of (a) studying *Judaism* and the observance of the commandments, (b) immersion in a ritual bath, and for males, (c) circumcision (although symbolic circumcision may be allowed by some sects).

One of the most important Jewish holidays is *Yom Kippur*, the Day of Atonement. It is a time set aside to atone for sins during the past year. Rosh Hashanah, the start of the Jewish New Year, is another High Holiday in *Judaism*. This holiday, celebrated 10 days before *Yom Kippur*, represents the creation of the world or universe. Even those who are not religious often attend *synagogue* services and spend time with family during these celebrations.

Within *Judaism*, the degree of adherence to religious tradition varies. Those who are traditional (*Orthodox Judaism*) follow all Jewish traditions. *Conservative Judaism* also seeks to preserve Jewish traditions and ceremonies but is more flexible in interpreting religious law. Many others are adherents of the *progressive* movement (*Reform Judaism*), which advocates the freedom of individuals to make choices about which traditions to follow (Altman, Inman, Fine, Ritter, & Howard,

2010; Rich, 2011). About one-third of U.S. Jews (35%) identify with the *Reform* movement, 18% with the *Conservative* movement, and 10% with Orthodox Judaism, including 6% who belong to Ultra-Orthodox groups (rejects modern secular society and believe they are the most religiously authentic Jews) and 3% who are Modern Orthodox (follows traditional practices but engages with the secular world to expand their spirituality). The remaining 37% do not identify with any particular Jewish denomination. With the exception of Orthodox Jews (who are very religious), Jews are less religiously committed than the U.S. public in general (Pew Research Center, 2013).

As previously noted, individuals need not actively practice *Judaism* in order to consider themselves Jewish. Many who are nonreligious but of Jewish parentage or upbringing identify as Jewish. About half who identify as Jewish adhere to *Judaism*, while many others celebrate only some Jewish holidays, deeming such celebration a cultural rather than a religious activity. These individuals consider themselves Jewish because of the commonality of history, culture, and experiences.

Friedman, Friedlander, and Blustein (2005) conducted interviews with 10 Jewish adults to understand their perspective on their own identity. All participants indicated a fluidity of identity over the years. One stated, "When I was a kid, it made me feel a little bit different in certain situations, but now I would be very proud to be associated with Jewish people and to be Jewish. I would say it has gotten stronger." Another commented, "[I]t's the dips and valleys in my life . . . it is pretty much a constant, but it does go up and down" (p. 79). Among the participants, childhood experiences, such as participating in Jewish holiday traditions with family members, eating in a kosher dining room, or engaging in discussions with parents about *Judaism*, influenced cultural identity.

As adults, some expressed feelings of guilt because they did not consistently practice religious customs. Some had a deep *Jewish identity* but did not engage in Jewish rituals. However, most expressed pride about being Jewish. From this phenomenological study, it appears that those who practice *Judaism* define *Jewish identity* differently from those individuals who are secular and do not engage in Jewish religious practices. For many, *Jewish identity* revolves around common experiences and history, rather than religion.

Cultural Strengths

> *Judaism is a guidebook on how to live your life and be a good person. . . . I keep Kosher because that's what I grew up with and it's*

something that is a comfort to me. . . My grandma and all my relatives went through and died for their religion. . . (Altman et al., 2010, p. 167)

Judaism is more than just a religion. It is a culture with a set of traditions and historical experiences that provide members with a sense of connection and commonality and feelings of acceptance (Schlosser, 2006). Some believe the sociocultural connection is even stronger than the religious aspects of *Judaism*, although the latter provide ideals that Jews can aspire to. Religious behavior and traditions, such as lighting Shabbat candles, can be calming, since they remind individuals of their history and their community (Altman et al., 2010). These aspects of *Judaism* serve as protective factors against the discrimination and prejudice that Jews face. Among orthodox Jews, higher levels of religious beliefs are associated with positive mental health. This may be due to emotional and spiritual support from having a personal relationship with God (Rosmarin, Pirutinsky, Pargament, & Krumrei, 2009).

The majority of Americans hold American Jews in high regard, stressing their strong religious faith, contributions to the cultural life of America, and strong emphasis on the importance of the family. Indeed, American Jews themselves are overwhelmingly proud to be Jewish and have a strong sense of being part of the Jewish community. Other aspects that are important to Jewish Americans' identity are leading an ethical life, working for justice and equality, and having a good sense of humor. However, only 19% indicated that following Jewish Law was an essential part of being Jewish (Pew Research Center, 2013).

SPECIFIC CHALLENGES

In the following sections we consider challenges often faced by those who are Jewish and consider their implications in treatment.

Historical and Sociopolitical Background

David Duke spoke to a group of Holocaust deniers at a conference on the Holocaust convened by Iran's president in 2006. During his speech, the former Imperial Wizard of the Ku Klux Klan and Louisiana State Representative claimed that the Holocaust was a hoax perpetrated by European Jews to justify the occupation of Palestine and the creation of Israel. (Fathi, 2006)

Since the Middle Ages, the Jewish people have experienced persecution, oppression, and second-class status, as well as being targeted for massacre or expulsion from their homes (e.g., during the Christian Crusades, the Spanish Inquisition, the *Holocaust*, and so on). For centuries, they have been stereotyped as hungry for wealth, power, and control and scapegoated during periods of financial distress. An older Jewish woman asked her therapist, "Have you heard of the *Holocaust*?" (Hinrichsen, 2006, p. 30). The *Holocaust* represents an incredibly traumatic period in Jewish history. During this period, Nazi Germans murdered approximately 6 million Jewish men, women, and children. There were many more who survived inhumane treatment after being imprisoned in forced labor and concentration camps and whose lives have been affected forever.

What constitutes *Jewish identity* is complex and highly personal. An important aspect is a sense of shared cultural and historical experiences. *Holocaust deniers*, individuals who do not acknowledge or who question the existence of the genocide that occurred during the *Holocaust*, not only invalidate the loss and suffering of *Holocaust* victims and their families but also strike at an important part of *Jewish identity*. It is distressing when this tragic history is ignored or invalidated. It is also hurtful when our society recognizes Christian holidays and religious expectations but ignores those of the Jewish faith.

A well-known mental health practitioner and educator, Stephen Weinrach (2002) was proud of his *Jewish identity* and became an outspoken critic of the mental health organization to which he belonged for being blind to the plight of Jewish Americans. He wrote:

> *Issues that have concerned Jews have failed to resonate with the counseling profession, including, for the most part, many of the most outspoken advocates for multicultural counseling. . . . The near universal failure of those advocates for multicultural counseling to rail against* anti-Semitism *and embrace the notion of Jews as a culturally distinct group represents the most painful wound of all.* (p. 310)

In his article, Weinrach made the following observations regarding the mental health profession:

- Counseling associations ignore requests from Jewish members to reschedule meetings when the meetings conflict with Jewish holidays (e.g., the National Board for Certified Counselors scheduled the National Counseling Exam on *Yom Kippur*, a day when work is not permitted).

- Texts on multicultural counseling often do not address Jewish Americans as a diverse group. Only 8% of multicultural courses in APA doctoral programs in counseling covered Jews as a distinct cultural group (Priester et al., 2008).

- Few articles in counseling journals have involved Jewish Americans, and, in some texts, Jewish Americans have been portrayed in a stereotypic manner.

In our opinion, Weinrach has made some valid points. In writing this chapter, we found very few articles on clinical issues involving Jewish Americans or their history of oppression, although numerous articles were easily located for the other diverse groups covered in this text. We must recognize the degree of prejudice and discrimination faced by Jewish Americans and reexamine policies that may be insensitive to their concerns.

Prejudice and Discrimination

> *The two 17-year-old girls told of repeated acts of anti-Semitic bullying—one girl had money shoved into her mouth, another kept seeing swastikas pervasively in school hallways and lockers . . . the Jewish students accused 35 students of anti-Semitic behaviors. They told of finding swastikas drawn on walls and lockers, sometime accompanied by messages like "Die Jew," of slurs like "Christ killer" and "disgusting Jew" . . . and of being shoved, punched, taunted and humiliated and of experiencing bus rides where classmates chanted "white power" and saluted Nazi-style. (Berger, 2015).*

> *Because of the targeting and killing of Jewish people in Paris and Copenhagen and the vandalism of hundreds of headstones at a cemetery in eastern France, Israeli Prime Minister Binyamin Netanyahu has asked Jewish individuals in European countries to migrate to Israel, saying "This wave of terror attacks can be expected to continue, including anti-Semitic and murderous attacks. We say to the Jews, to our brothers and sisters, Israel is your home and that of every Jew. Israel is waiting for you with open arms." (Politi, 2015)*

Prejudice and discrimination against Jews are found all over the world. A survey of over 100 countries revealed that anti-Semitic views and attitudes are held by 74% of the population in the Middle East and North Africa; 34% in Eastern Europe; 24% in Western Europe; 23% in Sub-Saharan Africa; 22% in Asia; 19%

in the Americas; and 14% in Oceania. The survey also showed that 35% of the world's population had never heard of the *Holocaust* and that among those who had, 32% believe it is either a myth or is greatly exaggerated. The most widely accepted anti-Semitic stereotypes worldwide are "Jews are more loyal to Israel than to this country/the countries they live in," "Jews have too much power in the business world," and "Jews don't care about what happens to anyone but their own kind" (ADL Global 100, 2013).

Jewish Americans have long been targets of discrimination and prejudice. That such prejudice continues to this day is revealed in the astonishing statistics that of the 1,163 hate crimes motivated by religious bias, the vast majority (more than 59%) have been anti-Semitic. The second highest were anti-Islamic (Federal Bureau of Investigation, 2013). Prejudicial reactions against Jews not only involve overt actions such as vandalism, assaults, or direct displays of *anti-Semitism* but also negative attitudes and beliefs. Such prejudice is revealed in personal statements such as that made by actor and director Mel Gibson in 2006: "Jews are responsible for all the wars in the world" (Gibson has since apologized for his statement); and a complaint purportedly made by Judith Regan, an editor at HarperCollins Publishers, that a "Jewish cabal" was against her—referring to members of the publishing firm and their decision not to publish a controversial book by O. J. Simpson that Ms. Regan had produced (Hall, 2006).

In a survey of Americans (Anti-Defamation League, 2013), it was found that 14% of the adults surveyed hold "hard-core" anti-Semitic beliefs. Many believe that Jewish Americans wield too much power in business, the news media, and the movie and television industries. In a national poll of American voters (Council for the National Interest, 2006), 39% of Americans believe that the "Israeli lobby" was a key factor responsible for the United States confronting Iran and going to war in Iraq. Among Jewish Americans, 77% disagreed with this view. Not surprisingly, anti-Semitic views toward American Jews often arise in conjunction with negative reactions to Israeli actions in the Middle East (Cohen, Jussim, Harber, & Bhasin, 2009).

Although Jewish individuals have achieved great success, it is evident that they remain targets of prejudice, discrimination, and even violence throughout the world. In the United States, about 43% of Jewish Americans report facing "a lot of discrimination" and 15% indicate that they have been called offensive names or have been snubbed socially because of being Jewish (Pew Research Center, 2013). Jewish Americans have reported being discriminated against at a rate similar to that reported by African Americans (Berkofsky, 2006; Goldberg, 2000).

Jewish undergraduates report experiencing microaggressions that involved suspicion from others and accusations or expectations that they were greedy or over-affiliated with their group. They also report that there is a lack of institutional cultural sensitivity for Jewish students (Na, Kleiman, Poolokasingham, & Spanierman, 2014). Additional examples of microaggressions against Jewish Americans include automatically assigning intelligence to a Jew; giving preference to Christians; lack of recognition of Jews during multicultural discussions; and assuming that Jews are wealthy and have control over U.S. policy and decisions in Hollywood (Schlosser, 2009a).

Cultural and Gender Issues

Orthodox Jews adhere strictly to the tenets of *Judaism*, which offer a comprehensive guide to living that includes rules and practices affecting one's entire life, such as what to do upon first waking up, what foods are allowed or forbidden, what attire and grooming are appropriate, what business practices should be followed, who to marry, and the proper way of observing holidays and the Shabbat (Rich, 2011). Some of these characteristics may make Orthodox Jews suspicious of therapy. Because of their strong faith in *Judaism*, they may be reluctant to seek treatment, since that might imply that their religion has failed them or that they are defective in some way. Orthodox Jewish communities tend to be very close knit, and the stigma associated with seeking therapy might reduce a person's opportunities to establish social relationships or marry within the community (Schnall, 2006).

Although Jewish denominations all arise from a patriarchal system, most Jewish Americans have moved toward an egalitarian relationship between spouses. However, those who are Orthodox are more likely to adhere to specific role divisions between males and females. Within the Orthodox tradition, women have the responsibility of taking care of the home, maintaining the health and happiness of the family, and nurturing the children. Because men are the ones who interpret the laws of *Judaism*, the women are subject to their husband's or father's interpretations of what constitutes appropriate behavior. The roles in marital relationships are seen to be complementary, with love and romance being less important than the task of raising a family (Schnall, 2006). Orthodox Jews are also much more restrictive about birth control and abortion than other Jewish Americans (Miller, Barton, Mazur, & Lovinger, 2014). Marital and family conflicts may occur as women move toward less rigid role divisions (Blackman, 2010).

Implications

It is evident that Jewish Americans continue to face a great deal of prejudice, even with the successes they have had in American society. For this reason, it is critical for therapists to be aware of the prejudice and discrimination that Jewish American clients may have experienced. A 78-year-old woman seeking treatment for depression asked the counseling intern, "Are you Jewish?" (Hinrichsen, 2006, p. 30). When the intern inquired about the question, the client stated that she had experienced discrimination from non-Jews and was uncertain whether the intern would understand her difficulties.

Anti-Semitic attitudes within ethnic minority populations may be especially troubling to those who are Jewish; that is, it can be especially hurtful when others who have experienced oppression, prejudice, and discrimination behave in a discriminatory manner toward Jews. There are several reasons for the anti-Semitic attitudes of some foreign-born Hispanic immigrants and African Americans toward Jewish Americans. First, many do not perceive Jews as a disadvantaged minority. Also, some may resent the fact that the Jewish community has historically opposed affirmative action policies and its members are more likely to favor advancement based on merit (Shapiro, 2006).

Orthodox Jews may be difficult to engage in therapy because of issues such as confidentiality and the concern that they will be asked to do things that are against their religious beliefs. Consulting with a *rabbi* on how to deal with issues such as confidentiality or how *Judaism* might affect counseling could be useful. Therapists can also work jointly with the client and the *rabbi* in defining the problem and developing interventions, so that these components of therapy do not conflict with religious beliefs. The *rabbi* may be helpful in developing culturally sensitive intervention strategies that incorporate religious principles (Schnall, 2006).

Ethnic Identity Issues

For many Jewish individuals, their identity is tied to historical events, such as the *Holocaust* and the oppression historically faced by the Jewish people. It can also involve cultural traditions and ancestry—not just religious beliefs. There is no single *Jewish identity*. Instead, there is a range: from individuals who are proud of their Jewish heritage, to those who have internalized *anti-Semitism* and hide their Jewish background from others, to those who feel confused and alienated from mainstream Jewish culture. While some do not publicly self-identify as Jewish, others are bicultural and take pride in both American and Jewish identities.

Schlosser (2009b) believes that Jews go through the following stages of ethnic identity development:

- Lack of awareness of one's *Jewish identity*

- Gradual awareness of *Jewish identity*

- Comparison of *Jewish identity* with other religions, such as Christianity

- Development of a sense of Jewishness

Counselors should recognize that American Jews may have identity concerns related to *anti-Semitism*, living under Christian privilege, the Shoah (*Holocaust*), and the invisibility of *Judaism*. Jews are highly diverse in regard to cultural and ethnic identity and adherence to religious orthodoxy. The counselor should not assume that all Jewish clients see *Jewish identity* or practice *Judaism* in the same manner (Schlosser, 2006).

 IMPLICATIONS FOR CLINICAL PRACTICE

In *Jewish Issues in Multiculturalism: A Handbook for Educators and Clinicians*, Langman (1999) indicates it is difficult to use culturally appropriate interventions because of the diversity of the Jewish culture. However, he does offer some guiding principles of importance for mental health providers. First, it is very important to be respectful of and knowledgeable about Jewish culture. Because most clinicians are from a Christian background, the traditions, values, and religious rituals that are important to Jewish Americans are often overlooked or dismissed. As we discussed in Chapter 6, therapists might inadvertently commit microaggressions due to their lack of understanding. For example, Langman describes a Jewish client who requested that an appointment not be scheduled during *Yom Kippur*, to which the therapist responded: "What? Do you need to pray or something?" The client felt humiliated, devalued, ashamed, and unsupported.

Second, therapists should strive to understand the full spectrum of Jewish identities within the Jewish population, including those of both religious and nonreligious Jews. As our prior section indicates, the therapist should have some knowledge of the history of *anti-Semitism*, its effects on identity, and the possible repercussions of internalized *anti-Semitism*. Langman (1999) discusses the latter as an insidious social conditioning process that makes some Jewish Americans ashamed of their ethnic and religious heritage. He views the sociopolitical process that defines Jewish differences as deviance to be the culprit and encourages counselors not to "blame the victim."

Third, as Langman makes clear, therapists need to be aware of any values, assumptions, and biases of their own that may be detrimental to their Jewish clients. He cites research that indicates that Jews are viewed as being "cold," "hostile," and "obstructive," whereas non-Jews (White) are seen as being more "warm," "friendly," and "helpful." He encourages counselors to explore any feelings of negativism toward Jewish Americans, Jewish culture, *Judaism*, and/or Israel.

Finally, although about two-thirds of Jewish Americans are not associated with a *synagogue* or have only slight connections to a Jewish congregation, it may be desirable to consult with a *rabbi* when working with clients who are strongly religious, particularly those who maintain Orthodox beliefs. In some cases, religious doubts or issues about religiously prohibited behaviors or behaviors associated with guilt or shame may be best addressed with guidance from religious leaders as part of the therapeutic process. Such consultation is easier when the counselor has spent time cultivating relationships with the Jewish community.

Counselors should also consider the following (Altman et al., 2010; Schlosser, Safran, Suson, Dettle, & Dewey, 2013):

1. As members of mental health professions, we must be aware of policies or expectations that do not take Jewish American concerns into consideration, such as scheduling meetings or appointments on Jewish holidays.

2. We need to examine our attitudes and beliefs in regard to Jewish Americans. Are their problems invisible to us? Is our failure to acknowledge the discrimination experienced by Jewish people due to a Christian-centered worldview, a lack of knowledge, or an unconscious *anti-Semitism*?

3. It is important for a counselor that Jewish Americans are the most targeted religious group for hate crimes and discrimination. Because many Jewish Americans are well educated and economically secure, we often do not understand that they may have experienced discrimination or hate.

4. Jewish American mental health professionals should also feel free to bring up their concerns when they are subjected to insensitivity or discrimination.

5. Jewish counselors should take care not to make assumptions about a client's *Jewish identity* and issues based on the counselor's own sense of identity or beliefs regarding *Judaism* (Schlosser, Safran, Suson, Dettle, & Dewey, 2013).

6. During assessment, it is helpful to ask clients about their sense of *Jewish identity* and life-affirming values, beliefs, and cultural norms (Miller et al., 2014).

7. The degree of receptivity to counseling and therapy may vary according to the degree of adherence to religious traditions. Orthodox versus non-Orthodox Jews are more likely to display treatment-seeking stigma and prefer individual to group therapy (Baruch, Kanter, Pirutinsky, Murphy, & Rosmain, 2014).

8. Among Orthodox Jews, women are expected to maintain the Jewish culture and raise Jewish children. For those who deviate from these expectations by, for example, being lesbian, remaining single, or preferring a career, conflicts may arise from opposing expectations (Ginsberg & Sinacore, 2013).

9. When working with Orthodox Jewish clients, determine how mental health issues are defined within their religious and cultural framework and develop appropriate, culturally adapted interventions based on this knowledge (Rosen, Rebeta, & Zalman Rothschild, 2014).

10. Although most Jewish Americans value psychotherapy and are receptive to traditional forms of therapy, any concerns or issues regarding therapy should be addressed during initial counseling sessions (Miller et al., 2014).

SUMMARY

Most Jewish individuals consider themselves to be a minority group and believe their heritage is important to them. Within *Judaism*, the degree of adherence to religious tradition varies from orthodoxy to *progressive* beliefs, practices, and decisions. *Judaism* is more than just a religion. It is a culture with a set of traditions and historical experiences that provide Jewish individuals with a sense of connection, commonality, and feelings of acceptance. As a result, mental health providers need to understand the importance of *Jewish identity*. Jews have suffered from *anti-Semitism* in all parts of the world. The *Holocaust* represents a deeply traumatic period in Jewish history. Jewish Americans have long been targets of discrimination and prejudice in the United States. The majority of hate crimes motivated by religious bias have been anti-Semitic. Cultural, gender, and identity differences also have major implications for issues likely to arise in work with Jewish clients. Nine clinical implications for counselor practice are identified.

GLOSSARY TERMS

Anti-Semitism	Orthodox
Conservative	Progressive
Holocaust	Rabbi
Holocaust denier	Reform
Jewish identity	Synagogue
Judaism	Yom Kippur

REFERENCES

ADL Global 100. (2013). *An index of anti-Semitism.* Retrieved from global100.adl.org/public/ADL-Global-100-Executive-Summary.pdf

Altman, A. N., Inman, A. G., Fine, S. G., Ritter, H. A., & Howard, E. R. (2010). Exploration of Jewish ethnic identity. *Journal of Counseling and Development, 88,* 163–173.

Anti-Defamation League. (2013). *A survey about attitudes towards Jews in America.* Washington, DC: Martila Communications.

Baruch, D. E., Kanter, J. W., Pirutinsky, S., Murphy, J., & Rosmain, D. H. (2014). Depression stigma and treatment preferences among orthodox and non-orthodox Jews. *Journal of Nervous and Mental Disease, 202,* 556–561.

Berger, J. (2015). Settlement over anti-Semitic bullying at Pine Bush Central Schools is approved. *New York Times.* Retrieved from http://www.nytimes.com/2015/07/10/nyregion/settlement-over-anti-semitic-bullying-at-pine-bush-central-schools-is-approved.html

Berkofsky, J. (2006). *National Jewish Population Survey: 2000. A snapshot of American Jewry.* Retrieved from http://www.myjewishlearning.com/article/national-jewish-population-survey-2000/

Blackman, M. (2010). *American Orthodox Jewish women and domestic violence: An intervention design.* Retrieved from https://ssa.uchicago.edu/american-orthodox-jewish-women-and-domestic-violence-intervention-design

Chua, A., & Rubenfeld, J. (2014). *The triple package: How three unlikely traits explain the rise and fall of cultural groups in America.* Toronto, Ontario: Penguin.

Cohen, F., Jussim, L., Harber, K. D., & Bhasin, G. (2009). Modern anti-Semitism and anti-Israeli attitudes. *Journal of Personality and Social Psychology, 97,* 290–306.

Council for the National Interest. (2006). *Poll: Forty percent of American voters believe the Israel lobby has been a key factor in going to war in Iraq and now confronting Iran.* Retrieved from http://www.cnionline.org/learn/polls/czand-lobby/index2.htm

Fathi, N. (2006, December 12). Iran opens conference on Holocaust. *New York Times.* Retrieved from http://www.nytimes.com/12/12/world/middleeast/12holocaust

Federal Bureau of Investigation. (2013). *Hate crime statistics, 2013.* Retrieved from http://www.fbi.gov/about-us/cjis/ucr/hate-crime/2013/topic-pages/incidents-and-offenses/incidentsandoffenses_final

Friedman, M. L., Friedlander, M. L., & Blustein, D. L. (2005). Toward an understanding of Jewish identity: A phenomenological study. *Journal of Counseling Psychology, 52,* 77–83.

Ginsberg, F., & Sinacore, A. L. (2013). Counseling Jewish women: A phenomenological study. *Journal of Counseling and Development, 91*, 131–139.

Goldberg, J. J. (2000, May 5). A portrait of American Jews. *Jewish Journal*, pp. 1–2.

Goldstein, L. (2013). Poll shows major shift in identity of U.S. Jews. *New York Times*. Retrieved from http://www.nytimes.com/2013/10/01/us/poll-shows-major-shift-in-identity-of-us-jews.html?pagewanted=print

Hall, S. (2006). *Judith Regan goes down fighting.* Retrieved from http://www.eonline.com/print/index.jsp?uuid=1486440990ae-45e6

Hinrichsen, G. A. (2006). Why multicultural issues matter for practitioners working with older adults. *Professional Psychology: Research and Practice, 37*, 29–35.

Jamieson, A. (2014). *Hate crimes spike against Jews, Muslims: NYPD.* Retrieved from http://nypost.com/2014/09/11/hate-crimes-spike-against-jews-muslims-nypd/

Langman, P. F. (1999). *Jewish issues in multiculturalism: A handbook for educators and clinicians.* Northvale, NJ: Jason Aronson.

Looft, C. (2015). *5 European Jews on the wave of anti-Semitic attacks, and what it means for their future.* Retrieved from http://nymag.com/daily/intelligencer/2015/02/5-european-jews-on-the-anti-semitic-attacks.html

Miller, L., Barton, Y. A., Mazur, M., & Lovinger, R. J. (2014). Psychotherapy with Conservative and Reform Jews. In P. S. Richards & A. E. Bergin (Eds.), *Handbook of psychotherapy and religious diversity* (2nd ed., pp. 257–283). Washington, DC: American Psychological Association.

Na, S., Kleiman, S., Poolokasingham, G., & Spanierman, L. (2014, August). *Examining the experiences of microaggressions among Jewish undergraduates.* Poster session presented at the annual convention of the American Psychological Association, Washington, DC.

Pew Research Center. (2013). *A portrait of Jewish Americans.* Retrieved from http://www.pewforum.org/2013/10/01/chapter-1-population-estimates/

Politi, D. (2015). *Israel's Netanyahu urges "mass immigration" of Jews after Denmark shooting.* Retrieved from http://www.slate.com/blogs/the_slatest/2015/02/15/benjamin_netanyahu_urges_mass_immigration_of_jews_to_israel_after_denmark.html

Priester, P. E., Jones, J. E., Jackson-Bailey, C. M., Jordan, E. X., Jana-Masri, A., & Metz, A. J. (2008). An analysis of content and instructional strategies in multicultural counseling courses. *Journal of Multicultural Counseling and Development, 36*, 29–39.

Rich, T. R. (2011). *Judaism 101.* Retrieved from http://www.jewfaq.org/

Rosen, D. D., Rebeta, J. L., & Zalman Rothschild, S. Z. (2014). Culturally competent adaptation of cognitive-behavioural therapy for psychosis: Cases of Orthodox Jewish patients with messianic delusions. *Mental Health, Religion & Culture, 17*, 703–713.

Rosmarin, D. H., Pirutinsky, S., Pargament, K. I., & Krumrei, E. J. (2009). Are religious beliefs relevant to mental health among Jews? *Psychology of Religion and Spirituality, 1*, 180–190.

Schlosser, L. Z. (2006). Affirmative psychotherapy for American Jews. *Psychotherapy: Theory, Research, Practice, Training, 43*, 424–435.

Schlosser, L. Z. (2009a). *Microaggressions in everyday life: The American Jewish experience.* Retrieved from http://bjpa.org/Publications/downloadPublication.cfm?PublicationID=5615

Schlosser, L. Z. (2009b). *A multidimensional model of American Jewish identity.* Retrieved from http://bjpa.org/Publications/downloadPublication.cfm?PublicationID=5620

Schlosser, L. Z., Safran, R. S., Suson, R. A., Dettle, K., & Dewey, J.J.H. (2013). The assessment, diagnosis, and treatment of mental disorders among American Jews. In F. A. Paniagua & A.-M. Yamada (Eds.), *Handbook of multicultural mental health: Assessment and treatment of diverse populations* (2nd ed., pp. 347–366). San Diego, CA.: Elsevier Academic Press.

Schnall, E. (2006). Multicultural counseling and the Orthodox Jew. *Journal of Counseling and Development, 84*, 276–282.

Shapiro, E. (2006). *Civil rights and wrongs.* Retrieved from http://www.myjewishlearning .com/history_community/Modern

Weinrach, S. G. (2002). The counseling profession's relationship to Jews and the issues that concern them: More than a case of selective awareness. *Journal of Counseling and Development, 80*, 300–314.

Weiss, P. (2013). *"I'm anti-Zionist," Helen Thomas declared, in twilight of long career.* Retrieved from http://mondoweiss.net/2013/07/helen-thomass -anti-zionist-statements#sthash.7x6gx0ei .dpuf

Younis, M. (2009). *Muslim Americans exemplify diversity, potential.* Retrieved from http:// www.gallup.com/poll/116260/Muslim- Americans-Exemplify-Diversity-Potential.aspx

Zollman, J. W. (2006). *Three waves of immigration.* Retrieved from http://www.myjewishlearning .com/history_community/Modern

PART VIII

Counseling and Special Circumstances Involving Other Multicultural Populations

Counseling Individuals with Disabilities

The mother of a child with Down syndrome explains how hurtful words can be. Use of expressions such as "spaz," "lame," "brain dead," "gimp," or "cripple" is demoralizing and communicates the message that it is okay to use this type of demeaning description. (Hertzog, 2010)

Members of the deaf community view deafness not as a disability but as a difference in human experience. Many have a positive attitude towards deafness and generally do not consider it a condition that needs to be "fixed" and, therefore, may oppose technological innovations such as cochlear implants. (Konig, 2013)

A 77-year-old woman has been on kidney dialysis for 10 years; she also has seizures, arthritis, and significant hearing loss. Communication with the social worker is not going well due to the woman's impaired hearing. The daughter explains that her mother has hearing aids but does not wear them because they hurt her ears. The social worker directs all her questions to the daughter, leaving the mother wondering what is being discussed. (Desselle & Proctor, 2000)

People often lack understanding and do not know how to respond to people with disabilities. Attitudes toward individuals with disabilities may be disdainful and dismissive, or overly protective or sympathetic. In the third vignette, the social worker was talking to the daughter as if the mother were not present. The daughter felt frustrated and responded,

You are not even trying to communicate with my mother. . . .She can understand you if you look at her and speak slowly and clearly. . . .Imagine how you would feel if you and your spouse went to the doctor to consult about a major surgery you were scheduled for and the doctor directed the conversation only to your spouse as if you were not intelligent enough to know what was being discussed. (Desselle & Proctor, 2000, p. 277)

There are about 56.7 million individuals with some level of disability (physical or mental), of whom over half have a disability that severely affects daily functioning (Brault, 2012). Of the 72.3 million families in the United States, about 21 million have at least one member with a disability. Rates of disability are higher among African Americans (22.2%) and American Indian/Alaska Native groups (27%) compared with non-Hispanic Whites (16.2%) (Cornish, Gorgens, Olkin,

Palomibi, & Abels, 2008). Because of the traumatic brain injuries incurred in the wars in Iraq and Afghanistan, the incidence of individuals with physical disabilities is increasing (Terrio, Nelson, Betthauser, Harwood, & Brenner, 2011).

Women are more likely to experience a physical disability than men; further, women with a physical disability are much more likely to experience depression than women in the general population (Brown, 2014) and are also at risk for abuse (Robinson-Whelen et al., 2010). In children, disability is more common in boys and children from low-income families (Sullivan, 2009). Children with disabilities are more likely to be subjected to maltreatment, including neglect; physical, sexual, or emotional abuse; or bullying (Jones et al., 2012; Zablotsky, Bradshaw, Anderson, & Law, 2014).

Individuals with severe disability have high unemployment and poverty rates (U.S. Census Bureau, 2010). Only 20% of those with disabilities are employed vs 69% of those without disabilities (U.S. Department of Labor, 2015). Individuals with disabilities have significantly lower rates of college completion compared to people without disabilities (Barber, 2012). Up to 90% of individuals with psychiatric disabilities are unemployed—the highest unemployment of all disability groups (Larson et al., 2011).

In the following sections we offer background information about individuals with disabilities, discuss the challenges often faced by these individuals, and consider their implications in treatment. Remember that disabilities vary greatly in terms of severity as well as the specific condition involved. Therefore, applicability of the information presented needs to be considered for each client.

CHARACTERISTICS AND STRENGTHS

In the following section, we will consider the *Americans with Disabilities Act,* myths regarding individuals with disabilities, models of disabilities, and characteristics and strengths associated with this population.

The Americans with Disabilities Act

In 1980, just five days before entering college, Fred Maahs sustained an injury while diving that left him paralyzed by his chest down. After months of recovery, he had to find a different college; it did not have wheelchair accessibility. On his first job located on the second floor with no elevator, two friends had to carry him up and down

> *the stairs. Maahs would find many fewer environmental restrictions today with curb cuts, ramps, elevators, and designated parking spots. (Associated Press, 2015)*

The *Americans with Disabilities Act* (ADA), signed into law in 1990, prohibits discrimination against people with disabilities in employment, transportation, public accommodation, communications, and governmental activities and ensures that buildings, facilities, and transit vehicles are accessible and usable by people with disabilities. Its passage was speeded up when hundreds of individuals with disabilities demonstrated in front of the Capitol building in Washington, D.C. To demonstrate the barriers they faced, dozens left their wheelchairs and crawled up the 83 steps to the building (Michaels, 2015).

The ADA defines *disability* as "a physical or mental impairment that substantially limits one or more of the major life activities of such individual." It protects individuals with intellectual impairment, hearing or vision impairment, orthopedic conditions, learning disabilities, speech impairment, HIV/AIDS, and other health or physical conditions. Psychiatric disorders covered include major depression, bipolar disorder, panic and obsessive-compulsive disorders, some personality disorders, schizophrenia, and rehabilitation from drug addiction.

Under the ADA, employers are allowed to inquire about candidates' ability to perform the job but not about their *disability*. Employers are not allowed to discriminate against an individual with a *disability* during the person's employment or in regard to promotion if the individual is otherwise qualified; similarly, employers cannot use tests that will cause individuals to be screened out because of a *disability*. Additionally, employers are required to make reasonable accommodations for people with disabilities.

Although the ADA has improved opportunities for employment by individuals with disabilities, the law has been whittled away by court decisions that have supported businesses rather than people with disabilities. For these reasons, the National Council on Disability has indicated a need to "restore the original intent" of the ADA (American Association of People with Disabilities, 2006).

Implications

Mental health professionals should keep abreast of federal and state *disability* laws, including statutes affecting the rights of individuals with disabilities in school and work settings. It is important for therapists to make sure that they do not provide unequal service or deny treatment to clients with disabilities; if the individual requires treatment outside your area of specialization, you can help facilitate a referral to a more qualified provider. Also, be alert for criteria that may screen out or disadvantage clients with disabilities, such as requiring a driver's license for payment by check. Policies, practices, and procedures in your office can be modified to take into consideration those with disabilities, such as ensuring that service animals are permitted in your building.

You may need to provide auxiliary aids and services, such as readers, sign-language interpreters, Braille materials, large-print materials, and videotapes or audiotapes to facilitate communication with some clients. Evaluate your office for structural and architectural barriers that prevent individuals from getting the services they need. Evaluate the accessibility of your office, including availability of ramps, parking spaces, reachable elevator control buttons, and wide doorways.

Myths Regarding Individuals with Disabilities

There are many myths associated with people with disabilities (Council for Students with Disabilities, 2006; LSU Office of Disability Services, 2011):

1. *Most are in wheelchairs.* Among the millions of people with disabilities, only about 10% use wheelchairs, crutches, or walkers. Most have more invisible disabilities, such as cardiovascular problems, arthritis and rheumatism, back and spine problems, hearing impairment, asthma, epilepsy, neurodevelopmental disorders (e.g., academic or intellectual impairment), and mental illness.

2. *People with disabilities are a drain on the economy.* It is true that many individuals of working age with disabilities are not working. However, the majority of those who are unemployed want to work. Discrimination often hampers their efforts to join the workforce.

3. *Employees with disabilities have a higher absentee rate than employees without disabilities.* Studies have found that employees with disabilities may actually have fewer attendance problems than nondisabled employees.

4. *The greatest barriers to people with disabilities are physical ones.* In actuality, negative attitudes and stereotypes are the greatest impediments and the most difficult to change.

5. *Persons who have disabilities are brave and courageous.* Individuals with disabilities react to situations like anyone else does. They demonstrate a variety of emotional reactions in adapting to their condition. Some adapt well, whereas others have more difficulty coping.

As mentioned previously, not all disabilities are apparent. Individuals with "invisible" disabilities (e.g., many mental disorders or physical conditions such as traumatic brain injury) may be responded to with frustration and resentment from friends, family members, and employers. When an individual looks healthy, others may not believe the person has a *disability* and may blame the individual for the difficulties that he or she displays. With a visible *disability*, prejudice and discrimination can occur, but accommodations are more likely to be made.

However, with a less visible disabling condition, such as a traumatic brain injury, misattributions are common (e.g., blaming difficulties in recovery on the individual's personality or unwillingness to cooperate). There may also be unrealistic hopes for full recovery. Invisible disabilities can be assessed by consulting with family and friends about the client's pre-injury behaviors, abilities, personality, and attitudes to determine whether the changes in these characteristics are due to the injury. If this is the case, the counselor can educate family members about the nature of the condition and explain how unrealistic expectations sometimes develop with unobservable injuries (McClure, 2011).

Models of Disability

There are three models of *disability*, each influencing societal perceptions of disabling conditions and possible treatment strategies (Artman & Daniels, 2010; Olkin, 1999). First, the *moral model* focuses on the "defect" as representing some form of sin or moral lapse. The *disability* may be perceived as a punishment or a test of faith. The individual or family members may respond with feelings of shame and responsibility. In some cultures, disabilities are believed to result from such factors as evil spirits, curses, or retribution from unhappy ancestors. Second, the *medical model* regards *disability* as a defect or loss of function that resides in the individual. Action is taken to cure or rehabilitate the condition. In some cultural groups, intervention targets rebalancing mind-body disharmony. The *medical model* has been responsible for many technological advances and treatments targeting a variety of conditions. Additionally, this approach dismisses the notion that moral issues have caused the *disability*. Third, the *minority model* views *disability* as an external problem involving an environment that is filled with negative societal attitudes and that fails to accommodate the needs of individuals with special needs. This perspective emphasizes the oppression, prejudice, and discrimination encountered by individuals who are disabled—experiences very similar to those of other minority groups.

Implications

Much of the research indicates that empowering individuals and caregivers increases life satisfaction. Unfortunately, the stress and prejudice associated with disabilities increase the risk for psychiatric or substance abuse problems (Turner, Lloyd, & Taylor, 2006). If mental health issues appear to be related to the *disability*, it is important to identify the way the *disability* is viewed by the client and by family members; such information may influence problem definition and intervention strategies. If the *disability* is seen as a moral issue (e.g., a test of faith), religious support may be an important component of the treatment process. Goals may include reducing guilt, giving meaning to the experience, generating support from the religious community, and developing problem-solving approaches.

From the *medical model* perspective, the client (or family) may want to focus on improving the client's condition, using technology or other interventions to help "normalize" functioning. Mental health professionals not only can help clients and family members obtain technological resources but can also enhance independent living skills and advocate for appropriate accommodations in school or work environments.

Incorporating perspectives from the *minority model* can be useful; counselors can emphasize how societal attitudes play a large role in the problems faced by individuals with disabilities and focus on environmental supports directed at maximizing the potential of the client. An emphasis on self-improvement and self-advocacy can help inoculate clients against societal prejudices and discrimination and help protect their self-esteem.

Life Satisfaction

> *I should have picked up the pieces and made the adjustment, and not dwell on it. . . . The problem is the rest of the world is dwelling on it. . . this place won't hire you and this company won't insure you and that potential lover won't look at you. . . . So that reopens the wound*

maybe twenty times a day and yet you're supposed to have made the adjustment. (Noonan et al., 2004, p. 72)

Because of an auto accident, Gary Talbot went from being an "able-bodied man to able-bodied wheelchair user." He evaluates his life this way: "I don't like the fact that I can't walk down the street or go jogging or climb a hill or ride a bike. [But] there's so much I can do and that I've been able to do that I just wouldn't change anything about my life." (Rosenbaum, 2010)

Ratings of life satisfaction among individuals with disabilities tend to be lower than those without disabilities. However, these ratings depend on the type of *disability* and the timing of the ratings. Some individuals adjust well, whereas others remain chronically distressed. In one study of the life satisfaction of people with traumatic spinal cord injuries, 37% indicated they were "very satisfied" and 31% "somewhat satisfied" with their lives. This compares to 50% "very satisfied" and 40% "somewhat satisfied" among the general population. An interesting aspect of the study was that those who perceived themselves as "in control" reported the greatest satisfaction (Chase, Cornille, & English, 2000). Similarly, in a longitudinal study of 307 individuals who were "severely" handicapped with a reduced capacity to work, life satisfaction was reduced in the first year but rose to preinjury levels by the fourth year. Those who were most likely to improve had the personality characteristic of "agreeableness," an attribute associated with the ability to access and cultivate social support. Thus, helping clients develop or maximize social skills may enhance recovery (Boyce & Wood, 2011).

Having close social relationships and paid employment are also associated with increased life satisfaction (Crompton, 2010). Individuals with disabilities often rate activities such as communication, thinking, and relating socially as more important than being able to walk or to dress oneself. Unfortunately, many health professionals display a negative attitude toward *disability*. Only 18% of physicians and nurses imagined that they would be glad to be alive if they had a high-level spinal cord injury; in sharp contrast, 92% of those with this condition reported satisfaction with their lives (Gerhart, Koziol-McLain, Lowenstein, & Whiteneck, 1994).

Implications

Mental health and health care providers often underestimate the potential quality of life for individuals with disabilities. They may accept signs of depression or suicidal thoughts as normal because of their low expectations regarding life opportunities for this population. The research seems to show that many individuals with disabilities feel satisfied with their lives and that increasing their sense of control is important. Self-efficacy can be enhanced by encouraging as much personal control and decision making as possible. If depressive or suicidal thoughts or wishes surface, they should be addressed. Some support the right of individuals with disabilities to engage in assisted suicide. However, other organizations argue that individuals with disabilities are an oppressed group and express concern that they may be coerced to end their lives (Coleman, 2015).

Sexuality and Reproduction

> In response to intrusive questions regarding her intimate experiences, poet Kelsey Warren, who uses a wheelchair, replied "Cripple copulation may be slightly more complicated, but it is always climactic" (Zeilinger, 2015).

Men and women with disabilities often express concerns over sexual functioning and reproduction. They worry about their sexual attractiveness and how to relate to or find a partner. Some may not know whether it is possible to have children or may have questions about the genetic implications of procreating. Mental health professionals who are uncomfortable with these topics may minimize or overlook these areas of concern.

Implications

Clearly, both clients and therapists need to be educated on these subjects as they relate to specific disabilities. Many individuals who have a *disability* receive the societal message that they should not be sexual or that they are sexually unattractive. This concern should be addressed and assessed both individually and, where applicable, for couples. Therapists can emphasize that sexual relationships are based on communication and emotional responsiveness to one another and can help individuals or couples develop new ways of achieving sexual satisfaction. Prior perspectives regarding sexuality may have to be replaced with new ones.

Sexual pleasure is possible even with the loss of sensation in the genitals that occurs with spinal cord injuries. Among men with spinal cord injuries, some are able to attain an erection and ejaculate, although they may have to learn new forms of stimulation (Klebine & Lindsey, 2007). Many women with spinal cord injuries are still capable of orgasms and sexual pleasure from stimulation of the genitals or other parts of the body (Perrouin-Verbe, Courtois, Charvier, & Giuliano, 2013). Such injury also does not preclude the ability to become pregnant or deliver a child.

Spirituality and Religiosity

Spirituality and religious beliefs can be a source of inner strength and support. One woman with a *disability* wrote, "It sort of helps me to identify myself, thinking I am a woman created by God and I am so precious and I am so loved and I have so much beauty inside of me" (Nosek & Hughes, 2001, p. 23). Religion and spirituality (connection to a higher power) are associated with increased life satisfaction and functional ability for individuals with traumatic brain injuries (Waldron-Perrine et al., 2011).

Implications

The mental health professional should determine the role, if any, that religious beliefs or spirituality play in the life of a client with a *disability*. The spirituality of the woman in the previous example enhanced her sense of self. Such beliefs can be a source of support for clients and their caregivers. Therapists can ask clients about their religious or spiritual beliefs and how their beliefs help them confront challenges; counselors can then incorporate these beliefs into treatment (Waldron-Perrine et al., 2011). In some cases, individuals may believe that their *disability* is a punishment from God or may blame God for not preventing the injury. These issues should also be addressed and resolved. Therapists can consult with or refer to religious leaders when working with clients who are attempting to come to terms with a *disability*.

Strengths

> *Many individuals with disabilities who have lived through natural disasters show resiliency and adaptation. Instead of responding, "Where were they when we needed them?" they were more likely to think, "What are my possibilities? What options do I have?" (Fox, White, Rooney, & Cahill, 2010, p. 237)*

Because of the variety of disabilities and because individuals with disabilities can come from any population, we will focus on personal characteristics that enhance daily living and satisfaction with life. Individuals with traumatic brain injuries who feel a connection to a higher power show greater life satisfaction and functional ability. Among those with spinal cord injuries, coping strategies, hope, and optimism are associated with a higher quality of life (Kortte, Gilbert, Gorman, & Wegener, 2010). Qualities such as creativity, resilience, self-control, self-advocacy and the ability to make positive connections with others and find meaning in life are strengths that can be tapped in the therapy process (Wehmeyer, 2014). Many individuals already possess these strengths; however, these attributes can also be developed or enhanced in counseling by focusing on changing the client's and the client's significant others' perceptions of the *disability*. Outcome is enhanced by improving self-confidence and finding and developing ways to empower the client (Shallcross, 2011) and encourage active decision making (Artman & Daniels, 2010).

For some, the development of a "*disability* identity" or a positive affirmation about the *disability* may enhance self-image. This may include association with the *disability* community; confronting discrimination and prejudice; and advocacy to reduce constraints—for example, by eliminating physical barriers that hamper access. Those with a *disability* identity often adapt to and view their *disability* as a valuable experience rather than a decrement. This perspective has been associated with lower distress levels among individuals with multiple sclerosis (Bogart, 2015). Others can have a positive self-identity even in the absence of an emotional and social connection to the *disability* community. Counselors need to listen to what their clients need rather than force clients into any specific direction in relation to their *disability* (Dunn & Burcaw, 2013).

In general, finding meaning in one's experience is associated with better adjustment and cognitive adaptation. Individuals facing a life-changing *disability* benefit when they embrace the opportunity to develop a new perspective on life, or view their changed life circumstances as a signal to slow down or a chance to change their lives for the better. In contrast, some individuals do not search for meaning in their experiences, yet still make a good adjustment to life. If a client is engaged in the search for meaning, a counselor can help the person with the process. However, attempting to encourage such inquiry in a client who is not searching for meaning may be counterproductive (Davis & Novoa, 2013).

SPECIFIC CHALLENGES

In the following sections we consider challenges faced by individuals with disabilities and consider their implications in treatment. Remember that these are generalizations and that their applicability needs to be assessed for each client.

Prejudice and Discrimination

Ableism is an all-too-common discriminatory practice in which individuals without disabilities are favored or given preferential treatment, thereby implying that those with a *disability* are somehow inferior (Keller & Galgay, 2010). Additionally, individuals who have disabilities may be evaluated based on an insidious deficit perspective (i.e., a belief that something is wrong with them). For example, employers believe that individuals with physical disabilities are less competent than individuals without a *disability* (Wang, Barron, & Hebl, 2010). Rohmer and Louvet (2009) make the point that "visible *disability* can be considered a superordinate social category" (p. 76); that is, *disability* appears to be a highly salient characteristic. For example, individuals with observable physical disabilities are often referred to using language such as "confined to a wheelchair" or "wheelchair bound" (Artman & Daniels, 2010).

Prejudicial terms such as *retarded*, *lame*, or *crazy* are also used without conscious awareness of the impact of these words on individuals with disabilities. Other reactions may be a result of not understanding the nature of specific disabilities. For example, most people without hearing loss do not understand that hearing aids can amplify all sounds, resulting in jumbled hearing, which is why individuals with hearing impairment may choose not to wear them. The public often has low expectations for individuals with disabilities and assumes that *disability* in one area also affects other skills. Additionally, able-bodied individuals often do not consider the structural and psychological barriers that individuals with disabilities have to face.

Implications

It is important for counselors to understand that individuals with disabilities are people first; like members of any group, they may demonstrate a wide range of functional difficulties as well as varying accomplishments. Mental health professionals need to actively assist individuals with disabilities to maximize their educational and employment opportunities. Approximately 9% of students enrolled in post-secondary educational institutions have some form of *disability* (Haller, 2006). Mental health professionals can prepare these students for success at the college level by teaching them to be self-advocates, encouraging them to alert their professors to their *disability* status and request course accommodations if needed.

The greatest prejudice may occur with hidden disabilities, such as psychiatric conditions. As a person with schizophrenia stated, "I don't want to tell anybody, because people who aren't ill, they do have a tendency sometimes to treat you different. . . We've got to disguise ourselves a lot" (Goldberg, Killeen, & O'Day, 2005, p. 463). Educating employers and workplace colleagues about specific conditions can sometimes allay fears (Law, 2011) as well as address false stereotypes associated with disabilities (Mizrahi, 2014). Independence for individuals with intellectual disabilities or severe mental health issues can be encouraged by teaching clients skills such as interviewing for jobs, managing money, doing laundry, or performing other daily living skills (Ericksen-Radtke & Beale, 2001).

Mental health professionals need to recognize that they are also subject to *disability* prejudice and address any discomfort they may have with disabilities. Several suggestions are helpful (American Psychological Association, 2001; Landsberger & Diaz, 2010):

1. Instead of thinking about a "disabled person," change the focus and use the phrase "person living with a *disability*." This emphasizes the individual rather than the limitation.

2. Do not sensationalize *disability* by referring to the achievements of well-known individuals with disabilities as "superhuman" or "extraordinary." Such references create unfair expectations. Most individuals with disabilities have the same range of skills as do individuals without disabilities

3. Avoid the use of phrases that evoke pity and conjure up a nonfunctional status, such as "afflicted with," "suffering from," or "a victim of."

4. Respond to individuals with a *disability* according to their skills, personality, and other personal attributes rather than their *disability*. Increase your understanding of the individual's specific condition and related resources, but take care not to assume that the *disability* is a primary concern. (See Table 22.1 for additional suggestions about working with clients with various disabilities.)

TABLE 22.1 Things to Remember When Interacting with Individuals with Disabilities

1. People with physical disabilities:

   - Ask if assistance is required before providing it; if your offer is accepted, ask for instructions on how to help and then follow them.

   - Do not use or move items such as wheelchairs, crutches, and canes without permission. They are considered part of the individual's personal space. Address the individual directly; it is important to attend to the client rather than someone who might have accompanied him or her.

   - Sit at eye level to facilitate comfort in communication.

   - Make certain there is easy access to your office.

2. People with vision loss:

   - Identify yourself and anyone else who is present when greeting the client. If the individual does not extend a hand, offer a verbal welcome.

   - Offer the use of your arm to guide—rather than steer or push—the individual.

   - Give verbal instructions to facilitate navigation.

   - If a service dog is present, do not pet or play with the dog.

   - Ask about the client's preference regarding presentation of information (e.g., large print, Braille, audiotapes).

   - Let the individual know if you are moving about or if the conversation is to end.

   - Give verbal cues when offering a seat. Place the individual's hand on the back of the chair, and he or she will not need further help.

3. People who are deaf or hard of hearing:

   - Ask about the individual's preferred communication (some use American Sign Language and identify culturally with the deaf community, whereas others may prefer to communicate orally, read lips, or rely on residual hearing).

   - Address the individual directly, rather than a person accompanying the client.

   - Realize that talking very loud may not enhance communication.

   - To get attention, call the person by name. If there is no response, lightly touch the individual on the arm or shoulder.

   - Do not pretend to understand if you do not.

   - Use certified interpreters to facilitate communication; their role is to relay information.

   - Try to avoid using family members as interpreters.

   - Make direct eye contact, and keep your face and mouth visible.

4. People with speech impediments:

   - Allow the individual to finish speaking before you speak.

   - Realize that communication may take longer, and plan accordingly. Do not rush.

   - Face the individual, and give full eye contact.

   - Address the individual directly.

   - Do not pretend to understand if you do not.

   - When appropriate, use yes-or-no questions.

   - Check with the client, if needed, to ensure understanding.

   - Remember that a speech impediment does not mean the client has limited intelligence.

Source: Adapted from United Cerebral Palsy (2001) and New York State Department of Health (2009).

Supports for Individuals with Disabilities

In the past, programs for persons with neurodevelopmental disabilities (e.g., autism, intellectual impairment, learning disabilities) were limited to efforts at "rehabilitation" rather than assistance in maximizing potential and developing independent living skills. There has been gradual recognition that deficiencies in experiences and opportunities can significantly limit an individual's development and that services are most effective when they enable independence, self-determination, and productive participation in society. To accomplish this task, it is important for students with disabilities to complete school and learn job skills. Many schools offer vocational educational programs and school-to-work transition programs. Such programs assess the student's skills and interests and provide a curriculum tailored to needed job skills as well as general vocational skills (Levinson & Palmer, 2005). Online sources such as the *Services for Adults with Disabilities* provide information on specific programs to help develop basic skills needed in employment and *DO-IT (Disabilities, Opportunities, Internetworking, and Technology)* seeks to increase participation of individuals with disabilities in academic programs and careers.

Many school-to-work transition programs, including those that provide students with disabilities the opportunity to learn work-related skills through local employment opportunities, have shown promising results (District of Columbia Public Schools, 2011). Some programs for individuals with moderate to severe intellectual or physical disabilities provide prevocational orientations for both the family and the student. Information on job preparation and job expectations is provided, followed by skills training and then an internship in a local business, where employers give feedback on the individual's performance. Such programs have been successful both in helping youth with disabilities make the transition to employment or further education and by opening doors in the business community. Mentors can also play an important role in helping college students with disabilities achieve academic success. Many graduates attribute their academic success to significant relationships with a faculty member or special services staff member (Barber, 2012).

Implications

There has been a shift in the orientation of programs for people with disabilities from remediation or "making them as normal as possible" to identifying and strengthening interests and skills. Mental health professionals working with individuals with disabilities should be aware of programs offering educational and employment assistance. For example, the *ParentCenterHub.org* website is a repository of different resources for individuals with disabilities, such as *Organizations and Agencies in Your State; Employment; Postsecondary Education; Recreation; Independent Living; Assistive Technology; and Disability Living Online.* Media such as *Ability Magazine, Disability Scoop, e-Bility, New Mobility* (magazine for active wheelchair users) also provide useful information and support for individuals with disabilities. It is also important for mental health professionals to be aware of the ways current technology is enhancing the quality of life and employment opportunities for many individuals with disabilities. Vocational and support group information is easily accessible via the Internet.

Counseling Issues with Individuals with Disabilities

Helping professionals often display the same attitude as the general public toward individuals with disabilities and may feel uncomfortable or experience guilt or pity when working with this population. As when working with other oppressed groups, counselors must examine their own views in regard to clients with disabilities and identify and question any prejudicial assumptions. A client's *disability* should not be the sole focus of counseling. However, environmental contributions to the problems a client is experiencing (e.g., frustrations with architectural barriers or with negative stereotypes or prejudices) should be identified and addressed in counseling.

Implications

As with all clients, comprehensive, nonbiased assessment is essential for those who have disabilities. Kemp and Mallinckrodt (1996) point out some of the errors that can occur in assessment and counseling relationships with individuals with disabilities. First, errors of omission may be made. The counselor may fail to ask questions about critical aspects of the client's life because the assumption is made that the issue is unimportant owing to the presence of the *disability*. For example, sexuality and relationship issues may be ignored because of the belief that the individual lacks the ability or interest to pursue these intimacies. Affective issues may also be avoided, since the counselor may be uncomfortable addressing the impact of the *disability* on the client. The counselor may also display lowered expectations of the client's capabilities.

Second, errors of commission may occur. In such cases, counselors make the unjustified assumption that certain issues *should* be important because of the *disability*, when, in fact, they are not important issues for the client. Further, a therapist might inaccurately assume that personal problems faced by the client result from the *disability*. Career and academic counseling may become a focus even when it is not what the client wants to discuss. Therapists also make errors by not addressing the *disability* at all, encouraging dependency and the "sick" role, or failing to confront countertransference issues (e.g., wanting to "rescue" the client).

It is generally appropriate to ask a client about the *disability*, including any related concerns. The therapist can also ask if there are ways that the *disability* is part of the presenting problem. Such an approach allows the therapist to address the *disability* directly. In doing so, it is important not to succumb to the "spread" phenomenon that often exists with disabilities: believing that the *disability* encompasses unrelated aspects of the individual. If the *disability* is of recent origin, factors such as coping strategies, recent challenges, the possibility of self-blame for the injury, and the amount of social support available can be assessed.

Family Counseling

Family caregivers now operate as integral parts of the health care system and provide services that were once performed by professional health care providers. It is, therefore, important to help reduce the impact of stressors on caregivers and other family members. Additionally, emotional issues, such as distress, guilt, self-punishment, or anger, may need to be considered. Family members may feel angry about their caretaking responsibilities or somehow feel responsible for the disabling condition (Resch et al., 2010).

Implications

Clients with a *disability* and their family members can work together to create positive changes that enhance both client well-being and family functioning. Among family caregivers, attributes such as positive problem-solving skills, positive problem orientation, and coping strategies are associated with greater satisfaction for themselves and the individual with the *disability* (Elliot, Shewchuk, & Richards, 1999). One effective approach employed by caregivers was using problem-solving strategies when encountering difficulties; these caretakers learned to define the problem, generate and evaluate alternatives, implement solutions, and assess outcomes. This approach helped increase self-efficacy among family members and improved their ability to cope with stress.

Reframing can also be useful. Albert Ellis, the founder of rational-emotive therapy, faced the challenges of diabetes, tired eyes, deficient hearing, and other physical handicaps but successfully used cognitive approaches, such as reframing, to deal with his disabilities. For example, because he could not keep his eyes open for any length of time, he focused on the positive aspects of conducting therapy sessions with his eyes closed, telling himself that with his eyes shut he could (a) focus "unusually well" on his clients' verbalizations (e.g., tone of voice, hesitations), (b) more easily identify their irrational thoughts, (c) help clients feel more relaxed, and (d) serve as a healthy model of an individual with a *disability* (Ellis, 1997). Ellis was thus able to redefine his *disability* as a useful feature in conducting therapy.

IMPLICATIONS FOR CLINICAL PRACTICE

1. Identify your beliefs, assumptions, and attitudes about individuals with disabilities.

2. Understand the prejudice, discrimination, inconveniences, and barriers faced by individuals with physical disabilities and the problems faced by individuals with "invisible" disabilities.

3. Assess the impact of multiple sources of discrimination on ethnic minorities and other diverse populations with disabilities.

4. Redirect internalized self-blame for the *disability* to societal attitudes.

5. Employ necessary modifications to enhance communication, and address the client directly rather than through conversation with an accompanying individual.

6. Determine whether the *disability* is related to the presenting problem and, if so, identify whether the client adheres to the *moral model* (*disability* results from a moral lapse), *medical model* (*disability* is a physical limitation), or *minority model* (*disability* results from societal failure to accommodate individual differences).

7. Determine whether the *disability* will influence assessment or treatment strategies. If this is not an issue, continue with your usual methods of assessment and case conceptualization.

8. If formal tests are employed, provide appropriate accommodations. Interpret the results with care since standardization does not take into account various physical disabilities.

9. Recognize that family members and other social supports are important. When possible, include them in your assessment, case conceptualization, goal formation, and selection of techniques, but try not to use family members as interpreters for those with communication difficulties. Be aware that family members may not fully understand psychiatric issues or may be part of the problem (Ali, 2012).

10. Identify environmental changes or accommodations that may be needed, and then assist the client or family with necessary planning to implement changes.

11. Help family members reframe the problem so that family and client strengths can be identified. Focus on and reinforce the positive attributes of the client and family members.

12. Help both the client and family members develop self-advocacy skills.

13. Realize that mental health professionals may need to serve as advocates or consultants to initiate changes in academic and work settings.

14. Be aware of web resources and provide links to *disability*-related products such as computer accessibility, clothing, augmentative communication devices, legal and advocacy resources, job training, and educational resources.

SUMMARY

There are approximately 56.7 million individuals with some level of *disability* (physical or mental); among this group, over half have a *disability* that severely affects daily functioning. People often lack understanding and do not know how to respond to people with disabilities. Attitudes vary from being disdainful and dismissive to overly protective or sympathetic. *Ableism* is an all-too-common discriminatory practice in which individuals without disabilities are favored or given preferential treatment, thereby implying that those with a *disability* are somehow inferior. The 1990 *Americans with Disabilities Act* extended the federal mandate of nondiscrimination to individuals with disabilities and to state and local governments and the private sector. Because of the number of myths and beliefs about those with disabilities, counselors need to be informed in areas such as sexuality and reproduction, worker capabilities, resources available to aid their clients, and especially their own feelings of discomfort or bias around those with disabilities. Fourteen clinical implications for counselor practice are identified.

GLOSSARY TERMS

Ableism

Americans with Disabilities Act

Disability

Medical model

Minority model

Moral model

Rehabilitation approach

REFERENCES

Ali, S. (2012). Providing interpreters for patients with hearing disabilities: ADA Requirements. *Innovations in Clinical Neuroscience, 9,* 30–33.

American Association of People with Disabilities. (2006). Bipartisan legislation introduced to restore ADA protections. *AAPD News*, pp. 1, 3.

American Psychological Association. (2001). *Aging and human sexuality resource guide.* Washington, DC: Author.

Artman, L. K., & Daniels, J. A. (2010). Disability and psychotherapy practice: Cultural competence and practical tips. *Professional Psychology: Research and Practice, 41,* 442–448.

Associated Press. (2015). *Disabilities act has changed lives of millions 25 years after passage.* Retrieved from http://www.newsday.com/news/nation/americans-with-disabilities-act-has-changed-lives-25-years-after-passage-1.10677392

Barber, P. (2012). *College students with disabilities: what factors influence successful degree completion? A case study.* Retrieved from http://www .heldrich.rutgers.edu/sites/default/files/content/College_Students_DisabilitiesReport.pdf

Boyce. C. J., & Wood, A. M. (2011). Personality prior to disability determines adaptation: Agreeable individuals recover lost life satisfaction faster and more completely. *Psychological Science, 22,* 1397–1402.

Bogart, K. R. (2015). Disability identity predicts lower anxiety and depression in multiple sclerosis. *Rehabilitation Psychology, 60,* 105–109.

Brault, M. W. (2012) *Americans with Disabilities: 2010.* Washington, DC: U.S. Census Bureau.

Brown, R. L. (2014). Psychological distress and the intersection of gender and physical disability: Considering gender and disability-related risk factors. *Sex Roles, 71,* 171–181.

Chase, B. W., Cornille, T. A., & English, R. W. (2000). Life satisfaction among persons with spinal cord injuries. *Journal of Rehabilitation, 66,* 14–20.

Coleman, D. (2015). *Why do disability rights organizations oppose assisted suicide laws?* Retrieved from http://www.advocacymonitor.com/why-do-disability-rights-organizations-oppose-assisted-suicide-laws/

Cornish, J.A.E., Gorgens, K. A., Olkin, R., Palomibi, B. J., & Abels, A. V. (2008). Perspectives on ethical practice with people who have disabilities. *Professional Psychology: Research and Practice, 39*, 488–497.

Council for Students with Disabilities. (2006). *Myths about people with disabilities.* Retrieved from https://www.msu.edu/~csd/myths.html

Crompton, S. (2010). *Living with disability series: Life satisfaction of working-age women with disabilities.* Retrieved from http://www.statcan.gc.ca/pub/11–008-x/2010001/article/11124-eng.htm

Davis, C. G., & Novoa, D. C. (2013). Meaning-making following spinal cord injury: Individual differences and within-person change. *Rehabilitation Psychology, 58*, 166–177.

Desselle, D. C., & Proctor, T. K. (2000). Advocating for the elderly hard-of-hearing population: The deaf people we ignore. *Social Work, 45*, 277–281.

District of Columbia Public Schools. (2011). *School-to-work programs nearly triple enrollment, increase capacity for DCPS Special Education students.* Retrieved from http://www.dc.gov/DCPS/In+the+Classroom/Special+Education/Special+Education+News/School-to-work+Programs+Nearly+Triple+Enrollment,+Increase+Capacity+for+DCPS+Special+Education+Students

Dunn, D. S., & Burcaw, S. (2013). Disability identity: Exploring narrative accounts of disability. *Rehabilitation Psychology, 58*, 148–157.

Elliott, T. R., Shewchuk, R. M., & Richards, J. S. (1999). Caregiver social problem-solving abilities and family member adjustment to recent onset physical disability. *Rehabilitation Psychology, 44*, 104–123.

Ellis, A. (1997). Using rational emotive behavior therapy techniques to cope with disability. *Professional Psychology: Research and Practice, 28*, 17–22.

Ericksen-Radtke, M. M., & Beale, A. V. (2001). Preparing students with learning disabilities for college: Pointers for parents—part 2. *Exceptional Parent, 31*, 56–57.

Fox, M. H., White, G. W., Rooney, C., & Cahill, A. (2010). The psychosocial impact of Hurricane Katrina on persons with disabilities and independent living staff living on the American Gulf Coast. *Rehabilitation Psychology, 55*, 231–240.

Gerhart, K. A., Koziol-McLain, J., Lowenstein, S. R., & Whiteneck, G. G. (1994). Quality of life following spinal cord injury: Knowledge and attitudes of emergency care providers. *Annals of Emergency Medicine, 23*, 807–812.

Goldberg, S. G., Killeen, M. B., & O'Day, B. (2005). The disclosure conundrum: How people with psychiatric disabilities navigate employment. *Psychology, Public Policy, and Law, 11*, 463–500.

Haller, B. A. (2006). Promoting disability-friendly campuses to prospective students: An analysis of university recruitment materials. *Disability Studies Quarterly, 26*, 1–10.

Hertzog, J. (2010). *"I just didn't know": The power of language.* Retrieved from http://blog.govdelivery.com/usodep/2010/i-just-didnt-know-the-power-of-language.html

Jones, L., Bellis, M. A., Wood, S., Hughes, K., McCoy, E., Eckley, L., . . ., Officer, A. (2012). Prevalence and risk of violence against children with disabilities: A systematic review and meta-analysis of observational studies. *Lancet, 380*, 899–907.

Keller, R. M., & Galgay, C. E. (2010). Microaggressive experience of people with disabilities. In D. W. Sue (Ed.), *Microaggressions and marginality* (pp. 241–267). Hoboken, NJ: Wiley.

Kemp, N. T., & Mallinckrodt, B. (1996). Impact of professional training on case conceptualization of clients with a disability. *Professional Psychology: Research and Practice*, *27*, 378–385.

Klebine, P., & Lindsey, L. (2007). *Sexual function for men with spinal cord injury.* Retrieved from http://www.spinalcord.uab.edu/show.asp?durki=22405

Konig, J. (2013). Cognitive processing therapy with a prelingually deaf patient suffering from posttraumatic stress disorder. *Clinical Case Studies*, *12*, 73–90.

Kortte, K. B., Gilbert, M., Gorman, P., & Wegener, S. T. (2010). Positive psychological variables in the prediction of life satisfaction after spinal cord injury. *Rehabilitation Psychology*, *55*, 40–47.

Landsberger, S. A., & Diaz, D. R. (2010). Communicating with deaf patients: 10 tips to deliver appropriate care. *Current Psychiatry*, *9*, 36–37.

Larson, J. E., Ryan, C. B., Wassel, A. K., Kaszynski, K. L., Ibara, L., & Boyle, M. G. (2011). Analysis of employment incentives and barriers for individuals with psychiatric disabilities. *Rehabilitation Psychology*, *56*, 145–149.

Law, N. (2011). *Disability discrimination in the workplace on the rise.* Retrieved from http://www.disabled-world.com/disability/discrimination/workplace-law.php

Levinson, E. M., & Palmer, E. J. (2005). *Preparing students with disabilities for school-to-work transition and postschool life.* Retrieved from http://www.nasponline.org/resources/principals/Transition%20Planning%20WEB.pdf

LSU Office of Disability Services. (2011). *Dispelling myths about people with disabilities.* Retrieved from http://appl003.lsu.edu/slas/ods.nsf/$Content/Myths?OpenDocument

McClure, J. (2011). The role of causal attributions in public misconceptions about brain injury. *Rehabilitation Psychology*, *56*, 85–93.

Michaels, S. (2015). The Americans with Disabilities Act is turning 25. Watch the dramatic protest that made it happen. *Mother Jones.* Retrieved from http://www.motherjones.com/mojo/2015/07/americans-disabilities-act-capitol-crawl-anniversary?

Mizrahi, J. L. (2014). False stereotypes of people with disabilities hold employers back. *Huffington Post.* Retrieved from http://www.huffingtonpost.com/jennifer-laszlo-mizrahi/false-stereotypes-of-peop_b_5353818.html

New York State Department of Health (2009). People First: Communicating with and about People with Disabilities. Retrieved from https://www.health.ny.gov/publications/0951/

Noonan, B. M., Gallor, S. M., Hensler-McGinnis, N. F., Fassinger, R. E., Wang, S., & Goodman, J. (2004). Challenge and success: A qualitative study of the career development of highly achieving women with physical and sensory disabilities. *Journal of Counseling Psychology*, *51*, 68–80.

Nosek, M. A., & Hughes, R. B. (2001). Psychospiritual aspects of sense of self in women with physical disabilities. *Journal of Rehabilitation*, *67*, 20–25.

Olkin, R. (1999). *What psychotherapists should know about disability.* New York, NY: Guilford Press.

Perrouin-Verbe, B., Courtois, F., Charvier, K., & Giuliano, F. (2013). Sexuality of women with neurologic disorders. *Progressive Urology*, *23*, 594–600.

Resch, J. A., Mireles, G., Benz, M. R., Grenwelge, C., Peterson, R., & Zhang, D. (2010). Giving parents a voice: A qualitative study of the challenges experienced by parents of children with disabilities. *Rehabilitation Psychology*, *55*, 139–150.

Robinson-Whelen, S., Hughes, R. B., Powers, L. E., Oschwald, M., Renker, P., & Curry, M. A. (2010). Efficacy of a computerized abuse and safety assessment intervention for women with disabilities: A randomized controlled study. *Rehabilitation Psychology*, *55*, 97–107.

Rohmer, O., & Louvet, E. (2009). Describing persons with disability: Salience of disability, gender, and ethnicity. *Rehabilitation Psychology*, *54*, 76–82.

Rosenbaum, P. (2010). *Amazing success fueled by act of discrimination*. Retrieved from http://www.cnn.com/2010/LIVING/07/26/ada.talbot/?hpt=Sbin

Shallcross, L. (2011). Seeing potential, not disability. *Counseling Today*, *54*, 28–35.

Sleek, S. (1998, July). Mental disabilities no barrier to smooth and efficient work. *Monitor*, p. 15.

Sullivan, P. M. (2009). Violence exposure among children with disabilities. *Clinical Child and Family Psychological Review*, *12*, 196–216.

Terrio, H. P., Nelson, L. A., Betthauser, L. M., Harwood, J. E., & Brenner, L. A. (2011). Post-deployment traumatic brain injury screening questions: Sensitivity, specificity, and predictive values in returning soldiers. *Rehabilitation Psychology*, *56*, 26–31.

Turner, R. J., Lloyd, D. A., & Taylor, J. (2006). Physical disability and mental health: An epidemiology of psychiatric and substance disorders. *Rehabilitation Psychology*, *51*, 214–223.

United Cerebral Palsy. (2001). *Etiquette tips for people with physical disabilities*. Portland, OR: Author.

U.S. Census Bureau. (2010). *20th anniversary of Americans with Disabilities Act: July 26*. Retrieved from http://www.census.gov/newsroom/releases/archives/facts_for_features_special_editions/cb10-ff13.html

U.S. Department of Labor (2015). *Current disability employment statistics*. Retrieved from http://www.dol.gov/odep/

Waldron-Perrine, B., Rapport, L. J., Hanks, R. A., Lumley, M., Meachen, S.-J., & Hubbarth, P. (2011). Religion and spirituality in rehabilitation outcomes among individuals with traumatic brain injury. *Rehabilitation Psychology*, *56*, 107–116.

Wang, K., Barron, L. G., & Hebl, M. R. (2010). Making those who cannot see look best: Effects of visual resume formatting on ratings of job applicants with blindness. *Rehabilitation Psychology*, *55*, 68–73.

Wehmeyer, M. L. (2014). *The Oxford handbook of positive psychology and disability*. New York, NY: Oxford University Press.

Zablotsky, B., Bradshaw, C. P., Anderson, C. M., & Law, P. (2014). Risk factors for bullying among children with autism spectrum disorders. *Autism*, *18*, 419–427.

Zeilinger, J. (2015). *This poem reveals what it's like to have sex when you have a disability*. Retrieved from http://mic.com/articles/122159/poet-destroys-stereotypes-about-having-sex-with-a-disability

Counseling LGBT Individuals

Chapter Objectives

1. Learn the demographics and issues faced by LGBT individuals.

2. Identify counseling implications of the information provided for LGBT individuals.

3. Recognize strengths that are associated with LGBT individuals.

4. Know the special challenges faced by LGBT individuals.

5. Understand how the implications for clinical practice can guide assessment and therapy with LGBT individuals.

> *On June 26, 2015, The Supreme Court ruled 5–4 that same-sex couples have the right to marry. With the ruling, gay marriage became legal in all 50 states, affecting not only the right to marry but also the right to be recognized as a spouse or parent on birth and death certificates and other legal documents. (Hurley, 2015)*

> *A surgeon who spots a wedding ring asks if the patient's wife can take care of him after surgery, not realizing the man's spouse is actually a husband. . . . Staff members in a long-term care facility express puzzlement and even disgust about same-sex sexuality. . . . Emergency room personnel are alarmed when they discover the woman the hospital just admitted was once a man. (Clay, 2014, p. 46)*

> *L.G.B.T. youth need support from their families—not derision. If you tell a child or teenager they're not good enough, that they're worthless, that who they are is broken or wrong, that's abuse. (Valenti, 2015)*

> *Zoey Tur, who was told that she would never work again in news if she transitioned to a female, has been hired as a reporter for the "Inside Edition" television program. Interestingly, she says the most difficult part of becoming a woman was the loss of "male privilege." (Soopermexican, 2015)*

In this chapter we will discuss *lesbian, gay, bisexual,* and *transgender* (LGBT) Americans—individuals who have an affectional and/or sexual attraction to a person of the same sex (*gay* men and *lesbians*); individuals who have an affectional and/or sexual attraction to members of both sexes (*bisexuals*); and individuals whose gender identification is inconsistent with the gender they were assigned at birth (*transgender*). The acronym *LGBTQ* is sometimes used with this population. The *Q* represents individuals who identify as "*queer*" or who are questioning their sexuality.

About 3.5% of U.S. adults or 9 million Americans identify as *lesbian, gay,* or *bisexual* and 0.3% as *transgender*. In addition, about 19 million Americans have engaged in same-sex behaviors and around one-fourth of the adult population acknowledges some same-sex attraction (Gates, 2011). Higher percentages for LGBT are reported among millennials between the ages of 18 and 35. Of this group, 4% identified themselves as *bisexual*, 3% as *gay* or *lesbian,* and 1% as *transgender* (Public Relations Research Institute, 2014).

The mood of the country reveals contradictory attitudes and actions toward sexual minorities. Overall, there appears to be increased acceptance of LGBT individuals and their lifestyles. In 1985, 89% of the public indicated that they would be upset if their child told them that he or she was *gay* or *lesbian*; 9% would not be. To the same question in 2015, 39% responded that they would be upset but 57% would not be. Also, in the same poll, 63% indicated that "homosexuality should be accepted by society." However, strong negative attitudes and feelings toward *gay* people continue among older adults and White Evangelicals (Pew Research Center, 2015).

Changes are also occurring in societal views regarding *transgender* individuals. Their issues are also being discussed more openly as represented by television shows with *transgender* characters—such as "Transparent" and "Orange Is the New Black" (Leitsinger, 2015). The Pentagon's current regulation banning *transgender* individuals from serving in the military is undergoing reevaluation (AP, 2015). When receiving the Arthur Ashe Courage Award, Caitlin Jenner made a plea that people should be respected and accepted, especially the "thousands of kids coming to terms with who they are" (Melas, 2015). New York City is making it easier for *transgender* individuals to change the sex listed on their birth certificates, even without undergoing sex-change operations. This is also true in Oregon, Washington, California, Iowa, Vermont, and Washington, D.C. (Wong, 2014). President Obama signed a memorandum indicating that hospitals participating in Medicare or Medicaid programs "may not deny visitation privileges on the basis of race, color, national origin, religion, sex, *sexual orientation*, gender identity, or disability" and California Governor Jerry Brown signed a bill requiring schools to modify the social studies curricula to include the contributions of LGBT individuals (Lin, 2011).

Even with progress occurring on these fronts, however, discrimination and violence against sexual minorities continue. In this chapter, we focus on the identity development and strengths of LGBT individuals, as well as some of the major issues and challenges facing sexual minorities, including the coming-out process, societal misconceptions, and the stress associated with ongoing prejudice and discrimination.

CHARACTERISTICS AND STRENGTHS

Cross-gender behaviors and appearance are highly stigmatized in schools and in our society. LGBT individuals live in a *heterosexual* and *cisgender* society (i.e., a culture expecting "normative" gender behavior) where they face the challenge of developing a healthy self-identity in the midst of societal norms that view their *sexual orientation* or gender identification as "abnormal." This disharmony can significantly affect the transition from childhood to adolescence to adulthood, as well as family relationships and personal identity development. In the following sections we will consider the issues faced by LGBT individuals in these areas as well as strengths found in this population.

Sexual Identity Issues

Once LGBT individuals recognize *heterosexual* and *transgendered* societal realities, the discovery of being "different" can be agonizing. As one individual observed: "No matter how open-minded I believed my companion to be, the coming-out conversation was always excruciating. I was a sweaty, self-conscious mess, having no idea what reaction I would get" (Diehl, 2013). Awareness of *sexual orientation* for *gay* males and *lesbians* usually takes place in the early teens, with sexual experiences and self-identification typically occurring during the mid-teens and same-sex relationships beginning during the late teens or early 20s (Pew Research Center, 2013). In a longitudinal study of 156 *gay*, *lesbian*, and *bisexual* youth, 57% consistently self-identified as *gay/lesbian* and 15% consistently identified as *bisexual*, while 18% of *bisexuals* transitioned to *gay/lesbian* (Rosario, Schrimshaw, Hunter, & Braun, 2006). *Bisexual* individuals are much less likely to say that *sexual orientation* is a big part of who they are or to have come out to important people. They also report few instances of discrimination (Parker, 2015).

Gender identity is an even more important aspect of one's total being. *Transgender* people feel a marked incongruence between the gender with which they self-identify and the gender assigned to them based on their physical characteristics at birth. They often report feeling "different" at an early age. The *sexual orientation* of a *transgender* individual can be *heterosexual*, same-sex, or *bisexual* (Wester, McDonough, White, Vogel & Taylor, 2010). *Gender dysphoria*, a mental health condition defined in *DSM-5*, occurs when there is significant distress and impairment resulting from an incongruence between a person's gender identity and assigned gender. One activist described *gender dysphoria* as "one of the greatest agonies . . . when your anatomy doesn't match who you are inside" (Wright, 2001). Although *gender dysphoria* is still considered a mental disorder (American Psychiatric Association, 2013), *transgender* individuals are hoping that they can follow the successful path taken by the *gay* and *lesbian* movement and eventually eliminate such classification.

Because *transgender* individuals have a long-standing conviction that nature somehow placed them in the wrong body, they often wish to replace their physical sexual characteristics with those of the appropriate gender. Therefore, sex reassignment surgery is frequently considered. Such surgeries have produced variable results; many females who undergo sexual reassignment express satisfaction with the outcome of surgery, whereas males who change to female are less likely to feel satisfied. This may be because adjusting to life as a man is easier than adjusting to life as a woman, or perhaps because man-to-woman changes are more likely to produce negative reactions (Lawrence, 2008).

Many LGBT individuals struggle with accepting their self-identity, which they may perceive to contrast with society's definition of what is healthy. The struggle for identity involves one's internal perceptions, which likely contrast with external perceptions and the assumptions made by others about one's *sexual orientation*. This process is particularly complex for *transgender* individuals because their *sexual orientation* may be *heterosexual*, same sex, or *bisexual* (Wester, McDonough, White, Vogel, & Taylor, 2010). LGBT individuals can overcome these stressors when they learn to identify and combat internalized heterosexism, homophobia, or transphobia (Chaney et al., 2011). A resolution often occurs when the individual ceases struggling to be "straight" and begins to establish a new identity, self-concept, and understanding of what constitutes an authentic and meaningful life. During this period, individuals (and members of their families) often deal with issues of grief over letting go of the old, sometimes idealized, identity (Adelson, 2012).

Implications

Adolescence and early adulthood is a time of exploration and experimentation. Heterosexual activity does not mean one is a *heterosexual*, nor does same-sex activity indicate homosexuality. Many LGBT individuals describe feeling "different" from early childhood. When they begin to acknowledge their sexual or *transgender* identity, they soon confront the stigma associated with being *gay*, *lesbian*, *bisexual*, or *transgender*. Because of the discrimination and prejudice they have faced or anticipate, it is important for mental health professionals to take an affirming position that validates and helps normalize the individual's identity. Often the stress and depression experienced by LGBT individuals is promulgated by the cisgender and *heterosexual* nature of our society (Chaney et al., 2011).

Because of fear of the consequences of disclosure during their struggle with identity issues, LGBT youth (and adults) often face this process alone, without the potential support and nurturance of peers, parents, and other family members, or of others who have gone through the same struggle. Many pretend to be straight or avoid discussing sexuality. Mental health professionals can help LGBT individuals develop coping and survival skills and expand environmental supports, but first the individual needs to be comfortable disclosing his or her struggles and seeking such support.

LGBT Youth

LGBT youth who are questioning their *sexual orientation* face a variety of stressors. Discrimination and harassment in the school environment is common. In a large survey of middle and high school students, over 80% of LGBT students reported experiencing harassment at school in the past year and about two-thirds reported feeling unsafe because of their sexual or gender orientation. Nearly 40% of LGBT students reported being physically harassed, and over 18% had been physically assaulted in school because of their *sexual orientation*. Further, 55% were exposed to cyberbullying through text messages, emails, and Internet postings on social networking sites. Safety concerns led one-third of the LGBT students surveyed to skip school (Kosciw, Greytak, Bartkiewicz, Boesen, & Palmer, 2012).

LGBT youth are more likely than their *heterosexual* peers to attempt suicide, especially when they live in an unsupportive environment (Hatzenbuehler, 2011). Even higher rates of suicide attempts are found among Black and Latina/o LGBT youth (Meyer, Dietrich, & Schwartz, 2008). LGBT youth also have increased risk for substance use and abuse (S. E. McCabe, Hughes, Bostwick, West, & Boyd, 2009), especially when there is also a history of childhood abuse or victimization (H. T. McCabe, Wilsnack, West, & Boyd, 2010).

Implications

Mental health professionals need to address the problems of LGBT youth at both the systems and individual levels. To improve the school environment, professionals can advocate for inclusion of *gay* and *transgender* issues in the curriculum. They can also promote opportunities for social skill development relevant to LGBT youth, provision of adequate social services, and a nondiscriminatory school environment. Although most schools have policies that prohibit antigay discrimination or harassment, only 30% offer any education regarding sexual and gender diversity and less than 30% of school districts provide training for teachers and staff regarding challenges facing LGBT students (Rienzo, Button, Sheu, & Li, 2006). It is essential to encourage school personnel to consistently enforce policies that protect LGBT youth from harassment and violence. Programs promoting gay-straight alliances and anti-bullying policies not only reduce harassment but also reduce the risk of suicide (Hatzenbuehler, 2011).

Support groups that allow LGBT students to discuss their concerns in a safe and confidential environment are also important. LGBT youth need safe places to meet others and to socialize. Community-based supports such as hotlines; youth clubs; and such groups as Parents, Families, and Friends of Gays and Lesbians (PFLAG), the Trevor project, and Gay-Straight Alliances can be helpful. The Gender Spectrum provides resources in working with children and youth with gender issues. Such organizations defuse possible harassment and violence in schools and allow LGBT students to gain support and openly express their sexual identities (Valenti, 2015).

On the individual level, bullying can lead to an internalization of negative attitudes by LGBT youth and the development of dysfunctional shame-focused coping strategies such as social withdrawal, self-criticism, or self-harm. The counselor can help their clients to realize that they are not responsible for the bullying and replace negative strategies and cognitions with self-affirmations and positive coping strategies (Greene, Britton, & Fitts, 2014).

LGBT Couples and Families

As opposition to gay marriage has eased over the past decade, the number of openly *gay* and *lesbian* couples has nearly doubled to about 650,000. Approximately one out of five same-sex couples are raising children (Yen, 2011). It is estimated that about 110,000 children lived with *gay* parents in 2012. This is less than 1% of children living in all households (Alper, 2012). Many LGBT couples and individuals have a keen interest in becoming parents, and their legal right to adopt a child is now supported by 63% of Americans according to a Gallop Poll (Swift, 2014).

However, the right of *gays* and *lesbians* to adopt children has been challenged in many states. Some religious agencies have gone so far as to discontinue adoption services to protest state laws allowing *gay* men and *lesbian* women to adopt children (Stern, 2014). Many adoption agencies still have discriminatory practices.

As one adoption worker observed, "I have seen a *gay* couple inquire about 30 children and not get one answer back of interest in their home. That just would not happen and it does not happen with the *heterosexual* couples we work with." Even when *gay* or *lesbian* applicants pass the required background checks, they still face the risk of being turned down if they do not meet agency "standards" (Graham, 2013).

Are children raised by LGBT couples or individuals harmed in any way? Despite myths to the contrary, children raised by same-sex parents have no increased likelihood of gender or sexual confusion or of developing a same-sex *sexual orientation* (Patterson, 2013). Research findings indicate that children raised by *gay* or *lesbian* parents are as mentally healthy as children with *heterosexual* parents and that there is no reason to believe that a *heterosexual* family structure is necessary for healthy child development. The relationships within *gay* and *lesbian* households appear to be similar to those of *heterosexual* individuals, although *lesbian* couples share a more egalitarian relationship than many *heterosexual* couples (Riggle, Whitman, Olson, Rostosky, & Strong, 2008). In fact, children raised by *lesbian* mothers perform better academically and have fewer behavioral problems than their peers (Gartrell & Bos, 2010).

Implications

In addition to the typical relationship difficulties faced by *heterosexual* couples and families, LGBT couples also face prejudice and discrimination from society. Conflicts sometimes occur when individuals in LGBT relationships differ in terms of internalized homophobia or the extent to which they are "out" to others in their social, work, or family networks. For example, one member of the relationship may be uncomfortable showing public displays of affection or may feel the need to hide the couple's *sexual orientation* or their relationship.

In work with LGBT parents or in determining their suitability as adoptive parents, mental health professionals should examine their own attitudes and beliefs about LGBT individuals. The empirical data indicate that LGBT parenting styles and child-rearing practices do not differ significantly from those of their *heterosexual* counterparts. In addition to normal developmental issues, children of LGBT parents may benefit from support when explaining their nontraditional family to peers. Many hope that changes in school curricula encouraging respect for diversity and diverse lifestyles will help with this challenge.

Strengths of LGBT Individuals

Queer people of color not only survive experiences of oppression, they develop resilience and coping skills in the process. (Singh & Chun, 2010, p. 38)

Although LGBT people face discrimination, prejudice, and disadvantaged status in society, many show considerable resilience in the face of adversity and effectively use such strategies as maintaining hope and seeking social support (Singh, Hays, & Watson, 2011). Many cite positive aspects of being a *lesbian* or a *gay* man, such as belonging to a supportive community, being able to create families of choice, serving as positive role models, living authentically, being involved in social justice and activism, and freedom from gender-specific roles (Orel & Fruhauf, 2014). Even going through the process of identity development can be a strength—many LGBT individuals move through the process of internalized heterosexism, identity confusion, and identity comparison toward identity tolerance, and finally identity acceptance, identity pride, and identity synthesis (Akerlund & Cheung, 2000). The egalitarian relationship frequently seen in *lesbian* couples not only promotes resilience in their children but also provides a positive model for respectful interpersonal relationships (Bos & Gartrell, 2010).

SPECIFIC CHALLENGES

In the following sections we discuss challenges faced by LGBT individuals and consider their implications in treatment. Societal pressures and related struggles are reflected in the higher incidence of substance abuse as well as anxiety and depressive disorders within this population. *Gay* youth are especially vulnerable because of pressures within the school and peer environment as well as struggles with "*coming out*" to family members. Adults face issues related to letting others know "who they really are" as well as settling down with a partner, getting married, and having children—things that *heterosexual* individuals take for granted.

Coming Out

Transgender teen Leelah Alcorn stepped in front of a semitrailer. In her suicide note, she said her family did not accept her when she came out to them. Her mother responded by stating that Leelah would

never be a girl and that God doesn't make mistakes; she continued to
refer to Leelah by her male name, Josh. (Helling, 2015)

The process of maintaining secrets about *sexual orientation* or gender identity issues can seriously affect relationships with friends and family. The decision to *come out* is extremely difficult and is often influenced by the overwhelming sense of isolation the individual feels. *Coming out* to parents and friends can lead to rejection, anger, and grief. This is especially difficult for adolescents who are emotionally and financially dependent on their family. *Coming out* is an ongoing process for LGBT individuals—each time they need to determine with whom and when to disclose. During initial stages of this process, self-esteem, life satisfaction, and happiness may decrease as they face negative reactions from others (Chaney et al., 2011). *Bisexual* individuals may encounter more difficulty since it is often assumed that they are "just going through a phase" or that they are *gay* or *lesbian*, but are unwilling to accept their *sexual orientation* (Schulman, 2014).

Coming out is often more difficult for ethnic minorities who face the stigma of being "multiple minorities." Asian, Black, and Latino/a *gay* and *lesbian* youth are more reluctant to disclose their *sexual orientation* than are their White counterparts and are less likely to be involved in gay-related social activities (Adelson, 2012). *Gay* Mexican American men have a greater degree of internalized homophobia, partly because of the cultural value of *machismo.* In Latino communities, there is strong negative reaction to *gay* men and frequent use of slurs such as *maricon* (sissy) and *joto* (fag) (Estrada, Rigali-Oiler, Arciniega, & Tracey, 2011). Further, Latino men who are *gay* report racism, discomfort, and rejection from the *gay* community; Latino men with darker skin or more Indian features are more likely to face such rejection (Ibanez, VanOss Marin, Flores, Millett, & Diaz, 2009).

Lindsey (2005), who is an African American, was asked to write a chapter on sexual diversity for the 2005 edition of *Our Bodies, Ourselves.* She notes, "In the mainstream media, both *gay* and straight, *coming out* is portrayed in an extremely idealized and simplistic way. The *gay* person, always white and middle class, decides he or she is *gay*, tells families and friends, who might experience a little homophobia. . .and ends up marching proudly down the main thoroughfare of a progressive major metropolitan area" (p. 186). The experience for people of color is often different when *coming out*—they frequently face both rejection from their communities and racism from the majority culture. Among the working poor, it also means the possibility of losing their jobs. *Transgendered* individuals face additional challenges as friends, family, children and coworkers adjust to their change in gender and physical appearance (Budge, Tebbe, & Howard, 2010).

Implications

The decision of "when" and "with whom" to come out should be carefully considered. Factors such as age, ethnicity, relationship status, and spiritual beliefs should be taken into account (Chaney et al., 2011). To whom does the individual want to reveal the information? What are the possible effects and consequences (both long and short term) of self-disclosure both for the individual and for the recipient of the information? What new sources of support are available if negative reactions are encountered? If the individual is already in a relationship, how will the disclosure affect his or her partner? In some cases, the client may conclude that it is not yet a good time to disclose. If a client has considered the implications of *coming out* and desires to take this step, the counselor can offer specific help and preparation in determining how this is best accomplished. Role-plays and the discussion of possible reactions can be practiced.

Clients needing support during the disclosure process may choose to disclose or pursue follow-up discussion during a counseling session. Disclosure to parents may provoke feelings of both grief (e.g., loss of their visions of their child's future, including weddings and grandchildren) and guilt (i.e., believing their parenting was responsible). Parents may need support in dealing with the societal stigma of having a LGBT family member and may benefit from receiving information and education about myths and stereotypes. If parents or other family members are rejecting, the individual must strengthen other sources of social support. This may be particularly important for ethnic minorities, who may be additionally affected by culturally based reactions. Prior to and during the coming-out process the counselor can help the client deal with both external and internalized heterosexism and other societal beliefs that are at the core of homophobia (Scott, 2011). Thus, rather than allowing clients to internalize self-blame, counselors can help them understand that it is societal prejudice that is the problem.

Prejudice, Discrimination, and Misconceptions

> *About one-quarter of LGBT staff, faculty, and students reported experiencing harassment. . . .with transgender individuals receiving even higher levels of harassment. . . About one-third have considered leaving their institutions. . . 43 percent of transgender students,*

> *faculty, and staff. . . .feared for their physical safety. (Rankin, Weber, Blumenfeld, & Frazer, 2010, p. 4)*

We have alluded to the overwhelming prejudice and discrimination facing LGBT youth and adults. Sexual assaults in adulthood were reported by 12% of *gay* men and 13% of *bisexual* men, compared to 2% of *heterosexual* men. Among women, the rates of sexual assault were 16% for *lesbians*, 17% for *bisexual* women, and 8% for *heterosexual* women (Balsam, Rothblum, & Beauchaine, 2005). More than 94% of LGBT adults reported hate crime victimization (Herek, Cogan, & Gillis, 2002). Such victimization was highlighted following the tragic suicide of a Rutgers University student who was victimized by antigay harassment and cyberbullying initiated by his college roommate, who secretly recorded and publicized a sexual interaction between the student and another man (Lederman, 2011). Further, *bisexual* individuals sometimes experience hostility both from *heterosexuals* and from the *gay* community (Brewster & Moradi, 2010). Mental distress is particularly pronounced among *bisexual* women (Ward, Dahlhamer, Galinsky, & Joestl, 2014). *Transgender* individuals face being viewed as mentally ill, delusional, or self-destructive not only by the public, but also by mental health workers (Mizock & Fleming, 2011).

In addition to openly antigay harassment, LGBT individuals often experience subtle heterosexism, such as the common practice of equating the word *gay* with *stupid* or automatically making the assumption that most people are *heterosexual*; practices such as these create distress and feelings of denigration (Burn, Kadlec, & Rexler, 2005). LGBT individuals face microaggressions that invalidate their *sexual orientation*, including the use of language and terms that demonstrate heteronormality and *heterosexual* privilege (Smith, Shin, & Officer, 2011). Perceived discrimination based on *sexual orientation*, especially among those who keep silent about their experiences, increases risk of depression (McLaughlin, Hatzenbuehler, & Keyes, 2010).

It is likely that societal stressors such as prejudice and discrimination account for the findings that LGBT youth report elevated rates of major depression, generalized anxiety disorder, and substance abuse (Rienzo et al., 2006) and that LGBT adults are at higher risk for substance- and alcohol-related problems (Ward, Dahlhamer, Galinsky, & Joestl, 2014). Although *gay* men report high rates of major depression, *lesbians* appear to fare better and report mental health equal to that of their *heterosexual* counterparts (DeAngelis, 2002).

A number of research studies reveal that bias continues to exist among mental health professionals (Shelton & Delgado-Romero, 2013). In one study, 97 counselors read a fictitious intake report about a *bisexual* woman seeking counseling, with no indication that the problem involved her *sexual orientation*. The problems involved career choice, issues with parents over independence, ending a two-year relationship with another woman, and problems with her boyfriend. Hence the issues involved were boundaries with parents, career choice, and romantic relationships. Counselors with the most negative attitude toward *bisexuality* believed her problems stemmed from her *sexual orientation* and rated her lower in psychosocial functioning (Mohr, Israel, & Sedlacek, 2001).

It is not uncommon for therapists to engage in biased and inappropriate practices or to hold beliefs that affect the therapeutic alliance with LGBT clients (Garnets, Hancock, Cochran, Goodchilds, & Peplau, 1998; Shelton & Delgado-Romero, 2013) including the following:

1. Assuming that a client is *heterosexual,* thereby making it harder to bring up issues around *sexual orientation.*

2. Believing that same-sex orientation is sinful or a form of mental illness.

3. Failing to understand that a client's emotional problems may result from experiences with discrimination or internalization of society's view of homosexuality.

4. Focusing on *sexual orientation* when it is not relevant.

5. Attempting to have clients renounce or change their *sexual orientation.*

6. Lacking an understanding of identity development in *lesbian* women and gay men, or viewing homosexuality solely as sexual activity.

7. Not understanding the impact of possible internalized negative societal pressures or homophobia on identity development.

8. Underestimating the consequences of *"coming out"* for the client, and making the suggestion to come out without careful discussion of the pros and cons of this disclosure.

9. Misunderstanding or underestimating the importance of intimate relationships for *gay* men and *lesbians.* One therapist reportedly advised a *lesbian*

couple who were having problems in their relationship to not consider it a permanent relationship and consider going to a *gay* bar to meet others.

10. Presuming that clients with a different *sexual orientation* cannot be good parents, and automatically assuming that their children's problems are a result of their *sexual orientation*.

11. Overidentifying with LGBT clients; offering excessive displays of acceptance or "understanding."

Implications

Although mental health organizations have acknowledged that homosexuality is not a mental disorder, it is recognized that a "need for better education and training of mental health practitioners" exists (Shelton & Delgado-Romero, 2013). *Heterosexist bias* in therapy needs to be acknowledged and changed. Fortunately, many mental health training programs have made curricular changes to increase their emphasis both on the concerns and challenges of LGBT individuals and on the positive characteristics and supportive relationships found in these groups.

It is important for therapists to continue to examine possible stereotypes or negative attitudes they may hold regarding LGBT clients and to monitor their behavior and interactions for possible microaggressions. LGBT clients report perceiving counselors more positively and feeling a greater willingness to disclose personal information, including *sexual orientation*, when a counselor refrains from heterosexist language (e.g., using the term *partner* instead of *boyfriend* or *girlfriend* or *husband* or *wife*). Workshops and training in the use of nondiscriminatory intake forms and identifying psychological and health issues faced by many LGBT clients are helpful means of increasing health care providers' effectiveness (Pachankis & Goldfried, 2013).

Aging

> *Kelly Glossip was accepted in a senior citizens home but turned it down, "I'm used to being out, so the idea of going into senior housing in a straight environment is horrifying. . . .I know that I would have to go completely back in the closet." (Watkins, 2010, p. 1)*

Because of anticipated or previous discrimination by health care providers, older LGBT individuals underutilize health care. Their concerns appear to be justified.

In a recent study, *heterosexual* male and female nurses showed a strong preference for *heterosexual* over *lesbian* and *gay* patients (Sabin, Riskind, & Nosek, 2015). Aging LGBT individuals are also fearful of having to go to retirement or assisted-living communities where prejudice may exist. In interviews, residents of these communities assumed that people living there were *heterosexual* and many expressed the view that it is "OK" to have LGBT residents as long as they did not talk about their orientation (Clay, 2014). Unless attitudes change, these types of problems will only increase, because up to 3 million LGBT individuals in the United States are older than age 65, and this number is expected to double in 15 years (Pearlman, 2006). In addition, as with other segments of U.S. society, ageism exists within *gay* and *lesbian* communities. All of these issues can produce a great deal of concern among older LGBT adults as they confront declining health and a diminishing social support system.

Implications

With older LGBT individuals, issues of *coming out* (or *coming out* again) may need to be addressed as their needs for health care or social services increase. Counselors can assist these clients to develop coping skills, expand their social support systems, and locate services for older LGBT adults. Advocacy groups for this population are increasing in number. One organization, Senior Action in a Gay Environment (SAGE), provides counseling, educational and recreational activities, and discussion groups for older LGBT individuals. The Gay and Lesbian Association of Retiring Persons (GLARP) operates retirement communities for LGBT individuals and provides them with support and education on aging (Donahue & McDonald, 2005). To promote a welcoming environment, some retirement communities use marketing materials that show same sex couples and other indications of diversity.

In addition to these services, LGBT-friendly teleconferences exist for homebound seniors. Project Visibility, a training program for staff and administrators of nursing homes and assisted-living facilities, incorporates culturally competent practices that counter stereotypes and foster compassionate care for older LGBT adults living in these facilities (Mellskog, 2011). Many organizations have added the *transgender* community to their mission statements. The mental health professional needs to be aware of these resources and advocate for laws that support LGBT partnership rights.

IMPLICATIONS FOR CLINICAL PRACTICE

1. Examine your own views regarding *heterosexuality*, and determine their impact on work with LGBT clients. Understand *heterosexual* and cisgender privilege. A way to personalize this perspective is to assume that some of your family, friends, or coworkers may be LGBT.

2. Read "Appropriate Therapeutic Responses to Sexual Orientation" in APA's *Multicultural Competency in Geropsychology* (2009a), the *Report of the APA Task Force on Gender Identity and Gender Variance* (APA, 2009b), and Adelson's "Practice Parameter on Gay, Lesbian, or Bisexual Orientation, Gender Nonconformity, and Gender Discordance in Children and Adolescents" (2012).

3. Develop partnerships, consultation, or collaborative efforts with local and national LGBT organizations.

4. Ensure that your intake forms, interview procedures, and language are free of *heterosexist bias* and include a question on sexual behavior, attraction, or orientation. Be aware that LGBT clients may have specific concerns regarding confidentiality.

5. Do not assume that presenting problems are necessarily the result of *sexual orientation*. Typical presenting problems may include relationship difficulties, self-esteem issues, depression, and anxiety (Lyons, Bieschke, Dendy, Worthington, & Georgemiller, 2010). Keep in mind that societal factors may play a role in these problems.

6. Remember that mental health issues may result from stress due to prejudice and discrimination; internalized homophobia; the coming-out process; a lack of family, peer, school, or community support; experiences of sexual victimization or physical assault; suicidal ideation or attempts; and substance abuse. Ethnic minority LGBT individuals may be dealing with rejection from their ethnic communities as well as marginalization within the LGBT community.

7. Realize that LGBT couples may have problems similar to those of their *heterosexual* counterparts but may also display unique concerns, such as differences in the degree of comfort with public demonstrations of their relationship or reactions from their family of origin.

8. Assess spiritual and religious needs. Many LGBT individuals have a strong religious faith but encounter exclusion. Religious support is available. For

example, for individuals of the Christian faith, the Fellowship United Methodist Church accepts all types of diversity and is open to *gay* congregation members. LGBT individuals who have strong religious beliefs but who belong to a nonaffirming church can explore different options, such as joining an affirming religious group, exploring more liberal sects of their own religion, or developing their own definitions of what it means to be *gay* or religious (Sherry, Adelman, Whilde, & Quick, 2010). It is much easier to adapt to a different religious group than to change one's *sexual orientation* (Haldeman, 2010).

9. Because many LGBT clients have internalized the societal belief that they cannot have long-lasting relationships, access to materials that portray healthy and satisfying long-term LGBT relationships can help counteract these stereotypes.

10. Recognize that a large number of LGBT clients have been subjected to hate crimes as well as microaggression. Depression, anger, post-traumatic stress, and self-blame may result. These conditions need to be assessed and treated. It can be helpful to ask questions such as, "Have you had incidences where you thought you were treated differently because you are a sexual minority person?" (Kashubeck-West, Szymanski, & Meyer, 2008, p. 617).

11. For clients still dealing with internalized homophobia, it may help to focus on assisting them to identify and replace heterosexist and cisgender messages with positive affirming messages about their identity. Many LGBT individuals avoid discrimination by assuming a *heterosexual* identity and avoiding the issue of sexuality with others, whereas others are able to reveal their true identity. The consequences of each of these reactions need to be considered both from individual and societal perspectives.

12. A number of therapeutic strategies can be useful with internalized homophobia, prejudice, and discrimination. Effective interventions may involve assisting clients to identify and correct cognitive distortions, practice coping skills, or expand social supports.

13. To increase awareness of internalized heterosexism, encourage LGBT clients who have expressed concerns related to *sexual orientation* to talk about their coming-out experiences; thoughts and feelings about their sexuality; feelings of homophobia; experiences with heterosexism in school, family, work, and religion; degree of interactions with other LGBT individuals; and the availability of support (Kashubeck-West et al., 2008).

14. Systems-level intervention is often needed in schools, employment situations, or religious organizations. Diversity workshops can help organizations acquire accurate information about sexual and gender diversity. Even with the Supreme Court decision legalizing same-sex marriage, counselors may need to be advocates for change and to assist clients who are facing discriminatory action in regards to legal matters such as adoptions.

15. *Transgender* individuals may need specific assistance making name changes, connecting with local support groups, or locating medical professionals who provide hormones or surgical options associated with a gender transition (Bess & Stabb, 2009).

16. Do not assume that *"coming out"* is the goal in all situations. Both counselor and client should carefully consider consequences, especially for younger individuals, and develop strategies to deal with possible negative reactions from family or friends.

SUMMARY

The acronym LGBT refers to individuals who have an affectional and/or sexual attraction to persons of the same sex (*gay* men and *lesbians*) or to members of both sexes (*bisexuals*), and individuals whose gender identity is inconsistent with their assigned gender (*transgender*). Overall, there appears to be increased societal acceptance of LGBT individuals and their lifestyles, especially among the young. Despite this change, prejudice, discrimination and violence against sexual minorities continues. Because of this fact, sexual identity issues and *"coming out"* are especially intense for adolescents. Suicide attempts are high among LGBT adolescents and young adults. *Heterosexist bias* in therapy needs to be acknowledged and changed. It is important for therapists to continue to examine possible stereotypes or negative attitudes regarding LGBT clients and to monitor their behavior and interactions for possible microaggressions. Sixteen clinical implications for counselor practice are identified.

GLOSSARY TERMS

Bisexual

Coming out

Gay

Gender dysphoria

Heterosexist bias

Heterosexual

Lesbian

LGBT (Q)

Queer

Sexual orientation

Transgender

REFERENCES

Adelson, S. L. (2012). Practice parameter on gay, lesbian, or bisexual sexual orientation, gender nonconformity, and gender discordance in children and adolescents. *Journal of the American Academy of Child & Adolescent Psychiatry*, *51*, 957–974.

Akerlund, M., & Cheung, M. (2000). Teaching beyond the deficit model: Gay and lesbian issues among African American, Latinos, and Asian Americans. *Journal of Social Work Education*, *36*, 279–291.

Alper, G. I. (2012). *Gay adoption statistics.* Retrieved from http://www.galperlaw.com/gay-law-report/gay-adoption-statistics/

American Psychiatric Association. (2013). *Diagnostic and statistical manual of mental disorders* (5th ed.). Washington, DC: Author.

American Psychological Association. (2009a). *Multicultural competency in geropsychology.* Washington, DC: American Psychological Association.

American Psychological Association. (2009b). *Report of the APA Task Force on Gender Identity and Gender Variance.* Washington, DC: American Psychological Association.

AP. (2015). *Pentagon readying plan to lift transgender ban.* Retrieved from http://www.msn.com/en-us/news/us/pentagon-readying-plan-to-lift-transgender-ban/ar-AAcVpjE

Balsam, K. F., Rothblum, E. D., & Beauchaine, T. P. (2005). Victimization over the life span: A comparison of lesbian, gay, bisexual, and heterosexual siblings. *Journal of Consulting and Clinical Psychology*, *73*, 477–487.

Bess, J. A., & Stabb, S. D. (2009). The experiences of transgendered persons in psychotherapy: Voices and recommendations. *Journal of Mental Health Counseling*, *31*, 264–282.

Bos, H., & Gartrell, N. (2010). Adolescents of the USA National Longitudinal Lesbian Family Study: Can family characteristics counteract the negative effects of stigmatization. *Family Process*, *49*, 559–572.

Brewster, M. E., & Moradi, B. (2010). Perceived experiences of anti-bisexual prejudice: Instrument development and evaluation. *Journal of Counseling Psychology*, *57*, 451–468.

Budge, S. L., Tebbe, E. N., & Howard, K.A.S. (2010). The work experience of transgender individuals: Negotiating the transition and career decision-making process. *Journal of Counseling Psychology*, *57*, 377–393.

Burn, S. M., Kadlec, K., & Rexer, B. S. (2005). Effects of subtle heterosexism on gays, lesbians, and bisexuals. *Journal of Homosexuality, 49,* 23–38.

Chaney, M. P., Filmore, J. M., & Goodrich, K. M. (2011). No more sitting on the sidelines. *Counseling Today, 34,* 37.

Clay, R. J. (2014). Double-whammy discrimination. *Monitor on Psychology, 45,* 46–49.

DeAngelis, T. (2002). New data on lesbian, gay, and bisexual mental health. *APA Monitor, 33,* 46–47.

Diehl, W. (2013). Yes, I really am bisexual. Deal with it. *New York Times.* Retrieved from http://www.nytimes.com/2013/04/28/fashion /yes-i-really-am-bisexual-deal-with-it.html ?pagewanted=all&_r=0

Donahue, P., & McDonald, L. (2005). Gay and lesbian aging: Current perspectives and future directions for social work practice and research. *Families in Society, 86,* 359–366.

Estrada, F., Rigali-Oiler, M., Arciniega, M., & Tracey, T.J.G. (2011). Machismo and Mexican American men: An empirical understanding using a gay sample. *Journal of Counseling Psychology, 58,* 358–367.

Garnets, L., Hancock, K. A., Cochran, S. D., Goodchilds, J., & Peplau, L. A. (1998). Issues in psychotherapy with lesbians and gay men: A survey of psychologists. In D. R. Atkinson & G. Hackett (Eds.), *Counseling diverse populations* (2nd ed., pp. 297–316). Boston, MA: McGraw-Hill.

Gartrell, N., & Bos, H. (2010). US National Longitudinal Lesbian Family Study: Psychological adjustment of 17-year-old adolescents. *Pediatrics, 126,* 28–36.

Gates, G. J. (2011). *How many people are lesbian, gay, bisexual, and transgender?* Retrieved from http://wiwp.law.ucla.edu/research/census-lgbt -demographics-studies/how-many-people -are-lesbian-gay-bisexual-and-transgender/

Graham, L. (2013). *How adoption agencies discriminate against hopeful LGBT parents.* Retrieved from http://michiganradio .org/post/how-adoption-agencies-discriminate -against-hopeful-lgbt-parents

Greene, D. C., Britton, B. J. & Fitts, B. (2014). Long-term outcomes of lesbian, gay, bisexual, and transgender recalled school victimization. *Journal of Counseling & Development, 92,* 406–417.

Haldeman, D. C. (2010). Reflections of a gay male psychotherapist. *Psychotherapy Theory: Research and Practice, 47,* 177–185.

Hatzenbuehler, M. L. (2011). The social environment and suicide attempts in lesbian, gay, and bisexual youth. *Pediatrics, 127,* 896–903.

Helling, S. (2015). *Suicide of transgender teen Leelah Alcorn sparks emotional debate.* Retrieved from http://www.people.com/article/leelah-al corn-death-sparks-emotional-debate-parents -speak

Herek, G. M., Cogan, S. C., & Gillis, J. R. (2002). Victim experiences of hate crimes based on sexual orientation. *Journal of Social Issues, 58,* 319–399.

Hurley, L. (2015). *U.S. Supreme Court rules in favor of gay marriage nationwide.* Retrieved from http://www.reuters.com/article/2015/06/26 /us-usa-court-gaymarriage-idUSKBN0P 61SW20150626

Ibanez, G. E., VanOss Marin, B., Flores, S. A., Millett, G., & Diaz, R. M. (2009). General and gay-related racism experienced by Latino gay men. *Cultural Diversity and Ethnic Minority Psychology, 15,* 215–222.

Kashubeck-West, S., Szymanski, D., & Meyer, J. (2008). Internalized heterosexism: Clinical implications and training considerations. *Counseling Psychologist, 36,* 615–630.

Kosciw, J. G., Greytak, E. A., Bartkiewicz, M. J., Boesen, M. J., & Palmer, N. A. (2012). *The 2011 National School Climate Survey: The experiences of lesbian, gay, bisexual and transgender youth in our nation's schools.* New York, NY: GLSEN.

Lawrence, A. A. (2008). Gender identity disorders in adults: Diagnosis and treatment. In D. Rowland & L. Incrocci (Eds.), *Handbook of sexual and gender identity disorders* (pp. 423–456). Hoboken, NJ: Wiley.

Lederman, J. (2011, February 2). Dharun Ravi wants Tyler Clementi case dismissed. *Huffington Post*. Retrieved from http://www.huffingtonpost.com/2011/07/26/dharun-ravi-wants-tyler-c_n_909451.html

Leitsinger, M. (2015). *Sex reassignment surgery at 74: Medicare win opens door for transgender seniors*. Retrieved from http://www.nbcnews.com/news/us-news/sex-reassignment-surgery-74-medicare-win-opens-door-transgender-seniors-n276986

Lin, J. (2011). *California Gov. Jerry Brown signs law requiring public schools to teach "gay history."* Retrieved from http://www.cnsnews.com/news/article/california-gov-jerry-brown-signs-law-requiring-public-schools-teach-gay-history

Lindsey, E. S. (2005). Reexamining gender and sexual orientation: Revisioning the representation of queer and trans people in the 2005 edition of *Our Bodies, Ourselves. NWSA Journal, 17*, 184–189.

Lyons, H. Z., Bieschke, K. J., Dendy, A. K., Worthington, R. L., & Georgemiller, R. (2010). Psychologists' competence to treat lesbian, gay and bisexual clients: State of the field and strategies for improvement. *Professional Psychology: Research and Practice, 41*, 424–434.

McCabe, H. T., Wilsnack, S. E., West, B. T., & Boyd, C. J. (2010). Victimization and substance use disorders in a national sample of heterosexual and sexual minority women and men. *Addiction, 105*, 2130–2140.

McCabe, S. E., Hughes, T. L., Bostwick, W. B., West, B. T., & Boyd, C. J. (2009). Sexual orientation, substance use behaviors and substance dependence in the United States. *Addiction, 104*, 1333–1345.

McLaughlin, K. A., Hatzenbuehler, M. L., & Keyes, K. M. (2010). Responses to discrimination and psychiatric disorders among Black, Hispanic, female, and lesbian, gay, and bisexual individuals. *American Journal of Public Health, 100*, 1477–1484.

Melas, C. (2015). *Caitlyn Jenner brought to tears at ESPYS after awarded Arthur Ashe award*. Retrieved from http://hollywoodlife.com/2015/07/15/caitlyn-jenner-speech-espys-video-espy-awards-2015/

Mellskog, P. (2011, June 5). LGBT program for seniors gets $100,000 grant. *Longmont Weekly*, p. 7.

Meyer, I. H., Dietrich, J., & Schwartz, S. (2008). Lifetime prevalence of mental disorders and suicide attempts in diverse lesbian, gay and bisexual populations. *American Journal of Public Health, 98*, 1004–1006.

Mizock, L., & Fleming, M. Z. (2011). Transgender and gender variant populations with mental illness: Implications for clinical care. *Professional Psychology: Research and Practice, 42*, 208–213.

Mohr, J. J., Israel, T., & Sedlacek, W. E. (2001). Counselors' attitudes regarding bisexuality as predictors of counselors' clinical responses: An analogue study of a female bisexual client. *Journal of Counseling Psychology, 48*, 212–222.

Orel, N. A., & Fruhauf, C. A. (2014). *The lives of LGBT older adults: Understanding challenges and resilience*. Washington, DC: American Psychological Association.

Pachankis, J. E., & Goldfried, M. R. (2013). Clinical issues in working with lesbian, gay, and bisexual clients. *Psychology of Sexual Orientation and Gender Diversity, 1*, 45–58.

Parker, K. (2015). *Among LGBT Americans, bisexuals stand out when it comes to identity, acceptance*. Retrieved from http://www.pewresearch.org/fact-tank/2015/02/20/among-lgbt-americans-bisexuals-stand-out-when-it-comes-to-identity-acceptance/

Patterson, C. J. (2013). Children of lesbian and gay parents: Psychology, law, and policy. *Psychology of Sexual Orientation and Gender Diversity, 1*, 27–34.

Pearlman, L. (2006). *Golden years.* Retrieved from http://www.bohemian.com/bohemian/02.22.06/fountaingrove-0608.html

Pew Research Center. (2013). *A Survey of LGBT Americans: Attitudes, experiences and values in changing times.* Retrieved from http://www.pewsocialtrends.org/2013/06/13/a-survey-of-lgbt-americans/

Pew Research Center. (2015). *Behind record support for same-sex marriage, differences endure.* Retrieved from http://www.people-press.org/2015/06/08/section-2-knowing-gays-and-lesbians-religious-conflicts-beliefs-about-homosexuality/#reactions-to-a-gay-child

Public Relations Research Institute, (2014). *Survey: A shifting landscape: A decade of change in American attitudes about same-sex marriage and LGBT issues.* Retrieved from http://www.the-dailybeast.com/articles/2015/03/31/millennials-are-the-gayest-generation.html

Rankin, S., Weber, G., Blumenfeld, W., & Frazer, S. (2010). *2010 state of higher education for lesbian, gay, bisexual & transgender people.* Retrieved from http://www.campuspride.org/Campus%20Pride%202010%20LGBT%20Report%20Summary.pdf

Rienzo, B. A., Button, J. W., Sheu, J.-J., & Li, Y. (2006). The politics of sexual orientation issues in American schools. *Journal of School Health, 76*, 93–97.

Riggle, E.D.B., Whitman, J. S., Olson, A., Rostosky, S. S., & Strong, S. (2008). The positive aspects of being a lesbian or gay man. *Professional Psychology: Research and Practice, 39*, 210–217.

Rosario, M., Schrimshaw, E. W., Hunter, J., & Braun, L. (2006). Sexual identity development among lesbian, gay, and bisexual youths:

Consistency and change over time. *Journal of Sex Research, 43*, 46–58.

Sabin, J. A., Riskind, R. G., & Nosek, B. A. (2015). Health care providers' implicit and explicit attitudes toward lesbian women and gay men. *American Journal of Public Health.* e-View ahead of print. doi: 10.2105/AJPH.2015.302631

Schulman, M. (2014). Bisexual: A label with layers. *New York Times.* Retrieved from http://www.nytimes.com/2014/01/05/fashion/Tom-Daley-Bisexual-LGBT.html?_r=0

Scott, D. (2011). *Coming out: Intrapersonal loss in the acquisition of a stigmatized identity.* Retrieved from www.yourtherapist.org/www/wp-content/uploads/coming_out.pdf

Shelton, K., & Delgado-Romero, E. A. (2013). Sexual orientation microaggressions: The experience of lesbian, gay, bisexual, and queer clients in psychotherapy. *Psychology of Sexual Orientation and Gender Diversity, 1*, 59–70.

Sherry, A., Adelman, A., Whilde, M. R., & Quick, D. (2010). Competing selves: Negotiating the intersection of spiritual and sexual identities. *Professional Psychology: Research and Practice, 41*, 112–119.

Singh, A. A., & Chun, K.S.Y. (2010). From "margins to the center": Moving towards a resilience-based model of supervision with queer people of color. *Training and Education in Professional Psychology, 4*, 36–46.

Singh, A. A., Hays, D. G., and Watson, L. S. (2011). Strength in the face of adversity: Resilience strategies of transgender individuals. *Journal of Counseling & Development, 89*, 20–27.

Smith, L. C., Shin, R. Q., & Officer, L. M. (2011, June 27). Moving counseling forward on LGB and transgender issues: Speaking queerly on discourses and microaggressions. *Counseling Psychologist, 40*, 385–408.

Soopermexican. (2015). *Transgender news reporter says hardest part of transition is "loss of male privilege."* Retrieved from http://therightscoop.com/transgender-news-reporter-says-hardest-part-of-transition-is-loss-of-male-privilege/

Stern, M. J. (2014). *Some conservatives would rather keep kids in foster care than let gays adopt them.* Retrieved from http://www.slate.com/blogs/outward/2014/08/01/conservatives_want_to_keep_gay_couples_from_adopting_or_fostering_kids.html

Swift, A. (2014). Most Americans say same-sex couples entitled to adopt. Retrieved from http://www.gallup.com/poll/170801/americans-say-sex-couples-entitled-adopt.aspx

Valenti, J. (2015). Telling an L.G.B.T. child they're worthless or broken is abuse. *New York Times.* Retrieved from http://www.nytimes.com/roomfordebate/2015/01/08/is-it-child-abuse-to-make-a-trans-child-change/telling-an-lgbt-child-theyre-worthless-or-broken-is-abuse

Ward, B.W., Dahlhamer, J. M., Galinsky, A. M., & Joestl, S. S. (2014). *Sexual orientation and health among U.S. adults: National Health Interview Survey, 2013.* Hyattsville, MD: National Center for Health Statistics.

Watkins, T. (2010). *Aging issues can be tougher on gays.* Retrieved from http://articles.cnn.com/2010–03–17/living/gays.aging.problems_1_couples-heterosexual-peers-social-security?_s=PM:LIVING

Wester, S. R., McDonough, T. A., White, M., Vogel, D. L., & Taylor, L. (2010). Using gender role conflict theory in counseling male-to-female transgender individuals. *Journal of Counseling and Development, 88,* 214–219.

Wong, C. M. (2014). New York's transgender residents will now be able to change birth certificate sex designation without surgery. *Huffington Post.* Retrieved from http://www.huffingtonpost.com/2014/12/08/new-york-transgender-birt_n_6290590.html

Wright, K. (2001). To be poor and transgender. *Progressive, 65,* 21–24.

Yen, H. (2011). *Census: Many gay couples say they're married—even if they technically aren't.* Retrieved from http://www.msnbc.msn.com/id/44690992/ns/us_news-life/#

Counseling Older Adults

Chapter Objectives

1. Learn the demographics and characteristics of older adult clients.

2. Identify counseling implications of the information provided for older adult clients.

3. Recognize strengths associated with older adult clients.

4. Know the special challenges faced by older adult clients.

5. Understand best practices in assessment and therapy with older adult clients.

An examination of Facebook comments revealed that older adults are often "vilified" and subjected to comments advocating that they be banned from public activities such as driving and shopping; some Facebook users even proposed the execution of older individuals. (Levy, Chung, Bedford, & Navrazhina, 2014)

. . . "gerontophobia" is harmful because we internalize it. Ageism has been described as prejudice against one's future self. It tells us that age is our defining characteristic and that, as midnight strikes on a milestone birthday, we will become nothing but old—emptied of our passions, abilities and experience, infused instead with frailty and decline." (Karpf, 2015)

Individuals aged 65 and older currently constitute 16.2% of the U.S. population. This group is growing and is expected to constitute more than 20% of the population by 2030. During the past decade, the age-85-and-older group, the fastest-growing segment of the adult population, has increased by 38%. Because females live longer than males, at age 85 there are only 39 men for every 100 women (Ortman, Velkoff, & Hogan, 2014). Because of the "graying" of adults, definitions of "old" are changing. Most baby boomers define old as being age 70 or older, although 25% believe that a person is not old until they reach the age of 80 (Carroll, 2011).

We are an aging society, yet we are poorly prepared to handle our current aged population and are certainly not equipped for the aging baby boomer generation. Information is lacking on therapies and medications for older individuals. As a group, older adults are less likely to receive new treatments for heart attacks or other illnesses, and older women are less likely to receive radiation and chemotherapy after breast cancer surgery. This is surprising, since a healthy person who is 65 years of age has an average life expectance of 19.3 more years (20.5 years for women and 17.9 years for men) (DHHS, 2014).

CHARACTERISTICS AND STRENGTHS

In the following sections we consider the characteristics and strengths of older adults and treatment implications. Remember that the applicability of this information needs to be considered for individual clients and their families.

Physical and Economic Health

> *She calls it "being sidelined." Greta Hale, an 82-year-old grand-mother of five, looks forward to visiting her large family but often feels like an outsider when she does. On holidays, she often sits alone while younger generations buzz about, preparing meals, tell-ing jokes, and engaging in lively debates. "My hearing is not so good anymore," she explains. Otherwise spry and healthy, Ms. Hale wants to participate but avoids doing so because, she admits, "I don't always understand what people are saying. I think maybe it's just easier for them to pretend I'm not there." She considers this one of the more difficult aspects of aging. (Wallhagen, Pettengill, & Whiteside, 2006, p. 40)*

Older adults often have physical impairments, such as hearing or vision loss or cardiovascular disease (McDonnall, 2011). About 30% of adults between the ages of 65 and 74 have some hearing impairment, and this increases to about half of those older than 75 (Wallhagen et al., 2006). Up to 25% of older adults have insomnia or difficulty falling asleep (Silvertsen et al., 2006). Ethnic minority older Americans tend to have more chronic, debilitating diseases, such as diabetes and heart disease (Costantino, Malgady, & Primavera, 2009).

The majority of older individuals, however, are quite healthy and able to live independent lives requiring only minimal assistance. Only 3.3% of adults 65 to 74 years need help with personal care from other persons; this percentage increases to 10.5% for those 75 and older (CDC, 2015). In all age categories, women are more likely to need assistance than are men (U.S. Census Bureau, 2005). The per-centage of adults requiring nursing home care is only 1% for those 65 to 74, 3% for persons 75 to 84, and 10% for persons 85 and older (DHHS, 2014).

Implications

When providing mental health services for older adults, counselors should con-sider the possibility that some will have physical limitations. To ensure that the counseling environment is appropriate for older clients, rooms should have ade-quate light and be free from extraneous noise, as well as any limiting environmen-tal barriers. If the client uses eyeglasses or hearing aids, make sure these are present during the session. Because of the frequency of physical illness (e.g., cardiovascular disease, hypertension), it is critical to work with medical providers to rule out the possibility that physical conditions, medications, or medication interactions are causing or contributing to emotional symptoms. Also, poverty, unemployment, poor living conditions, discrimination, or lack of receptivity among health care providers can significantly contribute to mental health concerns among older adults and may need to be addressed.

Sexuality in Later Years

> *The topic of sexuality and the aging process is often given little consideration. Underlying this neglect is the belief that sexuality should not be considered in the aged. Stereotypes of older adults as being asexual are incorrect. Romantic relationships are common in later life. In Internet personal ads, older men seek physical attractiveness and younger women, while older women are more selective, seeking status and security (Alterovitz & Mendelsohn, 2009).*

In our youth-oriented society, older adults are not expected to be interested in sex. One psychology intern remarked, "You never think the same about your older clients [or your grandparents] after you have an 80-year-old woman telling you how much she enjoys oral sex" (Zeiss, 2001, p. 1). Some consider sexual activity among older persons to be rare or even inappropriate. However, sexual interest and activity continue well into the 80s and 90s for many individuals. Among people 70 and older, 80% of men and 39% of women indicated that a satisfying sexual relationship is an important part of the quality of life (Fisher, 2010). In a study of over 3,000 older people, 53% between the ages of 65 and 74 were sexually active, as were 26% between the ages of 75 and 85. In fact, a study found that sexual frequency among married couples decreased over time but began to increase in those married for 50 years or more (Stroope, McFarland, & Uecker, 2015). Women reported significantly less sexual activity than men; in part, this was due to reduced likelihood of having a spousal or intimate relationship, as well as sexual problems such as low desire, difficulty with vaginal lubrication, and inability to reach orgasm. The most prevalent sexual problem in older men was erectile dysfunction (Lindau et al., 2007).

Changes do occur in sexual functioning in both older men and women. In men, erections occur more slowly and require continuous stimulation, although they can be maintained for longer periods without the need for ejaculation. The refractory period increases, so that it may take a day or two for the man to become sexually responsive again. Antihypertensive drugs, vascular diseases, and diabetes are common causes of impotence in men. For women, aging is associated with a decline in estrogen, resulting in decreases in vaginal lubrication. However, sexual responsiveness of the clitoris is similar to that of younger women. Sexual activities remain important for older men and women. Medical and psychological methods have been successful in treating sexual dysfunctions in older adults.

Age does not appear to be related to sexual satisfaction. In one survey involving 600 older women, most respondents voiced positive reactions to their sexual experiences, such as "Physical satisfaction is not the only aim of sex. . . .It is the nearness of someone throughout the lonely nights" and "I believe sex is a wonderful outlet for love and physical health and worth trying to keep alive in advancing age. . . .It makes one feel youthful and close to one's mate and pleased to 'still work'" (Johnson, 1995, p. A23).

Implications

Emotional stressors (retirement, caregiving, and lifestyle changes) as well as physical changes can produce problems in sexual functioning. As with younger adults, therapists should remain aware of possible sexual concerns. The mental health professional should determine the reason for any difficulties, encouraging the client to consult with medical professionals when appropriate. Many treatments and medications are now available to improve sexual functioning in older adults. Knowledge of these advances is important for those counseling this population.

Strengths

> *"There's an intimacy that comes later that is staggeringly wonderful,"* she said. *"You can hold hands with this person you love and adore, and somehow it's just as passionate as having sex at an earlier age. There is such a sense of connection and intimacy that grows out of a long relationship, that touch carries with it the weight of so many memories" (Hoffman, 2015).*

The majority of older adults have good emotional stability and high levels of affective well-being. Although they may have less control over their environment, many show flexibility in their ability to adjust to different situations. They also show greater facility in understanding and managing emotions than younger individuals (Scheibe & Carstensen, 2010). Most older adults are socially engaged and mentally alert. They also possess years of life and work experience. Interestingly, more than half of the individuals selected to serve as chief executive officers (CEOs) in Fortune 500 companies are over the age of 55 (Begley, 2010).

Many older adults, especially ethnic and minority group members, place a high value on religious beliefs, a factor contributing to a sense of hope and optimism, meaning and purpose in life, and better mental health (American Psychological Association, 2009b). In recent studies, older adults who believed they were resilient—had the ability to deal with stressors—tended to display successful aging regardless of physical or cognitive impairments. The same was true with those who rated themselves low on depression. Despite physical health status, self-ratings of successful aging were highly dependent on attitudinal qualities such as belief in one's ability to cope with challenges (Jeste et al., 2013). Similarly, in a 16-year longitudinal study involving adults aged 70 to 100, most were satisfied with aging, felt younger than their chronological age, and downgraded the importance of age-related changes. Only when they approached death did they become less satisfied with aging (Kotter-Gruhn, Kleinspehn-Ammerlahn, Gerstorf, & Smith, 2009).

SPECIFIC CHALLENGES

In the following sections we discuss challenges often faced by older populations and consider their implications in treatment.

Prejudice and Discrimination

> *Old people are a pain in the [expletive deleted] as far as I'm concerned and they are a burden on society. I hate everything about them, from their hair nets in the rain to their white Velcro sneakers . . . they are senile, they complain about everything, they couldn't hear a dumptruck. (Levy et al., 2014, p. 173)*

> *[The] "stereotype of being depressed, cranky, irritable and obsessed with their alimentary canal" constitute "no more than 10% of the older population. . . The other 90% of the population isn't like that at all," according to Paul Costa who has studied aging for over 30 years. (Tergesen, 2014)*

Older individuals are subject to negative stereotypes and discrimination (Altero-vitz & Mendelsohn, 2009). *Ageism,* defined as negative attitudes toward the pro-cess of aging or toward older individuals, is very common in our society. Older women, especially, are likely to be viewed negatively by society as a whole, and many internalize ageist norms involving qualities such as beauty (Clarke, 2011). In a review of negative attitudes toward older individuals, Palmore (2005) found that older adults were thought to be inflexible in their thought processes; lacking in health, intelligence, and alertness; and either having no sexual interest or, if they were sexually active, engaging in activity inappropriate for their age. Older adults are also viewed as "all alike," possessing such characteristics as being rigid, sickly, dependent, and depressed (APA, 2009b). Jokes about old age abound and are primarily negative in nature. The entertainment industry, news broadcasts, and advertising media are dominated by younger individuals. Information about older people is often presented by youthful reporters who may not understand the experiences of older generations.

Implications

Ageism influences how both the general public and mental health professionals perceive older persons. Negative stereotypes often result in older adults feeling invisible or less valued. Many older individuals come to accept ageist views and suffer a loss of self-esteem. In fact, many internalize negative societal beliefs. Unfortunately, mental health professionals also display age bias (Weiss, 2005), expressing reluctance to work with older adults and perceiving this population to be less interesting, having a poorer prognosis, more set in their ways, and less likely to benefit from therapy. Additionally, mental health problems in older adults may be inaccurately attributed to aging. Such beliefs can limit referrals for needed services.

Multiple Discrimination

Minority status in combination with older age can produce a double burden. Unfortunately, even minority members who have experienced discrimination themselves can display *ageism.* For example, older lesbian women may encounter discrimination based on both their age and sexual orientation. Some remain dis-tressed over their lack of acceptance from the heterosexual community and even family members. They observe that neighbors interact with them but do not invite them over. In addition, they may feel isolated from the lesbian community:

> *I was shocked and hurt when one of them [a young lesbian] who considers herself quite liberated didn't want to dance with me at a local lesbian bar, but she did dance with others. (Jacobson & Samdahl, 1998, p. 242)*

The woman attributed this rejection to her being older than the other woman. She points out that in lesbian newsletters or activities, there is seldom anything about older women. Because of institutionalized heterosexism, lesbian, gay, bisexual, or transgender (LGBT) older adults are often forced to hide their sexual or gender orientation from health providers (APA, 2009a).

Implications

The therapist should comprehensively assess for potential problems with discrimination when working with older adults who have a disability, who are from a different ethnic or cultural group, or who are members of a sexual minority. Counselors can help clients come to terms with factors associated with *ageism* and find different sources of social support. They can also actively work to change negative societal attitudes.

Mental Deterioration

> *Everyone knows that as we age, our minds and bodies decline—and life inevitably becomes less satisfying and enjoyable. Everyone knows that cognitive decline is inevitable. Everyone knows that as we get older, we become less productive at work. (Tergesen, 2014)*

A common view of older persons is that they are mentally incompetent. Although there is some cognitive slowing associated with normal aging (e.g., periodic minor memory difficulties, such as forgetting names or phone numbers or misplacing objects), the majority of older adults do not demonstrate significant mental decline. In fact, most are still mentally sharp and benefit from the store of knowledge they have acquired over a lifetime. Although they may show decrements on cognitive tests, their performance is much better in real-life situations that incorporate their skills and prior experiences (Salthouse, 2012). Even when cognitive slowing occurs, older adults often use various strategies to compensate for deficits (Krendl, Heatherton, & Kensinger, 2009). Multitasking involving activities that compete for attention (e.g., talking on a cell phone while crossing the street) becomes more difficult for many older adults, although passive tasks are not affected (Neider et al., 2011). Similarly, memory for perceptual information, highly practiced responses, and general knowledge hold up well even when working memory is compromised (Craik, 2008).

Approximately one in seven adults aged 71 or older have *dementia* (i.e., memory impairment and declining cognitive functioning), including the 5.2 million in this age group diagnosed with *Alzheimer's disease*. *Alzheimer's disease* is now the fifth leading cause of death among American adults aged 65 and older; the risk of *Alzheimer's disease* and other *dementias* increases with age (Alzheimer's Association, 2014). Women usually live longer than men, so they are more likely to develop *dementia*; among 65-year-olds, the lifetime risk of developing *dementia* is approximately 11% for men and 19% for women (Gatz, 2007).

Implications

Older adults who report a cognitive decline should undergo assessment to determine if these difficulties are associated with normal aging or due to pathological factors. For those with a "normal" decline, reassurance and strategies to improve cognitive functioning can be useful (American Psychological Association, 2014). Research has found that cognitive decline in older adults can be delayed or reduced through lifestyle changes such as the use of cognitive activities to stimulate the mind (e.g., chess, crossword puzzles, computer games, reading), engaging in physical activity, and better nutrition. These lifestyle interventions appear to improve neuroplasticity, increased neuronal connections in the brain, and increase cognitive reserve (Williams & Kemper, 2010). Normal cognitive declines may be reversed with specific training. In one study, older adults with declines in inductive reasoning or spatial orientation were given a five-hour training to improve these skills. Over two-thirds improved with the training and 40% reached the same performance level in these areas as they demonstrated 14 years previously. Such training may be useful for reversing specific types of cognitive declines (Schaie, Willis, & Caskie, 2004).

For older adults demonstrating significant cognitive decline and for those suspected of having a neurodegenerative condition such as *Alzheimer's disease*, the traditional mental status exam can provide some indication of problem areas. However, a more frequently used assessment is the Mini-Mental State Examination (MMSE). This test takes about 5 to 10 minutes to administer and has normative and validity data. The MMSE comprises eleven items that assess orientation, attention and calculation, recall, language, and visual motor integrity.

Early detection of cognitive decline allows for treatment and advanced planning involving legal matters or dealing with potential problems such as driving.

Other steps to take in evaluating cognitive changes include the following:

- Obtain a self-report from the client about possible changes in memory or other areas of cognitive function.

- Obtain reports from family members and friends regarding the client's cognitive performance. Be especially alert to discrepancies.

- Take a careful history of the onset and progression of the cognitive changes.

- Coordinate with medical professionals who can assess for possible side effects of medication or other physical conditions that may cause cognitive decline.

- Assess for depression, since it can also result in dementia-like performance or the overreporting of cognitive problems. Remember that depression and *dementia* often occur together.

Although *dementia* has a gradual progression, the effects of this condition can quickly affect both the client and family members. In the early stages, memory problems are often the primary concern. Delusions and hallucinations may develop as the *dementia* progresses. Family members may not understand that individuals with *dementia* do not always recall what they are told. They may become frustrated when the affected individual is forgetful or needs extra assistance following through with tasks. Some may believe the behavior is willful or may try to assume responsibility over all aspects of the person's life, even when the older person can perform effectively in some areas.

Self-identity and autonomy are important to older adults, including those with *dementia*. Adult children may infantilize or dominate a parent with a cognitive decline, assuming that their actions are in the best interest of their parent but failing to take the parent's own preferences or values into consideration. *Elderspeak*, such as "Are we ready for our bath?" or "You want to take your medicine now, don't you?" (Williams, Kemper, & Hummert, 2005, p. 15) is often used with exaggerated intonation and elevated pitch, along with terms such as *honey* or *good girl*. *Elderspeak* was commonly used by one group of certified nursing assistants when working with older adults with cognitive dysfunctions, especially when other individuals were not around (Lombardi et al., 2014). Many older adults consider *elderspeak* to be demeaning and even those with severe *dementia* may react negatively to its use by showing behavioral resistance (Williams, Herman, Gajewski, & Wilson, 2009).

Caregiving may be stressful and may increase conflict among family members. When working with families who care for a relative with *dementia*, mental health professionals should address the following:

1. The need for patience and understanding when working with individuals with *dementia*

2. Potential stresses on family members and the need to enhance coping strategies, including self-care

3. Education about specific neurological difficulties and their effects on cognition and behavior; available treatments; and strategies for dealing with agitation, wandering, and other safety issues

4. The family dynamics as they relate to the caregiving situation, including the allocation of caregiving responsibilities

5. Strategies for effective communication among family members, possibly including encouraging family members to avoid the use of *elderspeak*, oversimplification, or unnecessary repetition of requests

6. Financial and legal matters, such as power of attorney provisions

Elder Abuse and Neglect

> *She raises her hands to her snow-white hair in a gesture of frustrated bewilderment, then slowly lowers them to cover eyes filling with tears. The woman, in her 70s, is trying to explain how she wound up in a shelter that could well be where she spends the rest of her life. . . She says she was usually ordered to "go to bed," where she lay in a dark room, upset, unable to sleep. A family member "Just yelled at me all the time. Screamed at me, cussed me out," the woman says. "I don't know what happened. She just got tired of me, I guess."* (Sewell, 2013)

Maltreatment of older adults, including neglect and emotional, financial, physical, and sexual abuse, is a significant public health concern. Many cases of abuse or neglect go undetected, especially among those who are most vulnerable (e.g., individuals with *dementia*, depression, or significant health concerns). Family circumstances most commonly associated with abuse and neglect include (a) previous traumatic experiences and a pattern of violence in the family, (b) stress (including marital stress) resulting from accommodating an older parent or relative in the family home, (c) financial burdens, (d) overcrowded quarters, and (e) low levels of social support (Acierno et al., 2010). It is also important to be alert for client self-neglect (e.g., unsafe driving, failure to eat or take medications), another common concern that can have serious consequences (Mosqueda & Dong, 2011).

Implications

It is essential that counselors be familiar with best practice guidelines for treating older adults (APA, 2014; Molinari, 2011) and the complex ethical and legal issues pertaining to defining and reporting *elder abuse and neglect*, including self-neglect (Zeranski & Halgin, 2011). Counselors may see signs of bruising or malnutrition in older clients or indications that they are suffering from emotional abuse. Assessment may be difficult, since the client may have feelings of shame or dependency on the caregiver (Horning, Wilkins, Dhanani, & Henriques, 2013). Several steps can be taken to reduce the prevalence of *elder abuse and neglect* (APA, 2001). First, continued public education can bring the problem out in the open and increase awareness of the risk factors for abuse. Second, respite care (e.g., family members, friends, or hired workers to help with care giving) can help reduce caregiver burnout. Third, increasing social contact and support for caregivers helps keep stress more manageable. Assistance may also be possible from religious or community organizations, as well as organizations focused on particular medical conditions.

Substance Abuse

> *"I wouldn't get up in the morning," she said. "I realized I was using alcohol to raise my spirits. It raises your spirits for a little while, and then you become depressed . . . With people dying around you, you feel more lonely and isolated." (Wren, 1998, p. 12)*

Alcohol abuse can begin after a loss. Genevieve May, a psychiatrist, started abusing alcohol after the death of her husband. Finding that this was not a solution, Dr. May entered the Betty Ford Center and was successfully treated at age 83. There has been a dramatic increase in substance abuse and the nonmedical use of prescription medications among older adults. It is estimated that 11% of older adults abuse alcohol or prescription drugs; some of the misuse of prescription drugs may involve misunderstanding of dosing instructions. Drugs that have abuse potential include the benzodiazepines, opiates, and muscle relaxants. What is especially problematic is that aging produces physiological changes that may increase the potency of the drugs as well as of their interactions. Because of this, the National Institute of Alcohol Abuse and Alcoholism recommends that men 65 or older not have more than one drink daily and a maximum of two drinks on any occasion. Lower limits are recommended for women (Bogunovic, 2012). The misuse of drugs can produce conditions resembling organic or mental health conditions.

Between 1992 and 2008, the proportion of substance abuse treatment admissions involving older Americans for the abuse of heroin doubled from 7.2% to 16%, cocaine from 2.9% to 11.4%, prescription medications from 0.7% to 3.5%, and marijuana from 0.6% to 2.9% (Substance Abuse and Mental Health Services Administration, 2010). About 20% of seniors take pain medications several times per week; about 18% of these individuals abuse or become addicted to these drugs (Lowry, 2013).

Implications

Older adults rarely seek treatment for substance abuse problems because of shame and perhaps because they feel uncomfortable in programs that deal with "street" drugs, such as heroin or cocaine. Late-onset alcohol and drug abuse problems seem to be related to stressors such as the death of a spouse, family member, or friend; retirement issues; family conflicts; physical health problems; or financial concerns. Many of these stressors are typical issues faced in later life. Early intervention to identify and provide support for these situations can reduce substance abuse risk. As compared to younger substance abusers, older patients respond better to more structured programs, more flexible rules concerning discharge, more comprehensive assessment, and more outpatient mental health aftercare (Moos, Mertens, & Brennan, 1995). DHHS (2005) has published a comprehensive treatment manual for use by counselors that contains an evidence-based cognitive-behavioral group treatment for substance abuse in older adults. It contains modifications to therapy that incorporates physiological, cognitive, and social changes that are characteristic of this population. The manual is helpful in providing specific interventions in either a group or individual format.

Social Isolation, Depression, and Suicide

Depression and social isolation are common complaints among older adults. Although physical changes associated with aging (e.g., hearing or vision loss or cardiovascular disease) can sometimes lead to depression (McDonnall, 2011), depression is not a normal consequence of aging. Depression is more strongly associated with feelings of "being old" than with actual age or health status (Rosenfeld, 2004). The rate of depression increases with age for males, whereas the rate of depression in women decreases after the age of 60. Stressful life changes, such as the death of friends and relatives, increasing social isolation, or financial distress, can increase the risk of depression. Social isolation is not only related to depression but is also associated with other mental health conditions and physical complaints; between 10% and 43% of older adults living in the community report experiencing social isolation (Nicholson, 2012).

Among older men, the highest rates of depression are for those who never married (20.6%) or who are separated or divorced (19.2%). The prevalence of depression among older women is highest among those who are separated or divorced (23.1%) or widowed (15.4%). For males and females with partners, depression is most common among those in stressful relationships (St. John & Montgomery, 2009). Depression needs to be identified and treated, since it is also seen as an independent risk factor for cardiovascular and cerebrovascular disease. Not only does late-life depression significantly affect older adults' physical health, it can also affect social connections and overall functioning, and increase the risk of suicide (Beyer, 2007).

Baby boomers—those born in the '50s and '60s—have shown a dramatic spike in suicides, especially among Whites, Native Americans, and Alaskan men. This increase may be the result of coming from a youth-oriented and optimistic generation and an associated inability to deal with signs of aging or perceived lack of achievement (Bahrampour, 2013). Suicide rates are exceptionally high among older men, with the risk increasing with advancing age; White males aged 85 or older have the second highest suicide rate of any group. It is unclear whether this group has less resilience and fewer coping strategies or whether the high suicide rate is because life changes associated with advanced age (e.g., loss of employment, physical changes, loss of control) are a greater stressor for men. Factors associated with suicide include being separated, divorced, or alone; suffering depression; having an anxiety disorder; having physical or medical problems; and dealing with family conflict or loss of a relationship (American Foundation for Suicide Prevention, 2015).

Implications

It is important to avoid assuming that depression is a normal consequence of aging (APA, 2009b). Interestingly, in a sample of 139 people over 100 years of age, most were in good spirits even though they scored higher for depression than individuals in their 60s (Scheetz, Martin, & Poon, 2012). However, in many cases, major depression tends to be unrecognized in older adults and is a significant predictor of suicide. It is, therefore, essential to assess for depression and suicidality when working with older adults. A popular instrument for screening for depression is the Geriatric Depression Scale, which was developed for older adults. It has age-related norms and omits somatic symptoms that may be associated with physical problems rather than depression.

Because depression often co-occurs with physical illnesses, such as cardiovascular disease, stroke, diabetes, and cancer, health providers often believe that the mood disturbance is a normal consequence of these problems, so they are less likely to refer for mental health treatment. Many older individuals who committed suicide had visited a primary care physician very close to the time of suicide (45% within 1 week, and 73% within 1 month) (Juurlink, Herrmann, Szalai, Kopp, & Redelmeier, 2004). There is an urgent need to detect and adequately treat depression in order to reduce suicide among older individuals.

Because of the deleterious effects of social isolation on older adults, early assessment and intervention to prevent further isolation is important. Encouraging older adults to participate in senior centers or other social activities in their community may decrease social isolation (Nicholson, 2012). There is some evidence that the impact of loneliness and depression can be counteracted by helping older adults focus on positive emotions such as happiness, optimism, and resilience; in other words, happiness has been found to "undo" or negate the negative effects of loneliness or depression in older adults (Newall, Chipperfield, Bailis, & Stewart, 2013).

A number of biological and psychological treatments are effective in treating depression in older adults. Approximately 80% of older adults with depression show improvement when they are given appropriate treatment. Antidepressants such as certain selective serotonin reuptake inhibitors (SSRIs) have fewer side effects and are more likely to be continued, an important consideration since rates of noncompliance with medication are high among older adults (Cooper et al., 2005). Meta-analyses of evidence-based therapies, such as cognitive behavioral therapy, dialectical behavior therapy, and interpersonal therapy, indicate that these therapies are effective in reducing depression and dealing with issues such as loss, transitions, and cognitive decline in older individuals (Chand & Grossberg, 2013). Interpersonal therapy has been demonstrated to reduce suicidal ideation (Heisel, Duberstein, Talbot, King, & Tu, 2009).

IMPLICATIONS FOR CLINICAL PRACTICE

Many older adults develop meaningful support systems in the community and have positive contact with family members. Social contacts are important, and engaging in either paid or volunteer work can enhance the self-esteem and life satisfaction of older individuals (Acquino, Russell, Cutrona, & Altmaier, 1996). Issues that older adults face may include retirement and other changing roles; loss and illness of loved ones; more limited financial resources; caretaking responsibilities; social isolation; health and physical problems, including sensory impairment; and cultural devaluation of their group by society (Corna, Wade, Streiner, & Cairney, 2009).

A number of therapy approaches, such as helping clients improve coping skills and teaching them strategies to resolve interpersonal difficulties, can reduce depression in older adults (Reynolds et al., 2014). Cognitive behavioral therapy and interpersonal therapy are both evidence-based therapies that help older adults deal with the issues of grief, role transitions, interpersonal conflicts, and social skills deficits (Van Orden, Talbot, & King, 2012; Wyman-Chick, 2013). Reducing loneliness or social isolation by increasing social opportunities and developing positive emotions can also be effective in improving the mental and physical life of older adults.

Counseling can also significantly improve the quality of life for adults nearing the end of life, or help them resolve late-life issues. The American Counseling Association contains end-of-life care provisions (quality of care, counselor competence, and confidentiality) in its ethics code and should be consulted when working with terminally ill clients and their loved ones (Werth & Crow, 2009).

Following are some suggestions for offering mental health services to older adults (APA, 2014; Knight & McCallum, 1998; Pennington, 2004).

1. Acquire specific knowledge and skills in counseling older adults, and critically evaluate your own attitudes and beliefs regarding aging and older adults.

2. Remain knowledgeable about legal and ethical issues that arise when working with older adults (e.g., competency issues).

3. Determine the reason for evaluation and the social factors affecting the problem, such as recent losses, financial stressors, and family issues.

4. Show older adults respect, and give them as much autonomy as possible, regardless of mental status or the issues involved. When communicating with older adults:

- Give full attention to the individual.

- Talk to rather than about the person.

- Use respectful language (not *elderspeak*).

- Treat the person as an adult.

- Take the individual's concerns seriously.

5. Determine the older adult's views of the problem, his or her belief system, stage-of-life issues, educational background, and social and ethnic influences.

6. Assist in interpreting the impact of cultural issues, such as ethnic group membership, gender, and sexual orientation on the client's life and presenting problems.

7. Presume competence in older adult clients unless the contrary is obvious.

8. If necessary, reduce the pace of therapy to accommodate cognitive slowing.

9. Involve older adults in decisions as much as possible. If there are cognitive limitations, it may be necessary to use legally recognized individuals to assist with decision-making.

10. Use multiple assessments, and include relevant sources (client, family members, significant others, and health care providers).

11. Determine the roles of family caregivers, educate them about emotional or neurocognitive disorders, and help them develop strategies to reduce burnout.

12. When working with an older couple, help negotiate issues around time spent alone and together (especially after retirement) Arguments over recreation are common. There is often too much "couple time" and no "legitimate" reason for separateness

13. Recognize that it is important to help individuals who are alone establish support systems in the community.

14. Help older adults develop a sense of fulfillment in life by discussing the positive aspects of their experiences. Success can be defined as having done one's best or having met and survived challenges. A life review is often helpful.

15. Infections and medication side effects can be particularly troublesome for older adults. A physical evaluation may be needed to determine whether mental symptoms have physical causes.

16. Help adults very close to the end of their lives deal with their attachment to cherished objects by having them decide how heirlooms, keepsakes, and photo albums will be distributed and cared for.

SUMMARY

We are an aging society, and the older population has increased dramatically as the baby boomers retire and life span increases. Yet we are poorly prepared to handle our current aged population and information is lacking on therapies and medications for older individuals. Physical changes and economic concerns become increasingly important stressors in the life of this population. Counselors must become knowledgeable about how aging affects cognitive functioning, sexuality, and social isolation as friends and relatives pass away. Among older adults, special challenges present themselves: *elder abuse and neglect*, substance abuse, depression, and suicide. One of the greatest challenges facing this population is prejudice and discrimination directed at the elderly. Older individuals are subjected to *ageism*, defined as negative attitudes toward older individuals. Not only is less value placed on their lives, but they are often seen as a burden to society. Sixteen clinical implications for counselor practice are identified.

GLOSSARY TERMS

Ageism

Alzheimer's disease

Dementia

Elder abuse and neglect

Elderspeak

Multiple discrimination

REFERENCES

Acierno, R., Hernandez, M. A., Amstadter, A. B., Resnick, H. R., Steve, K., Muzzy, W., & Kilpatrick, D. G. (2010). Prevalence and correlates of emotional, physical, sexual, and financial abuse and potential neglect in the United States: The National Elder Mistreatment study. *American Journal of Public Health*, *100*, 292–297.

Acquino, J. A., Russell, D. W., Cutrona, C. E., & Altmaier, E. M. (1996). Employment status, social support, and life satisfaction among the elderly. *Journal of Counseling Psychology, 43,* 480–489.

Alterovitz, S. S.-R., & Mendelsohn, G. A. (2009). Partner preferences across the life span: Online dating by older adults. *Psychology and Aging, 24,* 513–517.

Alzheimer's Association. (2014). 2014 Alzheimer's disease facts and figures. *Alzheimer's & Dementia, 10,* 1–75.

American Foundation for Suicide Prevention. (2015). *Facts and figures.* Retrieved from https://www.afsp.org/understanding-suicide /facts-and-figures

American Psychological Association. (2001). *Elder abuse and neglect: In search of solutions.* Washington, DC: Author.

American Psychological Association. (2009a). *Insufficient evidence that sexual orientation change efforts work.* Retrieved from http:// www.apa.org/news/press/releases/2009/08 /therapeutic.aspx

American Psychological Association. (2009b). *Multicultural competency in geropsychology.* Washington, DC: Author.

American Psychological Association. (2014). Guidelines for psychological practice with older adults. *American Psychologist, 9,* 34–65.

Bahrampour, T. (2013). *Baby boomers are killing themselves at an alarming rate, raising question: Why?* Retrieved from http://www.washingtonpost .com/local/baby boomers are killing -themselves-at-an-alarming-rate-begging -question-why/2013/06/03/d98acc7a-c41f -11e2–8c3b-0b5e9247e8ca_print.html

Begley, S. (2010). *Science is reshaping what we know about getting older.* Retrieved from http:// www.newsweek.com/2010/06/18/this-is-your -brain-aging.html

Beyer, J. L. (2007). Managing depression in geriatric populations. *Annals of Clinical Psychiatry, 19,* 221–238.

Bogunovic, O. (2012). *Substance abuse in aging and elderly adults.* Retrieved from http://www .psychiatrictimes.com/geriatric-psychiatry /substance-abuse-aging-and-elderly-adults

Carroll, L. (2011). *Elderly ignore heat warnings—because they are not old.* Retrieved from http://www.msnbc.msn.com/id/43761917/ns /healthy-aging/

Centers for Disease Control and Prevention (2015). *Disability and dysfunction (adults).* Retrieved from http://www.cdc.gov/nchs/fastats /disability.htm

Chand, S. P., & Grossberg, G. T. (2013). *How to adapt cognitive-behavioral therapy for older adults.* Retrieved from http://www.currentpsychiatry .com/home/article/how-to-adapt-cogni tive-behavioral-therapy-for-older-adults /99ca3dc03cddedc62b20b672dcc4e56c.html

Clarke, L. H. (2011). *Facing age: Women growing older in anti-aging culture.* Toronto, Canada: Rowman & Littlefield.

Cooper, C., Carpenter, I., Katona, C., Scholl, M., Wagner, C., Fialova, D., & Livingston, G. (2005). The Ad-HOC study of older adults' adherence to medication in 11 countries. *American Journal of Geriatric Psychiatry, 13,* 1067–1076.

Corna, L. M., Wade, T. J., Streiner, D. L., & Cairney, J. (2009). Transitions in hearing impairment and psychological distress in older adults. *Canadian Journal of Psychiatry, 54,* 518–525.

Costantino, G., Malgady, R. G., & Primavera, L. H. (2009). Congruence between culturally competent treatment and cultural needs of older Latinos. *Journal of Consulting and Clinical Psychology, 77,* 941–949.

Craik, F.I.M. (2008). Memory changes in normal and pathological aging. *Canadian Journal of Psychiatry, 53*, 343–345.

DHHS (Department of Health and Human Services). (2005). *Substance abuse relapse prevention for older adults: A group treatment approach.* Rockville, MD: Substance Abuse and Mental Health Services Administration,

DHHS (Department of Health and Human Services). (2014). *A profile of older Americans: 2014.* Retrieved from http://www.aoa.gov/aging_statistics/Profile/

Fisher, L. L. (2010). *Sex, romance, and relationships: 2009 AARP survey of midlife and older adults.* Washington, DC: AARP.

Gatz, M. (2007). Genetics, dementia, and the elderly. *Current Directions in Psychological Science, 16*, 123–127.

Heisel, M. J., Duberstein, P. R., Talbot, N. L., King, D. A., & Tu, X. M. (2009). Adapting interpersonal psychotherapy for older adults at risk for suicide: Preliminary findings. *Professional Psychology: Research and Practice, 40,* 156–164.

Hoffman, J. (2015). *Married sex gets better in the golden years.* Retrieved from http://well.blogs.nytimes.com/2015/02/23/married-sex-gets-better-in-the-golden-years/

Horning, S. M., Wilkins, S. S., Dhanani, S., & Henriques, D. (2013). A case of elder abuse and undue influence: Assessment and treatment from a geriatric interdisciplinary team. *Clinical Case Studies, 12*, 373–387

Jacobson, S., & Samdahl, D. M. (1998). Leisure in the lives of old lesbians: Experiences with and responses to discrimination. *Journal of Leisure Research, 30*, 233–255.

Jeste, D. V., Savla, G. N., Thompson, W. K., Vahia, I. V., Glorioso, D. K., Martin, A. S., . . . Depp, C. A. (2013). Association between older age and more successful aging: critical role of resilience and depression. *American Journal of Psychiatry, 170,* 188–196.

Johnson, B. (1995, January 19). Elderly women need not abandon sexuality. *Seattle Post-Intelligencer.*

Juurlink, D. N., Herrmann, N., Szalai, J. P., Kopp, A., & Redelmeier, D. A. (2004). Medical illness and the risk of suicide in the elderly. *Archives of Internal Medicine, 164*, 1179–1184.

Karpf, A. (2015). *The liberation of growing old.* Retrieved from http://www.nytimes.com/2015/01/04/opinion/sunday/the-liberation-of-growing-old.html?_r=0

Knight, B. G., & McCallum, T. J. (1998). Adapting psychotherapeutic practice for older clients: Implications of the contextual, cohort-based, maturity, specific challenge model. *Professional Psychology: Research and Practice, 29*, 15–22.

Kotter-Gruhn, D., Kleinspehn-Ammerlahn, A., Gerstorf, D., & Smith, J. (2009). Self-perceptions of aging predict mortality and change with approaching death: Results from the Berlin aging study. *Psychology and Aging, 24*, 654–667.

Krendl, A. C., Heatherton, T. F., & Kensinger, E. A. (2009). Aging minds and twisting attitudes: An fMRI investigation of age differences in inhibiting prejudice. *Psychology and Aging, 24*, 530–541.

Levy, B. R., Chung, P. H., Bedford, T., & Navrazhina, K. (2014). Facebook as a site for negative age stereotypes. *Gerontologist, 54*, 172–176.

Lindau, S. T., Schumm, L. P., Laumann, E. O., Levinson, W., O'Muircheartaigh, C. A., & Waite, L. J. (2007). A study of sexuality and health among older adults in the United States. *New England Journal of Medicine, 357*, 762–774.

Lombardi, N. J., Buchanan, J. A., Afierbach, S., Campana, K., Sattler, A., & Lai, D. (2014). Is elderspeak appropriate? A survey of certified nursing assistants. *Journal of Gerontological Nursing, 40*, 44–52.

Lowry, F. (2013). *Opioid abuse in the elderly an urgent concern*. Retrieved from http://www.medscape.com/viewarticle/776128

McDonnall, M. C. (2011). Physical status as a moderator of depressive symptoms among older adults with dual sensory loss. *Rehabilitation Psychology, 56*, 67–76.

Molinari, V. (Ed.) (2011). *Specialty competencies in geropsychology*. New York, NY: Oxford University Press.

Moos, R. H., Mertens, J. R., & Brennan, P. L. (1995). Program characteristics and readmission among older substance abuse patients: Comparisons with middle-aged and younger patients. *Journal of Mental Health Administration, 22*, 332–346.

Mosqueda, L., & Dong, X. (2011). Elder abuse and self-neglect: "I don't care anything about going to the doctor, to be honest . . ." *Journal of the American Medical Association, 306*, 532–540.

Neider, M. B., Gaspar, J. G., McCarley, J. S., Crowell, J. A., Kaczmarski, H., & Kramer, A. F. (2011). Walking and talking: Dual-task effects on street crossing behavior in older adults. *Psychology and Aging, 26*, 260–268.

Newall, N. E., Chipperfield, J. G., Bailis, D. S., & Stewart, T. L. (2013). Consequences of loneliness on physical activity and mortality in older adults and the power of positive emotions. *Health Psychology, 32*, 921–924.

Nicholson, N. R. (2012). A review of social isolation: An important but underassessed condition in older adults. *Journal of Primary Prevention, 33*, 137–152.

Ortman, J. M., Velkoff, V. A., & Hogan, H. (2014). *An aging nation: The older population in the United States, current population reports, P25–1140*. Washington, DC: U.S. Census Bureau.

Palmore, E. (2005). Three decades of research on ageism. *Generations, 29*, 87–90.

Pennington, D. (2004, July). Until the "sunset": Helping persons who are older and their caregivers to cope with Alzheimer's, other forms of dementia. *Counseling Today*, pp. 22–23.

Reynolds, C. F. III, Thomas, S. B., Morse, J. Q., Anderson, S. J., Albert, S., Dew, M. A., . . . Quinn, S. C. (2014). Early intervention to preempt major depression among older Black and White adults. *Psychiatric Services, 65*, 765–773.

Rosenfeld, B. (2004). *Assisted suicide and the right to die*. New York, NY: Guilford Press.

Salthouse, T. (2012). Consequences of age-related cognitive declines. *Annual Review of Psychology, 63*, 201–226.

Schaie, K., Willis, S., & Caskie, G. (2004). The Seattle longitudinal study: Relationship between personality and cognition. *Neuropsychology of Cognition, 11*, 304–324.

Scheetz, L. T., Martin, P., & Poon, L. W. (2012). Do centenarians have higher levels of depression? Findings from the Georgia Centenarian Study. *Journal of the American Geriatrics Society, 60*, 238–242.

Scheibe, S., & Carstensen, L. L. (2010). Emotional aging: Recent findings and future trends. *Journal of Gerontology: Psychological Sciences, 65*, 135–144.

Sewell, D. (2013). *Aging America: Elder abuse on the rise*. Retrieved from http://vitals.nbcnews.com/_news/2013/01/27/16725913-aging-america-elder-abuse-on-the-rise?lite

Silvertsen, B., Omvik, S., Pallesen, S., Bjorvatn, B., Havik, O. E., & Nordhus, I. H. (2006). Cognitive behavioral therapy vs. Zopiclone for treatment of chronic primary insomnia in older adults. *JAMA, 295*, 2851–2858.

St. John, P. D., & Montgomery, P. R. (2009). Marital status, partner satisfaction, and depressive symptoms in older men and women. *Canadian Journal of Psychiatry, 54*, 487–492.

Stroope, S., McFarland, M. J., & Uecker, J. E. (2015). Marital characteristics and the sexual relationships of U.S. older adults: An analysis of National Social Life, Health, and Aging Project data. *Archives of Sexual Behavior, 44,* 233–247.

Substance Abuse and Mental Health Services Administration. (2010). *New nationwide study shows a dramatic rise in the proportion of older Americans admitted for substance abuse treatment from 1992 to 2008.* Retrieved from http://www.samhsa.gov /newsroom/press-announcements/201006161100

Tergesen, A. (2014). *Why everything you think about aging may be wrong.* Retrieved from http:// www.msn.com/en-us/news/us/why-every thing-you-think-about-aging-may-be-wrong /ar-BBgcIYn

U.S. Census Bureau. (2005). *65+ in the United States: 2005.* Washington, DC: U.S. Government Printing Office.

Van Orden, K. A., Talbot, N., & King, D. (2012). Using the interpersonal theory of suicide to inform interpersonal psychotherapy with a suicidal older adult. *Clinical Case Studies, 11,* 333–347.

Wallhagen, M. I., Pettengill, E., & Whiteside, M. (2006). Sensory impairment in older adults, Part 1: Hearing loss. *American Journal of Nursing, 106,* 40–48.

Weiss, I. (2005). Interest in working with the elderly: A cross-national study of graduating social work students. *Journal of Social Work Education, 41,* 379–391.

Werth, J. L. Jr., & Crow, L. (2009). End-of-life care: An overview for professional counselors. *Journal of Counseling and Development, 87,* 194–201.

Williams, K., Kemper, S., & Hummert, M. L. (2005). Enhancing communication with older adults: Overcoming elderspeak. *Journal of Psychosocial Nursing and Mental Health Services, 43,* 12–16.

Williams, K. N., Herman, R., Gajewski, B., & Wilson, K. (2009). Elderspeak communication: Impact on dementia care. *American Journal of Alzheimer's Disease and Other Dementias, 24,* 11–20.

Williams, K. N., & Kemper, S. (2010). Interventions to reduce cognitive decline in aging. *Journal of Psychosocial Nursing and Mental Health Services, 48,* 42–51.

Wren, C. S. (1998, June 5). Many women 60 and older abuse alcohol and prescribed drugs, study says. *New York Times,* p. 12.

Wyman-Chick, K. A. (2013). Combining cognitive-behavioral therapy and interpersonal therapy for geriatric depression with complicated grief. *Clinical Case Studies, 11,* 361–375.

Zeiss, A. M. (2001). *Aging and human sexuality resource guide.* Washington, DC: American Psychological Association.

Zeranski, L., & Halgin, R. P. (2011). Ethical issues in elder abuse reporting: A professional psychologist's guide. *Professional Psychology: Research and Practice, 42,* 294–300.

Counseling Individuals Living in Poverty

Laura Smith

Chapter Objectives

1. Learn the demographics associated with *poverty*.

2. Identify counseling implications of the information provided regarding impoverished clients.

3. Recognize strengths associated with experiences involving *poverty*.

4. Know the special challenges faced by impoverished clients.

5. Understand best practices for working with impoverished clients.

> *We're people with lives and things in our lives that are affecting our health . . . Talking about our mental health is not the same as someone who feels down sometimes. If you don't have a roof over your head, if you don't have your electric bill paid, then how are you going to take care of your mental health? There is not a traditional mental health strategy that gets at that. (Participant in the ROAD [Reaching Out About Depression] project, Goodman et al., 2007, p. 286)*

> *At least 12 states have passed legislation requiring drug testing for certain people receiving public assistance such as food stamps, public health care, and unemployment benefits. This reinforces the view that the poor do not want jobs and as one legislator argued "It reinforces the stigma that people who are in need, who are poor, are drug users." (Laine, 2015)*

> *[W]hen the therapist and client come from different class backgrounds, they do not always view situations, family relationships, nor solutions from the same viewpoint . . . I did not find that these therapists were particularly unsympathetic or knowingly unkind. What I did find was that the therapists . . . were unaware of their own class values. (Chalifoux, 1996, p. 32)*

Poverty does not constitute a cultural designation in the true sense of the word, yet the challenges and landmarks of life in *poverty* diverge enough from mainstream life to warrant consideration by counseling professionals. Part of this consideration requires that counselors who come from middle-class (and more affluent) backgrounds learn about the realities experienced by those living in *poverty*. Equally important, however, is learning about the class-related biases, attitudes, assumptions, and procedures that are often embedded in the worldviews of people who hold *social class privilege*, and the ways that these assumptions are manifested within psychological theory, research, and practice. Without an awareness of the social, cultural, and interpersonal discrimination that accompanies *poverty*, counselors may be unable to work effectively with low-income clients—and may even unintentionally contribute to their oppression.

These factors will be presented within the context of *social class stratification theory* (e.g., Beeghley, 2008). Many of us are not well acquainted with *social class* theory; we are much more familiar with numerical calculations like socioeconomic status (SES), and often think of *poverty* only in terms of inadequate financial resources. Financial resources are indeed critical to understanding life in *poverty*. A *social class* framework, however, positions *poverty* as more than a lack of purchasing power. Rather, *poverty* involves being on the bottom-most rung in a hierarchical system of sociocultural power relations that goes beyond differences in income. Within this hierarchy, *social class* oppression is called *classism* (Lott & Bullock, 2007), and it operates to limit access to many kinds of socially valued assets. As will be described in a subsequent section, these assets include the availability of essential services and resources (e.g., education and health care), entrée to mainstream opportunities and experiences, cultural inclusion/exclusion, and representation within our nation's system of participatory democracy (Smith, 2010).

CHARACTERISTICS AND STRENGTHS

The U.S. Census Bureau estimated that the American *poverty* rate was 14.5% in 2013, down from 15.0% in 2012 (DeNavas-Walt & Proctor, 2014). This was the first decrease in the *poverty* rate since 2006. The trends and data summarized below illustrate further a demographic snapshot of U.S. *poverty* today:

- The *poverty* rate for Whites was 9.6% in 2013. For African Americans, the 2013 *poverty* rate was 27.2%, while the rate for Latinas/os was 23.5%. For Asians, the 2013 *poverty* rate was 10.5% (DeNavas-Walt & Proctor, 2014). Because Whites are a larger population in the United States, they comprise 42% of those living in *poverty*. Further, 29% of those living in *poverty* are Latinas/o and 25% are African American.

- Children (at a *poverty* rate of 19.9%) continue to be the age group most likely to live in *poverty*, and the U.S. child *poverty* rate is one of the highest in the developed world (UNICEF, 2012). Unlike the overall *poverty* rate, the *poverty* rate for children did not decline from its 2012 levels (DeNavas-Walt & Proctor, 2014).

- Women are more likely to live in *poverty* than men. In 2013, 13.1% of males and 15.8% of females were impoverished, differences that are most pronounced among those aged 65 and older. For women aged 65 and older, the *poverty* rate was 11.6%, while it was 6.8% for men in this age group (DeNavas-Walt & Proctor, 2014).

- Among women, *poverty* rates are especially high among Black women (25.3%), Latinas (23.1%), and Native American women (26.8%); rates for

Asian American women are closer (11.0%) to the *poverty* rates for White women (10.7%). *Poverty* rates for all racial groups of adult women are higher than for their male counterparts (Entmacher, Robbins, Vogtman, & Morrison, 2014).

- Globally, one of the distinguishing features of American *poverty* is that it takes place in the wealthiest nation in the world. The United States continues to have one of the world's most unequal income distributions. As measured by the Gini coefficient—a statistic that reflects the disparity between the lowest and highest income levels in a nation—and after adjusting for taxes, the United States is second in global inequality (after Chile) (DeSilver, 2013). This inequality has grown steadily in recent decades: in the 1970s, the share of total income earned by the top 1% of families was less than 10%; however, their share exceeded 20% by the end of 2012 (Saez & Zucman, 2014).

- Similarly, the continuing escalation of wealth inequity in the United States is dramatic. The top 0.1% of American families—a group comprised of 160,000 families—by itself owned 22% of all U.S. wealth in 2012, up from 7% in the late 1970s (Saez & Zucman, 2014).

The statements above use the word *poverty* with reference to specific numerical criteria such as the federal *poverty* threshold. Different branches of the U.S. government compute such designations slightly differently, yet such calculations (hence, figures like the ones above) always underestimate the number of families who are struggling economically. For example, the Department of Health and Human Services guidelines (HHS, 2015) specify that a family of four must earn less than $24,250 per year to fall beneath the *poverty* line; therefore, a family of four attempting to live on $24,251 per year would *not* be counted among the poor. These data effectively illustrate a significant characteristic of American *social class* structure: positions of lower socioeconomic power and access—that is, life in *poverty*—intersect meaningfully with marginalization along other dimensions of identity such as race and gender.

Strengths

Presenting the strengths of people living in *poverty* is a somewhat self-contradictory undertaking. On the one hand, the question may seem to suggest that poor people are somehow inherently different from the rest of us. However, research evidence supports the opposite contention. Certainly, an individual *can* suffer a financial downturn for a variety of personal reasons. Nevertheless, the fact that particular cultural groups are consistently overrepresented among the poor supports the notion that *poverty* generally derives from people's historical and socio-political contexts rather than from individual peculiarities (e.g., Belle, 1990; Carmon, 1985; Costello, Compton, Keeler, & Angold, 2003). Similarly, the elevated levels of stress, deprivation, and physical wear-and-tear that are characteristically detected among poor people would theoretically be expected to affect almost anyone who was constrained to survive life in *poverty*.

On the other hand, when people *do* survive *poverty*, they demonstrate strengths that are not part of the stereotypical image that many people have of the poor. For example, Banyard (2008) wrote of the patience, persistence, and determination of homeless women as they struggled to make decent lives for their children—women who have often been stereotyped with the classist, racist label *welfare queen*. The words of these homeless mothers illustrate Banyard's characterization of them as not only surviving, but tenaciously creating survival strategies, solving problems, and maintaining hope as they prioritized their children and their roles as mothers:

> [Y]ou have an allotted time to get out of the [shelter]. That's stressful, knowing that the clock's ticking . . . You've worked all your life, and then you're stuck on welfare, and then your children ask for things. (p. 1)

> We just, we think of it again, and think of another route. You know, like taking another street. You know, it's not like you'll hit a highway . . . but it won't be a dead end street. (p. 2)

> You know, it's like I run this race, I fall down. I'm not just going to lay there. Even if I lose, I'm going to get up and still try to make it to the finish line. (p. 2)

Obviously, most of us would wish for a world in which mothers, fathers, and children did not have to demonstrate their ability to survive homelessness. However, it is important to take stock of the strengths that people in *poverty* demonstrate, as Banyard (2008) explained:

> If we assume that women in poverty are lazy and unmotivated (common stereotypes), we are likely to design policies that focus exclusively

on giving them, as individuals, penalties for not finding a job. If we, on the other hand, assume that many women possess the desire to make a better life for themselves and their families, and listen to their stories of how hard it is to feed and house a family on minimum wage or to find affordable childcare, then we design policies which encourage work by supporting a living wage and educational opportunities for low-income workers and increasing accessible, affordable childcare for their children. (p. 2)

Most of us can readily recognize how a scarcity of the essential resources and services that support life—healthy food, safe communities, good schools, adequate health care, a roof over one's head—may lead in obvious ways to discomfort, distress, and crisis for poor families. What may not be as obvious is the additional stress that results from institutional and cultural *classism*. As is the case with other forms of oppression, classist attitudes often exist at an unconscious level within the worldviews of well-intentioned individuals, and may be unintentionally perpetuated by counselors who are unaware of the implications of their actions. Understanding *classism*, therefore, is an essential component of multiculturally competent practice. The sections below profile some examples of classist discrimination.

SPECIFIC CHALLENGES

In this section, we consider the challenges faced by those living in *poverty* such as their invisibility, educational inequity, disparities in the judicial system, and health care inequities.

The Cultural Invisibility and Social Exclusion of the Poor

The American author and poet Dorothy Allison (1994), who was raised in *poverty*, observed, "My family's life was not on television, not in books, not even in comic books" (p. 17), a perception that has subsequently been borne out by the social psychological literature. Bullock, Wyche, and Williams (2001) found that poor people rarely appear within televised media representations, and when they do, they are often portrayed as lazy, promiscuous, dysfunctional, and/or drug-addicted. Similarly, the experiences of working-class people are largely without representation in popular culture, and there are few poor or working-class voices in the national discourse on public policy issues. When they are included, usually with regard to specific topics such as organized labor, they are often presented in a negative light.

Increasingly, the poor are being physically as well as metaphorically excluded from mainstream cultural life. A report entitled "Homes Not Handcuffs" documented the rise in civic ordinances that restrict the sharing of food, make it illegal to sit or sleep in public spaces, and drive homeless people away from public areas, often resulting in the loss of people's personal documents, medications, and other property (National Law Center on Homelessness and Poverty and National Coalition for the Homeless, 2009). Ehrenreich (2009) called this trend *"the criminalization of poverty"* (p. 2).

Educational Inequities

> *In 2013, 51% of public school students were considered low income (qualifying for free or reduced fee meals) as compared to 38% in 2000. As one educator warned "Without improving the educational support that the nation provides its low income students—students with the largest needs and usually with the least support—the trends of the last decade will be prologue for a nation not at risk, but a nation in decline"... (Southern Education Foundation, 2015, p. 4)*

Although education is often promoted as a pathway out of *poverty*, American educational disparities are such that the families with the greatest need are often relegated to the least adequate educational resources. Further, children in *poverty* often do not have proper nutrition, health insurance coverage, or necessary educational supplies.

The test score gap between affluent students and those from lower income families has increased by 40% since the 1960s, 22% of those from lower income families do not graduate from high school as compared to 6% of those from higher income families (Annie E. Casey Foundation, 2012). Jonathan Kozol has chronicled the interface of class, race, and schooling in America in books like *The Shame of the Nation* (2006), finding that children who attend public schools in poor communities are more likely to be taught by poorly-paid, uncertified teachers, and to have fewer computers, fewer library books, fewer classes, fewer extracurricular opportunities, and fewer teachers than those attended by wealthier students.

According to "Losing Ground," a report by the National Center for Public Policy and Higher Education (2002), the relatively small number of students from low-income families who make it to college campuses will find that the costs of a college education have escalated at a rate higher than both inflation and family income. As a result, the graduation rates of low-income students are reduced while students from middle-class and wealthy families continue to attend college in record numbers.

Up to 40% of low-income students who indicate that they will attend college fail to show up in the fall. This phenomenon is called "summer melt." Because they often lack role models from family members or friends, these students are unfamiliar with the process of completing paperwork for admission, financial assistance, choosing housing, or registering for classes. This is especially problematic when counselors are not available in the summer. Even after financial packages receive preliminary approval, there is a need for documentation regarding income and other resources. Unless assistance is available to help applicants respond to these requests, prospective students may become confused and give up.

Implications

Low-income students need assistance in navigating the application process for college admittance and follow-up support to ensure that enrollment proceeds successfully. Programs that have been effective in reducing summer melt attritions are bridge programs that facilitate the move from high school to college (Castleman & Page, 2014; Frey, 2014). Counselors play an important role in assuring successful entry into college. In one case, the manager of a college housing complex contacted a female student, informing her that she needed to immediately send in $1,700 to cover her deposit and rent. The mother then contacted a transition counselor, who was able to intervene until state financial assistance became available. Practical assistance such as this is often necessary to help low-income students navigate the complexities of the educational system (Frey, 2014).

Poverty and Mental Illness

> *Living in poverty for any significant length of time increases all sorts of risk factors for health and mental health problems. You are more stressed, worrying about money constantly, and how you're going to pay the bills or have enough money to eat . . . If you can still afford to live on your own, you will likely do so in a neighborhood more prone to violence, exposing you to more trauma and risk for personal violence. (Grohol, 2011)*

Poverty is related to and often precedes the development of emotional problems such as anxiety and depression (Hudson, 2005); it produces conditions conducive to the development of mental health issues. Individuals who live in *poverty* face a number of stressors, such as economic worries, discrimination, family conflict, inadequate housing, and frequent moves—all of which may result in psychiatric symptoms, including heightened physiological reactions to even minor anxiety-inducing events (Wadsworth & Achenbach, 2005; Wadsworth & Rienks, 2012). In addition, the living environment associated with *poverty* can increase the risk of exposure to violence and trauma, resulting in high rates of stress disorders such as PTSD, and other problems such as aggression, delinquency, substance abuse, and academic difficulties (Kearney, Wechsler, Kaur, & Lemos-Miller, 2010).

Implications

Many individuals living in *poverty* do not seek treatment because of practical problems such as limited transportation, inflexible work schedules, lack of health insurance, or other factors that affect their access to mental health services. Counselors working with low-income clients should develop a flexible schedule and style to meet the needs of individuals who may not be able to attend weekly or 50-minute sessions, address barriers that may affect attendance, and increase the outreach component in providing therapy (Santiago, Kaltman, & Miranda, 2013).

Environmental Injustice

Waste dumps, "dirty industries," and other pollution-producing operations are frequently located in the urban and rural areas where poor people and people of color live. U.S. Environmental Protection Agency (EPA) administrator Lisa Jackson called these neighborhoods "hot spots of emissions, hot spots of contamination" as she discussed efforts to address the resulting elevated risk of asthma and other pollution-related conditions (Filperin, 2010, para. 17).

Disparities in the Judicial System

Mentioned regularly in media descriptions of legal proceedings, bail represents one of the more overt forms of classist discrimination: the poor remain in prison cells while wealthier people accused of the same crimes go home. Moreover, funding for legal aid services is sufficient only to provide counsel to a small proportion of the Americans who need it, with the result that millions of poor people are priced out of the U.S. civil legal process for the vast majority of their legal concerns (Rhode, 2004). Reiman (2007) has argued that the criminal justice system itself is deeply classist in that it portrays crime as the misdeeds of the poor. In other words, street crimes like burglary, theft, and selling drugs are the contents of the typical police blotter and are detailed in national crime rate statistics. This practice serves to deflect attention from the crimes that actually cause the most death, destruction, and suffering in our country, crimes that derive from the actions of people with *social class privilege*: corporate fraud, the creation of toxic pollutants, profiteering from unhealthy or unsafe products, and risky high-level financial ventures where the American public ends up bearing the consequences of the risk.

Classism and the Minimum Wage

Without people working in minimum wage jobs, the lives of middle-class and wealthy Americans would come to a standstill. Our society relies upon the people who ring up our purchases, work in childcare, change hospital beds, clean offices, and serve food; yet the citizens who perform these necessary jobs cannot earn enough money to lift their families above the *poverty* line. The federal minimum wage of $7.25 per hour does not allow a full-time worker to lift his or her family of four out of *poverty*, a conclusion that emerges from examining the cost of living around the country via Penn State's Living Wage Calculator. This tool calculates the minimum cost of essential food, medical, housing, and transportation requirements in almost every U.S. city and county, and is available online at www.livingwage.geog.psu.edu. This observation goes hand-in-hand with a finding by the National Coalition for the Homeless (2005): as many as 25% of people in U.S. homeless shelters have jobs. The unlivable level of the minimum wage gives rise to inherent ethical contradictions, suggesting that classist attitudes toward the poor may influence public debate (or lack thereof) over this issue.

Health Care Inequities

The health disparities research is resoundingly clear: poor people face elevated rates of nearly every sort of threat to survival, including heart disease, diabetes, exposure to toxins, cognitive and physical functional decline, and homicide, among many other threats (e.g., Belle, Doucet, Harris, Miller, & Tan, 2000; Scott, 2005). In the first quarter of 2014, the number of Americans without health insurance has dropped to 41 million from 50 million in 2009 (Kaiser Foundation, 2010; Tavernise, 2014). This decrease is primarily because of enrollment via provisions of the Affordable

Care Act. Although this is an improvement, a substantial number of Americans remain uninsured. The majority of the uninsured come from low-income families, yet *61% come from families where one or more members work full-time.* Not surprisingly, people without access to medical care often have no choice but to allow preventable conditions to escalate into serious ones, and to leave serious problems untreated. Correspondingly, a 2009 Harvard study found that nearly 45,000 U.S. deaths annually are associated with a lack of health insurance (Wilper et al., 2009).

Negative Attitudes and Beliefs

> *Many states have passed laws restricting what food stamp recipients and people on other food nutritional programs can buy including items such as crab or other shellfish, energy drinks, soda, cookies, chips and steak (Kackley, 2015). Kansas politicians also proposed a $25 withdrawal limit from ATMs by welfare recipients to "help" these individuals manage their money better. (Paulson, 2015)*

> *My kids brought home a letter asking us to bring cookies or bars to a school potluck . . . buying ingredients for making cookies is expensive, so we used our food stamps to buy Oreos, self-consciously explaining our dilemma to the store clerk . . . Make no mistake: Forcing families to spend two-thirds of their benefits on approved foods is not about stemming growth in programs, teaching responsibility or curbing the extremely rare instances of abuse. It is about shaming. (Beyer, 2015)*

The current laws to restrict the "misuse" of government assistance to low-income individuals are based on the negative characterizations that have little basis in truth. The small amount of money that these families receive is spent on the necessities of life, not on buying expensive foods. The proposed $25 cap on money withdrawn from ATMs by welfare recipients would cause them to spend more money on fees and to travel more frequently to withdraw funds. The drug testing by states for welfare applicants has incurred a cost of nearly one million dollars. Very few drug users are found. Although the national drug use rate is 9.4%, the rate of positive drug tests for welfare applicants ranged from 0.002% to 8.3%. In fact, the positive drug rate for applicants for all states was under 1% except for one (Covert & Israel, 2015). These restrictive laws only serve to strengthen negative stereotypes of lower income individuals resulting in shame and stigmatization.

By contrast, wealthy people can become national celebrities on the basis of their wealth alone, with the media chronicling their everyday activities. Moreover, within popular culture, intellectualism and critical thinking are largely presented as the exclusive province of more affluent Americans. Although tax breaks for the wealthy contribute to the growing economic gap between the top 1% and the rest of the population, such inequities receive only minor criticism. Corporate welfare (grants, tax breaks, subsidies, or other special treatment for corporations) cost taxpayers hundreds of billions of dollar a year (Bennett, 2015). As Brunari (2014) writes, "The largest, wealthiest, most powerful organizations in the world are on the public dole . . . Boeing receives $13 billion in government handouts and everyone yawns . . . Where is the outrage?" By contrast, support for social programs for low-income individuals are carefully scrutinized, criticized, and considered a drain on society, and individuals using these programs are described as *irresponsible, drug addicts, spendthrifts,* and *lazy* (Johnson, 2014; Lott & Saxon, 2002).

IMPLICATIONS FOR CLINICAL PRACTICE

Collectively, the manifestations of *classism* discussed above operate to create a physically challenging, socially excluded life experience for men, women, and children living in *poverty*. Like other forms of oppression, therefore, *classism* can undermine the physical and emotional well-being of people withstanding its impact. The social exclusion of the poor was captured by psychologist Bernice Lott (2002), who described the primary characteristic of *classism* as *cognitive and behavioral distancing* from the poor. In particular, Lott linked this phenomenon to psychologists' lack of attention to *poverty*, which is often apparent even in the context of their consideration of other cultural issues. As a consequence, psychological theory, research, and practice tend to be largely inaccessible by poor people and are not particularly relevant to their experiences (Smith, 2010). In addition, counselors who offer services in poor communities may find that their work is compromised by previously unexamined classist assumptions. Aponte (1994), a family therapist who devoted his career to working with poor clients, suggested that "therapy with the poor must have all the sophistication of the best psychological therapies. It must also have the insight of the social scientist and the drive of the community activist" (p. 9). The following suggestions can help guide counselors in improving their skills in the context of *poverty* (Smith, 2005, 2009):

1. *Supplement your knowledge of social class, poverty, and related issues.* Although most counselors do not receive training experiences focused on *poverty*, helpful resources exist by which counselors, supervisors, and trainees can deepen their understanding of *social class*, the circumstances faced by poor Americans, and the implications of both for clinical work. Some useful starting points include the following:

   • *Psychology and Economic Injustice* (Lott & Bullock, 2007)

   • *The Color of Wealth* (M. Lui, Leondar-Wright, Brewer, & Adamson, 2006)

   • *Where We Stand: Class Matters* (hooks, 2000)

   • *Report of the Task Force on Resources for the Inclusion of Social Class in Psychology Curricula* (American Psychological Association [APA], 2008).

2. *Increase your understanding and awareness of social class privilege.* Many counselors-in-training receive multicultural training experiences that facilitate their awareness of ethnic- and race-related identities; enhancing class awareness is an analogous process, although it is seldom addressed as such. To aid counselors in this effort, Liu, Pickett, and Ivey (2007) developed a list of self-statements corresponding to White middle-class privilege. These statements included "I can be assured that I have adequate housing for myself and my family" and "My family can survive an illness of one or more members" (p. 205). The authors also present a case example to which counselors can refer in applying class-related considerations within counseling practice.

3. *Learn about the everyday realities of life in poverty.* Students in some professions (such as social work) receive training that educates them about welfare procedures, housing offices, food stamps, and other aspects of government bureaucracy; this training helps prepare them to work with clients who have nowhere to turn for health services, shelter, or childcare. Mental health counselors, who often lack this preparation, can find themselves disoriented by the unfamiliar deprivations of life in a poor community. Because such information is often locally specific and subject to change, city and state government websites and Internet searches are a good way to learn about available resources.

4. *Learn to see the everyday signs of social class stratification and bias.* Although *social class* is not often discussed openly in the United States, the signs of its existence are all around us if we begin to open our eyes to it. Sometimes these signs can be seen readily, as in the aforementioned public fascination with the

lives of wealthy people, or in people's interest in wearing clothing that features corporate or designer logos. Others are more subtle, such as those that are manifested through *classist microaggressions* (Smith & Redington, 2010). These expressions of class-based derogation are directly analogous to microaggressions based on other marginalized identities (Sue et al., 2007). Classist microaggressions include the use of class-referenced words to indicate favorable or unfavorable evaluations, such as describing an object or a person as *classy* or *high-class* in a complimentary fashion or describing it as *low-class* or *low-rent* to discredit it. Other classist microaggressions illustrate specific intersections with other identities. Hartigan (2005) discussed the meanings inherent in the name-calling directed toward poor White Americans such as *White trash, trailer trash, rednecks,* or *hillbillies,* whereas Rose (2008) analyzed a microaggression that derives from oppression according to race, class, and gender: *welfare queen.*

5. *Integrate a social justice framework within counseling practice.* Many counselors who go to work in poor communities will encounter bleak urban landscapes, crowded schools, and crumbling housing developments. How are counselors to incorporate the impact of such environmental and contextual dimensions within psychotherapeutic practice, which often seems concerned primarily with an individual's emotional interior? The application of a social justice model to counseling practice makes room within case conceptualization and treatment design for counselors' analyses of the systemic aspects and origins of client distress. Feminist and multicultural examinations of social justice practice can be found within other chapters of this book as well as in works by Aldarondo (2007); Goodman et al. (2004); Miller and Stiver (1997); and Nelson and Prilleltensky (2005).

6. *Adopt a flexible approach to treatment.* As multicultural psychologists have long contended, the conventional roles and behaviors of psychological practice are at best culture-bound and at worst oppressive to clients from marginalized groups (Sue et al., 1998). As mentioned, life in *poverty* can be vastly different from the middle-class existence portrayed in many counseling skills textbooks, and counselors must, therefore, be willing to use their skills flexibly. Dumont (1992) wrote about his experience with clients living in *poverty,* having come to practice in a community mental health center as a psychoanalytically trained psychiatrist. Contending with the pathological social and environmental forces—racism, pollution, involuntary unemployment, and malnutrition—that predominated in his clients' lives, he concluded that "the 50-minute hour of passive attention, of pushing toward the past, of

highlighting the shards of unconscious material in free association, just does not work" (p. 6).

Along these lines, when counselors are willing to learn from community members about the interventions that might be most useful, different kinds of supplementary (or alternative) modalities can emerge. These interventions might involve the development of new practices and modalities in accordance with local needs, such as group discussions offered as part of community gatherings, psychoeducational groups in local classrooms, and collaborative events with homeless shelters (Smith, 2005; Smith, Chambers, & Bratini, 2009). Other modalities might involve the formation of community partnerships that combine counseling practice with peer counseling and local social justice advocacy (Goodman et al., 2007). Participatory action research projects are also a means of enhancing the well-being of poor communities, in concert with social justice activism (Smith & Romero, 2010).

7. *Be willing to incorporate problem-solving and resource identification within sessions—but don't assume that this will be the focus of the work.* People living in *poverty* are often only a paycheck or an accident away from a health or housing crisis. Even in the absence of crisis, they may be constrained to devote time and energy to such exigencies as securing childcare and making food stamps last until the end of the month. Counselors have indicated that they often feel that discussion of such issues is not sufficiently "deep" and does not therefore qualify as the "real" work that they are there to do (Schnitzer, 1996). Such a response bears traces of class bias in that it discounts as superficial some of the most pressing realities of poor clients' lives. This bias can also work in the other direction—middle-class counselors can be so unsettled by their clients' lack of resources that they assume that clients' psychological realities are oriented entirely around securing them. The latter assumption undermines the therapeutic encounter as well, in that it can hinder counselors from engaging poor clients in exploring the same kinds of feelings, fears, hopes, or other emotional issues that clients in any setting are likely to find important (Smith, 2005). It should go without saying that many poor clients come to speak with counselors about precisely these issues. The suggestion that emerges from this balancing act has much in common with good multicultural counseling more generally: be accountable for understanding the unique aspects of clients' sociocultural context and be open to addressing them, but do not assume that this knowledge constitutes a "recipe" for working with them.

8. *Incorporate an advocacy role into your work.* Chen (2013) identified *advocate* as one of the systems intervention roles in which counselors should be competent, and at no time is that role more relevant than when working in the context of oppression. Moreover, given that research has conclusively demonstrated the damage that *poverty* exacts upon people's physical and emotional well-being, advocating for the eradication of *poverty* and the greater cultural inclusion of the poor *is* advocating for psychological well-being. Such advocacy can be expected to benefit a large portion of society, given that over half of Americans are likely to spend at least a year below the *poverty* line at some point during their lives (Hacker, 2006). Opportunities for advocacy include support for broadened access to mental and physical health care for poor families, and participation in the living wage movement, which would raise the minimum wage to a level that allows workers to lift their families out of *poverty*.

SUMMARY

Poverty does not constitute a cultural designation in the true sense of the word, but the challenges of a life in *poverty* are so different from mainstream life that it warrants consideration by clinicians. Counselors are likely to come from middle-class (or more affluent) backgrounds and lack understanding about how the assumptions of mental health and the process of counseling may be antagonistic and detrimental to their clients. Being familiar with the demographics of the poor and their strengths are important for informed work. The poor face many challenges in their lives: invisibility and social exclusion, educational inequities, poverty-related mental illness, disparities in the judicial system, wage and health care inequities, and negative attitudes and beliefs about the poor. Eight clinical implications for counselor practice are identified.

GLOSSARY TERMS

Classism

Cognitive and behavioral distancing

Poverty

Social class

Social class privilege

Social stratification theory

The criminalization of poverty

REFERENCES

Aldarondo, E. (2007). *Advancing social justice through clinical practice.* Mahwah, NJ: Erlbaum.

Allison, D. (1994). *Skin.* Ithaca, NY: Firebrand.

American Psychological Association. (2008). *Report of the task force on resources for the inclusion of social class in psychology curricula.* Retrieved from http://www.apa.org/pi/ses/

Annie E. Casey Foundation (2012). *Kid count data book.* Retrieved from http://www.aecf.org/resources/the-2012-kids-count-data-book/

Aponte, H. J. (1994). *Bread and spirit: Therapy with the new poor.* New York, NY: Norton.

Banyard, V. (2008). *Welfare queens or courageous survivors? Strengths of women in poverty.* Retrieved from http://www.unh.edu/discovery/sites/unh.edu.discovery/files/dialogue/2008/pdf/packet_banyard.pdf

Beeghley, L. (2008). *The structure of social stratification in the United States.* Boston, MA: Allyn & Bacon.

Belle, D. (1990). Poverty and women's mental health. *American Psychologist, 45*(3), 385–389.

Belle, D., Doucet, J., Harris, J., Miller, J., & Tan, E. (2000). Who is rich? Who is happy? *American Psychologist, 55*, 1160–1161.

Bennett, J. T. (2015). *Corporate welfare and the crony capitalism that enriches the rich.* Piscataway, NJ: Transaction Publishers.

Beyer, M. G. (2015). *Don't shame food stamp recipients.* Retrieved from http://host.madison.com/news/opinion/column/guest/maria-gaie-beyer-don-t-shame-food-stamp-recipients/article_13e12dee-a5f3-52c5-a1b6-b5779a7f35f0.html

Brunari, D. (2014). *Where is the outrage over corporate welfare?* Retrieved from http://www.forbes.com/sites/taxanalysts/2014/03/14/where-is-the-outrage-over-corporate-welfare/

Bullock, H. E., Wyche, K. F., and Williams, W. R. (2001). Media images of the poor. *Journal of Social Issues, 57*, 229–246.

Carmon, N. (1985). Poverty and culture: Empirical evidence and implications for public policy. *Sociological Perspectives, 28*, 403–417.

Castleman, B. L., & Page, L. C. (2014). *Summer melt: Supporting low-income students through the transition to college.* Cambridge, MA: Harvard Education Press.

Chalifoux, B. (1996). Speaking up: White working class women in therapy. In M. Hill & E. D. Rothblum (Eds.), *Classism and feminist therapy.* (pp. 25–34). New York, NY: Harrington Park.

Chen, E. C. (2013). *Multicultural competence and social justice advocacy in group psychology and group psychotherapy.* Retrieved from http://www.apadivisions.org/division-49/publications/newsletter/group-psychologist/2013/04/multicultural-competence.aspx

Costello, E. J., Compton, S. N., Keeler, G., & Angold, A. (2003). Relationships between poverty and psychopathology: A natural experiment. *JAMA, 290*(15), 2023–2029.

Covert, B., & Israel, J. (2015). *What 7 states discovered after spending more than $1 million drug testing welfare recipients.* Retrieved from http://think-progress.org/economy/2015/02/26/3624447/tanf-drug-testing-states/

DeNavas-Walt, C., & Proctor, B. (2014). *Income and poverty in the United States: 2013.* Retrieved from https://www.census.gov/content/dam/Census/library/publications/2014/demo/p60-249.pdf

DeSilver, D. (2013). *Global inequality: How the US compares.* Retrieved from http://www.pewresearch.org/fact-tank/2013/12/19/global-inequality-how-the-u-s-compares/

Dumont, M. P. (1992). *Treating the poor: A personal sojourn through the rise and fall of community mental health.* Belmont, MA: Dymphna Press.

Ehrenreich, B. (2009). Is it now a crime to be poor? *New York Times.* Retrieved from http://www.nytimes.com/2009/08/09/opinion/09ehrenreich.html?

Eilperin, J. (2010). Environmental justice issues take center stage. *Washington Post.* Retrieved from http://www.washingtonpost.com/wp-dyn/content/article/2010/11/21/AR2010112103782.html?sid=ST2010112104098

Entmacher, J., Robbins, K., Vogtman, J., & Morrison, A. (2014). *Insecure & unequal: Poverty and income among women and families 2000–2013.* Retrieved from http://www.nwlc.org/sites/default/files/pdfs/final_2014_nwlc_poverty_report.pdf

Frey, S. (2014). *Programs target crucial summer before college.* Retrieved from http://edsource.org/2014/programs-target-crucial-summer-before-college/66896#.VN4rvy4sDoa

Goodman, L. A., Liang, B., Helms, J. E., Latta, R. E., Sparks, E., & Weintraub, S. (2004). Training counseling psychologists as social justice agents: Feminist and multicultural perspectives. *Counseling Psychologist, 32,* 793–837.

Goodman, L. A., Litwin, A., Bohlig, A., Weintraub, S. R., Green, A., Walker, J., . . . Ryan, N. (2007). Applying feminist theory to community practice: A multilevel empowerment intervention for low-income women with depression. In E. Aldarondo (Ed.), *Advancing social justice through clinical practice* (pp. 265–290). Mahwah, NJ: Erlbaum.

Grohol, J. M. (2011). *The vicious cycle of poverty and mental health.* Retrieved from http://psychcentral.com/blog/archives/2011/11/02/the-vicious-cycle-of-poverty-and-mental-health/

Hacker, J. S. (2006). *The great risk shift: The new insecurity and the decline of the American dream.* New York, NY: Oxford University Press.

Hartigan, J. (2005). *Odd tribes: Toward a cultural analysis of White people.* Durham, NC: Duke University Press.

HHS. (2015). *Poverty guidelines.* Retrieved from http://aspe.hhs.gov/poverty-guidelines

hooks, b. (2000). *Where we stand: Class matters.* New York, NY: Routledge.

Hudson, C. G. (2005). Socioeconomic status and mental illness: Tests of the social causation and selection hypotheses. *American Journal of Orthopsychiatry, 75,* 3–18.

Johnson, D. (2014). *7 common myths about people on welfare.* Retrieved from http://everydayfeminism.com/2014/11/common-myths-people-welfare/

Kackley, R. (2015). *Chew on this: Should food stamp recipients have their shopping lists limited?* Retrieved from http://pjmedia.com/blog/chew-on-this-should-food-stamp-recipients-have-their-shopping-lists-limited

Kaiser Foundation. (2010). *The uninsured: A primer.* Retrieved from http://www.kff.org/uninsured/upload/7451-06.pdf

Kearney, C. A., Wechsler, A., Kaur, H., & Lemos-Miller, A. (2010). *Posttraumatic stress disorder in maltreated youth: A review of contemporary research and thought. Clinical Child and Family Psychology Review, 13,* 46–76.

Kozol, J. (2006). *The shame of the nation.* New York, NY: Broadway Books.

Laine, S. (2015). *Drug testing for welfare recipients: Wisconsin poised to join other states.* Retrieved from http://www.csmonitor.com/USA/USA-Update/2015/0123/Drug-testing-for-welfare-recipients-Wisconsin-poised-to-join-other-states

Liu, W. M., Pickett, T., & Ivey, A. E. (2007). White middle-class privilege: Social class bias and implications for training and practice. *Journal of Multicultural Counseling and Development, 35,* 194–206.

Lott, B. (2002). Cognitive and behavioral distancing from the poor. *American Psychologist, 57,* 100–110.

Lott, B., & Bullock, H. E. (2007). *Psychology and economic injustice.* Washington, DC: American Psychological Association.

Lott, B., & Saxon, S. (2002). The influence of ethnicity, social class and context on judgments about U.S. women. *Journal of Social Psychology, 142,* 481–499.

Lui, M., Leondar-Wright, B., Brewer, R., & Adamson, R. (2006). *The color of wealth.* Boston, MA: New Press.

Miller, J. B., & Stiver, I. P. (1997). *The healing connection.* Boston, MA: Beacon Press.

National Center for Public Policy and Higher Education. (2002). *Losing ground: A national status report on the affordability of American higher education.* Retrieved from http://www.highereducation.org/reports/losing_ground/ar.shtml

National Coalition for the Homeless. (2005). *Who is homeless? NCH Fact Sheet #3.* Retrieved from http://www.ncchca.org/files/Homeless/NCH_Who%20is%20Homeless_07.pdfNational

National Law Center on Homelessness and Poverty and the National Coalition for the Homeless (2009). *Homes not handcuffs.* Retrieved from http://nlchp.org/content/pubs/2009HomesNotHandcuffs1.pdf

Nelson, G., & Prilleltensky, I. (Eds.). (2005). *Community psychology: In pursuit of liberation and well-being.* New York, NY: Palgrave Macmillan.

Paulson, A. (2015). *Why is Kansas pursuing tougher welfare rules?* Retrieved from http://www.csmonitor.com/USA/Society/2015/0407/Why-is-Kansas-pursuing-tougher-welfare-rules-video

Reiman, J. (2007). *The rich get richer and the poor get prison.* New York, NY: Pearson.

Rhode, D. (2004). Access to Justice. *Georgetown Journal of Legal Ethics, 17*(3), 369–422.

Rose, T. (2008). *The hip-hop wars.* New York, NY: Basic Books.

Saez, E., & Zucman, G. (2014). *The explosion in U.S. wealth inequality has been fuelled by stagnant wages, increasing debt, and a collapse in asset values for the middle classes.* Retrieved from http://blogs.lse.ac.uk/usappblog/2014/10/29/the-explosion-in-u-s-wealth-inequality-has-been-fuelled-by-stagnant-wages-increasing-debt-and-a-collapse-in-asset-values-for-the-middle-classes/

Santiago, C. D., Kaltman, S., & Miranda, J. (2013). Poverty and mental health: How do low-income adults and children fare in psychotherapy? *Journal of Clinical Psychology: In Session, 69,* 115–126.

Schnitzer, P. K. (1996). "They don't come in!" Stories told, lessons taught about poor families in therapy. *American Journal of Orthopsychiatry, 66,* 572–582.

Scott, J. (2005). Life at the top in America isn't just better, it's longer. In *Correspondents of the New York Times, Class Matters* (pp. 27–50). New York, NY: Times Books.

Smith, L. (2005). Classism, psychotherapy, and the poor: Conspicuous by their absence. *American Psychologist, 60,* 687–696.

Smith, L. (2009). Enhancing training and practice in the context of poverty. *Training and Education in Professional Psychology, 3,* 84–93.

Smith, L. (2010). *Psychology, poverty, and the end of social exclusion.* New York, NY: Teachers College Press.

Smith, L., Chambers, D. A., & Bratini, L. (2009). When oppression is the pathogen: The participatory development of socially-just mental health practice. *American Journal of Orthopsychiatry, 79,* 159–168.

Smith, L., & Redington, R. (2010). Class dismissed: Making the case for the study of classist microaggressions. In D. W. Sue (Ed.), *Microaggressions and marginalized groups in society: Race, gender, sexual orientation, class and religious manifestations* (pp. 269–286). Hoboken, NJ: Wiley.

Smith, L., & Romero, L. (2010). Psychological interventions in the context of poverty: Participatory action research as practice. *American Journal of Orthopsychiatry, 80,* 12–25.

Southern Education Foundation. (2015). *A new majority: Low income students now a majority in the nation's public schools.* Retrieved from http://

www.southerneducation.org/Our-Strategies/
Research-and-Publications/New-Majority-Di-
verse-Majority-Report-Series/A-New-Majori-
ty-2015-Update-Low-Income-Students-Now

Sue, D. W., Capodilupo, C. M., Torino, G. C.,
Bucceri, J. M., Holder, A.M.B., Nadal, K. L.,
& Esquilin, M. (2007). Racial microaggressions in everyday life: Implications for clinical
practice. *American Psychologist, 62,* 271–286.

Sue, D. W., Carter, R. T., Casas, J. M., Fouad, N.
A., Ivey, A. E., Jensen, M., . . . Vazquez-Nutall,
E. (1998). *Multicultural counseling competen-
cies.* Thousand Oaks, CA: Sage.

Tavernise, S. (2014). Number of Americans without health insurance falls, survey
shows. Retrieved from http://www.nytimes
.com/2014/09/16/us/number-of-americans
-without-health-insurance-falls-survey-shows
.html?_r=0

UNICEF. (2012). *Tens of millions of children living in poverty in the world's richest countries.*
Retrieved from http://www.unicef.org/media
/media_62521.html

Wadsworth, M. E., & Achenbach, T. M. (2005).
Explaining the link between low socioeconomic status and psychopathology: Testing two
mechanisms of the social causation hypothesis.
*Journal of Consulting and Clinical Psychology,
73,* 1146–1153.

Wadsworth, M. E., & Rienks, S. L. (2012). *Stress
as a mechanism of poverty's ill effects on children:
Making a case for family strengthening interventions that counteract poverty-related stress.*
Retrieved from http://www.apa.org/pi/fami
lies/resources/newsletter/2012/07/stress-mech
anism.aspx

Wilper, A. P., Woolhandler, S., Lasser, K. E.,
McCormick, D., Bor, D. H., & Himmelstein,
D. U. (2009). Health insurance and mortal-
ity in US adults. *American Journal of Public
Health, 9,* 1–7.

Counseling Women

Diane M. Sue and David Sue

Chapter Objectives

1. Review gender demographics and societal expectations affecting women.

2. Identify counseling implications of the information provided.

3. Recognize strengths that are associated with women.

4. Know the special challenges faced by women.

5. Understand how best practices can guide assessment and therapy with women.

Microsoft CEO Satya Nadella stated during a conference on women and technology that female employees should not ask for raises because it would be "good karma" not to do so, that "the system" will compensate them over time, and that being patient for raises was one of women's "superpowers." He later admitted that he was "completely wrong." (R. Smith, 2014)

Women get pregnant. This is a real disadvantage and risk for any project leader. I witnessed myself that a project leader hired a woman . . . but she got pregnant . . . she promised to keep working, but then left . . . So given the same qualifications, I would rationally go for the man. (Moss-Racusin, Molenda, & Cramer, 2015, p. 5)

Nearly 40 million Americans provide unpaid care to an adult friend or relative, and of those caregivers 60% are women, including 38% who report feeling highly stressed. The typical caregiver in the United States is a 49-year-old female who balances a full-time job with at least 20 hours each week of helping an older or sick family member who lives nearby. (Gurnon, 2015)

There were 160,593,445 females in the United States in 2013, compared to 155,535,384 males. The ratio of women to men increases with age; among those aged 85 or older, there are about twice as many women as men (U.S. Census Bureau, 2014). Although women constitute more than half of the population, we include them in the special populations section because within the patriarchal nature of U.S. society, women have been historically subjected to prejudice and *discrimination* as well as a disadvantaged status. For centuries, governmental leadership and legal decision makers (e.g., the Supreme Court) as well as religious leaders have been primarily male—such power imbalances are deeply ingrained in the social context of our society. Contemporarily, women continue to face oppressive conditions and experience high levels of economic and psychological stress.

In this chapter we focus on many feminist issues. *Feminism,* a frequently misunderstood term, refers to efforts directed toward gender equality—equal economic, social, and political rights and opportunities for women. Early feminists focused on voting and property rights, whereas contemporary feminists advocate for reproductive rights; parental leave and quality childcare; psychosocial safety for women (e.g., targeting domestic violence and sexual assault); and ending wage disparity, sexist power structures, and other forms of *discrimination*. Many feminists focus on the social forces that contribute to gender oppression as well as related socialization practices.

Feminist therapists believe that the patriarchal nature of U.S. society contributes to many of the problems faced by women and that psychological symptoms are often the result of women's subordinate status in society; feminist case conceptualizations incorporate the intersection between multicultural influences and other forms of oppression. Interventions based on a feminist perspective focus on goals such as empowerment, identifying personal strengths, and discovering areas for self-growth outside of traditional roles (Diaz-Martinez, Interian, & Waters, 2010).

CHARACTERISTICS AND STRENGTHS

In the following sections we discuss issues faced by women such as their prescribed roles and socialization experiences and their implications in treatment. We conclude with a discussion of women's strengths. Remember that these are generalizations and their applicability needs to be assessed for each client.

Societal Roles and Expectations

Historically, women have taken on caregiving roles while simultaneously fulfilling stereotyped feminine social roles in which they are evaluated according to physical beauty, modesty, and their potential as marriage partners. Currently, the large number of women employed outside the home must balance expectations of traditional female roles within the home with varying work expectations outside the home. Although the "marriageability" focus has lessened in recent years (i.e., more women view marriage as an option rather than an economic or social necessity), females are still socialized based on these historic cultural values and realize that women who delay having children or who have no children are often viewed negatively and characterized as selfish (Chrisler, 2013).

Ongoing socialization experiences affect women's self-perceptions. For example, the more women are treated as sexual objects (e.g., subjected to sexualized evaluation such as erotic gazes or overt visual inspection and related sexual comments), the more they feel devalued and trivialized (M. S. Hill & Fischer, 2008). Such objectification is pervasive. Melissa Farley, a clinical psychologist who conducted a study on the buying of sex (broadly defined as purchases such as prostitution, pornography, phone sex, lap dances, etc.) found that it was exceedingly difficult to locate men who do not participate in at least some of these activities. She voices concern about the burgeoning demand for (and proliferation of) such products and services, with the resultant dehumanization and commoditization of women (Bennetts, 2011). Some are concerned that films that associate physical violence and pain with sex (such as *Fifty Shades of Grey*) will result in the "erotic normalization of violence against women" (Thistlethwaite, 2015).

There are ongoing concerns about the film industry's sexualization and marginalization of females, even in family-oriented films (S. L. Smith & Choueiti, 2011). The stereotyped standards of beauty expressed through advertisements and the mass media also have a strong impact on the health and self-esteem of girls and women. The sexualization of young girls, sometimes as early as the preschool years, is particularly troublesome (Machia & Lamb, 2009). When females are exposed to stereotyped societal messages via toys (e.g., dolls), television, music videos, song lyrics, magazines, and advertising, they begin to (a) believe that their primary value comes from being attractive, (b) define themselves according to media-influenced body standards, and (c) see themselves as sexualized objects (American Psychological Association, 2010; Moffitt & Szymanski, 2011).

Additionally, societal pressure for females to be thin leads to the internalization of an unrealistic "thin ideal," with resultant body dissatisfaction, disordered eating patterns, and frequent dieting (Fallon, Harris, & Johnson, 2014; M. S. Hill & Fischer, 2008). In one sample of 4,745 middle and high school students, many more females than males were unhappy with their bodies (42% of females versus 25% of males) and reported self-esteem issues due to body shape or weight (36% of females versus 24% of males) (Ackard, Fulkerson, & Neumark-Sztainer, 2007). The need to meet societal standards for thinness or beauty becomes more intense when girls experience the physical changes associated with puberty. Underweight models and digitally "enhanced" photos further convey unrealistic messages about ideal body size and shape. Exposure to such photos is strongly associated with increased depression, body dissatisfaction, and disordered eating in young women (Grabe, Ward, & Hyde, 2008; Moffitt & Szymanski, 2011).

In addition to the focus on physical attributes, females are socialized to prioritize the needs of others, taking on the role of nurturer and caregiver. They are influenced by beliefs that "good mothers" should stay home with their children or be available if needed by their children during work hours. Women often experience "role overload" and exhaustion due to disproportionate responsibility for childcare, household chores, and care of elders. For example, women are 2.5 times more likely than men to do housework, and among couples with children, women spend nearly three times as much time on childcare than men (Bureau of Labor Statistics, 2015). Such family responsibilities can affect women's employment status as well as career commitment (Bertrand, Goldin, & Katz, 2010). Further, women are also more likely to take on primary caretaking responsibilities for older or disabled family members (National Alliance for Caregiving, 2009).

Implications

Interventions directed at changing the unrealistically thin female image promoted by advertisers, magazines, and other mass media can help reduce body dissatisfaction in females. Programs aimed at preventing or altering disturbed eating patterns generally involve (a) learning to develop a more positive attitude toward one's body; (b) becoming aware of unhealthy societal messages of "what it means to be female" (e.g., girls must be thin, pretty, and sexy); (c) understanding the consequences of internalized gender-related societal messages (e.g., distorted expectations and negative self-statements); (d) developing healthier eating and exercise habits; (e) increasing comfort in expressing feelings to peers, family members, and significant others; (f) choosing appropriate self-care messages (e.g., "Being healthy is important, so I will eat and exercise appropriately"); (g) developing plans to implement health-based changes; and (h) identifying healthy strategies to deal with stress and pressure (Richardson & Paxton, 2010).

Similarly, women can be encouraged to develop as much balance as possible in their lives by emphasizing the importance of maintaining personal well-being while meeting the various role demands. Counselors can also help women who are overwhelmed with caretaking responsibilities to negotiate more equal sharing of responsibilities, including seeking support from other family members or outside sources.

Gender Strengths

Women tend to display affiliative qualities, such as sensitivity, nurturance, kindness, and being concerned with relationships (dePillis & dePillis, 2008), characteristics often undervalued in our society. Such relationship strengths result in effective teamwork and better rapport within family systems and within society. Women have a strong capacity for developing and maintaining robust social support networks. Many women also demonstrate skill at understanding how others are feeling, and responding accordingly; thus, they are skilled at anticipating emotional consequences of decisions. Women often show talent in terms of creativity, problem solving, and mental flexibility and are frequently guided by strong values. A recent poll (Pew Research Center, 2015) revealed that Americans believe women are just as creative and intelligent as men and that women are more honest, ethical, compassionate, organized, and able to work out compromises compared to men.

Gender-based characteristics such as emotional self-regulation and an orientation to relationships are assets in work settings (Raffaelli, Crocket, & Shen, 2005). Women employees and leaders are more likely to display an open, consensus-building, and collegial approach to work; to encourage participation, teamwork, and cooperative efforts among colleagues; and to share power (Caliper, 2005). These qualities are increasingly recognized as important attributes in a work environment (Rosette & Tost, 2010). Women are also more likely than men to display a transformational leadership style—an energetic, passionate approach to projects and the ability to energize others to work toward clearly articulated goals (Vinkenburg, vanEngen, Eagly, & Johannesen-Schmidt, 2011).

SPECIFIC CHALLENGES

In the following sections we consider the challenges often faced by women and consider implications for treatment.

Discrimination, Harassment, and Victimization

Women continue to experience both *sexism* and gender-based *discrimination* in social and professional settings, with the vast majority of women reporting experiences with *sexual harassment*, being disrespected due to their gender, or being subjected to sexist behavior by strangers (Lord, 2010). Nearly two-thirds of women believe that their gender faces *discrimination* in today's society (Pew Research Center, 2015). As mentioned in our discussion of microaggressions in Chapter 6, *sexism* can be overt (i.e., blatantly unequal and unfair treatment), covert (i.e., unequal, harmful treatment conducted in a hidden manner, such as gender-biased hiring practices), or subtle (i.e., unequal treatment that is so normative that it is unquestionably accepted).

Sexual harassment (broadly defined as verbal or physical conduct of a sexual nature, sometimes with explicit or implicit expectations that a woman submit to sexual requests) continues to be quite prevalent in school and work environments. Intimidating, hostile, or sexually offensive work environments (e.g., where sexually suggestive pictures are displayed or sexual jokes are told) are also examples of *sexual harassment.* A national survey indicates that *sexual harassment* in the schools remains a significant concern—one that affects not only girls' psychological well-being but also their learning (American Association of University Women, 2011). Women feel threatened and devalued by these unwanted sexual experiences (E. Smith, 2012). In a study involving waitresses working in U.S. restaurants, it was found that sexual objectification experiences can lead to depression and negative job satisfaction (Szymanski & Feltman, 2015). The more women are treated as sexual objects (e.g., subjected to sexualized evaluation such as erotic gazes or overt visual inspection and related sexual comments), the more they feel devalued and trivialized. Although harassment can be extremely distressing and can influence academic and work performance, many women are hesitant to report such behavior.

Sexual and physical assault is also a significant concern for women. During their lifetime, an estimated 31.5% of American women are subjected to intimate partner violence, 19.3% have been raped, 43.9% have suffered some other form of sexual violence, and 15.2% have been victims of violence outside of the home. These statistics are higher among certain groups of women. It is estimated that 32.3% of multiracial women, 27.5% of American Indian/Alaskan women, and 21.2% of Black women have been raped sometime during their lifetime. Additionally, 65% of multiracial women and 55.0% of American Indian/Alaska Native women have experienced sexual violence other than rape (Breiding et al., 2014). Up to half of one sample of college women reported experiencing some form of sexual aggression (Yeater, Treat, Viken, & McFall, 2010).

Sexual *victimization* and intimate partner violence disproportionately affect women and account for 27% of the violence experienced by females (U.S. Department of Commerce, 2011). Many women affected by intimate partner violence report significant ongoing psychological distress (Zahnd, Aydin, Grant & Holtby, 2011). Such abuse or harassment can have long-term effects, including chronic headaches, pelvic pain, gastrointestinal distress, and other physical symptoms, as well as emotional symptoms such as anxiety, depression, disordered eating, and post-traumatic stress disorder (Chen et al., 2010; Steiger et al., 2010).

Implications

Violence and *sexual harassment* against females can lead to a number of mental health problems. It is important for counselors to ask about experiences with *discrimination*, harassment, or gender-based violence and to consider the effect of such events in case conceptualization. Even among adolescents, screening should be performed for intimate partner abuse, especially in cases where suicidal thoughts, use of drugs, or disordered eating patterns exist.

The American Psychological Association (2007) recommends support for policy initiatives, including legal and legislative reform addressing the issue of violence against women; improved training for mental health workers to recognize and treat those affected by such violence; dissemination of information regarding violence against women to churches, community groups, educational institutions, and the general public; and the exploration of psychoeducational and sociocultural interventions to change male objectification of women. California and New York have passed the "yes means yes" law, legislation that clearly conveys that consent to sexual activity requires an "an affirmative, conscious, and voluntary agreement." State-supported colleges must adhere to this definition when investigating sexual assaults (Garrido, 2014; McDermid, 2015).

Students and employees can benefit from knowing how to identify harassment and exactly what steps to take if harassment occurs (e.g., request that the behavior stop; seek help from parents, counselors, or administrative staff; record details of the event). Prevention strategies targeting dating violence are sometimes implemented in high school and college settings (Yeater et al., 2010). Similarly, strategies for assertively reacting to overt or covert *sexism* can empower women who are confronted with offensive or discriminatory behaviors. Additionally, therapists can help women who have been subjected to violence decrease self-blame (Szymanski & Feltman, 2014).

Educational Barriers

> *You never see someone that looks like me as a scientist. No matter how long I stay here. When I walk through the campus, no one's ever gonna look at me and just think that I'm a physicist . . . I guess the things that made other people find it hard to see me as a scientist are making it hard for me to see myself as a scientist, too. (Soffa Caldo, Chicana college senior, quoted in Ong, 2005, p. 593)*

Although women make up 51% of the U.S. population, they are affected by implicit bias, gender stereotyping, and *discrimination* and are thus underrepresented in positions of power. Further, the National Coalition for Women and Girls in Education (2008) reports that girls and women continue to be underrepresented in such areas as math and science, and female students continue to receive less attention, encouragement, and praise than male students do. Teachers are often unaware that they may be promoting *sexism* by providing differential responses to male and female students (Frawley, 2005). In one study of third-grade teachers who believed they had a gender-free style, it was found that boys were allowed to speak out of turn, whereas girls were not; boys were less likely to be confronted when involved in disagreements; and when girls spoke out of turn, they were reminded to raise their hands (Garrahy, 2001).

Some progress has been made in promoting gender equality, but inequities continue. In many cases, the culture of masculinity (including images of dominance and forcefulness) is deeply entrenched in "masculine" fields of study within institutions of higher education (dePillis & dePillis, 2008). Women face particular barriers in the fields of science, math, technology, and engineering (Moss-Racusin et al., 2015).

Implications

In the educational arena, mental health professionals can advocate for changes at the system levels. Coursework for teachers can include demonstrations and discussion of responses that may inadvertently convey gender-restrictive messages. Attitudes and negative gender stereotypes do affect performance (Johns, Schmader, & Martens, 2005). One study investigating the influence of *stereotype threat* found that female engineering students who interacted with men behaving in a sexist manner prior to taking an engineering test performed more poorly than women exposed to a nonsexist male prior to the test. This effect was found for engineering tests but not for English tests (i.e., an area not expected to be affected by *stereotype threat*) (Logel et al., 2009).

Attitudes and expectations regarding stereotyped personality characteristics and appropriate career choices need to be addressed in educational programs and with individual clients. Small changes in the culture of mathematics, science, or engineering departments (e.g., hiring female faculty, providing mentoring systems for female staff and students, combating negative stereotypes) can help attract women to these fields as well as maintain their interest, enthusiasm, and sense of belonging (C. Hill, Corbett, & St. Rose, 2010).

Economic and Employment Barriers

Although women make up 55% of college students and account for a greater percentage of associate, bachelor's, and master's degrees, women earn less than their male counterparts across all racial groups. Hispanic women showed the largest gap, making only 54 percent of the earnings of White men (American Association of University Women, 2014). This gap affects not only women but also the families they are supporting. The poverty rate for single mothers with children is 37%—the highest of any demographic group in the United States. Women with a low income are especially at risk for depression or domestic violence (Levy & O'Hara, 2010).

Many organizations continue to operate under a value system that emphasizes power and control rather than relationship skills. Nontraditional career fields are often not hospitable to women; thus many women remain in "feminine" careers. Women are underrepresented not only in fields such as science and engineering but also in managerial and executive-level jobs—occupations associated with "masculine" qualities, such as being assertive and independent and influencing others, rather than "feminine" qualities, such as sensitivity, nurturance, kindness, and being concerned with relationships (dePillis & dePillis, 2008).

College women are also aware that when a woman behaves in a manner that is not considered feminine, negative consequences may result. For example, if a woman displays a task-oriented style of leadership that violates the gender norm of modesty, she may be rated as competent but only at the expense of lower social attraction and likability ratings; men displaying the same leadership style are rated high in both competence and likeability (Rudman, 1998).

Women leaders often confront divergent expectations—they are expected to be assertive and in control but are simultaneously criticized for these same traits. Even successful businesswomen report barriers to advancement on the corporate ladder, including the following (Lyness & Thompson, 2000):

1. Women were made to feel that they somehow needed to change, that they were hired or promoted due to "token-hiring practices," and that they were not a "good fit" for senior management.

2. Male coworkers heightened cultural boundaries by emphasizing male camaraderie and differences from women, often relying on a "good old boys network," and withholding from women information necessary for job performance.

3. Women executives received less frequent and less effective mentoring than their male counterparts, including limited access to potential mentors, mentors unwilling to work with them, and the misinterpretation of a mentorship request as a sexual invitation.

A study involving 610 women of different races working in the fields of science, technology, engineering, and math (Williams, Phillips, & Hall, 2014) found the following forms of gender bias that may contribute to the underrepresentation of women in nontraditional fields:

- Prove-it-again—Two-thirds of the women indicated that they have to repeatedly demonstrate a higher level of competence than their male colleagues. African American women were most likely to experience this type of bias.

- The tightrope—Over three-quarters of women reported having to walk a fine line between being seen as "too feminine" to be competent or "too masculine" to be likeable. Asian American women were much more likely to report a backlash from being assertive whereas African American women were given more "leeway" in behaving in a "dominant" manner.

- The maternal wall—Nearly two-thirds of the participants with children faced the assumption that motherhood would reduce their competence and commitment to work.

- Tug of war—Women may also be biased against other women in these fields. Although most reported that female colleagues supported one another, about half believed that some women demonstrate considerable gender bias toward other women.

- *Sexual harassment*—Over one-third reported *sexual harassment* with White women being much more likely to be victims of this behavior.

Implications

Counselors can encourage continued education and job training for women working in minimum-wage jobs and, when needed, provide information on quality childcare as well as assistance locating food, clothing, and affordable housing. Counselors should consider the worldview of women living in poverty and the web of stress with which low-income women contend. Therapists can use multicultural therapy models such as *feminist relational advocacy*, a therapeutic approach focused on listening to women's narratives, recognizing the role of oppression in creating emotional distress, recognizing strengths, and providing advocacy as well as emotional and practical support (Goodman, Glenn, Bohlig, Banyard, & Borges, 2009). When possible, mental health services should be provided in convenient locations serviced by public transportation. Childcare and other on-site programs for family members can increase participation in the mental health system.

Mental health professionals should also help expand the career choices available to women. In doing so, a comprehensive, skills-based approach is most effective. One program for college women (Sullivan & Mahalik, 2000) focused on increasing career self-efficacy by enhancing understanding of the impact of gender socialization on career choice and development; learning about the career paths of successful women (e.g., reading about and discussing women's unique career development and observing successful women and interviewing them about their career decision-making processes and insights); promoting skills to manage anxiety through relaxation and adaptive self-talk; and counteracting internalized stereotypes by identifying and challenging self-defeating thoughts.

Ageism

The number of women aged 65 and older is expected to double and reach 40 million by 2030 (U.S. Census Bureau, 2011). Given the emphasis on youth and beauty that exists in our society, women face additional barriers as they age, including age *discrimination* at work; preferential treatment of younger females in stores, restaurants, and other public establishments; reduced dating opportunities (e.g., men often prefer to date younger women); and a sense of being "invisible" (Committee on Women in Psychology, 1999). In addition, older women often confront changing roles (e.g., an "empty nest," loss of career, increased caretaking of aging family members, accommodating a partner's retirement). Responses to midlife changes such as menopause can be influenced by both *ageism* and *sexism*, as well as by the cultural meanings ascribed to menopause (e.g., beliefs that sexual attractiveness and youthful qualities such as enthusiasm and high energy are lost at menopause).

Many women report that midlife transitions were not as stressful as they anticipated. Among women between the ages of 40 and 59, nearly three-fourths reported feeling "very happy" or "happy." Most were enjoying midlife because of increased independence, freedom from worrying about what others think, freedom from parenting, and the ability to define their own identity based on their own interests (McQuaide, 1998). Instead of being concerned about a midlife crisis, aging, the empty nest syndrome, or menopause, many middle-aged women report going through a midlife review process, as well as having confidence, a strong sense of identity, and a sense of power over their lives (Gibbs, 2005). These findings indicate that transitions through midlife may be easier than previously assumed. Different transition experiences may occur for women experiencing the stress of poverty or caretaking responsibilities.

Implications

It is important not to assume that all women experience a "midlife crisis" and to be aware that women may differ significantly in how they experience life transitions. The life path of women is quite variable. For example, some women are grandmothers in their late 30s or early 40s; other women delay childbearing until their 40s or never have children. Thus, women may experience various midlife transitions at significantly different ages. The personal meaning of and reaction to these events are different for each individual. Counselors can help women negotiate the loss of prior roles by affirming new commitments in life and by assisting women to develop the personal meaning of their life experiences through self-exploration. It is helpful to normalize feelings of anxiety or doubt associated with life transitions and to reframe such experiences as opportunities for greater personal and spiritual development.

Depression

Depression is one of the most prevalent psychiatric disorders and a leading cause of worldwide disability (Andrade et al., 2010); women have a 70% greater lifetime risk of experiencing a major depressive episode compared with men (Kessler, Chiu, Demler, & Walters, 2005). Various stressors such as sexual abuse and unequal *gender roles* (Chen et al., 2010; Vigod & Stewart, 2009), as well as perceived *discrimination* based on gender, especially among those who do not talk to others about their experiences (McLaughlin, Hatzenbuehler, & Keyes, 2010), contribute to the high prevalence of depression in women. The following three additional factors encountered by females are also linked with the development of depression:

- The presence of stress, especially acute stress and stress involving interpersonal problems and the need to depend on others (Muscatell, Slavich, Monroe, & Gotlib, 2009).

- Work environments that involve chronic stress and few decision-making opportunities, conditions experienced by many women in the workplace (Verboom et al., 2011).

- Exposure to targeted rejection involving active, intentional social exclusion or rebuff (Slavich, Way, Eisenberger, & Taylor, 2010).

Gender-specific socialization practices can influence females' feelings of self-worth. Although males are socialized to value autonomy, self-interest, and achievement-oriented goals, females are taught to value interdependent functioning and social goals such as behaving in a caring or nurturing manner. The opinions of others, therefore, often influence women's self-perceptions. Women frequently try to maintain relationships at the cost of their own needs and wishes. Failures in relationships are often viewed as personal failures, compounding stress and affecting mood. Additionally, gender role expectations can decrease women's sense of control over life situations and diminish their sense of personal worth. Women are often affected by interpersonal stress, particularly stressors involving close friends or family. Ruminating (i.e., repeatedly thinking about concerns or events) further increases depressive symptoms among females (Hankin, 2009). Additionally, adolescent girls experiencing depression are more likely to generate interpersonal stress, which in turn can result in ongoing depressive symptoms (Rudolph, Flynn, Abaied, Groot, & Thompson, 2009).

Women who are also subject to stressors such as racism, *ageism*, or exposure to poverty have increased vulnerability to depression. For example, among African American women, everyday encounters with *discrimination* are linked with increases in depressive symptoms (Wagner & Abbott, 2007). Community-based focus-group discussions involving African American women with histories of violent *victimization* underscored the role of interpersonal violence in the development of depression among these women (Nicolaidis et al., 2010).

Implications

In therapy it is important to address the stressors faced by clients, identifying societal and cultural factors as well as individual influences. Counselors should assess for environmental factors, such as poverty, racism, economic conditions, and abusive relationships, as well as specific experiences with overt, covert, or subtle *sexism*. Women often benefit from psychoeducation regarding the power differential in society, unrealistic gender expectations, and the impact of these expectations on mood. Identifying internalized stereotypes and related self-defeating thoughts and substituting more positive self-statements can reduce depression. Establishing strong social support networks and locating sources of assistance with specific needs (e.g., financial, health, childcare) can help women who are experiencing stressful life circumstances.

Evidence-based therapies involving exposure to positive activities; facilitating social interactions; improving social, communication, and assertiveness skills; and identifying role conflicts can help women decrease depressive symptoms and find relationships more satisfying (Lejuez, Hopko, Acierno, Daughters, & Pagoto,

2011; Levenson et al., 2010). Similarly, learning strategies to alter negative, self-critical thoughts and negative self-biases can reduce depressive symptoms (DeRubeis, Siegle, & Hollon, 2008). Using mindfulness strategies involving calm awareness of present experiences, thoughts, and feelings and developing an attitude of acceptance rather than being judgmental, evaluative, or ruminative can disrupt the cycle of negative thinking (Gilbert & Christopher, 2010). Therapy focused on improving interpersonal relationships and enhancing social support has been helpful in decreasing depression in women affected by intimate partner violence (Zlotnick, Capezza, & Parker, 2011).

Gender Bias in Therapy

It is important for counselors to recognize the sexist nature of our society and to be aware of possible biases when working with female clients (Diaz-Martinez et al., 2010). For example, does the counselor believe there are certain attributes associated with a healthy feminine identity? In past research, qualities such as being more submissive, emotional, and relationship-oriented were identified as positive qualities in women (Atkinson & Hackett, 1998). If counselors consciously or unconsciously adhere to these stereotypic societal standards, they may convey these attitudes to clients during counseling. For example, one study of family therapy sessions revealed that counselors interrupted women more often than they interrupted men (Werner-Wilson, Price, Zimmerman, & Murphy, 1997). The therapists, unaware of their behavior, were engaged in subtle *sexism*. *Gender-based microaggressions* such as this are not only destructive to the therapeutic alliance, but can also significantly affect a female client's sense of empowerment (Owen, Tao, & Rodolfa, 2010).

Biases can also occur during diagnosis, especially for ethnic minority women (American Psychological Association, 2007). Some researchers and clinicians contend that certain personality disorders are based on exaggerated gender characteristics. Self-dramatization and exaggerated emotional expressions; intense fluctuations in mood, self-image, and interpersonal relationships; and reliance on others and the inability to assume responsibilities are characteristics of histrionic, borderline, and dependent personality disorders, respectively. Not surprisingly, women are much more likely to be diagnosed with these disorders.

Many psychological theories are gender biased. For example, the concepts of "codependency" and "enmeshment," descriptors more frequently applied to women, involve behaviors such as devotion to home and relationships, connectedness, nurturance, and placing the needs of the family over personal needs—behaviors that are strongly influenced by cultural expectations and gender-based socialization practices. Gender bias is also inherent in family systems therapeutic models: these approaches generally fail to recognize the effects of gender-based power imbalance, including unequal distribution of power within families. Also, disturbances are often interpreted as problems in the system rather than as troubles due to stressors experienced by individual family members. Under this theoretical conceptualization, women who are abused are seen as contributors to the system dysfunction.

 IMPLICATIONS FOR CLINICAL PRACTICE

Both male and female counselors should self-assess for possible sexist beliefs, assumptions, or behaviors and take care not to limit client growth by fostering traditional *gender roles*. Each female client should be provided the opportunity to choose the life path that is best for her, despite societal gender expectations or political correctness. Problems identified by female clients should be viewed within a societal context in which devaluation of women is a common occurrence; gender-based considerations should be understood as integral aspects of problem conceptualization and treatment planning. Guidelines for counselors working with female clients include the following (American Psychological Association, 2007; Szymanski, Carr, & Moffitt, 2011):

1. Remain aware of potential biases in the diagnosis and treatment of women.

2. Recognize that many counseling theories and practices are male-centered and may require modifications when working with women. For example, cognitive-behavioral therapeutic approaches can be modified to include a focus on internalized societal messages or unrealistic standards of beauty.

3. Possess up-to-date information regarding the biological, psychological, and sociological issues that affect women, including a strong understanding of the physiological and social implications of reproductive processes such as menstruation, pregnancy (including unplanned pregnancy), birth, infertility and miscarriage, and menopause.

4. Assess sociocultural factors to determine their role in the presenting problem; consider the influence of gender role socialization; overt, covert, and subtle *sexism*; *discrimination* and harassment; and economic, educational, and employment barriers.

5. Help clients realize the impact of power imbalances, gender expectations, and societal definitions of attractiveness on mental health.

6. Emphasize the unique strengths and talents that women bring to work and interpersonal relationships, including the effectiveness of democratic, people-oriented leadership styles.

7. Help clients correct cultural misperceptions that men are superior in math, science, and technology, and discuss women's achievements in leadership positions and in nontraditional fields for women (e.g., science, math, technology, engineering) as well as strategies women have used to overcome barriers in these fields. Exposure to successful female role models is important for both girls and women.

8. Encourage females to take challenging coursework in math and science and to recognize that academic achievement is an ongoing, cumulative process.

9. Assess for the possible impact of abuse or trauma-related experiences. If necessary, help the client mobilize resources, such as support from friends and family, and develop plans to leave (see Hays, 2013).

10. Clients may need assistance developing financial independence and other supports necessary to leave unhappy marriages or abusive relationships.

11. Do not allow traditional definitions of "good leadership" to mask the talents and strengths women bring to the workplace. Systems-level intervention may be needed to create work environments that optimize the contributions of female leaders and employees.

12. Counselors can educate women about how negative gender-based stereotypes and *stereotype threat* undermine women's confidence and lead to lower performance—such knowledge can reduce the influence of negative stereotypes (Johns et al., 2005).

13. Be alert for signs of depression. Keep in mind that women tend to internalize problems and that maternal depression can have a significant effect on children's behavior and well-being (Tully, Iacono, & McGue, 2008).

14. Encourage women to identify and address their own needs and to practice assertively setting boundaries when confronted with unrealistic demands.

15. Be ready to take an advocacy role in initiating systems-level changes as they relate to *sexism* and *sexual harassment*.

SUMMARY

Women constitute over half the population of United States, but because of the patriarchal nature of society, they occupy a disadvantaged status. For centuries, governmental leadership and legal decision makers as well as religious leaders have been primarily male—such power imbalances are deeply ingrained in the social context of our society. Contemporarily, women continue to face oppressive conditions and experience high levels of economic and psychological stress. Effective work with female clients requires understanding gender-based societal pressures, sexual objectification, stereotyping, harassment, *victimization*, *discrimination*, educational/employment barriers, depression, and *ageism*. Gender bias in therapy is a reality. *Feminism*, a frequently misunderstood term, refers to efforts directed toward gender equality—equal economic, social, and political rights and opportunities for women. Feminist therapy represents a school of thought and action directed at addressing these inequalities. Fifteen clinical implications for counselor practice are identified.

GLOSSARY TERMS

Ageism

Discrimination

Feminism

Gender microaggressions

Gender roles

Sexism

Sexual harassment

Stereotype threat

Victimization

REFERENCES

Ackard, D. M., Fulkerson, J. A., & Neumark-Sztainer, D. (2007). Prevalence and utility of *DSM-IV* eating disorder diagnostic criteria among youth. *International Journal of Eating Disorders, 40*, 409–417.

American Association of University Women. (2011). *Crossing the line: Sexual harassment at school.* Retrieved from http://www.aauw.org/learn/research/crossingtheline.cfm

American Association of University Women. (2014). *The simple truth about the gender pay gap.* Retrieved from http://www.aauw.org/research/the-simple-truth-about-the-gender-pay-gap/

American Psychological Association. (2007). Guidelines for the psychological practice with girls and women. *American Psychologist, 62*, 949–979.

American Psychological Association. (2010). *Report of the APA Task Force on the sexualization of girls.* Retrieved from http://www.apa.org/pi/women/programs/girls/report-full.pdf

Andrade, P., Noblesse, L. H., Temel, Y., Ackermans, L., Lim, L. W., Steinbusch, H. W., & Visser-Vandewalle, V. (2010). Neurostimulatory and ablative treatment options in major depressive disorder: A systematic review. *Acta Neurochirugia, 152,* 565–577.

Atkinson, D. R., & Hackett, G. (1998). *Counseling diverse populations* (2nd ed.). Boston, MAc: McGraw-Hill.

Bennetts, L. (2011, July 25). The John next door. *Newsweek,* pp. 60–63.

Bertrand, M., Goldin, C., & Katz, L. F. (2010). Dynamics of the gender gap for young professionals in the financial and corporate sectors. *American Economic Journal: Applied Economics, 2,* 228–255.

Breiding, M., Smith, S. G., Basile, K. C., Walters, M. L., Chen, J., & Merrick, M. T. (2014). Prevalence and characteristics of sexual violence, stalking, and intimate partner violence victimization—National Intimate Partner and Sexual Violence Survey, United States, 2011. *Morbidity and Mortality Weekly Report, 63,* 1–18.

Bureau of Labor Statistics. (2015). *America time use survey summary.* Retrieved from http://www.bls.gov/news.release/atus.nr0.htm

Caliper. (2005). *The qualities that distinguish women leaders.* Retrieved from http://www.calipercorp.com/cal_women.asp

Chen, L. P., Murad, M. H., Paras, M. L., Colbenson, K. M., Sattler, A. L., & Zirakzadeh, A. (2010). Sexual abuse and lifetime diagnosis of psychiatric disorders: Systematic review and meta-analysis. *Mayo Clinic Proceedings, 85,* 618–629.

Chrisler, J. C. (2013). Womanhood is not as easy as it seems: Femininity requires both achievement and restraint. *Psychology of Men & Masculinity, 14,* 117–120.

Committee on Women in Psychology. (1999). *Older psychologists survey.* Washington, DC: American Psychological Association.

dePillis, E. G., & dePillis, L. G. (2008). Are engineering schools masculine and authorarian? The mission statements say yes. *Journal of Diversity in Higher Education, 1,* 33–44.

DeRubeis, R. J., Siegle, G. J., & Hollon, S. D. (2008). Cognitive therapy vs. medications for depression: Treatment outcomes and neural mechanisms. *National Review of Neuroscience, 9,* 788–796.

Diaz-Martinez, A. M., Interian, A., & Waters, D. M. (2010). The integration of CBT, multicultural and feminist psychotherapies with Latinas. *Journal of Psychotherapy Integration, 20,* 312–326.

Fallon, E. A., Harris, B. S., & Johnson, P. (2014). Prevalence of body dissatisfaction among a United States adult sample. *Eating Disorders, 15,* 151–158.

Frawley, T. (2005). Gender bias in the classroom: Current controversies and implications for teachers. *Childhood Education, 81,* 221–227.

Garrahy, D. A. (2001). Three third-grade teachers' gender-related beliefs and behavior. *Elementary School Journal, 102,* 81–94.

Garrido, E. (2014). *California adopts "yes means yes" sex-assault rule.* Retrieved from http://news.msn.com/us/california-adopts-yes-means-yes-sex-assault-rule

Gibbs, N. (2005). Midlife crisis? Bring it on! *Time.* Retrieved from http://www.time.com/time/magazine/article/0,9171,1059032,00.html

Gilbert, B. D., & Christopher, M. S. (2010). Mindfulness-based attention as a moderator of the relationship between depressive affect and negative cognitions. *Cognitive Therapy and Research, 34,* 514–521.

Goodman, L., Glenn, C., Bohlig, A., Banyard, V., & Borges, A. (2009). Feminist relational advocacy processes and outcomes from the perspective of low-income women with depression. *Counseling Psychologist, 37,* 848–876.

Grabe, S., Ward, L. M., & Hyde, J. S. (2008). The role of the media in body image concerns among women: A meta-analysis of experimental and correlational studies. *Psychological Bulletin, 134*, 460–476.

Gurnon, E. (2015). *Who America's caregivers are and why it matters.* Retrieved from http://www.nextavenue.org/who-americas-caregivers-are-and-why-it-matters/

Hankin, B. L. (2009). Development of sex differences in depressive and co-occurring anxious symptoms during adolescence: Descriptive trajectories and potential explanations in a multi-wave prospective study. *Journal of Clinical Child and Adolescent Psychology, 38*, 460–472.

Hays, B. E. (2013). Women's resistance strategies in abusive relationships. Retrieved from: http://sgo.sagepub.com/content/3/3/2158244013501154

Hill, C., Corbett, C., & St. Rose, A. (2010). *Why so few? Women in science, technology, engineering, and mathematics.* American Association of University Women. Retrieved from http://www.aauw.org/learn/research/upload/whysofew.pdf

Hill, M. S., & Fischer, M. S. (2008). Examining objectification theory. *Counseling Psychologist, 36*, 745–776.

Johns, M., Schmader, T., & Martens, A. (2005). Knowing is half the battle: Teaching stereotype threat as a means of improving women's math performance. *Psychological Science, 16*, 175–179.

Kessler, R. C., Chiu, W. T., Demler, O., & Walters, E. E. (2005). Prevalence, severity, and comorbidity of 12-month *DSM-IV* disorders in the National Comorbidity Survey replication. *Archives of General Psychiatry, 62*, 617–627.

Lejuez, C. W., Hopko, D. R., Acierno, R., Daughters, S. B., & Pagoto, S. L. (2011). Ten-year revision of the brief behavioral activation treatment for depression: Revised treatment manual. *Behavior Modification, 35*, 111–161.

Levenson, J. C., Frank, E., Cheng, Y., Rucci, P., Janney, C. A., & Fagiolini, A. (2010). Comparative outcomes among the problem areas

of interpersonal psychotherapy. *Depression and Anxiety, 27*, 434–440.

Levy, L. B., & O'Hara, M. W. (2010). Psychotherapeutic interventions for depressed, low-income women: A review of the literature. *Clinical Psychology Review, 30*, 934–950.

Logel, C., Walton, G. M., Spencer, S. J., Iserman, E. C., vonHippel, W., & Bell, A. E. (2009). Interacting with sexist men triggers social identity threat among female engineers. *Journal of Personality and Social Psychology, 96*, 1089–1103.

Lord, T. Y. (2010). The relationship of gender-based public harassment to body image, self-esteem, and avoidance behavior. *Dissertation Abstracts International: Section B: The Sciences and Engineering, 70*(8–B), 5171.

Lyness, K. S., & Thompson, D. E. (2000). Climbing the corporate ladder: Do female and male executives follow the same route? *Journal of Applied Psychology, 85*, 86–101.

Machia, M., & Lamb, S. (2009). Sexualized innocence: Effects of magazine ads portraying adult women as sexy little girls. *Journal of Media Psychology, 21*, 15–24.

McDermid, R. (2015). *All NY colleges to adopt "yes means yes" sex assault policy.* Retrieved from http://www.reuters.com/article/2015/07/07/us-usa-new-york-sexcrimes-college-idUSKCN-0PH23Y20150707

McLaughlin, K. A., Hatzenbuehler, M. L., & Keyes, K. M. (2010). Responses to discrimination and psychiatric disorders among Black, Hispanic, female, and lesbian, gay, and bisexual individuals. *American Journal of Public Health, 100*, 1477–1484.

McQuaide, S. (1998). Women at midlife. *Social Work, 43*, 21–31.

Moffitt, L. B., & Szymanski, D. M. (2011). Experiencing sexually objectifying environments: A qualitative study. *Counseling Psychologist, 39*, 67–106.

Moss-Racusin, C. A., Molenda, A. K., & Cramer, C. R. (2015). Can evidence impact attitudes?

Public reactions to evidence of gender bias in STEM fields. *Psychology of Women Quarterly, 39,* 1–16.

Muscatell, K. A., Slavich, G. M., Monroe, S. M., & Gotlib, I. H. (2009). Stressful life events, chronic difficulties, and the symptoms of clinical depression. *Journal of Nervous and Mental Disease, 197,* 154–160.

National Alliance for Caregiving. (2009). *Caregiving in the U.S.* Retrieved from http://www.caregiving.org/data/Caregiving_in_the_US_2009_full_report.pdf

National Coalition for Women and Girls in Education. (2008). *Report from the National Coalition for Women and Girls in Education: Title IX at 35: Beyond the headlines.* Retrieved from http://www.ncwge.org/pubs-reports.html

Nicolaidis, C., Timmons, V., Thomas, M. J., Waters, A. S., Wahab, S., & Mitchell, R. (2010). "You don't go tell White people nothing": African American women's perspectives on the influence of violence and race on depression and depression care. *American Journal of Public Health, 100,* 1470–1476.

Ong, M. (2005). Body projects of young women of color in physics: Intersections of gender, race, and science. *Social Problems, 52,* 593–617.

Owen, J., Tao, K., & Rodolfa, E. (2010). Microaggressions and women in short term therapy: Initial evidence. *Counseling Psychologist, 38*(7), 923–946.

Pew Research Center. (2015). *Women and leadership.* Retrieved from http://www.pewsocialtrends.org/2015/01/14/women-and-leadership/

Raffaelli, M., Crocket, L. J., & Shen, Y. (2005). Developmental stability and change in self-regulation from childhood to adolescence. *Journal of Genetic Psychology, 166,* 54–75.

Richardson, S. M., & Paxton, S. J. (2010). An evaluation of a body image intervention based on risk factors for body dissatisfaction: A controlled study with adolescent girls. *International Journal of Eating Disorders, 43,* 112–122.

Rosette, A. S., & Tost, L. P. (2010). Agentic women and communal leadership: How role prescriptions confer advantage to top women leaders. *Journal of Applied Psychology, 95,* 221–235.

Rudman, L. A. (1998). Self-promotion as a risk factor for women: The costs and benefits of counter-stereotypical impression management. *Journal of Personality and Social Psychology, 74,* 629–645.

Rudolph, K. D., Flynn, M., Abaied, J. L., Groot, A. G., & Thompson, R. D. (2009). Why is past depression the best predictor of future depression? Stress generation as a mechanism of depression continuity in girls. *Journal of Clinical Child and Adolescent Psychology, 38,* 473–485.

Slavich, G. M., Way, B. M., Eisenberger, N. I., & Taylor, S. E. (2010). Neural sensitivity to social rejection is associated with inflammatory responses to social stress. *Proceedings of the National Academy of Sciences, 107,* 14817–14822.

Smith, E. (2012). *Hey baby! Women speak out against street harassment.* Retrieved from http://www.cnn.com/2012/10/06/living/street-harassment/index.html

Smith, R. (2014). The career advice Microsoft's CEO should have given to women. *Forbes.* Retrieved from http://www.forbes.com/sites/ricksmith/2014/10/27/the-3-things-microsofts-ceo-should-have-said-to-women/

Smith, S. L., & Choueiti, M. (2011). *Gender inequality in cinematic content? A look at females on screen & behind the camera in top-grossing 2008 films.* Retrieved from http://annenberg.usc.edu/News%20and%20Events/News/~/media/PDFs/smith_rpt_apr11.ashx

Steiger, H., Richardson, J., Schmitz, N., Israel, M., Bruce, M. I., & Gauvin, L. (2010). Trait-defined eating-disorder subtypes and history of childhood abuse. *International Journal of Eating Disorders, 43,* 428–432.

Sullivan, K. R., & Mahalik, J. R. (2000). Increasing career self-efficacy for women: Evaluating a group intervention. *Journal of Counseling and Development, 78,* 54–62.

Szymanski, D. M., Carr, E. R., & Moffitt, L. B. (2011). Sexual objectification of women: Clinical implications and training considerations. *Counseling Psychologist, 39,* 107–126.

Szymanski, D. M., & Feltman, C. E. (2014). Experiencing and coping with sexually objectifying treatment: Internalization and resilience. *Sex Roles, 71,* 159–170.

Szymanski, D. M., & Feltman, C. E. (2015). Examining sexually objectifying environments and experiences among female waitresses and their links to psychological and job related outcomes. *Psychology of Women Quarterly.* doi: 10.1177/0361684314565345

Thistlethwaite, S. B. (2015). #50ShadesIs Abuse: The erotic normalization of violence against women. *Huffington Post.* Retrieved from http://www.huffingtonpost.com/rev-dr -susan-brooks-thistlethwaite/50shadesis abuse-the-eroti_b_6640884.html

Tully, E. C., Iacono, W. G., & McGue, M. (2008). An adoption study of parental depression as an environmental liability for adolescent depression and childhood disruptive disorders. *American Journal of Psychiatry, 165,* 1148–1154.

U.S. Census Bureau. (2011). *Age and sex composition: 2010.* Retrieved from http://www.census .gov/prod/cen2010/briefs/c2010br-03.pdf

U.S. Census Bureau. (2014). *USA people quick facts.* Retrieved from http://quickfacts.census .gov/qfd/states/00000.html

U.S. Department of Commerce. (2011). *Women in America.* Washington, DC: U.S. Government Printing Office.

Verboom, C. E., Sentse, M., Sijtsema, J. J., Nolen, W. A., Ormel, J., & Penninx, B. W. (2011). Explaining heterogeneity in disability with major depressive disorder: Effects of personal and environmental characteristics. *Journal of Affective Disorders, 132,* 71–81.

Vigod, S. N., & Stewart, D. (2009). Emergent research in the cause of mental illness in women across the lifespan. *Current Opinion in Psychiatry, 22,* 396–400.

Vinkenburg, C. J., vanEngen, M. L., Eagly, A. H., & Johannesen-Schmidt, M. C. (2011). An exploration of stereotypical beliefs about leadership styles: Is transformational leadership a route to women's promotion? *Leadership Quarterly, 22,* 10–21.

Wagner, J., & Abbott, G. (2007). Depression and depression care in diabetes: Relationship to perceived discrimination in African Americans. *Diabetes Care, 30,* 364–366.

Werner-Wilson, R. J., Price, S. J., Zimmerman, T. S., & Murphy, M. J. (1997). Client gender as a process variable in marriage and family therapy: Are women clients interrupted more than men clients? *Journal of Family Psychology, 11,* 373–377.

Williams, J. C., Phillips, K. W., & Hall, E. V. (2014). *Double jeopardy: Gender bias against women of color in science.* Retrieved from http://www.toolsforchangeinstem.org/tools /double-jeopardy-report

Yeater, E. A., Treat, T. A., Viken, R. J., & McFall, R. M. (2010). Cognitive processes underlying women's risk judgments: Associations with sexual victimization history and rape myth acceptance. *Journal of Counseling and Clinical Psychology, 78,* 375–386.

Zahnd, E., Aydin, M., Grant, D., & Holtby, S. (2011). The link between intimate partner violence, substance abuse and mental health in California. *UCLA Center for Health Policy Research* (PB2011–10), 1–8.

Zlotnick, C., Capezza, N. M., & Parker, D. (2011). An interpersonally based intervention for low income pregnant women with intimate partner violence: A pilot study. *Archives of Women's Mental Health, 14,* 55–65.

Glossary

Chapter 1

Antiracist: A person with a nonracist identity who advocates and actively intervenes when injustice makes its presence felt at the individual, institutional, and societal levels

Behavioral resistance (to multicultural training): Resistance that entails paralysis or inaction in the presence of discrimination from majority group individuals

Cognitive resistance (to multicultural training): A form of intellectual denial in which individuals from the majority group provide alternative reasons or excuses to explain incidences of racism, oppression, or discrimination

Cultural competence: Cultural competence is the awareness, knowledge and skills needed to function effectively with culturally diverse populations

Emotional affirmation: Occurs when individuals from marginalized groups feel their lived experiences of oppression and discrimination has been heard, acknowledged, understood, and validated

Emotional invalidation: When individuals negate or dismiss the lived experiences of oppression and discrimination of marginalized groups

Emotional resistance (to multicultural training): A defensive maneuver that entails emotions such as guilt, anger, defensiveness, or helplessness that block self-exploration

Microaggressions: Microaggressions are the everyday slights, put-downs, invalidations, and insults directed to socially devalued group members by well-intentioned people who may be unaware that they have engaged in such biased and harmful behaviors

Multiculturalism: Multiculturalism is the integration, acceptance, and embracing of cultural differences that include race, gender, sexual orientation, and other sociodemographic identities

Nested/Embedded emotions: Unacknowledged emotions such as anger, anxiety, defensiveness, or guilt regarding one's thoughts about race, culture, gender, and other variables of culture

Nonracist: Individuals who own up to their biases, and acknowledge their past oppressive attitudes and actions

Self-reflection: Self-reflection entails truthfully taking stock of one's emotions, beliefs, values, thoughts, and actions and how those impact the self and others

Worldview: Worldviews are composed of people's attitudes, values, and beliefs that affect how people think, define events, make decisions, and behave

Chapter 2

Awareness: Being conscious and mindful of one's own worldview, and the possible differences between culturally diverse clients, and other group identities

Collectivism: A philosophy that the psychosocial unit of identity resides in the family, group, or collective society

Cultural competence: Cultural competence is the awareness, knowledge and skills needed to function effectively with culturally diverse populations

Cultural humility: A complementary component to cultural competence associated with an open attitudinal stance or a multiculturally open orientation to work with diverse clients

Cultural incompetence: When counselors unwittingly impose their standards of normality and abnormality upon culturally diverse clients without consideration of cultural differences

Cultural relativism: The belief that the manifestation and treatment of mental disorders must take into consideration cultural differences

Culture bound syndromes: Mental disorders unique to various cultures

Emic (culturally specific): The belief that cultural differences must be considered in the diagnosis and treatment of culturally diverse groups

Etic (culturally universal): The belief that human beings share overwhelming commonalities and that the manifestation and treatment of disorders are similar across all cultures and societies

Group level of identity: Identity associated with group membership such as race, gender, sexual orientation, religious affiliation and so on

Individual level of identity: Identity which acknowledges that no two individuals are alike, because people are unique and do not share the same experiences in life, not even identical twins

Knowledge: The presence of accurate information about diverse groups

Multicultural counseling/therapy: A helping role and a process that uses modalities and defines goals consistent with the life experiences and cultural values of diverse clients

Multiculturalism: Multiculturalism is the integration, acceptance, and embracing of cultural differences that include race, gender, sexual orientation, and other sociodemographic identities

Personalismo: A Latino/a cultural orientation whereby people relationships are more valued over institutional obligations and responsibilities

Skills: Specific expertise and ability to effectively utilize therapies and knowledge to help clients from cultures different from the therapist

Social justice: Active engagement and action in working toward equal access and opportunity for all people and in fighting injustice in all its forms

Universal level of identity: Identity that acknowledges people have a universal level of identity, are similar to one another, originate from the same species, and share qualities that make them human

Worldview: Worldviews are composed of people's attitudes, values, and beliefs that affect how people think, define events, make decisions, and behave

Worldview: Worldviews are composed of people's attitudes, values, and beliefs that affect how people think, define events, make decisions, and behave

Chapter 3

Communication styles: Characteristics of communication associated with race, gender and other group identities often manifested in verbal and nonverbal communication language

Cultural values: Values held in common by a cultural group which often help shape worldview and the perceptions of individuals of that culture

Historical stereotypes: Stereotypes which are fueled by the historical relationship between cultural groups

Interracial/interethnic bias: This is the bias that a person of one racial/ethnic group harbors for members of another racial/ethnic group which can be fueled by erroneous stereotypes or negative experiences with a member of the other racial/ethnic group and can cause cognitive dissonance or denial by the holder of the bias

Interracial/interethnic conflict: These are differences and conflicts between interracial/interethnic groups that are infrequently publicly aired because of possible political ramifications for group unity

Interracial/interethnic discrimination: This is discrimination that is extended to a racial/ethnic group or member by another racial/ethnic group or member

Interracial/interethnic group relations: This pertains to the historical and current relationships between racial/ethnic groups

Model minority: A model minority is a socially marginalized group that is deemed to have been successful in U.S. society, such as Asian Americans

Multicultural counseling: A helping role and a process that uses modalities and defines goals consistent with the life experiences and cultural values of diverse clients

Racial/Ethnic identity: The identity one forms as a member of a racial or ethnic group

Socially marginalized groups: These are groups that are excluded from the dominant social order and are often linked to culture and social status

Stereotype threat: When an individual of a marginalized group fear inadvertently confirming a mistaken notion (stereotype) about their group

Who's more oppressed game: When one uses his or her own group's oppression to negate, diminish, and invalidate that of another socially devalued group

Chapter 4

Abnormality: A term used to describe a deviation from some standard or norm considered to be desirable

Antiracism: When people, organizations, or social movements work toward the eradication of racism

Cultural deprivation: The belief that groups of color are "culturally deprived" because they lack White middle-class values

Cultural encapsulation: Counselors who are culturally unaware and who operate in isolation from a broader cultural context

Cultural paranoia: A term used to describe the guardedness, suspiciousness and mistrust of marginalized group members toward majority group members

Culturally deficient model: Belief that people of color are inferior because they were culturally disadvantaged, deficient, or deprived of a White middle-class upbringing

Culturally diverse model: Belief that all cultures are valued and that diversity should not indicate whether one group's cultural heritage is better than another's

Culture-bound training: Multicultural training that reflects only one cultural perspective, usually the White, EuroAmerican, middle-class perspective

Emic (culturally specific): The belief that cultural differences must be considered in the diagnosis and treatment of culturally diverse groups

Ethnocentricity: The belief that one's culture is superior to other cultures

Etic (culturally universal): The belief that human beings share overwhelming commonalities and that the manifestation and treatment of disorders are similar across all cultures and societies

Genetically deficient model: Belief that people of color are inferior by virtue of their biological makeup

Paranorm: A term used to describe the norm of cultural paranoia, which has proven to be a survival mechanism among people of colo

Scientific racism: Racist attitudes and beliefs expressed under the guise of science and scientific findings

Social justice counseling: Counseling that operates from an active philosophy and approach to producing conditions that allow for equal access and opportunity

Chapter 5

Attractiveness: Attractiveness based upon how similar the client is to the counselor

Color blindness: When Whites profess to not see the "color" of persons of color

Credibility: People who perceived as possessing expertness and trustworthiness

Cultural oppression: When members of the dominant culture impose their standards upon culturally diverse populations without regard for differences

Ethnocentric monoculturalism: Refers to a belief in the superiority of one's group's cultural heritage over another, and the imposition of those standards upon the less powerful group

Expertness: Typically a function of reputation, evidence of specialized training, and behavioral evidence of proficiency/competency

Institutional racism: A set of institutional policies, practices, and priorities, designed to subjugate, oppress, and force dependence of individuals and groups on the larger society

Invisible veil: The invisibility of people's values and beliefs (worldviews) which are outside the level of conscious awareness

Locus of control: Locus of control refers to people's beliefs about the degree of control they have over their life circumstance

Locus of responsibility: Locus of responsibility refers to the degree of responsibility or blame placed on the individual or system

Playing it cool: A survival mechanism to appear serene while concealing one's true feelings of anger and frustration toward oppressors

Stereotype: A common but inaccurate belief and perception about a cultural group

The authority set: A psychological orientation that attributes higher credibility to people who occupy a particular legitimate position

The consistency set: A psychological orientation toward accepting or rejecting information based upon whether it is consistent with other opinions, beliefs, or behaviors

The economic set: A psychological orientation most concerned with the perceived rewards and punishments that a source is able to deliver

The identity set: A psychological orientation that makes information credible if it is consistent with one's group identity

The problem-solving set: A psychological orientation toward obtaining correct information (solutions and skills) that has adaptive value in the real world

Trustworthiness: The degree to which people perceive the communicator as motivated to make valid or invalid assertions

Uncle Tom Syndrome: A survival mechanism used by people of color to appear docile, nonassertive, and happy-go-lucky

Unintentional racism: Racism and unconscious bias that is invisible to those who perpetuate it

Victim blaming: Explanations that attribute blame to marginalized group members for their status in life when the cause is due to external barriers such as bias and discrimination

White privilege: The unearned advantages and privileges that accrue to people of light-colored skin (usually White European descent)

Worldview: this was defined in chapter one

Chapter 6

Ableism: Negative bias toward people with disabilities reflecting societal assumptions and practices people who are able bodied

Aversive racism: A form of subtle and unintentional racism

Covert sexism: Unequal and harmful treatment of women that is conducted in a hidden manner

Heterosexism: Cultural ideology that assumes heterosexuality to be the societal norm and distinctively superior to homosexuality

Homonegativity: Includes homophobia, or phobia of homosexual individuals, and cultural attitudes that devalue sexual minorities

Islamaphobia: Prejudice directed toward Muslim individuals or followers of Islam

Microaggression: Brief, everyday exchanges that send denigrating messages to a target group

Microassault: Blatant verbal, nonverbal, or environmental attacks intended to convey discriminatory and biased sentiments

Microinsult: Behaviors or verbal comments that convey rudeness or insensitivity or demean a person›s group identity heritage

Microinvalidation: Verbal comments or behaviors that exclude, negate, or dismiss the psychological thoughts, feelings, or experiential reality of the target group

Overt sexism: Blatant unequal and unfair treatment of women

Racism: Blatant and overt acts of discrimination that are epitomized by White supremacy, that denies people of color their equal rights and opportunities, and can include having hate crimes perpetuated against

Religious discrimination: Discrimination against individuals of certain religious affiliations, usually non-Christians

Subtle sexism: Unequal and unfair treatment of women that is embedded in our culture and often perceived as normal appropriate behaviors

Transphobia: Prejudice against transgendered individuals

Chapter 7

Activity dimension: A reference to how different cultural groups lie in their action orientation from one of "doing" and influencing the world, to one of "being" or living in harmony with nature

Biculturalism: When an individual ascribes to and values two different cultures

Class-bound values: Socioeconomic values that permeate counseling and psychotherapy (middle and upper class) and may prove disadvantageous to clients from poverty or less affluent situations

Collectivism: The psychosocial unit of operation resides in the family, group, or collective society rather than the individual

Culture-bound values: Traditional western counseling and therapy are seen to possess the values of the dominant culture

Ebonics: Often referred to as "Black language or Black English," it references a certain distinct pattern of speech used by some African Americans

Egalitarian roles: When roles are based on equality between genders

Emotional expressiveness: The value placed upon clients who are encouraged to express their feelings and to verbalize their emotional reactions

Extended families: Families that include others outside of the nuclear unit such as godparents, aunts, uncles, cousins, or fictive kin

Family systems: This comprises the system that makes up the family and includes structural alliances and communication patterns

Individual-centered: A culture-bound value in mental health practice in which the individual is the psychosocial unit of operation and independence and autonomy are the primary goals to treatment

Individualism: One of the primary values of U.S. culture and society and refers to valuing individualism

Insight: A generic characteristic of counseling that values the attainment of insight in mental health and treatment

Linguistic barriers: Language barriers often place culturally diverse clients at a disadvantage because counseling is usually provided in standard English

Minority standard time: A reference to how people from situations of poverty often perceive time, and the resultant effects it has on behavior

Nature of people dimension: A reference to how different culture groups view human nature ("good, neutral, or bad")

Nuclear families: A reference to the family unit composed of only the husband, wife, and biological children

Patriarchal roles: A division of roles where males are given greater status, prestige and influence in the family and society

QUOID: An acronym for clients less preferred by mental health professionals and stands for quiet, ugly, old, indigent, and dissimilar culturally (QUOID)

Relational dimension: A reference to cultural group relations and whether they are more collateral or individualistic in orientation

Scientific empiricism: Western value placed on empiricism which involves objective, rational, linear thinking as the means to define and solve problems

Self-disclosure: In counseling, the value and desire for clients to talk about the most intimate aspects of their life and to share it with the counselor

Social class: Refers to where one falls on the socioeconomic spectrum and are usually classified as upper, middle, and lower class

Time dimension: How different societies, cultures, and people view time can be divided into being past, present or future oriented

YAVIS syndrome: An acronym meant to indicate counselor preference for clients who are young, attractive, verbal, intelligent, and successful (YAVIS)

Chapter 8

Communication style: An acknowledgment that race, culture, and gender influence strongly how people communicate

High context cultures (HC): Communications that rely more on the context to interpret the meaning of messages

High-/low-context communication: Reference to whether a person relies more on the context to interpret the meaning or the content of the message

Kinesics: The study of how bodily movements that include facial expression, posture, characteristics of movement, gestures, and eye contact orientation affect interpersonal transactions

Low-context cultures (LC): Communications that rely more on the content of what is said to interpret the meaning of the message

Nonverbal communication: Nonverbal communication includes such things as body language, vocal tone, or vocal inflection

Nonverbals as reflection of bias: Nonverbal behaviors that are likely to reflect the unconscious biases or attitudes of the person

Nonverbals as triggers to bias: Nonverbal behaviors that may trigger racist stereotypes and fears in the individual

Paralanguage: The study of how vocal cues such as loudness of voice, pauses, silences, hesitations, rate of speech, and inflection affect communication

Playing the dozens: Considered by many Blacks to be the highest form of verbal provocation and impromptu speaking

Proxemics: The study of how sociodemographic identities affect the use of conversing distances and their meanings

Therapeutic style: The helping style of the therapist as influenced by their theoretical orientation, race, gender and other variables

Verbal communication: Spoken or written language and communication in which the content of what is said is important

Woofing: Among some Black Americans, it refers to a form of verbal banter which is an exchange of threats and challenges to fight

Chapter 9

Cognitive empathy: Cognitively understanding the client's predicament associated with others or his or her life circumstance

Countertransference: Involves the therapist's emotional reaction to the client based on the therapist's own attitudes, beliefs, values, or life experiences

Cultural adaptations: The counseling process of attempting to incorporate culture specific variables and factors into specific treatment strategies, thereby making them more culturally relevant

Emotional bond: The strength of the therapeutic relationship is often due to the emotional understanding or emotional connection with the client

Emotional empathy: An emotional understanding or emotional connection with the client

Empathy: The ability to place oneself in the client's world, to feel or think from the client's perspective, or to be attuned to the client

Empirically supported relationships: Therapeutic interventions that possess empirical support for the efficacy of the therapeutic relationship, client values and beliefs, and the working alliance between client and therapist

Empirically supported treatments: Treatments that have empirical evidence regarding their effectiveness

Evidence-based practices: Counseling interventions based on research evidence from qualitative studies, clinical observations, systematic case studies, and interventions delivered in naturalistic settings

Goal consensus: An agreement on goals between the therapist and the client

Multicultural counseling: This was defined in Chapter 2.

Positive regard: The quality of therapists that focuses on and acknowledges the strengths and positive aspects of the client, including appreciation for the values and differences displayed

Self-disclosure by counselor: The therapist's revealing personal thoughts or personal information

Therapeutic alliance: Refers to the importance of the interpersonal bond such as collaboration, empathy, warmth, and genuineness which are all factors known to be critical for effective multicultural counseling

Therapeutic bond: The strength of the working relationship between client and therapist

Universal–diversity orientation: The therapist's orientation that balances the universal and diversity perspective

Chapter 10

Afrocentric perspective: Teaches that human beings are part of a holistic fabric—that they are interconnected and should be oriented toward collective rather than individual survival

Băt Gió: Southeast Asian massage treatment called Băt Gió means "catching the wind" and involves using both thumbs to rub the temples and massaging toward the bridge of the nose at least 20 times

Brain fag: This culture-bound disorder is usually manifested by students in West Africa in response to academic stress

Cao Gió: Southeast Asian massage treatment, Cao Gió means "scratching the wind," or "coin treatment" and involves rubbing the patient with a mentholated ointment and then using coins or spoons to strike or scrape lightly along the ribs and both sides of the neck and shoulders

Enlightenment: Asian psychologies states of consciousness in which attaining the highest level enhances perceptual sensitivity and clarity, concentration, and sense of identity, as well as emotional, cognitive, and perceptual processes

Espiritismo: Puerto Ricans believe in espiritismo (spiritism), a world where spirits can have major impacts on the people residing in the physical world

Giác Hoi: Southeast Asian massage treatment, Giác Hoi means "pressure massage," or "dry cup massage" and involves steaming bamboo tubes so that the insides are low in pressure, applying them to a portion of the skin that has been cut, and sucking out "bad air" or "hot wind"

Hmong Sudden Death Syndrome: A culture-bound mental disorder or phenomenon observed among the Hmong of Southeast Asian whereby individuals die suddenly in their sleep from unknown causes

Ho'oponopono: A healing ritual of Native Hawaiians that attempts to restore and maintain good relations among family members and between the family and the supernatural powers

Holistic outlook: Most non-Western indigenous forms of healing make minimal distinctions between physical and mental functioning and believe strongly in the unity of spirit, mind, and matter

Indigenous healing: Helping beliefs and practices that originate within the culture or society

Mahiki: The actual work that occurs during the Native Hawaiian healing ritual of Ho'oponopono begins through mahiki, a process of getting to the problems

Oia'i'o: The Native Hawaiian healing ritual of Ho'oponopono elicits 'oia'i'o or (truth telling), sanctioned by the gods, and makes compliance among participants a serious matter

Pani: Following the closing prayer of the Native Hawaiian healing ritual of Ho'oponopono, the family participates in pani, the termination ritual in which food is offered to the gods and to the participants

Pule weke: The opening prayer of the Native Hawaiian healing ritual of Ho'oponopono

Shaman: The name given to many healers in different cultures who are believed to possess special powers to cure troubled individuals through their ability to communicate with the spirit world via divination skills

Spirituality: The life force that resides within individuals which makes them inherently worthy, and connects them to other living creatures

Sweat lodge ceremony: A form of healing and purification that involves rituals filled with American Indian cultural and spiritual symbolism and meaning that takes place in a sweat lodge

Thuốc Nam: Among the Vietnamese, Thuốc Nam, or traditional medicine, involves using natural fruits, herbs, plants, animals, and massage to heal the body

Universal shamanic tradition: Refers to the centuries-old recognition of healers (shamans) such as those called witches, witch doctors, wizards, medicine men or women, sorcerers, and magic men or women

Western healing: Interventions based upon Western European science and empiricism

Chapter 11

Asian American identity development models: Models of identity development that focused on the development of Asian ethnic identity

Black identity development models: Models proposed to explain how African Americans develop their racial identities through a process of racial awakening

Conformity: A characteristic of the Racial/Cultural Identity Development model (RCID), distinguished by an unequivocal preference for dominant cultural values over their own

Dissonance: Under the Racial/Cultural Identity Development model (R/CID), people of color become more aware of inconsistencies between dominant-held views and those of their own group resulting in a sense of dissonance

Encounter: The second stage of the Cross black identity development model where African Americans encounter situations which challenge their previous acceptance of White ways

Identity synthesis: The process of successfully integrating multiple identities such as ethnicity, sexual orientation, gender and so forth

Immersion-emersion: The third stage of the Cross black identity development model is characterized by a withdrawal from the dominant culture and immersion in African American culture

Integrative awareness: Under the Racial/Cultural Identity Development model (R/CID), people of color develop an inner sense of racial security and can own and appreciate unique aspects of their culture as well as those in US culture

Internalization-commitment: The last stage of the Cross black identity development model characterized by commitment to social change, social justice, and civil rights

Internalization: The fourth stage of the Cross black identity development model characterized by resolution of conflicts between the old and new identities and a movement toward becoming more bicultural/multicultural

Internalized racism: The term used to describe the process by which persons of color absorb and internalize the society's racist messages about their own group, and other groups of color

Introspection: Under the Racial/Cultural Identity Development model (R/CID), the introspection stage includes self-reflection and rethinking of rigidly held racial beliefs and its relationship to whiteness

Latino/Hispanic American identity development models: Models of identity development that focus on the development of Latino/Hispanic ethnic identity

Marginal person: A person caught between two cultural traditions who attempts to assimilate into the dominant culture because of negative attitudes held toward one's own group, but not fully accepted by the majority population

Nigrescense: Nigrescense is the process of becoming "Black" and formulating a Black identity

Preencounter: The first stage of the Cross black identity development model characterized by anti-Black attitudes and a positive White orientation

R/CID model: A racial/cultural development model that attempts to integrate the racial/cultural development of groups of color

Race salience: The degree to which race is an important and integral part of a person's approach to life

Racial awakening: An individual's understanding of themselves as racial/cultural beings and how it impacts their perception of the world and relationships with others

Resistance and immersion: Under the Racial/Cultural Identity Development model (R/CID), the primary orientation of these individuals is they tend to endorse minority-held views completely and to reject the dominant values of society and culture

Chapter 12

Antiracist white identity: The complementary identity to a nonracist one in that the person is likely to take direct action to eradicate its manifestation in individuals, institutions and society

Commitment to antiracist action phase: In the Sue and Sue White identity development model, this phase is most characterized by social action and increased commitment toward eradicating oppression

Conformity phase: In the Sue and Sue White racial identity development model, it refers to beliefs that White culture is the most highly developed and that all others are primitive or inferior

Dissonance phase: In the Sue and Sue White identity development model, it refers to how Whites are forced to deal with inconsistencies in their racial attitudes and behaviors as they encounter information/experiences at odds with their racial denial and naiveté

Ego statuses: Reference to the different levels of ethnic identity development and the traits and defenses associated with them

Hardiman White racial identity development: The White racial identity development model formulated by Rita Hardiman

Helms White racial identity development: The White racial identity development model formulated by Janet Helms

Information-processing strategies: These are strategies that White people use to avoid or assuage anxiety and discomfort around the issue of race

Integrative awareness phase: In the Sue and Sue White identity development model, this phase is marked by an understanding of self as a racial/cultural being, being aware of sociopolitical influences regarding racism, appreciating racial/cultural diversity, and becoming more committed toward eradicating oppression

Introspective phase: In the Sue and Sue White identity development model, the introspective phase is characterized by a state of relative quiescence, self-reflection, introspection, and reformulation of what it means to be White

Naiveté phase: The Naiveté phase of the Sue and Sue White racial identity development is characterized by racial naiveté, and innocence

Nonracist white identity: An identity associated with the Whites recognizing their own racial biases, and an internal commitment to eradicating prejudice and commitment

Resistance and immersion phase: In the Sue and Sue White identity development model, the White person begins to question and challenge his or her own racism and begins to become aware of the existence or racism in society

Unintentional racism: Racism and unconscious bias that is invisible to those who perpetuate it

White privilege: The unearned advantages and privileges that accrue to people of White European descent

White racial identity development descriptive model: The White Racial Identity Model developed by Sue and Sue

White racial identity development: The process and accompanying stages or phases by which Whites achieve various racial identities

White supremacy: A belief that individuals of White European descent are superior to people of color

Whiteness: A reference to the light skin tone of European Americans and the surrounding assumptions and norms associated with it used to judge all other groups

Chapter 13

Attribution errors: Attribution errors occur when the therapist holds a different perspective of the problem than that of the client and uses it to define problems and to propose solutions

Collaborative approach: When the therapist and client work together to construct an accurate definition of the problem and the contextual background

Collaborative assessment: The clinical approach that values and obtains clients' input regarding social and cultural elements that may be associated with presenting problems

Collaborative conceptualization: Developing a joint definition of the problem and treatment through formulating and testing hypotheses from both the clinician's clinical experiences and perspectives of the client

Confirmatory strategy: Confirmatory strategy involves the search for evidence or information supporting one's hypothesis and ignoring data that is inconsistent with this perspective

Contextual viewpoint: An approach or viewpoint that acknowledges the client and therapist are both embedded in systems such as family, work, and culture

Culturally competent assessment: Culturally competent assessment integrates traditional assessment methods within a cultural competency framework

Culturally sensitive intake interviews: Intake interviews that take into consideration situational, family, sociocultural, or environmental issues that impact the client and includes other areas of diversity and identity

Diagnostic overshadowing: Misdiagnosing a problem by focusing on a salient characteristic that has nothing to do with the problematic issue

Ethnographic inquiry: Scientific inquiry based upon a qualitative approach that seeks to understand an individual from his or her point of view and experiences and observes the individual in his or her natural environment

Judgmental heuristics: Judgmental processes commonly used to make quick-decisions by short-circuiting the ability to engage in self-correction

Stereotypes: Stereotypes are inflexible generalizations based on limited or inaccurate information that can create biases and discriminatory treatment towards marginalized groups in our society

Therapeutic alliance: Refers to the importance of the interpersonal bond such as collaboration, empathy, warmth, and genuineness which are all factors known to be critical for effective multicultural counseling

Chapter 14

Afrocentric: An ideology that focuses on the Black experience, history, culture and traditions

Cultural mistrust: When a person of one culture develops a mistrust of someone from another culture due to personal or historical experiences between the two groups

Extended family: Families that include others outside of the nuclear unit such as godparents, aunts, uncles, cousins, or fictive kin

Healthy cultural paranoia: A term used to describe the guardedness, suspiciousness and mistrust of marginalized group members toward majority group members

Kinship bonds: Bonds between relatives

Prejudice: An erroneous preconceived judgment about another person based on one's group membership

Racial identity: The identity one forms as a member of a racial or ethnic group

Racial socialization: The process by which parents of color inform and educate their children about the realities of racism in society

Racism: Blatant and overt acts of discrimination that are epitomized by White supremacy, that denies people of color their equal rights and opportunities, and can include having hate crimes perpetuated against

Spirituality: The life force that resides within individuals which makes them inherently worthy, and connects them to other living creatures

Chapter 15

Acculturation: The process of internalizing the values, beliefs and traditions of the larger society

Cooperation: A cultural value of Native Americans where harmony and betterment of the tribe holds precedence over individual needs

Extended family: Families that include others outside of the nuclear unit such as godparents, aunts, uncles, cousins, or fictive kin

Noninterference: A Native American value and outlook in life associated with living with nature and people rather than attempts to change it or others

Nonverbal communication: Nonverbal communication includes such things as body language, vocal tone, or vocal inflection

Reservation: A legally designated place under the U.S. Bureau of Indian Affairs, upon which a Native American people reside

Sharing: A cultural value of Native Americans in which honor and respect are gained by sharing and giving, in contrast with the dominant culture where status is gained by the accumulation of material goods

Spirituality: The life force that resides within individuals which makes them inherently worthy, and connects them to other living creatures

Sweat lodge: A form of healing and purification that involves rituals filled with American Indian cultural and spiritual symbolism and meaning that takes place in a sweat lodge

Tribe: An indigenous social grouping and unit connected by heritage, history, and culture and important for individual and group identity

Vision quest: A rite of passage among many Native American nations and is often used to reestablish connections between the mind, body, and spirit and to seek spiritual guidance

Chapter 16

Acculturation: The process of internalizing the values, beliefs and traditions of the larger society

Assimilation: This entails an individual seeking to become part of the dominant society to the exclusion of one's own cultural group

Co-construction: Co-construction involves the client and the counselor working together to identify problems and solutions

Collectivistic orientation: A philosophy that the psychosocial unit of identity resides in the family, group, or collective society

Emotionality: A term used to describe the degree to which an individual or group is taught to express or restrain emotional displays

Hierarchical relationships: A family structure whereby males and older individuals are given higher status in decision making and females and children are expected to defer to the authority of males and their elders

Integration/biculturalism: Entails an individual retaining many Asian values while simultaneously learning the necessary skills and values for adaptation to the dominant culture

Model minority: A term used to describe the myth of Asian American success in U.S. society

Somatic complaints: Within the meaning of this term, bodily or physical symptoms are means by which Asian clients may express their emotional distress

Chapter 17

Acculturation: The process of internalizing the values, beliefs and traditions of the larger society

Bicultural orientation: When an individual ascribes to and values two different cultures

Extended family: Families that include others outside of the nuclear unit such as godparents, aunts, uncles, cousins, or fictive kin

Familismo: Reference to the importance of the extended family kinship system and its importance to a sense of connectedness, support, and identity of members

Fatalismo: Latinos often believe that life's misfortunes are inevitable and feel resigned to their fate (fatalismo)

Latina/o Americans: Describes individuals of Mexican or Latin descent

Machismo: In traditional Latino/a culture, men are expected to be strong, dominant, and the provider for the family (machismo)

Madrina: Refers to the godmother (madrina) sanctioned through a baptismal ceremony

Marianismo: In traditional Latino/a culture, women are expected to be nurturing, modest, virtuous, submissive to the male, and self-sacrificing (marianismo)

Padrino: Refers to the godfather (padrino) sanctioned through a baptismal

Personalismo: A Latino/a cultural orientation whereby people relationships are more valued over institutional obligations and responsibilities

Respecto: Respecto is the act of showing respect

Simpatico: The relational style displayed by many Latinos—a style emphasizing social harmony and a gracious, hospitable, and personable atmosphere

Chapter 18

Biracial: Individuals who are come from two racial heritages

Biracial/multiracial identity development: A model of identity development used to describe the stages of biracial identity development in contrast to the monoracial development models

Hypodescent: Also known as the "one drop rule," which is a class-based social system that maintains the myth of monoracialism by assigning the person of mixed racial heritage to the least desirable racial status

Miscegenation: This term describes the "mixing" of two or more different races

Monoracial: Individuals who are, or who are perceived to be, of just one racial heritage

Multiracial: Individuals who are of mixed racial heritage

One Drop rule: Describes the racist practice of classifying individuals as African American even if they possess minimal African American blood in their heritage

Racial/ethnic ambiguity: Racial/ethnic ambiguity occurs when people are not easily able to distinguish the monoracial category of the multiracial individual from phenotypic characteristics

Chapter 19

Arabs: Individuals who originate from countries located in the Middle East and North Africa and whose primary language is Arabic

Islam: Islam is the religion of Muslims and it means "submission to God"

Mosques: A mosque is a place of worship for followers of Islam

Muhammad: Muhammad is the messenger of God according to the Muslim religion and its holy book the *Quran*

Muslim religion: Muslims are followers of Islam or the Quran, the Islamic holy book

Qur'an: The *Quran* is the Islamic holy book and it is considered to be the literal word of God

Ramadan: An annual event of Muslims that involve fasting during daylight hours throughout the holy month of Ramadan—a time for inner reflection, devotion to God, and spiritual renewal

Shiite: Shiites compose 10% of the Muslim population worldwide

Sunni: Sunnis are the largest group of Muslims, accounting for about 90% of Muslims

Chapter 20

Asylum: Asylum can be granted to certain classes of refugees due to political persecution

Bilingualism: This term describes individuals who speak two languages

"Illegal" immigrants: People who have immigrated to a country illegally, meaning they did not go through the proper procedures according to the host country's laws

Immigrant: People who have moved from their country of origin to the United States in which they now reside

Interpreters: Bilingual individual who acts as a language translator between two individuals who do not speak each other's language

Migration: The movement of groups of people from one geopolitical area to another

Naturalized citizens: Naturalization is the process by which an immigrant can obtain citizenship in the United States after he or she meets the criteria set by the U.S. Congress

Post-traumatic stress disorder (PTSD): A mental health condition that often accompanies someone who has been subjected to trauma or terror in which the individual thought he or she would die or that another individual would or did die

Refugees: In contrast to other immigrants who voluntary left their country of origin, refugees are individuals who flee their country of origin in order to escape persecution or oppression

Survivor's guilt: The guilt associated with surviving atrocities in their country of origin and the necessity of leaving other family members behind

Undocumented immigrants: This is the less stigmatized term for individuals who are foreign born and have immigrated to a country without following the host country's laws

Chapter 21

Anti-Semitism: Anti-Semitism is prejudice, discrimination, and hatred of people of Jewish descent

Conservative: Politically conservative Jews who generally support the Republican party

Holocaust denier: Individuals who do not acknowledge or who question the genocide that occurred during the Holocaust

Holocaust: An incredibly traumatic period in Jewish history in which Nazi Germans murdered approximately 6 million Jewish men, women, and children

Jewish identity: Refers to a highly complex and personal sense of shared cultural and historical experiences among Jews

Judaism: Judaism is a religion with a belief in an omnipotent God who created humankind; it is one of the earliest monotheistic religions

Orthodox: Jews who follow strictly all Jewish rules and traditions of Judaism

Progressive: These are individuals of Reform Judaism, which advocates the freedom of individuals to make choices about which traditions to follow

Rabbi: A religious leader of the Jewish faith

Reform: Reform Judaism advocates the freedom of individuals to make choices about which traditions to follow

Synagogue: A place of worship for individuals who follow traditional Judaism

Yom Kippur: Yom Kippur, the Day of Atonement, is a major holy day of the Jewish religion set aside to atone for sins during the past year

Chapter 22

Ableism: An all-too-common discriminatory practice in which individuals without disabilities are favored or given preferential treatment, thereby implying that those with a disability are somehow inferior

Americans with Disabilities Act: The Americans with Disabilities Act (ADA) was signed into law in 1990, extending the federal mandate of nondiscrimination to individuals with disabilities and to state and local governments and the private sector

Disability: The ADA defines disability as "a physical or mental impairment that substantially limits one or more of the major life activities of such individual

Medical model: Regards disability as a defect or loss of function that resides in the individual

Minority model: Views disabilities as an external problem involving an environment that is filled with negative societal attitudes and that fails to accommodate the needs of individuals with special needs

Moral model: Regards the "defect" as representing some form of sin or moral lapse

Rehabilitation approach: The rehabilitation approach has historically been a drive to remediate the individuals with disabilities and "make them as normal as possible"

Chapter 23

Bisexual: This is a term that describes individuals who have an affectional and/or sexual attraction to members of both sexes

Coming out: The process of when a gay, lesbian, bisexual, or transgendered person reveals his or her gender or sexual orientation to others

Gay: This is a term that describes a man who has an affectional and/or sexual attraction to another man

Gender Dysphoria: A mental health condition defined in *DSM-5* as significant distress and impairment resulting from an incongruence between a person's gender identity and assigned gender

Heterosexist bias: The assumption that everyone is a heterosexual and its manifestation in societal practices

Heterosexual: This is a term that describes a person who has an affectional and/or sexual attraction to a person of the opposite sex

Lesbian: This is a term that describes a woman who has an affectional and/or sexual attraction to another woman

LGBT (Q): This is an acronym that stands for Lesbian, Gay, Bisexual, Transgender, and Queer (or Questioning)

Queer: An umbrella term that encompasses many categories of sexual minorities and reclaimed by activists to remove its' stigma

Sexual orientation: The term that describes how one identifies in terms of which gender he or she has an affectional and/or sexual attraction

Transgender: The term describes individuals whose gender identification is inconsistent with their assigned gender

Chapter 24

Ageism: Negative attitudes and behaviors toward the process of aging or toward older individuals

Alzheimer's disease: A form of dementia that generally strikes older adults and is currently incurable

Dementia: Memory impairment and declining cognitive functioning as a result of brain disease

Dementia: Memory impairment and declining cognitive functioning usually associated with increasing age

Elder abuse and neglect: The abuse and/or neglect of an elderly person

Elderspeak: A derogatory way of speaking to someone of the geriatric generation

Multiple discrimination: Discrimination based on more than one aspect of diversity

Chapter 25

Classism: Social class oppression is called classism and it operates to limit access to many kinds of socially-valued assets

Cognitive and behavioral distancing: The social exclusion of the poor is captured by society's cognitive and behavioral distancing from them

Poverty: A condition in which individuals possess chronic inadequate financial resources and occupy the bottom-most rungs of society

Social class privilege: This describes the social, economic and cultural privileges afforded to the upper class population that does not apply to those of other classes

Social class: Social class refers to where one falls on the sociocultural continuum most often described as upper class, middle class, or lower class

Social stratification theory: A description of a hierarchical system that not only positions poverty and economic characteristics of groups in our society, but involves sociopolitical relationships as well

The criminalization of poverty: Perceiving poverty as undesirable (criminalization of poverty) and that the poor should be excluded from mainstream cultural life

Chapter 26

Ageism: Negative attitudes and behaviors toward the process of aging or toward older individuals

Discrimination: Negative or prejudicial treatment toward a person or group of people usually based on biased beliefs and stereotypes

Feminism: A philosophical stance that refers to beliefs and practices directed toward gender equality—equal economic, social, and political rights and opportunities for women

Gender microaggressions: The everyday slights, put-downs, invalidations, and insults directed toward a specific gender, typically women

Gender roles: Societal and cultural expectations and rules governing gender role definitions of acceptable behaviors, values and beliefs for males and females

Sexism: Unequal and unfair treatment of women that is embedded in our culture and often perceived as normal appropriate behaviors

Sexual harassment: Verbal or physical conduct of a sexual nature, sometimes with explicit or implicit expectations that a woman or a man submit to sexual requests

Stereotype threat: When an individual of a marginalized group fear inadvertently confirming a mistaken notion (stereotype) about their group

Victimization: The experience of becoming a victim of a negative act such as of crime, discrimination, or another aversive event

Index

A

Abaied, J. L., 738
Abbott, G., 738
Abels, A. V., 636–637
Ableism, 186, 187, 646, 653
Abnormality, 114, 116–118, 751
Aboud, F. E., 414–415
Abrams, E. M., 10, 23, 267, 392, 396, 409
Abu-Salha, Razan Mohammad, 574
Acculturation, 480, 503, 506, 511, 513, 519, 529, 531, 536–538, 540, 541
Achenback, T. M., 713
Acierno, R., 694, 738–739
Ackard, D. M., 728
Ackerman, S. J., 296, 297, 304
ACLU, 592
Acquino, J. A., 698
ACREP, 366
Acs, G., 459
Activity dimension, 242–243, 275, 755
ADA. *See* Americans with Disabilities Act (ADA)
Adams, E. M., 129
Adamson, R., 717
Addison, J. D., 465–466
Adelman, A., 675
Adelson, J., 112
Adrian, S. L., 60, 663, 664
ADL Global 100, 623
Advocacy counseling roles, 136–137
Affordable Care Act, 599–600, 714–715
African Americans, counseling: and characteristics and strengths of African Americans, 459–461; and cultural strengths, 468; and D (case study), 463; and educational characteristics, 464–465; and ethnic and racial identity, 460–461; and family structure, 461; and interaction of four sets of factors in Jones model, 471; and Jackie (case study), 464; and Johnny (case study), 461–462; and Leajay Harper (case study), 465; and Michael (case study), 467; overview, 458–459; and racism

and discrimination, 469–472; and spiritual and religious values, 463–464; youth, 465–467
Afrocentric perspective, 338, 460
Ageism, 689, 736
Aguiar, L. J., 41
Aguilera, A., 293, 528
Ahmad, F. Z., 503
Ahn, A. J., 511, 513
Ahn, S., 470
AhnAllen, J., 557
Ahuvia, A., 116
Ai, A. L., 534
AI/NA/AN populations (Alaska), 493, 495
Aisenberg, E., 534
Ajamu, A., 44, 74, 113, 156, 225, 275
Akerlund, M., 667
Al Harahsheh, S., 578
Al Quaeda, 582
Alcohol/substance abuse, 491–492
Aldarondo, E., 718
Alegria, M., 290, 298, 472, 609
Alexander, C., 339
Alexander, R., 129
Ali, A., 130, 131
Ali, S., 653
Alleccia, J., 578
Allen, A., 405
Allen, T. J., 58, 458
Allison, D., 710
Allport, G. W., 414
Allyne, R., 112–113
Alper, G. I., 665
Alpert, E., 552
AlterNative Education Program, 489
Alterovitz, S. S.-R., 686, 689
Altmaier, E. M., 698
Altman, A. N., 618–620, 627
Alzheimer's Association, 691
Alzheimer's disease, 691
American Association of People with Disabilities, 638

N